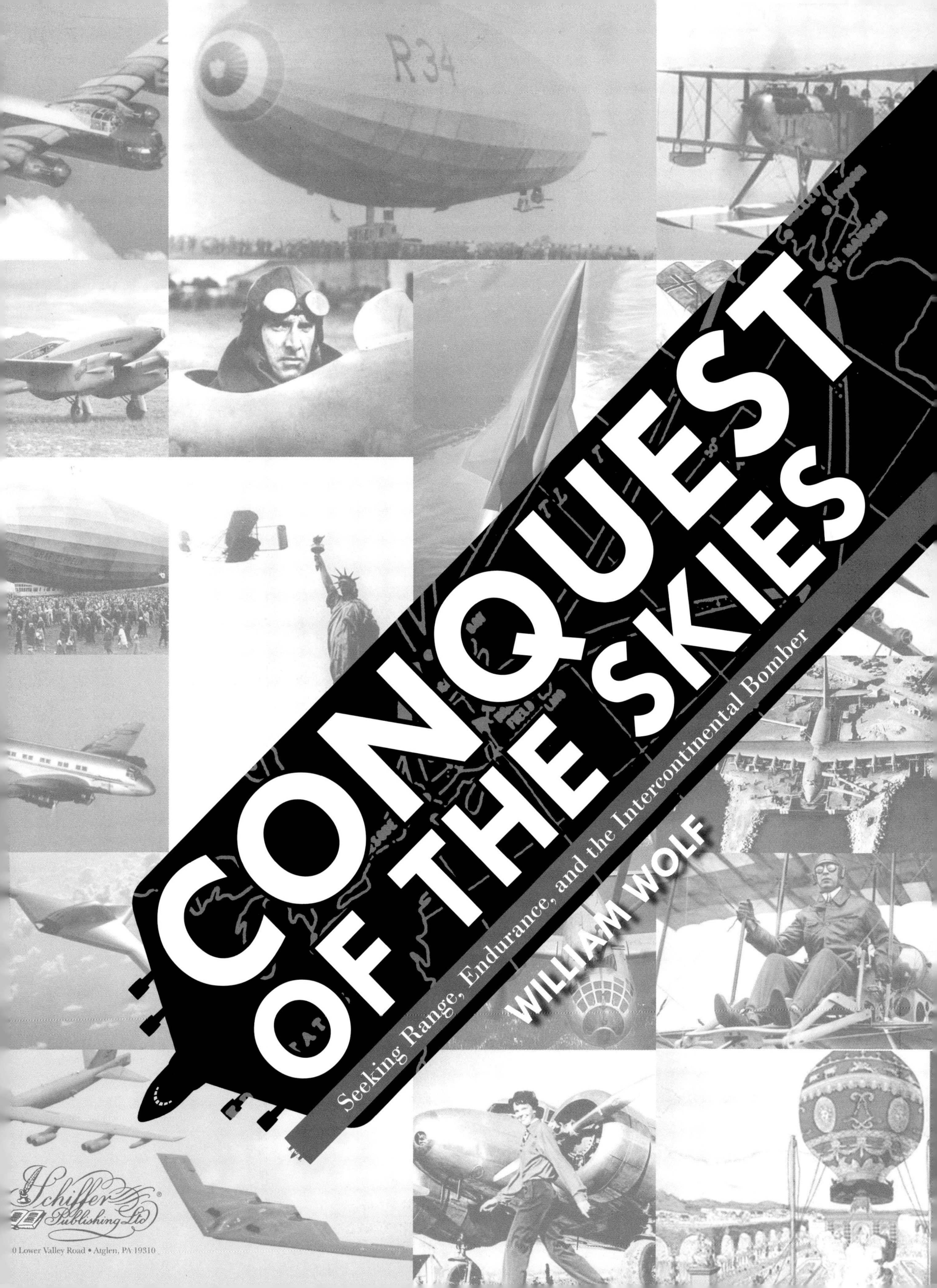
CONQUEST OF THE SKIES
Seeking Range, Endurance, and the Intercontinental Bomber
WILLIAM WOLF
R34
Schiffer Publishing Ltd
0 Lower Valley Road • Atglen, PA 19310

Library of Congress Control Number: 2017940407

Designed by Danielle D. Farmer
Cover design by Justin Watkinson

Type set in Tw Cen MT/Bodoni MT

ISBN: 978-0-7643-5321-5
Printed in China

Published by Schiffer Publishing, Ltd.
4880 Lower Valley Road, Atglen, PA 19310
Phone: (610) 593-1777; Fax: (610) 593-2002
E-mail: Info@schifferbooks.com
Web: www.schifferbooks.com

DEDICATION

To all the aviators, such as my dad, who flew the 1920s and '30s in aircraft which were primitive by today's standards, for the sheer fun and exhilaration of flying.

CONTENTS

FOREWARD 6
ACKNOWLEDGMENTS 7
NOTE TO READERS 8

PROLOGUE: QUEST FOR PROOF OF CONCEPT AND DISTANCE: 1903–1914 9
Chapter 1: The Wright Brothers and Other Early Fliers: 1903-1909 10
Chapter 2: 1909-1912: Crossing the English Channel 22
Chapter 3: Early and Yearly Air Meets and Races 25
Chapter 4: 1911: A Glorious Year 37
Chapter 5: 1912: New Meets Begin, Old Meets Continue 42
Chapter 6: 1913: More Competitions and Records 48
Chapter 7: 1914: The Age of Innocence Ends 51

AXIS: QUEST FOR SIZE AND DISTANCE: AN OVERVIEW 1914–1945 58
Part 1: Italian Long-Range Aircraft 59
Chapter 1: Italian Interwar Giants 59
Chapter 2: Savoia-Marchetti Long-Distance Record Setters 61
Chapter 3: Italian Passenger and Military Long-Range Aircraft 63

Part 2: Japanese Long-Range Aircraft 70
Chapter 1: Japanese Long-Range Aircraft of the 1930s 70
Chapter 2: Japanese Long-Range Private/Military Aircraft of the 1930s 73
Chapter 3: Japanese Wartime Long-Range Military Aircraft 76
Chapter 4: *Project Z* and Steps Toward an Intercontinental Bomber 80

Part 3: German Long-Range Aircraft 84
Chapter 1: German Giants of World War I 84
Chapter 2: German Interwar Long-Range Aircraft and Pilots 86
Chapter 3: The Ural Bomber Concept 97
Chapter 4: Late 1930s Luftwaffe Long-Range Bomber Concepts 100
Chapter 5: The Amerika Bomber Projekt 103

ALLIED: QUEST FOR SIZE AND DISTANCE: AN OVERVIEW 1914 ONWARD 116
Part 1: French Long-Range Aircraft 117
Chapter 1: Farman Goliath 117
Chapter 2: Breguet Br.19 GR 118
Chapter 3: Bleriot 110 121
Chapter 4: Bernard 80/81 GR 122
Chapter 5: Dewoitine D33 and D332 123
Chapter 6: The Great Trans-Atlantic Mystery of the *L'oiseau Blanc* 125
Chapter 7: Maryse Bastie: France's Amelia Earhart 126
Chapter 8: Challenge International de Tourisme 1929-1934 127

Part 2: British Long-Range Aircraft 143
Chapter 1: British World War I Long-Range Aircraft 143
Chapter 2: British Long-Range Aircraft and Flights of the 1920s 144
Chapter 3: British Long-Range Aircraft and Flights of the Late 1920s and 1930s 156
Chapter 4: British World War II Long-Range Bomber Development 181
Chapter 5: British Postwar Long-Range Bomber Development 182

Part 3: Soviet Long-Range Aircraft 184
Chapter 1: Sikorsky Soviet Postwar Giants 184
Chapter 2: Tupolev and Other Soviet Giants 186
Chapter 3: Towards a Soviet Postwar Intercontinental Bomber 195

Part 4: America's Pioneering Pilots and the Realization of the Intercontinental Bomber 198
Chapter 1: Quest for Distance and Endurance: The Flying Fuel Tanks: 1911-1927 198
Chapter 2: Lindbergh and the Golden Age of Long-Distance Flights: 1927-1932 208
Chapter 3: In-Flight Refueling: Extending Range and Endurance 237
Chapter 4: American Transcontinental and Other Records: 1929–1934 248
Chapter 5: Flying Boats: Quest for Size and Distance: 1930-1946 256
Chapter 6: The Military Bomber: Quest for Distance and Size: 1920-1932 262
Chapter 7: Quest for Long-Range Bombers Begins 268
Chapter 8: R-40-B Very Long-Range Bomber Specification 286
Chapter 9: The Postwar US Intercontinental Bomber Is Realized 295

EPILOGUE: LONG DISTANCE CIVILIAN AND MILITARY AIRCRAFT FROM THE COLD WAR AND BEYOND 312
Chapter 1: Post World War II Civilian Aircraft and Military Fighters 313
Chapter 2: Intercontinental Bombers of the Cold War and Beyond 366
Chapter 3: The Future: Intercontinental to Interstellar 381

APPENDIX 386
INDEX 393

FOREWORD

While researching my book, *The Douglas XB-19: America's Would-Be Intercontinental Bomber*, I became fascinated with the civil and military attempts at setting long distance flight and endurance records from WWI onward. My father, William "Bill" Wolf, was one of the youngest licensed pilots in the US in 1929, when he graduated from high school at sixteen. He used his college money to make a partial payment on a De Havilland Gypsy Moth and spent the next decade in the Milwaukee area teaching flying and giving weekend rides (until he married my mother and she made him get a real job!). In nostalgic moods he told me that while flying in air shows in the Midwest he met many of the famous record-setting pilots that I describe in this book. These pilots virtually flew fuel tanks with wings in their attempts to set new distance and endurance records. I have tried to incorporate and link their flights and the flights of foreign pilots to the development and evolution of the long-range military aircraft of their nations.

TOP RIGHT/ Author with a painting of his father's De Havilland Gypsy Moth.

ABOVE/ What the dapper eighteen-year-old flier (my dad) wore in 1931.

ACKNOWLEDGMENTS

My lifelong hobby has been WWII aerial combat, and over the past thirty-five years I have collected over 24,000 books and magazines, along with hundreds of reels of microfilm, on the subject. I probably have nearly every book written on WWII aviation and complete collections of every aviation magazine published since 1939. Also included in my collection are hundreds of aviation unit histories; intelligence reports; pilot, crew, flight, and training manuals; and technical, structural, and maintenance manuals for aircraft ordnance, armament, engines, and equipment. My microfilm collection includes vintage intelligence reports; hundreds of USAF, USN, and USMC group and squadron histories and After Combat Reports; the complete Japanese Monograph series; and complete US Strategic Bombing Surveys, as well as complete USAF Historical Studies. Over the years I have been fortunate to meet many fighter aces, other pilots, and fellow aviation buffs who have shared stories, material, and photographs with me (I have over 5,000 photos of fighter aces alone). I have made many multi-day expeditions to various military libraries, museums, and photo depositories with my copy machine and camera, accumulating literally reams of information and thousands of photographs. I also once had a photo darkroom where I developed thousands of rare photos from microfilm negatives.

The author wishes that every person who contributed photos and materials during the past forty years could be specifically mentioned. Over the years the origin of many of the photos I have been lent to copy, or have copied, or that I have collected have become obscured. Most are from military and government sources, but many are from private individuals, and I apologize in advance if some of the photos are miscredited. Also, some of the photos are not of the best quality because of their age and sources, especially those copied from microfilm and contemporary newspapers and magazines at a time before digital cameras and Photoshop, but they were used because of their importance to the book.

Again, at my publisher, Schiffer, thanks go to my helpful and talented editor, Ian Robertson, who reads through my manuscript with a "fine tooth comb" and patiently places the hundreds of photos and drawings I submit for each book. Ultimately, the content and final editing of this book is solely my responsibility as the author, and hopefully after many days and months of research I am somewhat the authority on the subject.

For yet another time thanks go to my persevering wife, Nancy, who allows me to spend many hours researching and writing, and patiently (especially if there is a nearby mall) waits while I browse bookstores and visit air museums in search of new material and photos. Also, I thank her because her car sits out in the hot Arizona sun as my WWII library luxuriates in our remodeled, air-conditioned three-car garage.

NOTE TO READERS

Although "range" is often qualified, in this context it indicates how far an aircraft can fly non-stop under given operating conditions from the moment of take-off to the time when its fuel supply is exhausted. The "combat radius" is the radius of action for any given aircraft on a combat mission with a specified load and flight plan. The "radius of action" differs from "range" in that the combat aircraft is always considered to have to return to the point at which it takes off (unless on a kamikaze mission!). It can be compared to the radius of a circle and represents the maximum distance (point of no return) at which a given aircraft can operate, under given conditions, from the center of the circle and still return to the center. This distance, under combat conditions, is considerably less than one-half the distance the aircraft can fly under non-combat conditions, as possible interception by the enemy has to be factored.

Until the early 1950s, the range and speed of aircraft were usually shown in statute miles. Afterward, the Air Force began to measure speed in knots and range in nautical miles. Speed records continued to be in miles per hour and distances were expressed in kilometers. (A knot nautical mile per hour is 1.152 times faster than a statute mile per hour. A nautical mile represents approximately 6,080 ft. and is 800 ft. more than the statute mile.) In this book all speeds, distances, and weights are reported in mph and feet/miles, and lbs., respectively (except for specific metric records); for this reason there appear to be some odd figures, for instance, a specification of 100 km/h would be reported as 62.5 mph or a 1,000 kg bomb load would be reported as 2,200 lb. Flight times of hours, minutes, and seconds are recorded as 00:00:00. All fuel and oil readings are in US gallons. Many of the record distance and endurance records described in this book were documented and verified by the Swiss-based Federation Aeronautique Internationale (FAI, the World Air Sports Federation), which is the established body (1905) for "air sports, aeronautics, and astronautics world records."

PROLOGUE

QUEST FOR PROOF OF CONCEPT AND DISTANCE

1903–1914

1 THE WRIGHT BROTHERS AND OTHER EARLY FLIERS: 1903–1909

BEFORE THE WRIGHT BROTHERS: PRETENDERS AND NOT?

SAMUEL LANGLEY

After a distinguished career as an astronomer and shortly before becoming secretary of the Smithsonian Institution, Samuel Langley began investigating aerodynamics, and in 1891, published *Experiments in Aerodynamics* detailing his research. Utilizing his research he then began building his designs, concentrating on achieving automatic aerodynamic stability, but in doing so, he gave little consideration to control in-flight. On 6 May 1896, Langley's Aerodrome No. 5 made the first successful sustained flight of an unmanned, engine-driven heavier-than-air craft of sizeable dimension. It was launched from a spring-actuated catapult mounted on the top of a houseboat anchored in the Potomac River near Quantico, Virginia. The Aerodrome No. 5 was intended to land in the water, as there was no landing gear installed to save weight to help it get into the air. Two flights were made that afternoon—one of 3,297 ft. and a second of 2,300 ft.—at a speed of approximately 25 mph. On 28 November 1896, another successful flight of 4,790 ft. was made by the significantly modified Aerodrome No. 6 version of No. 4 that was witnessed and photographed by Alexander Graham Bell. With the successes of Aerodromes No. 5 and No. 6, Langley was granted the then large sum of $50,000 by the US government to develop a manned flying machine for aerial reconnaissance in the ongoing Spanish-American War. Langley planned on building a scaled-up version known as the Aerodrome A and started with the smaller Quarter-scale Aerodrome, which flew twice on 18 June, but with a problematic engine in 1903. Langley needed to find a suitable engine for his successful basic design. However, finding an acceptable engine would take years before a five-cylinder water-cooled radial 52 hp engine could be installed in the Aerodrome. Once the new engine was installed, Langley became extremely disappointed when he found that the up-scaled Quarter-scale Aerodrome was just too fragile and the aircraft's control system was insufficient to allow quick pilot responses and had no method of lateral control, making the Aerodrome's stability marginal. The two launches in late 1903 ended with the Aerodrome immediately crashing into the water. Langley's attempts to gain further backing failed, terminating his quest. Nine days after his last unsuccessful launch the Wright brothers successfully flew their Flyer on December 8.

Samuel Langley's Aerodrome about to crash into the water.

GUSTAVE WHITEHEAD

German Gustave Weiskopf, who changed his name to Whitehead upon immigrating to America, designed and built flying machines and engines from 1897–1915. On 14 August 1901, Whitehead claimed to have flown about a half mile at 50 ft. in a controlled, powered flight in his Number 21 monoplane in Fairfield, Connecticut. The aircraft had fabric-covered 36 ft. span wings ribbed with bamboo and supported by steel wires very similar in shape to the wings of Lilienthal's gliders. The craft was powered by two engines: a 10 hp ground engine intended to propel the front wheels to reach take-off speed and a 20 hp acetylene engine powering two propellers designed to counter-rotate for stability. Whitehead claimed two more flights on 17 January 1902, using his Number 22 monoplane. For many years the Whitehead claims were ignored or dismissed by aviation historians, but recent research has found over 250 compelling newspaper reports of Whitehead's 1901/1902 flights. Influential *Jane's All the World's Aircraft* in a March 2013 editorial and prominent, independent chief aviation historians at the Library of Congress and Smithsonian have accepted Whitehead's flight as the first manned, powered, controlled flight of a heavier-than-air craft before the Wright Brothers.

On 14 August 1901, Gustave Whitehead's Number 21 monoplane was probably the first aircraft to fly.

Orville Wright runs alongside Wilbur during their historic first flight of the Wright Flyer at Kill Devil Hills, North Carolina, on 17 December 1903.

1903: THE WRIGHT BROTHERS FIRST HEAVIER-THAN-AIR FLIGHT

After their exasperating glider experiments on the Kill Devil Hills of the Outer Banks of North Carolina, the Wright Brothers finally solved the problem of sustained lift, and more significantly, they were able to control an aircraft while in flight using double tails and elevators. But the difficult problem of powering their aircraft remained, so when they were unable to find a suitable lightweight commercial engine they designed and built their own engine, then also designed the first efficient propeller. Returning to Kill Devil Hills, they mounted their new engine on the 40 ft., 605 lb. Flyer airframe. The engine drove two pusher propellers with chains, one crossed to make the props rotate in opposite directions to counteract a torquing (twisting tendency) in flight. The brothers tossed a coin to determine who would fly first and Wilbur won, but he lost his chance when he oversteered after leaving the launching rail. The Flyer dove into the sand and the world's first flight would not come until after repairs were completed three days later on 17 December 1903. The Flyer was ready for the second attempt and at 1035, Orville released the restraining wire and Wilbur steadied the wings as the Flyer moved down the rail. Orville overcompensated with the controls, but he kept the Flyer aloft for twelve seconds until it skidded on the sand about 120 ft. from the rail. The brothers took turns flying three more times that historic day, increasing their distance with each flight, with Wilbur's second flight—the fourth and last of the day—reaching a notable 852 ft. in fifty-nine seconds. From the Wright brothers' first manned twelve second flight on 17 December 1903, it would be only a little over a decade before an airplane could stay in the air for over a day without refueling.

1904–1908: THE WRIGHTS CONTINUE TO DEVELOP THE FLYER

The Wrights continued developing their flying machines in 1904–05 at Huffman Prairie, a large meadow near Dayton. During April and May 1904, Wilbur and Orville built a new heavier and stronger machine with a more powerful motor, and with these significant design changes the Flyer III became the first practical aircraft, flying consistently under full control and landing safely without damage back at the starting point. Beginning 15 September, the Wrights flew practice flights in their new Wright Flyer at Huffman Prairie totaling forty-nine minutes flying time, with Wilbur flying the first complete circle on 20 September. The longest flight of the year was 5:04 minutes covering 2.75 miles, which was almost four circles around the field. On 5 October 1905, Wilbur would fly the longest flight ever: 24.2 miles in 39:24 minutes, which was more than twenty-nine times around the field, at an average speed of 38 mph. The Wrights conducted these trials in secrecy while trying to file their patents and further develop their Flyers.

The Wright Flyer III set one record after another in 1905.

1908: WRIGHTS GO TO EUROPE

By 1908, the Wright brothers had filed their patents and nearly concluded their negotiations with the US military and decided it was time to demonstrate their Flyers and piloting talents for the public. While Henry Farman had been laboring to fly but a kilometer in his Voisin, he and other Wright challengers were beginning to appear in America and Europe, but were not yet significant. Due to the Wrights' secrecy there was a prevalent skepticism about their accomplishments, and in May 1908, Wilbur Wright and his crated 1905 Wright Flyer arrived on the docks at Le Havre. By June, Wilbur had established his base at the auto racing course at Le Mans and meticulously prepared the Flyer to prove the naysayers wrong. It would not be until late afternoon on August 8, that he and the Flyer would be ready for their first public flight in Europe before a large crowd that included Ernst Archdeacon, Louis Bleriot, Leon Delagrange, Hubert Latham, and many other interested members of the French Aero-Club. Wilbur and the Flyer had not flown for almost three years, but all skepticism was removed during the 1:45 minute flight that climbed to 30 ft., made three smooth sweeping circuits around the racecourse, and then landed easily within 150 ft. of his take-off point. Despite his reticent and aloof character, Wilbur Wright became a celebrity in France and his flying prowess spoke for him. On September 3, he flew for more than 10 minutes; on September 16, he flew 29:18 minutes, and then flew a passenger (Ernest Zens) over a measured flight of an implausible 41 miles in 1:32 hours on September 22. By October 15, he had flown thirty awestruck passengers, which was more than the number of all the European aviators! Many of these passengers were aviators or aviator want-to-bes who Wilbur would give flying lessons: among his first pupils were the Comte de Lambert, Paul Tissandier, and Capt. Lucas-Girardville. Before the end of 1908, Wilbur had set the altitude record at 375 ft. (December 18) and the distance/duration at 76.5 miles in 2:19 hours (December 31). After the turn of the year Wright moved to Pau, in southwest France, and "taught Europe to fly"; among his pupils were Louis Bleriot and the Comte de Castillon de Saint-Victor. In 1909, brother Orville joined Wilbur in Europe after demonstrating the Flyer for the US Army at Fort Myers, which included the first ever hour-long flight on 9 September 1908. Unfortunately, these flights had also included the first fatal aircraft crash when Lt. Thomas Selfridge, flying as passenger with Orville, was killed.

Wilbur went to Rome and Orville to Berlin to demonstrate and train those countries' Army officers, hoping to obtain large government orders for their Flyer. They declined to participate in the race for crossing the English Channel or the Reims Meeting as they viewed such contests as sensational and stunts, although they could have undoubtedly made greater sales to civilian enthusiasts if they had participated and probably won. Instead, Louis Bleriot would garner the publicity as Europe's and probably the world's greatest (i.e., well-known) aviator. In 1910, the brothers founded the Wright Company and retired from active participation in the flying world, but Wilbur's astonishing demonstrations in summer 1908 had left an enduring mark on European aviation.

Wilbur Wright demonstrating the Flyer III to King Alfonso of Spain on his European tour.

WRIGHT BROTHERS QUEST FOR DISTANCE: 1903–1909

Date	Miles	Km	Pilot	Aircraft	Location
17 Dec 1903	120 ft.		Orville Wright	Wright Flyer biplane	Kitty Hawk, NC
17 Dec 1903	852 ft.	0.1	Wilbur Wright	Wright Flyer biplane	Kitty Hawk, NC
20 Sept 1904	4,080 ft.	0.5	Wilbur Wright	Wright Flyer No 2 biplane	Huffman Prairie, OH
9 Nov 1904	2.7	4.3	Wilbur Wright	Wright Flyer No 2 biplane	Huffman Prairie, OH
26 Sept 1905	11.2	18.0	Wilbur Wright	Wright Flyer No 3 biplane	Huffman Prairie, OH
29 Sept1905	12.0	19.3	Orville Wright	Wright Flyer No 3 biplane	Huffman Prairie, OH
3 Oct 1905	15.25	24.5	Orville Wright	Wright Flyer No 3 biplane	Huffman Prairie, OH
4 Oct 1905	20.75	33.4	Orville Wright	Wright Flyer No 3 biplane	Huffman Prairie, OH
5 Oct 1905	24.25	39.0	Wilbur Wright	Wright Flyer No 3 biplane	Huffman Prairie, OH
9 Sept 1908	40.0	64.4	Orville Wright	Wright A biplane F	Fort Myer, VA
10 Sept1908	43.5	70.0	Orville Wright	Wright A biplane	Fort Myer, VA
12 Sept 1908	53	85	Orville Wright	Wright A biplane	Fort Myer, VA
18 Dec 1908	62	100	Wilbur Wright	Wright A biplane	d'Auvours, France
31 Dec 1908	77	124	Wilbur Wright	Wright A biplane	d'Auvours, France

Time	Date	Location	Pilot	Aircraft
02:18:34	December 31, 1908	Camp d'Auvours Le Mans, France	Wilbur Wright	Wright Model A
01:54:00	December 18, 1908	Camp d'Auvours Le Mans, France	Wilbur Wright	Wright Model A
01:31:26	September 21, 1908	Camp d'Auvours Le Mans, France	Wilbur Wright	Wright Model A
01:14:20	September 12, 1908	Fort Myer, VA	Orville Wright	Wright Model A
01:10:24	September 11, 1908	Fort Myer, VA	Orville Wright	Wright Model A
01:05:52	September 10, 1908	Fort Myer, VA	Orville Wright	Wright Model A
01:02:15	September 9, 1908	Fort Myer, VA	Orville Wright	Wright Model A
00:59:24	October 5, 1905	Huffman Prairie, OH	Wilbur Wright	Wright Flyer III
00:33:17	October 4, 1905	Huffman Prairie, OH	Orville Wright	Wright Flyer III
00:26:11	October 3, 1905	Huffman Prairie, OH	Orville Wright	Wright Flyer III
00:19:56	September 29, 1905	Huffman Prairie, OH	Orville Wright	Wright Flyer III
00:18:11	September 26, 1905	Huffman Prairie, OH	Wilbur Wright	Wright Flyer III
00:05:41	September 12, 1905	Huffman Prairie, OH	Wilbur Wright	Wright Flyer III
00:05:04	November 9, 1904	Huffman Prairie, OH	Wilbur Wright	Wright Flyer II
00:01:38	October 14, 1904	Huffman Prairie, OH	Orville Wright	Wright Flyer II
00:01:36	September 20, 1904	Huffman Prairie, OH	Wilbur Wright	Wright Flyer II
00:00:59	December 17, 1903	Kitty Hawk, NC	Wilbur Wright	Wright Flyer
00:00:12	December 17, 1903	Kitty Hawk, NC	Orville Wright	Wright Flyer

1906: SANTOS DUMONT: FIRST HEAVIER-THAN-AIR FLIGHT IN EUROPE

Alberto Santos Dumont was born in Brazil of a wealthy coffee plantation family, and immigrated to France in 1891. During the late 1890s, he became well-known for his work with dirigibles and in 1901, he piloted his *Airship No. 6* around the Eiffel Tower, winning a huge prize of 100,000 Francs. In 1904, a year after the Wright Brothers' first powered flight, Santos Dumont began his work on heavier-than-air flying machines, and by 1906, he built a biplane based somewhat on the Wright biplane design. Its box-like elevator and rudder protruded in front of the wings like the head of a duck in flight, which gave rise to the aviation term *canard* (French for duck). To fly the strange-looking aircraft Santos Dumont had to stand up in a wicker basket under the duck's head. Santos Dumont named the airplane the *14-bis*, meaning "14-encore," since it made its first appearance suspended from the belly of Santos Dumont's *No. 14 Dirigible*. On 13 September 1906, he made an "unofficially observed test hop" of about 23 ft. at two feet altitude on the Bagatelle Meadows outside Paris. On 23 October 1906, Santos Dumont flew 197 ft. at a height of 10 ft. for the first "officially observed powered European flight" and was awarded the Deutsch-Archdeacon Prize of 3,000 Francs for surpassing 25 m (about 80 ft.). On 12 November, with members of the Aero-Club du France observing, the *14 bis* flew 722 ft. in 21.5 seconds, climbing to about 20 ft., which won Santos Dumont a prize of 1,500 Francs for making the first flight in Europe of over 100 meters. Santos Dumont last flew the *14-bis* briefly on 4 April 1907, and then abandoned it as a technological dead end. His next design was the *15 bis* biplane, which was also abandoned in favor of a monoplane design that required five models before the hard copy, *Demoiselle*, was flown successfully in 1909, and was then considered the first practical light aircraft. Santos Dumont offered the plans for the *Demoiselle* gratis, enabling young men to afford to get into the air inexpensively and helping to fuel the remarkable growth of aviation in the years before WWI. Santos Dumont would not create another airplane as popular or as influential as the *Demoiselle* before being diagnosed with multiple sclerosis. Once stricken, he withdrew from aviation and retired to Brazil in 1916, dying there in 1932.

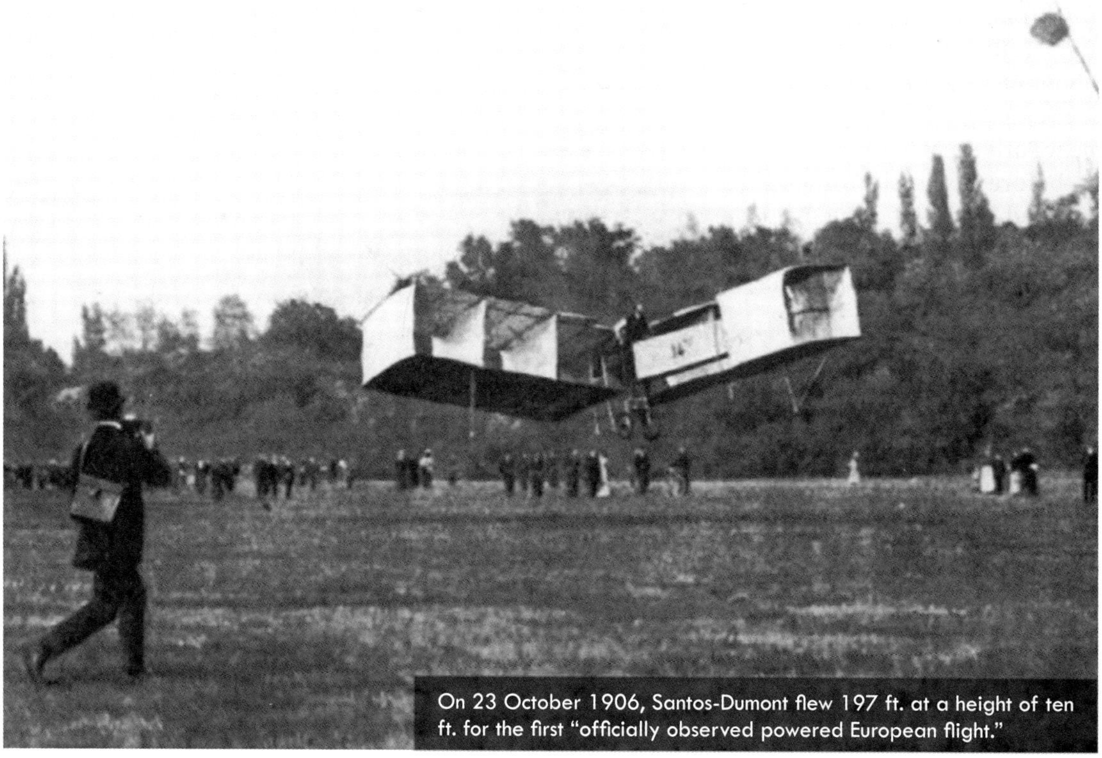

On 23 October 1906, Santos-Dumont flew 197 ft. at a height of ten ft. for the first "officially observed powered European flight."

1906: TRAJAN VUIA: FIRST TRACTOR MONOPLANE TO FLY

Trajan Vuia was a Romanian inventor and aviation pioneer who designed, built, and tested the first aircraft to demonstrate the ability to take off from a flat surface, running on wheels on a standard road without assistance such as an incline, rails, or catapult, unlike the Wright Brothers, who flew their first *Wright* Flyer at Kitty Hawk from level ground using a dolly undercarriage running on a guide rail. Vuia's basic framework consisted of a pair of triangular frames, the lower components forming the sides of the rectangular chassis that carried four wheels on pneumatic tires, with the front pair steerable. The wings resembled those of Otto Lilienthal's gliders and were covered in varnished linen. Pitch control was achieved by varying the angle of attack of the wing and a trapezoidal rudder was mounted behind and below the wing. The *Vuia I* was powered by a 25 hp carbonic acid gas engine adapted by Vuia driving a single tractor propeller. The fuel supply was enough for a running time of about five minutes at full power. On 8 March 1906, at Montesson, France, Vuia flew his *Vuia 1* for the first time, traveling about 39 feet at an altitude of about three feet. He flew four more times during the day: one flight traveled about 66 ft. at an altitude of about three ft. and his longest flight was 79 ft. Then, on 9 August 1906, at Issy-les-Moulineaux, near Paris, Vuia flew almost 79 ft. at a height of just over eight ft. before his tractor monoplane—without any controls—crashed, damaging the propeller. Though unsuccessful in sustained flight, Vuia's design influenced Louis Bleriot's monoplane designs. Later Vuia also designed helicopters.

Romanian Traijan Vuia in his Vuia I monoplane, 1906.

1907: LEON DELAGRANGE AND HENRI FARMAN: "A SPORTING RIVALRY"

After the Wright's flight, Henri Farman and Leon Delagrange were Europe's most prominent aviators, both of whom had purchased and were learning to fly a standard Voisin biplane, and soon a "sporting rivalry" developed. On 16 March 1907, Delagrange flew his Voison *Delagrange I* for 30 ft. at Chateau de Bagatelle, near Paris, and on 5 November 1907, he flew 984 ft. in a semicircle there before crash landing. Meanwhile, on 30 September, Farman made his first flight in his modified Voisin-Farman outside Paris at Issy-les-Moulineaux (Issy), flying approximately 262 ft., and then completed a 2,541 foot flight on 26 October that was farther than the official world record held by Europe's first pilot, Albert Santos Dumont. In 1904, French oil tycoon Henri Deutsch de la Meurthe, in collaboration with wealthy Parisian lawyer Ernest Archdeacon, created the *Grand Prix d'Aviation* (also known as the Deutsch-Archdeacon Prize), awarding a prize of 50,000 Francs ($10,000 then and equal to about $1.2 million today) for the first pilot to fly to a marker 500 meters from his take-off point and return without touching the ground. Farman made a practice flight on 9 November without observers present, but then the weather deteriorated. Farman was poised to break the prized one kilometer mark.

1908: HENRI FARMAN: FIRST EUROPEAN FLIGHT OVER ONE KILOMETER

The Wrights had always been secretive of their flights, but when they claimed flights of more than 39 km during 1905, and also the first flight with a passenger, Parisian newspapers almost went as far as to call them liars, and even the respected *Scientific American* refused to publish an article about the Ohio flight. In early January 1908, Henri Farman returned to the parade grounds at Issy-les-Moulineaux outside Paris, where he had made his first flight in his Voisin only three and a half months earlier. On the eleventh he flew 1,800 m (almost 6,000 ft.) in 1:45 hours. For the One Kilometer attempt, Aero-Club officials marked the starting and finishing line with two posts and flags set up 500 meters away. Farman accelerated to a take-off and crossed the starting line at an altitude of 12 to 15 ft. Once he reached the 500 meter flags Farman made a skidding wide turn with his rudder, maintaining level flight. While the Wright Flyers used wing warping to bank their aircraft, to turn his Voisin, which lacked either wing warping or the ailerons used today, Farman had to rely entirely on the rudder. Once through the turn Farman descended and crossed the finish poles 1:28 minutes later to the ovation of the small group of onlookers who had gathered in the cold. In all, Farman probably flew about 1,500 m due to his wide, flat turn, winning the 10,000 Franc Grand Prix d'Aviation prize and establishing the "official" (the French did not consider the Wright's flights as official) world record for time, distance, and speed, averaging just over 25 mph.

Henri Farman passing the finish pole in his Voisin after completing the first 1 km flight in Europe on 13 January 1908.

THE FARMAN-DELAGRANGE RIVALRY CONTINUES

After Farman's one kilometer record coup Delagrange migrated south to Italy to demonstrate his flying skills, while Farman moved north to Belgium. Delagrange was flying the new *Delagrange II* that incorporated the modifications made to Farman's aircraft.

On 14 January 1908, Farman flew 1,500 m in 1:33 minutes.

On 21 March, Farman set a duration and distance flight of 2,004.8 meters (1.25 miles) in 3:31 minutes, doubling the previous official circular flight that was bettered by Delagrange, first with a flight of 2.5 km (1.6 miles) on 10 April, and the next day with a flight of 3.95 km (2.44 miles). On 30 May, while giving a series of demonstration flights in Italy, Delagrange succeeded in making a flight of 12.75 km (7.92 miles) lasting 15:25 minutes. At the end of May, Farman had also made the first flights in Europe with a passenger, carrying Ernest Archdeacon 1,242 m (4,075 ft.) at Ghent. On 23 June, Delagrange set an endurance record of 18:30 minutes at Milan. On 6 July 1908, Farman flew 20:19.6 at Ghent, winning the Armengaud Prize (10,000 Francs) for the first aircraft to fly 15 minutes in France. On 6 September, Delagrange flew 25 km (15 miles) at Issy, which Farman unofficially bested on 29 September, flying 42 km in 43 minutes at Mourmelon, but then officially flew 40 km (25 miles) at Champ de Chalons on 2 October.

After making 260 flights, flying 1,300 km, and setting six speed, distance, and duration world records, Delagrange was killed in a flying accident on 4 January 1910 at Pau when the port wing of his Bleriot XI collapsed while trying to win the Michelin Cup.

Leon Delagrange and his Voisin biplane

GABRIEL VOISIN

Ernest Archdeacon employed Gabriel Voisin to construct gliders, after which Voisin and Louis Bleriot formed *Ateliers d' Aviation Edouard Surcouf, Bleriot et Voisin* in 1905. Voisin bought out Bleriot, and on 5 November 1906, he founded the *Appareils d'Aviation Les Frères Voisin* with his brother, Charles. The new company, based outside Paris, was the first commercial aircraft factory in the world. Like many early aircraft companies, to support their own designs the Voisins built aircraft to customers' designs or specifications. They built an aircraft for Leon Delagrange powered by a 50 hp Antoinette engine that was first successfully flown by Charles Voisin on 30 March 1907, achieving a straight-line flight of 200 ft. Delagrange then referred Henri Farman, who ordered an identical aircraft, and these aircraft were referred to by their owners' names as the *Voisin-Delagrange No. 1* and the *Voisin-Farman No. 1*. After Farman won the Grand Prix de l'aviation these aircraft became the foundation of the Voisins' company and about sixty were built. Voisin got a late start on military manufacturing, but his *Voisin VIII* was the French Army's main night bomber in 1916–1917, with over 1,000 built. After the war, in 1918, Voisin left the aviation industry for automobile construction under the brand Avions Voisin.

Henri Farman (L) and Gabriel Voisin

1908: ALEXANDER GRAHAM BELL AND THE AERIAL EXPERIMENT ASSOCIATION

In 1908, Alexander Graham Bell created the Aerial Experiment Association (AEA) along with Canadian engineers John Douglas and Alexander McCurdy. The AEA hired Thomas Selfridge to design the aircraft and Glenn Curtiss, an American motorcycle designer and manufacturer and recognized expert on gasoline engines, to design and build the lightweight engines. The AEA quickly produced several different aircraft, with each member acting as principal designer for at least one. The group introduced key technical innovations, notably wingtip ailerons and the tricycle landing gear. The *Red Wing* (or *Aerodrome #1*) was an early aircraft designed by Selfridge, while Curtiss designed and built its 40 hp Curtiss B-8 air-cooled V8 engine. The biplane was named for the bright red color of its silk wings so it could be seen by spectators and photographers. On 12 March 1908, Frederick Baldwin first piloted the skate-equipped aircraft off frozen Lake Keuka in upper New York State. Since the Wrights had been so secretive and this flight was observed by a fairly large crowd of onlookers and invited aerial observers, it is considered the first public demonstration of a powered aircraft flight in the United States, as well as the first flight by a Canadian pilot. The aircraft flew 319 ft. at a height of about 20 ft. before crashing twenty seconds after take-off; it was damaged but repaired, only to be destroyed in a crash on its second flight on 17 March, with only the engine salvaged. On 19 May, Selfridge became the first US military officer to pilot a modern aircraft when he flew solo in AEA's newest aircraft, *White Wing*, traversing 100 ft. on his first attempt and 200 ft. on his second. Between 19 May and 3 August, he and Curtiss flew a number of flights at Hammondsport, culminating in a flight of 1:30 seconds at 75 ft. The next day his final solo flight of 50 seconds traveled 2,400 ft. Selfridge was the first US military officer to fly any aircraft solo. (Note: Selfridge would become the world's first person killed in an aircraft while flying with Wilbur Wright on 17 September). The third AEA design would be Glenn Curtiss' *June Bug*, which would fly over one kilometer (described next). Their fourth aircraft was the *Silver Dart* (also built in 1908), which flew the first controlled powered flight in Canada on 23 February 1909 by McCurdy, who was one of its designers. On 10 March 1909, McCurdy set a record when he flew the *Silver Dart* on a circular course over a distance of more than 20 miles, which the Wrights had previously accomplished in 1905. The Association made the first passenger flight in Canada on 2 August, also in the *Silver Dart*. After Curtiss unexpectedly formed a new commercial aircraft company in March 1909, relations became strained between Curtiss and the Association's other members, and Bell discontinued his support. The association was disbanded on 31 March 1909.

The *Red Wing* during the first public demonstration of a powered aircraft flight in the United States.

1908: GLENN CURTISS: FIRST "RATIFIED" US FLIGHT OVER ONE KILOMETER

In 1908, *Scientific American* offered a prize of $2,500 and a silver trophy for an official US flight of over one kilometer to be ratified by the Aero Club of America. The Wright Brothers' almost unobserved 2.75 mile flight on 9 November 1904 had already by far surpassed this goal and the Aero Club had offered the Wright brothers the first chance at setting the "official" record on Independence Day, but Orville declined on 30 June, as the Wrights were busy completing their deal with the government. Glenn Curtiss had tested his pusher *June Bug* and flew it successfully three out of four tries on 21 June, at distances of 456 ft. (139 m), 417 ft. (127 m), and 1,266 ft. (386 m). On 25 June, *June Bug* flew 2,175 ft. (663 m) and 3,420 ft. (1,040 m), which encouraged Curtiss to contact the Aero Club about trying for the Scientific American Cup. Curtiss was accepted on 1 July, and transported the aircraft to Hammondsport, New York. He tested it on 3 July, but it crashed on a trial flight, damaging the wing and rudder. After hours of overnight repair it was ready the next day, but the weather was windy and rainy, delaying the attempt. Finally, in the late afternoon the weather cleared and in front of a large crowd that included twenty-two members of the Aero Club, Curtiss rolled the *June Bug* out of its tent. The aircraft was supposedly named by Alexander Graham Bell because of its large stiff outer wings used for gliding that resembled those of the June Bug insect. The aircraft started slowly down the muddy grass pathway and climbed steeply before quickly settling back to the ground. Curtiss and his crew hauled it back to the starting area, made an adjustment to the horizontal stabilizer, and Curtiss tried again. The aircraft ascended more surely and steadily as it passed the half mile marker and then the red flag that represented the full kilometer, but Curtiss continued to fly down the valley fifteen to twenty ft. above the ground, turning right and then left above the local vineyards and finally, after 1:42.5 minutes, landed effortlessly almost a mile from the starting point. The next day Curtiss successfully flew over the course again to prove his point. *Scientific American* not only awarded him the prize and trophy, but Curtiss also received the Aero Club of America's Pilot's License No. 1, the first US pilot's license.

On 4 July 1908, Glenn Curtiss flies the *June Bug* to complete the first official 1 km flight in America.

FIRST AIR PASSENGERS

EUROPE

On 28 March 1908, Henri Farman became the first air passenger in Europe, ironically carried by his rival Leon Delagrange in his Voisin biplane at Issy during a "simple straight line flight of several hundred meters."

On 30 May 1908, Farman flew Ernest Archdeacon over one kilometer at Ghent, Belgium, for the longest passenger flight to date. The next day Farman was reported to have flown a Mlle. P. Van Pottelsberghe de la Potterie, daughter of the mayor of Desteldonk.

On 8 July 1908, Therese Peltier officially became the first woman to fly in an airplane, flying with

Leon Delagrange pilots Henri Farman as the first air passenger in Europe.

Leon Delagrange at Turin on an exhibition tour. By September 1908, Peltier soloed, but when Delagrange died in an airplane accident on 4 January 1910, she gave up aviation.

First woman passenger Therese Peltier and pilot Leon Delagrange

During the first months of his visit to France, Wilbur Wright flew a large number of passengers (without mishap) to garner enthusiasm and contracts for his Wright biplanes.

On 28 July 1909, Henri Farman flew 10 km in 10:39 minutes with two passengers for the first time.

During February–March 1911, Leon Lemartin, a pilot/engineer for Bleriot, flew a Bleriot XIII *Aerobus* with seven passengers, then eight, and finally thirteen, although on the last flight some of the passengers were young boys.

On 23 March 1911, Louis Breguet flew eleven passengers over three miles at Douai, but the following day Sommer flew twelve passengers over a half mile.

Louis Breguet flies eleven passengers

AMERICA

On 14 May 1908, Charles Furnas, a Wright mechanic, became the first air passenger in the US when he accompanied Wilbur Wright in a Wright 1905 Flyer equipped with modified seats for the pilot and passenger over approximately 2,000 ft. in 28.6 seconds. Later Orville Wright flew Furnas over approximately 2.6 miles in 4:02 minutes.

First passenger in America Charles Furnas and Wilbur Wright

On 17 September 1908, during flight trials to win a contract from the US Army Signal Corps, pilot Orville Wright and passenger and Army pilot Lt. Thomas Selfridge were aloft in a Wright Flyer at Fort Myer, Virginia. After completing three circuits in four minutes Wright heard a tapping sound and shut the engine off, shouting to Selfridge that he was going to land. As Wright began the final turn there was a loud crack as a piece of a propeller broke and fell to the ground. The Flyer immediately tipped sharply to the left and Wright responded by pulling hard on the front rudder lever. The plane appeared to recover briefly, climbing about ten feet, but then dove from seventy-five feet, hitting the ground with an almost complete somersault. Wright was injured and Selfridge became the first passenger and person to die in an airplane accident (Selfridge Field, Michigan, was named in his honor).

Wreck of the Wright Flyer, in which Lt. Thomas Selfridge became the first aviation casualty.

Eugene Lefebvre was the first pilot killed in a powered airplane.

NOTE:
The first pilot to be killed in a powered airplane was Eugene Lefebvre, who died on 7 September 1909, at Juvisy, France, when his controls jammed. His death was closely followed by Capt. Ferdinand Ferber, who was killed on 22 September at Boulogne-sur-Mer when he overturned while taxiing his Voisin. On 21 July 1911, Denise Moore, France, fell 150 ft. from her capsized aircraft to become the first woman pilot killed in an airplane accident. The first three pilots to die in unpowered aircraft (gliders) were Otto Lilienthal (10 August 1896), Percy Pilcher (2 October 1899), and Daniel Maloney (18 January 1905).

1908: FIRST UK AIRCRAFT FLIGHT, ONE MILE, CROSS-COUNTRY, AND PASSENGER FLIGHT: SAMUEL CODY

Samuel Cody was born in America and was a well-known Wild West showman, but not *the* Buffalo Bill Cody whose surname he took and personal appearance he emulated. During a Wild West tour of England he remained in the country and became interested in aviation. After working on and flying on Britain's first powered airship, he assisted with the development of Britain's first powered airplane, *British Army Aeroplane No 1*, driven by a 50 hp Antoinette engine. He learned to fly and tested the aircraft in September 1908, and on 16 October, at Farnborough, Samuel Cody became the first man to fly in Britain, flying for 1,391 ft. from the take-off point at an altitude of approximately 30 ft. Unfortunately, his turn on landing was too sharp and he crashed and was slightly injured. Later, on 14 May 1909, Cody completed the first flight in the UK longer than one mile in British Army Aeroplane No. 1. By August 1909, Cody had completed the last of his long series of modifications to the aircraft and carried passengers for the first time on 14 August 1909. On 8 September, Cody flew from Aldershot to Farnborough and back (46 miles) in 1:03 hours for the first recorded cross-country flight in the UK and Europe. Cody is well known for his work on large kites known as Cody War Kites that were used by the British in WWI as a smaller alternative to balloons for artillery spotting.

Samuel Cody

1907–1910: EUROPEAN FIRST FLIGHTS

Germany: 28 June 1908: J. C. H. Ellenhammer (Danish) in his biplane at Kiel and 12 January 1909: Hans Grade (German) in his triplane at Magdeburg
Austria: 23 April 1909: Legagneaux in a Voisin at Vienna
Italy: 23 May 1908: Leon Delagrange (French) at Rome and September 1909: Lt. Mario Calderara (Italian) at Rome
Denmark: February 1908: J. C. H. Ellenhammer
Holland: Summer 1909: Comte de Lambert in a Wright biplane near the Hague
Switzerland: 13 March 1910: Rapp and Armand Defaux

Jacob Ellenhammer, first to fly in Germany and Denmark.

Sweden: 29 July 1909: Georges Legagneaux in a Voisin at Stockholm
Rumania: 30 October 1909: Louis Bleriot at Bucharest
Russia: 25 July 1909: Van den Schrouff in a Voisin at Odessa
Spain: March 1910: Francois Gaudart and Edmond Poillot at Barcelona
Portugal: December 1909: Armand Zipfel and April 1910

Henri Farman in his Voisin biplane on his first European cross-country flight.

Georges Legagneaux, first to fly in Sweden and Austria.

1909: FIRST EUROPEAN CROSS-COUNTRY AND OTHER RECORDS: HENRI FARMAN

On 30 October 1909, after completing the first one kilometer flight, Farman made the first cross-country flight over continental Europe, flying from Chalons and landing on a cavalry parade grounds at Reims over 27 km (17 miles) at an altitude of 150 ft. in twenty minutes in his Voisin biplane. On 3 November, he flew 232 km (145 miles) in 4:18 hours at Mourmelon. At the end of 1909, Farman became so angered at Gabriel Voisin, who sold an aircraft built to Farman's specifications to John Moore-Brabazon, that he started manufacturing aircraft to his own design. The first, the *Farman III*, became an instant success and was widely copied.

1909: FIRST CIRCULAR MILE FLIGHT IN BRITAIN USING A BRITISH AIRCRAFT: JOHN MOORE-BRABAZON

John Moore-Brabazon learned to fly in France in late 1908, in a Voisin "boxkite" biplane. In April 1909, he flew another Voisin, called *The Bird of Passage*, in what was considered the first flight by a British subject in England, although A. V. Roe also claimed this first. (American Samuel Cody made this first flight.) On 30 October 1909, flying a *Short*, he won the Daily Mail £1,000 prize for the first circular one mile flight in Britain using a British aircraft. The next year he flew his *Short* with a piglet as passenger to show that "pigs can fly" (i.e., reflecting considered possibility of the chances of man ever flying in the 1800s). Moore-Brabazon was awarded British pilot's certificate No. 1 and remained involved in aviation all his life; he received a peerage for his services in 1942, becoming Lord Brabazon of Tara.

John Moore-Brabazon

2
1909–1912: CROSSING THE ENGLISH CHANNEL

1909: HUBERT LATHAM AND LOUIS BLERIOT VIE TO CROSS THE ENGLISH CHANNEL

Hubert Latham joined the Antoinette Company in February 1909, and was taught to fly by the company's pilots, becoming proficient after several weeks. In May 1909, he at last realized his potential and flew for 37.5 minutes at a speed of 45 mph at a height of just over 98 ft., followed a week later by a European non-stop flight record at 1:07 hours that seriously challenged the Wright's record. On 6 June 1909, Latham won the Prix Ambroise Trophy for flying a straight-line course of 6 km in 4:13 minutes. These successes convinced Leon Levavasseur—co-director, designer, and chief engineer of the Antoinette—that Latham was his best pilot, and was satisfied that his Antoinette IV monoplane was sufficiently reliable for a 45 minute to one hour continuous flight required to cross the Channel to win a £1,000 (US $5,000 in 1910) prize offered by the *Daily Mail*. On 9 July 1909, while based near Calais, on the French coast of the English Channel, Latham officially informed the *Daily Mail* that he intended to cross the Channel by air and claim their prize. Within four days Comte Charles de Lambert, a Franco-Russian aviator, also notified the *Daily Mail* of his intent to cross the Channel and established his base near Calais, bringing two French-built Wright Flyers with him. On 19 July, Latham took off from Cap Blanc-Nez, but after only eight miles his Antoinette IV suffered engine failure and Latham had to make the world's first ditching. The Antoinette's fuselage was undamaged and remained afloat, and Latham and his aircraft were towed ashore by a French torpedo destroyer that was following the flight. The salvage operation damaged the aircraft so badly that a second aircraft, an Antoinette VII, was shipped from the Paris factory on 21 July.

A day later, Louis Bleriot and his Bleriot XI monoplane set up base only about two miles away from Latham. The three contestants had to wait for better weather to fly, but de Lambert damaged one of his Flyers during a test flight shortly after Bleriot's arrival and decided to withdraw from the competition. At about 0300 in the morning of 25 July 1909, Bleriot's crew noticed a break in the weather, awakened him, prepared the aircraft, and waited for dawn to make the attempt if favorable conditions continued. Latham's crew slept through the night while Bleriot took off just at dawn (0441) to begin the first successful crossing of the English Channel by airplane. Levavasseur woke up just in time to see Bleriot's monoplane leaving the French coast and he rushed to wake Latham and his crew, hoping it was possible to catch Bleriot or overtake him should he not succeed in crossing. At the time the Antoinette VII was in position atop the cliffs and was unable to take off in the now gusty winds and rain. Flying without the aid of a compass Bleriot deviated to the east of his intended course, but nonetheless saw the English coast to his left. Fighting blustery winds he made a heavy landing, nearly collapsing the undercarriage and shattering one blade of the propeller, but he was unhurt and on English soil. The flight had taken 36.5 minutes and had made Bleriot a celebrity, immediately resulting in numerous orders for his aircraft. The aircraft never flew again and was quickly repaired and put on display at Selfridge's Department Store in London, and was later displayed outside the offices of the French newspaper *Le Matin*; eventually it was bought by the Musee des Arts et Metiers in Paris. On 27 July, Latham made a second attempt to cross the Channel. He was within minutes of Dover when engine failure again forced him into the sea, seriously damaging the aircraft, and Latham suffered severe lacerations to his forehead. For the next two years he competed at aviation meets throughout Europe and America, setting records and winning prizes, earning him celebrity on both sides of the Atlantic flying the Antoinette monoplane.

Between 1909 and the beginning of WWI, Bleriot manufactured about 900 aircraft; most were variations of the Type XI model. Bleriot monoplanes and Voisin-type biplanes and its Farman derivatives ruled the pre-war aircraft market, despite safety concerns. From 1910, Bleriot and five other European aircraft builders were involved in a five-year legal battle with the Wright brothers over the latter's wing warping patents, but the Wrights' claim was dismissed in French and German courts. From 1913, Bleriot's aviation activities were handled by Bleriot Aeronautique, based at Suresnes, which continued to design and produce aircraft up to the nationalization of most of the French aircraft industry in 1937, when it was absorbed into SNCASO. (Note: Bleriot was the first person in France to gain a pilot's license and was followed by the American Glenn Curtiss and Leon Delagrange.)

Hubert Latham and his Antoinette IV suffered engine failure on his Channel crossing and Latham had to make the world's first ditching.

Louis Bleriot made the first successful crossing of the English Channel on 25 July 1909 in his Bleriot monoplane to become Europe's first aviation celebrity.

1910: DOUBLE CROSSING OF THE CHANNEL: CHARLES ROLLS

On 2 June 1910, Charles Rolls became the first pilot to make a non-stop double crossing of the English Channel, flying his Wright *Flyer* for ninety-five minutes. His flight included the first east-bound aerial crossing of the English Channel, from Swingfield Downs, Kent, to Sangatte, France, returning to Eastchurch, Kent, for which Rolls was awarded the Gold Medal of the Royal Aero Club. Together with Henry Royce he co-founded the Rolls-Royce automobile manufacturing company, which would later develop the incomparable Rolls-Royce aero engine. On 12 July 1910, thirty-two-year-old Rolls was the first Briton killed in a powered aviation accident when the tail of his Wright *Flyer* broke off during a flying display held at Southbourne, England.

Charles Rolls, first return crossing of the English Channel

1910: FIRST PASSENGER TO CROSS THE ENGLISH CHANNEL: JOHN MOISANT AND ALBERT FILEUX

On 23 August 1910, American John Moisant flew across the English Channel to complete the first flight with a passenger, his mechanic Albert Fileux. Moisant took off in the face of a gale but made the trip in thirty-seven minutes at an average height of between 300 and 400 ft. High winds and hail drove him to land at Deal, a few miles north of his intended landing point at Dover.

John Moisant (R) and Albert Fileux

1912: FIRST WOMAN TO CROSS THE CHANNEL: HARRIETT QUIMBY

On 16 April 1912, American Harriett Quimby took off from Dover, England, en route to Calais, France, and made the flight in 59 minutes, landing on a beach about twenty-five miles from Calais. She had become the first woman to pilot an aircraft across the English Channel, but her accomplishment received little media attention due to the sinking of the *RMS Titanic* the day before. On 1 July 1912, Quimby flew in the Third Annual Boston Aviation Meet at Squantum, Massachusetts, and flew out over Boston Harbor in her new two-seat Bleriot monoplane with passenger, William Willard, the organizer of the event and father of aviator Charles Willard. When she returned and circled the airfield at 1,500 ft. the aircraft unexpectedly pitched forward and Willard and Quimby were ejected from their seats and fell to their deaths.

NOTE: On 2 April 1912, Eleanor Trehawke Davies was actually the first woman to fly across the Channel, albeit as a passenger, flying with British pilot, Gustav Hamel, to whom Quimby had earlier confided her desire to be the first woman to cross the Channel.

1910: CROSSING THE ALPS: JORGE (GEO) CHAVEZ

After the English Channel was crossed, the crossing of the Alps became European aviation's next great challenge. Franco-Peruvian Jorge Chavez received his pilot's license at Henry and Maurice Farman's school of aviation and first flew in Reims on 28 February 1910. He then participated in several aviation competitions throughout France and Europe. On 8 August, he flew his Bleriot monoplane to Blackpool, England, where he climbed to a notable altitude of 5,405 ft., and on 6 September, climbed to 8,700 ft. over Issy, France. After these successes Chavez believed his Bleriot could gain enough altitude to be the first to cross the Alps and win the $20,000 prize offered by the Aero Club of Italy. As part of the Crossing Alps Gran Prix he took off from Ried-Brig, Switzerland, on 23 September 1910, and made his way through the Simplon Pass; fifty-one minutes later he arrived at Domodossola, Italy, on the other side of the pass, but his plane crashed on landing. The severely injured Chavez suffered for four days before dying of massive blood loss. According to his friend and fellow aviator Juan Bielovucic, his dramatic last words were, "Higher. Always higher."

Harriett Quimby

1913: FIRST CHANNEL CROSSING AND RETURN WITH A PASSENGER: GUSTAV HAMEL

In April 1913, Gustav Hamel made the first cross-channel return flight carrying a passenger: Frank Dupree, an *Evening Standard* journalist. Hamel disappeared over the English Channel on 23 May 1914, while returning from Villacoublay flying a new Morane-Saulnier monoplane he was to compete with in the Aerial Derby the same day.

Jorge Chavez (above) in his Bleriot for take-off and his fatal crash (below).

3
EARLY AND YEARLY AIR MEETS AND RACES

1909: THE PRIX DE LAGATINERIE: THE FIRST AIR RACE

The Prix de Lagatinerie, held at the Port-Aviation Airport south of Paris on 23 May 1909, was arguably the first heavier-than-aircraft air race. The event was widely publicized in newspapers and on posters that encouraged an estimated crowd of between 30,000 and 60,000 to gather, expecting to see the most famous aviators compete for the 5,000 Franc prize. The prize was to be awarded to the pilot who covered ten laps of a 1.2 km (0.75 mile) course marked by two pylons 600 meters apart in the shortest time, and if no one completed the full course—which was not unexpected—the winner would be decided by the longest distance covered. Only four pilots entered the race: two started and no one was able to get into the air even long enough to fly past one pylon. Non-starter contestant Leon Delagrange made a second effort after his Voisin experienced broken elevator controls. Delagrange got approval from a local flying school to use one of their Voisins on the condition that he paid 4,000 Francs of the prize money to the LNA if he won. Delagrange managed to fly almost five laps, covering 5,800 m (3.6 miles) in 10:19 minutes at an average speed of 33.75 km/h (21 mph).

The Prix de Lagatinerie: Leon Delagrange

1909: GRANDE SEMAINE D'AVIATION DE LA CHAMPAGNE: THE FIRST INTERNATIONAL AIR RACE

The Grande Semaine d'Aviation de la Champagne (Champaign's Grand Week of Aviation) was a seven-day aviation meet held near Reims, France, 22–29 August 1909. The Grande Semaine was sponsored by many of the leading champagne producers, including Moet et Chandon and Mumm, who offered six prizes of 50,000, 25,000, and 10,000, and three prizes of 5,000 Francs. It is considered the first international public flying event and denoted the coming of age of heavier-than-air aviation, as nearly all of the leading aviators of the time took part. The event was viewed by a huge crowd estimated to be as many as 250,000 that packed into large grandstands constructed for the event on the grounds. A row of sheds to accommodate the aircraft and an area intended for taking off and landing were constructed in front of the grandstands, opposite which was the timekeeper's hut, provided with a signaling system to indicate to the spectators which event was under way. The 10 km (6.2 mile) course was rectangular and marked by four pylons, and was mostly over nearby farmland on the Betheny Plain. The fields were to be cleared of crops to expedite forced landings, but on race day many fields still had standing crops and many more had sheaves of drying wheat and barley, a hazard for emergency landings which were to occur often during the week.

Grand Prix de Champagne et la Ville de Reims

The competition for this award resulted in the world record for distance being broken three times in three days, with the prize eventually being won by Henri Farman with a flight of 180 km (110 miles) flying a Farman III biplane. Farman eventually landed because the competition was stopped at the mandatory 1930 hours and any distance flown after that time was not valid.

Prix du Tour de Piste

The Circuit Prize of 7,000 and 3,000 Francs for the fastest single lap was held by Louis Bleriot flying his *Type XII* monoplane with a speed of 76.95 kph (47.8 mph).

Prix des Passager

A single prize of 10,000 Francs given to the aviator whose aircraft carried the most passengers over one lap (in case two contestants carried the same number of passengers the prize was awarded to the fastest). Henri Farman won by being the only pilot to carry two passengers.

Prix de l'Altitude

The 10,000 Francs prize for altitude was won by Hubert Latham flying an *Antoinette VII* with an altitude of 155 m (509 ft.)

GORDON BENNETT TROPHY

The Gordon Bennett Trophy was the most prestigious event of the *Champagne* meet. After the success of his balloon competition, which had become the most important prize for ballooning, tycoon Gordon Bennett—publisher of the *New York Herald*—announced a competition for powered aircraft in December 1908. Like Michelin, Bennett enlisted the Aero Club de Franc (AeCF) to administer and formulate the rules. Held on the last day of the event, the race consisted of a time trial over two laps of the 10 km (6.25 miles) circuit, rather than a direct race, and each nation was allowed three entrants. The Sunday morning qualification trials for the French team were hampered by poor weather conditions, with the most successful competitor, Eugene Lefebvre, flying a French-built Wright biplane, narrowly failing to complete two laps of the course. The only other pilot to make a successful flight was Louis Bleriot, and the third place was later given to Hubert Latham, flying an *Antoinette* monoplane, due to his performance in trials for the Prix de la Vitesse held later that day. Other nations were represented by the American aviator Glenn Curtiss and Brit George Cockburn flying a French Farman III biplane, while the authorized Italian and Austrian entries did not appear. On the last day of the event Curtiss made the initial flights, first making an attempt for the Circuit Prize and lowering the record to 7:55.4 minutes. Encouraged by this, he then made his attempt for the Trophy, completing the two laps in 15:50.4 minutes. Cockburn made the next attempt, but was unable to complete one lap. Lefebvre then made the first attempt by the French team, only managing a time of 20:47.6 minutes. Flying next, Latham's time was 16:32 minutes. Bleriot, flying last, flew a first lap time in the same time as Curtiss' second (faster) lap, but during the second round he was hindered by a squall and his total time was 15:56.1 minutes. The premier event, the first Gordon Bennett Trophy competition, was won by Glenn Curtiss in his *Reims Racer*, who beat second place finisher Louis Bleriot by five seconds and broke the 50 mph barrier, setting a new speed record of 52.6 mph.

After Curtiss' slim victory over Bleriot, spectators were next anticipating an exciting thirty kilometer race in the Grand Prix de la Vitesse for the fastest time over three laps of the circuit. The propeller on Bleriot's *Type XII* monoplane experienced an in-flight structural failure, forcing him to make an immediate forced landing that somersaulted the aircraft onto its back. The fuel tank ruptured in the crash and burst into flames from which Bleriot was able to escape with only his clothes catching on fire. The close call probably caused Bleriot to reconsider flying, as he seldom flew competitively after Reims. Curtiss was named "Champion Air Racer of the World." Under the rules of the Trophy Curtiss' victory meant the next race would be held in America.

The Grande Semaine d'Aviation de la Champagne was the first international air race and would become commonly referred to as the Reims Air Race of 1909. It was considered a great success and an important milestone for heavier-than-air craft, making the public aware of the airplane as a viable flying machine with impressive memorable flights such as Farman's 112-mile flight, Curtiss' exciting battle with Bleriot in the Gordon Bennett Cup, and Latham's altitude record. Bleriot's twenty-two-mile Channel crossing record was far surpassed in only a month.

Glenn Curtiss: "Champion Air Racer of the World"

GORDON BENNETT CUP: AFTER 1909

The Bennett Cup competitions were not a direct race but a time trial, with competitors taking off separately. As aircraft became faster and their engines more reliable, the distance to be covered was increased each year. The 1914 race was to have been held at Reims 19–28 September, but was canceled due to the outbreak of WWI. There was no contest in 1919, but the competition was resumed in 1920.

BENNETT COMPETITION WINNERS

Location	Winning Pilot	Aircraft Type	Distance	Time	Speed
1909 Reims, France	Glenn Curtiss	Curtiss No. 2	20 km (12 miles)	15:50.6 m	75.27 km/h (46.77 mph)
1910 Belmont Park, NY	Claude Grahame-White	Bleriot XI	100 km (62 miles)	1:01: 4.74 h	98.23 km/h (61.04 mph)
1911 East-church, UK	Charles Weymann	Nieuport II	150 km (93 miles)	1:11: 36.2 h	125.69 km/h (78.10 mph)
1912 Clearing, IL	Jules Vedrines	Deperdussin Monocoque	200 km (124 miles)	1:10:56 h	169.7 km/h (105.4 mph)
1913 Reims, France	Maurice Prevost	Deperdussin Monocoque	200 km (124 miles)	59:45:45.6m	200.8 km/h (124.8 mph)
1920 Orleans/Etampes	Joseph Sadi-Lecointe	Nieuport 29	300 km (186 miles)	1:06 :17.2 h	271.55 km/h (168.73 mph)

1910: THE SECOND GORDON BENNETT RACE

When Glenn Curtiss won the first Gordon Bennett Race, according to the Bennett by-laws the US was obligated to stage the next race, which was scheduled 22–30 October at Belmont Park, Long Island, New York. It was wrongly billed as the "first air race in America"; the first was the Dominguez, California, race during January 1910 (Lesseps, Roland Garros, Edmund Audemars, and others represented France, while Claude Grahame-White represented England). The late October dates for the meet to be held on an island adjacent to the Atlantic Ocean all but guaranteed cold and windy conditions. The meet was to be flown in two parts: the Bennett Race for the $5,000 prize and the "Statue of Liberty Race" for the Thomas Fortune Ryan $10,000 prize. Alfred Le Blanc, Hubert Latham, Jacques De Lesseps, Grahame-White, James Radley, Alec Ogilvie, and William McCardle were among the English fliers participating. Glenn Curtiss, John Moisant, Armstrong Drexel, Walter Brookins, Frank Coffyn, Archibald Hoxsey, Ralph Johnstone, Duval La Chappelle, and other capable pilots flew for America.

This Bennett Race was to be twenty laps around the 5 km (3.1 mile) pylon-marked course for the $5,000 prize. Claude Grahame-White of England, who flew first in his new, modified French 100 hp Bleriot XIbis monoplane, recorded a total time of 1:10:04.74 and a speed of 61 mph, which was a new world record for that distance. Next aloft was Frenchman Alfred LeBlanc, flying a stock Bleriot XI. Each of his lap times was faster than Grahame-White's and all were much more consistent; by the end of lap 19, LeBlanc was leading by more than five minutes and had broken every world's record from 5–100 km.

Claude Grahame-White, winner of the 1910 Bennett Trophy

But then LeBlanc ran out of gas on the last lap, and while making a dead-stick landing he crashed into a telegraph pole, demolishing his airplane but escaping with minor injuries. Almost an hour behind in second place was American John Moisant, whose Bleriot XI averaged 33.7 mph. Walter Brookins flew the new Wright Baby Grand, a clipped wing V-8 powered Flyer. While flying past the grandstand during the official timing the aircraft lost half its cylinders and crashed, ejecting Brookins and leaving him with bruised ribs. Ralph Johnstone shattered the world's record for altitude by flying to 9,714 ft. in a later competition.

THE "STATUE OF LIBERTY RACE"

The race was to be flown from Belmont Horse Race Track over the New York City shoreline and around the Statue of Liberty. Wilbur Wright told reporters he was "strongly opposed to flying over cities. While it is an aviator's own business whether he decides or not to risk his own neck, he has no right to endanger the lives of others." Only three pilots entered the race: Count Jacques de Lesseps, a French aristocrat; Claude Grahame-White, who had just won the Bennett International Aviation Cup the day before; and American John Moisant. Count de Lesseps took off first and completed the course in forty-one minutes, followed by Grahame-White, once again piloting his 100 hp Bleriot monoplane. The Englishman had the best time, completing the course in 35:21 minutes and seeming to have won, but then John Moisant surprised him at the last moment. Earlier in the week Moisant had heavily damaged his Bleriot IX and was attempting to purchase another aircraft even as Grahame-White was on his way to an apparent victory. At the last minute Moisant acquired a 50 hp Bleriot and took off, trying to best Grahame-White's time. Using a new navigational system and by flying a more direct route than the Englishman, Moisant, much to the delight of the American multitude below, returned in 34:38 minutes, bettering Grahame-White's mark by forty-three seconds and becoming the meet's star. Afterward, Grahame-White protested Moisant's victory because the American had started the race twenty-one minutes after the close of allowable start times. The mostly American Meet officials nevertheless sided with Moisant, but after appealing his case all the way to the Federation Aeronautique Internationale (aviation's main ruling body at the time), Grahame-White finally realized his victory when the FAI reversed the Belmont Park Meet officials' decision in 1912. Grahame-White collected the race's prize money and an additional $500 in interest.

Eventual Statue of Liberty Race winner Claude Grahame-White flying over Miss Liberty.

1911: THE THIRD GORDON BENNETT RACE

The 1911 race was held in July at Eastchurch, England, and provided the closest finish in any race to date. The surprise winner was Charles Weymann, an American born in Haiti whose clean 100 hp Nieuport completed the twenty-five laps of the 6 km (3.7 mile) course in 1:11:36.2 hours at an average speed of 78.11 mph. Close behind was Bennett's 1910 hard-luck pilot Alfred LeBlanc, flying his Bleriot in 1:13:40 hours at 75.91 mph. Third was Edward Nieuport flying one of his own airplanes, finishing in 1:14:37.2 hours at 74.98 mph. Gustave Hamel's Bleriot was the first ever race-modified aircraft, having severely clipped wings that theoretically made the aircraft faster by reducing the effectiveness of the wing warping roll control. Hamel failed to complete his first pylon turn and crashed, demolishing his airplane, but he escaped with no serious injuries.

American Charles Weymann, winner of the 1911 Bennett Cup.

1912: THE FOURTH GORDON BENNETT RACE

The second Gordon Bennett Race to be held in America occurred on 9 September at Clearing, near today's Midway Airport in Chicago. The race was to be thirty laps over the 4.14-mile course. The French team entered the very promising Bechereau Deperdussin Racers, powered by the 160 hp Gnome 14-cylinder, air-cooled rotary engine. They were considered many years ahead of their time due to their new and innovative airframe streamlining. The American team entered the Defender, which was an improved Bleriot, but it was not ready in time, and only Paul Peck and his Columbia biplane remained in the competition, though at take-off it had a flat tire on the starting line. As expected, the French Deperdussin monoplanes completed the race with a clean sweep. Jules Vedrines finished the course in 1:01:51 hours and became the first pilot to average over 100 mph with a record speed of 105.5 mph. Maurice Prevost was second in an identical Deperdussin at

1:15:25 hours at 103.8 mph. Andre Frey, flying a Hanriot monoplane, dropped out late in the race while averaging 94 mph. Led by the Deperdussins, speed was fast becoming the preserve of the French, who would set most of the important world records over various distances.

Emile Vedrines with his Deperdussin won the 1912 Bennett Cup.

1913: THE FIFTH BENNETT RACE

The race was held on 29 September at Reims, site of the historic first Bennett Race in 1909. The race consisted of twenty laps over the 10 km (6.2 mile) course for a total of 124.25 miles. After Great Britain, Germany, and the US had withdrawn only Belgian Henri Crombez remained in an all-French field. Eight of the nine entries flew monoplanes, and the Gnome-powered Deperdussins were again expected to dominate the race. But it became a very close race, with Maurice Prevost winning at a record 124.78 mph to become the first to fly over 200 km in less than one hour. Just a minute behind him was Emile Vedrines—brother of Jules—flying a Ponnier at 122.53 mph, and another minute behind him was Eugene Gilbert in a second Deperdussin at 118.51 mph. Crombez, in a third Deperdussin, finished fourth at 106.73 mph. The superiority of these streamlined monoplanes was proven beyond a doubt.

1913 Bennett Cup Competitors (L-R) Guillaume Busson, Rene Vidart, Jules Vedrines, and winner Maurice Prevost.

1914: THE SIXTH BENNETT RACE

The 1914 race was to have been held at Reims 19–28 September, but was canceled due to the outbreak of WWI.

1920: THE FIRST POSTWAR BENNETT RACE

There was no postwar contest in 1919, but it was resumed in 1920. Because of the increasing speed of aircraft, unlike the races held before the war that were over short courses marked by pylons, the competition was held between two points 50 km (31 miles) apart between the French towns Orleans and Etampes. Joseph Sadi-Lecointe, flying a Nieuport-Delage, won in a time of 1:06:17 hours, while another French aviator, Bernard de Roumanet, finished second with a time of 1:39:7 hours. After the war Sadi-Lecointe became a test pilot for Nieuport-Delage, flying their aircraft in a number of races and also using them to set seven speed and three altitude records. His win of the 1920 Gordon Bennett race gave permanent possession of the trophy to the Aero Club de France. During WWII he was a member of the French Resistance and was tortured to death by the Gestapo in Paris 15 July 1944.

Joseph Sadi-Lecointe flying a Nieuport-Delage to Bennett Cup victory in the resumed postwar 1920 Bennett Cup Race.

POMMERY CUP

The Pommery Cup was awarded with a 7,500 Franc prize given twice a year on 30 April and on 31 October (1911–1913) by Pommery Champagne to the aviator who traveled the greatest straight line distance in one day at a speed of not less than 50 km/h between the award dates.

Pommery Cup Winners

- 28 March 1911: Julcs Vedrines: Paris to Poitiers (Morane, 50 hp Gnome engine), 293 km
- 22 May 1911: Jules Vedrines: Paris to Angouleme (Morane, 50 hp Gnome engine), 400 km
- 30 April 1912: Rene Bedel: Villacoublay to Biarritz (Morane, 80 hp Gnome engine), 750 km
- 6 October 1912: Pierre Daucourt: Valenciennes to Biarritz (Borel, 50 hp Gnome engine), 852 km
- 27 April 1913: Maurice Guillaux: Biarritz to Kollum (Clement-Bayard 50 hp Clerget rotary engine), 1,229 km
- 10 June 1913: Marcel Brindejonc Moulinais: Villacoublay to Warsaw (Morane, 80 hp Gnome engine), 1,382 km. During this race Maurice Guillaux, a previous winner of the Pommery Cup, claimed to have covered 1,386 km, but this distance was not ratified after de Moulinais appealed: the claim was the result of a "mistake" over where Guillaux claimed he had landed and he was banned from flying in the competition for ten years.

Several Pommery Cup flights were made in early 1914, but pilot and public interest was fading, as the public was more interested in aerobatics or actual races held over several days. It was the outbreak of the war that ended the Pommery competition.

1910: FIRST US CROSS-COUNTRY FLIGHT: GLENN CURTISS

When the 1910 flying season began, Glenn Curtiss was looking forward to flying again after his previous year's triumph at Reims. To compete for the $10,000 prize that Joseph Pulitzer's *New York World* was offering Curtiss and his staff built the *Hudson Flier*, a new aircraft with a larger airframe and longer wingspan than his Reims aircraft and was equipped with flotation gear to land safely on water. The *New York World* contest called for flying 152 miles (245 km) along the Hudson River from Albany, New York, to Governors Island in New York City within a twenty-four hour period with two landings allowed during the flight. On Sunday morning, 29 May 1910, hundreds of thousands of people congregated along the Hudson River to watch Curtiss fly past to New York City. He took off from Albany, and after flying eighty-seven miles made one planned landing in an open field near Poughkeepsie, New York, where he had to solicit oil and gas from motorists. After an oil leak threatened to freeze the engine Curtiss was forced to make an unplanned landing on a large lawn in Manhattan. The lawn was part of the estate of leather merchant William Isham, whose daughter sent a servant to retrieve gas and oil from their boathouse. At 1142, Curtiss took off from the Isham lawn and once again headed west for the Hudson River, again cheered by thousands of spectators lining its shores. In New York Harbor he circled the Statue of Liberty, then landed on Governor's Island at almost exactly noon after flying 2:51 hours, averaging nearly 52 mph. On the flight he carried the first piece of US airmail, a letter from the mayor of Albany to the mayor of New York City. Curtiss received the $10,000 cash prize, permanent possession of the *Scientific American* trophy, and wide public acclaim, as the *New York Times* dedicated six full pages with photos—the most the newspaper had ever devoted to a single news event. After this well-publicized success, Curtiss built aircraft for the US Army and Navy, and during the years leading up to WWI, the Curtiss Aeroplane and Motor Company led the way in advances in naval aviation. Curtiss' civil and military aircraft were predominant in the interwar and WWII eras, and the Curtiss Aeroplane Company would become the world's largest aircraft manufacturer during the war. Sadly, in 1930, while having surgery for appendicitis, Curtiss suffered a small cerebral blood clot that ended his life at fifty-two.

Glenn Curtiss, First US Cross Country Flight

1910: HARVARD-BOSTON AERO MEET

After the Bennett/Statue of Liberty Races of 1910, the next significant American airshow was the Harvard-Boston Aero Meet held 3–13 September 1910 at Harvard Aviation Field in Atlantic, Massachusetts. It was the first major air event on the east coast and offered aviators more than $90,000 in prizes and appearance fees. Both the Wright Brothers and Glenn Curtiss exhibition teams made presentable showings, but it was the Englishman Claude Grahame-White who won several contests, including the speed race. He also won prizes for the most accurate landing and the shortest take-off. He gave a bombing demonstration by dropping plaster-of-Paris "bombs" on a mock warship. The most prestigious event he won was the thirty-three mile race from Squantum, Massachusetts, around Boston Light, and back. His winner's purse was $10,000 of the approximately $22,000 in prizes he won during the meet.

Claude Grahame-White won the thirty-three mile 1910 Harvard-Boston Aero Meet.

1910: DOMINGUEZ, CALIFORNIA: THE FIRST AMERICAN AIR MEET

Shortly after the Reims airshow Charles Willard and Roy Knabenshue, the very first pilots that Glenn Curtiss taught to fly, resolved to stage the first air show in America during winter 1909–1910, choosing Southern California, as it was their winter aerial demonstration headquarters. After receiving a pledge of participation from Glenn Curtiss, Knabenshue enlisted Dick Ferris, a Los Angeles athletic promoter and balloon enthusiast, who then solicited local businesses and formed an organizing committee. Railroad magnate Henry Huntington's pledge of $50,000 gave final credence to the event, which was to be held in Los Angeles 10–20 January 1910. A field near Santa Anita Park was initially considered as the site of the race, but obstructions such as tall trees led them to select Dominguez Field, atop a small hill outside Los Angeles. Once the site was selected promotion of the meet began and grandstands with a capacity of between 50,000 and 60,000 were erected; an aviators' camp was also built nearby.

Organizers invited pilots of monoplanes, biplanes, balloons, and dirigibles, and drew many famous aviators, most of whom were American. Glenn Curtiss was the most well-known, having won the Reims race over European champion Louis Bleriot and being named "Champion Air Racer of the World." To highlight the event's "international" hype, French aviator Louis Paulhan, a celebrity from the 1909 Reims Meet, was invited to fly his Farman biplane and was guaranteed an appearance fee. Other participants included Americans Knabenshue and Willard, Lincoln Beachey, Charles Hamilton, Howard Warfield Gill, and Clifford Harmon, and Frenchman Didier Masson. The Wright brothers did not fly in the meet, but were there with their lawyers in an attempt to prevent Paulhan and Curtiss from flying with ailerons that infringed on Wright patents; nonetheless, Paulhan and Curtiss flew their infringing aircraft. Forty-three flying machines entered; sixteen showed up but not all flew.

An estimated 254,000 tickets were sold and gate receipts were roughly $137,500. During the event streetcars ran to Dominguez Field every two minutes from the Pacific Electric Station in Los Angeles. The great crowd turn-out, averaging more than 20,000 spectators per day, included then thirteen-year-old Jimmy Doolittle, who saw his first airplane, and nine-year-old Florence Lowe, later known as "Pancho" Barnes, who was brought by her grandfather, aviation pioneer Thaddeus Lowe. By the end of the event the backer announced a profit of $60,000 after disbursing the $75,000 cash prize money allotted for competitive events in altitude, speed, and endurance. Aviators competed for the prizes according to a standard procedure in which aviators would first "notify the judges for which prize they were about to compete" and then fly around the 1.61 mile course, always in a counterclockwise direction. Aviators were informed that under threat of a penalty they "must not fly over the grand stand or any place where a crowd is assembled without permission of the judges."

ABOVE / Frenchman Louis Paulhan dominated the 1910 Dominguez Air Meet in his Farman.

LEFT / Glenn Curtiss flying his Wright patent infringing biplane at the Dominguez Meet.

All flights taking place between 1400 and sunset counted toward scoring for prizes, and aviators were encouraged to fly as many times per day as possible, and to make as many record attempts in the competitive events as possible. In fact, if a contestant did not make one complete circuit every day between 1400 and 1700, those contestants would be penalized five percent of their best time for the prize. Only the best time was counted during the judging at the end of the meet. Ballooning competitions and events were also held in the Los Angeles suburb Huntington Park throughout the week. These events included attempts to reach a new altitude record and passenger flights.

The following prizes (1910 $US) were offered at the air meet:

$10,000 for "the machine which, carrying two or more persons, breaks all world's records for duration, altitude, distance, and speed."
$7,500 for "the machine making the best general average in all events."
$5,000 for setting a new height record
$5,000 for setting a new endurance record.

Paulhan dominated the meet, winning $19,000 in prize money for the following performances:

New flight endurance record, carrying a passenger almost 110 miles in his Farman III biplane in 1:49 hours.
New altitude record of approximately 4,164 ft.

He also performed several aerial feats during the week and carried US Army 1Lt. Paul Beck aloft on 19 January to demonstrate one of the first tests of aerial bomb dropping.*

Glenn Curtiss set a new air speed record of approximately 55 mph and in all, he won approximately $6,500.

The long term effect of the meet was its introduction of aviation to a completely new and enthusiastic West Coast audience and the resultant quick expansion of aircraft building and pilot training there.

1910: MOISANT'S INTERNATIONAL AVIATORS LTD.: THE BIRTH OF BARNSTORMING

During a time when aviation became especially popular in Europe, flying in America was basically limited to a few local aviators who performed at county fairs and carnivals. The first earnest attempt to organize and promote performances at local events was a direct result of the 1910 Bennett/Statue of Liberty Meet. John Moisant, the popular and still de facto winner of the Statue of Liberty Race, gathered a group of race contestants who had no real prospects to afford their passion to fly and joined Moisant's "Flying Circus," a la Barnum and Bailey. Moisant hired a special train equipped with a built-in repair shop to transport his entourage, including a tent, a dozen roustabouts, a dozen ticket sellers and press agents, a dozen airplanes and their mechanics, and eight "death-defying" aviators. The nomadic troupe left New York, opened in Richmond, and continued on to Chattanooga, Memphis, Tupelo, New Orleans, Dallas and Fort Worth, and Oklahoma City; then back to Texas with shows in Waco, Temple, Houston, San Antonio, and El Paso; across the border to Monterrey, Mexico City, and Vera Cruz; and finally to Havana, Cuba. Publicity-minded Moisant chose the last day of the year to set a new Michelin non-stop distance mark that had been set only the day before when Frenchman Maurice Tabuteau flew 362.7 miles in 7:48:21 hours flying a Farman biplane. To begin the attempt Moisant flew a short hop to a nearby racetrack, but when he was landing a gust upended the Bleriot's tail and Moisant was pitched forward and out of the aircraft; he broke his neck and was killed. After Moisant's death his older brother, Alfred, took control of the show and successfully toured Mexico and Cuba; when the tour was over the show disbanded early in 1911. Moisant's enterprise is considered the birth of barnstorming.

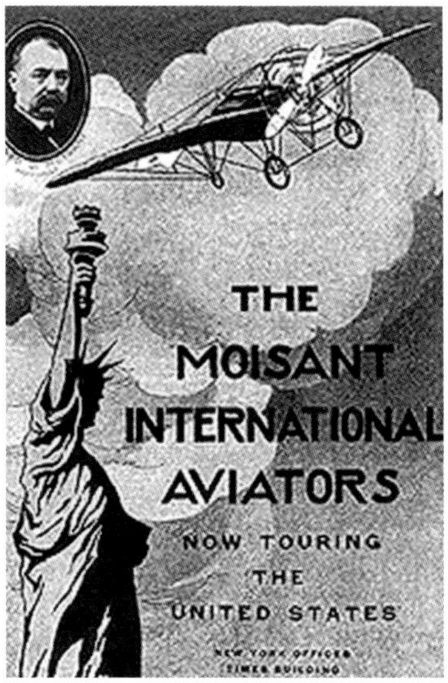

1910: CIRCUIT DE L'EST

The *Circuit de l'Est* was sponsored by French news magazine *Le Matin*, which offered a huge 100,000 Francs prize to the pilot who could complete the full circle from Paris to Troyes (130 km/81 miles), to Nancy (150 km/93 miles), to Mezieres (125km/78 miles), to Douai (65 km/40 miles), to Amiens, and return to Paris (110 km/68 miles)—an extremely long 805 km (503 mile) course. Only two years previous this distance would have been impossible, but now it seemed a distinct possibility, and soon thirty-five pilots entered. Along the route a series of individual

*See *U.S. Aerial Armament in World War II, the Ultimate Look. Volume 2: Bombs, Bombsights, and Bombing* (Schiffer Publishing) for a description of Beck's bombing demonstration.

competitions were also scheduled at the bidding of local sponsors who had scheduled numerous paid admission events and competitions. Each competition (i.e., the longest flight, highest flight, etc.) had its own prize money. The competitors were to arrive at each of the cities within a few hours of each other, followed by an evening of festivities. The winner would be the pilot who completed the greatest number of legs and, in the event of a tie, the prize was awarded to the pilot who achieved the distance in the least time. If a pilot could complete the entire circuit first the prize would be his; if not, then the sum would be half.

At the start from Issy on Sunday, 7 August 1910, instead of the scheduled thirty-five pilots—well known names like Latham, Nieuport, Breguet, Picard, Morane, Leblanc, Sommer, Wallon, and Mamet—only ten were present to start, of which eight would manage to take off. By the second leg to Nancy only three arrived: Albert Leblanc (Farman biplane), Emile Aubrun (Bleriot XI), and Georges Legagneux (Bleriot XI). Day after day, the three pilots arrived at each stop more or less successfully, with Leblanc usually arriving first. Legagneux failed to complete one of the legs in the required time, but continued the following day; he was out of the race for the prize money, but could participate in the lucrative local competitions. Each day the competitions put more stress on the three airplanes and pilots, especially when local pilots were allowed to compete for the prize money, adding to the interest in the event for local crowds. The local competitors, looking for fame and fortune, took big risks to outshine the three race competitors, who in turn also had to up their game for the local prizes and the bigger prize at the completion of the race. As the remaining three flyers left Amiens on the last leg of the Circuit de l'Est, an estimated crowd of 250,000 formed at dawn at Issy to watch Alfred Leblanc's Bleriot come into view and land, and Leblanc was carried away by the crowd. Soon after, Emile Aubrun arrived in his Bleriot to take second place in the competition.

Only Leblanc and Aubrun had completed all of the arduous ten-day circuit, flying the full 805 kilometer distance: Leblanc in 12:01:14 hours, while Aubrun had recorded a time of 13:31:09 hours. Legagneux had only completed four stages of the course, flying 510 km in 17:21:14 hours. Of the other three pilots who had completed the first stage from Paris to Troyes at the beginning (Lindpaintner, Weymann, and Mamet), none had made it past Troyes. Alfred Leblanc became a wealthy man after the ten-day competition, being awarded 100,000 Francs in prize money from *Le Matin* (approximately $550,000 US/£350,000/400,000 Euros). In addition, the aviators won prize money from the afternoon competitions at each of the stops and local aviators, such as Paul de Lesseps and Henri Bregi, joined the Circuit de l'Est to compete in these local competitions, even if they had not completed any of the full legs of the circuit itself on any of the days within the times allotted. Leblanc and Legagneux were the biggest winners, each winning 27,000 Francs during the local competitions. These huge prizes offered by Le Matin, the *Daily Mail*, Michelin, Bennett, and others were enough to lure the aviators of the day to risk their lives for the advance of aviation and aeronautics.

Alfred Leblanc at the Circuit de l'Est

1910: THE LONDON-TO-MANCHESTER RACE: THE FIRST TRUE CROSS-COUNTRY RACE

In 1910, the *London Daily Mail* offered a prize of £10,000 for the pilot who completed the first true air cross-country race of over 185 miles from London to Manchester, England. The first to try was Claude Grahame-White, taking off from London on 23 April 1910 in his Farman biplane. He made his first planned stop at Rugby at just after 0715 and was met by one of his support autos that left London and arrived about ten minutes before he landed. His mechanics serviced the biplane, which subsequently experienced engine problems that forced a landing near Lichfield. High winds made it impossible to continue the flight and the aircraft was further damaged on the ground when it was not tied down and was blown over, then hauled back to London. While Grahame-White's aircraft was being repaired in London, Louis Paulhan had arrived at Dover from the Dominguez Air Show in California. Another contestant, Emile Dubonnet, also officially entered the cross-country contest and was scheduled to take off a few days later. On 27 April 1910, Paulhan's Farman biplane, which was a newer model than Grahame-White's, arrived at Hendon and was assembled in less than eleven hours; at 1720 Paulhan took off for Hampstead Cemetery, his official starting line. Soon after he arrived there he flew on to Harrow and began to follow the tracks of the London and North Western Railway. The LNW Railway Company had whitewashed the tops of its sleeper cars along the route for Paulhan to follow and also supplied a special car carrying Mme. Paulhan and Henry Farman, while other members of the party followed by car.

After spending two days directing the restoration of his Farman Grahame-White wanted to make a test flight earlier in the day, but the huge crowds prevented him from taking off

Louis Paulhan's Farman biplane at the London-to-Manchester Race

and he retired to a nearby hotel. At about 1800, he was made aware that Paulhan had begun his attempt and he decided to immediately pursue; by 1830, he had passed the starting line. Almost an hour later he flew over Leighton Buzzard, just as Paulhan was passing over Rugby. As night approached, Grahame-White landed his Farman in a field near the railway line at Roade, in Northamptonshire. Fifteen minutes later Paulhan reached Lichfield, where at about 117 miles into his journey he ran out of fuel. He managed to land the biplane in a field near Trent Valley railway station. After his Farman was secured for the night Paulhan left to stay overnight at a nearby hotel with Mme. Paulhan and Henry Farman. Meanwhile, Grahame-White landed fifty-seven miles behind Paulhan and stayed at the house of a Dr. Ryan. Both aviators intended to restart at 0300 the following day. More concerned with winning than with the obvious dangers of nighttime flying, Grahame-White took off again at 0230 the next morning in an unprecedented nighttime take-off, guided by the head lamps of his ground support automobiles. Within minutes of becoming airborne he almost crashed, as while he was leaning forward to make himself more comfortable his jacket caught the engine ignition switch and accidentally shut down the engine. He quickly restarted the engine and was able to continue using the lights of railway stations to guide him through the darkness. Within forty minutes he reached Rugby, and at 0350 he passed Nuneaton, but despite making good progress he was carrying a large load of fuel and oil, and his engine was not powerful enough to climb the Farman over the hills ahead. He landed at Polesworth, about 107 miles from London and only ten miles behind the Frenchman, who had not yet resumed his flight. A few minutes later Paulhan, unaware of Grahame-White's progress, resumed his flight. He flew over Stafford and Crewe, and at 0530 landed at Barcicroft Fields—within five miles of the Manchester office of the *Daily Mail*—winning the £10,000 prize after flying 4:12 hours at an average speed of 44 mph. Grahame-White attempted to resume his flight to Manchester and reached Tamworth, but he later abandoned the flight, being forced down after less than two hours by high winds and being overweight. Paulhan repeated the journey in April 1950—the fortieth anniversary of the original flight—this time as a passenger aboard a British jet fighter.

1910: On 2 July 1910, "amateur" flier Clifford Harmon broke all American air endurance records at Mineola, Long Island, New York, flying his Farman biplane for 2:05 hours and covering about sixty-eight miles. Due to high afternoon winds he took off late and only descended in darkness when

Clifford Harmon in his Farman, in which he set a new endurance record.

his fuel ran out. His flight bested Louis Paulhan's 1:58 hours set in Los Angeles in January, but Paulhan was carrying a passenger in his Farman.

1910: In 1909, Maurice Arnold de Forest offered the Baron de Forest Prize of £2,000 to the first Englishman who could fly across the English Channel in an English-built airplane. When Frenchman Louis Bleriot successfully crossed the Channel in July 1909, de Forest doubled the prize to £4,000. On 18 December 1910, Thomas Sopwith flew his Howard-Wright biplane 169 miles (272 km) in 3:40 hours from Kent, England, to Beaumont, Belgium, landing in rough weather that almost threw him out of the cockpit in the days with no seat beats. Sopwith returned by steamer and used the winnings to set up the Sopwith School of Flying in Brooklands.

Thomas Sopwith in his Howard-Wright biplane

1910–1911: FIRST SEAPLANES: HENRI FABRE, HENRI VOISIN, AND GLENN CURTISS

Henri Fabre

French engineer and son of a prominent family of ship owners, Henri Fabre developed the first successful seaplane, the *Hydravion*, which he flew three times on the Etang de Berre, near Marseilles, on 28 March 1910. The *Hydravion's* two wings, which could be furled like sails, were each supported by a single cellular exterior spar and were united by two beams (one above the other), with the pilot seated on the middle of the upper beam. The aircraft was powered by a 50 hp Gnome engine mounted in the rear and it sat on three floats invented by Fabre. The longest of the first day's three flights was 2,700 ft. at a height of 15 ft., but the next day Fabre flew 3.5 miles. On 18 May, Fabre flew about one-half mile at 65 ft., but landed too hard and the aircraft broke up, throwing Fabre into the water unharmed. Glenn Curtiss and Gabriel Voisin used Fabre's floats to develop their own seaplanes. The *Hydravion* was reconstructed and is displayed in the *Musee de l'Air* in Paris.

Fabre Hydravion Seaplane

Henri Voisin

In early 1911, Voisin added Fabre floats to his curious land plane *Canard* (named due to its duck-like shape) per an order by Prince George Bibesco, who intended (but did not) to use it to make a flight across the Black Sea. It was first flown by Maurice Colliex from the water at Issy on 25 April 1911, and landed on the River Seine. Voisin did not delete the wheels, making it the first amphibian. One *Canard* was purchased by the French Navy in March 1912 to equip the seaplane tender *La Foudre*, the world's first seaplane carrier; a second was delivered to the Navy in December 1913.

Voisin Canard Amphibian

Glenn Curtiss

During winter 1910, Curtiss developed a float based on Fabre's design and adapted them to a Model D biplane, enabling him to take off and land on water. On 26 January 1911, he flew the first seaplane from the water in the United States. On 24 February 1911, Curtiss made his first amphibian aircraft demonstration in North Island, California, by taking off and landing on land and water. In July 1911, the US Navy purchased their first aircraft from Curtiss, the A-1 *Triad*, which was primarily a seaplane equipped with retractable wheels, also making it the Navy's first amphibian. Curtiss won the Collier Trophy for designing the revolutionary *Triad*, which was purchased by the navies of Britain, Germany, Russia, and Japan. Curtiss trained the Navy's first pilots and built their first aircraft; he is considered the "Father of Naval Aviation."

Curtiss Triad Amphibian

1910–1914: FIRST MILITARY AVIATION MISSIONS

During 1909, an intensive rivalry developed in France between the Army's Artillery and Engineers; at the time each was developing its own air force. In April, General of the Engineers Pierre Roques formed the first aeronautics unit, and on 9 June 1910, Capt. Marconnet and Lt. Fequant flew from Chilons to Vincennes. That year the French Army took control of aviation and a military pilot's license test was initiated that included a sixty-mile cross-country flight; soon there were thirty-nine pilots available to fly twenty-nine aircraft. The first military maneuvers took place at Picardy using aircraft that included fourteen airplanes and four dirigibles. The Army then sponsored a competition for new designs for more military-oriented aircraft. On 20 August 1909, Lt. Jacob Fickel fired a Springfield rifle from an airplane piloted by Glenn Curtiss at a target on the ground over Sheepshead Bay Speedway, Brooklyn, New York, scoring a hit for the first time a gun was fired from an aircraft. On 22 October 1911, Capt. Carlo Piazza (Italy) made a reconnaissance flight in a Bleriot monoplane, taking off from Tripoli and observing the Turkish army near Benghazi for the first record of an airplane being used for a wartime mission. On 1 November, Lt. Giolio Gavotti and his passenger conducted the first wartime aerial bombardment, bombing Turkish forces in Libya. On 7 June 1912, Capt. Charles Chandler fired the Lewis machine gun from a Wright Model B piloted by Lt. Thomas de Witt Milling at College Park, Maryland, for the first time a machine gun was fired from an airplane. Despite the success of the test, the US Army rejected the gun and inventor Isaac Lewis took it to England, where it became the standard armament on British aircraft. On 30 November 1913, during the Mexican Revolution, American mercenary pilots Dean Ivan Lamb, flying for the Carrancistas (supporters of Venustiano Carranza), and Philip Rader, flying for then-President Victoriano Huerta, exchanged (ineffective) pistol shots over Naca, Mexico, in the world's first aerial combat. On 17 August 1914, Capt. Lewis Goodier tested a bomb dropping device designed by Lt. Riley Scott in a Martin Model T at the Signal Corps Aviation School, North Island, California. On 5 October 1914, French Corp. Louis Quenalt, an observer flying in a Voisin piloted by Sgt. Joseph Frantz, shot down a German Aviatik with a Hotchkiss machine gun for the first air-to-air victory. On 31 October 1914, Lt. Francis Humphreys of the Royal Flying Corps conducted the first recorded strafing attack, firing 250 rounds at a German convoy.

4
1911: A GLORIOUS YEAR

1911: FIRST NON-STOP FLIGHT FROM LONDON TO PARIS: PIERRE PRIER

On 12 April 1911, Pierre Prier, chief instructor of the Bleriot school at Hendon, completed the first non-stop flight between London (Hendon) and Paris (Issy), flying 290 miles in 4:55 hours in a Bleriot XI. During 1911, Prier designed the British and Colonial Aeroplane Company's fast single-seat Bristol Prier monoplanes.

Pierre Prier

JEAN CONNEAU/ANDRE BEAUMONT

French Navy Lt. Jean Conneau had to fly under the pseudonym Andre Beaumont, because as an active member of the French armed forces he was not allowed to use his own name while flying in non-military air events. This deceived no one, as his real name and rank were often mentioned in the newspapers. During 1911, he won three of the year's most demanding races against his great rival, Jules Vedrines: the Paris-Rome Race in May, the first *Circuit d'Europe* (Tour of Europe) on 7 July 1911, and the Daily Mail Circuit of Britain Race (England and Scotland) on 26 July 1911, all while flying a Bleriot XI. He also participated in the ill-fated 1911 Paris to Madrid air race in May the same year.

1911: PARIS TO ROME: ANDRE BEAUMONT

At 0543 on 28 May 1911, twelve pilots of the scheduled twenty entered took off from Buc (Paris) to commemorate the fiftieth anniversary of Italian independence. Andre Beaumont (Conneau) was leading the race on the last day despite having changed his engine in Nice on the fourth day and falling behind Roland Garros. While Beaumont was having his engine changed, Garros would also encounter bad luck after he left Pisa on 31 May, when his engine failed; he was not harmed, but his aircraft's propeller and engine were damaged. Garros had to obtain a new aircraft to continue the race and returned to Pisa by rail. Fortunately, Garros had landed close to a rail line as a train was passing and the engineer stopped the train to offer help to the possibly injured aviator. Garros got on the train and arrived in Pisa at 0820, where he telegraphed for the immediate dispatch of another monoplane, allowing Beaumont to catch up from his engine change in Nice. Beaumont was well rested for the last day's flight to Rome and took off on 1 June at 0350, flying over Genoa and landing at Pisa at 0925, then taking off for Rome and landing at Campo dei Parioli at 1610, after flying over 922 miles in 28:05 hours at 44 mph. Meanwhile, Garros had obtained another aircraft and took off at 1036, landing for the first time in Castiglion della Pescaia to refuel, but he had to land a second time in Palo because of a malfunctioning carburetor, which he was able to quickly correct. He then set out again at 1648 and landed at Parioli at 1720—only 1:10 hours behind Beaumont—but was unable to catch him. Andre Frey would finish third, reaching Rome on 3 June, and Rene Vidart would finish fourth, arriving in Rome on 9 June. Beaumont was awarded 109,000 Liras, Garros 45,000, Frey 23,000, and Vidart 20,000.

Lt. Jean Conneau, flying under the name Andre Beaumont, won the Paris to Rome.

1911 PARIS TO MADRID AIR RACE

After the success of *Le Matin* sponsoring the Circuit de l'Est air race of August 1910, rival French newspaper *Le Petit Parisien* decided to sponsor the three-stage 1911 Paris to Madrid air race. The first stage was to start at Paris Issy and end 400 km (250 miles) to the south-southwest in Angouleme; the challenging second stage from Angouleme was to be flown over the Pyrenees to the Spanish town of San Sebastian on the Atlantic Ocean; and the final leg of 462 km (287 miles) from San Sebastian over the Sierra de Guadarrama Range to Madrid. The first prize was 100,000 Francs, with 30,000 Francs as second prize and 15,000 Francs for third place. An estimated 200–300,000 spectators congregated in the pre-dawn hours of Sunday, 21 May 1911, to watch competitors take off at five-minute intervals beginning at 0500. The first competitor to take off at 0510 was Andre Beaumont (Conneau), followed by Roland Garros and Eugene Gilbert. Soon the other competitors began having problems leaving. Andre Frey took off at 0535, made a circuit of the field, and landed. After some adjustments he tried again at 0600, but damaged a wheel and had to delay his attempt for repairs. The next competitor was not ready, and the following aviator only made a short flight before returning. Then Jules Vedrines immediately returned after take-off to land, as his aircraft was not handling correctly. At this time the crowd had begun to leave the stands and come on to the air field, and in an effort to avoid spectators Vedrines crashed, escaping injury, but severely damaging his aircraft. Le Lasseur de Ranssay took off at 0622, and at 0630 Andre Train taxied to the starting line, but had engine problems soon after take-off. When he returned to land he saw a military detachment crossing the field, and when he turned to avoid them his engine failed; while he was able to fly over the troops, he dropped on an unseen group of spectators on the field, including a number of French officials. Among the casualties were French Prime Minister Ernest Monis, who was unconscious with a broken leg, and French Minister of War Henri Berteaux, who lost an arm and suffered a fatal head injury. Monis' son and millionaire aviation patron Henri Deutsch de la Meurthe were also injured. The crowd panicked, causing more injuries, and the race was suspended. The injured Monis approved the continuance of the race the next day, but only four competitors continued, while the remaining competitors withdrew. Eugene Gilbert, while flying his Bleriot XI over the Pyrenees, was attacked by a large eagle which he repelled by firing his revolver. Andre Beaumont (Conneau) landed his Bleriot XI at Loches for engine maintenance but then crashed on take-off. Andre Frey, flying a Morane-Saulnier, only flew as far as Etampes before damaging his aircraft. The only competitor to finish was the very stressed-out Jules Vedrines, flying a borrowed Morane-Borel monoplane and winning after a total time of 37:30 hours (12:18 hours in the air). He was awarded the $30,000 prize and Spanish King Alfonso bestowed the Cross of the Order of Alfonso XII on Vedrines, who in the best of times was never known for his good disposition.

Andre Train's wrecked aircraft after it crashed into a group of French officials at the Paris to Madrid Air Race.

Jules Vedrines was the only competitor to finish the Paris to Madrid Air Race.

1911: CIRCUIT OF BRITAIN RACE

Immediately after Louis Paulhan's victory in the London to Manchester competition, the *London Daily Mail* announced another £10,000 prize to the pilot flying the fastest time either between London and Edinburgh and return or London and Paris and return. The *Daily Mail* then decided the race would be a tour around Great Britain and that a committee of the Royal

Aero Club would administer the race, to be held between 22 July and 5 August 1911. The 1,010 mile (1,625 km) route of the Circuit of Britain would start and finish at Brooklands, site of the world's first paved auto race track, and fly north from London to Edinburgh, then west to Glasgow, south to Bristol, and finally back to London; it was to be completed in twenty-four hours flying time with eleven compulsory stops. All competing aircraft were required to carry ten official "marks" on important components, such as the tail, wings, and engine, and as many as six of these components could be replaced during the race, but at least four had to be in place at the finish. Repairs were allowed, but a complete re-build was not. The pilots were supplied with a twenty-two foot strip map of the route designed by Claude Grahame-White and Alexander Cross. It displayed the country on either side of the route to a depth of seven miles, compass headings for each leg, spot terrain heights, and a cross-section of the terrain. The original large field of thirty competitors was soon reduced, as nine competitors withdrew before the start for various reasons. Of the twenty-one pilots that started nineteen headed for Hendon—only twenty miles away—and seventeen arrived. After five stages with eleven compulsory stops only four pilots completed the course. The first, and winner of the prize, was Frenchman Andre Beaumont (Conneau), flying a Bleriot and completing the course in 22:28 hours at an average speed of 45 mph on 26 July. Emile Vedrines (1:10 hours behind) was second in a new type—the Deperdussin monoplane—as was the third place plane flown by James Valentine, who arrived on 4 August, followed the next day by Samuel Cody, who was the fourth and last to arrive at Brooklands as the top British finisher.

Lt. Jean Louis Conneau (Beaumont) won the Circuit of Britain.

1911 CIRCUIT OF EUROPE RACE

Le Journal scheduled the Circuit of Europe Race (*Circuit d'Europe*) for 18 June to 7 July, starting in France, going on to Belgium, then to the Netherlands, back to Belgium and France, across to England, and finally back to France for a total of 990 miles/1,600 km. A prize of £8,000 ($90,000) was offered for the entire circuit, with additional prizes for the individual stages:

Paris-Liege: Prize £1600.
Liege-Spa-Liege: Prize £400.
Liege-Utrecht: Prize £1,200, plus £400 for the first Dutch aviator to finish the stage.
Utrecht-Brussels: Prize £1,600 (£1,000 for Paris to Brussels and £600 for Utrecht-Brussels).
Brussels-Roubaix: Prize £600
Roubaix-Calais: Prize £400
Calais-London (Hendon Aerodrome): Prize £2,500 by the standard for the overall time between Paris and London and £400 offered by Shoreham for the daily stage.
London-Calais: Prize £400.
Calais-Paris: Prize £800, in addition to the £8,000 for the whole circuit

Of the forty-two entrants who started, fewer than half even flew to the end of the first leg, with one competitor and one observer killed in a crash at the start. Eight pilots completed the entire circuit back to Paris, though only one was flying an airplane that had not been completely rebuilt or even replaced. Winner Andre Beaumont (Conneau) flew a Bleriot, completing the distance in 58:30 hours at a speed of 17 mph and winning by more than three hours.

Lt. Jean Louis Conneau (Beaumont) won the Circuit of Europe Race.

1911: FIRST US TRANSCONTINENTAL FLIGHTS: THE PIONEERS VIE FOR THE HEARST PRIZE

During 14–25 August 1911, Harry Atwood flew his Wright Model B 1,265 miles from St. Louis to New York in nine days for the longest cross-country flight to date. On 10 October 1910, newspaper tycoon William Randolph Hearst announced a very handsome $50,000 prize to the first pilot who completed a transcontinental flight, either west to east or east to west. He set only three conditions: finish in the original airplane; finish the trip in thirty days or less; and follow a route through Chicago and other cities with Hearst newspapers. Eight pilots entered, but only three actually took off: James Ward, Cal Rodgers, and Robert Fowler.

JIMMIE WARD: DOES NOT GET OUT OF NEW YORK

Jimmie Ward was a star during the brief early period of barnstorming (1910–1914), an era marked by dangerous limitations in airplane materials and designs. During his heyday sensational exhibition flights featuring speed and feats of derring-do helped popularize aviation and promoted its technical development. On 13 September 1911, Ward started the challenge when he flew a Curtiss Model D pusher biplane (the *Hurst Pathfinder*) from Governors Island, New York, toward California. After a series of misdirections, accidents, and mechanical problems the Curtiss' engine failed and Ward crashed in Addison, New York, ending his transcontinental quest on 22 September.

CALBRAITH RODGERS: FIRST TRANSCONTINENTAL FLIGHT (EAST TO WEST)

After only learning to fly in June 1911 at the Wright School in Dayton, Ohio, Calbraith "Cal" Rodgers quickly became a skilled pilot. In August he won the $11,000 World's Grand Endurance Aviation Contest in Chicago by staying in the air for twenty-seven hours at intervals over a nine-day period. Rodgers interested J. Ogden Armour of Armour and Company in sponsoring the flight and named his Wright Model EX *Vin Fiz* after Armour's grape soft drink. The EX was a small, fast, single-seat version of the Wright Model B Flyer powered by a 4-cylinder, 35 hp engine and modified to reduce drag, increasing its airspeed to 55 mph. Wright built the biplane for exhibition flying—the EX stood for "Exhibition." The entrepreneurial Rodgers tried to interest the Post Office Department with the idea of airmail but was rebuffed. Undeterred, he initiated his own transcontinental airmail service and had the help of his wife, the world's first airmail postmistress.

Calbraith "Cal" Rodgers (C) posing with his Wright Model EX, *Vin Fiz*.

Rodgers left from Sheepshead Bay, New York, on 17 September 1911, and the *Vin Fiz* would make seventy intentional and accidental stops crossing the continent, with Rodgers using railroad tracks as his guide and making landings and take-offs anywhere convenient, including roads, parks, and pastures. Rodgers reached Chicago after twenty days and endured the first of a succession of sixteen major and near fatal crashes he was to experience. During the trip the foresighted Rodgers had paid the Wright brothers' mechanic, Charles Taylor, a generous $70 per week to follow the flight by train to maintain the *Vin Fiz* for the next day's flight and repair any damage. Taylor earned his salary not only for maintenance, but for frequent repairs, and sometimes after nearly rebuilding the *Vin Fiz*, allowing Rodgers to continue west. When he reached Kansas City on 14 October, his sponsors directed him to sidetrack his original planned route and fly to the more populated Southwest US. He arrived in Texas on 17 October, and he slowly crossed that state over two weeks, making twenty-nine stops. Before reaching California Rodgers made a stop at the University of Arizona in Tucson, where he met another Hearst Prize contender, Robert Fowler, who was headed east, but with no hope of winning the Prize, since Rodgers was so close to Los Angeles. Rodgers continued on nearly uneventfully until he arrived over California's Imperial Valley, where his engine exploded, its metal fragments wounding him and forcing him to land. After this major repair he reached Pasadena, California, on 5 November in the late afternoon and was greeted by 20,000 people. He was nineteen days too late to claim the Hearst Prize, but on his arrival the de facto US postmaster delivered the first transcontinental US Mail pouch. On 10 December, he landed in Long Beach, California, and ceremoniously taxied his plane into the Pacific Ocean. The feat made him a national celebrity, but he was killed in a crash a few months later during an exhibition in California.

ROBERT FOWLER: SECOND TRANSCONTINENTAL FLIGHT (FIRST WEST TO EAST)

Robert Fowler was the second (to be a non-) contender for the Hearst Prize, leaving San Francisco on 11 September 1911 flying a Wright biplane equipped with a Cole Motor Car Company engine. Fowler's route was to traverse the Donner Pass, but near Colfax high winds overturned his aircraft and stranded the biplane in the treetops. Fowler escaped injury and his aircraft was repaired in ten days. After a number of delays he left Los Angeles on 19 October, and four days later he landed in Tucson, where he met Cal Rodgers, who was headed to Pasadena. Already without any hope of crossing the continent in the required thirty days, Fowler pressed east, taking a month to cross Texas. Twice he had railway men use their railroad handcar as a means to get his Wright into the air after engine problems forced him down near rails: once when he landed in a sandy desert near El Paso, Texas, and once when he landed in a Louisiana rice field. He landed in Jacksonville, Florida, on 8 February 1912, to become the first person to fly coast-to-coast (west-to-east), flying 2,800 miles in 45 days with 66 stops. In April 1913, Fowler was also the first man to fly a non-stop transcontinental flight, flying from the Pacific to the Atlantic across the Isthmus of Panama in 57 minutes.

Robert Fowler using a railway hand car to take off on his way to flying the American Continent from west to east.

MARCH 1911: THE HENDON AND BROOKLANDS LONDON AIRDROME RACE

The owners of Hendon and Brooklands offered a prize for the fastest return flight between their two London aerodromes. On 11 March, four pilots were ready to fly from Hendon. First to take off was Clement Gresswell flying a Bleriot XI, but he was forced down by fog near Staines. Next off was J. V. Martin flying a G. W. Baby, who reached Brooklands, but became hopelessly lost on the return leg, landing at St. Albans (fifteen miles away) before finding Hendon again. Maurice Ducrocq, flying a Farman III, was forced to turn back to Brooklands by fog. Only Gustav Hamel in his Bleriot XI was able to navigate the course without problems, making the 40 mile round trip in 49:35 minutes.

In December 1912, Pierre Verrier (pilot) and Lt. Gilbert Mapplebeck (passenger) began a daring winter flight from Hendon to Brooklands (only 20 miles), but the flight was made into a 45 mph gale. Since their Maurice Farman MF.7 *Longhorn* with its 70 hp Renault engine had a top speed of 55 mph, the flight took 2:10 hours, for an average ground speed of 9 mph! An automobile following them was forced to stop several times to allow the Farman to catch up.

5
1912: NEW MEETS BEGIN, OLD MEETS CONTINUE

HENRI DEUTSCH DE LA MEURTHE

Henri Deutsch de la Meurthe was a French oil tycoon known as the "Oil King of Europe," who recognized that future petroleum sales would be determined by the development of small internal combustion engines, so he encouraged the development of the automobile and aircraft. He and Ernest Archdeacon founded the Aero-Club de France to sponsor the new technologies and used his wealth to create a number of monetary prizes as incentives for aviators to achieve milestones in aviation. He was also active in investing in aircraft research and manufacturing.

In April 1900, Henri offered the Deutsch de la Meurthe Prize (the Deutsch Prize) of 100,000 Francs to the first flying machine capable of flying a round trip from Parc Saint Cloud to the Eiffel Tower in Paris and back in less than thirty minutes. The winner of the prize needed to maintain an average ground speed of at least 22 km/h (14 mph) to cover the round trip distance of 11 km (6.8 miles) in the allotted time. The prize was to be available 1 May 1900–1 October 1903. Alberto Santos Dumont won the prize in his Santos Dumont No. 5 airship on 19 October 1901.

In 1904, Deutsch de la Meurthe, in collaboration with Ernest Archdeacon, established the Grand Prix d'Aviation Prize (the Deutsch-Archdeacon Prize) of 50,000 Francs for the first person to fly a circular one-kilometer course in a heavier-than-air craft, which was won by Henry Farman on 13 January 1908.

Henri Deutsch de la Muerthe (with mustache second from left)

At the end of May 1909, Deutsch de la Meurthe endowed the University of Paris with the huge sum of 500,000 Francs and an annual pension of 15,000 Francs for the creation and maintenance of the Institute Aerotechnique at Saint-Cyr-l'Ecole, which would continue the theoretical research and development of air transport aircraft.

Although an enthusiastic promoter of heavier-than-air flight, de la Meurthe did not make his first flight in an airplane until May 1911, when he was taken for a flight in a Bleriot monoplane piloted by Alfred Leblanc. On 21 May 1911, Deutsch was injured and French Minister of War Maurice Berteaux was killed when a Train monoplane crashed at the beginning of the 1911 Paris to Madrid air race. De la Meurthe died in 1919 at seventy-three.

1912–1914: THE COUPE DEUTSCH DE LA MEURTHE RACE

Emmanuel Helen, 1912 Coupe Deutsch de la Muerthe Race winner

Eugene Gilbert, 1913 Coupe Deutsch de la Muerthe Race winner

The *Coupe Deutsch de la Meurthe* Race was the first of three planned separate series of races sponsored by Henri Deutsch de la Meurthe. The first race was to be a single 124 mile (200 km) lap around Paris on 1 May 1912. The winner was Emmanuel Helen, flying a 70 hp Nieuport, who covered the course in 1:36 hours, averaging 77.85 mph. The second race in the first series of Coupe Deutsch Races was held 27 October 1913, on a course around Paris. The winner was Eugene Gilbert in a Deperdussin Monocoque at an average speed of 101.94 mph. This was the last run for the highly successful make of air racers, as manufacturer Armand Deperdussin was imprisoned for establishing his company with embezzled money and his company then became part of SPAD. The 1914 de la Meurthe Race was suspended due to the war and were then held intermittently 1920–1936, with 20,000 Francs offered first by Deutsch and later by the Aero-Club de France.

MICHELIN CUP

The Michelin Cup, announced in March 1908, was a number of long distance aircraft flight competitions sponsored by French tire manufacturer Michelin, and the administration and determination of the conditions for each year's race were allocated to the Aero Club de France. The major annual prize was a bronze trophy (valued at 10,000 Francs) and a monetary prize of 20,000 Francs. The air club of the winner was also to receive a replica of the trophy if they had not already won one previously. Concurrently, a special prize of 100,000 Francs was offered for the first flight by an aircraft carrying a passenger taking off from either the department of Seine or Seine-et-Oise, flying over the Arc de Triomphe and the Cathedral of Clermont-Ferrand, and landing on the summit of the 1,456 m (4,777 ft.) Puy de Dome within six hours starting from the time at the Arc de Triomphe. Eugene Renaux and Albert Senouque won this prize on 7 March 1911 by landing on the Puy de Dome flying a Maurice Farman biplane. In 1909, a second award, the British Empire Michelin Cup, was announced for flights made by aviators who were citizens of the British Empire flying aircraft of all-British manufacture, after which the original Michelin award became known as the International Michelin Cup.

Michelin Cup

Eugene Renaux and Albert Senouque won the 1911 Michelin Prize by landing on the Puy de Dome.

1908

On 31 December 1908, the International Michelin Cup was won by Wilbur Wright at Le Mans with a flight of 124.7 km (77.5 miles) over a triangular course with two sides of 1 km and a third of 200 m, totaling 2.2 km. The flight had to be completed before sunset and only complete circuits were tallied. Wright took off at 1400 and completed 56 circuits before sunset to set a new world distance record of 124.7 km.

Wilbur Wright wins the 1908 International Michelin Cup.

1909

Henry Farman flew 234.21 km (145.53 miles) in 4:06:25 hours on 3 November at Chalons.

1910

Maurice Tabuteau, flying a Maurice Farman biplane, won with a flight of 584.75 km (363.34 miles) taking 7:48:36 hours flown at Buc on 30 December.

1911

On 8 September, Emmanuel Helen, flying a Nieuport II monoplane, traveled 1,252.8 km (778.5 mi) in 14:07 hours.

1912

The rules for the 1912 competition were charged to a large extent. The flight had to be flown over a three-circuit course, with each circuit different, but each starting from the same point. The first and third circuit, each of about 500 km (310 miles), had three or four compulsory landing areas, and the second circuit, measuring 255 km (158 miles), was to have one or two landing points. Refueling was only permitted at the start of each circuit. The circuits had to be flown in sequence, and if a participant landed somewhere other than the correct airfield, they had to begin that circuit again. For every 75 kg

(165 lbs.) of useful load (passengers or ballast) carried, not including the pilot's weight and fuel, a bonus of twenty-five percent was allowed on the time, up to a maximum of one hundred percent. Each aircraft had to carry a sealed barograph and an average speed of at least 40 km/h (25 mph) had to be sustained. No aircraft was able to complete the course and the prize money was added to the prize for the following year.

1913
The Aero-Club de France changed the 1913 race course again, with the prize being awarded for the maximum distance flown on a series of consecutive days flying over a 100 km (62 mile) course, with a compulsory landing after each circuit. The Cup was won by Emmanuel Helen flying a Nieuport monoplane, with 16,096.6 km (10,002.0 miles) flown between 22 October and 29 November.

1914
The course was changed again for the 1914 competition, the prize being awarded for the fastest time over a circuit of about 3,000 km (1,900 miles). Eugene Gilbert, flying a Morane-Saulnier monoplane, won the prize by starting from Villacoublay at 0304 on 8 June; he ran out of fuel before reaching Pau. The next day he flew via Pau back to Villacoublay, landing at 1837 and having covered a distance of 2,970 km (1,850 mi) in 39:35 hours, thus wining the last International Michelin before the war.

BRITISH MICHELIN CUP

In 1909, Michelin established a United Kingdom Cup administered by the Aero Club of Great Britain, offering an annual award of a trophy and £500. The competition was limited to British subjects flying aircraft of British manufacture.

1909–10
The inaugural flight was to be flown around a closed circuit consisting of two or more markers and a minimum distance of 5 miles (8 km) was specified. The race was won by J. T. C. (John Theodore Cuthbert) Moore-Brabazon, flying the Short Biplane No. 2 over 18.75 miles (30.18 km) at Eastchurch on 1 March 1910. (The closing date for the race was 31 March.)

John Moore-Brabazon flying the Short Biplane No. 2.

1910
The rules for the 1910 Cup race (the closing date was 31 December 1910) were the same as previous, except that the minimum qualifying distance was raised to 38 miles (61 km).

The Cup was won by Samuel Cody flying the Cody Michelin Cup Biplane at Laffan's Plain, Farnborough, with a flight of 185.46 miles (298.47 km), requiring 4:47 hours in 1911.

Cody Michelin Cup biplane

1911
Michelin announced a separate prize of a trophy and a cash prize of £400 for 1911, £600 for 1912, and £800 for 1913 for the fastest time over a cross-country circuit. On 29 October, the Michelin Cup No. 1 was again won by Samuel Cody, flying his *Circuit of Britain* biplane 261.5 miles (420.8 km) in 5:15 hours at Laffan's Plain and also setting a new British duration record. On 11 September, Cup No. 2 was also won by Cody, with a flight on a circuit starting at Laffan's Plain on to Farnborough taking 3:06:30 hours to complete the 125 mile (201 km) course.

1912
For the 1912 competition the rules were changed: the No. 1 Cup and cash prize of £5,000 was for endurance—all flying was to be completed between sunrise and sunset—while the No. 2 Cup and prize of £600 was for distance covered over a cross-country course of approximately 186 miles (299 km) of the competitor's choosing. Entering the competition were Harry Hawker flying a Sopwith-Wright biplane, R. L. Charteris flying an AVRO biplane, S. F. Cody in a Cody biplane, Arthur Knight in a Vickers monoplane, I. G. Vaughan Fowler in a Wright machine, and F. P. Raynham in another AVRO biplane.

Due to the change in rules to have the longest time aloft, Harry Hawker's plan to win was uncomplicated: he would fly to the highest possible altitude and lean the engine to a minimum, then he would pull the throttle back and glide down gently, only to restart and very slowly and judiciously climb back to altitude, hoping to considerably extend the plane's endurance. On 16 October, Hawker was first in the air, setting an early time of 3:31 hours aloft, but would have until the close of competition on October 31 to improve his technique and times. He flew twice more over the next week, but could not increase his time. On 22 October, Raynham took off in his AVRO biplane and posted a time of 3:48 hours, surpassing Hawker by 17 minutes. By 24 October, Raynham had bettered his own record, passing the five hour mark and then the six hour mark, while Hawker remained a few hours behind, but was honing his technique. Then Raynham passed the seven hour mark, but his 60 hp Green engine failed and he was forced to land. He had been in the air an incredible 7:31:30 hours. That same day Hawker was in the air climbing and gliding, and as nightfall rapidly approached he passed seven hours in the air and then passed Raynham's recent mark and continued flying, but the Michelin rules required all flying conclude within one hour after sunset. On landing he had broken Col. Cody's 5:15 hour mark from 1911 by nearly three hours, setting a new time of 8:23 hours, and Hawker had beaten Raynham and had still not exhausted his fuel.

Harry Hawker, 1912 British Michelin Cup winner

1913

Michelin Cup No. 1 was to be awarded for the longest distance flight round the course Brooklands–Hendon–Farnborough, plus one section (e.g., starting from Brooklands the competitor would pass Hendon, Farnborough, Brooklands, and land at Hendon) with a minimum distance of 300 miles. Competitors had to make periodical stops of not less than five minutes with their engine stopped. The prize had not been won by the closing date of 31 October 1913, so the Aero Club extended the closing date to 14 November. The No. 1 Cup was won by Reginald Carr and his engineer as a passenger, flying the Grahame-White *Charabanc*, with a flight of over 300 miles (480 km). The No. 2 Cup, for the fastest time round a circuit of the competitor's choice of around 450 km, was not awarded. Although the prize was carried over to the next year, competition was terminated by the outbreak of WWI.

Reginald Carr (R), 1913 British Michelin Cup winner

THE *DAILY MAIL* AERIAL DERBY

The Aerial Derby was a United Kingdom air race sponsored by the *Daily Mail* in which the competitors flew a circuit around London. It was first held in 1912, with subsequent races in 1913 and 1914; after being suspended during WWI the event was revived in 1919, with a "Victory Aerial Derby." Further races were held in 1920, 1921, 1922, and 1923. Although a race was scheduled for 1924, there were insufficient entries and the event was canceled. It was never held again.

1912 Aerial Derby

Held on 8 June, the first Aerial Derby consisted of a single circuit of an 81 mile (130 km) course, starting and finishing at Hendon Aerodrome with control points at Kempton Park, Esher, Purley, and Purfleet. The contestants had to fly low enough for the judges to see the race number painted on their aircraft. Due to sponsor *Daily Mail's* publicity a large turnout of about 45,000 people paid to view the start and finish at Hendon, and huge crowds congregated along the route. Fifteen aviators were expected to start the race, but due to bad weather only seven started (six monoplanes and one biplane). Thomas Sopwith, flying in a two-seat Bleriot for 1:23:08 hours at a speed of 58.46 mph, was the first to finish, but was then disqualified for missing the control point at Purley. He appealed and was later pronounced the winner, as visibility was so poor that Sopwith had in fact passed well outside the marker, unseen by the

Thomas Sopwith, 1912 Aerial Derby winner

judges. Sopwith, later famous for his biplane scouts and pursuits, received the *Daily Mail* Gold Cup and $1,250. Gustave Hamel was second in an identical airplane in 1:38:46 hours with Miss Eleanor Trehawke Davies as passenger, and W. B. Rhodes-Morehouse was third in Radley-Morehouse, which resembled a Bleriot, but had a fully enclosed fuselage.

1913: The Aerial Derby

The second Aerial Derby, held at Hendon Aerodrome on 20 September, was flown over a longer one lap 94 mile (151 km) course than the first Derby (81 miles) and had five turning points. The course alterations were made because the original route crossed areas prohibited under the recently passed Air Navigation Order. In addition to the *Daily Mail* trophy and £200 prize, a trophy and three prizes of £100, £70, and £25 were given by Shell for the winners of a handicap competition. Eleven of the original fifteen entries started the race, with the winner being Gustave Hamel, flying a clipped-wing Morane-Saulnier with an 80 hp Gnome engine, with a scratch handicap and a winning time of 1:15:49 hours. Harold Barnwell finished second, flying a Martin-Handasyde at 72.5 mph (with a 6:39 minute handicap) over 1:18:44 hours, while in third was Frederick Raynham, flying the prototype Avro 504 at 66.5 mph.

Gustave Hamel, 1913 The Aerial Derby

1914: The Aerial Derby 1914

The Derby was to be originally held on 23 May, but was postponed to 6 June due to poor weather. While the weather on race day was somewhat better, some contestants were unable to fly to the starting line at Hendon. The overall winner of the race was American Walter Brock, flying a Morane-Saulnier with a time of 1:18:54 hours at 71.9 mph to win the *Daily Mail* and Shell Trophies, along with 300 gold sovereigns ($1,500). Following him were Reginald Carr and Pierre Verrier in Farman biplanes.

The Derby was suspended during WWI, but was revived in 1919, when it was flown over the same course as the 1914 event; due to the increased speed of aircraft over the war years it was flown over two circuits rather than one. G. Gathergood, flying a considerably modified D.H.4R with a reduced-span lower wing, won with a speed of 129.34 mph. M. C. Hammersley flying an Avro Baby won the handicap race.

OTHER HIGHLIGHTS

31 March: The Mortimer Singer Army prize of £500 for distance by a British Army pilot with a passenger was won by Lt. B. H. Barrington-Kennett in a Nieuport monoplane flying at 249 miles (401 km) at Salisbury Plain.

9–12 June:

Hellmuth Hirth (pilot) and Lt. Schoeller won the Berlin-Vienna Race.

Hellmuth Hirth (R) and Lt. Schoeller

16–17 June:

Roland Garros, flying a Bleriot XI, won the 75,000 Franc prize of the French Aero Club's *Prix d'Anjou* in very poor weather. The race started on 16 June as the annual Grand Prix de l'Aéro-Club de France over a 190 km (120 miles) triangular course Angers–Cholet–Saumur, but conditions were so harsh that the rules had to be changed overnight and the race was shortened in the interest of safety. Of the six starters only two completed the first day's flying. Garros, flying a 50 hp Gnome Bleriot XI, had taken off in a 43 mph gale, flown through a torrential downpour, and been pummeled by a hail storm. Each lap of the course took him about 2.5 hours to complete. The second day the weather was better, and Garros was able to complete a further four laps to claim the 75,000 Franc prize.

19 August:

Swiss pilot Edmond Audemars completed the first flight from Paris to Berlin, flying a Bleriot XI monoplane on a 590 mile (949 km) two-day flight, landing at Berlin's Johannisthal airfield.

11 September:
Alexandre (Geo) Fourny completed the first round trip of 1,000 km (625 miles) and the first flight lasting more than 12 hours (631 miles in 13:18 hours) at Etampes. Fourny flew a Farman with an extra bay which increased its wingspan and thus endurance.

Edmond Audemars

1912:
Baronne Raymonde de Laroche was born as Elise Roche, but assumed her aristocratic stage name to benefit her career as an actress. Reputably inspired by Wilbur Wright's 1908 demonstrations in Paris and being acquainted with several aviators, including Leon Delagrange, who was alleged to be the father of her son Andre, de Laroche resolved to leave her theater career and engage in flying. De Laroche first became an experienced balloonist and then, in October 1909, after instruction by Charles Voisin, became arguably the world's first woman airplane pilot (there are proposals that during 1908 P. Van Pottelsberghe flew with Henri Farman and Therese Peltier had flown with Delagrange). On 8 March 1910, de Laroche was granted the world's first pilot's license (No. 36 France) for a woman. In July, she competed in the *Prix des Dames* at the 1910 Reims Week, but was seriously injured in a crash. Two years later she was fit again and returned to flying. After finally recovering, on 26 September 1912, she and Charles Voisin were involved in a car crash in which Voisin was killed and she was again severely injured. After she recovered on 25 November 1913 de Laroche won the Aero-Club of France's Femina Cup for a non-stop long distance flight of more than four hours. After not being allowed to fly during the war, in 1919, she would set both the female altitude (4,800 m/15,750 ft.) and distance (323 km/200 miles) records before being tragically killed in July while co-piloting an experimental aircraft.

Geo Fourny

Baronne Raymonde de Laroche

6
1913: MORE COMPETITIONS AND RECORDS

1913: FIRST FLIGHT OVER THE PYRENEES AND ALPS: OSCAR BIDER

In November 1912, Swiss native Oskar Bider entered flight training at the Bleriot school in Pau, at the foot of the Pyrenees in southwest France. Once he had soloed, he purchased a Bleriot and painted Swiss crosses on the wings and tail. As his first flying adventure he decided to fly from Pau to Madrid, crossing the Pyrenees en route. Having trained at Pau, he knew the Pyrenees well and scouted out the route to Madrid by taking the train to Madrid to visually familiarize himself with the landmarks along the way. On 24 January 1913, he left Pau at 0645 on the 190 mile leg to Guadalajara, climbing 11,500 ft. over the Pyrenees. After landing at Guadalajara he flew on to Madrid and was hailed there as an international hero, as well as in Switzerland. On 7 July 1913, he flew over the Alps from Bern to Milan and returned to Bern to become the first aviator to cross the Alps both ways. On 7 July 1919, an inebriated Bider insisted on demonstrating his aerobatic talents in his Nieuport 21, stalled the plane, and spun it into the ground, dying instantly.

Oscar Bider, first flight over the Pyrenees

1913: FIRST NON-STOP FLIGHT FROM BRITAIN TO GERMANY: GUSTAV HAMEL

On 17 April, Brit Gustav Hamel made the first non-stop flight from Britain to Germany in 4:18 hours, flying from Dover to Cologne in his Bleriot XI. The flight, which carried a passenger, was sponsored by the *Evening Standard*, and was intended to demonstrate Britain's need for military aircraft.

1913: THE RECORD FLIGHTS OF MARCEL-GEORGES BRINDEJONC DES MOULINAIS

By 1913, Marcel-Georges Brindejonc des Moulinais was as famous in France as Roland Garros, having competed in many races and flown across Europe. Between 25 and 27 February 1913, des Moulinais' flight from Paris to London—crossing the Channel to Brussels, crossing of the Channel, and returning to Paris (650 miles)—was flown in a Morane-Saulnier C monoplane powered by an 80 hp Gnome engine. His circuit (Paris-Bordeaux-Burgos-Madrid-Barcelona-Perpignan-Lyon-Paris) was flown 24 March–12 April 1913. Between 10 June and 2 July, des Moulinais flew a tour of the European capitals, beginning with an impressive one-day first leg from Villacoublay (Paris)-Berlin-Warsaw of 845 miles, then arriving at St. Petersburg on 18 June, crossing the Baltic to arrive in Stockholm on 25 June. His route back to Paris took him through Copenhagen on 29 June and the Hague (Holland) on 1 July, arriving back at Paris on 2 July having covered more than 3,000 miles (4,800 km). On 3 July 1913, he received the Great Gold Medal of the Aero-Club de France for this flight. On 11 August 1913, at the age of twenty-one, he became the youngest holder of the Legion of Honour and then, on 23 December 1913, he received the Medal of the Academy of Sport. During 1913, he was decorated in Saint Petersburg by Grand Duke Alexander with the order of Sainte-Anne; in Stockholm with the order of Gustav Vasa; and in Copenhagen by the Danish king with the Order of Daneborg. During WWI he flew reconnaissance missions over the Battle of the Marne and was shot down and killed on 18 August 1916 over Vadelaincourt, near Verdun.

Marcel-Georges Brindejonc des Moulinais

1913: THE FIRST SCHNEIDER CUP RACE

Jacques Schneider was the wealthy heir to a French industrial empire, a balloonist, and an aircraft enthusiast who created the Schneider Trophy, a race for seaplanes, which had only flown for the first time two years before. His Schneider Cup Race series was designed to stimulate technical progress in seaplanes by offering cash prizes and a trophy that would soon be coveted as a major achievement in aviation. Contestants had to fly a distance of at least 150 miles (240 km), and the winner was to be rewarded with 25,000 Gold Francs and a cup worth as much as the prize. If a nation won the cup three times in five years the cup would belong to them. The first race was held over the Mediterranean, just offshore of Monaco, on 14–16 April. Of the six seaplanes entered, four were ready to start the 28 lap race around a 20 km (12.5 mile) closed course, with each lap being 10 km long. The Schneider Cup was not a traditional race, but rather a set of time trials where the seaplanes would try to finish in the quickest time over a long course consisting of multiple turns. The shortest leg was just 260 yards long and the longest was about 3.5 km. The tightest turn was at Cap Martin, which reversed the racers' course by 165 degrees. To prove the seaworthiness of the aircraft, every racer had to land on the water twice during the first lap. The racers took off one by one. Roland Garros, flying a Morane-Saulnier, was delayed in starting. Of the remaining three starters (Charles Weymann, Gabriel Espanet, and Maurice Prevost), the winner was Maurice Prevost in a Deperdussin Monoplane, which was much larger than the company's land plane racers. Prevost had originally finished while on the water, then had to take off again and complete a flying finish, being timed at 2:50:47 at 45.7 mph. Neither of the other two starters finished, as Weymann and Espanet experienced oil leaks in their Nieuports and dropped out.

Schneider Cup

Maurice Prevost, 1913 Schneider Cup Race winner

1913: *DAILY MAIL* WATERPLANES CIRCUIT OF GREAT BRITAIN COMPETITION

The 1913 race, offering prize of £5,000, was for "Waterplanes" (float planes) of all-British construction. The course, totaling 1,540 miles (2,480 km), had to be completed in 72 hours, but since no flying was allowed on Sundays this period was in practice a day longer. The race was divided into nine stages, landing at the ports Southampton to Yarmouth to Scarborough to Aberdeen to Oban to Dublin to Falmouth, and back to Southampton. Entrants included Samuel Cody, who was killed during a test flight of his design on 7 August, when his aircraft broke up in flight; the Radley-England Waterplane that was damaged during trials before the start of the race; Francis McClean's Short biplane, which was delayed by engine problems that kept it from competing; and the Sopwith biplane flown by Australians Harry Hawker and his mechanic, Harry Kauper, as passenger, which was the only aircraft to start. When Hawker and Kauper reached Great Yarmouth Hawker collapsed shortly after landing, supposedly due to sunstroke, but the cause may have been carbon monoxide poisoning from the exhaust. The aircraft was returned to Southampton by rail for a second attempt that began when Hawker and Kauper took off on Monday, 25 August. The flight went well until after take-off from Scarborough on the third day, when they were forced to land with engine problems that were corrected, and the flight continued to Aberdeen to Oban. On the leg to Dublin Hawker decided to land a few miles from their destination to make adjustments to the engine valves. On the landing approach Hawker's foot slipped from the rudder bar and the aircraft crashed into the water, breaking Kauper's arm and demolishing the aircraft. Although they had only covered two-thirds of

Harry Hawker and Harry Kauper, 1913 Circuit of Great Britain

the course, Hawker was awarded a prize of £1,000 and was later also awarded the Royal Aeronautical Society's silver medal; Kauper was awarded a bronze medal.

The 1914 race, also offering a prize of £5,000, was to have been held 1–15 August, but was canceled due to the outbreak of WWI.

1913: GARROS CROSSES THE MEDITERRANEAN

At 0547 on 23 September 1913, Roland Garros took off from near Cannes, in the south of France, piloting a Morane-Saulnier monoplane powered by the reliable 60 hp Gnome rotary engine. He flew over water to Corsica and intended to land at Cagliari, the capital of Sardinia, to top off his fuel, but decided the flight was going so well that he continued along those island's coastlines until he crossed the Mediterranean's open water. After a flight of almost 460 miles he landed at 1353 hours at Bizerta, Tunisia, with less than two gallons of the more than fifty-five gallons of fuel he began with remaining. During WWI Garros was credited with perfecting the first metal deflector wedges attached to tractor propeller blades, enabling him to shoot down several German aircraft. On 18 April 1915, Garros' aircraft was downed and he was taken prisoner by the Germans, but he escaped on 14 February 1918 and resumed combat flying. On 5 October 1918, he was shot down and killed near Vouziers, Ardennes, only a month before the end of the war.

Roland Garros, first to Cross the Mediterranean at Bizerte.

7
1914: THE AGE OF INNOCENCE ENDS

1914: THE SECOND SCHNEIDER CUP RACE

The second race in this series was held on 20 April off Monaco—the same location as the first, conducted over the same course, and for the same number of laps (twenty-eight). Eleven seaplanes were entered of which all were standard aircraft, many of them land planes with added pontoons. Only five aircraft started and just two finished, and it was an easy win for Englishman Howard Pixton in the special float-equipped Sopwith Baby land plane powered by a 100 hp Gnome Monosoupape rotary engine and dubbed the *Sopwith Schneider*. Pixton's 87 mph speed was almost twice the race record and could not be approached by any known seaplane. The other finisher was Ernest Burri of Switzerland in an F.B.A. who finished more than an hour behind, due in part to having to land and refuel. All other entries either failed to start the race or dropped out.

The competition was suspended during WWI, then resumed in 1919. Nine more races were held until the competition was permanently suspended in 1931. The races did not achieve Schneider's objective of furthering commercial aviation by developing large long-range seaplanes. Instead, they became an object of intense national competition, with powerful, sleek designs built only to win the cup.

Howard Pixton, 1914 Schneider Cup Race winner

1914: THE LONDON-PARIS-LONDON RACE

Longer cross-country races were increasing in popularity, and one of the most interesting was a 500 mile race known as the "International Correspondence Schools London-Paris-London Air Race." The race between the two European capitals began on 11 July at Hendon Aerodrome and flew to Paris BUC Aerodrome, where each participant would land and wait for two hours before returning to Hendon; a round-trip flight of 502 aerial miles. The pilot completing the course in the least amount of time would be the winner and receive £800 from the sponsors, plus £300 from the Royal Aero Club (about $5,500). Second and third place finishers would receive £300 each. Fourteen pilots were registered to fly and would take off in their handicap position, which were kept secret by race officials until take-off on the day of the race. At 0630, seven pilots (six French) in five monoplanes and two biplanes took off from Hendon Aerodrome at ten-minute intervals to fly to Paris, navigating by dead reckoning. As each aircraft landed in Paris the pilot was informed of his take-off time to occur in two hours. At 1704, American Walter Brock landed in his Morane-Saulnier-G monoplane in Paris with a record speed of 71.5 mph and a time of 7:03. Later Roland Garros, flying another Morane-Saulnier-G monoplane, landed at Hendon to place second, while Eugene Renaux, flying a Farman biplane, came in third the following day. Out of the fourteen entries these three were the only ones to finish.

Walter Brock, 1914 London-Paris-London Race winner

1913–1914: FLIGHTS TO MIDDLE EAST

In 1913, Paris newspaper *Le Matin* and the French Aero Club offered a prize to the flyer to complete the first flight from Paris to Peking, China, but that route was changed because of the perils involved. Cairo became the new destination and two routes would be flown: one by way of North Africa, and the other 3,500 miles across central Europe, over the Balkan States, and mountains before crossing into Asia at Constantinople. Europe in 1913 was a complexity of alliances and rivalries, and the pilots would have to wend their way through this political landscape almost as carefully as through the physical one.

Pierre Daucourt

The first pilot to attempt the route was Pierre Daucourt and his mechanic, J. Roux, when they took off from Issy, Paris, on 20 October 1913, in a Gnome-powered *Borel* monoplane. Their first leg took them to Sens (fifty miles from Paris) and then to Belfort, near the German border, where they obtained permission to fly into Germany at a time of mounting tension between the two countries. They landed in Munich, where they negotiated permission to cross the Austro-Hungarian/Serb border to fly to Aspern, Austria, on 31 October. From Aspern they passed through Vienna and arrived in Budapest on 2 November, after which they needed to cross the Transylvanian Alps and the Balkans—where the Second Balkan War had just ended and they had no permission to land. Daucourt solved the political problem by flying over but not landing on Serbian territory; the Alps altitude problem was solved by arranging for Roux to travel by rail to lighten the aircraft while Daucourt flew around the western foothills of the mountain range to Krajova, Romania, where he met Roux. The reunited pair then flew to Bucharest on 5 November, and from Bucharest, the next leg took the fliers to Varna, Bulgaria, and then down the Black Sea coast toward Constantinople (Istanbul). Due to a head wind they were forced to land in the Bulgarian town Burgas when their fuel ran low, and they had to spend several hours scouring the town for gasoline. Almost immediately after leaving they were forced down again by bad weather and had to land just over the Turkish border in a small town whose citizens mistook them for Bulgarians and refused to give them any shelter. Daucourt and Roux were forced to spend a cold night under the wing of their plane. After flying over 1,500 miles and about two-thirds of the way to Cairo, the pair finally arrived in Constantinople on 9 November, where they took a week's rest. On 17 November, the fliers left Constantinople and crossed the Bosporus from Europe into Asia. The route across Turkey followed the Constantinople-Baghdad railway across Turkey, and by the end of November the terrain had become increasingly mountainous, so Daucourt was forced to leave Roux to travel by rail again to lighten the monoplane and climb over the Anatolian Plateau and Taurus Mountains. At the Taurus Mountains Daucourt ended navigating by the railway line to try to find a way through the range via a mountain pass, but he crashed in the mountains on 26 November and his Borel was destroyed (he was unhurt). Daucourt and Roux resumed their flight through the Taurus Mountains in another aircraft at the end of December, and on 7 January 1914, they finally reached Cairo.

Pierre Daucourt

Bonnier and Barnier

Marc Bonnier set out with his mechanic, Joseph Barnier, flying an 80 hp Gnome-engined Nieuport monoplane on 10 November 1913, in an attempt to fly "as far East as possible." Once they learned of Daucourt's crash in Turkey they changed their plans and decided to attempt the Cairo flight, closely following the Daucourt route, and reached Constantinople by 5 December. They experienced mechanical problems that seriously delayed them and allowed experienced racing pilot Jules Vedrines to gain on them. They did not fly over the Taurus Mountains until 31 December, and although they became the first aviators to visit Jerusalem, when they finally reached Cairo on New Year's Day 1914, they found Vedrines had beaten them by three days.

Marc Bonnier (L) and mechanic Joseph Barnier

Jules Vedrines

Veteran and very eccentric long distance pilot Jules Vedrines left Paris during mid-November 1913 on a long distance flight east—possibly to Baghdad—but he had no carefully planned route, few maps, and relied on refueling wherever able. On his first stop in the French-German border town Nancy he was placed under arrest for flying in a military "no fly zone" near the frontier with Germany. On 20 November, he negotiated his release on the stipulation that he return to Paris and did not try to cross into Germany. Vedrines took off west toward Paris, but then banked round to the east and disappeared over the German frontier, although he could not land there without risking another arrest. He crossed Germany during one seven-hour leg, landing in Prague, in Austria-Hungary, during the afternoon. Although he did not have permission from Austria-Hungary to cross into Serbia, he landed in the capital, Belgrade, on 2 December, and by 4 December, he was in Sofia, the Bulgarian capital. Here Vedrines heard that Daucourt had crashed a week earlier and realized he could catch Bonnier and Barnier, who were already in Constantinople. While in Sophia he contacted France and succeeded in gaining the support of influential Rene Quinton—co-founder of the Aero-club de France and president of the *Ligue Nationale Aerienne*—and the French government, which would be of great assistance crossing the Ottoman Empire. Upon reaching Constantinople clever Vedrines flew low over the imperial palace, dropping an Ottoman flag and a letter ingratiating himself to the Sultan. He left Constantinople on 17 December, and continued southeast across Turkey along Daucourt's route to the Mediterranean, where he flew 180 miles across the Gulf of Alexandretta directly to Syria, then flew down the coast to Jaffa (modern Tel Aviv) via Beirut. On 29 December, he set off on the final leg from Jaffa to Cairo via Kantara, and just after 1300, he was greeted by a small crowd at Heliopolis, just outside Cairo, after joining three continents in a single extraordinary flight. Three days later Bonnier and Barnier arrived in Cairo. After Daucourt and Roux arrived in Cairo Vedrines became involved in a public argument with Roux (Daucourt's mechanic), accusing him of having authorities hinder his progress to Cairo, and actually slapped him. Roux immediately demanded "satisfaction" in the form of a duel, which Vedrines refused. When Rene Quintin heard of the incident he advised Vedrines to fight Roux, and Vedrines cabled back that he would not, but he would fight his benefactor Quintin on his return instead!

Jules Vedrines

1914: UP THE NILE: FRANK MCCLEAN AND MARC POURPE

While Vedrines was continuing toward Cairo, a band of British fliers and their aircraft had arrived in Egypt by sea from England: Frank McClean (pilot), Alec Olgivie (reserve pilot and rigger), and Gus Smith (mechanic), along with their Short Brothers' Hydro-aeroplane. The Short S.70 chosen for this flight was an enlarged version of the standard four-place Short military seaplane with its wing span elongated to 70.5 ft. and was powered with new 140 hp Gnome engines. During a test flight on 10 August 1912, McClean flew the Short Seaplane up the Thames and under Tower Bridge to gain publicity for a proposed first flight that would take a flying machine into the heart of Africa. In preparation for the 1,500 mile flight up the Nile river from Cairo to Khartoum, capital of Anglo-Egyptian Sudan, McClean organized petrol dumps all along the river and sent a supply of spare parts to the Sudan. On 3 January 1914, the fliers took off from Alexandria Harbor on the start of their expedition on a route that would first take them over the sea to Rosetta, then inland across the Nile Delta, and up river to Cairo, which they reached just after noon, settling on the river near Cairo's center city.

Meanwhile, young French pilot Marc Pourpe had arrived in Cairo and, compared to the McClean team, was very well-prepared for his endeavor, having the financial backing of the Ligue Nationale Aerienne. He was flying the same long range

60 hp Morane-Saulnier monoplane Roland Garros had flown across the Mediterranean. Pourpe had extensive experience flying in tropical conditions, as during 1913 he was a demonstration pilot for Bleriot in the Far East. In 1912, while barnstorming in Calcutta in a Bleriot, Pourpe met Raoul Lufbery, whom he hired as his mechanic. He also taught Lufbery how to fly and the two then began travelling together, continuing Pourpe's tour of Asia, Europe, and now Africa. Meanwhile, the inexperienced McClean was flying an untested aircraft equipped with an experimental engine and could only land on water.

On 4 January, while McClean conducted test flights over the Nile, Pourpe took off from Cairo, hoping to reach Khartoum first. His first stop was Luxor, 400 miles upriver, but engine problems forced him to land at Menshah, about one hundred miles from Luxor. A mechanic was sent from Cairo by train with spare parts, and Pourpe began making repairs. On 6 January, McClean took off from Cairo, flying one hundred feet above the Nile, and arrived at Minia, about 150 miles upriver. The next day McClean flew to Assuit, but during a routine inspection a cylinder and piston needed replacement. These parts were shipped by train from Cairo, and McClean dragged the seaplane onto a sand bank for repairs, which were not completed until 14 January.

Meanwhile, Pourpe had arrived at Luxor on 6 January and Wadi Halfa on the seventh, and had reached the first great bend of the Nile. Because he was flying a land plane, he could leave the river behind and cut across the desert to Abu Hamid, following the railway line. If the need arose he could always land and await rescue, though it was still a daunting prospect. Pourpe landed safely at Abu Hamid just after noon on 8 January, and his progress left little doubt that a Frenchman was going to reach Khartoum before a Brit, restoring French prestige in the Sudan. On 12 January, he arrived in Khartoum in the early afternoon, flying 1,350 miles in just nine days with a total flying time of less than 19 hours. Pourpe rested at Khartoum for a week before heading back north to Cairo.

In the meantime, McClean completed repairs on 14 January and arrived at Luxor that day after refueling on the way. On 16 January, they touched down in Aswan near the Savoy Hotel on Elephantine Island and were greeted by an enthusiastic crowd. After resting a few days they took off again on 19 January toward Wadi Halfa, but were forced to turn back after thirty-five miles with a malfunctioning engine that needed four cylinders replaced and other repairs, during which time Pourpe visited the McClean team on his way back to Cairo. Finally, almost a month later on 17 February, McClean was able to continue south to Wadi Halfa, reaching the great Nile Bend that Pourpe's land plane had been able to bypass. Because their seaplane could only land on the river and nowhere else, flying along the Nile meant adding hundreds of miles to their flight. On 19 February, they passed Delgo, where they were forced to land to avoid a threatening "dust devil," but during the landing a wingtip was torn off and a spar broken. Mechanic Olgivie fixed the damage "with remarkable ingenuity" and the Short Seaplane was ready to fly again by 24 February; they made good progress, reaching Abu Hamid on 28 February. On 4 March, while flying between Abu Hamid and Atbara, a large section of the engine's timing wheel detached and damaged two of the four tail booms. During the harried emergency landing McClean also damaged a float and two undercarriage struts. Fortunately the railway was nearby, so spare parts could be quickly transported by train from Cairo. With the help of Sudan Railway workshops the damage was repaired in only ten days. Atbara was reached on 14 March, and after repairing a broken connecting rod at Kabushiya, McClean was ready to fly the final leg to Khartoum on 22 March. After a prolonged eighty-five days from their take-off in Alexandria they landed at Khartoum. Justifiably, the fliers decided not to make the return leg by air and instead traveled back to Cairo in the comfort of a river steamer and train.

POSTSCRIPT: When WWI broke out Pourpe joined the French Air Service, serving with Escadrille No. 23, and was killed when his fighter was shot down by a German Fokker near Villers-Bretonneux in 1914. McClean joined the Royal Naval Air Service and carried out patrols over the English Channel before becoming chief instructor at Eastchurch.

Frank McClean (R) and mechanic Gus Smith repair their Short S.70 Hydro-aeroplane on the Nile.

Marc Pourpe and his Morane-Saulnier monoplane in the Sudan

TURKISH CAIRO EXPEDITION

The Ottoman Turks also wished to demonstrate their long distance flying abilities, so the Cairo Expedition was announced at the beginning of 1914. On 8 February 1914, a flight of two airplanes—a Bleriot XI and a Deperdussin—was planned to fly about 1,500 miles from Constantinople, Turkey, to Alexandria, Egypt, through Lebanon, Syria, and Palestine. During the trip the Bleriot crashed near the Lake of Galilee and its two pilots were killed. The Deperdussin reached Palestine and landed near Jaffa on 9 March, but upon taking off it crashed into the Mediterranean; one pilot drowned in the accident while the other survived. Despite these setbacks another Bleriot named *Edremit* was flown by Salim and Kemal Bey, and finally landed in Alexandria, successfully completing the Cairo Expedition in mid-May 1914.

1914: GERMAN ENDURANCE RECORDS

With German militarism rising toward war the German Air Service set a number of endurance records:

3 February: Bernard Langer flew for 14:07 hours in his Roland biplane.

7 February: Karl Ingold left Mulhouse in an Aviatik biplane powered by a 100 hp Mercedes engine and landed in Munich after flying for 16:20 hours, covering 1,000 miles.

11 February: Bernard Langer flew from Berlin to Posen in 16 hours in a Roland biplane.

4 May: France regained the endurance record when Etienne Poulet flew his Cauldron for 16:28 hours at Etampes.

23 June: Taking off at the same time, Gustav Basser, in a Rumpler, flew for 18:12 consecutive hours without landing, while Werner Landmann's 17:17 hours in an Albatros fell short of the new record.

27–28 June: Werner Landmann followed his failed flight with a record endurance flight of 21:50 hours. During 1923, Landmann would be the test pilot for the first flight of the large Rohrbach Ro II Seaplane, attempting to set load carrying records.

Werner Landmann and his Albatros

10–11 July: Reinhold Boehm left Johannistahl flying a 75 hp Albatros carrying 132 gallons of fuel to become the first pilot to break the twenty-four hour endurance barrier with a non-stop flight of 24:12 hours without refueling. This one-man flight record would last until 1920, when Lucien Boussoutrot and Jean Bernard broke his record by seven minutes.

Etienne Poulet lands his Cauldron after regaining the endurance record.

Reinhold Boehm and his Albatros

AIRCRAFT DURATION IN THE AIR 1909–1914

Duration (H/M/S)	Date	Location	Pilot(s)	Aircraft
24:12:00	July 10–11, 1914	Johannisthal AF, Berlin, Germany	Reinhold Buehm	Albatros biplane
21:49:00	June 28–29, 1914	Johannisthal AF, Berlin, Germany	Werner Landmann	Albatros biplane
13:22:00	September 11, 1912	Etampes Airfield, France	Alexandre Fourny	Maurice Farman MF-2
11:01:29	September 1, 1911	Buc, France	Alexandre Fourny	Maurice Farman biplane
08:12:45	December 18, 1910	Etampes Airfield, France	Henri Farman	Maurice Farman biplane
06:01:00	October 28, 1910	Buc, France	Maurice Tabuteau	Maurice Farman MF-2
05:03:05	July 10, 1910	Reims, France	Jan Olieslagers	Bleriot monoplane
04:17:35	November 3, 1909	Mourmelon-le-Grand, France	Henri Farman	H. Farman

AIR LEGACY OF WWI AND INTO THE INTERWAR PERIOD

The gunshots fired in Serbia in August 1914 brought aviation's years of innocence to a sudden end. Trailblazing across new continents and the quest for new height and distance records would have to wait until the bloody conclusion of the Great War. The courage and imagination of early pioneers was to be replaced by the courage and reality of harsh warfare faced by combat pilots. The airplane would be used as a weapon for the first time, and specialized aircraft and techniques had to be developed for its use. With the infusion of massive government funding pursuit and bombardment aircraft technology made developmentally exponential leaps. As the war progressed, aircraft had far greater importance than just aerial reconnaissance and two entirely different forms of aircraft developed: the fighter and bomber. By the Armistice in November 1918, there was no comparison of the makeshift warplanes that were on hand at the start of the war and those that finished the war. Four short (in time, not blood) years of war had brought huge changes.

Strategic bombing was primarily employed by the Entente Powers, the United Kingdom and France, and Central Power Germany, but eventually all belligerents developed strategic and tactical elements for their fledgling air forces. The strategic component was developed on the belief that a long-range heavy bomber would have the ability to breach distant enemy air defenses and inflict heavy damage on their industries and degrade civilian morale, greatly reducing their ability to produce arms and materials to field and supply ground and naval forces. As aircraft technology increased almost exponentially the use of larger aircraft for strategic bombing was investigated, particularly by the British and Germans. The war ended before the concept of strategic bombing could be tested and proven.

Meanwhile, early fighters were very small, lightly armed, and by later standards, easy to manufacture. Most were biplanes built with a wooden frame covered with fabric and limited to about one hundred miles per hour. As control of the air became increasingly imperative, all of the major powers continually developed fighters to support their military operations, but they typically became obsolete within a year. A technological advantage held by the enemy demanded an immediate response to design entirely new, larger, and more complex fighters and alter the tactics to combat them. This trend continued between the wars, albeit much more slowly, as wood was largely replaced by steel tubing, then aluminum tubing, and finally aluminum stressed skin structures began to predominate.

With the 1918 Armistice and the Treaty of Versailles, only the victorious Allies (Britain, France, and America) and secondary and neutral nations were allowed to continue aircraft development and manufacture and expand strategic bombing concepts. During the interwar years many civilian and military flights took place in these nations that would lead to the development of large long-range bombers capable of flying missions to even the most distant enemy targets. In these nations large or long distance aircraft sponsored mostly by military and government factions, or smaller specialized aircraft built by manufacturers whose market was to be civilian pilots, were developed in an attempt to set endurance and distance records that would eventually culminate in an intercontinental bomber. Particularly in America, long distance record flights were predominately flown by civilians such as Lindbergh, Earhart, and Post flying small non-military aircraft for the highly personal achievement of setting a flying record.

During the two-decade period between world wars aircraft technology, particularly aircraft engines, propellers, and airframes, became comparatively more developed than any other military weapons systems. The other two major weapons developed in WWI, the tank and submarine, made no similar giant strides in technology during that period. Aircraft engines increased in horsepower from the 1918 Spad's 220 hp to the Spitfire's 1,030 hp in 1936. Propellers developed from fixed pitch that were adjusted on the ground to variable pitch that could be altered in flight by the pilot to increase performance at different altitudes and for different circumstances. A propeller on a multi-engine aircraft could also be feathered if the engine became inoperative. Previously the prop of a disabled engine continued to windmill, further diminishing the aircraft's performance. Airframe development was the most apparent of the new technology. Monoplanes appeared with all metal flush riveted construction, enclosed crew compartments, enhanced engine cowlings, and retractable landing gear. Another innovation was the wing flap, increasing wing area, lift, and drag, and allowing heavier aircraft to take off and land at slower airspeeds and in shorter distances.

Many advocates of strategic bombing during the interwar period, such as America's Billy Mitchell, Italy's Giulio Douhet, and Britain's Hugh Trenchard, had commanded aircraft during WWI and realized the great potential of the warplane. Improvements in aircraft technology during and after the war convinced many air authorities that the "bomber will always get through," and this popular belief influenced planning for strategic bombing in WWII. From the early 1920s until the outbreak of WWII—the so-called "Golden Age of Aviation"—civilian and military pilots of the future combatants (the Allies: British, French, Russian, and American; and the Axis partners: Italian, Japanese, and German) set a number of long-range and endurance records which—only for America—would culminate in an intercontinental bomber.

After WWI, pilots in Europe and particularly in America, whose manpower and economics had not been ravaged by the war, took to the air, and the era of barnstormers and stunt fliers was born. Higher, faster, and farther, these daring pioneering pilots added immeasurably to the scope of aviation. Open cockpit, fabric-covered biplanes gave way to the streamlined, metal monoplanes with enclosed cockpits. Flying across the Atlantic and Pacific Oceans and across continents in airplanes became the rage and a nationalist enterprise, especially throughout the 1930s, after Lindbergh's famous first Atlantic flight. The public became entranced with airplanes and, more slowly, flying in them as passengers. If between 1927 and 1930 there were more failures than successes in trans-Atlantic crossings and other long-range objectives, after 1930, there would be more successes than failures, and these competitions led to incremental advances in aircraft technology. Throughout the 1930s, civil aviation far surpassed military aviation in capturing the public's attention and imagination, but during the six years of WWII military aviation was in the world headlines every day. After WWII civilian aviation, primarily as the rapidly emerging airline industry, vied with jet-propelled Cold War military fighters and bombers for the public's attention.

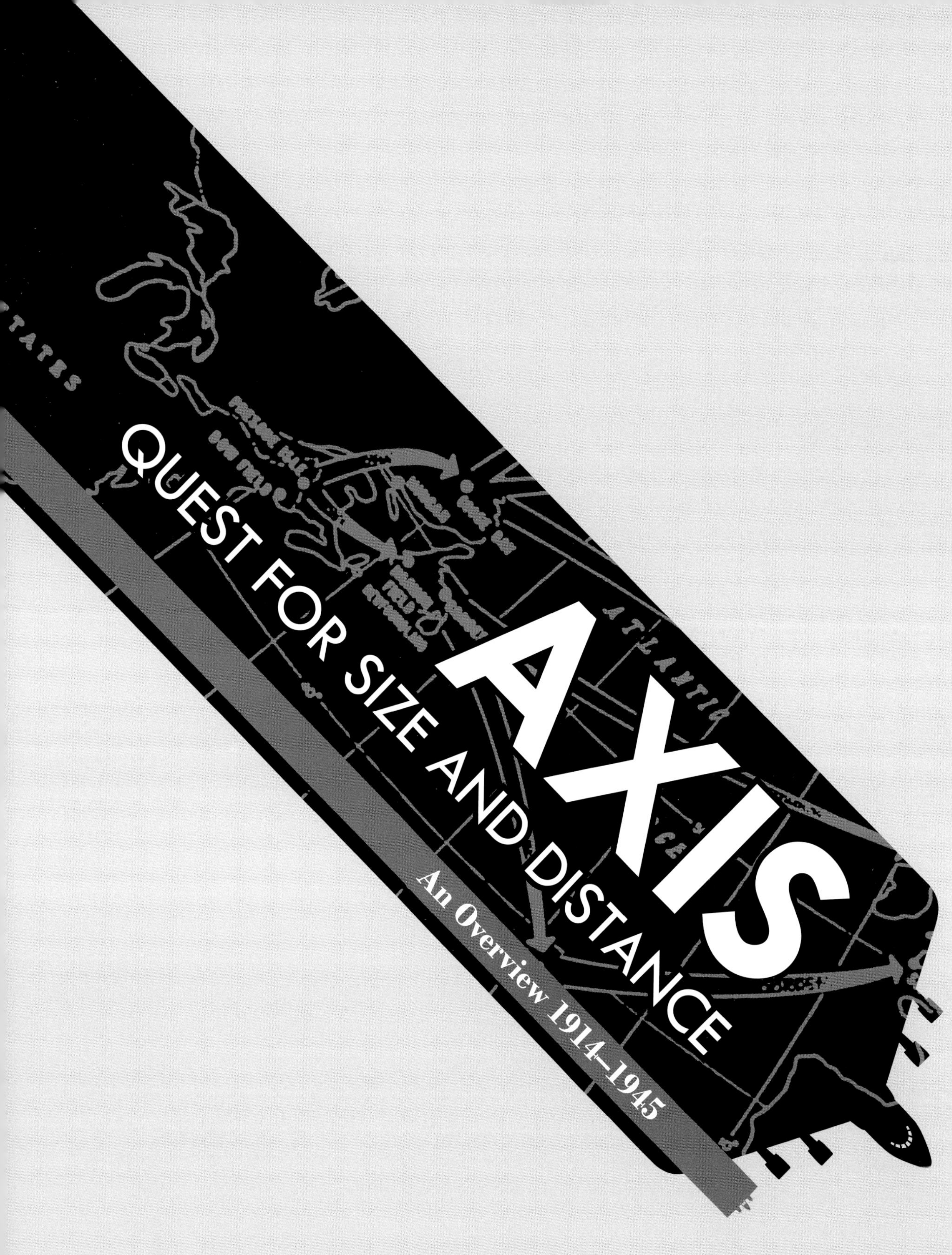

AXIS

QUEST FOR SIZE AND DISTANCE

An Overview 1914–1945

PART 1:
ITALIAN LONG-RANGE AIRCRAFT

During the interwar years two of Italy's most distinguished aircraft designers dominated that country's aviation arena. Prolific designer Gianni Caproni conceived and built large bombers that rivaled the later Soviet Tupolev giants, while Savoia-Marchetti chief designer, Alessandro Marchetti, designed and built the long distance record setting S.64 series and the SM 75.

1
ITALIAN INTERWAR GIANTS

COUNT GIANNI CAPRONI

In 1908, while in his early twenties, Caproni founded a factory in Milan, Italy, to manufacture biplanes. In 1910, he designed and built his first powered aircraft, the experimental Caproni Ca.1 biplane, which was the first aircraft built in Italy, but was destroyed during its first flight on 27 May 1910. In 1911, the newly renamed *Societa de Agostini e Caproni* converted to successful monoplane construction. In 1914, Caproni tested Italy's first multi-engined aircraft, the Caproni Ca.3, a three-engine biplane. After Italy entered the war in 1915, Caproni concentrated on designing and constructing bombers and renamed his company Societa Caproni e Comitti. Ca.4s were tested by the Italian Air Force in 1917, and began operations in 1918. In April 1918, Caproni was an early advocate of passenger aircraft and developed a variant of the Ca.4 bomber into the Ca.48 airliner, which crashed near Verona, Italy, on 2 August 1919, after its wings apparently collapsed in mid-flight at an altitude of 3,000 ft., killing everyone (15–17?) onboard in Italy's first commercial aviation disaster. In 1921, he built the prototype of a giant transatlantic passenger seaplane, the Caproni Ca.60 *Noviplano*, with a one hundred passenger capacity. Between WWI and WWII, most of Caproni's efforts were concentrated on the design and production of bombers and light transport aircraft, and his company manufactured the early Stipa-Caproni and Caproni Campini N.1 ducted fan experimental aircraft, which were precursors of true jet aircraft. Seventy-three-year-old Caproni would pass on 27 October 1957.

Count Gianni Caproni

Ca.4 and later Ca.40/50 Series

After designing the successful Caproni Ca.3 WWI biplane bomber, Caproni designed a much larger version that had an unusual, atypical tri-plane layout, rather than the more common biplane, with twin booms containing a single elevator and

Caproni Ca.4

three fins. The Ca.4 was powered by a push-pull engine configuration, with one pusher engine at the rear of a central nacelle and two tractor engines in front of twin booms. The engines were three 400 hp V-12 water-cooled piston American Liberty L-12s. The main landing gear was fixed and consisted of two sets of four wheels each. All the variants had a ninety-eight-foot wing span, a wing area of 2,200 sq. ft., a length of forty-three ft., an empty weight of 14,780 lbs., and a maximum take-off weight of 16,535 lbs. The huge new bomber was accepted by the Italian Army under the military designation Ca.4, but was produced in several variants, differing in factory designations in the Ca.40–Ca.50 series. Various publications provide different production figures, but the most likely number is thirty-eight examples of all Ca.4 variants, including the Ca.40 (single prototype), Ca.41 (production variant), Ca.42 (re-engined), Ca.43 (floatplane), Ca.48 (airliner conversion), Ca.51 (enlarged, re-engined version), Ca.52 (built for the RNAS), Ca.58 (re-engined), and Ca.59 (export version).

Caproni Ca.60

It is not documented why Gianni Caproni, the designer and builder of some very good aircraft, chose to build a grotesque "Trans-Atlantic" one-hundred-passenger giant flying boat, the Caproni Ca.60 *Noviplano*. The outlandish aircraft had nine wings in three tri-wing sets positioned above and along a giant fuselage that resembled a luxury houseboat. It had no tail surfaces, two pontoons mounted on each side to give the aircraft stability, and was powered by eight 400 hp American Liberty L-12 liquid-cooled V12 engines. To make Caproni's Capronissimo even more bizarre was he intended it to be a prototype for an even larger version! The three sets of triple wings measured 98.5 ft. each, while the aircraft was 77 ft. long. Only one Ca.60 was built, and it only made one short flight on 4 March 1921, over Lake Maggiore, in northern Italy. The 55,000 lb. (loaded weight) aircraft lumbered off the lake's surface, attaining an altitude of about 60 ft. before diving and crashing, breaking up on impact and with its lucky pilot escaping unharmed. There was speculation that previous testing had shown the need for heavy lead ballast that had shifted in flight, causing the disastrous crash. Caproni had the wrecked giant towed to shore and announced it would be rebuilt, but that night it was destroyed by a "mysterious" fire that ended the count's trans-Atlantic (pipe)dream.

Caproni Ca.60

Caproni Ca.90

The Caproni Ca.90 was a large prototype biplane heavy bomber designed and built by Caproni that first flew in 1929. Although Italians considered it the largest aircraft in the world at the time, the German Dornier Do X flying boat that flew later in 1929 had a larger wingspan and was heavier, so the Ca.90 would be the largest land plane until the introduction of the Russian Tupolev ANT-20 in 1934. It was a six-engined inverted sesquiplane (a biplane having one wing with not more than half the surface area of the other wing). The upper wing had a span of 114.5 ft., while the span of the lower wing was just under 153 ft. Total wing area was 5,345.4 sq. ft. Empty weight was 33,069 lbs., and maximum take-off weight was 66,139 lbs. It was powered by two tandem pairs of 1,000 hp Isotta-Fraschini Asso 1000 W-18 inline piston engines mounted above the lower wing, with each pair driving a four-bladed pusher and a two-bladed tractor propeller. Another pair of engines was mounted above the fuselage. Its maximum speed was 127 mph, range was approximately 700 miles, its service ceiling was about 14,750 ft., and its bomb load was eight tons.

Caproni Ca.90

2
SAVOIA-MARCHETTI LONG-DISTANCE RECORD SETTERS

The initial company was founded in 1915 as *Societa Idrovolanti Alta Italia* (SIAI, Seaplane Company of Northern Italy). After WWI the name Savoia was added when it acquired the *Societa Anonima Costruzioni Aeronautiche Savoia*, an Italian aircraft company founded by Umberto Savoia in 1915. The name Marchetti was added when Chief Designer Alessandro Marchetti joined the company in 1922. Savoia-Marchetti became famous for its flying boats and seaplanes, which set numerous endurance and speed records.

Savoia-Marchetti S.64 and S.64bis
S.64

After Charles Lindbergh's New York to Paris trans-Atlantic flight in May 1927, the Italian Air Ministry decided to build a long distance record setting aircraft to display the expertise of Italian aviation to the world. Savoia-Marchetti chief designer Alessandro Marchetti was chosen to design this record breaking aircraft without any design stipulations and was given comprehensive control of the aircraft's configuration. The result was the unorthodox Savoia-Marchetti S.64, which was similar to Marchetti's earlier unusual pod-and-boom designed S.55 flying boat, with the empennage carried on two open truss structures that extended aft from the wings. The single 550 hp FIAT A.22T V-12 liquid-cooled pusher engine was mounted on a set of struts above the wing center and turned a two-blade wooden propeller with a streamlined, pointed spinner. Coolant from the engine flowed down tubes in the supporting struts into a radiator under the rear of the wing. This radiator was semi-retractable, so it could be extended below the wing for increased airflow. A pod-like fuselage nacelle protruded below the wing, extending beyond its leading edge and was part of the wing's center structure. The pilot and co-pilot sat side-by-side inside a fully enclosed stubby wooden fuselage pod skinned with plywood. The pilots were provided a rest area in the rear of the fuselage for long distance flights. The S.64's large, thick, wooden/plywood-skinned cantilever wing had a 70.5 ft. span and a 646 sq. ft. area that housed twenty-seven fuel tanks holding 1,717 gallons of fuel. The 34.1 ft. long S.64 had an empty weight of 5,291 lbs. and a maximum weight of 15,432 lbs.—nearly three times its empty weight—resulting in a useful load of 10,141 lbs., much of which was fuel, giving the aircraft an estimated range of 7,146 miles. Two duralumin frame booms extended behind the wing and supported the S.64's slab horizontal stabilizer from underneath on both sides of the single vertical stabilizer. The fixed main gear was faired, and was suspended via struts under the wing while a tail skid was attached to the end of each boom.

Savoia-Marchetti S.64

The Italian Air Ministry ordered two S.64s: the first example was flown by Alessandro Passeleva on 3 April 1928, at Cameri Airfield, in northern Italy. On 10 April, Arturo Ferrarin and Carlo del Prete conducted flight tests that revealed the aircraft had a high take-off speed, requiring a long, smooth runway, and a special 4,265 ft. concrete-paved runway was constructed at Guidonia Montecelio, near Rome. Flight testing continued with progressively larger fuel loads and the installation of a larger 9.8 ft. diameter propeller replacement. On 31 May, Ferrarin and del Prete took off with 921 gallons of fuel in an attempt to set a new closed circuit distance record. The duo made fifty-one triangular round trips between Montecelio, to Torre Flavia, to Anzio, and back to Montecelio. When they landed on 3 June after 58:34 hours they had flown 4,791 miles for a new world distance record over a closed circuit, and they also set the world record for top speed over a distance of 5,000 km (3,110 mi) at 87 mph. The S.64 had surpassed the endurance record set by Americans Edward Stinson and George Haldeman, who flew for 53:35 hours in a Stinson Detroiter in late March 1928. After setting the record the air ministry announced that this flight was only a "proving exercise" for a future Rome to New York trans-Atlantic flight.

Arturo Ferrarin (L), Carlo del Prete, and their Savoia-Marchetti S.64

The S.64 was salvaged and taken by ship to Rio and donated to Brazil. The Italians' endurance record would be short-lived, as later in July a German Junkers W33 flown by Johann Risztics and Wilhelm Zimmermann flew non-stop for 65:25 hours.

S.64bis

The second, improved S.64 (it had a longer windscreen and a variable-pitch metal propeller), designated the S.64bis, was prepared to regain the endurance record. In mid-December 1929, while S.64bis flight testing was being delayed by bad weather, French pilots Dieudonne Costes and Paul Codos eclipsed the S.64's distance record, flying 4,989.26 miles in their Breguet 19. On 29 May 1930, Umberto Maddalena and Fausto Cecconi took off from Montecelio in their S.64bis and flew the same closed circuit course the S.64 had traveled. When they landed on 2 June (the second anniversary of Ferrarin and del Prete's S.64 flight), Maddalena and Cecconi became the new endurance and distance record holders with their 67:13:55 hour flight that covered 5,088.28 miles. Unfortunately, the S.64bis would set no other records, as on 19 March 1931, while preparing to regain the endurance record, an undetermined failure occurred near Pisa, about halfway into their flight from Cinisello (near Milan) to Montecelio. The S.64bis crashed into the sea, killing Maddalena and Cecconi and radio operator Giuseppe Da Monte. The S.64bis' wreckage was too widely scattered to determine the cause, but the commission of inquiry suspected that the FIAT engine's crankshaft may have broken, causing the propeller to cut into the wing and fuselage nacelle.

Umberto Maddalena (L), Fausto Cecconi, and their Savoia-Marchetti S.64 bis after a record 67:13:55 hour flight that covered 5,088.28 miles.

The S.64 returned to Montecelio to prepare for its next record flight: not trans-Atlantic to New York, but a straight-line flight of over 5,800 miles from Montecelio to Rio de Janerio, Brazil. That destination was changed to fly 5,280 miles to Bahia, Brazil, due to the high temperatures in Montecelio, which would have necessitated an even longer take-off run with the same fuel load. The S.64 departed Montecelio the evening of 3 July, flying over Sardinia overnight and then passing Gibraltar early the next morning. During 4 July, their course headed south down the northeast coast of Africa, and by that evening they were over the Cape Verde Islands and proceeded for Brazil. The afternoon of 5 July, Ferrarin and del Prete crossed the Brazilian coastline and flew south toward Bahia, only to discover thick fog below. After searching for a landing strip without success they turned back north for another one hundred miles, and after 49:15 hours made a forced landing on a beach at Touros, damaging the S.64's landing gear and fuselage. Nonetheless, the S.64 set a new straight-line distance record of 4,466.58 miles (not accounting for the distance flown searching for a landing strip). After repairs to the S.62, Ferrarin and del Prete flew the S.64 to Natal and then Rio de Janeiro, where they remained for weeks. During this time Ferrarin and del Prete crashed during a demonstration flight in a S.62 on 11 August, with del Prete dying from his injuries five days later.

3
ITALIAN PASSENGER AND MILITARY LONG-RANGE AIRCRAFT

1920: LTS. ARTURO FERRARIN AND GINO CAPPANNINI FLY ROME TO TOKYO

In post-WWI Italy, a plan was approved for a goodwill flight to Tokyo called the *Rome-Tokyo Raid.* The plan was to send two Ansaldo SVA-9 two seat trainers, each with a pilot and mechanic, ahead as route pathfinders (called "Hares") for a formation flight of three Caproni Ca.3 tri-motor bombers and five additional SVA-9s to follow later. The logistics of the flight were almost overwhelming, including the procurement, organization, and transportation of fuel, oil, spare parts, and aircraft, and then organizing, staffing, and often protecting the route and resting/refueling stops.

Two SVA-9s were to leave first, and were to be followed by the other aircraft. One was piloted by Arturo Ferrarin, who served as a fighter pilot in the war, and his mechanic Gino Cappannini, while the other was piloted by five-victory ace Lt. Guido Masiero and his mechanic Roberto Maretto. As the two aircraft left Rome's Centocelle Airport on 14 February 1920, what began as a flight to Japan was to become a "friendly" race. Ferrarin flew to Baghdad without a problem, but there his aircraft malfunctioned and he had to land on a soccer field during a match. After leaving Rome Masiero was forced to make several unscheduled repair stops, putting him three days behind in Baghdad. After Ferrarin had some en route problems Masiero finally overtook him before Karachi, but Ferrarin, arriving behind Masiero after dark in Delhi, made a hard landing and damaged the undercarriage. While Ferrarin's SVA was being repaired Masiero took off for Calcutta, but underwent engine failure on the climb out and crashed heavily, destroying his plane without injury to himself or Maretto. Ferrarin, his plane repaired, flew on to Calcutta while Masiero and Maretto continued on to Calcutta by train. After a fuel stop at Allahabad and a diversion to Agra to sightsee the Taj Mahal from the air Ferrarin and Cappannini arrived safely in Calcutta. The Italian ground crew at Calcutta severely damaged Ferrarin's plane while servicing it, and he and Masiero were forced to fly spare SVA-9s that had been pre-positioned there for that eventuality. During the next stop, while flying into Rangoon Ferrarin's overheated engine seized upon landing, forcing a dead stick landing and another delay for an engine change. Masiero went on ahead to Bangkok, where he was joined a day later by Ferrarin. The next leg to Ubon and Hanoi was uneventful, but en route to Canton from Hanoi both pilots became lost and landed in Portuguese Macao to wait for better weather, then continued on to Canton. Rainy weather and flooding made the take off from Canton for Foochow treacherous; Ferrarin got off, but Masiero crashed, destroying his aircraft; both he and Maretto were unhurt and continued to Shanghai by boat. Ferrarin's departure from Foochow for Shanghai was delayed for a week by a typhoon, and when Farrarin/Cappannini joined Masiero/Maretto in Shanghai they were feted in a week-long celebration. There was another spare SVA in Shanghai for Masiero and Maretto, and the two SVAs took off for Tsingtao and encountered another typhoon en route. At the time Tsingtao was a Japanese mandate of the Versailles Treaty, and the Japanese gave them an unwanted four-day celebration there, which was insured because the Japanese refused to refuel their aircraft for the next leg of the flight to Peking until the revelry was over. The Italians were given seven more days of celebrations

Lts. Arturo Ferrarin and Gino Cappannini in Japan

on their arrival in Peking, China. After a fuel stop at Mukden they flew on to Sinuiju, in Japanese mandate Chosen (Korea), and then flew to Seoul and Taegu before crossing the Sea of Japan to Osaka, where they were greeted by a huge crowd. The two SVAs were cleaned and serviced for the last leg of the trip to Tokyo, where they landed at 1330 on 31 May 1920.

To celebrate the conclusion of their amazing flight, an imperial decree proclaimed forty-two days of extraordinary festivities, including a special imperial audience with the empress as surrogate for the emperor, who was ill. As a gesture of friendship the Italian government presented Ferrarin's SVA to the Japanese, who placed it in the Imperial Munitions Museum in Tokyo, where it remained displayed until destroyed by B-29 raids in 1945. At the end of the forty-two-day celebration the fliers boarded the Italian liner *Pilsna* and were greeted at Bari, not with forty-two days of festivities, but with bills from the Italian Ministry of Finance for their fare and meals on the voyage! The crews had been en route from Rome to Tokyo for 106 calendar days, of which only twenty-three were actual flying days due to weather delays, logistics problems, and celebrations.

Ferrarin died at age forty-six in a crash while testing a prototype aircraft in Rome in 1941; Masiero at age forty-seven in a mid-air collision over Milano in 1942; Cappannini at age forty in combat over Tobruk in 1940; and Maretto at fifty of illness in Padua in 1942. All men died while serving in the Italian Air Force.

1925 AND 1927: THE EPIC FLIGHTS OF FRANCESCO DE PINEDO

1925: Rome-Australia-Tokyo-Rome

During WWI, Naples Nobleman (Count Francesco De Pinedo) served in the Royal Italian Navy's air division, mostly flying reconnaissance. After the war he took part in milestone flights to the Netherlands and Turkey, establishing his technical talents and organizational skills, and in 1924, he was transferred from the navy to help structure the newly created *Regia Aeronautica*. Soon he was assigned to organize and pilot a flight to Australia and beyond. The aircraft he selected was a Savoia S-16ter, a five-seat biplane flying boat he named the *Gennariello*, after San Gennaro, Naples' patron saint. The seaplane was powered by a single Fiat A.12bis engine. The Savoia had a wingspan of 50.9 ft., a length of 32.5 ft., and was 12 ft. high. Three of the seats were removed to make room for additional supplies, spare parts, and fuel. Provisions were made with Shell Oil Company, the British government, and local suppliers for refueling along the well-planned route. On 20 April 1925, after preparations were completed, de Pinedo and his mechanic Ernesto Campanelli took off from the Savoia factory heading east over the Middle East and India, gradually falling behind schedule due to bad weather and lengthy repairs. Their flight to Australia was during the monsoon season, and they encountered near-constant rain and gale-strength winds until they reached the Australian coast on 31 May. In Australia their tour circumnavigated the continent, including stops in Melbourne, Sidney, and Brisbane. The next objective was to explore the first air route between Australia and Japan, and they landed in Tokyo on 26 September to a tumultuous week-long welcome. After the *Gennariello's* engine was changed de Pinedo returned to Rome on 7 November, after flying 34,000 miles.

Count Marquis Francesco de Pinedo (in cockpit), mechanic Ernesto Campanelli, and their Savoia S-16ter seaplane

1927: ROME-SOUTH AMERICA-UNITED STATES-ROME

Count de Pinedo planned a route that would begin in Rome, followed by an Atlantic crossing to Brazil from Portuguese Guinea, on Africa's jutting western coast, offering the narrowest distance between the continents. From Brazil he would proceed with a lengthy tour of South America and make his way to North America, visit major US and Canadian cities, then finish the voyage with a second Atlantic crossing back to Italy. In choosing his aircraft, de Pinedo opted to employ an S.55 flying boat designed by Alessandro Marchetti as a torpedo bomber for the Regia Aeronautica that had recently set fourteen world records in its class for speed, distance, altitude, and load capabilities. The *Santa Maria's* two sleek hulls were joined by a single broad and sweeping wing. The cockpit was situated in the center of the wing, above which perched two tandem-mounted 1,000 hp Isotta Fraschini V-6 engines. The S.55 was equipped with top quality navigational instruments and in case of an emergency landing at sea: a saltwater distiller, a life raft, and fishing gear. For his crew de Pinedo chose navy friend and navigation expert Capt. Carlo del Prete and skilled mechanic Sgt. Vitale Zacchetti.

The *Santa Maria* left on its voyage the early morning of 13 February, skirting the Algerian coast and Morocco, the Gibraltar Strait, and over the desolate beaches of the Spanish Sahara. The next morning, the *Santa Maria* reached Bolama, in Portuguese Guinea, where they prepared for the Atlantic crossing on 16 February. The weather was so hot that the engines rapidly overheated whenever the overloaded plane tried to lift off and they then flew back north to the Cape Verde Islands with less fuel, where cooler weather was reported. They were able to take off on 23 February, but only after the fuel load was limited to the calculated minimum required and every item that was not absolutely necessary was left behind. During the crossing the *Santa Maria's* engine overheated and the crew's drinking water had to be used before the overheating stopped. Then the S.55 was buffeted by storms, and when nearing the Brazilian coast de Pinedo had to set the aircraft down on rough seas and was towed by a Brazilian cruiser that damaged its aileron before reaching Natal. After repairs the *Santa Maria* visited cities on the Brazilian coast until it reached Rio de Janiero, and then continued on to Buenos Aires, Montevideo, and four days of difficult navigation across the continent over Brazil's vast Matto Grosso region's dense jungles. They landed at Manaos, in northeastern Brazil, and followed the Amazon River 1,000 miles east to Para, near the Atlantic coast.

With the most rigorous part of their voyage behind them, they were ready to take on the second half of their tour and headed for Georgetown, Guyana, their final South American stop. The next day they crossed the Caribbean Sea, making brief visits at Pointe-a-Pitre, Port-au-Prince, and Havana, and made American landfall in New Orleans, landing on the Mississippi River the afternoon of 29 March and claiming to be the first foreign airplane to fly to the United States. The US tour got underway on 2 April, with the Italians making a five-hour flight to Galveston, then flying on to San Antonio. Over the next few days their route took them along the course of the Rio Grande, into New Mexico, and over the Rockies, where they used the Southern Pacific Railroad tracks as a guide. By 6 April, they headed to San Diego, and on the way the S.55 landed on Roosevelt Reservoir, Arizona, to refuel. During the refueling a helper with a cigarette set the *Santa Maria* on fire and it was destroyed after journeying 18,000 miles. Italo Balbo, the new secretary of state for air, ordered the construction of an exact duplicate and arranged for its shipment by sea to New York; on 1 May, the *Santa Maria II* arrived in New York. Ostensibly to return to Italy on schedule, de Pinedo revised his itinerary by eliminating all stops west of the Mississippi. At the time the Orteig Prize "mania" and to be the first to cross the Atlantic was at its crescendo and de Pinedo, not wanting to see his achievements of the past four months become obscured by the more sensational feat of an Atlantic crossing, decided that he would be the first to cross. First, de Pinedo and his crew decided on a shakedown trip with their new aircraft by finishing their East Coast tour with stops in Boston, Philadelphia, and Charleston, before returning to New Orleans for a token tour of the Midwest. From the Midwest they planned to fly to Newfoundland by way of the Great Lakes and St. Lawrence Seaway to be ready to cross the Atlantic by 21 May at the latest. The schedule was kept and they arrived at Trepassey Bay, Newfoundland, on 20 May, the same day Lindbergh flew east toward Paris in the *Spirit of St. Louis*. The S.55's range was only 1,300 miles, so the Newfoundland-Azores-Portugal route flown by the US Navy planes in their 1919 crossing was chosen by de Pinedo as the logical route, since it provided the indispensable midway refueling point. After take-off weather caused them to drift off course and de Pinedo determined there was not enough fuel to reach the Azores. A Portuguese fishing boat was sighted and de Pinedo landed the plane near the vessel; the fishermen offered to tow the aircraft the remaining miles to the Azores.

During the tow the *Santa Maria II* sustained damage which took a week to repair. Conscientious de Pinedo resumed the flight by returning to the same spot where he began his tow. After stops in Portugal and Spain, on 16 June, de Pinedo concluded his flight in Ostia harbor, just west of Rome.

After his 1927 flight, Benito Mussolini christened de Pineda the "Lord of Distances" and promoted him to general, after which de Pinedo became an involved bureaucrat in the Regia Aeronautica. Meanwhile, the government would not support any future long distance flights by individual aircraft, but would sponsor goodwill tours by squadrons of aircraft to demonstrate fascist Italy's growing military strength. De Pinedo resigned from the Regia Aeronautica in 1933 to pursue long distance flying and sailed to the US under the unimaginative pseudonym "Mr. Smith." He purchased a Bellanca monoplane and planned to fly from New York to Baghdad to set a new non-stop solo distance flight record of 6,300 miles. At dawn on 3 September the attempt ended tragically when de Pinedo lost control during take-off from Floyd Bennett Field, and the Bellanca, laden with more than 1,000 gallons of fuel, skidded off the pavement and crashed into a steel fence adjacent to the runway. The impact ejected de Pinedo from the cockpit unhurt and he quickly returned to shut off the engine of the smoldering Bellanca. Just as he climbed up to reach the control panel the fuel vapors ignited and de Pineda died in a flaming explosion.

Francesco de Pinedo and mechanic Sgt. Vitale Zacchetti with their Savoia-Marchetti S.55 seaplane

Savoia-Marchetti S.55 Seaplane

The S.55 seaplane presented many innovative design features. All the passengers or cargo were placed in the twin hulls, but the pilot and crew flew the plane from a cockpit in the thicker section of the wing between the two hulls. The S.55 had two inline counter-rotating propellers turned by twin, sharply upward canted, 880 hp Isotta-Fraschini *Asso* 750V engines mounted back to back (pusher/tractor). Two wire-braced booms connected the triple-finned tail structure to the twin hulls and wing. The seaplane had a wingspan of 74.8 ft. and a wing area of 1,001 sq. ft., a length of 55 ft., and a height of 16.4 ft. During 1926, the S.55P prototype set fourteen world records for speed, altitude, and distance with a payload, but the S.55's greatest successes were its flights between Europe and the Americas. The TAM Museum in Sao Carlos, Brazil, contains the last example of the S.55 painted in Joao Ribeiro de Barros' markings (see below).

1927: JOAO RIBEIRO DE BARROS CROSSES THE SOUTH ATLANTIC

In 1926, Brazilian Joao Ribeiro de Barros decided to attempt a "raid"—as transatlantic air crossings were known at the time—from Italy to Brazil without using support ships. After having his request for help from the Brazilian government denied his brothers bought his inheritance and traveled to Italy, where he purchased a damaged Savoia-Marchetti S.55 seaplane, the *Alcione*; it had previously been used by Count Casagrande during a failed attempt to complete the Italy-Brazil transatlantic crossing when, at Casablanca, it was determined that the aircraft was not capable of the ocean crossing. De Barros and mechanic Vasco Cinquini refurbished the aircraft and convinced Joao Negrao (co-pilot), Newton Braga (navigator), and Vasco Cinquini (mechanic) to accompany them in the renamed *Jahu*, in honor of De Barros' home town. The *Jahu* left Genoa, Italy, on 18 October 1926 for the Cape Verde Islands to begin its crossing of the Atlantic. An emergency stop was needed in Alicante, Spain, when it seems their aircraft was sabotaged in Genoa, as water, sand, and soap were found in the engine. They were also arrested in Spain, accused of landing there without permission, but the Brazilian consul in Spain intervened. Another emergency caused a stop in Gibraltar, where new repairs were made. After a few days they reached the Cape Verde Islands, where, due to disagreements, co-pilot Arthur Cunha was discharged. While preparing to make the crossing de Barros contracted malaria and had to wait, giving him the opportunity to ready and repair the *Jahu*. While waiting he received a telegram from the Brazilian government, which had supplied him no aid, ordering him to discontinue his attempt to cross the Atlantic and dismantle the aircraft and ship it to Brazil. The outraged de Barros ignored the order, but suffered more bouts of malaria; it was not until the morning of 28 Apri 1927 that the *Jahu* took-off from Praia, on Santiago Island (Cape Verde), and crossed the Atlantic, landing triumphantly at 1700 in the northern cove of Fernando de Noronha and establishing a record for speed that was only surpassed a number of years later. Afterward, de Barros landed at each of the great Brazilian coastal cities—Natal, Recife, Salvador, Rio de Janeiro, Santos, and Sao Paulo—where he was received with great adulation. Today the *Jahu* is on display at the TAM Museum in Sao Paulo.

Joao Ribeiro de Barros on the wing above the rear cockpit of the S.55 Jahu/Ja Volto

ITALO BALBO LEADS LONG DISTANCE FLIGHTS FOR THE GLORY OF ITALY

After serving in WWI, Balbo became a leading fascist organizer and was one of the principals that brought Mussolini and the fascists to power in 1922. On 6 November 1926, with only a modicum of aviation experience, Balbo was appointed secretary of state for air and began building the Regia Aeronautica Italiana (Italian Royal Air Force), and took a leading role in popularizing aviation in Italy and promoting Italian aviation to the world. On 19 August 1928, he became general of the air force, and on 12 September 1929, minister of the air force. Balbo became famous for organizing a squadron of S.55 seaplanes, and led two trans-Atlantic flights for the glory of Italy and for the glory of Italo Bilbo.

Balbo's first trans-Atlantic crossing was flown between 17 December 1930 and 15 January 1931, when he led twelve Savoia-Marchetti S.55 flying boats 6,500 miles from Orbetello, Italy, to Rio de Janeiro, Brazil. Balbo's most notable trans-Atlantic flight culminated when he led twenty-four S.55s to Chicago's Century of Progress International Exposition. On 1 July 1933, Balbo commanded the flight of S-55s from Orbetello, Italy, and completed the 6,100 mile flight in 47:52 hours, maintaining a tight "V" formation sometimes called a "Balbo." The flight had seven legs: Orbetello-Amsterdam-Derry, Ireland-Reykjavík, Iceland-Cartwright- Labrador-Shediac-Montreal, and landing on Chicago's Lake Michigan shore. In honor of the flight Mussolini donated a column to the city of Chicago which stands today somewhat south of Soldier Field. During Balbo's time in America President Roosevelt invited him to lunch and presented him with the Distinguished Flying Cross. Later he was awarded the 1931 Harmon Trophy.

On Balbo's return to Rome he was also honored as he and his airmen paraded under Constantine's Arch and Balbo was promoted to air marshal. Mussolini and other fascist leaders became aware of his popularity, especially among the young, and were irritated by his coarse manners and impertinence. Balbo was then exiled to Libya as its colonial governor in January 1934, where he remained 1933–1940, transforming Libya from a backward colony to an ideal Italian province. During early WWII he brazenly appealed for Italy to side with Great Britain, further raising Mussolini's ire. Nonetheless, Balbo remained loyal to Italy and led air patrols against the British over North Africa. On 28 June 1940, he was killed by friendly fire while landing in Tobruk, Libya, several minutes after a British air attack. Although the fascist government contended his death was due to friendly fire, Balbo's closest friends and family strongly asserted that it was an assassination on Mussolini's orders.

During July 1933, Italo Balbo commanded a flight of S-55s.Jahu/Ja Volto.

Savoia-Marchetti SM.75

The tri-motor Savoia-Marchetti SM.75 Marsupiale (Marsupial) was the last of a series of Italian passenger and military transport aircraft that Alessandro Marchetti designed and manufactured in the early 1930s. The Italian airline Ala Littoria, which had been flying the Savoia-Marchetti SM.73, was seeking a modern, middle-to-long-range airliner and cargo aircraft as a replacement. During its first flight in November 1937, the SM.75 proved to be a fast, durable aircraft capable of long-range flight that could carry a four-man crew and up to twenty-four passengers for 1,000 miles. Because of its short take-off run (1,100 ft.) and even shorter landing distance (920 ft.), it could operate from short runways on ancillary airfields. Three 750 (or 860) hp Alfa Romeo 126 radial engines powered the aircraft. With the SM.75, Marchetti retained the general configuration of the low-wing, tri-motor SM.73 monoplane, but introduced a retractable main landing and tail wheel gear to reduce aerodynamic drag. The SM.75's 70.8 ft. long airframe was constructed of a steel-tube frame with fabric and plywood covering, while the control surfaces were plywood covered. It had a wingspan of 97.4 ft. and a wing area of 1,276 sq. ft.

In Italian commercial service with Ala Littoria beginning in 1938, the SM.75 was employed on routes within Europe and to South America, as well as establishing the Rome-Addis Ababa route during the Italian invasion and conquest of Abyssinia. During the late 1930s, the SM.75 established a number of world records for speed-over-distance-with-payload and closed-circuit transport aircraft distance. After Italy entered WWII on 10 June 1940, the civil SM.75s continued to fly supply operations to Italy's overseas territories and also operated its services to South America until December 1941, when Italy declared war on the United States. Civil operations declined as the war progressed and ceased with the Italian armistice on 8 September 1943.

Savoia-Marchetti SM.75

Special missions

Because of its long range the SM.75 flew several notable missions, mainly for propaganda purposes.

Leaflet mission to Asmara

In January 1942, Regia Aeronautica Commander-in-Chief Gen. Rino Corso Fougier became interested in a long-range flight from Rome to Tokyo and consulted with experienced civilian SM.75 pilots who had previously flown long-range flights to South America and East Africa. The consultations determined that the SM.75 was more suitable than the SM.82 because of its superior endurance, notwithstanding the expense of deleted defensive armament and self-sealing fuel tanks. The SM.75 aircraft selected for the flight (s/n MM.60537) was modified to become the first long-range SM.75 GA (*Grande Autonomia*/Long-range) aircraft. The SM.75 GA was powered by three 860 hp Alfa Romeo 128 engines and had auxiliary fuel tanks to increase its range to 4,350 miles carrying a 2,430 lb. load or 4,971 miles with a four- or five-man crew and only a 441 lb. load.

Pilot Lt.Col. Amadeo Paradisi flew a Savoia-Marchetti SM.75 from Rome to Benghazi to Eritrea and back to Rome on a twenty-eight hour leaflet dropping mission in May 1942.

The first mission of the SM.75 GA was to drop propaganda leaflets over British-held territory in East Africa occupied by Italian colonists, assuring them, "Rome is not forgetting you. We shall come back!" At 1730 on 7 May 1942, a five-man crew led by pilot Lt.Col. Amadeo Paradisi flew from Rome to Benghazi, Libya, on the 1,700 mile first leg. Despite some bad weather, after 10:20 hours in the air the SM.75 GA arrived over Asmara, in Eritrea, and released the leaflets, but instead of returning as planned to Benghazi, Paradisi flew directly to Rome at high altitude (17,060 ft.) on the last portion of the twenty-eight-hour mission to optimize fuel consumption. On 11 May 1942, two days after arriving in Rome, this SM.75GA suffered a simultaneous failure of all three of its engines during a thirty-mile ferry flight from Rome to Montecelio. Paradisi skillfully glided the SM.75 to an emergency landing that destroyed the aircraft; he lost a leg, although the rest of the crew escaped injury.

ROME-TO-TOKYO FLIGHT

After the first SM.75 GA was a total loss, a second SM.75 (s/n MM.60539) was modified to the SM.75 GA standard for a wartime flight from Rome to Tokyo and was designated the SM.75 GA RT (Rome-Tokyo). The mission was not only to demonstrate Italian aviation competence, but to carry new codes for communications between Japan, Italy, and Germany, as the Italians supposed the British had broken established codes. The flight was not only to be difficult due to the extreme distance involved, but also because many miles were flown through enemy Soviet territory, causing the flight to be postponed due to military and political considerations. Nonetheless, it remained viable for its propaganda value. The Japanese, who were not at war with the Soviets, requested that the flight be kept secret and that the aircraft carry no documents nor correspondence that could embarrass the Japanese if captured; its crew were ordered to burn the aircraft if forced down in Soviet territory.

At 0530 on 29 June 1942, the mission was ready, and was to be led by Lt.Col. Antonio Moscatelli assisted by two other pilots—Capts. Mario Curio and Dr. Publio Magni; radio-navigator Lt. Ernesto Mazzotti; and engineer Sgt. Ernesto Leone. In the meantime, although its load had been steadily reduced, the still-overloaded aircraft weighed 47,400 lbs., including 24,250 lbs. of fuel, and had trouble getting airborne even from the extended runway at Montecelio. Once airborne Moscatelli headed for the Italian occupied base at Zaporozhye, in German-occupied Ukraine, which was the easternmost airfield available to Axis aircraft. The SM.75GR RT landed later that day for refueling after flying 1,260 miles in 14:10 hours. Hoping to avoid Soviet fighter interception, the SM.75 took off on 30 June 1942 at 1800, flying in the safety of darkness. Moscatelli guided the again overloaded SM.75 off the challenging 2,300 ft. grass Russian runway. With the heavy load the SM.75 was unable to climb above 2,500 ft. and at a greatly reduced speed, rendering the aircraft vulnerable to fighter interception or anti-aircraft fire. Observing strict radio silence, Moscatelli piloted the aircraft safely through Soviet ground defenses, poor weather, and evaded a Soviet fighter while flying north of the Caspian Sea. From there the SM.75 flew over the north coast of the Aral Sea, near Lake Baikal, over the Tarbagatai Mountains that separate Russia and China, and then over the Gobi Desert. Because their maps of Soviet positions were found to be erroneous Moscatelli had to climb to 16,500 ft. to avoid detection, causing the aircraft's oxygen supply to deplete earlier than scheduled. A sandstorm over Mongolia caused navigation problems, but fortunately the crew sighted the Yellow River at 2200 on 30 June 1942. With the SM.75's fuel almost exhausted after flying 3,700 miles in 21:14 hours, Moscatelli landed on the 4,270 ft. runway at Pao Tow Chien, in Japanese occupied Inner Mongolia, at 1720 on 1 July 1942.

At Pao Tow Chien the aircraft was painted with provisional Japanese "Rising Sun" markings for safe passage in Japanese airspace, which was especially important after the Doolittle Raid on Tokyo two months earlier that heightened Japanese air defenses. The SM.75 left for Tokyo at 0700 on 3 July on its final 1,700 mile leg under the guidance of a Japanese navigator and landed at Tachikawa Air Force Base, near Tokyo, at 1704 on 5 July.

After several days of festivities and return route planning the SM.75 departed Tokyo on its return journey at 0520 on 16 July 1942. It arrived at Pao Tow Chien at 1540, where its Japanese markings were removed and replaced with Italian symbols. It took off at 2145 on 18 July 1942, retracing its route over Soviet territory, and after 29:25 hours in the air and having covered 3,950 miles, it landed in Odessa, in the Ukraine, at 0210 on 20 July. Moscatelli took off the same day at 1100, flying to Montecelio, landing at 1750, and finding Mussolini waiting to greet the crew. Despite the Japanese insistence that the flight be kept secret, Italian/Mussolini ego publicized it on 2 August 1942, causing the Japanese to cancel the proposed second flight in August which was to investigate a more southerly route.

Lt.Col. Antonio Moscatelli and his crew pose in front of their SM.75 after landing in Tokyo on 5 July 1942, after flying 5,400 miles from Rome.

Bombing Mission to Abyssinia

In 1943, a proposal was tendered for two SM.75 GAs to carry out a bombing mission intended to destroy American bombers stored at an airbase in Gura, in Abyssinia. The mission would entail a 1,900 mile flight and would be the only bombing mission made by a SM.75. The two S.75 GAs had their civil registrations, *I-BUBA* and *I-TAMO,* redesignated with military serial numbers MM.60539 and MM.60543, respectively. These GAs were greatly modified to carry 24,250 lbs. of fuel and specially equipped with a Jozza bomb aiming system and a bomb bay capable of carrying a bomb load of 2,650 lbs.

The mission, led by experienced officers Alberto Villa and Max Peroli, took off at 0630 on 23 May 1943 from the island of Rhodes in the Aegean Sea, which at the time was the easternmost Regia Aeronautica base. The aircraft, which weighed 22,490 lbs. empty, had a take-off weight of 52,910 lbs. Because the bomber's Alfa Romeo engines were enhanced for endurance and economy rather than power, take-off with the heavy load of fuel and bombs was difficult. After initially being forced to fly at low altitude for 3:30 hours until some of the fuel load was burned off, the SM.75 GAs climbed to 9,850 ft. Because Peroli had used an extreme amount of fuel he had to divert to bomb Port Sudan instead and returned safely to Rhodes at 0530 on 24 May 1943, after 23 hours in the air. Meanwhile, Villa flew on alone and arrived over heavily defended Gura Airbase at 1845. Villa dropped his bombs, and although one bomb hung up on board, Villa's mission was considered successful and he returned to Rhodes safely 1:15 hours after Peroli, landing at 0645 on 24 May 1943, after flying 4,100 miles during 24:15 hours in the air.

Savoia-Marchetti SM.82

The Regia Aeronautica needed aircraft to maintain contact with Italy's imperial possessions in East Africa (Abyssinia, Italian Somaliland, and Eritrea), which were surrounded by British controlled territories and military forces. The Regia Aeronautica Savoia-Marchetti SM.82 *Canguru* (Kangaroo), powered by three Alfa Romeo 128 RC.21 engines, could carry up to twenty-four troops over long distances with the same performance as the airliner version. This aircraft had no windows in the passenger cabin and had a greater cargo capacity than the SM.75. It had a reinforced panel in the cabin for the installation of a 12.7 mm Breda-SAFAT machine gun mounted in a dorsal Caproni-Lanciani gun turret for a fifth crewman to man it. The SM.82 began its career by setting two records: a closed-circuit distance record of 8,083 miles, remaining in the air for 56:30 hours; and a speed record over 6,250 miles (10,000 km) with an average speed of almost 150 mph in August 1939, which bettered the record of 7,239 miles set by the Japanese Koken-Ki on 15 May 1938. The SM.82 was Italy's largest three-engine aircraft and constituted about eighty percent of the Italian Air Force transport fleet.

Savoia-Marchetti SM.82

PART 2:
JAPANESE LONG-RANGE AIRCRAFT

In the 1930s, Japanese aircraft designers had made maximizing the range of their aircraft a high priority to link the Japanese home islands with the Japanese Empire's overseas possessions in Taiwan, Korea, Manchuria, and the South Pacific Mandates. Long-range capabilities also had implications for the development of military aircraft for future conflicts in China and over the Pacific Ocean, potential war theatres which offered few airfields for aircraft to refuel.

1
JAPANESE LONG-RANGE AIRCRAFT OF THE 1930s

KOKEN-KI

The Koken-Ki (also known as the Gasuden Koken) was a project to design and build a long-range research aircraft originally intended to break the world closed-circuit distance record of 5,018 miles previously set by French pilots Codas and Costes in a Breguet 19 in December 1929, and the straight-line record of 7,155 miles recently set in July 1937 by Russian pilot Gromov flying an ANT-25.

In 1931, the Japanese government funded the Aeronautical Research Institute of Tokyo Imperial University with $125,000 to initiate studies to design and develop a diesel engine and airframe for long distance flights within two years. Dr. Suhara was the director of the program, with Dr. Iwamoto as staff director, Hidemasa Kimura as head airframe designer, Ichiro Tani as the aero-dynamist, and Keikichi Tanaka developing the power plant. The institute had limited experience designing a full-scale aircraft, and the design for production was not completed until August 1934. The final design submitted by Head Designer Kimura was a three-seat (two pilots and an engineer), single-engine, all-metal fuselage, low-wing cantilever monoplane with a retractable undercarriage. It had fabric-covered outer wings and control surfaces. The wingspan was 91.6 ft., with a wing area of 939.7 sq. ft.; it was 49.4 ft. long and weighed 9,314 lbs. empty and 20,317 lbs. loaded, with a fuel capacity of 1,281 gallons. The originally specified diesel engine was inefficient and provided insufficient power for heavily loaded take-offs, so a modified version of the 715 hp German BMW-VIII water-cooled V12 gasoline engine license-built by Kawasaki was selected. The 13.5 ft. propeller was a wooden, two-blade Sumitomo. The new engine was projected to provide a maximum speed of 155 mph (sea level) and a cruising speed of 211 mph (at 6,600 ft.). Its range was to be about 7,250–7,550 miles with a service ceiling of 11,200 ft. The design for production was completed in 1934, but there was a problem as to where to produce the aircraft, since the demand for military aircraft was very large at the time and the cost of production was well over the cost of the $125,000 production budget.

Despite having only limited resources, only twenty-five available workers, and previously building only small numbers of light wooden aircraft, the Tokyo Gas and Electric Industry (known as Gasuden) was selected to construct the aircraft. Construction lagged due to the company's inexperience in metal processing and fabrication, along with tool maintenance. The fabric wing was covered with the finest Egyptian cotton, eleven coats of paint were applied to the aircraft, the metal surfaces were given a high polish, and flat rivet heads were used to reduce air resistance. The wing was painted crimson to help find the downed aircraft during rescue and gave the aircraft its popular name *Crimson Wing*. The landing gear folded and was completely retractable, and only during take-off and landing was the folded windshield raised above the cockpit. The Koken-Ki was not completed until 31 March 1937, and was first flown from Haneda Airport on 25 May 1937, piloted by Maj. Yuzo Fujita of the Army Aviation Technology Laboratory, with co-pilot Fukujiro Takahashi and engineer Kinkichi Sekine. Flight tests were conducted for the next six months before the first attempt to break the distance record was made on 13 November, which ended in failure due to landing gear complications. The next attempt at the record was made on 10 May 1938, and was aborted due to autopilot problems.

At 0455 on 13 May 1938, after some last minute repairs, the Koken-Ki took off for a third attempt on the record from 4,000 ft. Kisarazu Airfield. The aircraft weighed 10,275 lbs. at take-off, of which 1,538 gallons was fuel. The aircraft flew a three-sided course totaling 249 miles. After twenty-nine laps of the circuit the weather began to deteriorate and several minor mechanical problems arose, so at 1921 on 15 May, a national broadcast reported its landing at Kisarazu as having flown a distance of 7,239 miles for a new world closed-circuit distance record and a speed record of 116.25 mph over 10,000 km. After the Koken-Ki landed 132 gallons of fuel remained, which could have added 750 miles to the record. This record, which is the only aviation record ever set by Japan recognized by the Federation Aeronautique Internationale (FAI), was not broken until August 1939, when it was reset by an Italian Savoia-Marchetti SM.82 that flew 8,038 miles. After it set the record the Koken-Ki was used for sporadic test flights, last flying in 1939, and survived WWII. After the war it was stored in a hangar at Haneda AF near Tokyo, but was reported as destroyed by fire. A replica of the Gasuden was completed in 2002 and is on display at Oyanagi Museum, Japan.

ABOVE / Koken Ki

LEFT / Pilot Yuzo Fujita (L), co-pilot Fukujiro Takahashi (C), and engineer Kinkichi Sekine (R) pose with their Koken Ki.

KAWANISHI K-12

After Lindbergh's illustrious 1927 Trans-Atlantic flight Japan decided to initiate a project for the first non-stop crossing of the Pacific, again to bring attention to Japan's emergence as the technological and industrial power of Asia. The Imperial Aeronautics Association (IAA) heralded the spectacular scheme by announcing that a Japanese pilot, flying a Japanese-built aircraft, would be the first to fly cross the Pacific. Tokyo newspaper *Mainichi Shimbun* sponsored the project and ordered an exact replica of Lindbergh's long-range monoplane *Spirit of St. Louis* from manufacturer Ryan. This replica was not to be used for the 4,500 mile trans-Pacific crossing because it did not have the required range, as it had been purposely designed to fly Lindbergh only the 3,600 miles between New York and Paris. The Great Circle Route was chosen as it curved northeast from Japan, along the Aleutian Island chain, before turning southeast toward the American mainland.

The Kawanishi Company was chosen to re-engineer the aircraft and to build two similarly configured trans-Pacific monoplanes (one a backup), designated the K-12. Kawanishi designer Eiji Sekiguchi's proposal was a larger version, using the "greater the size, the greater the range" aviation precept popular at the time. The K-12, known as the *Nichi-Bei-Go* (Japan to America Model) or the *Sakura* (Cherry Blossom), emerged as an "overstuffed" *Spirit of St. Louis* with twice the wing area and a massive landing gear to support its huge, boxy fuselage that accommodated two crew members and the vast quantities of fuel required for the Pacific crossing. The K-12's 500 hp water-cooled engine produced over twice the horsepower of the *Spirit's* 223 hp Wright Whirlwind.

By May 1928, the K-12 was ready for flight testing, painted silver with red-striped wings to make the aircraft more visible if the crew ditched.

When the K12 was fully loaded, it weighed twice the Lindbergh plane at 11,300 lbs. After extensive inspection and testing by the Civil Aviation Bureau, it was determined that when fully fueled, the K-12's weight significantly exceeded the aircraft's safe design limit and would not fulfill a minimum rate-of-climb requirement; moreover, even with its excess fuel capacity there would be insufficient fuel to complete the proposed flight. The Bureau forced Kawanishi to grudgingly agree to modify the second K-12 by strengthening its airframe to accommodate a greater fuel load. The *Cherry Blossom II's* entire design concept was faulty, and it, too, was finally rejected by the Imperial Aeronautics Association, which calculated that maximum range was only 3,782 miles, more than 1,000 miles less than required to complete the trans-Pacific flight. The IAA suspended the Trans-Pacific Project on 7 July 1928, and afterward the long-suffering aircraft was unable to even qualify for civil registration. The K-12 project so dishonored the Kawanishi

Company that it signaled an ignominious end to the company's last private, non-military aircraft venture.

By this time Australian Charles Kingsford Smith and his crew had completed the first trans-Pacific flight from Oakland, California, to Brisbane, Australia, in the Fokker tri-motor *Southern Cross* in June 1928 on a three-stage island hopping flight. The Japanese Imperial Aeronautics Association, hoping to seduce non-stop trans-Pacific participants with a large financial enticement, offered a then enormous prize of $100,000 for the first Japanese pilot to fly the Pacific, while Tokyo's *Asahi Shimbun*, one of Japan's leading newspapers and promoters of Japanese aviation, added a further $50,000 (half that amount for a successful foreigner). All of which would amount to a very substantial $2,130,000 today (2017) and about $350,000 for foreigners. Soon Japanese and American contestants appeared to vie for the prize.

In February 1931, another rival Tokyo newspaper, *Hochi Shimbun*, announced it was sponsoring a trans-Pacific flight to be piloted by Seiji Yoshihara, who had just completed an extraordinary light plane flight from Berlin to Tokyo in a very small, open-cockpit Junkers A-50 Junior powered by a single 85 hp Armstrong Siddeley Genet air-cooled radial engine. Since this flight would mainly be flown over water floats were installed on the Junkers A-50 for water take-offs and landings. Yoshihara took off on 18 May 1931, following the Great Circle Route and hoping to fly to and land somewhere on the American West Coast. He had flown almost 1,000 miles when his little Junkers float plane developed engine trouble off the Russian Kuril Islands and he was forced to ditch; incredibly, he was rescued by a passing ship seven hours later.

Hochi Shimbun then purchased a Junkers W33 transport, which was similar to the W33 Bremen that had made the first east-west Atlantic crossing in 1928. The all-metal Junkers monoplane was powered by a reliable 300 hp Junkers L 5 engine and was well-regarded for its sturdy construction and load carrying ability. The Junkers was sent to Mitsubishi for further conversion for long-range operations and Eiichiro Baba of the Japan Air Transport Research Institute was selected as the pilot, while Cdr. Kiyoshi Homma and Master Sgt. Tomoyoshi Inoshita of the Navy were appointed navigator and radio operator, respectively.

During that year several American crews had arrived in Japan to contest for the trans-Pacific flight but were unsuccessful. On 2 October 1931, self-proclaimed "King of the Barnstormers" Clyde Pangborn and his wealthy co-pilot/backer Hugh Herndon had left New York in their Bellanca *Miss Veedol* in an attempt to break Wiley Post's round-the-world record. By the time they were over Russia they were too far behind schedule to break Post's record and when they arrived in Tokyo, the duo decided to collect the $25,000 dollar Trans-Pacific "foreigner's prize" instead. After taking off from Sabishiro Beach they jettisoned their Bellanca's landing gear to extend its range, and 41 hours and 4,860 miles later belly-landed in Wenatchee, Washington, to complete the first non-stop trans-Pacific flight

Even though Americans had collected the *Asahi Shimbun* foreigner's prize, Japan continued to be determined that one of its pilots should make the Pacific non-stop crossing, and the burden was on the *Hochi Shimbun* Junkers W33 team to complete its flight safely. To minimize the danger and increase the chances of success, two support aircraft were to be provided to join the Ju 33, flying together across the Pacific. Rescued Seiji Yoshihara was sent to England to ferry the Saunders-Roe Cutty Sark flying boat back to Japan while two army flyers were sent to the US to ferry back a Bellanca similar to Pangborn's triumphant *Miss Veedol*. Soon the project encountered problems when both support aircraft crashed. In March 1932, the Trans-Pacific Bellanca *Rising Sun* crashed at New York's Floyd Bennett Field, killing its pilot, Capt. Yoshinori Nagoya, and six weeks later Yoshihara crashed the Cutty Sark during a test flight in Oakland, California, reducing the project to its original Junkers W33. The Japanese Trans-Pacific project finally got under way on 24 September 1932, when pilot Eiichiro Baba set out on the Great Circle Route. After five hours radio operator Inoshita reported their position as south of Iturup Island, in the Russian Kurils, being on course and making good time. The Junkers' radio transmission for the next position report never came, and Baba and his crew vanished without a trace. After five years since Lindbergh's inspiring flight, four Japanese Trans-Pacific projects had failed and the *Asahi Shimbun* prize would go unclaimed by a Japanese pilot and crew.

Kawanishi K-12

2

JAPANESE LONG-RANGE PRIVATE/MILITARY AIRCRAFT OF THE 1930s

MITSUBISHI KI-15 KAMIKAZE-GO

Development of the Ki-15 began on 11 July 1935, when Capt. Yuzo Fujita and Engineer Masao Ando of the Technical Department of the Koku Hombu issued specifications for a fast reconnaissance aircraft to the Mitsubishi Company. The specification called for a two-seat reconnaissance aircraft with a maximum speed of 280 mph (at 9,845 ft.); an operating altitude of 6,560 ft.–13,125 ft.; an endurance of one hour at a combat rating at 250 miles from base; a loaded weight of less than 5,291 lbs.; and armament comprising a single flexible 7.7 mm machine gun in the rear cockpit. The aircraft was to be powered by a single engine in the 700–800 hp class.

To meet the Koku Hombu performance requirements Mitsubishi's Fumihiko Kono, assisted by Tomio Kubo and Shokichi Mizumo, designed a small, aerodynamic, low-wing cantilever monoplane with a spatted, non-retractable undercarriage, a 39.4 ft. wing span with a 219.1 sq. ft. wing area, and a length of 27.8 ft. The 750 hp Nakajima Ha-8 nine-cylinder air-cooled radial engine powered the aircraft to a very speedy (for the time) maximum speed of nearly 300 mph (200 mph cruising) and a range of 1,491 miles. Construction of the prototype began in December 1935, and the first aircraft was completed within five months, flying for the first time in May 1936, with the first production aircraft delivered in May 1937.

While the first Ki-15 was undergoing flight trials *Asahi Shimbun* received authorization from the Army to purchase the second Ki-15 prototype from Mitsubishi to be a communication aircraft. It was built under the civil designation *Karigane I* (Wild Goose I) and was completed on 19 March 1937, then registered as J-BAAI. It was delivered to *Asahi Shimbun* on 25 March and named *Kamikaze-go* after a patriotic slogan referring to the Divine Wind, the typhoon that saved Japan from a Mongolian invasion in the thirteenth century, while the *go* meant "the one and only." The right side of the silver aircraft, trimmed with medium blue, carried its name *Kamikaze* in Japanese language characters, the Japanese Rising Sun flag, and J-BAAI, while the left side carried the English language characters Kamikaze, the flag, and J-BAAI. The underside carried large and colorful markings to aid reporters on the ground to identify the aircraft when it flew overhead.

The newspaper's original intent was to use the aircraft to fly to the sites of developing news stories to gather information and aerial photos and then return home. Although it carried a radio to communicate with the ground and other aircraft, the observer's position was also equipped with a telegraph key to send Morse code signals to the ground via large red lights mounted on the top and bottom of the fuselage.

When a French newspaper offered considerable prize money to the first aircraft to fly between Paris and Tokyo within one hundred hours, the Tokyo newspaper decided to use its aircraft in an attempt to complete a record flight between Japan and England (with a Paris stop) to celebrate the coronation of HM King George VI. Many aviators had previously failed in the Paris-Tokyo attempt, including Andre Japy, the French aviator who survived when his Caudron Simoun crashed into the mountains of Japan's Kyushu Island on 15 November 1936, with only hours remaining on the last leg of his record attempt from Paris to Tokyo after flying 75:15. Previously, on 16 December 1935, Japy had successfully completed a solo flight from Paris to Saigon in 98:52 hours.

French aviator Andre Japy (C) and his Caudron Simoun

With much fanfare the *Kamikaze-go* took off from Tachikawa Airfield near Tokyo at 1612 on 6 April 1937. The aircraft flew from Tokyo via Taipei to Hanoi and Vientiane, in French Indochina, then via Calcutta and Karachi in British India, Basra and Baghdad in Iraq, and then over Athens, Rome, and

Mitsubishi Ki-15 Kamikaze-Go after landing in London

Paris in Europe. Between 6–9 April 1937, Masaaki Iinuma (pilot) and Kenji Tsukagoshi (flight mechanic and navigator) flew J-BAAI from Tachikawa to London, covering 9,542 miles in 94:17:56 hours with the actual flying time being 51:17:23 hours, at an average speed of 101.2 mph (according to the FAI, which officially recognized the record).

The *Kamikaze-go* remained in England for about a month before the 12 May coronation, carrying English officials and dignitaries and Japanese Prince Chichibu and Princess Chichibu, who were visiting England for the coronation. On the day of the coronation the aircraft filmed the ceremonies from the air. The *Kamikaze-go* was then flown back to Japan, duplicating its original route in the opposite direction, departing London on 14 May and arriving in Japan/Osaka on 20 May and Tokyo's Haneda Airport the next day.

After the record flight pilot Masaaki Iinuma became a national hero, being acclaimed as the "Japanese Lindbergh." Both the pilot and navigator Kenji Tsukagoshi were awarded the Legion d'honneur by the French government. Iinuma later served as chief test pilot for the Kayaba Ka-1 Autogiro, but was later killed in combat in the Pacific War in December 1941 near Phnom Penh, Cambodia. In 1943, the *Kamikaze*'s former navigator, Tsukagoshi, set off from Singapore for Germany in the prototype Tachikawa Ki-77, but disappeared over the Indian Ocean. After its return to Japan the *Kamikaze-go* continued to actively fly in an assortment of capacities for *Asahi Shimbun.* On a return flight from south China it had to be ditched in southern Taiwan due to bad weather. It was later recovered and put on display at a "Kamikaze Memorial Center" in the city Ikoma, but the display was destroyed in an air raid during the war. Later a small number of Ki-15-Is were transferred to civilian operators, including J-BAAL *Asakaze* (Morning Breeze) and J-BAAM *Sochikaze* (Providential Wind). The 500 Ki-15s, code-named Babs by the Allies, would serve the Imperial Japanese Army (Ki-15) and Navy (C5M2), and for a brief time in 1937, it was the fastest production aircraft in the world. It served with distinction in the early war in China and the Pacific, but by 1943 was relegated to second line roles. They were finally expended as real Kamikazes at the end of the war.

Post card of Kamikaze-Go record flight with Masaaki Iinuma (L) and flight mechanic Kenji Tsukagoshi

MITSUBISHI G3M NIPPON

The Mitsubishi G3M's forerunner, the Ka-9 (manufacturer's designation) was designed to a 1933 naval specification for a land-based bomber to support naval units. When first flown in April 1933, the bomber had an extremely clean airframe that had exceptional handling and maneuverability and a long range capability of 3,750 miles. The success of this prototype in testing led to the 9-Shi Specification for a Ka-15 production attack bomber with a wider fuselage, space for three retractable turrets, and two more powerful Kinsei radial engines. The aircraft was put into production in June 1936 as the Navy G3M1 and saw service during 1940 as the G3M2, operating from mainland bases in China, where they suffered heavy losses due to poor defensive armament.

In the late 1930s, Japan had few high-performance transports, and several modifications of the G3M series were developed to fulfill military and civil needs. Beginning in 1938, about twenty-five G3M2s were converted to Mitsubishi Twin-Engine Transports for civil operators, with most used by Nippon Koku K.K. (Japan Air Lines) and its successor, Dai Nippon Koku K.K. (Greater Japan Air Lines). This variant is best known for their goodwill, flag-waving flights: J-BEOA flew from Tokyo to Tehran, J-BEOC from Tokyo to Rome, and the most famous, J-BACI *Nippon* (G3M2 No. 328), would attempt a round-the-world flight.

The *Nippon* aircraft, sponsored by *Mainichi Shimbun* (Mainichi Press), had a wing span of 82 ft. with a wing area of 810 sq. ft., a length of 54 ft., an empty weight of 10,945 lbs. (it had its armament removed), and a gross weight of 17,637 lbs., including 1,143 gallons of fuel enabling it to fly continuously for twenty-four hours. Two 1,061 hp Mitsubishi Kinsei 9-cylinder air-cooled radial piston engines powered the *Nippon*.

During a ceremony before the epic flight Mainichi President Nobutaro Okumura named the aircraft *Nippon* and introduced the crew: pilot Sumitoshi Nakao, co-pilot Shigeo Yoshida, navigator Hajime Shimokawa, flight engineer Hiroshi Saeki, and radio operators Chosaku Yaokawa and Nobusada Sato. The official Japanese envoy and goodwill ambassador for this round-the-world flight was its only passenger, Takeo Ohara. The *Nippon*, equipped with the latest autopilot and navigation equipment, took off for its first stop, flying north on 26 August 1939. The route itinerary included Alaska, Canada, the US West Coast (Seattle-Oakland-Los Angeles), across the US (Albuquerque-Chicago-New York-Washington, DC-Miami), south through Latin America (San Salvador-Columbia-Chile-Argentina-Brazil), across the Atlantic to Morocco, Spain, Italy, Greece, Iraq, Pakistan, India, and Formosa, and finally landing at Haneda Airport (Tokyo) on 20 October, covering a distance of 32,850 miles in 194 flying hours in 55 days.

During the war the G3M was most famous for its role with Mitsubishi G4M Betty bombers in the sinking of British battleships *HMS Prince of Wales* and *Repulse* (Force Z) near the Malayan coast on 10 December 1941. After the bombing of Pearl Harbor in 1941 the G3M, known as the Nell by the Allies, was by this time considered antiquated, but three front-line units continued flying 204 G3M2s in four *Kokutai* (Naval Air Corps) in the Central Pacific. During the war Mitsubishi twin-engine transports were operated by Dai Nippon Koku on their military contract routes throughout the war zone. By 1943, the Nell's combat usefulness had run its course and the remaining aircraft were placed in second-line duties, such as transport, bomber and navigation trainers, and paratrooper platforms.

Mitsubishi G3M Nippon

Pilot Sumitoshi Nakao and the Mitsubishi G3M Nippon are greeted at Haneda Airport.

G3M2 "Nell" military version of the Nippon

3
JAPANESE WARTIME LONG-RANGE MILITARY AIRCRAFT

TACHIKAWA A-26/ARMY KI-77

In late 1939, *Asahi Shimbun* was in an acrimonious competition with rival newspaper *Mainichi Shimbun*, which had recently sponsored a round-the-world- flight by the modified Mitsubishi G3M2 J-BACI *Nippon* and previously vied for long distance records, sponsoring the Junkers W33 and Ki-15 *Kamikaze*. In February 1940, the newspaper announced the funding of a new ultra-long distance flight to commemorate 2,600 years of the founding of the Japanese Imperial Dynasty (660 BC). For the flight *Asahi Shimbun* required an aircraft that would have a range exceeding 15,000 km (9,321 miles), more than a non-stop distance from Tokyo to New York City via San Francisco. To meet these needs the newspaper sponsored the construction of two extraordinary aircraft designed by the Tachikawa Aircraft Company to be designated the Tachikawa A-26 (the A referring to Asahi and the 26 to the first two digits of the year, 2600). Later the Japanese Army Air Force designated it the Ki-77. The newspaper's specifications for the all-metal, twin-engine monoplane called for a minimum range of 9,325 miles, a maximum speed of 275 mph (at 15,000 feet), a cruising speed of at least 186 mph, a service ceiling of 28,000 ft.—an altitude at which the aircraft would benefit from the high-speed west-to-east Jet Streams—and a range of 11,185 miles. (The odd specification figures are due to metric to English conversion.)

An all-civilian team from the University of Tokyo's Aeronautical Research Institute headed by Dr. Hidemasa Kimura (of the Koken-Ki) worked on the design, while the Tachikawa Hikoki Aircraft Company selected Ryokichi Endo, assisted by Munesaburo Oguchi, as their chief project engineers responsible for the engineering drawings and manufacture. The design revolved around an innovative high aspect ratio wing with a laminar-flow airfoil chosen to minimize drag, although it would be very difficult to achieve the workmanship required to attain the marked smoothness required by this wing type. By utilizing a laminar wing loaded with fuel the ailerons would be less effective, thus sixty percent of the trailing edge was committed to the ailerons, because on landing most of the fuel had been used and the need for large flaps would be minimized. The wing, designed by Dr. Fukazu of the University of Tokyo, had a 6° dihedral and an aspect ratio of 11 (12.5 was judged the most efficient), which he considered to be the best compromise for long-range operation and to facilitate production (an aspect ratio of 8 had been the most Fukazu had previously attempted). The wing had a span of 96.6 ft. with an area of 856.4 sq. ft. and seventy percent of the enormous 2,454 gallon fuel load was carried internally in the wings. The fuel load would more than double the aircraft's 15,955 lbs. empty weight to 36,872 lbs. The two power plants were 1,170 hp Nakajima Ha-115 14-cylinder, two-row, air-cooled radials driving three-bladed constant-speed metal propellers. The aircraft was streamlined with a seamlessly rounded fuselage featuring a bullet-shaped nose and curved windshield. The curved windshield glass created a problem, as it produced a pronounced refraction, causing the horizon to appear curved. Since take-offs and landings were the most important visual portion of flight, a white line was painted down the center of the runway to aid the pilot in maintaining orientation.

Tachikawa worked on developing a design for a pressurized "sealed oxygen cabin" for use in high-altitude aircraft by the five-man crew. This cabin's purpose was to maintain air pressure for the crew when operating at altitudes above 10,000 ft., at which outside air pressure was much lower and the air thinner. The new cabin did not require the use of oxygen masks and flight gear to protect the crew against the cold, hypoxia, barotrauma, and altitude sickness. In the A-26 Dr. Kimura utilized a "sealed" crew cabin, but one that was not pressurized, anticipating that sealing the cabin would retain the oxygen supplied by liquid oxygen cylinders; in testing it failed to meet expectations, as the metering of the oxygen was very unreliable and the crew had to wear their oxygen masks constantly for as much as fifty hours.

The aircraft's layout was finalized in Fall 1940, with two of the aircraft to be completed by November 1941, and ready for their first flight on 3 November, to commemorate the birth date of Emperor Meiji. This target date was postponed, due to design and manufacturing delays, to 11 February 1942, the 2,602nd anniversary of the National Foundation. The recent outbreak of the Pacific War and the associated reallocation of Japan's priorities caused the project to be canceled and the uncompleted aircraft were placed in storage.

In summer 1942 the Japanese Army Air Force directed Tachikawa to complete the two A-26s under the JAAF designation Ki-77, as it was thought their range would make them ideal for special flights between Japan and Germany to maintain communication between the Axis partners. Engine cooling problems on the ground delayed the first flight until 18 November 1942, when pilots Kamila and Nagatomo took off from the Tachikawa Company Airfield for flight testing. Powered by the two Nakajima engines that were similar to those powering the Zero fighter, the Ki-77 showed excellent handling and long-range performance, but the engine cowlings required several modifications due to continued engine overheating. While resolving this problem the second Ki-77 prototype was completed.

The bomber's first long-range flight began on 30 June 1943, when the second Ki-77 prototype took off from Fussa, near Tokyo, reputedly on a clandestine *Seiko* ("Success") mission to Berlin under the directive of Col. Saigo. The more straightforward Great Circle northern route over Russia was overruled because of concern it might imply violation of Soviet airspace, even though Japan was not at war with the Soviets. Instead, the K-77 was to be routed 3,312 miles first to Singapore, where it refueled for the long, dangerous non-stop flight over the Indian Ocean, Arabian Sea, Persian Gulf, Middle East, over Southern Europe, and on to Berlin. The aircraft's crew was pilot Juukou Nagatomo, co-pilot Hajime Kawasaki, and a flight engineer, radio operator, and a navigator, along with three Japanese Army passengers, including two attachés. To insure a safe take-off by the fuel-overloaded Ki-77, the Singapore airfield required a lengthening of 3,300 ft. The Ki-77 took off at 0710 on 7 July with 16,000 lbs. of fuel—an ample supply to take them to the captured German airfield at Sarabus, Crimea, Ukraine. That day, somewhere over the Indian Ocean, contact was lost with the Ki-77. The reason for its disappearance was never established; strong tropical storms were in the area, but it seems probable that the unarmed aircraft was shot down by British fighters, as RAF records reveal an unidentified Japanese aircraft was destroyed over the Indian Ocean that day. Earlier that month the RAF "Y" Service had intercepted an ULTRA intercepted and decrypted signal from Berlin to Luftwaffe 6/VI Airfield Regional Command in Sarabus, Crimea, which stated: "On 8/7 an Allied aircraft will fly via air grid squares 3420, 2560, and 2510 to Sarabus. It is a two-engined low-wing monoplane, wing span 30 metres, metal fuselage, natural colour, wings grey. The aircraft must not be fired on under any circumstances." The ULTRA signals intelligence analysts at Bletchley Park who decoded intercepted German communications then attached the following note: "This presumably refers to undertaking GOA in which an aircraft was flying to Sarabus from Tokio via Singapore" and set the trap for the Ki-77 departing Singapore.

Interest in the remaining A-26 aircraft diminished as the fortunes of war changed for Japan, but the Japanese made an inexplicable decision to resurrect the Ki-77 to challenge the world distance record. The original New York destination was obviously not feasible, and a closed course over Japan could not be used, as turning points were over blacked out areas caused by American air raids. In Spring 1944 a secret 537 mile closed-circuit was chosen over Manchuria, which was isolated from the war. The aircraft was flown to Hsinking, 250 miles north of the Korean border, which had a 3,940 ft. concrete runway extending on to grass that could accommodate the almost 37,000 lb. fully loaded (3,052 gallons of fuel) aircraft, which was ten percent over gross weight on take-off. On 2 July, after an agonizing forty-eight-second take-off run that used almost 500 more ft. on the grass runway, the aircraft lifted off and slowly climbed to initial 10,000 foot altitude. This altitude was dictated by the initial fuel load, but as fuel was burned off it would climb to 20,000 ft., where it was to circle over a course until it had surpassed the record distance. Soon after take-off the autopilot failed and the two pilots had to take turns flying the aircraft over the next three days over 11,000 miles. Japanese crew records are unclear, but show that Komata and Tanaka were the two pilots, Shimozaki and Morimatsu were the engineers, Habiro was radio operator, and the observer Sakamoto chronicled the particulars of the record attempt. Conditions in the cabin became very uncomfortable, and by the second day, with no air circulating in the sealed cockpit, the crew had problems staying awake. With sun streaming through the Plexiglas nose windows the interior became disagreeably warm and their breath condensed into ice on the windows and metal frames. Throughout the flight their oxygen masks became increasingly more uncomfortable. By 1000 on the third day the crew was entering the sixteenth lap and had been aloft 8,550 miles for more than forty-eight hours, and was virtually assured of surpassing the record on the nineteenth lap. Later in the day, sensing the crew was nearing exhaustion, the ground team commanding officer ordered them to land after the completion of the nineteenth circuit. At 1859 on 4 July, Ki-77 landed safely after a flight of 57:11 hours over an amazing 10,248 miles—the distance flown exceeded a Tokyo to New York flight by more than 3,000 miles—and with over 200 gallons of fuel remaining that would have added more than 1,120 miles to the record. The Japanese military was in turmoil and did not announce the record, as two weeks later Japanese Warlord

Tachikawa A-26/Army Ki-77

Hideki Tojo resigned. The record was eventually revealed in September 1946, when the Lockheed P2V-1 *Truculent Turtle* flew an unofficial (non-FAI) 9,720 miles from Perth, Australia, to Columbus, Ohio, in 55:17 hours. In December 1945, Tachikawa's A-26 was shipped to the US aboard the carrier *USS Bogue* for evaluation, but unfortunately, oblivious of its record, it was scrapped. It would not be until 12 November 1975 before a direct flight from Tokyo to New York was flown. Aboard the Boeing 747SP that day was Dr. Hidemasa Kimura, design leader of the splendid A-26.

TACHIKAWA KI-74

In spring 1939, the Ki-74 was designed by Dr. Hidemasa Kimura to meet the requirements of a specification issued by the Koku Hombu calling for a long-range reconnaissance aircraft capable of operating from Manchurian bases. The twin-engine, five-man aircraft was to have a wingspan of 88.6 ft. with an area of 862 sq. ft., a length of 57.8 ft., and its weight empty was 22,487 lbs. and loaded 42,770 lbs. The aircraft was to have a range of 3,107 miles (5,000 km) at a cruising speed of at least 280 mph. To meet these performance requirements, Kimura planned to use a pair of 2,400 hp Mitsubishi Ha-214M radials turning six-blade propellers. A pressurized cabin was planned to maintain constant pressure when flying above 10,000 ft. without the need of oxygen or flight gear for use against the cold. While awaiting the development of the pressurized cabin system being tested on the Tachikawa SS-1 (a licensed version of the Lockheed *Super Electra*, Thelma) and the Ki-77, the Ki-74 project was temporarily suspended in its design stage.

In late 1941, the project was revived as a long-range, high-altitude, mid-wing monoplane bomber reconnaissance aircraft capable of bombing the American mainland by adding bombing equipment, self-sealing fuel tanks, and armor to the original design and replacing the Ha-214M engines with a pair of 2,200 hp Mitsubishi Ha-211-1 radials. In September 1942, the new design was approved by the Koku Hombu and construction of three prototypes was authorized, with the first prototype to be ready in March 1944, and to be followed by two externally identical aircraft powered by 2,200 hp turbo-supercharged Ha-211-1 Ru radials. During the flight test program both versions of the Mitsubishi Ha-211 engine encountered initial problems and the decision was made to replace these engines on the pre-production aircraft with the lower-powered but more reliable turbo-supercharged Mitsubishi Ha-104 Ru.

The five-man crew was accommodated in the pressurized cabin that comprised most of the front of the aircraft, with the large bomb bay underneath. The crew consisted of the bombardier in the nose; the pilot and co-pilot on the flight deck, which was offset to the port side of the fuselage; and the navigator/radio operator and gunner in stations behind the flight deck. The windows of the pressurized cabin were smaller than standard glazing. In its intended bomber and reconnaissance role it carried 2,205 lbs. (1,000 kg) of bombs, and because it was expected to operate at high altitude where interception would be difficult, it was equipped with a very minimal armament consisting of a tail-mounted 12.7 mm Ho-103 machine gun remotely controlled by the gunner. After a number were built it was decided they were to be formed into a flight of three aircraft (*shotai*) to conduct bombing missions against B-29 *Superfortress* airbases on Saipan.

As the war progressed badly for the Axis, communication, especially maritime, between Japan and Germany was severely curtailed by the Allies, so the fourth pre-production Ki-74 was to be prepared for non-stop flights to Germany and return in late 1944. Ha-211-1-Ru engines with more horsepower were installed and fuel capacity was increased to permit the aircraft to fly up to 7,456 miles (12,000 km)—ample to fly from Tokyo to Berlin. Additional modifications were the removal of all non-essential equipment and the lengthening and reallocation of the flight deck to the middle of the fuselage. This modified Ki-74 would never fly to Berlin, as Germany surrendered beforehand.

The Ki-74s were never flown in combat because flight testing of the twelve remaining pre-production aircraft was not completed before VJ-Day. Before the end of the war two additional variants of the Ki-74 were proposed. The first variant was to be a transport but was soon abandoned, while the second was the Ki-74-II bomber powered by two Mitsubishi Ha-104-Ru engines. All five crew members of this bomber version were seated in a small pressurized cabin in the fuselage forward of the wings, which furnished more space for a deeper bomb bay needed to carry the planned increased 4,410 lb. (2,000 kg) bomb load, which also necessitated a front landing gear equipped with two tires. This aircraft would weigh more,

Tachikawa Ki-74

reducing its operating range to an estimated 4,439 miles compared to the 4,971 miles of the Ki-74. For its high-altitude operation, the Ki-74-II's wings were to be more slender than those of the Ki-74. In place of the single tail mounted remote machine gun two machine guns or cannons were to be used. Like the transport concept, the Ki-74-II was also abandoned and did not progress beyond the design stage.

Although never encountering the Ki-74 during the war, the Allies were wrongly aware of its long development as a "super-range, high-speed fighter" intended for long-range escort duty and accordingly assigned to it a male codename *Pat*; when its correct role was learned the codename was appropriately changed to *Patsy*.

NAKAJIMA G5N SHINZEN (MOUNTAIN RECESS)

In 1938, the Japanese naval staff initiated a study for a large bomber with a range of 3,450–4,030 miles that would require the installation of four engines, but the Japanese aircraft industry lacked experience in the design and manufacture of such a large aircraft. In late 1939, the front company for the Japanese Navy, Mitsui Trading, purchased the solitary prototype of the four-engined Douglas DC-4E transport, officially for use by Dai Nippon Koku (Greater Japan Air Lines). The navy also instructed Nakajima to be prepared to develop a long-range heavy bomber based on the DC-4E.

The Douglas Company shipped the DC-4E from California, and shortly after its arrival in Japan, it was secretly transferred to Nakajima, which examined it; by the beginning of 1940, they had constructed the first prototype of the Experimental 13-Shi Attack Bomber Shinzen (Mountain Recess) G5N1. Meanwhile, to conceal their real use of the DC-4E, the Japanese reported it had crashed. The new aircraft retained many of the features of the Douglas transport, but added a new fuselage with glazed nose and ventral bomb bay, new tail surfaces with twin fins and rudders, and powered it with four 1,870 hp Nakajima NK7A Mamoru 11 14-cylinder radial engines. It was the Japanese Navy's first four-engine land-based aircraft and the first Japanese aircraft with a retractable tricycle undercarriage.

Ill advisedly, Nakajima engineers had based their G5N design on the DC-4E prototype that was found unacceptable by United Air Lines and was canceled by Douglas to begin work on the more promising DC-4/C-54. The Nakajima design suffered from the same original poor DC-4E airframe and overweight design problems, and from the addition of unreliable Japanese engines. The result was very poor performance, including a low maximum speed of 262 mph, a low operating altitude (13,450 ft.), and a short range (2,757 miles) with a 4,409 lb. bomb load.

Only three additional G5N1 prototypes were built, but the Navy attempted to save the project by building two further prototypes (designated G5N2) equipped with four 1,530 hp Mitsubishi *Kasei 12* engines. Nonetheless, the aircraft was underpowered and airframe problems continued, causing the project to finally be canceled. The projected Japanese Army versions were the Nakajima Ki-68 and the Kawanishi Ki-85, which were also canceled.

Nakajima G5N Shinzen

NAKAJIMA G8N RENZAN (MOUNTAIN RANGE)

By late 1942, the worth of long-range, land-based Japanese Navy bombers supporting the Imperial Fleet and conducting deep penetration offensive missions against enemy bases had been established. The Imperial Navy Staff was investigating the intended performance of the Mitsubishi G7M1 and the Kawanishi K-100, which were to have a specified maximum speed of 368 mph, a range of 4,605 miles, and a bomb load of 8,816 lbs., to replace the then ubiquitous operational Mitsubishi G4M *Betty.* Since the G7M1 and K-100 were twin-engine aircraft the Navy concluded that their specifications would not be met. Consequently, in February 1943, Nakajima was contracted to design a four-engine, all-metal, seven-seat monoplane with retractable main and nose landing gear as an attack bomber to be designated as the Navy Experimental 18-Shi Attack Bomber *Renzan* (Mountain Range) G8N1.

To meet specifications Nakajima chose a mid-mounted 106.8 ft. wing of comparatively small area (1,205 sq. ft,) and high aspect ratio with a laminar flow section. Four 2,000 hp Nakajima NK9K-L *Homare 24* engines with Hitachi 92 turbo-superchargers were adopted and cooled by fans rotating in the opposite direction to the propellers. Defensive armament was provided by a power-operated nose turret with two 13.2 mm machine guns; dorsal, ventral, and tail turrets equipped with two 20 mm cannon each; and two flexible 13.2 mm machine guns in each side of the fuselage. The Renzan could carry as much as 8,818 lbs. of bomb load, with this load decreasing with increasing range. It was projected that forty-eight G8Nls, including sixteen prototypes and service trial aircraft, could be produced by September 1945.

The first prototype was completed in October 1944, and first flown on 23 October, with three additional aircraft completed in December 1944, and March and June 1945, respectively. Apart from minor turbo-supercharger problems flight tests were satisfactory, but were continually interrupted by American air attacks, with the third G8NI prototype destroyed on the ground by strafing US Navy aircraft. The critical shortage of light alloys and the Japanese Navy's more defensive role forced the cancellation of the proposed production program. The bomber was codenamed *Rita* by the Allies.

Nakajima G8N Renzan

4
PROJECT Z AND STEPS TOWARD AN INTERCONTINENTAL BOMBER

Like the Germans, the Japanese delayed the design and production of an authentic intercontinental bomber. The main cause of their apathy was their early success in China, where their short and medium range bombers adequately fulfilled the combat requirements of the time. It was not until America entered the war that the Japanese realized the Pacific Ocean placed the US war industry and its population out of range of any bomber in their inventory.

KAWASAKI KI-91

By May 1943, the Nakajima G5N was an utter failure, and in turn led to the termination of the Ki-68 program (proposed Army version of the G5N1 that was discontinued in 1941) and Ki-85 program (Kawanishi had a full-scale mockup of this proposed Army version of the G5N1 constructed by November 1942, but the project was discontinued in May 1943), and left the Imperial Japanese Navy without a four-engine long-range bomber project. In June 1943, Kawasaki decided to begin one as a private venture and directed engineers Takeo Doi and Jun Kitano to begin initial research. By October, work was under way on the first design concept for the Ki-91 long-range bomber, which was slightly larger than the Boeing B-29 *Superfortress*, which was optimistically planned to be in mass production in late 1943. Like the B-29, the Ki-91 was to have a tricycle landing gear, with the nose gear using a single tire (vs. two on the B-29), and the main landing gear was fitted with dual tires and a semi-recessed tail wheel. The wingspan was to be 157.5 ft. (vs. the B-29's 141.3 ft.) with an area of 2,411.1 sq. ft. (vs. 1,736 sq. ft.); its length was up to

116 ft. (vs. 99 ft.). Its empty weight was to be 74,957 lbs. (vs. 74,500 lbs.), and its loaded weight was to be 127,868 lbs. (vs. 120,000 lbs.). It was to carry up to a 16,500 lb. bomb load (vs. 20,000 lbs.) and was heavily armed with twelve 20 mm cannons in five power-operated turrets: one in the nose, one on the underside of the forward fuselage, one above and below the aft portion of the fuselage, and the last in the tail. The bottom turrets were remotely controlled, while the remainder were manned. The tail turret was to mount four cannons, while the other turrets were armed with two cannons each.

Because the Ki-91 was to operate at high altitude, four Mitsubishi Ha-214 18-cylinder, radial, supercharged engines were chosen to power the bomber to its projected maximum speed of 360 mph over an anticipated 6,214 mile range. To achieve this range each wing carried eight fuel tanks, with a further two mounted in the fuselage above the bomb bay. Like the B-29, the Ki-91 was to be equipped with a pressurized cabin for the eight-man crew. This large pressurized cabin was in the developmental stage, and the Ki-91 prototype would fly without pressurization to avoid delaying its development and flight testing.

A full-scale wooden mockup was not completed until April 1944, when Kawasaki requested that Japanese Navy representatives consider their Ki-91, and in May, the Navy inspected the Ki-91 mockup and immediately ordered production of the first prototype. Kawasaki planned to construct the Ki-91 at a new plant to be built in Miyakonojo, but the navy could not wait for the construction of a new factory and instructed Kawasaki use their established factory in Gifu Prefecture. By June 1944, Ki-91 prototype manufacture had begun at the Gifu Factory, in conjunction with the purchase and installation of the essential tools and jigs to produce additional aircraft.

Although June would see the first B-29 raids over Japan, attacks were infrequent and work on the Ki-91 continued, despite Japan's deteriorating manufacturing and raw material situation. The sporadic B-29 raids of 1944 would become ever more frequent once the Superfortresses began operations from bases in the Marianas. In February 1945, an attack heavily damaged the Gifu Factory in which the Ki-91 prototype was still under construction, causing extensive damage to it and the destruction of the jigs and tools necessary for future Ki-91 production. This damage, together with diminishing stores of aluminum, forced the navy to place a higher priority on producing fighter aircraft to ward off B-29s than continuing with the Ki-91, which was only sixty percent completed; the project was officially canceled in February 1945.

If the Ki-91 had become operational there were plans prepared to attack the US industrial West Coast mainland from temporary bases on the Kurile Islands. Another early plan (mid-1943) to strike Hawaii was prepared using bases in the Marshall Islands, but the Japanese lost these islands in February 1944.

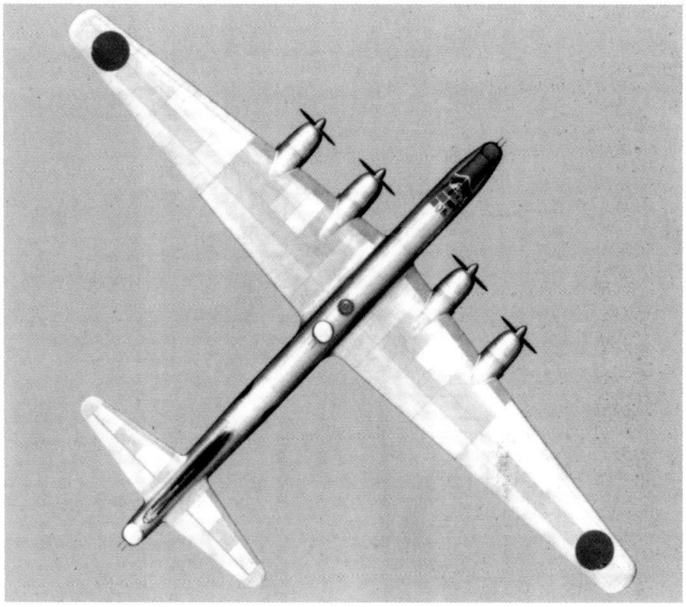

Kawasaki Ki-91

PROJECT Z

As the war situation worsened, the Japanese became more resolute to develop an intercontinental bomber similar to the Nazi *Amerika Bomber Projekt*, which was capable of reaching America. Japan, like Germany, was slow to grasp the strategic bombing concept involved in reaching America. The one-way distances involved from Japan/Honshu were vast, as New York was 6,700 miles distant, Los Angeles was over 5,300 miles, and Seattle was approximately 4,700 miles. On the easterly outbound trip from Japan a heavily loaded bomber would have to climb to 30,000 ft. to reach the prevailing tailwinds of the Jet Stream and take advantage of higher ground speeds at high altitude. Then the return trip would be against these prevailing winds, but the bomber would be lighter after using fuel and dropping its bombs. The shortest route for a feasible attack on Seattle was 3,500 miles from Paramushiro, in the northern Kuril Group (which had four air bases, most with 4,000 ft. runways).

NAKAJIMA G10N FUGAKU: PROJECT Z INTERCONTINENTAL BOMBER

At the end of January 1943, company President and Chief Designer Chikuhei Nakajima began gathering analyses and preliminary drafts for the design and production of an intercontinental bomber. In April 1943, Nakajima presented his data and preliminary design proposal to the Imperial

Japanese Army and Navy, but the problem was the rival services had contradictory views of the bomber's requirements and design.

The Army sought a bomber that could operate at 32,800 ft. and have heavy defensive armament, while the Navy wanted a bomber able to fly at a very noteworthy 49,200 ft., where enemy fighter interception would be minimal and heavy defensive armament would be unneeded, which would also reduce the aircraft's weight. The two services also differed on the mission objective: the Navy wanted to take off from Japan, bomb any American target, continue east, and land in German-occupied France, then make an identical return sortie, while the Army wanted to fly the shorter Japan-American West Coast-Japan round trip route. The Army design proposal bore some resemblance to German designs and used a "tail dragger" undercarriage, had dual vertical stabilizers, and had a rounded, bullet nose similar to the Boeing B-29 Superfortress and Messerschmitt Me 264 Amerika bomber. The Navy's design proposal sat on a tricycle landing gear and also had a rounded nose, but had a single vertical stabilizer. Nakajima's proposal also kept the single vertical stabilizer, but had a stepped nose very similar to that used on the company's previous G5N Shinzan. On 9 August 1943, after the two services submitted their conflicting input to Nakajima, the Army and Navy Aviation Technical Committee was created to continue research and agree on the development of a finalized Project Z aircraft.

In August 1943, Chikuhei Nakajima prepared a proposal, "Strategy for Ultimate Victory," recommending ways to change Japan's existing war strategy to regain the initiative. The proposals' six chapters explained Nakajima's "bold vision" for defeating the US, as well as defending Japan. His main premise was that the proposed Project Z bomber would be used to destroy US airfields as a method to prevent America's ability to launch raids against Japan. Another major aspect of the proposal was the use of the Z Bomber to attack the US homeland war industry and deny it the materials and oil to produce aircraft, tanks, and other weapons. Nakajima also added that as a way to support Germany, the Japanese should provide her Axis partner with this long-range bomber to help destroy the Soviet military industry. Nakajima printed fifty copies of his thesis and approached not only military officials, but also politicians, including Prime Minister Hideki Tojo. Nakajima additionally initiated an Air Defense Research Workshop to promote the program. Although Nakajima's "bold vision" was rather improbable in reality, it was the only means by which Japan could begin to reverse its military position in August 1943.

The selected Project Z design was a huge all-metal, mid-wing bomber 147.6 ft. long with a wing span of 213.2 ft. and a huge wing area of 3,789 sq. ft. The proposed power plant was the prototype D.BH Nakajima Ha-54, 36-cylinder radial engine, which was two Ha-44 18-cylinder radials mated together. Its maximum projected horsepower was 5,000 hp, and six Ha-54s would swing two 14.7 ft. diameter contra-rotating, three-bladed propellers each to a substantial maximum speed of 422 mph. However, the Ha-54 engine would not be available for "some time" (actually, by the end of the war it remained a prototype due to problems with cooling the power unit through the use of a ducted cowling). Consequently, Nakajima had to compromise on the experimental Ha-53 NK11A, which was anticipated to be available for trials. Since the Ha-53 was projected to produce only 2,500 hp, the bomber's performance estimates would be certainly reduced, necessitating the revision of the Project Z airframe to the final G10N Fugaku version, which was a smaller, less powerful aircraft with performance less than proposed.

Designers presumed the bomber's estimated ceiling of almost 50,000 ft. and high speed would confer protection from enemy interceptors and make heavy defensive armament unnecessary. Consequently, the bomber would only carry four Type 99 20 mm cannons. But having to settle for the less powerful NK11A engines driving four-bladed 15.7 ft. diameter propellers meant this speed/altitude defensive advantage would have been lost and the armament array would have to be increased to protect the bomber with two cannon mounted in the tail, two in the nose, two twin-cannon dorsal turrets in the front and rear of the fuselage, and at least one ventral turret with variations, including waist gunner stations. The proposed normal bomb load was expected to be up to 44,092 lbs. of bombs, but for attacks on the US, the bomber would carry only up to 11,023 lbs. of bombs (for anti-shipping missions torpedoes could be carried).

Construction of the new Project Z production plant began during Autumn 1943. By January 1944, the Project Z designation and specifications were changed to the *Fugaku* (Mount Fuji) derivative. At the time the Nakajima Company was burdened by more urgent defense projects, and work on the Fugaku diminished to a point that the probability of a completed prototype appearing was nil and the Army would be abandoning the project.

Once the Japanese-held Marianas fell in August 1944, the Japanese air forces no longer needed a super long-range bomber and demanded that more relevant fighter aircraft be produced to protect the homeland. Nonetheless, at the same time the *Gunjusho* (the Ministry of Munitions) also recognized that the Fugaku would never be realized and directed Kawanishi to design a new long-range bomber known as the TB. The Gunjusho failed to inform Nakajima, the Army, or the Navy of its decision to build a new bomber, so when the new TB bomber project was revealed, the hoopla and protests that followed not only halted the development of the Fugaku, but all long-range bomber projects, including the TB, which was soon canceled. All work on plans for the proposed Fugaku was halted, and work on the future production facility was also stopped and left unfinished. Upon the Japanese surrender almost all Fugaku documentation had been destroyed.

There were to be three specified Fugaku airframe variations: a heavy long-range bomber, a long-range transport capable of carrying 300 troops, and a ground attack gunship armed with forty downward-firing machine guns in the fuselage, each raining fire on enemy infantry and positions below. The design idea suggesting a long-range Fugaku transport carrying 300 soldiers with full equipment (the equivalent to one infantry rifle company with a heavy weapon platoon) was a most interesting operational concept. Chikuhei Nakajima proposed a fantastic plan for a raid against America in which 400 Fugaku transports would convey 120,000 troops to land on and capture Seattle-Tacoma Airport in Washington State. After landing the troops would move overland to attack and destroy Boeing's Renton Factory, which produced B-29s, and then return to Japan.

The differences in the Project Z specification bomber and the Fugaku specification were as follows:

Crew: Six to ten vs. seven to eight
Engines: Six 5,000 hp Nakajima Ha-54 36-cylinder, air-cooled radials, each driving two alternating stroke, contra-rotating three bladed 14.7 ft. diameter propellers vs. six 2,500 hp Nakajima NKI1A Ha-53 18-cylinder, air-cooled radials each driving an alternating stroke, four-bladed 15.7 ft. diameter propeller.
Dimensions: (Z-Project on left and Fugaku on right)
Wing Span: 213.2 ft. vs. 207 ft.
Wing Area: 3,789 sq. ft. vs. 3,552.1 sq. ft.
Length: 147.6 ft. vs. 131.2 ft.
Height: 28.8 ft. vs. 28.8 ft.
Weight Empty: 143,300 lbs. vs. 74,516
Weight Loaded: 298,963 lbs. vs. 92,594 lbs.
Weight Maximum: 352,793 lbs. vs. 354,323 lbs.
Max. Speed: 422 mph vs. 484 mph (both at 32,808 ft.)
Ceiling: 49,212 ft. vs. 49,212 ft.
Range: 10,252 miles vs. 10,252 miles
Maximum Range: 11,184 miles vs. 13,054 miles

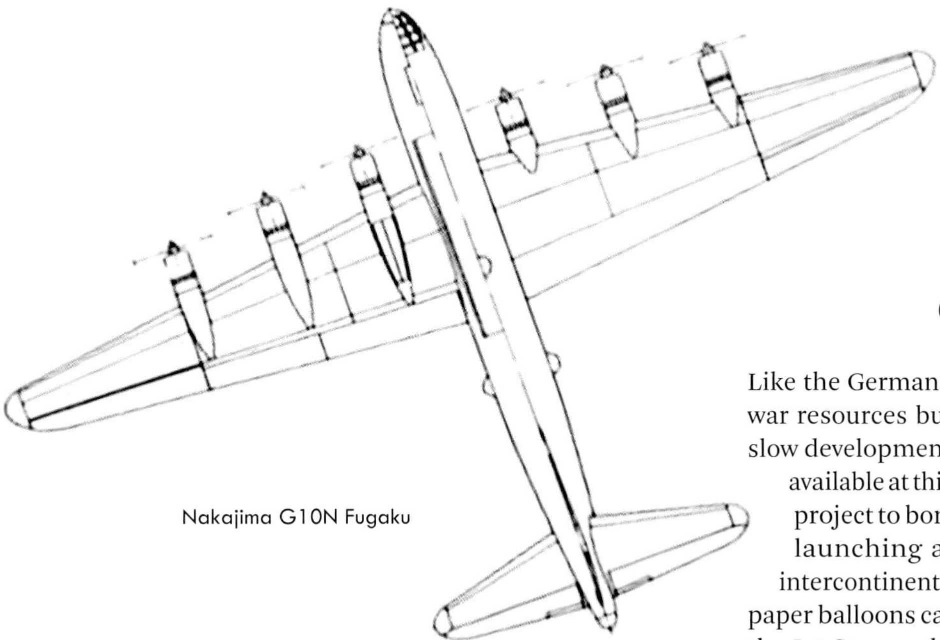

Nakajima G10N Fugaku

CONCLUSION

Like the Germans, the Japanese would unwisely use critical war resources building these complex large aircraft whose slow developmental progress made it unlikely they would be available at this juncture of the war for an uncertain, fanciful project to bomb America. The Japanese would succeed in launching air attacks against America without an intercontinental bomber, launching unsophisticated *Fu-Go* paper balloons carrying small incendiary bombs to float with the Jet Stream, hoping to set fires to the forests along the American West Coast. Early in the war the Japanese initiated isolated attacks by float planes launched off the US West Coast from submarines that carried them in containers on their decks. Except for forest fires these "intercontinental" bombings all caused little or no damage and were not divulged to the American public.

PART 3:
GERMAN LONG-RANGE AIRCRAFT

The German Air Service of WWI produced a number of large bombers with significant technology and range, considering this early era in aircraft development. The Treaty of Versailles virtually stripped the interwar German aviation industry, and it was not until Hitler and the Nazis regained power that the Luftwaffe began its initial clandestine program to revive the German aircraft industry.

1
GERMAN GIANTS OF WORLD WAR I

GOTHA G.IV AND G.V

The Gotha bomber was introduced by the Imperial German Air Service in Autumn 1917, when the limitations of the Zeppelin as a raider over London had become obvious and to serve as the counterpart to the RNAS/RFC's Handley Page O/400 heavy bomber. The Gothas had a 78 ft. wingspan and could carry up to 1,100 lbs. of bombs for up to six hours at speeds as high as 80 mph over a range of 500 miles. The IV model had a major defect, as its fuel tanks were built into the engine nacelles. Most operational G.IV losses (seventy-five percent) occurred during a hard landing, when the remaining fuel in the engine compartments would ignite, as the fuel would regularly spill on to the very hot engines. While the fuel tank problem was solved in the Gotha V, its increased weight combined with engines of the same power as the IV meant it could only be operated at low altitudes, making it vulnerable to attack. Even though the Gotha had many flaws, it has become legendary in the annals of WWI air war history, but the reputation of the Gotha is somewhat more impressive than its actual operational record. After earlier raids on London were successful, the GVs took part in the largest aerial attack on England on 19 May 1918, as part of *Operation Türkenkreuz*, when thirty-eight GVs attacked London. Nearly twenty percent of all the aircraft in the raid were destroyed; an unacceptable attrition rate, causing all remaining Gothas to be used in support of German ground forces on the Western Front instead of bombing London.

Gotha G.IV

ZEPPELIN-STAAKEN R.VI

The largest operational WWI bomber was the four-engine Zeppelin-Staaken R.VI biplane, the most numerous of the R-Bombers (twenty-nine built) and allegedly the largest production wooden aircraft of the war. It had a crew of seven: commander, pilot, copilot, radio operator, and fuel attendant in the cockpit, with one mechanic in each engine nacelle. It had a wingspan of 138 ft., which was only about three feet shorter than the WWII B-29 bomber. It was one of the earliest closed-cockpit military aircraft (the first was the Russian Sikorsky *Ilya Muromets*). Four 245 hp Maybach Mb.IVa 6-cylinder, water-cooled, in-line piston engines powered four propellers mounted in tandem pairs in the nacelle. R.VI (R.30/16) was the earliest known supercharged aircraft to fly, with a fifth Mercedes D.II installed in the central fuselage driving a Brown-Boveri four-stage supercharger at 6,000 rpm. Internal racks could accommodate up to eighteen 220 lb. bombs; the bomb load varied with the fuel load, but it could carry as much as 4,400 lbs. of bombs as far as 500 miles. It could also carry 660 lbs. of bombs externally. With an average of five R.VIs available for missions, eleven raids/thirty sorties on Great Britain were conducted between 28 September 1917–20 May 1918, dropping thirty tons of bombs. The bombers flew individually on the 340-mile round-trip seven-hour missions to their targets on moonlit nights, using directional bearings by radio after take-off; once nearing

London they used the Thames as a navigational aid. None were lost in combat over Great Britain (compared to twenty-eight Gotha G bombers shot down over England), but two crashed while returning to base in the darkness.

Zeppelin-Staaken R.VI

LINKE-HOFMANN R.II

Both Linke-Hofmann R.I biplane prototypes showed unsatisfactory performance and handling characteristics, and both crashed due to structural weaknesses. The company took a completely different approach designing their R.II *Riesenflugzeug* (giant aircraft), making it an approximately three-fold upscale of the single-engined R.I biplane. The R.II, first flown just after the Armistice, had a wing span of 135 ft. and a length of 76.4 ft., and was driven by a huge single 22.7 ft. diameter duo-engine tractor propeller, the largest single propeller ever used to propel any aircraft in aviation history. The huge propeller was powered through clutches, shafts, and gearboxes by four 260 hp Mercedes power plants arranged in pairs in the central fuselage. Flight testing demonstrated acceptable performance and handling, being able to fly with only two engines driving the enormous propeller with a cruising speed of 74 mph. It had a normal endurance estimated to be seven hours, but with adjustment of load it was estimated the R.II could stay aloft for thirty hours. There were plans to convert the R.II into a twelve-passenger airliner, but the restrictions of the Versailles Treaty ended further development.

Linke-Hofmann R.II

SIEMENS-SCHUCKERT R.VIII

The war's largest aircraft was the Siemens-Schuckert R.VIII, designed by Harald Wolff in 1917. The biplane bomber had wooden four-bay wings that spanned a record 157.5 ft. and had an area of 4,734 sq. ft. The bomber was 70.8 ft. long, 24.3 ft. high, and weighed 35,060 lbs. loaded, making it the heaviest plane in the world. Its estimated performance included a 78 mph top speed, 13,120 ft. ceiling, and 560 mile range. The huge bomber was powered by six 300 hp Basse and Selve engines mounted in the fuselage, where they could be serviced by mechanics in flight. Transmission shafts from the forward power plant pair turned two outboard, two-bladed tractor propellers, while the remaining four were coupled to two four-bladed pusher propellers. Gun mounts were to be provided in the nose, two rear cockpits, and floor, with a cockpit placed in the top wing's center. Two aircraft were to be built by 1 March 1918, but only the first (the R23/16) was completed after the Armistice; ground trials for commercial application would not commence until 1 March 1919. A gearbox failure on 6 June resulted in a propeller breaking up, causing extensive damage, and the new German government canceled the project on June 26 due to Treaty of Versailles restrictions, so the world's largest aircraft never flew.

Siemens-Schuckert R.VIII

MANNESMANN POLL TRI-PLANE

The first intercontinental bomber proposal was likely the gigantic ten-engine (260 hp Mercedes or Maybach) Mannesmann Poll Tri-plane, actually designed to attack America. It was to have five engine-carrying gondolas, each with engines paired back to back, with four gondolas mounted on the mid-wing and the other gondola mounted below the fuselage, on the middle of the lower wing. The 40 ft. high Tri-plane had a middle wingspan of 165 ft. and top and bottom wingspans of 102 ft.; its fuselage length was 150 ft., which was only seven feet shorter than the wingspan of the Siemens-Schuckert. The aircraft, crewed by four or five, was to be unarmed except for its bomb load. It was projected to fly for eighty hours with its 48,000 lb. fuel load, which would have given it the theoretical range to cross the Atlantic, bomb New York City, and then return. The bomber encountered many problems during construction due to its size, weight, the engine power required, and the availability of airframe materials. When the war ended the mostly unfinished bomber was discovered by the Allied Control Commission and parts were sent to England, including the 7.75 ft. diameter solid wooden wheel.

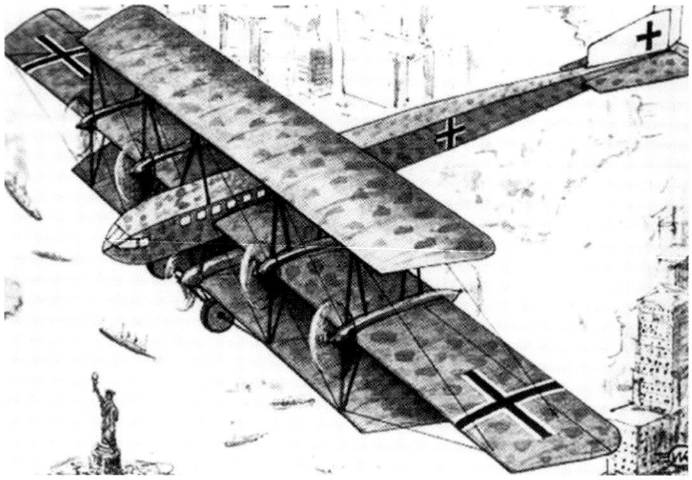

Mannesmann Poll

2

GERMAN INTERWAR LONG-RANGE AIRCRAFT AND PILOTS

DORNIER DO X: POSTWAR GERMAN GIANT

When it rolled off the Dornier Altenrhein assembly line on the Swiss portion of Lake Constance in 1929, the Do X was the largest, heaviest, and most powerful flying boat in the world; only the Russian Tupolev ANT-20 *Maxim Gorki* land plane that appeared a few years later was physically larger, but its maximum take-off weight was not as heavy as the Do X's.

The Do X was financed by the German Transport Ministry and a factory was expressly designed and built in Altenrhein, Switzerland, to sidestep conditions of the Versailles Treaty, which prohibited any aircraft exceeding established speed and range limits to be built by Germany after WWI. The Do X *Flugschiff* ("Flying Ship") was a semi-cantilever monoplane with an all-duralumin hull and wings composed of a steel-reinforced duralumin framework covered in heavy linen fabric covered with aluminum paint. The physical particulars of the Do X included a wing with a 157.4 ft. span and 4,844 sq. ft. area; a length of 131.3 ft., a height of 33.7 ft., an empty weight of 62,280 lbs., and a maximum take-off weight of 123,460 lbs.

Do X designer Dr. Claude Dornier is known for his unique concepts in multiple aircraft engine installations, with his aircraft often utilizing paired propellers in a push-pull configuration. The Do X flying boat was initially powered by twelve 524 hp Siemens license-built British Bristol Jupiter radial engines (six tractor propellers and six pushers) mounted in six tower nacelles on the wing. The nacelles were joined by an auxiliary wing used to stabilize the mountings. The engines were supervised by an engineer who also controlled the throttle, and the pilot would request the engineer to adjust the power; a similar method to that used by maritime vessels. The air-cooled Jupiter engines were subject to overheating and were unable to propel the Do X to altitudes over 1,400 ft. After 103 flights in 1930, the Do X was refitted with 610 hp American Curtiss V-1570 Conqueror water-cooled 12-cylinder inline engines, enabling the Do X to attain the 1,650 ft. altitude necessary to cross the Atlantic.

Dr. Dornier designed the flying boat to carry sixty-six passengers on long distance flights or one hundred passengers on short flights. The passenger accommodation was so luxurious that they nearly met the criteria of trans-Atlantic ocean liners. The main deck included a smoking room with its own wet bar, a dining salon, and seating for the sixty-six passengers, which could also be converted to sleeping berths for night flights. Aft of the passenger spaces was an all-electric galley, lavatories, and a cargo hold. The cockpit, navigational office, engine control, and radio rooms were situated on the upper deck. The lower deck held fuel tanks and nine watertight compartments.

A crew of fourteen was aboard the Flugschiff when it was launched for its first test flight on 12 July 1929. On its seventieth test flight on 21 October, there were 169 (including ten aircrew) persons on board to set a world record for the number of persons carried on a single flight; a commercial aircraft record that would stand for thirty years, until the Boeing 707-120 carried 189 on a revenue flight. After a long fifty-second take-off run the Do X slowly climbed to an altitude of only 650 ft., and because of its size and weight the passengers were requested to crowd together on one side or the other to aid in making turns. To introduce the airliner to the potential American market the Do X took off from Friedrichshafen, Germany, on 3 November 1930, under the command of Friedrich Christiansen, for a trans-Atlantic test flight to New York via the Netherlands, England, France, Spain, and Portugal, where, on 29 November, the flight was interrupted at Lisbon. A tarp had contacted a hot exhaust pipe and started a fire that demolished much of the port wing, requiring six weeks for new parts to be fabricated and to get the damage repaired. The Do X then continued (with several further interruptions) along the western coast of Africa, crossing the Atlantic at its narrow African-Brazilian waist to Natal, then continuing north to the United States, finally reaching New York on 27 August 1931, nearly nine months after departing Germany. The Do X and crew then remained at Glenn Curtiss Airport (now LaGuardia) for the next nine months for engine overhaul, during which time thousands of visitors toured the "leviathan of the air." The effects of the Depression scuttled any marketing plans for the Do X and it departed from New York on 21 May 1932, flying via Newfoundland and the Azores to Berlin, where it arrived on 24 May, and was met by an enthusiastic crowd of 200,000.

Financially beleaguered Dornier was unable to continue to operate the aircraft, and the original Do X was delivered to German national airline Deutsche Lufthansa, which conducted a successful 1932 tour of German coastal cities. During a planned 1933 tour to Vienna, Budapest, and Istanbul, the journey ended after nine days when the Do X's tail section detached during a failed too-steep landing on a reservoir near Passau, in Bavaria. The Do X was permanently out of service and then became the centerpiece of Germany's new aviation museum Deutsche Luftfahrt-Sammlung, at the Berlin Bahnhof, where it remained on exhibit until it was destroyed in an RAF air raid during the night of 23–24 November 1943. Fragments of the torn-off tail section are now on display at the Dornier Museum in Friedrichshafen.

While never a commercial success, the Dornier Do X was the largest heavier-than-air aircraft of its time and a pioneer in demonstrating the potential of an international passenger air service. Three Do Xs were constructed by Dornier: the original Do X operated by Dornier and two others ordered by Italy. The X2, named *Umberto Maddalena*, entered service in August 1931, and claimed to be the largest aircraft in the world at that time. The X3, named *Alessandro Guidoni*, entered service in May 1932. These Italian variants were basically identical to the original, except for being slightly larger, using Fiat A-22R V12 water-cooled power plants, and the six engine mounts being covered by a streamlined fairing. Both Italian Do X orders originated with SANA—then the Italian state airline—but were requisitioned and used by the Italian Air Force primarily for maneuvers, prestige flights, and public exhibitions. Only a month after Lufthansa's Do X lost its tail section, the Do X2 also lost its tail in an identical landing accident. During 1934, the Italians reduced flights and crew complements, and then mothballed the two Dorniers at Marina di Pisa in 1935; the two were scrapped in 1937. A successor, the Do XX, was envisioned by Dornier, but never advanced beyond the design study stage.

Dornier Do X

Engineering compartment of the Do X, with the engineer controlling the engines on command of the pilot, marine vessel style.

JUNKERS W33

The Junkers W33 was a transport development of the very advanced 1919 four-seat Junkers F13 airliner and closely mimicked it in size and structure. Like all other Junkers designs, the W33 was an aerodynamically clean, all-metal, cantilever, unbraced monoplane, with only Anthony Fokker's designs being of comparable modernity. Also, like all Junkers designs it used a Duraluminium structure covered with Junkers' signature corrugated Dural skin. The W33's wingspan was 58.2 ft. with a wing area of 462.8 sq. ft.; length was 34.5 ft.; height was 11.6 ft.; and it had an empty weight of 2,689 lbs. and a maximum take-off weight of 5,511 lbs. The 310 hp Junkers L5 upright, inline, water-cooled engine was also the same as the F 13FE and propelled the W33 at a maximum speed of 120 mph and a cruising speed of 93 mph to a service ceiling of 14,100 ft. with a range of more than 620 miles. While the Junkers "W" designated the W33 as a seaplane, it was also a land plane. From 1927–1934, the Junkers Dessau Plant manufactured 198 W33s. The W33 set several records:

Johann Risztics:

Feldwebel Johann Risztics was the Austro-Hungarian WWI flying ace credited with seven confirmed aerial victories.

On 3–5 August 1927, Cornelius Edzard and Johann Risztics flew circuits over Dessau, Germany, setting records for 52:22:3 hours and a distance of 2,896 miles.

On 3 August 1927, Johann Risztics and Cornelius Edzard flew their W33 over 2,923 miles (4,660 km) in 52:22 hours, a new distance world record.

On 14 August 1927, Risztics, Edzard, and American journalist Hubert Renfro Knickerbocker, on board the Junkers W33 *Europa*, attempted the first east to west crossing of the Atlantic. They left from Germany, but bad weather and engine problems soon ended their flight.

On 5–7 July 1928, Johann Risztics and Wilhelm Zimmermann surpassed both the unrefueled and refueled endurance records by staying in the air for 65:25:00 hours.

Freiherr von Hunefeld, et. al. Flights

The W33 is most well known for the first heavier-than-air west to east trans-Atlantic flight. The east to west trans-Atlantic flight had always been more challenging due to prevailing headwinds. On 12–13 April, 1928, W33 D-1167 (the *Bremen*), crewed by Hermann Kohl, Freiherr von Hunefeld (a.k.a the "Crazy Baron"), and James Fitzmaurice flew from Baldonnel, near Dublin, Ireland, and headed for New York, but strong westerly head winds and a faulty magnetic compass drove them north of their intended destination. As a result, their forward progress had been too slow, and to avoid the head winds they descended to only a few hundred feet, but saw no landmarks, nor signs of civilization. A crash landing meant they might never be found, so after flying for several more hours they finally spotted a lighthouse on an island and several people below. They circled and landed on a flat area, damaging the *Bremen*, but coming to a safe stop after thirty-seven hours in the air. They learned they had landed on Greenly Island, Canada, off Labrador, and calculated they were 1,200 miles from New York; with the headwinds and the fuel they had available they would never reach New York and would have landed in the Atlantic.

Famed pilots Floyd Bennett and Bernt Balchen flew a Ford Trimotor to provide relief to the downed pilots. Bennett developed pneumonia following a previous crash and flying with a fever succumbed while in flight on 25 April 1928. Balchen flew the remaining eight hours and was paid $10,000, which he donated to Bennett's widow. The three trans-Atlantic pioneers were rescued, and were later the subject of a jubilant reception on 17 May in New York City, where two million people turned out to greet them. President Calvin Coolidge presented them with the Distinguished Flying Cross, making them the first non-Americans to receive that honor. The original *Bremen* is owned by the Henry Ford Museum in Detroit and is currently on display at Bremen Airport in Germany.

During Fall 1928, Freiherr von Hunefeld purchased the other Junkers W33 (sister ship of the *Bremen*, which he had named *Europa*) and engaged Swedish pilot Karl Gunnar Lindner to attempt an around-the-world flight. After leaving Berlin on 18 September 1928, the Europa headed west over southern Europe, across the Middle East, then crossed the Indian Ocean to India before skirting the coast of Asia and China. Since they were not trying to set a speed record they made multiple rest stops along the way, arriving in Tokyo on 20 October. While there they had to wait for favorable weather to cross the Pacific, but as the wait prolonged von Hunefeld's health began to deteriorate and he was forced to cancel the remainder of the flight. In February 1929, von Hunefeld died of stomach cancer in Berlin.

Other Notable W33 Feats

Flying a greatly modified W33 (sometimes referred to as a W34), Willy Neuenhofen established a world altitude record of 41,800 ft. on 26 May 1929.

On 2 February 1930, Lufthansa and DVL tested in-flight fueling of a W33 by a DVL Fokker F II tanker aircraft via a sixty-five foot hose connection.

Junkers W33 *Bremen*

Bremen was crewed by Hermann Kohl (L), James Fitzmaurice (C), and Freiherr von Hunefeld (R).

Johann Risztics (L) and Wilhelm Zimmermann (R) with Hugo Junkers

FRIEDRICK VON KOENIG-WARTHAUSEN'S RESOURCEFUL ROUND-THE WORLD "FLIGHT"

German-born, English-educated Friedrick Karl Baron von Koenig-Warthausen had an early passion for aviation that was sated in 1929 at age twenty-two, when he purchased a Klemm monoplane he named *Kamerad* powered by a Daimler 20 HP motorcycle engine.

That year German president von Hindenburg created the Hindenburg Cup to be awarded to the amateur pilot completing the best sporting flight of the year, and Koenig-Warthausen decided to compete for this honor by flying from Berlin to Moscow. His Klemm had the basic instruments (an altimeter, fuel gauge to measure gasoline in the fifty gallon tank, oil pressure gauge, and a thermometer to measure outside air temperature), which he supplemented with a minimum of equipment, including a few maps and charts, a portable compass, an emergency flare gun, and a few tools.

On 9 August 1929, he took off from Berlin's Tempelhof Airport and fourteen hours later landed in a small village about ten miles outside Moscow; the next day he continued on to Moscow's Chodinka Aerodrome. Flushed with success, Koenig-Warthausen decided to continue flying eastward, and on 15 August he left Moscow, crossed the Caucasus Mountains, landed in Baku, on the Caspian Sea, and then continued south along the western coast of the Caspian Sea and landed in Pachlevi, Iran, on his way to Tehran. On 23 September, he made a forced landing in Isfahan, Iran, and three days later he took off for Shiraz, Iran, where he made another forced landing. He and some locals built a runway (it took four days to complete) before he could take off for Bushire, Iran. Unfortunately he ran out of gas, but made another forced landing on the way, finally arriving at Bushire, where he was informed he had been awarded the Hindenburg Cup and also met fellow Germans Baron von Huenefeld and K. G. Lindner (see text), who were on their way to Tokyo on their round-the-world flight attempt. Koenig-Warthausen continued flying east and on the way made forced landings and repairs before landing in Karachi, where he remained for five weeks. He took off from Karachi on 17 December, flying the Indian Uterlai, Jodhpur, Nasirabad, and Agra route, and spent Christmas in Calcutta, India.

Koenig-Warthausen spent two months in Calcutta, making a visit to Tibet and meeting Gandhi, and finally decided to cancel his return trip to Europe by steamer. He departed Calcutta on 5 February 1930 and continued flying toward Singapore, spending five days in Rangoon and five weeks in Bangkok. On 25 March, he continued toward Singapore, flying with Tanim—a Siamese cat given as a gift from the wife of the crown prince. He made several landings on the Malay Peninsula and remained in Singapore for three weeks, making a short flight south to cross the equator. It was here that he finally committed himself to continue east and "flying" round-the-world, rather than taking a steamer to return to Europe.

From Singapore he and the Klemm boarded a steamer headed for Hong Kong and then Shanghai, China, from where he took a short flight to Nanking, where he visited with General Chang Kai Check, after which he and the Klemm boarded a steamer for Kobe, Japan. He waited in Kobe for ten days for the weather for a flight to Tokyo, where he spent three weeks before embarking from Yokohama on 25 May aboard the steamer *Siberia Maru* headed for America, stopping in Honolulu, Hawaii, before arriving in San Francisco on 8 June 1930. Here Koenig-Warthausen learned of the death of his pilot friend Baron von Huenefeld. To honor his comrade he changed the name of his Klemm from *Kamerad* to *Huenefeld*.

After ten days in San Francisco, on 19 June he left for Los Angeles and San Diego, with two side flights from there into Mexico before heading for El Centro, California, Tucson, Arizona, and El Paso, Texas. The "Baron's" trip was well publicized by the American press and Tanim was referred to as Felix after the popular cartoon character *Felix the Cat*. On 12 July 1930 in El Paso, while traveling in a taxi to the airport, he was involved in a serious traffic accident, requiring a two-month convalesce. On 15 September, Koenig-Warthausen took off heading east toward New York City, but while taxiing over the muddy airfield at Sweetwater, Texas, his Klemm sunk in the mud, damaging his left wing, so his plane was transported by road to Dallas, where it was repaired. He then flew to Oklahoma City, Saint Louis, and Chicago without incident, but on 17 October, when landing in Detroit, he found his Daimler engine had a broken valve, delaying his departure four days. To shorten his flight path to New York he chose to fly over Canada, but water in his fuel and constant bad weather delayed his landing at Roosevelt Field, Long Island.

On 15 November 1930, he sailed from New York City with his Huenefeld lashed on the deck of the steamer *Bremen*, arriving in Germany on 22 November and welcomed by a special delegation of German pilots. He was to fly to Berlin, but fog forced him to land in Hanover, where he left the Klemm and traveled to Berlin by train and car, arriving on 23 November 1930 to ceremoniously receive the Hindenburg Cup and recognition for his resourceful solo round-the-world flight in his single-engine, open-cockpit Klemm in 15 months covering 20,000 miles during 450 flying hours and using less than 1,000 gallons of gas.

Friedrick Karl Baron von Koenig-Warthausen and Tanim

Hans Bertram

On 29 February 1932, Hans Bertram (pilot), (?), Thom (co-pilot), Adolph Klausmann (mechanic), and Alexander von Lagorio (cameraman) departed in their Junkers W-33D floatplane from Cologne, Germany, on their attempted round-the-world flight, with the intention to visit German communities along their route and to locate potential markets for Germany's aviation industry. Other than a forced landing in Porto Fossone, Italy, because of a blinding snowstorm and engine problems, their flight continued without problems until they were forced to land in the Syrian desert when they encountered a sand storm that clogged their carburetor. On the flight from Cocanada, India, to Batavia, Indonesia, the plane needed to be lighter and co-pilot Thom continued by rail and boat to meet them there. After they met it was further decided that Bertram and Klausmann would continue their flight together and Thom and von Lagorio would meet them in Shanghai, China. After an engine overhaul at the Dutch naval aerodrome in Soeeabaja, Indonesia, they refueled at Kupang and headed for Port Darwin, on the northwest coast of Australia, on 15 May. On the way they flew into a ferocious storm and lost direction; finally, low on fuel, they were forced to land on the remote northwest Australian coastline with little water and no food. Since there was no official record of their flight no search party was initially organized. They were stranded after their routine water crossing had become "a flight to hell," which became the title of Bertram's 1936 book on this adventure. Finally, on 23 June 1932, they were rescued by a search party and transported to Perth for recuperation. Klausmann returned to Germany by steamer but never entirely recovered. Bertram had the W33 repaired, removed the floats, and for the next four and a half months visited several cities around Australia, giving talks. On 17 April 1933, he returned to Berlin to a tumultuous welcome and joined the Nazi Party and the SS in 1934, when he began a career making propaganda films. During WWII he was shot down over Libya, taken POW, and sent to Australia in 1941. He had a successful career and wrote ten films (1938–1985). He also directed six films (1939–1952), including a four-part Australian television miniseries named *Flight into Hell* based on his book.

Hans Bertram

ELLY BEINHORN, GERMANY'S AMELIA EARHART

Using a small inheritance, twenty-one-year-old Elly Beinhorn moved to Berlin, where she took flying lessons and soloed in a small Klemm KL-20, after which she gave weekend aerobatic displays to finance her appetite for flying. Long-distance flying was her passion, and in 1931, she signed on as the pilot for a scientific expedition to West Africa. On 4 January 1931, she began the African journey, flying the Klemm Kl 25 previously flown by Theo Osterkamp at the 1930 Challenge International de Tourisme. Soon she was forced to land with oiled spark plugs on a Black Forest snowfield, and continued after a Klemm factory mechanic arrived to clean the plugs. She then flew over Spain and Gibraltar to Rabat, Casablanca, and Cape Juby, and flew along the African coast to Dakar, where she joined the expedition and explored the surrounding area, taking aerial photographs. To avoid the rainy season Beinhorn left the expedition team on 15 March, but on the return flight to Germany a broken oil line occurred on the way to Timbuktu and caused an emergency landing. Led by locals, she spent three days on foot and by boat before arriving exhausted in Timbuktu. After a few day's rest she went back to retrieve her aircraft, but found that it was beyond repair, so a military aircraft returned Beinhorn to Bamako, from where she traveled by rail and ship to Casablanca. By this time her plight became known in Germany and a Berlin newspaper sent Theo Osterkamp and a reporter with another aircraft to meet Beinhorn in Casablanca. They left Africa on 23 April, and after an emergency landing on the way to Oran because of contaminated fuel they finally arrived in Rome. Beinhorn then flew back to Germany alone via Vienna, where she was escorted to Berlin by a fighter escort and landed on 29 April 1931, where she was greeted as a celebrity by a large crowd. Beinhorn's African adventure made her Germany's Amelia Earhart, and she no longer had problems financing future escapades.

After her African flight Beinhorn spent six months preparing for her next venture: a solo world tour. To finance the flight she gave lectures and interviews and sought out backers.

During the morning of 4 December 1931, Beinhorn took off from Berlin-Staaken toward India, flying an open cockpit Klemm Kl 26 with an 80 hp Argus engine. She flew over Pol About, Wroclaw, Budapest, Belgrade, Sofia, and Istanbul, landed in Syria because of a storm, then completed a night flight to Aleppo, where her Klemm was repaired by French military airmen. She flew to Baghdad, then made an emergency landing on the north coast of the Persian Gulf because of clogged carburetors and gas lines. Continued mechanical problems developed near Bushire, Iran, where she met pilot Moye Stephens and travel adventure writer Richard Halliburton, who helped her repair her aircraft. Stephens and Halliburton were flying around the world in a Stearman C-3B named *Flying Carpet* (see text). Later, Halliburton wrote a foreword to her book, *Flying Girl,* about these and other of her adventures in the air. Beinhorn joined them and they flew to Karachi and on to Delhi to spend Christmas together. Beinhorn stayed for six days in Delhi and flew to the Taj Mahal, where she and Stephens thrilled the Maharajah of Nepal with a daring aerobatic display, and then the two aircraft flew over Mount Everest, with Halliburton standing in the *Flying Carpet's* open cockpit to take the first aerial photograph of the mountain. Meanwhile, Beinhorn decided to cancel the planned flight to Tokyo because of the uncertain political situation there and instead travel to Australia, which involved long, risky flights over open water. She left for Bangkok, where she met the Thai royal couple, on to Siam for a week, and to Singapore, where she met Stephens and Halliburton again. They flew to Borneo, crossing the Equator on their way to the Philippines, where they separated and Beinhorn continued to Java. In Batavia she was invited to numerous receptions and lectured and toured the area. On her way to Timor she was grounded by a strong tropical storm and then flew on to Darwin, Australia, accompanied by three English seaplanes. She arrived on 22 March 1932 without incident in Darwin, where an enthusiastic crowd welcomed only the second woman after Amy Johnson (see text) to fly solo from Europe to Australia. Two days later Beinhorn flew toward Sydney, arriving on 2 April, where an honorary squadron including Kingsford Smith met them. Beinhorn spent almost a month in cordial Sydney, lecturing, being endlessly interviewed, socializing, and organizing her onward flight to New Zealand. Because the distance was too far for her single-engine Klemm it was disassembled and shipped to New Zealand, and then a one-month voyage to Panama. After arriving in Balboa she learned it was not possible to fly from Panama along the 2,000 km (1,250 miles) of the mountainous South American West Coast, as there were few airports and little available gasoline. Not to be deterred, Beinhorn enlisted the aid of US airmen at a military airfield who helped her rebuild her Klemm to accept six auxiliary tanks, which would allow her eleven hours of uninterrupted flight. She flew to Cali, Columbia, and Lima, Peru, then stopped in Arica and Ovalle to Santiago, on the long Chilean coast. At Santiago she prepared to cross the Andes Mountains through a dangerous pass, sending her baggage by land and equipping her aircraft with oxygen. She arrived safely in Mendoza, Argentina, and continued on to Buenos Aires, hoping to continue on to Rio de Janeiro, where she would again disassemble the Klemm and sail to Europe. Bad weather forced her to sail from Buenos Aires instead. During the next three weeks Beinhorn began to write for her later bestseller *A Girl Flies Around the World*. She landed in Bremerhaven, where she was welcomed by a large crowd. On 26 July 1932, Beinhorn reassembled the Klemm, first flew to Hanover, and finally back to the starting point, Berlin. There Beinhorn was not only greeted by large crowds, but also by news that her purse was 16,000 Reichmarks, which was partially decreased by German President Paul von Hindenburg's presentation of 10,000 Reichmarks, and the Hindenburg Cup for the best sport flying performance of the year. The National Federation of German

Aviation Industry covered the remaining balance so the widely celebrated Beinhorn could begin further flight planning.

1933 Trans-African Flight: Beinhorn's immense popularity after her world tour enabled her to finance her following flights. With the money earned from lectures, interviews, magazine articles, and her films and photos, she accumulated the necessary funds within a few months, and Heinkel made a new aircraft available to her. Heinkel had specifically designed the experimental model He 71 for that flight: it was a smaller version of the two-seat Heinkel He 64 modified with an enclosed cockpit, a 78 hp Hirth HM 4 engine, and additional fuel tanks to increase its range. Beinhorn began her African circumnavigation from Berlin in summer 1933, flying to Istanbul, Aleppo, and Cairo, then along the Nile river to Khartoum, Juba, Nairobi, Johannesburg, and finally to Cape Town. Along the way she encountered bureaucratic colonialism that prohibited women from traveling without a male escort. When these escorts were forced to leave her she was arrested in Juba, where she was forced to remain until she finally received an exception from the British colonial administration and was able to continue and complete the flight as scheduled. She described the 28,000 km (17,400 mile) journey in the book *Berlin-Cape Town-Berlin*.

1934 American Sojourn: During 1934, Beinhorn acquired the much faster Klemm Kl 32 powered by a 160 hp Siemens Sh 14a engine. The cabin had three seats, one of which was replaced by an additional fuel tank. The original intention of the trip was to visit the historic Central American Mayan cities, but to pay for the trip Beinhorn had to do a promotional tour in the United States. During her Central American tour she received the aid of a Maj. Lewis Brereton in Panama. Subsequently Beinhorn flew to Los Angeles, where she met Stephen Moye again and spent several weeks in California with Moyes' family. Afterward, she visited Amelia Earhart in Kansas, then Jimmy Doolittle and other acquaintances while giving lectures and showing films.

1935 Record Flight Across Two Continents in 24 Hours: During 1935 Beinhorn tested Bayerische Flugzeugwerke's (BFW) BF 108, which she believed would be a more comfortable and better long-distance aircraft with its four seats, air-cooled Hirth engine, and retractable landing gear than her Klemm. She flew it to London and then convinced BFW to lend her the aircraft for an attempted record flight from Germany to Asia in twenty-four hours and back. She contended that the flight would place the aircraft in the world aviation spotlight and christened it *Taifun* (Typhoon). At 0340 on 13 August 1935, she took off from Gliwice, trying to keep the distance as short as possible to meet the twenty-four hour time constraint. She crossed Hungary, traversed the Transylvanian Alps, and by 0600 had crossed five countries, reaching Asian Istanbul—the turning point—at 0920. The return flight was 450 km (280 miles) longer, and over the High Tatras she flew blind through dense clouds, but finally arrived in Gliwice at 1808, flying 3,470 kilometers (2,100 miles) to set a new record. Until the war Beinhorn became a Taifun spokesperson, flying each of the seven or eight of the latest models.

In September 1935, Elly attended the Grand Prix of Czechoslovakia, where she met racing driver Bernd Rosemeyer, who had just won his first victory. They soon began a relationship, with the smitten Rosemeyer accompanying Beinhorn on her lectures. The reluctant Beinhorn was at the height of her career and had reservations about the relationship—she had planned to fly three continents in one day in the new model Bf 108. The Taifun's delivery was delayed, causing Beinhorn to remain in Germany until its delivery, and she married Rosemeyer on 13 July 1936. The day after their wedding the Bf 108 was delivered and Beinhorn readied the aircraft for its trip. Meanwhile, Rosemeyer won the Grand Prix of Germany at the famous Nurburgring, and in the following months would drive to continuous victories, making him extremely popular. On 6 August 1936, Beinhorn-Rosemeyer took off from Berlin at 0200 and by sunrise landed in Cairo, then flew about 1,000 km (625 miles) across the Mediterranean over Asian Istanbul to Athens. When she tried to take off from there to Berlin stones ripped her rudder, but Deutsche Lufthansa technicians quickly repaired the damage and Beinhorn continued the flight on schedule; after 3,750 km (2,330 miles) she landed safely in the evening in Berlin-Tempelhof. Rosemeyer was entered in the Grand Prix of South Africa and Elly flew the couple in eight daily stages to Johannesburg. After another race in Cape Town they had a belated honeymoon, visiting and sightseeing on their way to Cairo and encountering a cracked propeller, a broken tail wheel, and an emergency landing in Budapest. Rosemeyer also became seduced by flying, took lessons, and bought a Klemm Kl 35. On 12 November 1937, son Bernd Rosemeyer Junior was born. On 28 January 1938, Rosemeyer attempted a speed record on the Frankfurt-Darmstadt motorway, and at about 430 km/h (267 mph) he was hit by a side wind, rolled over several times, and was killed.

In the following six months Beinhorn wrote a biography which sold more than 200,000 copies. She then began to fly again, delivering new aircraft and flying VIPs and dignitaries for the company. In 1939, Beinhorn flew to Asia to deliver an aircraft to an Indian maharaja, visiting friends along the way, and returned two months before the outbreak of WWII. Sport flying was no longer possible in Germany and Beinhorn's Taifun was commandeered as a Luftwaffe courier. On 26

September 1941, she married industrial buyer Karl Wittmann and they had a daughter; all survived the war.

After WWII German citizens were forbidden to fly, but in Spring 1951, she obtained a Swiss pilot's license and became a flying journalist and photographer for an illustrated magazine, flying to various areas in Europe and Africa. In 1959, when private flying was allowed again in Germany, Beinhorn renewed her license and flew in thirteen Powder Puff Derbys (see text) and won the Gold Medal in the European Star Flight. In 1963, she was first in the Women in Europe flights and second in the Alps Star Flight. In 1979, the then seventy-two-year-old pilot voluntarily surrendered her pilot's license. She died on 28 November 2007, at age one hundred.

Elly Beinhorn

GRAF ZEPPELIN (LZ-127) AIRSHIP LONG-RANGE DIVERSION

Although the Zeppelin bombing raids on the United Kingdom during WWI showed that the dirigible would never become a viable aerial weapon, its potential as a trans-Atlantic passenger carrier would be explored and proven in the early 1930s. The Graf Zeppelin (LZ-127) was completed in 1928 by the Zeppelin Company, and its commercial flights pioneered the first trans-Atlantic air service.

At 776 ft. long and 100 ft. in diameter, and with a total gas volume of 3,707,550 cu. ft.—of which 2,648,585 cu. ft. was hydrogen carried in seventeen "lift gas" cells and 1,059,435 cu. ft. was Blau gas (an artificial illuminating gas similar to propane) in twelve "power gas" cells—the Graf was the largest airship in the world at the time. It was powered by five Maybach VL-2 12-cylinder 550 hp engines that could burn either Blau gas or gasoline. Although the Graf Zeppelin had a maximum airspeed of 80 mph, its normal operational airspeed was 73 mph. Some flights were flown using only Blau gas, enabling the airship to cruise for up to 100 hours. By only using gasoline it was able to cruise for 67 hours, and up to 118 hours using both. The Graf Zeppelin had a total lift capacity of 191,800 lbs. with a usable payload of 33,000 lbs. on a 6,200 mile flight.

A gondola was built into the forward third of the airship's ventral surface and contained the flight deck and operational spaces, common areas, passenger cabins, and public toilet facilities. The forward operational spaces consisted of the flight deck, a map/navigation room with two large open access hatches to allow the command crew to communicate with the navigators, radio room, galley, and a short passage to the main entrance/exit door space.

The three radio operators were provided with the most modern radio equipment available, enabling communication with ground stations and ships, performing radio navigation, receiving weather reports, and sending private telegrams for passengers. A ladder in the map room allowed access up into a keel corridor inside the hull. Behind the operational spaces were the main dining and sitting room, with four large windows that connected via a long corridor to ten passenger cabins capable of sleeping twenty-four, two washrooms, and two lavatories. The sofa in the passenger cabins converted to two beds—one above the other—at night. The quarters for the forty crew were inside the hull and were accessed by a catwalk. The galley was equipped with an electric oven with two compartments and hot plates on top for cooking.

From 1928–1932, the airship was used primarily for experimental and demonstration purposes to prepare for subsequent regular commercial trans-Atlantic passenger "voyages." After making six domestic shake-down flights, the Graf Zeppelin departed Friedrichshafen, Germany, on 11 October 1928, on its first trans-Atlantic crossing to Lakehurst, New Jersey. On 14 May 1929, Graf Zeppelin left Friedrichshafen to begin the first flight around the world by an airship. Since William Randolph Hearst paid a sizeable $100,000 ($1,420,000 in 2017) to finance this round-the-world trip, he stipulated that the trip's beginning was to be when it passed over the Statue of Liberty. So, on 8 August 1929, the Graf departed Lakehurst piloted by Dr. Hugo Eckener for its return flight to Friedrichshafen, arriving there on 10 August and completing Leg #1, carrying forty crew, twenty-two passengers, and thousands of pieces of mail. On 15 August, the Graf then left Germany on Leg #2 (6,988 miles) for Tokyo, arriving on 18 August. On 23 August, the Graf proceeded toward the United States on Leg #3 (5,998 miles), arriving in Los Angeles on 26 August. The next day it departed Los Angeles for Lakehurst, completing Leg #4 (2,996 miles) on 29 August, then returned to Friedrichshafen, arriving on 4 September to complete the fifth and last Leg (4,391 miles). (Note: Lady Grace Drummond-Hay was a passenger on this around-the-world trip and became the first woman to fly across the Pacific Ocean.) Later demonstration flights included the Europe-Pan American flight in 1930, a polar expedition in 1931, two round trips to the Middle East, and an assortment of other flights around Europe. In 1932, the Graf began five years of providing regularly scheduled passenger, mail, and freight service between Germany and South America, mainly Brazil. Commercial service was immediately withdrawn the day after the loss of the Hindenburg in May 1937, after having made sixty-four trips to Brazil. During its operating life the airship made 590 flights covering more than a million miles. It was scrapped in 1940 for the manufacture of fighter plane parts.

Do J (Do33) Wals (Whale) seaplane

Graf Zeppelin

1932: DORNIER DO J WALS

The Friedrichshafen Dornier Works on Lake Constance were building a freight/passenger twin-engine Do J (Do33) seaplane called *Wals* (Whales). Because the Treaty of Versailles restricted German aviation after WWI, production took place in Italy until 1932, when Dornier transferred Wals production to Germany until 1936. The Do J made its first flight on 6 November 1922. The Do J was distinguished by its high-mounted strut-braced monoplane wing with two piston engines mounted in tandem in a central nacelle above the wing: one engine powered a tractor and the other powered a pusher propeller. The Wals were crewed by three and could carry eight to ten passengers. It had a wingspan of 72.1 ft. and a wing area of 1,030 sq. ft., a length of 56.8 ft., an empty weight of 8,000 lbs., and a maximum take-off weight of 15,432 lbs. Its varied twin engines could power it to a maximum speed of 115 mph and a cruising speed of 90 mph over a range of 500 miles. Because of their reliability and durability, foreign-flagged Wals were flown on a number of long distance flights during the mid-1920s.

1925: ROALD AMUNDSEN AND LINCOLN ELLSWORTH: FARTHEST NORTH BY AN AIRCRAFT (DO J WALS)

Roald Amundsen

By the 1920s, the evolution of the airplane was such that it opened a new dawn of aerial exploration of the polar regions, with numerous expeditions setting aerial "firsts." In mid-May 1925, Roald Amundsen, accompanied by Lincoln Ellsworth, directed a polar expedition that took two Dornier Do J flying boats (N-24 and N-25) to 87° 44' north; the northernmost latitude reached by an aircraft to that time. The Wals landed several miles apart with N-24 damaged. Despite not having radio contact the crews managed to join up, but it took Amundsen and Ellsworth and the four other crew members more than three weeks to prepare an airstrip for take-off from the ice. Since N-24 could not be repaired all six men climbed into N-25 and pilot Hjalmar Riiser-Larsen expertly lifted the overloaded Wal off the ice to a jubilant landing at their Spitzbergen base, where it was assumed they had vanished forever.

1926: CAPT. RAMON FRANCO: CROSSING THE SOUTH ATLANTIC (DO J WALS)

Ramon Franco was a Spanish aviation pioneer, a notable political personality, and brother of Francisco Franco, future dictator of Spain. In 1920, he joined the Spanish Air Force, and in 1926 became a national hero when he piloted the Dornier Do J flying boat *Plus Ultra* (Ever Further) on a trans-Atlantic flight with co-pilot Julio Ruiz de Alda Miqueleiz and other crew members, Juan Manuel Duran and mechanic Pablo Rada. On 22 January, the *Plus Ultra* took off from Huelva, Spain, and arrived in Buenos Aires, Argentina, on 26 January. The flight approximately followed the 1922 first trans-Atlantic flight route flown by Portuguese aviators Sacadura Cabral and Gago Coutinho, stopping over at Gran Canaria, Cape Verde, Pernambuco, Rio de Janeiro, and Montevideo. The 6,381 (6,419 from other sources) mile flight was completed in 59:39 hours. In 1929, Franco attempted another trans-Atlantic flight, but ditched in the ocean. He and the crew were rescued days later by the Royal Navy aircraft carrier HMS *Eagle*. Franco was killed in an air accident on 28 October 1938, when his hydroplane crashed near the coast of Majorca while attempting to bomb republican-controlled Valencia during the Spanish Civil War. Franco's Wals was subsequently donated to the Argentine Navy, which used it to deliver airmail, and is currently on display in a museum in Lujan, Argentina.

Capt. Ramon Franco (in cockpit)

1927: SARMENTO DE BEIRES: FIRST NIGHT CROSSING THE SOUTH ATLANTIC (DO J WALS)

The night of 17 March 1927, Portuguese Army aviator Sarmento de Beires and his crew—Duvalle Portugal (co-pilot), Jorge de Castilho (navigator), and Manuel Gouveia (mechanic)—flew a Dornier Wals J named *Argos* on the first night air crossing of the South Atlantic from Portuguese Guinea to Brazil. The *Argos* took off from the Tagus River, Portugal, on 7 March 1927, and arrived in Casablanca, Morocco, the same day. From Casablanca it flew to Bolama, Portuguese Guinea, where the Wal experienced mechanical and weight problems that prevented take-off. Co-pilot Duvalle Portugal remained behind so the *Argos* could continue. At 1808 on 16 April, *Argos* headed to Brazil; on the way mechanic Gouveia fixed engine problems twice while navigator Castilho skillfully directed the aircraft over the

Sarmento de Beires (3R)

prominent Brazilian landmark the Rocks of Saint Peter and Saint Paul, from which he navigated to Fernando de Noronha Island, where they arrived at 1220 hours after flying 1,622 miles on an 18:12 hour flight. The flight then continued with Brazilian stops in Recife, Natal, and finally Rio de Janeiro.

1932: WOLFGANG VON GRONAU: AROUND-THE-WORLD FLIGHT (DO J WALS)

WWI naval pilot Wolfgang von Gronau ended the war as the adjutant to the commander of aviation in the German High Seas Fleet, and was responsible for the introduction of several innovations for German flying boats and floatplanes. After the war he was able to find a place in postwar German commercial aviation, and by 1926, he directed the Lufthansa Seaplane School on the North Sea island Sylt. Here he became convinced that the Dornier Wals could be used to establish a commercial air route between Germany and the US, as the aircraft had a proven reputation for reliability and endurance on long distance flights.

During training exercises von Gronau began reconnoitering routes to Iceland from northwestern Europe. At the time Germany's Graf Zeppelin airship program, the giant Do X Flying Boat, and pioneering Lufthansa commercial air services were gaining international prestige, and there was little interest in the unproven Wal. During 18–26 August 1930, von Gronau led his first trans-Atlantic flight, flying Amundsen's old Dornier Amundsen-Wal from Sylt over Iceland, Greenland, Labrador, and Newfoundland. Von Gronau continued on to New York City, arriving on 26 August, finishing the first complete transit of the northern trans-Atlantic Great Circle Route since the 1924 US Army Air Service around-the-world flight. The Wal crew arrived in New York to great fanfare, and several days later, was feted by President Hoover at the White House. From 8 August–7 September 1931, von Gronau repeated this flight, flying the new twin-engine Dornier seaplane *Gronland-Wal* (Greenland Whale) over the Greenland Ice Cap, landing in Chicago, and then visiting several American cities afterward. This flight led von Gronau to contemplate an around-the-world flight.

On 21 July 1932, von Gronau—piloting the same Gronland-Wal as the previous year—accompanied by co-pilot Gerth von Roth, mechanic Franzl Hack, and radio operator Fritz Albrecht, began his third Atlantic crossing to be followed by an around-the-world flight. The crew flew for more than three months, making forty-four stops en route, including the initial flight from Sylt to Chicago on 2 August that crossed the Greenland Ice Cap. The Dornier then traveled across Canada, Alaska, the Aleutian Islands, Japan, China, Manila, Indonesia, India, Iraq, Cyprus, Greece, and Italy, then finally back to Germany on 10 October as a national hero after being in the air 270 hours over 27,750 miles. After visiting Japan as part of this around-the-world flight von Gronau decided to accept an appointment to the German Embassy in Tokyo in 1939 as part of a self-imposed disenchantment with the Nazis. After the war von Gronau became part of the reorganized Lufthansa airline.

The largest and last versions of the Wal were operated by Lufthansa on their South Atlantic airmail service from Stuttgart, Germany, to Natal, Brazil. Wals made more than 300 crossings of the South Atlantic in regular mail service. Two Dornier Wals also played an important role in the Third German Antarctic Expedition of 1939.

Wolfgang von Gronau (in cockpit)

JU G.38

The Junkers Company specialized in durable, long-range aircraft, and the massive G.38, a four-engine thirty-passenger airliner, was one of its first, flying in late 1929. Two prototypes were built, and at the time were the largest commercial land-based planes in the world with a 144.3 ft. wingspan, a 76.2 ft. length, and a 53,000 lb. gross weight. The fuselage and cantilever wing was covered in stressed, corrugated Duralumin. The G.38's biplane tail—also found on other contemporary large aircraft—was intended to reduce rudder forces; initially there were three rudders with only a central fixed fin. The landing gear was fixed, with double tandem main wheels that were originally enclosed in very large, distinctive spats. The G.38 carried a crew of seven, with onboard mechanics able to service the engines in flight due to the G.38's blended wing design that provided access to all four power plants. Blended Wing Body (BWB, or Hybrid Wing Body, HWB) aircraft have no distinct dividing line between the wings and the main body of the craft, with the body form composed of distinct and separate wing structures, though the wings are smoothly blended into the body (unlike a flying wing, which has no distinct fuselage). Passenger accommodation was luxurious, and was intended to compete with Zeppelin service. The G.38 was unique, in that passengers were seated in the wings, which were 5.7 ft. thick at the root. The leading edge of each wing had sloping windscreens, giving the passengers a forward-facing view like the pilot's. There were three eleven-seat cabins, plus smoking cabins and wash rooms. There were also two seats in the extreme nose. In flight tests the G.38 set four world records, including speed, distance, and duration for airplanes lifting a 5,000 kg (11,000 lb.) payload. Both G.38s were in service concurrently with Lufthansa until 1936, when the first crashed and was written off. The second G.38 flew with Lufthansa for nearly a decade and was destroyed on the ground during an RAF air raid on Athens on 17 May 1941. During the 1930s the design was licensed to Mitsubishi, which constructed and flew six in a military bomber/transport configuration designated the Ki-20.

Junkers G-38

3
THE URAL BOMBER CONCEPT

While the victorious Allied powers and secondary nations continued to develop large and long-range aircraft, the Treaty of Versailles and the economics of being a defeated nation severely handicapped German aviation aspirations in the interwar years. When the new militaristic Nazi regime came into power, it began to improvise means to revitalize and develop an air force. German air tacticians focused their new air force on one that would engage in a revolutionary new type of rapid maneuvering ground warfare called Blitzkrieg. The vital strategic component of air warfare was neglected, as Blitzkrieg doctrine required the extensive use of Luftwaffe resources in a tactical role, which would profoundly influence the outcome of the Battle of Britain and the war on the strategic bombing of Soviet Russia.

In the early 1930s, Walther Wever was an aggressive advocate of strategic bombing, desiring to build the Luftwaffe's strategic air arm. In the interwar years Wever quickly rose in the Luftwaffe's ranks, and in early 1932 was appointed Germany's Air Command Officer, putting him in command of Germany's new Luftwaffe air arm. In this position Wever recognized that the next air war would be a strategic as well as a tactical one, necessitating the development of a viable four-engine bomber, and he urged the German air industry into developing one. Wever also understood that the Soviet communists would become fascist Nazi Germany's enemy, and to destroy the Soviet manufacture and supply of aircraft, tanks, artillery, and munitions he would need a bomber able to fly beyond the Ural Mountains to bomb Stalin's relocated war factories. The bomber Wever proposed was to carry a payload of two tons over at least 1,240 miles.

Despite his farsightedness, Wever's views were in the minority in the Luftwaffe, as most senior Luftwaffe leaders did not appreciate the need for a strategic heavy bomber. Nonetheless, during secret talks Wever was able to influence German aircraft companies Junkers and Dornier to begin to develop plans for the design and production of a heavy bomber.

Walther Wever

During 1934, the RLM (*Reichsluftfahrtministerium*, Ministry of Aviation) requested that the Dornier and Junkers Companies tender proposals for a bomber capable of carrying a bomb load in excess of 4,000 lbs. over a distance of 1,550 miles.

On 3 January 1935, given a heads up by Wever, Junkers Chairman Dr. Heinrich Koppenberg informed Col. Wilhelm Wimmer, chief of the Luftwaffe Technical Department (T-amp) and a zealous Wever supporter, that Junkers had completed its preliminary design for the new bomber. The Dornier Company then completed its preliminary studies, and in late 1935, each company received an order for three prototypes under the respective designations Dornier Do 19 and Ju 89. Despite the Junkers head start, the Dornier entry (Do-19) flew first on 28 October 1936, with the Ju 89 following six months later.

On 3 June 1936, while in Dresden meeting with Luftwaffe cadets, Wever was informed of the death of a WWI German hero, and while taking off for the funeral in his He 70 one wing clipped the ground, causing a fiery crash and killing Wever and his flight engineer. With Wever's death the fate of the Ural Bomber, the Do 19, and the Ju 89 was ultimately sealed, as was his vision of a Luftwaffe with a strategic air component.

DO 19

The first Dornier Do 19 prototype (VI) was a nine-place (pilot, co-pilot, bombardier, navigator, radio operator, and five gunners) cantilever mid-wing (114.8 ft. span/1,744 sq. ft. area) monoplane with a length of 83.5 ft. It was equipped with four underpowered 650 hp BMW/BRAMO 322H nine-cylinder radials that gave the bomber a slow maximum speed of 196 mph, a mediocre range of about 1,000 miles (insufficient for a round trip to bomb Ural factories), a ceiling of 18,370 ft., and the ability to carry a bomb load of much less than the required 4,000 lbs. When the bomber first flew from Lowental on 28 October 1936, it was more advanced than its RAF contemporaries (i.e., the Armstrong Whitworth *Whitley*), as the RAF was just then in the process of formulating its first specifications for a modern long-

Dornier Do 19

range bomber. After Wever's death the Do 19's numerous test flights showed disappointing performance statistics, and the RLM finally decided to scrap the only Do 19 prototype and cancel the other two prototypes on order.

JU 89/JU 90

Development and production contracts for the Ju 89 were awarded to Junkers on 24 January 1935, but due to seriously underpowered engines the first Ju 89 V1 did not take off on its maiden flight until 7 December 1936, followed a few weeks later in early 1937 by the second Ju 89 prototype, the V2. The Ju 89 was a five-seat, cantilever, mid-wing (115.7 ft. span/1,979 sq. ft. area) monoplane with a length of 87 ft. It was powered by four 750 hp Daimler-Benz DB 600A engines which gave the aircraft a very good maximum speed of 241 mph, a very good range of 1,862 miles, and a ceiling of 22,920 ft., but its ability to carry a bomb load of 3,520 lbs. did not meet specification.

Meanwhile, the assembly of Ju 89 V3 was progressing, and it was to be the first armed prototype, with nose and tail armament installed. When it was almost completed the RLM ordered work stopped and further construction was to be redirected toward completing it as a heavy transport with lower-powered engines; designated the Ju 90 VI, it took off for the first time on 28 August 1937 and demonstrated satisfactory performance.

On 29 April 1937, the RLM, without issuing any reasons, ordered an immediate termination to all construction and development work on the Ju 89 and Do 19. Because the Ju 89 was considered the better performing of the two Ural Bomber prototypes its VI and V2 prototypes then continued testing as part of the Ju 90 transport program, and were then reported (unconfirmed) to have briefly served with a transport unit during the invasion of Norway and then scrapped. Ironically, the Ju 90 later served as a patrol aircraft, as it was one of the few long-range types available. The Ju 90 design resulted in the small production series of the Junkers Ju 290 four-engine maritime patrol and long-range reconnaissance aircraft.

Junkers Ju 89

Junkers Ju 90

THE URAL BOMBER CONCEPT DIES WITH WEVER

After Wever's death, his replacements would be a succession of former Army ground officers who tried to administer a new and unfamiliar type of weapon, and would also have to contend with the persistent meddling of the incompetent Hermann Goering. Wever's replacement as chief of staff was Albert Kesselring, a former army artillery officer and an advocate of the prevailing credo that the air arm's mission was to support ground forces. Kesselring was much more concerned about building a larger number of smaller, twin-engine tactical aircraft and fighters and canceled the strategic bomber program entirely on 29 April 1937. Shortly after Wever's death Goering personally removed Wilhelm Wimmer, an advocate of Wever's strategic bomber program, as chief of the Luftwaffe Technical Department (T-amp) and selected an "air force man" in Ernst Udet, Germany's second-highest scoring ace after von Richtofen with sixty-two victories. Udet's agenda endorsed Kesselring's tactical air force decision.

Udet had become enamored with the dive bomber during a visit to America, when he toured the Curtiss-Wright aircraft factory in Buffalo, New York, on 27 September 1933. While there he was invited by Glenn L. Curtiss to fly one of his new US Navy carrier-based F2C Hawk biplane dive bombers. During his flight Udet realized this aircraft was the solution to bombing moving shipping. The enthusiastic Udet immediately contacted Berlin for authorization to purchase two Hawks which would become the basis for future German dive-bombers and ultimately become the Luftwaffe's Achilles heel. As director of the technical department, Udet required that all bombers be able to carry out their role in a dive, later including the much proclaimed and anticipated four-engine He 177 long-range heavy bomber, which was seriously delayed in production when Udet informed He 177 manufacturer Dr. Ernst Heinkel that his bomber "had no future unless it could operate as a dive-bomber." So the focus of the Luftwaffe was first on the dive bomber and then on the design and production of "practical" medium bombers (He 111, Ju 88, and Do 215) and fighter aircraft.

Albert Kesselring

Hans Jeschonnek

Ernst Udet

Kesselring continued as Luftwaffe chief of staff for just over a year, then would go on to distinguish himself as the Army commander of the defense of Italy; he was replaced by Gen. Hans-Jurgen Stumpff, another former infantry officer. On 1 February 1939, Stumpff was replaced by a former cavalry officer, ardent Nazi, and dive bomber devotee, Gen. Hans Jeschonnek, who had transferred to the Luftwaffe as a staff officer in 1933. Jeschonnek would linger as the chief of staff of a declining Luftwaffe until August 1943, when he committed suicide after Hitler blamed him, rather than Goering, for the Luftwaffe's continuing failure. Jeschonnek was the wrong man for several reasons, one of which was his belief in the infallibility of Adolf Hitler, but even worse was his adherence to the obsessive belief in dive bombers held by subordinate Lt.Gen. Ernst Udet.

Meanwhile, Luftwaffe Ural Bomber development resources were redirected to the development of Udet's favored dive bombers. Like many Nazi leaders, Hermann Goering was a numbers man who could have two and a half He 111s—the backbone of the Luftwaffe bomber force—built for the same cost and resources as one heavy bomber. This was the same numbers mentality displayed by the US Army Air Corps when it decided to build three Douglas B-18s—the bomber version of the DC-3—for the cost of one much superior B-17, whose prototype had crashed in testing. Consequently, at the time of Pearl Harbor there were more B-18s in AAC inventory than any other US bomber.

Without Wever, the Luftwaffe would remain a tactical air force, while the RAF and USAAF would flourish as a balanced force, both tactical and strategic, its fighters and fighter bombers destroying Germany in the air and on the ground, while its heavy bombers would devastate the German populace, cities, and war industry. The Luftwaffe would have one last chance for a long-range heavy bomber in the Heinkel He 177.

ON TRACK TO THE AMERIKA BOMBER

No matter the tack the Luftwaffe followed after Wever's death, Hitler would determine the ultimate fate of Germany and the Luftwaffe. Der Fuhrer had always been entranced by large, heavy, long-range bombers capable of bombing far-flung enemy targets and then returning safely. Reichmarshall and Luftwaffe Commander Hermann Goering, always eager to showcase German aircraft, urged a record-setting flight between Berlin and America with his new airliner/future bomber. Hitler heartily endorsed the project as the possible first step in seeing New York City in flames. The same day as Wever's death, the RLM issued the Bomber A heavy bomber specification of 3 June 1936 and a design competition that would culminate in the Heinkel 177, the Luftwaffe's only wartime heavy bomber in production and frontline service.

Hermann Goering

4
LATE 1930S LUFTWAFFE LONG-RANGE BOMBER CONCEPTS

FW 200 KONDOR 1938 NON-STOP FLIGHT FROM BERLIN TO NEW YORK

Focke Wulf FW 200 Kondor

At a time when airlines flew seaplanes to travel across long over-water routes, Kurt Tank, technical director of Focke-Wulf Flugzeugbau of Bremen, sent a proposal to Dr. Rudolf Stuessel of the Deutsche Lufthansa Airline to develop a land plane to carry passengers across the Atlantic Ocean to the US. Tank's FW 200, ostensibly an airliner, was designed to cruise economically over long distances at an altitude of over 10,000 ft., which was as high as possible without using a pressurized cabin (existing airliners/seaplanes were designed to cruise at altitudes below 5,000 ft.). For a short time the FW 200 was the most modern airliner in the world, until the appearance of the Boeing 307 in 1940 and the Douglas DC-4 in 1942. The twenty-six-passenger *Kondor* was designed as a civilian airliner—for commercial and propaganda purposes—to be the first airliner capable of non-stop trans-Atlantic flight. Although originally intended as a civilian airliner, the FW 200 principally saw military service as a long-range maritime bomber and reconnaissance aircraft during WWII. The aircraft had a wing span of 107.75 ft. with a wing area of 1,290 sq. ft., a length of 76.9 ft., an empty weight of 37,490 lbs., and a maximum take-off weight of 50,057 lbs. Its four 1,200 hp BMW/Bramo 323R-2 nine-cylinder, single-row, air-cooled, radial engines gave it a range of 2,212 miles and an endurance of 14 hours.

In an attempt to set distance and endurance records the first prototype, the FW 200 V1, was enhanced with additional fuel tanks and redesignated the FW 200 S-1 *Brandenburg*. On 10/11 August 1938, only two weeks after its first flight on 27 July 1937, it became the first heavier-than-air craft (i.e., non-Zeppelin) to fly non-stop between Berlin and New York City, making the flight of 4,075 miles against strong headwinds from Berlin-Staaken to New York's Floyd Bennett Field in 24:56 hours at an average speed of 164 mph. The return trip on 13 August 1938, taking advantage of prevailing tail winds, was flown in 19:47 hours at an average speed of 205 mph. On 28 November 1938, the *Brandenburg* flew from Berlin to Tokyo via Basra, Karachi, and Hanoi in only 46:18 hours, but on the return flight it ran out of fuel and was forced to ditch in the ocean near Manila. German Foreign Minister Joachim von Ribbentrop used a specially equipped FW 200 *Grenzmark* on his two flights to Moscow in 1939, as he negotiated and signed the infamous Non-Aggression Treaty between Germany and the Soviet Union.

BLOHM & VOSS LONG-RANGE FLYING BOATS

Blohm & Voss built a number of very large, ponderous flying boats that were too large and too slow to be bombers, but their spacious hulls provided ample room for all the equipment needed for long-range naval reconnaissance, including search radar and power-operated gun turrets, or for use as transports for carrying troops and large quantities of supplies. Their importance was marked by their use of six engines that were vital in achieving long range in large bombers.

Blohm & Voss BV 222

The double-decked Blohm & Voss BV 222 was the largest flying boat to see combat in WWII with a ten man crew, a wing span of 150.8 ft., a wing area of 2,745 sq. ft., a length of 121.4 ft., a height of 35.75 ft., and a take-off weight of 101,064 lbs. The first six were initially powered by six 1,000 hp BMW/Bramo 323R radial engines, and the remaining twenty-three had Junkers Jumo 207-C diesels installed. BV Chief Designer Richard Vogt designed the aircraft for Lufthansa trans-Atlantic routes, as it had a projected range of between 3,726 and 5,589 miles depending on the load. The BV 222 V1 was first flown on 7 September 1940, and served as a Luftwaffe transport.

Blohm & Voss BV 222

Blohm & Voss BV 238

Blohm & Voss also built the largest German flying boat of the war as a development and replacement for the BV 222. It had a wing span of 188.9 ft. and 3,896 sq. ft. of area, a length of 150.9 ft., a towering height of 50.8 ft., an empty weight of 120,470 lbs., and a loaded weight of 207,936 lbs. The BV 238 V1 was powered by six 1,750 hp Daimler-Benz DB 603V inline engines which carried it over a range of 2,320–4,099 miles depending on the load. It was heavily armed with twelve machines guns. The prototype of the BV 238 V1 flying boat was first flown on 10 March 1944 as a long-range patrol and reconnaissance aircraft, but saw limited use on seas and large lakes. The design succumbed to the German emergency fighter production program and the lone example floated well-camouflaged on Lake Schaal; after only four test flights it was destroyed by strafing American fighters.

Blohm & Voss BV 238

Blohm & Voss BV 250

Simultaneously with the BV 238 V1 flying boat design, a land-based transport version was under development by Richard Vogt, initially designated the BV 238 Land and then the BV 250. The six-engine (1,950 hp Daimler Benz DB 603Es) aircraft had the general layout of the BV 238 and was projected to have a wing span of 189.5 ft. with a wing area of 3,735.2 sq. ft., a length of 151 ft., a height of 22.1 ft., and a take-off weight of 238,100 lbs. To become a land-based aircraft, the BV 238 Land had the entire bottom portion of its fuselage replaced and modified to accommodate wheel wells housing twelve wheel bogies (three rows of four wheels) in tandem under the central section, additionally supported by the nose wheel and two stabilizing wheels retracting into the wings. The main aircraft consisted of a rectangular wing center section and tapered outer sections.

The BV 250 transport was to be capable of carrying a load of nearly 100,000 lbs. over a distance of about 1,400 miles. The bomber variant, carrying a huge bomb load of 45,000 lbs. and armed with MG 151 cannon and MG 131 machine guns in six turrets on the sides, top, and at the rear of the fuselage, could fly 4,200 miles, and with a 8,400 lb. bomb load the range was projected to be as far as 6,250 miles. The lighter weight reconnaissance variant could extend its range to almost 9,400 miles. The BV 250 remained a paper design, as had other large redundant German aircraft, due to the war situation. The project was revived and briefly examined at the time of the Amerika Bomber Projekt, but its performance failed to match that of other bomber contestants.

HEINKEL HE 177 GREIF (GRIFFIN)

The 3 June 1936 RLM Bomber A Specification called for a bomber able to carry 4,400 lbs. of bombs over 1,000 miles or, alternatively, 2,200 lbs. over 1,800 miles with a maximum speed of about 335 mph at altitude, essentially making it an advanced Ural Bomber. Paradoxically, the proposal was issued the same day that Gen. Walther Wever, the Luftwaffe's main advocate for a strategic bomber force, was killed in a flying accident. This formidable specification (for the time) basically called for a bomber able to outrun fighters and substantially outperform any bomber then in service. Blohm & Voss, Heinkel, Henschel, Junkers, and Messerschmitt showed interest in the project. At Heinkel, Chief Engineer Heinrich Hertel assigned Siegfried Gunther as project engineer on Project P 1041 to build a mockup with unique features that would meet the challenging specifications, including the ability to dive as dictated by Udet!

On 5 November 1937, the mockup was assigned RLM airframe number 8-177 and was contracted by the RLM for manufacture as the Heinkel 177 on 12 November 1938, for an initial eight prototypes. As part of the contract the big bomber was now to have sufficient structural strengthening of the wings and installation of large dive brakes, enabling it to carry out sixty-degree diving attacks and fulfilling Udet's wish for a "Big Stuka!"

As there were no engines of sufficient power available at the time of its development, Heinkel persuaded Daimler-Benz to develop a compound power plant consisting of two DB 9-601 engines coupled side-by-side in each nacelle to drive a single propeller to minimize drag. Designated DB 209-606, this 2,700 hp power plant would attain series production. This new "double" power plant was exhaustively tested in the Heinkel He 119 experimental single-engine monoplane and showed excellent results. On 22 November 1937, the fourth prototype, He 119 V4, flew a world class record flight in which it recorded an airspeed of 314 mph carrying a payload of 2,200 lbs. (1,000 kg) over a distance of 620 miles (1,000 km). Only eight prototypes were completed, and the promising He 119 did not see production primarily because of the shortage of Daimler-Benz DB-601engines.

This engine configuration was the direct result of the RLM's insistence that the He 177 should be capable of dive bombing, as the use of only two propellers (vs. four) on a heavy bomber offered a substantial reduction in drag and a noticeable improvement in maneuverability. The initial He 177 prototypes and pre-production models had airspeed and maneuverability comparable to many heavy fighters of the time. The DB 606 engine had a very close fitting, low drag, surface evaporation system installation in the He 177 nacelles that caused significant overheating, resulting in in-flight engine fires and even upper wing distortion that caused unairworthiness, resulting in a temporary pause in flight testing. The installation of conventional larger but higher drag radiators had little effect, except to increase weight and decrease speed and range. Another catch-22 fix was to maintain range specifications by adding more fuel, further increasing the bomber's weight.

The first V1 prototype was flown in November 1939 at Rostock by Carl Francke. The bomber, while large by Luftwaffe standards, was not very large, having a wing span of only 105 ft., a wing area of only 1,076.4 sq. ft., a length of 72.2 ft., an empty weight of 37,000 lbs., and a loaded weight of approximately 70,000 lbs. While its maximum speed was high at 350 mph at altitude, its combat radius was a disappointing 950 miles.

All of the first six prototypes were destroyed during testing, either due to engine fires or accidents associated with the aircraft's weight. The required dive bombing capability necessitated a substantial strengthening of the airframe and wings, which with the installation of dive brakes caused an important increase in overall weight. The He 177 that went into production had a take-off weight of about 70,000 lbs., as opposed to the loaded weight of about 62,000 lbs. per the original specification. Other serious problems occurred, particularly the weakness of the wings under heavier loads and weight associated braking problems.

Heinkel attempted to prevent the frequent engine fires by moving the engines forward, relocating the oil and fuel lines to safer positions, and installing contra-rotating propellers. Heinkel's alternative proposed remedy was to use four separate engines, but it was rejected by the RLM. The problems of the coupled engine arrangement and its related overheating would remain a chronic and major cause of unreliability and accidents plaguing the He 177 design throughout its life. These problems, plus the large number of modifications required, at times led to a complete cessation of production. In late 1943, the RLM ordered the entire production program to be terminated and the scrapping of all existing airframes. Heinkel and some front line units were slow to comply and the Ministry for Armaments and War Production then issued a similar order on 8 July 1944. Despite these commands to halt production and scrap all completed aircraft, Heinkel continued secret developmental work on the He 177, culminating in the He 177B—the four separate DB 603 engine version—with three prototypes contributing to the company's eventual four-engine development programs: the Heinkel He 274 high-altitude design and the paper-only BMW 801 radial powered Heinkel He 277 Amerika Bomber.

Heinkel He 177 Greif (Griffin)

5
THE AMERIKA BOMBER PROJEKT

BACKGROUND

Hitler's vision was to build a bomber that could fly from Berlin, bomb targets in the United States, and return to Europe without stops for refueling. Meanwhile, American air planners considered the same mission in reverse, but from a different developmental perspective. While the Luftwaffe plan was to develop a single aircraft with extraordinary range to fly this mission non-stop, the USAAF concentrated on a two-step developmental and design approach, with the first step resulting in the long-range B-29 and the second step finalized in the first true intercontinental B-36.

The specifications for a very long-range bomber with extraordinary performance (for the time) were first prepared in 1937 and expanded the following year. The bomber, known to German insiders as the Amerika Bomber or the "New York Bomber," was to be multifunctional, being able to deliver a five ton bomb load to New York City and a smaller bomb load to targets in the Central US, and also fly reconnaissance patrols as far as the American West Coast. The Amerika Bomber concept then languished as the Luftwaffe concentrated on the Stuka Ju 87 dive bomber and "more practical" medium bombers, such as the He 111 and Ju 88 designs.

Hitler's fascination with the Amerika Bomber never died, and on 27 April 1942, the RLM completed specifications for a long-range strategic bomber for the Luftwaffe that would be capable of flying 3,600 miles to bomb the United States from Germany. On 12 May 1942, the Amerika Bomber Plan was submitted to Hermann Goering. The plan specifically mentioned using the Portuguese Azores as a transit airfield to reach the United States. At the time enigmatic Portuguese Prime Minister Antonio Salazar had allowed German U-boats to refuel there, but from 1943 onward he leased bases in the Azores to the British, allowing the Allies to provide aerial coverage in the middle of the Atlantic.

The plan cited the following bombers having the capability to reach American targets (with tons of bombs carried):

Willy Messerschmitt (L), Erhard Milch (C), and Albert Speer (R)

Tri-motor men: Hugo Junkers (L) and Henry Ford

Heinkel He 277 (5 tons), Junkers Ju 390 (5 tons), and the Messerschmitt Me 264 (6.5 tons). The plan was then submitted to Field Marshall Erhard Milch for evaluation. Milch had commanded Luftflotte 5 in Norway and was promoted to field marshal after the French surrender, appointed as air inspector general overseeing aircraft production. After cursory consultations and deliberations it was almost a forgone conclusion that the Me 264 design of Hitler favorite Dr. Willy Messerschmitt was the most plausible design of becoming the Amerika Bomber. For personal reasons Milch did not embrace the Me 264 selection and considered the Junkers or Dornier designs more worthy.

As was common in Nazi Germany, politics and personalities often hindered aircraft technological developments. Milch directed Nazi aircraft production as his personal fiefdom and did not tolerate any opposition. Dr. Hugo Junkers was a well known, longtime German aircraft designer and manufacturer, but was also a socialist and pacifist. When the Nazis gained control in 1933, Milch secured his position as state secretary of the newly formed RLM, answering directly to Goering, and in this position he quickly settled personal animosities with other aviation industry figures, including Junkers and Willy Messerschmitt. In 1933, Goering and Milch wanted to make the Junkers Company part of Nazi re-armament and demanded ownership of Hugo Junkers' patents and the majority of shares of his remaining companies. When the seventy-two-year-old resisted he was threatened with prison and was forced to comply. A year later he was placed under house arrest, and died the following year, having the satisfaction of never having colluded with the Nazis or Luftwaffe. The Milch and Messerschmitt feud began in 1928, when Milch's close friend, pilot Hans Hackmack, was killed on 26 February 1928—flying the Messerschmitt M20 on its first flight—when the surface stripped from part of the wing. At the time Milch was a director of Lufthansa, for which the M20 was intended. Milch became agitated by Messerschmitt's lack of apparent concern and retaliated by ensuring that Messerschmitt would receive no government contracts; to remain solvent Messerschmitt sold the M37 and M36 transports to Rumania. When Milch discovered this he publicly denounced Messerschmitt as a traitor. Messerschmitt was detained by the Gestapo, and it was only his association with top Nazis Rudolf Hess and Hermann Goering that saved him. Milch eventually canceled all contracts with Messerschmitt and forced BFW into bankruptcy in 1931. However, the German re-armament programs and Messerschmitt's high echelon friendships allowed his career and BFW to revive in 1933. Milch then banned Messerschmitt from submitting a design in the competition for a new fighter aircraft, but Messerschmitt managed to sidestep this ban and successfully submit his design for the illustrious Bf 109, which made him a favorite of Hitler. (Bf 109 and not Me 109 until July 1938, when Bayerische Flugzeugwerke AG became part of Messerschmitt AG and Willy Messerschmitt was appointed chairman and managing director.)

Four of Germany's iconic aircraft manufacturers vied for the Amerika Bomber contract: Messerschmitt (Me 261 and Me 264), Junkers (Ju 390), Heinkel (He 277), and Focke-Wulf (FW 300/Ta 400).

MESSERSCHMITT ME 261

In 1937, Messerschmitt began the P.1064 Projekt, which was a specialized long-range maritime reconnaissance aircraft designed with the sole intended purpose of being a Nazi "prestige" aircraft to showcase the resurgent German aircraft industry by setting new flight records. The aircraft was envisaged to fly the Olympic Torch non-stop from Garmisch-Partenkirchen, Germany (site of the 1936 Winter Olympics), to Tokyo for the 1940 Summer Olympic Games in what would be a record breaking non-stop flight of 5,870 miles. Hitler became interested in the Olympic plan, and the German Air Ministry approved the project and gave it the designation 8-261J. Three prototypes were ordered under designation Me 261 and because of Hitler's interest it was given the unofficial nickname *Adolfine*.

The Me 261 took the basic design of the Me 110 twin-engine heavy fighter as its source, having a long, slim fuselage with two wing-mounted engines. Since the main consideration of the Me 261 design was long range, the aircraft was to have the greatest possible fuel capacity at the expense of a very limited payload. A substantial quantity of fuel was carried by sealing the maximum internal volume of the single-spar wing to act as tanks; its depth at the wing root was only slightly less than the height of the fuselage. The strength of the heavily loaded wing was increased by the use of stressed metal skin and a thick profile section.

The slender fuselage was nearly rectangular in section with space for five (seven in the V3) crew members, consisting of two pilots seated side-by-side with the radio operator directly behind in the front compartment, while a navigator and a flight engineer were contained in the rear fuselage under a stepped, glazed station. The slender fuselage was planned to have space for crew bunks.

The Me 261 was to be powered by two 2,700 hp Daimler-Benz DB 606A/B, 24-cylinder engines spinning two variable pitch 15.2 ft. in diameter four-blade propellers. The DB 606 "power system" engine was two Daimler-Benz DB 601 engines coupled in pairs. Each DB 606 derived its high power by the side-by-side coupling of two DB 601 12-cylinder, liquid-cooled engines with drive gears connected to the single propeller shaft. Each DB 606 engine was mounted in a flattened nacelle, having two separate oil coolers underneath and two separate radiators mounted outboard beneath the wing trailing edge. The twin DB 606 power systems were originally developed for the single-engine Heinkel He 119 high-speed reconnaissance aircraft and the twin engine Heinkel He 177 strategic heavy bomber. The Me 261's design lodged the DB 606 power systems in nacelles that had significantly more maintenance and cooling space than the overheating vexed Heinkel 177 heavy bomber, and the design did not experience overheating problems.

The Me 261 featured unusually large and wide main gear low-pressure tires—resembling today's Alaskan bush aircraft tires—which prevented the aircraft from becoming bogged down on rough grass landing strips. The main gear's design had main struts that rotated through ninety degrees during their rearward retraction sequence, which had the large main wheels resting atop the retracted struts, resembling those of the Junkers Ju 88 twin-engine bomber. The conventional, fully retractable tail wheel also had larger tires.

The construction of three prototypes began at Messerschmitt's Augsburg facility during Spring 1939, but was of low priority and progressed unhurriedly, as a war was threatening and Japan had canceled the Olympics in July 1938 due to the war in China. The Me 261 was viewed as non-strategic and all work stopped in August 1939. However, the Air Ministry recognized that the aircraft could be a useful instrument for evaluating long-range missions and work was resumed during summer 1940.

Me 261 V1

The first flight of Me 261 V1 on 23 December 1940 was flown by renowned Messerschmitt test pilots Karl Baur and Fritz Wendel. In early 1941, Willy Messerschmitt informed Ernst Udet of the results of the first flight, predicting an overly optimistic range of over 12,000 miles. The decision to use the DB 606 engine was a problem, because only a few were available for development projects, as most were needed for types already in production, such as the Heinkel He 177. Messerschmitt realized that the fuel-carrying nature of the aircraft's wings excluded armament installation, so both prototypes were tested for endurance through to 1943. The Me 261 V1 was seriously damaged during an Allied bombing attack on Lechfeld in 1944 and was eventually scrapped.

Me 261 V2

The first flight of Me 261 V2 occurred spring 1941. Further testing was ordered to test the V2 as a long-range maritime reconnaissance aircraft. The V2 differed from the V1 in having a dorsal fuselage clear-view dome instead of a rear fuselage glazed step. There are some reports that one or both V1 and V2 prototypes were to be used to drop propaganda leaflets on New York City, but V2 was damaged during the same bombing attack as V1 and was also later scrapped.

Me 261 V3

Messerschmitt Me 261 after capture by Allied troops.

V3 differed from its predecessors in being propelled by two more powerful 2,950 hp DB 610 "power system" engines using two DB 605s each, instead of the paired 601s. These engines were housed in a modified nacelle, were easier to maintain, and were not prone to overheating. V3 also had increased room for two additional crew members. The first flight of Me 261 V3 occurred in early 1943, and this aircraft conducted the longest series of flight tests of any of the prototypes. On 16 April 1943, Me 261 V3 was flown by Karl Baur over a distance of 2,800 miles in an elapsed time of ten hours, setting an unofficial endurance record which could not be confirmed due to war conditions. In May 1943, Me 261 V3's hydraulics failed on landing and the port undercarriage leg collapsed. V3 was transported to Oranienburg for repairs and afterward was used on a few long-range missions for the Luftwaffe's reconnaissance division. Its ultimate fate is unknown.

The only data specification available on the Me 261 concerns the V3 prototype: wingspan was 88.2 ft. with a wing area of 817.8 sq. ft., a length of 54.8 ft., and a height of 15.5 ft. The two DB 610A coupled 24-cylinder, inverted-V engines produced 2,900 hp, giving V3 a speed of 385 mph (at 3,840 ft.) and a service ceiling of 27,100 ft. over a range of 6,800 miles.

MESSERSCHMITT ME 264

Birth of the Me 264

The original concept work for the Me 264 originated in 1937, from Bavarian Aircraft Works' (Bayerische Flugzeugwerke BFW) long-range P.1061 (Project 1061), intending to build a four-engine aircraft capable of operating at a range of 12,428 miles. Work on the project at BFW was sporadic due to increased Luftwaffe demands for its new standard single-seat, single-engine Bf 109 fighter and the Luftwaffe's new multi-purpose, twin-engine Bf 110 fighter.

In August 1940, the *Kriegsmarine* (Navy) informed Goering of the intended occupation of the Central African colonies, which would require a bomber/transport aircraft with a range of 3,728 miles. This request was released at the same time as the Air Ministry's new requirements for a long-range aircraft capable of flying 7,457 miles round trip from bases in occupied France to bomb America. In late December, Messerschmitt assigned three designers to Project 1061 (Wolfgang Degel, Paul Konrad, and Waldemar Voigt) with instructions that the aircraft was to have the originally planned range requirement of 12,428 miles and be able to carry at least 11,000 lbs. of bombs in an internal bomb bay, as well as an additional assortment of small underwing bombs.

The Heinkel He 177 Greif (Griffin) was a leading candidate for the long distance bomber project.

In January 1941, Messerschmitt was awarded a contract to build six prototypes, and if all performance claims were met, an additional twenty-four were to be ordered for "harassing missions against the United States." Project 1061 was redesignated Me 264. Meanwhile, Messerschmitt continued to work on a six-engine version of the Me 264 as Project 1075, but a portion of the design effort was allocated to Amsterdam Fokker Works, as the Messerschmitt design offices were functioning at capacity.

On 22 January 1941, the Luftwaffe General Staff requested testing on a selection of proposed long distance aircraft able to operate over the Atlantic Ocean in support of the U-boat campaign against shipping between the United States and Great Britain. In addition to the Me 264, three other candidates were to be compared for this task: the He 177, the six-engine float plane BV 222, and the Focke-Wulf Fw 200. The RLM chose the Me 264 because of its performance and weight data, which were the best of the other candidates, but seemed to be overly optimistic as stated by the company.

Me 264 V1/V2

The 69.75 ft. long, 14 ft. high Me 264 V1 was an all-metal, high-wing, four-engine heavy bomber of conventional construction with a circular cross section throughout. V1's exterior was puttied and completely sanded for the smoothest possible finish. The cabin had an extensively glazed nose and cockpit comprising a stepless cockpit design without a separate windscreen section for the pilots, which was usual for most of the later German bomber designs and very similar in design to that used for the B-29. Just behind the cockpit was a galley, crew rest area, and walkway to the rear of the aircraft above the enclosed bomb bay. The tapered, shoulder-mounted wing had a slightly swept leading edge, a straight trailing edge, a span of 141 ft., and an area of 1,376 sq. ft. All control surfaces were conventional, including split flaps on the inner wing. The wings contained a single main spar and one auxiliary spar, with the wing loads being transferred through the main spar and two auxiliary bulkheads into the fuselage. Me 264 V2 was to have extended wing tips. The entire fuel supply was stored in the large wings. The empennage had twin-tail fins and rudders that were electrically adjustable during flight. A retractable tricycle landing gear with large-diameter wheels on the wing-mounted main gear and a single nose wheel was unusual for such a large aircraft at this time. Because of the aircraft's ever increasing weight, the main landing gear had to be strengthened so frequently that a droppable auxiliary main gear was also considered. The aircraft weighed 46,630 lbs. empty, 100,400 lbs. loaded, and had a maximum take-off weight of 123,000 lbs. It was to have a maximum speed of 350 mph, a cruising speed of 217 mph at a service ceiling of 26,000 ft., and a range of 11,000 miles. The planned armament consisted of guns in remotely operated turrets and in positions on the sides of the fuselage, but generally it carried very little armor protection and few guns to increase fuel capacity and range. The first Me 264 prototype was initially equipped with four Junkers Jumo 211 inverted V12 engines that powered the Ju 88A-4 and used the then-new *Kraftei* "power-egg" installation feature. The power egg was a completely unitized modular Junkers Jumo engine installation, consisting of the engine and all auxiliary equipment, which could be installed as a unit using standardized quick-changing attachment points and connectors. Thus, the complete Ju 88A-4 power egg engine unit could be installed in the Me 264, and to save more time the Ju 88's nacelles and radiators were also utilized. But the Jumos were found wanting and led to their replacement on the Me 264 V1 with four similarly unitized BMW 801G engines.

Messerschmitt Me 264

This first prototype was not fitted with weapons or armor, but of the following two prototypes, the Me 264 V2 had 2,200 lbs. of armor for the engines, crew, and gun positions, although it was decided to complete Me 264 V2 without defensive armament and vital equipment, and Me 264 V3 was to be armed and have the same armor.

Messerschmitt Me 264 cockpit

Continued Trials and Tribulations

To achieve the 11,247 mile range and 11,023 lb. bomb load (16,405 miles without bombs) specification, the Messerschmitt Design Bureau proposed several methods to increase the Me 264's range, including adding two more engines (totaling six) and using rocket pods for overloaded take-off conditions. A more esoteric suggestion was the towing of one Me 264 by another to altitude and then using in-flight refueling by the second Me 264 when the first was low on fuel. In early 1942, due to the deteriorating war situation (the US entry into the war and the defeats at Stalingrad and North Africa), Milch canceled or reduced numerous development projects, including reducing the number of Me 264 prototypes from six to three. On 28 February 1942, Me 264 development was to be temporarily transferred to Dornier, but that company declined, as it was operating at capacity. On 24 April 1942, on Milch's orders, a commission directed by Lt.Col. Petersen, who was present at the Messerschmitt Augsburg Plant to assess the always questionable performance figures of the Me 264, announced that the test data was found to be "about 90%" of what Messerschmitt had been stating, and Petersen estimated the Me 264 could be ready for attacks against America by Fall 1943. Coincidentally or probably not, 24 April was the same day shrewd Willy Messerschmitt was visiting the RLM, expounding his idea of using the Me 264 on the so-called "Atlantic Missions"—the harassing attacks on the American East Coast.

On 7 May 1942, yet another detailed report was submitted stating that the Me 264, with a take-off weight of 99,207 lbs. and powered by four Jumo 211J engines, could achieve a range of 8,078 miles, and equipped with four BMW 801 engines reach a range of 8,700 miles. Then, on 16 May 1942, at a meeting concerning all long-range aircraft, it was decided that any flights over 8,389 miles would require in-flight refueling, although Jeschonnek had previously vetoed this option in February of the same year. The resulting confusion for a time ended all further consideration of harassing attacks against American targets and the proposed reconnaissance missions over the Trans-Siberian railroad and Equatorial Africa.

V1 Prototype Ready for Testing

Meanwhile, amidst the paper confusion on mission refueling and objectives, the construction of the first prototype (V1) was progressing very slowly at Augsburg. Finally, on 23 December 1942, Karl Baur flew Me 264 V1 for twenty-two minutes on its first test flight with its landing gear down due to safety concerns. On landing, the airframe was damaged when the aircraft continued off the end of the runway due to brake failure. To accommodate the large Me 264, later test flights were conducted at Lechfeld's longer concrete runway, but the base only had one hangar large enough to house the Me 264 V1.

Me 264 Fate in Limbo

As flight testing continued during the first half of 1943, there was no decision made on the future of the Me 264. Grand Admiral Karl Doenitz and the Supreme Naval War Staff favored the Focke-Wulf Ta 400, but since this aircraft would not be ready until 1946, it was decided that the Ju 290, He 177, and Ju 390 were to be produced in the interim to provide maritime reconnaissance. In May 1943, Messerschmitt was informed that the Me 264 was to be discontinued, even though just a week earlier the RLM had supported the completion of the Me 264 prototypes. In June 1943, hoping that Hitler would intercede, a desperate Willy Messerschmitt contacted the Fuehrer to personally enlighten him on the good progress of the Me 264's development. At a meeting at Supreme Headquarters on 8 July 1943, Hitler pledged his support for continued Me 264 production, but only for maritime use, and canceled his decision to bomb the American East Coast. Then, only a day later, Milch agreed to continue the construction of the three Me 264 prototypes but for study only.

Goering, Milch, and Messerschmitt met on 14 October 1943, to discuss further development of the Me 264. Messerschmitt stated that the components for the first five prototypes were completed, but due to Me 410 production he lacked necessary space and facilities in which to assemble them. All of the Me 264 jigs in the final assembly building were to be moved from the Augsburg plant and stored at Gersthofen. However, that day Milch stated he wanted to halt Me 264 development completely to concentrate on the Me 262 jet fighter and was supported by Goering. The next day Focke-Wulf Ta 400 production orders were also canceled, largely because Focke-Wulf facilities and resources were needed for Fw 190D-9 and Ta 152 production. While further production was canceled, Me 264 V1 remained a viable venture.

On 11 August 1943, Me 264 V1 had been taken out of service to be re-engined with the BMW 801 twin row radial. V1, with its new engines, returned to Lechfeld in spring 1944, only to be slightly damaged in an air raid, but was quickly repaired to renew testing with its new engines. During the first test roll out with the new engines the brake shoes tore off and soon V1 tests at Lechfeld were discontinued and were transferred to Memmingen, where further testing continued until the end of June 1944.

Me 264 Death Knell

On 29 June 1944, the Trial Establishments Headquarters stated the Me 264, as well as the Ju 390, were now definitely considered unsuitable for operational deployment since the installation of their entire military equipment and payload would excessively increase take-off weight and wing loading to unsafe limits. The final blow to the Me 264 program occurred on 18 July 1944, when the only complete Me 264 prototype was destroyed in an air raid, along with the assembled components of the other two prototypes and eighty percent of the production facilities. Me 264 V2 was reported to be nearly ready for flight testing at the time of its demise. Although numerous attempts were made to save the Me 264 program, on 23 September 1944, G.Adm. Doenitz convinced Hitler to agree to halt all work on the Me 264. Then, on 18 October 1944, Reichsmarschall Technical Order Nr. 2 made the cancellation official, ending the eight-year development program that produced only one test aircraft that never came close to attaining operational status.

Other Drawing Board Versions

There were other Me 264 prototypes and concepts on the drawing board from 1937, but after September 1944, the continuing design work was underway mainly as a means to safeguard Messerschmitt employees from being conscripted into the army. Among the drawing board Me 264s were the following:

The Me 264A, an armed long-distance reconnaissance version using Jumo 222 engines with the GM-1 boost system then under development, would have been equipped with three cameras and could reach distant areas in Russia, Iran, Lagos, and New York, but also targets in America's Midwest. There were also plans to base some Me 264s on Japanese fields on islands in the Philippines to fly reconnaissance missions as distant as Australia and India.

The Me 264B long-range bomber version was projected to be powered by four BMW 801E radial engines and an additional two Jumo 004C jet engines. Its total weight was to be 105–110,000 lbs. with a 7,208 mile range with a 6,614 lb. bomb load without the Jumo jets and 5,282 miles with the jets. The maximum speed with the jets was to be 407 mph at 21,981 ft. A maximum ceiling of 47,572 ft. could be reached with the pressurized cockpit and was beyond the ceiling of most interceptors.

There was also a high-altitude bomber version on the drawing board which would have been equipped with four BMW 801 E/F radial engines with superchargers. The cockpit was planned to be pressurized, with remote controlled defensive armament installed in the non-pressurized portion of the fuselage.

Me 264 Conclusion

The Me 264 and Hitler's fantasy that his favorite aircraft designer, Willy Messerschmitt, would design and build a fleet of ultra-long-range bombers capable of attacking America was ended. It was stymied by chronic infighting among the Luftwaffe, the Luftwaffe with the Nazis, and both with Willy Messerschmitt, as well as a lack of cooperation between the Luftwaffe and the Kriegsmarine. However, the primary cause was Germany's failure to develop and build the required engines and the airframes under an unrelenting Allied bombing campaign that reduced already short material supplies and eventually destroyed the only working model that had been built.

JUNKERS JU 290

While Willy Messerschmitt struggled to have his version of the Amerika Bomber selected, the Junkers Company worked on its version. After Hugo Junkers lost control of his company to the Nazi government in 1933, the company came under total and direct Luftwaffe control, and as such was a preferred Luftwaffe manufacturer.

Junkers' experience in building its Ju 89 version of the Ural Bomber led to the conversion of the partially completed third Ju 89 to become the first Ju 90, a series of very successful forty-seat passenger airliners used by Lufthansa. Improvements and enlargement of the Ju 90 design and engines eventually led to its last two prototypes (V7 and V8), leading directly to the development of the new Ju 290 reconnaissance and transport models. The various models of the Ju 290 served as long-range maritime reconnaissance/bombers, heavy transports, and heavy bombers. Although the Ju 290's wingspan was only 137.75 ft., it was a large aircraft at almost 94 ft. long, was 22.4 ft. high, and had a maximum take-off weight of nearly 100,000 lbs. Its four BMW 801 14-cylinder engines drove it at 273 mph (max.) over 3,843 miles. The bomber versions could carry up to 6,600 lbs. of bombs or up to three HS 293 guided missiles. In March 1943, FM Erhard Milch agreed to have three Ju 290s modified at the Junkers factory for flights connecting Germany with Japan. After the invasion of the Soviet Union in June 1941 the trip was no longer possible by Lufthansa commercial aircraft or too dangerous by vessels or U-boats. The Germany-Japan itinerary selected was a Great Circle Route over north Finland, along the Arctic Ocean, then across eastern Siberia to refuel in Manchuria before completing the flight to Japan. In February 1944, tests began on a Ju 290 loaded with forty-five tons of fuel and cargo, but the plan was put on hold after the Japanese failed to agree on a course that would not provoke the Soviet Union by an overflight and these three aircraft were eventually transferred to KG 200. In December 1944, plans for the Berlin-Tokyo flights were revived, mainly to transport Luftwaffe Gen. Ulrich Kessler to Japan as a replacement for the German air attaché in Tokyo. A Ju 290 A-3 was flown to Travemunde for the necessary modifications, but work was delayed and Kessler was transported aboard U-boat *U-234* instead. This aircraft was destroyed on 3 May 1945. There are sources that claim the trips to Japan took place, taking off from Odessa, southeast Russia, and Mielec, southeast Poland, and landing in Manchuria, but there is no reliable evidence.

Junkers Ju 290

JUNKERS JU 390

Junkers was awarded a contract to build two working models of the Ju 390 using components of the Ju 290 that were available and tested. The basic Ju 290 airframes led directly to the development of the even larger Ju 390 by attaching an extra pair of inner wing segments on the Ju 290 airframe and adding new sections to lengthen the fuselage. As a result, Ju 390 construction moved forward relatively quickly.

The Ju 390 was a very large aircraft with a wingspan of 165 ft. (vs. 137.75 ft. for the Ju 290) and wing area of 2,730 sq. ft. (vs. 1,291), a length of 112.2 ft. (vs. 94), a height of 22.7 ft. (vs. 22.4), and an empty weight of 87,100 lbs., a loaded weight of 117,100 lbs., and a maximum take-off weight of 166,400 lbs. (vs. 99,141). It had a maximum speed of 314 mph, a range of 6,030 miles, and a service ceiling of 19,700 ft.

Compared to the USAAF B-29, the Ju 390's wingspan was 24 ft. longer (165 vs. 141), its length was 13 ft. longer (112 vs. 99), and it weighed 31,000 lbs. more (166,000 vs. 135,000 take-off weight).

It was relatively heavily armed with three to five 20 mm MG 151/20 cannon and four 13 mm MG131 machine guns. There is no known record of internal bomb load capacity and there were no hard points. There are indications the bomber could have carried the Messerschmitt Me 328 parasite fighter for self defense, and some test flights are believed to have been performed by a Ju 390 prototype equipped with the anti-shipping *Fritz X* guided glide bomb.

There were two prototypes ordered and three planned variants:

Ju 390 V1: First prototype.
Ju 390 V2: Second prototype.
Ju 390 A-l: Planned heavy transport version.
Ju 390 B: Planned maritime patrol version.
Ju 390 C: Planned long-range heavy bomber version.

First Prototype Ju 390 V1

The first prototype (Ju 390 V1, the so-called "bomber" version) was modified at Merkersberg using the Ju 90 V6 airframe. The first test flight was on 20 October 1943, by Chief Project Pilot Hans Joachim Pancherz, and the aircraft performed well, resulting in an Air Ministry order for twenty-six more to be built and designated Ju 390 A-l.

On 26 November 1943, Ju 390 V1, along with many other new Luftwaffe aircraft and prototypes, were exhibited for Adolf Hitler in Insterburg, East Prussia. According to former Ju 390 V1 test pilot Hans-Joachim Pancherz' logbook, Ju 390 V1 was flown to Prague immediately after it was displayed in Insterburg, and while there was test flown until March 1944, including tests of in-flight refueling.

During late June 1944, Rechlin was testing the Ju-390 for an intended role as the Ju-390C bomber to carry three Me 328 parasite aircraft or large rocket-powered glide bombs to New York. The Ju 390C's wing was too weak to carry the weight of these weapons. For the transport role the wing was strong enough, as it was very lightly loaded and the weight of fuel was evenly distributed across its span, and on the ground the transport version had four sets of main undercarriage. (Note: The Me 328 was originally conceived in 1941 as a simple, cheap wooden escort fighter powered by pulse jets to either be towed aloft by a He 177 or Ju 388 or carried on a Me-264 or Ju 390 in a piggyback/Mistel-type fashion. Due to the lower air pressure the pulse jets performed poorly at high to medium altitudes where most combat would take place and thus were deemed unsuitable.)

None of the ordered twenty-six Ju 390 A-1s were built by the time that project, along with Ju 290 production, was canceled on 20 June 1944. Testing was continued on V1, which was returned to Dessau during November 1944, where it was stripped of parts. It was finally destroyed, along with the V2 prototype, in late April 1945, either by Allied bombing or by retreating German troops, to keep them from falling into enemy hands as the American Army approached.

Ju 390 V2

The second prototype (V2) was an unarmed transport version with a longer fuselage than the V1, because it was constructed from a Ju 290 A-1 airframe, rather than a Ju 90 like the V1. The fuselage forward of the wing appears to have been shortened.

Different sources present various accounts of the history of Ju 390 V2. Griehl and Dressel state in their definitive book *Heinkel He 177, 277, and 274*, that Ju 390 V2 was assembled in Bernburg and first flown in October 1943 (or that the V2 was first flown from Bernburg in August 1943 by Capt. Hans Werner), and that it was configured for a maritime reconnaissance role. Its fuselage had been extended by 8.2 ft., and it was to be equipped with FuG 200 Hohentwiel ASV (Air to Surface Vessel) radar and defensive armament consisting of five 20 mm MG 151/20 cannon, or per William Green four 20 mm MG 15 l/20s and three 13 mm (.51 caliber) MG 131 machine guns.

Kossler and Ott state in their book on the Ju 89, 90, 290, and 390 that Ju 390 V2 was completed during June 1944, with flight tests beginning at the end of September 1944. After the war, Ju 390 Project Pilot Hans Pancherz claimed only one Ju 390 was ever flown. At an inquiry before British authorities on 26 September 1945, Professor Heinrich Hertel, Junkers' chief designer and technical director, also affirmed that Ju-390 V2 had never been completed. Test Pilot Oberleutnant Eisermann recorded in his logbook that he flew the V2 prototype on 9 February 1945 at Rechlin for one handling flight. A second twenty-minute flight was used to ferry Ju-390 V2 to Rechlin. But this aircraft may have been V1.

Ju 390 V3

Another controversial aircraft, the V3 was apparently converted from Ju 90 V10 to become a flying tanker for air-to-air refueling trials at Prague with Ju 390 V1 in early 1944. Construction of V3 appears to have halted in May 1944, when all Luftwaffe aircraft construction was converted to fighter production.

The Ju 390's Controversial Intercontinental Flights

France to New York Flight

Over the years numerous aviation magazines and books have perpetuated the story of the Ju 390's alleged flight from France to within a dozen miles of New York City in 1944. The first public reference to the flight appeared in a letter published in the November 1955 issue of *British RAF Flying Review* magazine, of which respected aviation writer William Green was an editor. Dr. Robert Werrell, in an excellent article, "World War II German Distance Flights: Record or Fraud?" appearing in the Summer 1988 issue of *Aerospace Historian*, writes a comprehensive analysis of the flight and concludes: "The modest and numerous questions attending the New York flight strongly suggest that they did not take place." Werrell does acknowledge that the Ju 290 flights to Manchuria were "possible....German aircraft could have been adequately modified, and if flown by skilled and well-trained crews, could have flown these distances. Clearly, the Germans had both the required skills and technology."

Flight to South Africa

A Ju 390 is claimed to have made a test flight from Germany to Cape Town in early 1944. The sole source for the story is a speculative article that appeared in the *Daily Telegraph* in 1969 titled "Lone Bomber Raid on New York Planned by Hitler." This flight has even less credence than the France to New York flight.

Ju 390 Export to Japan

The Imperial Japanese Army Air Force showed considerable interest in this ultra-long-range aircraft as part of their Project Z development of the long-range Nakajima G10N Fugaku version of the Amerika Bomber. In autumn 1944, the Japanese government acquired a manufacturing license agreement for the Ju 390A-1 that included detailed manufacturing drawings scheduled to be delivered to Japanese Army representative Maj.Gen. Otani by 18 February 1945. There is no record of this part of the agreement having been fulfilled.

Junkers Ju 390

JUNKERS JU 488

In September 1943, the RLM granted a contract to Junkers for a four-engine high-altitude reconnaissance bomber. Except for part of the wing section, which had to carry four instead of two engines, Junkers utilized their proven Ju 188 airframe; by using components from their Ju 88s, 188s, 288s, and 388s, the company was able to quickly produce the 488. Due to the lack of capacity at the Junkers Dessau Works, two of the six scheduled prototypes were to be constructed by the French Latecoere aircraft manufacturing company near Toulouse.

The aircraft had a wingspan of 102.7 ft. with a wing area of 947 sq. ft., a length of 76.2 ft., and a take-off weight of 79,350 lbs. Four 2,500 hp BMW (powering the first two prototypes) and then four Jumo 9 engines were to drive the Ju 488 to 430 mph, and to 37,000 ft. over a range of about 2,800 miles. With the first two prototypes unarmed, the other four were to carry 11,000 lbs. of bombs and be armed by a dorsal and tail turret carrying a single FDL 151 machine gun.

The Ju 488 project was virtually terminated by an attack on the factory by the French Resistance on 7 July 1944 that destroyed the nearly completed first prototype. The 488 Project ended several weeks later when German forces retreated from the area and left the second and third prototypes, which were under their initial stages of construction, to be captured by the Allies.

Junkers Ju 488

HEINKEL HE 277

The Heinkel He 277 was a four-engine, long-range heavy bomber derivative of the He 177 that became Heinkel's contender in the Amerika Bomber competition. Like the Me 274 entrant, the He- 277 also has a murky history, but even more so.

As early as November 1938, Ernst Heinkel made his first of three separate efforts to develop "true four-engine versions" of the He 177A-series:

1) The He 177B, which culminated in four prototypes being built, with three having flown before the war's end;
2) The He 274, of which only two prototypes were in the manufacture stage before the end of war and were completed and flown in France after the war. Partly to allow Heinkel to devote company engineering and production staff resources on other projects like the He 277 and the Heinkel He 343 jet medium bomber, work on the He 274 had already been outsourced to the French Farman firm by the end of 1941;
3) And the manufacture of the He 277's two V-series prototypes.

The seven-man He 277 had a wingspan of 131.25 ft., a wing area of 1,431.6 ft., a length of 75.4 ft., a height of 19.8 ft., an empty weight of 48,060 lbs., and a maximum take-off weight of 98,105 lbs. The main crew compartment consisted of a heavily glazed greenhouse framed clear-view, unstepped cockpit, which was a common feature among late-war German bomber airframes and new designs. The cockpit's fully glazed front section was said to somewhat resemble an "aerodynamically refined, rounded-off, well-framed version of the Bristol Blenheim's fully-glazed unstepped nose shape." A pressurized cockpit was considered. Immediately aft of the heavily glazed nose, the cockpit glazing over the crew and pilot compartment enclosing the upper section was merged with the nose glazing's contours. This configuration "somewhat resembled that of the RAF Lancaster heavy bomber," protruding above the 277's forward dorsal fuselage decking level, with a rearward extension atop the fuselage that faired in the forward upper dorsal turret's forward surface, extending rearward to just forward of the inner engine cowls. The fuselage was large and almost slab-sided in cross section, with its general side view profile very suggestive of Heinkel's smaller He 219 night fighter; this similarity with the 219 extended to the He 277's fuselage mounted defensive armament positions, with one forward and two aft facing steps along the slightly rounded dorsal and ventral surfaces of the fuselage similar to the smaller night fighter's earliest prototypes for the 277's manned aft dorsal and remote aft ventral turret defensive guns. The first prototype was to have the He 177's conventional vertical stabilizer, but wind tunnel testing soon discovered that the four new "regular" DB 603E engines created new turbulence on the tail, reducing the stability of the bomber. Several tail configurations were wind tunnel tested before the twin fin rudder layout was chosen. The He 277's twin tail empennage was also similar to the He 219, and added aerodynamic stability compared to the 177A's single vertical tail, making mounting a powered traversable tail turret easier.

Rather than the two fire-prone twin Daimler-Benz DB 606s, the first He 277 prototype was to be powered by new "regular"

DB 603E engines, and the second prototype by four 1,973 hp (take-off) BMW 801E 14-cylinder, twin-row, radial engines each mounted in an individual nacelle and each turning a three-blade, 13.2 ft. diameter propeller. The He 277B-6 production series was projected to be equipped with 2,060 hp Jumo 213 F engines, while the He 277B-7 was to have 24-cylinder Jumo 222As. The engines were supplied by a maximum of 4,478 gallons of fuel for an Amerika Bomber mission. The maximum speed was 354 mph at 18,700 ft., the cruising speed was 286 mph, the service ceiling was 30,000 ft., and the range was 3,728 miles up to 6,900 miles for the Amerika Bomber.

The undercarriage was to be either a fully retracting conventional tail dragger type or tricycle nose wheel landing gear. Both main gear assemblies had twin main wheels on each unit, retracting forward into the inner engine nacelles for the nose wheel version and rearward for the tail wheel gear assembly.

The armament included eight remotely operated 20 mm MG 151/20 auto-cannon and four 13 mm MG 131 machine guns in a quad-mount manned tail turret. The bomb load was as much as 6,612 lbs. for the Amerika Bomber trans-Atlantic missions and a maximum of 12,345 lbs. internally for shorter ranges, with a 2,670 mile combat radius.

End of the He 277 project

In an October 1943 report to the RLM, Ernst Heinkel compared his He 277 four-engine design to the Messerschmitt Me 264, Ju 390, Ta 400, and the six-engine BV 222:

> In our opinion, the Me 264 is a record-breaking aircraft, but does not come up to service requirements for operations in large numbers. The BV 222 and Ju 290 are far too big and are not bombers, in addition to which the Ju 290 has to be altered to Ju 390 [six engines]. This would make the construction effort bigger still. Thus, only the Ta 400 and the He 277 remain as useful operational aircraft.

That same month the Ta 400 project was canceled and six months later, on 18 April 1944—simultaneously with the four He 177B prototypes (the completed He 177 V101 to V103 or nearly completed V104)—the RLM ordered Heinkel to terminate any further work on the He 277 project, and all components were also ordered scrapped. No He 277s were ever completed. On 3 July 1944, the *Jagernprogramm* (Fighter Program) assumed all German military aircraft production and the RLM only allowed Heinkel's He 162 *Volksjager* lightweight jet fighter to be manufactured by the Heinkel Company.

Despite many repeated accounts that two He 277 prototypes were completed and flown, Heinkel historians Manfred Griehl and Joachim Dressel state in their book *Heinkel He 177, 277, and 274* that the two prototypes were never completed when the RLM suspended work on the He 277 and He 274 on 20 April 1944. It appears the RLM-approved development of the original He 177 aircraft line was not in any way directly related to the entirely separate He 277 advanced bomber design project, which by the summer of 1943 was considered to be Heinkel's Amerika Bomber aviation contract contender. The first He 277 prototype was underway, with the second prototype scheduled to be the "pattern" aircraft for the future production B-series beginning with the He 277B-5. The two He 277s in the program were in rudimentary bits and pieces condition before being canceled.

Heinkel He 277

HEINKEL 274: HE 277 EPILOGUE

The Heinkel He 274 was a four-engine, high-altitude variant of the Heinkel He 177. The He 274 was first intended to be in the He 177's eventual line of development as the He 177H ("H" probably an abbreviation for "Hohe," meaning high-altitude in German). The developing incompatibility of parts led to its redesignation to He 274. The usual Luftwaffe numbering system of a major new version would add 100 to the original model number, but the He 277 was already another different version of the He 177, which was itself being developed as early as September 1943 into the He 177B four-engine bomber, whose four prototypes were converted from He 177A airframes with different wings. The main differences between the He 274 and He 177 were the discarding of the twin coupled engines for four independent turbocharged units, an extended fuselage with a modified wingspan, a twin-tail empennage, and a more conventional twin-wheel main gear, abandoning the awkward four-strut main gear scheme of the He 177A. It was originally designated He 177H on 11 October 1941, as the He 274 high-altitude development of the He 177 A-3. The coupled engines were abandoned for four independent DB 603A-2 *Kraftei* power egg unitized engine installations (engines cooled by annular radiators) to provide room for the installation of DVL exhaust driven TK 11B turbo-superchargers. To accommodate its four-man crew at high altitudes at a maintained equivalent 8,200 ft., the He 274 had a heavy gauge alloy double-walled pressurized compartment with hollow sandwich-type windows and inflatable rubber seals. The only defensive armament was a single forward firing 13 mm (.51 in) MG 131 machine gun and remotely controlled dorsal and ventral gun turrets, each containing a pair of 13 mm MG 131s remotely controlled from a slightly offset Plexiglas dome in the roof of the flight deck or the rear of the ventral Bola gondola.

During 1941, Heinkel was engaged by other vital projects that left the company critically deficient of detail design and manufacturing capability, so the He 274 Project was reallocated to SAUF in Suresnes, France. (In 1941, the Farman brothers reestablished their company as the *Societe Anonyme des Usines Farman* [SAUF], and only three years later it was absorbed by Sud-Ouest.) Construction of the two prototypes (He 274 V1 and V2) did not start until 1943, and He 274 V1 was not ready for flight testing at Suresnes until July 1944, when the approach of Allied forces imposed the evacuation of Heinkel personnel working on the project. The virtually completed prototype He 274 V1 was to be transferred to Germany, but as Allied troops closed on Suresnes new orders were issued to destroy the aircraft. The scuttling of V1 caused only minor damage to the airframe and repairs were begun after the Allied occupation. He 274 V1 was repaired in December 1945, and renamed AAS 01A by Ateliers Aeronautiques de Suresnes; it was used by the *Armee de l'Air* for several years as a high-altitude research plane. In December 1947, He 274 V2 was also eventually completed as AAS 01B by the French SNCASO aviation conglomerate. Both reconstituted He 274s served as "mother ships" for the aerial launching of several early French advanced jet and rocket test aircraft mounted on top of the fuselage pick-a-back style, including models of the Sud-Ouest SO.4000, France's first jet bomber. The two French He 274s were eventually scrapped in late 1953.

Heinkel He 274 as a postwar French test bed renamed the AAS 01A.

FOCKE-WULF TA 400

Focke-Wulf Aircraft Construction was founded in 1924 by Professor Heinrich Focke, Georg Wulf, and Dr. Werner Neumann in Bremen, Germany, and was somewhat successful, producing a series of light passenger aircraft used by several European airlines. In 1931, Kurt Tank became head of the company's design department, and as such changed the fortunes of the company while becoming one of the world's leading aircraft designers and engineers, with the superlative FW 190 fighter being his signature aircraft design.

In 1942, the RLM issued its Amerika Bomber specification, and at the time Focke-Wulf had Tank's successful FW 200 Kondor long-range reconnaissance aircraft in service and was working on the FW 300 very long-range pressurized bomber as its replacement. The FW 300 design was begun in 1941, and was to have a cantilevered low-wing design with a rounded forward fuselage and nose. It was to be powered either by four 1,800 hp Daimler-Benz DB 603 12-cylinder engines or by four unproven experimental 2,500 hp Jumo 222 24-cylinder, multi-bank, inline engines. It was to be armed with twelve 20 mm MF151/20 cannon in six remotely controlled turrets and was to carry guided missiles on anti-shipping missions of up to 5,500 miles. The FW 300 was a paper project only and no prototype was built, as the RLM and Focke-Wulf moved on to other projects.

In response to the RLM guidelines of 22 January 1942, the Focke-Wulf Ta 400 was to be a six-engine, long-range bomber and reconnaissance aircraft designed by Kurt Tank as Focke-Wulf's contender for the Amerika Bomber Projekt. Since Focke-Wulf was encumbered with contracts for Tank's exceptional FW 190 fighter, the Ta 400 development program was transferred to the former French SNCASO works in Chatillon sur Bagneux, a suburb near Paris. Subcontracts for the design and construction of major components were awarded to German, French, and Italian firms in an effort to begin constructing the first prototypes as quickly as possible.

Because no prototype of the Ta 400 was ever built and the design never advanced beyond the wind tunnel stage, performance ranges and dimensions are based on Focke-Wulf estimates. It was to have a shoulder-mounted wing with a 4° dihedral, with a long straight center section extending to the middle engine on each wing, and highly tapered outer wing panels. It would have had a span of about 150 ft. with an area of 1,832 sq. ft. The Ta 400 was to have twin vertical stabilizers mounted at the tips of the tail plane. Its overall length was to be about 94 ft., height 21 ft., and its gross weight was to be about 132,277 lbs. (60,000 kg). It was expected to achieve a maximum speed of 332 mph (395 mph with the projected Jumo auxiliary jet engines). Tank's original Ta 400 design was to use six 1,750 hp BMW 801D 14-cylinder, two-row radial engines. The power of a later variant was to be boosted by 8.9kN Jumo

004B jet engines installed into the nacelles of the former two outboard BMW engines. The aircraft carried 7,133 gallons of fuel contained in thirty-two fuel tanks: twelve in each wing and eight in the fuselage. The Ta 400 with six DB 603 engines was estimated to have a range of 7,500 miles in its reconnaissance role while cruising at 202 mph. The two bomber versions would have estimated ranges of 2,800 miles and 6,600 miles, respectively, depending on bomb and fuel loading. The projected Jumo jet-powered aircraft would have had a maximum range of 8,700 miles for long-range reconnaissance and 8,100 miles as a bomber.

The crew of eight or nine men were to be housed in a pressurized cockpit in the front, followed aft by a long bomb bay, pressurized armament operator's compartment, fuel tanks, and equipment bays. Two versions of the pressurized forward fuselage were designed: one was to have a common cockpit with glazed nose, while the other included a standard cockpit with separate canopies for the pilots and the bombardier. The tricycle undercarriage, with a single nose wheel and four main wheels, was to retract into the fuselage and engine nacelles.

Defensive armament was to be in remotely controlled turrets on the spine of the fuselage, underneath the body, and in the tail. It consisted of twin 30 mm MK 103 cannon in the FDL103Z turret, three twin 20 mm MG 151 cannon in two HD 151Z turrets, and one FDL 151Z turret, as well as twin 13 mm MG 131 machine guns in the HL 131V position.

The Ta 400 bomber version was to carry an impressive bomb load, but not to New York. The typical internal bomb load was to be four SC 2500 (2,500 kg) bombs weighing 5,500 lbs. each or four SC 1800 (1,800 kg) weighing 3,968 lbs. each, or four SC 1000 (1,000 kg) weighing 2,200 lbs. each for a bomb load that ranged from a maximum load of 22,000 lbs. Two Fritz X guided bombs weighing 2,150 lbs. each could also be carried internally. A maximum bomb load of nine SD 1000 bombs weighing 19,841 lbs. and 12 SD 550FE bombs weighing 13,277 lbs. could also be specially accommodated. Typical combat loads to be carried on racks under the engine nacelles were to consist of bombs and missiles in the following configurations: assorted bomb loads ranging from two SC 2500 bombs to two SC 1800 and two SC/SD 1000 bombs; two 4,850 lb. Hs 294 radio-controlled rocket-propelled missiles; two 3,417 lb. Hs 293 radio-controlled rocket-propelled missiles; two 2,150 lb. Fritz X guided bombs; and two 4,850 lb. naval mines.

The Ta 400 was considered to be a backup to Messerschmitt's Me 264 and was assigned a very low priority, so work continued slowly, but without any major interruptions. A number of wind tunnel models were fabricated and tested, and a possible mockup of the forward fuselage and some components may have been completed. As the Ta 400 required more materials and labor than the Me 264, the RLM decided that further development of the Ta 400 was to be discontinued on 15 October

Kurt Tank

Focke Wulf Ta 400 wind tunnel model

1943 and notified Focke-Wulf that the program would be terminated. There is some evidence Kurt Tank continued to work on the project and proposed the cooperation of Italian subcontractors continue their part on the project.

HORTEN HO 18 SERIES

The Horten brothers (Reimar and Walter) were considered design mavericks of the German aviation industry, pursuing tailless, flying wing fighter aircraft designs. The Hortens were not included among the four original designers requested to submit ideas to the Air Ministry for an America Bomber. When they found the America Bomber contenders were experiencing problems achieving the specified range they decided to present an innovative tailless design of their own.

Ho 18A

The Horten design—completed in ten days in complete secrecy—was the Ho 18A (Ho XVIIIA), and had many similarities to their earlier Ho 229 design, which was based on the brothers' favored flying wing design that decreased drag by deleting all unnecessary control surfaces. The Ho 229 was built by Hermann Goering's request for light bomber designs capable of meeting his "3 × 1000" requirement, namely to carry 1,000 kg (6,200 lbs.) of bombs a distance of 1,000 km (625 miles) at a speed of 1,000 km/h (625 mph). Aircraft with jet engines were the only contenders able to provide the required speed, but they also demanded huge amounts of fuel to meet the 1,000 km range specification. The Ho 18A was a bomber with a clean flying wing layout, with the engines—either six Jumo 004H jet engines or HeS 011 Ajets—inside the wing center section with exhaust nozzles on its upper surface. These engines produced a maximum speed of 559 mph and a range of 6,835 miles. The Ho 18 had a wingspan of 131.2 ft. with an area of 1,614.6 sq. ft., a length of 63.3 ft., a height of 19 ft., an empty weight of 24,250 lbs., and a take-off weight of 70,548 lbs. The cockpit was at the front, along with remotely controlled turrets armed with 30 mm MK 213 cannon. The tricycle undercarriage retracted into the fuselage/wing and the main undercarriage had multiple wheels. The Ho 18 bomb bay could accommodate up to 11,000 lbs. of bombs. While the Ho 18 design was innovative, it was considered too expensive to manufacture.

Horten brothers (Reimar and Walter)

Ho 18B-1/B-2

The Hortens then proposed a less complicated design in two versions, designated the Ho 18B (Ho XVIIIB) models. The first version was the Ho 18B-1, combining the wings of the Ho 18A (without the engines) with an unusual eight-wheel undercarriage. The wheels, in sets of four, were in tandem on a special system of struts covered completely with huge spats enclosed at the bottom after take-off. Four (instead of the six in the Ho-18A) HeS 011A jet engines were mounted at the joint of the spat with the wing. These jet engines gave the B-1 a projected maximum speed of 535 mph over a range of 4,089 miles. The B-1 was to have a wing span of 98.4 ft., a wing area of 1679.2 ft., a height of 19 ft., an empty weight of 40,000 lbs., and a take-off weight of 73,000 lbs. It had a three-man crew housed under a bubble canopy. This version was unarmed, as armament was considered unnecessary due to its high speed and high maximum ceiling beyond effective enemy interceptor capabilities.

Their second version (Ho 18B-2, Ho XVIIIB-2) was completely unlike B-1, having a traditional tricycle undercarriage retracting into the wings. The B-2 was larger than the B-1, with a wingspan that was 41 ft. longer than the B-1 (139.4 ft. vs. 98.4 ft.), and was heavier, with its take-off weight being 93,153 lbs. vs. 73,000 lbs. The aircraft was to be a compromise between the pure flying wing layout and the aircraft with advantages of a tail. The huge tail was rather unusual, as it merged into the fuselage, which in side view had a triangular shape. The front of this triangle housed the cockpit, while the rear section was the rudder. Remote controlled gun positions with MG 151 cannon were at the front or the rear of the aircraft. Four Jumo 004H jet engines were in pairs housed in two cowlings under the wing center section and propelled the B-2 at a projected 566 mph over a range of 5,592–to 7,456 miles. An option of six BMW 003 turbojets were slung under the wing (designed by Junkers and Messerschmitt). There was also a variant that was projected to be powered with piston engines in the rear part

Horton Ho 18 Flying Wing

of the wing center section driving two sets of contra-rotating eight-bladed propellers.

On 23 March 1945, the Hortens were granted a contract for their Ho 18B-1 prototype equipped with conventional landing gear, with construction to begin on 1 April 1945 in the underground Kahla factory in Thuringen. The war ended in a month and the Horten flying design ended with it, until their flying wing designs were resurrected forty-five years later with America's B-1 Stealth bomber.

AMERIKA BOMBER CONCLUSIONS

For all the reasons discussed, including personality differences, jealousies, and political maneuvering, and the limitations of time and materials, Germany never built the Amerika Bomber Hitler fantasized about during the early years of the war. The project was only seriously initiated at a time when Allied air attacks were beginning to have an adverse effect on German industrial production and morale. The Amerika Bomber was calculated as a means of retaliation on American industry and populace, but the crescendo of Allied bombing increased, causing the Nazis to change their priorities to building V-Weapons to punish the British and fighters to defend against bombers which ultimately destroyed or stopped Amerika Bomber production and destroyed its prototypes and Hitler's dream.

ALLIED

QUEST FOR SIZE AND DISTANCE

An Overview 1914 Onward

PART 1: FRENCH LONG-RANGE AIRCRAFT

1
FARMAN GOLIATH

The Goliath was initially designed by the Farman Aviation Works in 1918 as a fixed undercarriage biplane heavy bomber of fabric-covered wood construction. The bomber had a wingspan of nearly 87 ft. with a wing area of 1,730 sq. ft., a length of 47 ft., and a loaded weight of 10,510 lbs., and could carry 2,200 lbs. of bombs. It was powered by two relatively powerful 424 hp Salmson Z.9 water-cooled radial engines that provided a maximum speed of 87 mph, a cruising speed of 75 mph, a service ceiling of 13,100 ft., and a range of 250 miles. It was undergoing initial testing when WWI ended and the three Farman brothers (Richard, Henri, and Maurice) realized there would be no orders for their design, so they modified the Goliath's big, box-like fuselage into an airliner configuration. With the new passenger cabin arrangement the Goliath could carry up to twelve or fourteen passengers, and began regular Paris-London flights on 8 February 1919.

Lucien Boussoutrot

At midnight on 10 August 1919, a Farman Goliath piloted by Lucien Boussoutrot carrying six crewmen and a passenger took off from Toussus-le-Noble (Paris) and arrived at Casablanca at 1725 hours and 1,273 miles later, setting the record for a non-stop passenger flight. At 1100 on 14 August, the Goliath then took off for a flight across the Sahara to Dakar. On the way it landed overnight in Mogador and took off the next morning, but was last seen at Port Etienne, about 470 miles from Dakar. Search parties were deployed and their disappearance was news throughout Europe. On the sixteenth, the right propeller fell off the Goliath and shortly thereafter the left engine overheated and Boussoutrot was forced to land on a beach, where the Goliath slid into the ocean and was broken up by waves. The crew was able to salvage some equipment and provisions and build a shelter in the dunes. With no civilization in sight and being cut off from land by a series of lagoons, Boussoutrot decided to head south the next morning. After traveling about thirteen miles they became exhausted and thirsty and headed back to their aircraft landing site to await rescue. On the twenty-first two natives appeared and the next day the Emir of Trarza arrived with Arab scouts, and the French crew and passengers were led to safety.

Farman Goliath used by Lucien Boussoutrot on the first Paris to London flight.

The Farman would set several other records:

On 3–4 June 1920, a Goliath flown by Lucien Boussoutrot and J. Bernard flew 1,196.9 miles for a closed circuit record.
On 16–17 July 1924, Etiene Coupet and Maurice Drouhin flew their Farman F.60 for 37:59:10 hours on a closed course over Chartes, France, to set a new world's endurance record. Their record also surpassed the re-fueled record.
On 7–9 August 1925, a Goliath F.62 flown by Maurice Drouhin and Jules Landry covered 2,750 miles in 45:11:59 hours, flying from Floyd Bennett Field, New York, to Rayak, Syria, to set a new world's endurance record.

Maurice Drouhin

2
BREGUET BR.19 GR

The Breguet 19 (also known as Breguet XIX, Br.19, or Bre.19) was a light bomber and reconnaissance biplane manufactured for the French Armee de l'Air with several civilian variants, many used for long distance flights. The aircraft was designed by Breguet Chief Engineer Marcel Vuillerme to be a replacement for the successful Breguet 14 WWI light bomber. The prototype was ready in November 1921 and equipped with a troublesome experimental Bugatti power plant comprised of two eight-cylinder Bugatti engines coupled to drive a single four-bladed propeller. In March 1922, a new design appeared with a more conventional layout powered by a single, less complicated 450 hp Renault 12Kb inline engine. After successful evaluation trials aircraft with the new engine were ordered by the Armee de l'Air in September 1923.

The Br.19 biplane had a conventional layout with an ellipsoid cross section fuselage. The two-spar, Duraluminium-framed wings were of sesquiplane design (biplane having one long wing and one short one above or below it). The tail, featuring horn-balanced elevators, was also framed with Duraluminium. The landing gear of the production aircraft was a simple cross-axle type, having a single tapered strut on each side with cable cross-bracing, and had a rear skid rather than a tail wheel. It seated a crew of two in an open, tandem cockpit with dual controls. It had a wingspan of 48.7 ft. and a wing area of 538 sq. ft., a length of 31.5 ft., a height of 12.2 ft., and its range depended on the engine used: Lorraine 497 miles or Renault 746 miles.

The Br.19 was employed by the air forces of many nations, including Spain, Belgium, Poland, Romania, Greece, Yugoslavia, Turkey, Persia, and South American countries Venezuela, Uruguay, Bolivia, Brazil, and Argentina. The French began operating their Br.19 A2s in Fall 1924, the B2 in June 1926, and the C2 and CN2 later. In the later 1920s and early 1930s, the

Breguet Br.19 GR

Br.19 was the most numerous French combat aircraft. The Br. 19 is most well known for the long distance records set by standard and modified aircraft during the mid-1920s. The first record was set by the prototype, which won the military aircraft speed contest in Madrid on 17 February 1923; on 12 March 1923, it set an international altitude record of 19,660 ft. while carrying a load of 1,100 lbs.

THE BR.19 GR LONG-DISTANCE VARIANT

The Br.19 GR was a long distance sport variant built in France in 1925 and equipped with a large 526 gallon fuel tank. During 1926, the Br.19 GR underwent modification to the Bidons variant of the GR, especially developed for long-range flights. The Br.19 GR (Grand Raid) was a specially modified variant used for long distance flights after early long-range attempts were made using the "regular" Br.19 A2 (no. 23) equipped with additional fuel tanks for long distance flights. Many world records were set by the Br.19 and its variants, mostly long-distance, non-stop flights:

On 24 April 1924, Georges Pelletier d'Oisy—a five-victory fighter ace in WWI—and Lucien Besin flew from Paris in an attempt to fly around the world aided by additional fuel tanks mounted at the Br.19's bomb mounts. Their attempt ended when they crashed on a golf course near Shanghai after flying 10,580 miles in 26 days. Afterward, d'Oisy was in Hong Kong and borrowed a Breguet 14 leased by Col. Tsuo Kse-Tiang, Republic of China Air Force commander and WWI pilot who fought with the French, and departed for Tokyo, arriving on 17 July 1924. The entire trip from Paris to Tokyo had taken 120 hours in the air over 84 days.

Georges Pelletier d'Oisy (R cockpit) and Lucien Besin (upper cockpit)

On 12 February 1925, Belgian Edmond Thieffry, a WWI ten-victory ace and a founder of Sabena Airlines (1923), took off with co-pilot Leopold Roger and mechanic Joseph de Bruycker from Brussels to scout an air route to Leopoldville, Belgian Congo. The seven-day flight plan called for seven stops, but strong winds, bad weather, and a broken propeller that took weeks to replace ended the troubled 5,500 mile flight 51 days later on 3 April. On 11 April 1929, during his second test flight in the Congo flying an Avimeta C.92, the thirty-six-year-old Thieffry and co-pilot Gaston Julian were killed in a crash near Lake Tanganyika.

Edmond Thieffry (R) and Jef De Bruycker in Paris upon their return from the Congo.

H. Abe and K. Kawachi (1/2R)

Ludovic Arrachart and Henry Lemaitre flew 1,967 miles from Paris to Villa Cisneros (Dakhla, Morocco, today) in 24.5 hours on 2–3 February, 1925.

In 1925, the Osaka and Tokyo *Asahi Shimbun* newpaper sponsored two Japanese Army flight officers, Abe Hiroshi and Kawachi Kazuhiko, to fly two company Breguet Bre. 19 A.2 aircraft (with extra-capacity fuel tanks)—the *Hatsukaze* (First wind) and *Kochikaze* (East wind), respectively—to Rome. On 25 July, the two pilots left Tokyo and landed in Moscow (6,025 miles) in mid-August after crossing Siberia. They proceeded to Paris on 27 September, then London (8,575 miles) on 12 October, and Rome on 27 October.

On 14–15 July 1926, Andre Girier and Francois Dordilly flew 4,928 miles from Paris to Omsk, southwest Siberia (1,390 miles east of Moscow).

During August–September 1926, the Pole Boleslaw Orlinski flew the Warsaw-Tokyo route of 6,400 miles and back in a modified Br.19 A2.

From 31 August–1 September 1926, Leon Challe and Rene Weiser flew 3,274 miles non-stop from Paris-Le Bourget to Bandar Abbas, on the south coast of Iran on the Persian Gulf.

On 26 September 1926, Dieudonne Costes (a six-victory WWI fighter ace, airline pilot, and test pilot for Breguet since 1925), with Rene de Vitrolles, attempted to set the world non-stop distance record, but were well short, flying 2,546 miles from Paris to Assuan, on the south Nile River, Egypt. On 28 October, Costes, with Jean Rignot, broke the world distance record, flying 3,351 miles non-stop from Paris to Jask, Persia, as part of a 12,187 mile Paris-India-Paris flight.

BR.19 GR "3,000 LITER"

In 1926, three further aircraft (no.1685–1687) were modified to Br.19 GR "3,000 Liter" specifications. They had larger fuel tanks installed in the fuselage with a total capacity of about 790 gallons; the cockpit was moved slightly aft; and the wingspan was increased three feet to 48.7 ft., with the wingtips being rounded. The three aircraft were each equipped with different engines: the first one (no.1685) had a 500 hp Hispano-Suiza 12Hb, the second had a 550 hp Renault 12K, and the third had a 520 hp Farman 12Wers engine. In 1927, no.1685 received a new 600 hp Hispano 12Lb engine, its fuel capacity was increased to 920 US gallons, and its wingspan was further increased by 3.3 ft. It was named *Nungesser et Coli* for the two airmen who disappeared on a trans-Atlantic flight attempt in May 1927, two weeks before Lindbergh succeeded. Between 10 October 1927 and 14 April 1928, pilot Capt. Dieudonne Costes and navigator Joseph le Brix, both WWI veterans, flew this aircraft to complete a 35,418 mile round-the-world flight (they crossed the Pacific between San Francisco and Tokyo on board ship) and made the first non-stop aerial crossing of the South Atlantic Ocean on 14–15 October 1927, flying between Saint Louis, Senegal, and Natal, Brazil. While in South America they visited every country on that continent.

Dieudonne Costes (R) with Jean Rignot in their Breguet Br.19 GR

BR.19 TR BIDON

The Br.19 TR Bidon was built in 1927, incorporating various aerodynamic related refinements for long distance flight. The fuselage tanks held 987 gallons of fuel, augmented by an additional 103 gallon tank in the wing, giving the aircraft a total fuel capacity of 1,090 gallons. Five were built by Breguet and two by the Spanish company CASA. Three of the French aircraft were powered by 600 hp Hispano-Suiza 12Lb engines, one by a 550 hp Renault 12K, and the other by a 450 hp Lorraine 12Eb. The first Hispano Bidon was sold to Belgium; the Renault Bidon was sold to China after a Paris-Beijing flight. The third Hispano Bidon would become the French Br.19 TF Super Bidon. During 15–17 December 1928, Dieudonne Costes, with Paul Codos, set a world distance record in a closed circuit of 4,986 miles flying the Bidon.

BR.19 TF SUPER BIDON

In 1929, the last and most advanced Br. 19, the French Super Bidon long distance variant, was completed especially for trans-Atlantic flight. It was the third Br.19 TR Hispano and had a modified fuselage, a wingspan of 60 ft., and a fuel capacity of 1,420 gallons. It was powered by a 600 hp Hispano-Suiza 12Lb engine, later replaced by a 650 hp Hispano-Suiza 12Lb. This Super Bidon was named *Point d'Interrogation* (Question Mark) and was mostly flown by Dieudonne Costes and Maurice Bellonte while setting several records.

Dieudonne Costes (L) and navigator Joseph le Brix in their Br.19 GR 3,000 Liter

On 13 July 1929, Costes and Maurice Bellonte attempted to complete the first westbound crossing of the Atlantic Ocean, but returned after seventeen hours due to bad weather.

On 27–29 September 1929, Costes and Bellonte set the world distance record, flying 4,909 miles from Paris to Qiqihar, in northeast China, near Manchuria.

On 1–2 September 1930, Costes with Bellonte flew the Super Bidon from Paris Le Bourget Airport to New York as the first heavier-than-air, fixed wing aircraft to cross the North Atlantic in the more difficult westbound direction. They flew 3,633 miles (or 3,850 miles?) in 37:18 hours.

Dieudonne Costes (R) with Maurice Bellonte in their Br.19 GR Super Bidon

The *Cuatro Vientos*, the second specially built Super Bidon, was purchased by the Spanish government for long distance flights. Mariano Barberan, Joaquin Collar Serra, and Sgt. Modesto Madariaga flew from Seville, Spain, to Camaguay, Cuba, on 10–11 June 1933, on a 4,575 mile flight that took 39:55 hours. On 20 June 1933, the aircraft departed for Mexico City without Madariaga and disappeared near Villahermosa, Mexico, without a trace.

3
BLERIOT 110

In 1929, the Breguet 19 TR *Point d'Interrogation* regained the world straight-line and closed circuit distance records for France. French Air Minister Albert Claquot therefore announced a prize of one million Francs for the prototype of an aircraft that could fly for 10,000 km (6,215 mi) against a 35 km/h (22 mph) headwind. Both non-stop flights in this open cockpit aircraft covered about 5,000 miles, and it was obvious longer flights would require better crew protection. Three manufacturers responded, resulting in the Bleriot 110, Dewoitine 33 *Trait d'Union*, and the Bernard 80 GR *L'Oiseau Tango*.

The Bleriot 110 was built specifically at the request of the French government with the intention of setting new world aerial distance records in 1930. It was a large high-wing cantilever monoplane with a wingspan of 86.9 ft. and a wing area of 872 sq. ft., a length of 47.75 ft., a height of 16.1 ft., an empty weight of 5,808 lbs., and a gross weight of 19,783 lbs. It was powered by a 600 hp Hispano-Suiza 12L engine that gave it a maximum speed of 137 mph and a range of 7,838 miles with additional fuel tanks. For its long distance record attempts the Bleriot was equipped with six fuel tanks in the wings and four in the fuselage, containing a total of 1,585 gallons of fuel. Because the pilot and co-pilot's seats were behind the huge fuselage fuel cells, a unique mirror system was devised for take-offs and landings. Also a sleeping couch was provided behind the co-pilot's station to allow one of the two crew to sleep on long distance flights.

After the loss of the purpose-built long distance D.33s, the French government placed a ban on straight-line flight record flights, so further record attempts had to be made from Algeria as closed-circuit bids. The aircraft's first flight on 16 May 1930 was terminated early by a fuel supply problem, and after repairs it was flown to Oran, Algeria, to attempt to set the closed-circuit distance record.

Between 15 November and 26 March 1932, Bleriot 110 pilots Lucien Boussoutrot and Maurice Rossi tried eight times to set world records for distance on the closed circuit over Algeria and broke this record three times. In 1932, Boussoutrot and

Lucien Boussoutrot and Maurice Rossi with their Bleriot 110

Paul Codos (R) and Maurice Rossi by their Bleriot 110

Rossi surpassed the previous record for a continuous flight set by Italian airmen Maddalena and Cecconi on 2–4 June 1930, when they flew for 67:13 hours over 5,118 miles. They flew a Bleriot named *Joseph Le Brix* in honor of the record-setting aviator who died in 1931 flying the 110's challenger, the Dewoitine D.33, which set a distance record on its first flight. The Bleriot carried approximately 1,400 gallons of fuel but took off easily from Senia, near Oran, at 0719 on 16 February, and flew in good weather for the first sixty hours of the planned eighty-five-hour flight. The night of the third day bad weather and violent squalls violently pommelled the *Joseph Le Brix*, increasing fuel consumption considerably and causing the pilots to reduce their speed. After battling the storm for hours they finally decided to land after setting the third record for a closed circuit, staying airborne for 76:34 hours over a distance of 6,587 miles.

It was the straight-line record the Frenchmen coveted, and finally, in 1933, the French government relented on its ban on straight-line record flight attempts and also offered one million Francs to the new record setter. Codos and Rossi packed up their Bleriot 110 and traveled to New York by ship. The pair took off from Floyd Bennett Field, New York, to Syria on 5 August 1933, flying in shifts for more than three and a half days with 1,770 gallons of fuel aboard—enough for over seventy-five hours of flight. They flew north to Nova Scotia, across the Atlantic, and after a day and a half in mostly overcast weather, they made landfall in Cherbourg, France, and made a low pass over Le Bourget to celebrate. After 33:40 hours they overflew Munich and turned south over the Aegean over Rhodes in good weather and finally, over French Syria, they landed in Rayak, Syria, after flying 5,657 miles in just over 55 hours.

During 27–28 May 1934, Paul Codos and Maurice Rossi completed the second non-stop aircraft crossing from continental Europe, landing at Floyd Bennett Field. The flight, which began in Paris, was an attempt to exceed their 1933 New York to Syria non-stop distance record of 5,657 miles with a scheduled destination of Los Angeles. The aging Le Brix was straining under 12,540 lbs. of fuel and Codos and Rossi had to land in New York after 38:27 hours.

Further record flights were attempted over the next two years, but when all proved unsuccessful the Bleriot 110 was subsequently scrapped. Thus ended the French claim to long distance flight recognition, and the country would continue in its role as a secondary player in the aviation community and virtually a bombardment aircraft non-player during the short 10 May–22 June 1940 war against the Nazi blitzkrieg.

4
BERNARD 80/81 GR

The Bernard 80 GR *L'Oiseau Tango*, powered by a 650 hp water-cooled Hispano-Suiza, was built in response to a French government appeal for an aircraft capable of setting new long distance records. The GR designation used by both Bernard designs and by other long-range French aircraft stood for *Grand Raid*, or extreme long distance flight, while the *Tango* referred to the orange color of the aircraft. The French government had imposed restrictions on straight-line long distance flights from France due to the recent Dewoitine 33 fatal crash and the Bernard 80 had to attempt to set the closed circuit record, which at the time of the 80 GR's first flight was held by Italians Madallena and Cecconi, who had flown 5,089 miles in a Savoia-Marchetti S.64. In February 1931, the two-man, single-engine 80 GR *Tango* monoplane was flown to Oran, Algeria, which was then part of metropolitan France. In a first attempt at the record Antoine Paillard and Louis Mailloux flew 5,076 miles over a 9.3 mile circuit for more than 50 hours, but fell short of the record due to propeller problems. While waiting for propeller changes a new record of 5,483 miles was set on 1 March 1931 by Maurice Rossi and Lucien Boussoutrot in the Bleriot 110. The Bernard 80GR *Tango* took off again, piloted by Jean Marmoz and Antoine Paillard, from the La Senia (Oran) aerodrome, French North Africa, at 1835 on 30 March, and flew over a closed course, encircling Oran for 59:16 hours at an average speed of 95 mph and landing in Oran at 0544 on 2 April, covering 5,682.7 miles. They landed with fuel remaining, but encountered coolant loss; during the last part of the flight legend has it that they pumped Champagne, eau de Vittel, and coffee into the radiator. The record was short-lived, for on 10 June 1931, Doret and Le Brix flew the Dewoitine 33 over 6,446 miles.

After the successful record flight of March 1931, the GR 80 returned to the factory at Bourget to be modified for further record attempts as the GR 81. The GR 81 was re-engined with a Hispano-Suiza 12 Nbr driving a three-bladed (later four-bladed) propeller and re-named *L'Oiseau Canari II*. After completing the transformation in August, planning began for an attempt at the straight-line record with a flight from Oran to South America, which would also win a one million franc prize. The French government continued its ban on straight-line flights and the GR 81 attempted to regain the closed-circuit record. On 29 December 1931, the GR 81, carrying 2,245 gallons of fuel and piloted by Jean Marmoz and Louis Mailloux, attempted to take off. On take-off the large propeller hit the ground, the undercarriage collapsed, and the 81 GR skidded on its belly, fortunately without its huge fuel load catching fire and with Mermoz and Mailloux unharmed. After repairs the 81 GR made a second attempt to regain the record, but during take-off from Istres on 18 October 1932, Marmoz encountered aileron control problems, dumped fuel, and returned to land safely.

Almost a year later, the ban on long-range flights was lifted and *L'Oiseau Canari II* was ready to make another attempt at the straight-line record. By this time the record was held by Rossi and Codos in the Bleriot 110 at 5,658 miles. *L'Oiseau Canari II* left Oran on 4 October 1933, flown by Jean Assolant and Rene Lefevre, intending to land in Saigon. After twenty-four hours they realized the engine's fuel consumption would put the record just out of reach and landed in Karachi after having flown 4,100 miles in 27 hours. The GR 81 was subsequently re-engined and was designated the 84 GR, but never flew again, putting an end to the Bernard's long distance aspirations.

Louis Mailloux (L) and Jean Mermoz with the Bernard 81

5
DEWOITINE D33 AND D332

During Summer 1931, chief pilot Marcel Doret, co-pilot Joseph Le Brix, and engineer/mechanic Rene Mesmin formed the crew of the first prototype Dewoitine D33 *Trait d'union* (Hyphen) in an attempt to break the straight-line distance record, flying from Paris Le Bourget to Tokyo. The D33's flight was funded by multi-millionaire French perfumer and businessman Francois Coty.

The D33 was a single-engine, all-metal cantilever monoplane with a fixed main undercarriage, with its wheels covered by conspicuous spats and the typical Dewoitine strutted tailplane. The pilot and co-pilot sat side-by-side, with the engineer directly behind them. The D33 was powered by a single Hispano-Suiza radial (a license-built version of the Wright Cyclone) turning a huge three-bladed Ratier prop.

In March, before attempting the Paris-Tokyo flight, the D33 set seven international records for load, distance with loads, and speed with loads. In June, the D33 established the distance closed-circuit record, flying more than 70 hours and 6,444 miles over Provence. On 12 July 1931, the Doret, LeBrix, and Masmin trio attempted to break the straight-line distance record, flying from Paris Le Bourget to Tokyo. While flying over Siberia the engine iced up and Le Brix and Mesmin parachuted safely, while Doret managed to land the *Trait d'union* in the trees unharmed, but the aircraft was destroyed.

The French Aeronautics Technical Branch had built a second D33 which Coty purchased. The *Trait d'union II* made its maiden flight over Toulouse on 10 August 1931, and on 11 September, it was ready to leave Le Bourget for another attempt to set the straight-line record while flying to Tokyo. That same day Paul Codos and Henri Robida took off on board their Breguet Super Bidon *Le Point d'interrogation* (Question Mark) to set the record by flying from Paris to Hanoi. While near Düsseldorf, their Breguet encountered mechanical problems, and Codos set it down safely in a field. The *Trait d'union II* continued, but after about 1,900 miles, near the Russian and Siberian border, they ran into a pre-dawn storm and fog, then the engine failed. Doret parachuted to safety, but for unknown reasons Le Brix and Mesmin remained in the doomed aircraft, which crashed near Ufa, killing both.

In 1933, about three years after the fatal crash of the D33, its basic design was developed into the D332 *Emeraude* (Emerald), an all-metal cantilever low-wing eight-passenger monoplane with an aerodynamic design and a rigid undercarriage. The aircraft was powered by three Hispano-Suiza 9V radials (a license-built version of the Wright Cyclone) that powered it to a best speed of over 155 mph. The aircraft first flew on 11 July 1933, and proved successful during initial tests flown by test pilot Marcel Doret, who survived the D33 crash. During demonstration flights around European capitals *Emeraude* gained a world class record on 7 September 1933, when it flew a 620 mile course with a useful 4,410 lb. load.

The D.332 was designed to meet an Air France requirement for use on the route to French Indochina, and on 21 December 1933, the *Emeraude* left Le Bourget for Saigon on a proving flight. The aircraft flew uneventfully and arrived in Saigon on 28 December. On the return flight and only 250 miles from Paris, the *Emeraude* flew into a hill near Corbigny in an intense snowstorm and was destroyed, killing all ten crew and passengers. Despite the accident, Air France decided to order three of an improved version designated the D333.

A postcard of Marcel Doret (L), co-pilot Joseph Le Brix (C), and engineer/mechanic Rene Mesmin (R) with the D33 overhead.

6
THE GREAT TRANS-ATLANTIC MYSTERY OF THE *L'OISEAU BLANC*

The *L'Oiseau Blanc* (White Bird) was a French Levasseur PL.8 biplane flown by French WWI aviation heroes Charles Nungesser and Francois Coli that disappeared in 1927, during an attempt to make the first non-stop trans-Atlantic flight between Paris and New York to compete for the Orteig Prize. The disappearance of *L'Oiseau Blanc* is considered one of the greatest mysteries in the history of aviation.

With the $25,000 Orteig Prize as an incentive, Francois Coli, a WWI veteran who lost an eye as the commander of *Escadrille des Coqs*, had been planning a trans-Atlantic flight since 1923 with his wartime friend, twelve-victory ace Paul Tarascon. In late 1926, Tarascon was badly burned in an accident that destroyed their Potez 25. Charles Nungesser, the third highest scoring French ace with forty-three victories, also had been planning a solo crossing to win the Orteig Prize, but aircraft designer Pierre Levasseur insisted that Coli be considered as the navigator in a new two-seat version of the production Levasseur PL.4 designated the PL.8, a conventional, single-bay, wood- and fabric-covered biplane that carried a crew of two in a side-by-side, open cockpit. The main alterations included increasing the wingspan to 49 ft., reinforcing the plywood fuselage, and removing two of the forward cockpits to widen the main cockpit so Nungesser and Coli could be seated side-by-side. Two additional fuel tanks were mounted aft of the firewall, giving the PL.8 three fuel tanks with a total fuel capacity of 1,056 gallons. To reduce the aircraft's weight, the fixed undercarriage was to be jettisoned on take-off. The watertight underside of the fuselage had a boat-like shape for Nungesser and Coli's planned water landing in New York, in front of the Statue of Liberty. The aircraft was powered by a 460 hp W-12 Lorraine-Dietrich engine. No radio was installed, and celestial navigation—a Coli specialty—was to be relied on. The white-painted *L'Oiseau Blanc* had the French tricolor markings with Nungesser's personal WWI skull and crossbones, candles, and a coffin on a black heart painted on the fuselage.

Nungesser and Coli took off on the planned forty-two-hour flight at 0517 on 8 May 1927 from Le Bourget Field near Paris, heading for New York with their heavily loaded PL.8-01 barely clearing the trees at the end of the field before jettisoning its main undercarriage. The intended route was a Great Circle Route, which was to take them across the English Channel, over the southwestern part of England and Ireland, across the Atlantic to Newfoundland, then south over Nova Scotia, to Boston, and finally to a water landing off New York City. The last verified reports of the *L'Oiseau Blanc* were over Ireland. Tens of thousands gathered at Battery Park to view the landing at the Statue of Liberty, but after forty-two hours and then more time had passed it became apparent the *L'Oiseau Blanc* had been lost. An international search to find Nungesser and Coli was launched that included the French, US, and Royal Canadian Navies, and many aircraft that combed the lost aircraft's proposed route. *Aviation Digest* sponsored renowned pilot Floyd Bennett to search the area between New York and Newfoundland for nine days. Finally, the search was discontinued.

The International Group for Historic Aircraft Recovery (TIGHAR) has called the *L'Oiseau Blanc*, "History's Most Important Missing Airplane." Considering how difficult the 2014 search for the missing Malaysian airliner was, the 1926 search for the *L'Oiseau Blanc* was hopeless. There were storms

Charles Nungesser (R), Francois Coli, and their *L'Oiseau Blanc*

and squalls over the area that day, and initial speculations were that the aircraft was caught in a storm and went down at sea. Unsubstantiated rumors and sightings spread in the northeast and Canadian maritimes that the *L'Oiseau Blanc* had crashed in the inaccessible forests there and, in fact, Nungesser and Coli were the first to cross the Atlantic. Conspiracy theorists believed the flight and its disappearance could have been covered up by US and French authorities so as not to distract from Lindbergh's achievement. In the 1980s, interest in the mysterious disappearance was revived. Clive Cussler, well known author of very popular nautical thrillers and his National Underwater and Marine Agency (NUMA) research organization, made multiple visits in the 1980s, searching for the aircraft in Maine and in Newfoundland and interviewing dozens of elderly witnesses. While not finding any wreckage, NUMA concluded that Nungesser and Coli could have possibly reached North America. Writer Gunnar Hansen did extensive research, as did the self-serving French government, but only added to the mystery with embellishments of the many rumors, memories, and sightings without confirming anything substantial. Today, the *L'Oiseau Blanc* mystery remains unsolved; the landing gear is the only confirmed part remaining and is on display at the French Air and Space Museum at Le Bourget Airport, Paris.

7
MARYSE BASTIE: FRANCE'S AMELIA EARHART

Maryse Bastie married early, had a child, then divorced, but then married WWI pilot Louis Bastie, who became an instructor at an aero-club in Bordeaux. Maryse became captivated by flying and was determined to become a pilot, earning her pilot's license in September 1926. After her husband was killed in an October 1926 aircraft crash she moved to Paris and began doing aerobatics and flying advertising signs to earn money to continue flying; in 1927, she purchased a Caudron C.109. She gained a reputation as a pilot and in 1928, with Maurice Drouhin, set the world record straight-line distance for light two-seat aircraft between Paris and Trepton (Pomerania) with 1,058 km (657 miles); then in 1929, the French record for women's duration of flight at 10:30 hours; and then the international women's duration record at 26:44 hours. That record was soon surpassed by Lena Bernstein, flying for 35:44 hours. Bastie was determined to regain this record, and taking off the evening of 2 February 1930, she landed after flying for 37:55 hours. Finding endurance flying very demanding, she decided to break the record straight distance for light aircraft. On 28 June 1931, she took off from Paris Le Bourget and landed in Yurino (Russia) after 30:30 hours flight and 2,976 km (1,850 miles) to break the international straight distance record for single-seat light aircraft, for which she received the Knight's Cross of the Legion of Honor and the American Harmon Trophy. In 1935, Australian Jean Batten crossed the South Atlantic in 13:30 hours and prompted Bastie to attempt breaking this record . She took off solo from Dakar on 30 December 1936, and landed in Natal, Brazil, after a crossing of 12:05 hours, for which she was promoted to Officer of the Legion of Honor. In 1935, she founded her own flying school at Orly Airport. During 1937, she published an account of her aviation adventure, *Ailes Ouvertes: Carnet d'une Aviatrice*. During the war she was active with the Red Cross and Resistance, and after the liberation of Paris, she enlisted in the women's air force auxiliary as a lieutenant before being demobilized in 1946. In 1947, she was made a Commander of the Legion of Honor for "exceptional war titles and acts of resistance." Bastie served in the postwar French Air Force, rising to the rank of captain while logging more than 3,000 hours flying time. On 6 July 1952, following a conference in Lyon, Bastie was killed when she was aboard a military aircraft that crashed on take-off.

Maryse Bestie

8
CHALLENGE INTERNATIONAL DE TOURISME 1929–1934

The FAI International Tourist Plane Contest, better known as the Challenge International de Tourisme, consisted of four contests held 1929–1934, and were major aviation events in prewar Europe. The contest was conceived by the Aéro-Club de France, inspired by the International Light Aircraft Contest in France in 1928. The concept of a tourist plane contest was approved by the Fédération Aéronautique Internationale (FAI, the World Air Sports Federation), and the first challenge was organized by the French to take place in August 1929.

It consisted of two parts: technical trials of aircraft and a rally over Europe. Since one of the purposes of the challenge was to engender progress in aircraft building, it was not only a pilots' competition, but technical trials also included construction evaluation to build more advanced tourist planes. In 1929, the contestants flew the popular sport planes of the late 1920s, with two-man crews: pilot and passenger or mechanic. But the prestige of the challenge and the rising national fever in Europe led participating countries, especially Germany, to design new aircraft to meet the contest's demands.

The technical portion included a technical evaluation of competing aircrafts' construction. Since it was a touring plane contest, features like comfortable cabs with a good view, the presence of third and fourth side-by-side seats, a comprehensive set of twin controls, ease and time of engine starting (in which aircraft equipped with a starter were at an advantage), take-off and landing on a short field (which required flying over an 8.5 m [28 ft.] high gate consisting of two masts with a stretched tape, with each crew having two training attempts and two trials), flying a long distance with a good cruise speed, fuel consumption, quick wing folding (which was a feature to save space in hangars with aircraft dimensions and the method of folding was awarded points), and safety devices (anti-fire devices and places for parachutes and water safety equipment) were also awarded. The view was evaluated by placing a lamp in the cabin while the aircraft was in a dark hangar and examining the light area.

Wing folding was part of the technical evaluation of competing aircraft's construction (an Avia BH-11 is seen).

Despite the attempts by many of the competing pilots to be first in each leg of the rally portion, the challenge was not a race, but a reliability test. A "regularity of flight" (covering at least one stage daily and spending nights at appointed airfields) was the most important factor, the second being a cruise speed (minimal cruise speed had to be 80 km/h [49 mph] for Class I aircraft or 60 km/h [29 mph] for lighter Class II aircraft). Cruise speeds above 175/155 km/h (108/96 mph), respectively, were not worth extra points. The average speed was judged on flying time, so a competitor had to have his log book signed as soon after landing as possible. During the 1930 competition a competitor was given seventy-five points for "regularity," and points were deducted for spending nights off the control airfield or not covering any stage in a day. One night outside the control or arrival after the official closing time (8 pm) cost fifteen points, two nights cost forty-five points, and three failures to reach the control resulted in disqualification. Also, for failing to fly any stage in a day a competitor would lose ten points, and for the second time another twenty points. Apart from seventy-five points for regularity, up to 195 points could be gained for a high cruise speed. Points were also awarded for "reliability" and lack of repairs.

At the end of the competition the technical and rally points were added to determine an overall winner. In the four challenges the rally points always totaled twice as many as the technical points.

CHALLENGE INTERNATIONAL DE TOURISME 1929

The first of the four challenges took place 4–16 August 1929 in Paris, with fifty-five aircraft entered from six countries: Germany (twenty-four crews), Italy (twelve crews), France (nine crews), United Kingdom (five crews), Czechoslovakia (three crews), and the Swiss (two crews). All aircraft flew with two-man crews: pilot and passenger or mechanic.

Aircraft

The aircraft in the contest were popular sport planes of the late twenties and had mostly open cabs built in low-wing, high-wing, or biplane layouts. Unlike in the following years, there were no aircraft built specially for a challenge. All aircraft in the contest had fixed landing gear and no wing mechanization. The most numerous were German wooden low-wing, open two-seater tandem cabin BFW M.23bs (nine aircraft) and Klemms (six of the L.25 Ia model, including two on the Swiss team, and two L.26).

BFW M.23

The BFW M.23, sometimes known as the Messerschmitt M.23, with the "M" signifying its designer, Willy Messerschmitt, was a late 1920s two-seat sporting aircraft produced by *Bayerische Flugzeugwerke* (BFW). BFW developed the M.23 as its response to a 1929 specification issued by the German Aero Club for the *Ostpreussenflug* (East Prussian Circuit) competition. The small conventional low-wing cantilever monoplane M.23 design was an improved version of the M.19, with seating for two and wings that could be folded for transport or storage. It had a fixed undercarriage, with the main wheels mounted on a cranked axle, plus a tail skid. The fin and rudder assembly was broader and shorter than the M.19, although its form varied with sub-types. An assortment of engines were installed, ranging from the 38 hp, two-cylinder ABC Scorpion to the 150 hp, seven-cylinder Siemens Sh 14a radial. The M.23a—the first of three production variants—was equipped with low-powered engines and was distinguished by its very angular vertical tail. The M.23b was distinguished by a curved upper fuselage decking and a more rounded tail, and was powered by a large variety of inline and radial engines, causing the M.23b's length to vary. At least one M.23b was a floatplane. The M.23c was the final M.23 version, displaying an enclosed cockpit, the most powerful engines, slightly larger wings, and an increased length. Its tail identified it as a model M.23c, being more rounded at the top and missing the elevator cut-away of the earlier models. Production numbers are not certain, but seventy-four are listed on the German civil aircraft register: fifty-three M.23bs and eleven M.23cs. Fourteen M.23bs were built by Romanian ICAR (Intreprinderea de Constructii Aeronautice Romanesti) under Messerschmitt license. Many were bought by flying clubs for basic and acrobatic training. M.23bs won the 1929 Ostpreussenflug (Genet-powered version) and the Circuit of Europe (Siemens Sh 13-powered) races. The M.23c was developed for, and won, the Circuit of Europe the following year, with seven of them entered. Other M.23s were purchased by individual owners, with some familiar Nazi names among them like Ernst Udet (who made well publicized flights to Africa and Greenland, the latter with Leni Riefenstahl as a passenger) and Rudolph Hess. In 1933, Erwin Aichele and his wife flew trouble free for 13,000 km (8,000 mi) around the Mediterranean.

BFW M.23

Klemm L.25

The Klemm L.25 (later Klemm Kl 25) was a successful German light leisure, sports, and training monoplane developed in 1928. More than 600 were built in Germany 1929–1936, flying with various flight training establishments on either wheels, skis, or floats. Before WWII, fifteen were sold to Britain and equipped with a variety of domestic engines, while twenty-eight more were built by the British Klemm Aeroplane Company as the B.A. Swallow. American production—about 120 of all models—was performed by the Aeromarine-Klemm Company, which was relatively successful and also independently developed models for the American market. Hanns Klemm developed the wooden fuselage, low-cantilever wing, fixed landing gear Klemm L.25 with two open cockpits using his previous Klemm Kl 20 design as a basis. It was initially powered by a 20 hp Mercedes engine, but about thirty different Kl 25 versions were equipped with engines ranging from 43 to 94 hp, giving the aircraft a low take-off speed of only 31 mph and a maximum speed of 93–99 mph. Depending on the model, the aircraft's weight varied between 1,367 to 1,587 lbs. and its wingspan from 34 to 43 ft.

Klemm 25

Technical Trials

The first part of the contest was technical trials, starting on August 4. Unlike the following challenges, it was not too complicated and consisted of a technical evaluation, quick engine start test, quick wing folding test, and fuel consumption trials. Germany took eight of the top ten places (five by Klemm L.25 Ias). There was a three-way tie for first place with 32.5 points: Johannes Nehring of Germany, Hans Wirth of Switzerland, and Frantisek Kleps of Czechoslovakia. Eight crews withdrew during technical trials, mostly due to engine malfunctions during the last trial.

1929 Rally over Europe

The second part of the contest was a 5,942 km (3,692 mile) rally over Europe on a route Paris to Basil, to Genoa, to Lyon, to Marseille, to Saint Raphael, to Turin, to Milan, to Venice, to Zagreb, to Belgrade, to Bucharest, to Turnu, to Severin, to Budapest, to Vienna, to Brno, to Prague, to Breslau, to Warsaw, to Poznan, to Berlin, to Hamburg, to Amsterdam, to Brussels, and back to Paris. Main waypoints were Belgrade, Warsaw, and Paris. It was not an ordinary rally, but a trial of aircraft capability, with the important factors being maintaining a good cruise speed, a regularity of flight (covering at least one stage daily and spending nights at appointed airfields), and lack of major repairs. The maximum number of points to obtain in a rally was 119 (70 for cruise speed, 35 for regularity, and 14 for reliability).

The rally started at 0900 on 7 August, from Orly airfield in Paris. Two crews dropped out during start, including the Czech Josef Novak flying Aero A.34, whose engine failed and the aircraft turned over during landing. In the rally a maximum speed was not important; nonetheless, most crews tried to make their best time and a group of the nine fastest crews reached Belgrade on 8 August at noon: Hubert Broad (DH-60), Winifred Spooner (DH-60), Frantisek Kleps (Avia BH-11), Johannes Nehring (D-18), Raymond Delmotte (Caudron C.191), and John Carberry (RK-25). This group was also at the lead at the next airfields. Other groups were five German crews with Fritz Morzik (BFW M.23b) and two groups of Italians; most other crews flew separately. Some crews dropped out on the way, mostly due to faults and accident landings.

On 9 August, after starting at 0900, most crews took off from Belgrade; only a few crews had not arrived at their next stops. On 11 August, the leading group took off from Brno and arrived at Warsaw. Flying to Poznan, Johannes Nehring had a landing accident that damaged his Darmstadt D-18, one of the fastest aircraft. Some other crews dropped out as well.

Since competitors were not allowed to land in Paris before 1500 on 14 August, the leading group took off from Brussels and flew over Orly airfield minutes before 1500. A few minutes later nineteen aircraft landed in Paris, the first being Italian Batista Botalla flying his Fiat AS.1. That day four more crews arrived. On 15 August three crews finished, and the next day the remaining crews arrived. Only thirty-one crews from the original forty-seven finished the rally. Only two crews attained the maximum 119 points for the rally: German Fritz Morzik (BFW M.23b) and Canadian John Carberry (RK-25), with Brit Hubert Broad (DH-60G) in third place with 109 points. Five of the top ten teams (99–104 points) were Italian crews flying in a group.

1929 RALLY FINAL RESULTS

1) Fritz Morzik	Germany/ BFW M.23b	119 points
2) John Carberry	Canada/ RK-25	119 points
3) Hubert Broad	UK/DH-60	109 points
4) Wolf von Dungern	Germany/ BFW M.23b	106.5 points
5) Umberto Gelmetti	Italy/RO-5	104 points
6) Federico Guazetti	Italy/RO-5	99 points
7) Winifred Spooner	UK/DH-60	99 points
8) Gustavo Castaldo	Italy/RO-5	99 points
9) Francesco Lombardi	Italy/ Fiat AS.1	99 points
10) Batista Bottalla	Italy/ Fiat AS.1	99 points

1929 Challenge International de Tourisme Final Results

The first prize in the challenge was 100,000 French francs, second was 50,000 FRF, and third was 25,000 FRF, with the sixteen other crews receiving 7,350 FRF. German Fritz Morzik was first flying a BFW M.23 with 19.5 technical points and a perfect 119 rally points for a total of 138 points. Brit Hubert Broad, flying a DH-0G, was second with 135.25 points (26.25+109), while Canadian Jonn Carberry was third, flying for the Germans in a RAKA RK-25 for 131 points (12+119). In all, the contest was a German success (including John Carberry), but only twelve out of twenty-four German crews finished the contest. The Italian team had nine of twelve crews finish with high placings.

TOP 10 FINAL RESULTS

1) Fritz Morzik	Germany/BFW M.23b	138.5 points (19.5+119)*
2) Hubert Broad	UK/DH-60G	135.25 points (26.25+109)
3) John Carberry	Canada-Germany/RK-25	131 points (12+119)
4) Robert Lusser	Germany/Klemm L.25 1a	128.25 points (30.5+97.75)
5) Federico Guazetti	Italy/Romeo RO-5	127.25 points (28,25+99)
6) Wolf von Dungern	Germany/BFW M.23b	126.75 points (20.25+106.5)
7) Frantisek Kleps	Czech/ Avia BH-11	126.5 points (32.5 + 94)
8) Gustavo Castaldo	Italy/ Romeo Ro-5	124.25 points (25.25 + 99)
9) Umberto Gelmetti	Italy/ Romeo Ro-5	122 points (18 + 104)
10) Winifred Spooner	UK/DH-60G	121.5 points (22.5 + 99)

**(Technical + Rally points)*

Friedrich-Wilhelm "Fritz" Morzik

Morzik trained as a pilot and served with the flying detachment of the Asia Corps during WWI. After the war he served with a police flying unit in Silesia until 1921, after which he was an instructor with the German Air Transportation School in Brunswick. In 1928, he became a vice-director in Staaken, then its director. He was connected with Deutsche Lufthansa, the German national airline at that time. Fritz Morzik was also an active sports pilot. He was a winner in the first International Tourist Plane Contest Challenge and the second Challenge in 1930. In the third challenge in 1932 he was second before he was forced to withdraw. He took part in the fourth challenge in 1934, but did not finish due to engine breakdown; he was the only pilot to participate in all challenges. In 1935, he joined the emerging German Air Force as a commandant of the pilot's school. During WWII *Generalmajor* Morzik became a head of Luftwaffe Transport Command and was captured in May 1945 by American troops, then held until 1947. After the war he wrote two academic histories of the Luftwaffe Transport Command in WWII.

Fritz Morzik on his KL26

CHALLENGE INTERNATIONAL DE TOURISME 1930

Because German pilot Fritz Morzik won the previous 1929 contest, Germany was to organize the next 1930 challenge to take place 18 July–8 August 1930 at Berlin-Staaken airfield. The challenge was again based upon FAI rules, but the particulars of the event were to be arranged by the German Aero Club. Ninety-eight crews applied, but eventually sixty aircraft entered from six countries: Germany (thirty crews), Poland (twelve crews), United Kingdom (seven crews), France (six crews), Spain (three crews), and Switzerland (two crews). The strong German team featured Fritz Morzik, Reinhold Poss, Willy Polte, and Oskar Notz, among other talented pilots. The British team was led by Capt. Hubert Broad (2nd place in 1929), John Carberry (3rd place in 1929), and two women: Winifred Spooner and Lady Mary Bailey. The Spanish team highlighted Prince Antonio de Habsburgo-Borbon. The contest roster also featured many other skilled and well known aviators of that time.

Aircraft

Forty aircraft were assigned to Class I with a net weight up to 400 kg (881 lbs.) plus fifteen percent, while the remaining twenty were Class II aircraft with a net weight up to 300 kg (661 lbs.) plus fifteen percent. The Class II aircraft were eleven German BFW M.23s and five Klemm L.25s and L.25Es (apart from two L.25 IVas), three Polish RWD-2s, and one French PM XI. The classifications only influenced the awarding of points for cruise speed and fuel consumption.

The majority of the entered aircraft were popular sport planes that had participated in the 1929 Challenge. These aircraft had mostly open cockpits, mostly all-wooden (fifty-five, with five all-metal), low-wing (twenty-nine), or high-wing (seventeen) monoplanes, with only thirteen biplanes and one mid-wing. All aircraft had fixed conventional landing gear and no wing mechanization (e.g., slats or flaps). The new 1930 Challenge regulations placed more emphasis on the technical portion, compelling the appearance of more special, advanced aircraft more capable of meeting challenge demands. The lighter category German BFW M.23c and Klemm L 25E were new variants of the successful 1929 models with closed canopies and equipped with more powerful Argus engines, giving them a better chance in technical trials. The ten BFW M.23cs were the most numerous entries, followed by six de Havilland DH.60G Gipsy Moths, four Klemm L.25s, and four Arado L IIs.

de Havilland DH.60G Gipsy Moth

The DH.60G Gipsy Moth evolved from the Cirrus-powered DH 60 Moth first flown by Geoffrey de Havilland in 1925. The Moth was a two-seat wooden biplane with a plywood-covered fuselage and fabric-covered surfaces with folding wings. Three aircraft were modified for the 1927 King's Cup Race with internal modifications and a Cirrus II engine on a lowered engine mounting. Cirrus Aero-Engines Ltd.'s poor workmanship on its engine caused de Havilland to replace the Cirrus with the new in-house built Havilland Gipsy I engine in 1928. The new engine was placed in a prototype designated the DH.60G Gipsy Moth, which was virtually a standard DH.60. Except for changes to accommodate the new engine the fuselage remained the same, and the Moth's signature exhaust still ran alongside the left side of the cockpit with the *De Havilland Moth* logo on the right side. The fuel tank was accommodated in the bulging airfoil that formed the center upper wing section. The folding wings had de Havilland's patented differential ailerons on the bottom main planes and no ailerons on the top ones. The new

DH.60G Gipsy Moth was inexpensive and reliable, and quickly became the mainstay of British flying clubs, as by 1929, it was estimated that eighty-five of every one hundred British aircraft were some type of Moth, mostly the Gypsy variety. While most Gypsy Moths belonged to flying clubs, after the Prince of Wales purchased one as his private aircraft the Gipsy Moth became popular with high society and was used for many record flights. Sir Francis Chichester flew his Gipsy Moth from England to Australia, further to New Zealand, and then across the Pacific to Japan (see text). In March 1928, Mary Bailey flew her Cirrus Moth solo from Croydon to Cape Town (see text), Amy Johnson flew her Gipsy Moth to Australia (see text), and Jean Batten (see text) flew a Gipsy Moth for her flights from England to India and England to Australia. (Author's note: as mentioned in this book's foreword, my father owned a Gipsy Moth).

De Havilland DH.60G Gipsy Moth

For the contest the aircraft had alphanumerical starting numbers: the German from a range A2–A9, B3–B9, C1–C9, D1–D8, E1–E9, and F1–F2; British: K1–K8; French: L1–L3, and M1–M6; Polish: O1–O9 and P1-P5; Swiss: S1–S2; and Spanish: T1–T7 (numbers were painted in a circle with the inscription *Challenge International* and *1930*).

1930 Rally over Europe

The 1930 Challenge was the only one in which the rally was the opening segment. It was a 7,560 km (4,697 miles) circuit over Europe, with compulsory stops in Berlin, Braunschweig, Frankfurt, Reims, Saint-Inglevert, Bristol, London, Saint-Inglevert, Paris, Poitiers, Pau, Zaragoza, Madrid, Seville, Barcelona, Nimes, Lyon, Lausanne, Bern, Munich, Vienna, Prague, Breslau, Poznan, Warsaw, Kaliningrad, Danzig, and Berlin. The distances between stops ranged from 77.5 km (48 miles, Lausanne-Bern) to 410 km (254 miles, Danzig-Berlin). In spite of attempts by many pilots to be the first to arrive it was not a race, but rather a reliability test. A regularity of flights was the most important factor, the second was cruise speed (minimal cruise speed had to be 80 km/h [49 mph] for Class I aircraft or 60 km/h [37.3 mph] for lighter Class II aircraft. Cruise speeds above 175/155 km/h [108/96 mph] respectively did not award extra points). The average speed was judged on flying time, so a competitor had to have his log book signed as soon after landing as possible. A competitor was given seventy-five points for regularity, stipulated similar to the first challenge. The original time limit for the return to Berlin was 1600 on July 31, but it got extended later for some crews due to bad weather in Pau. Apart from seventy-five points for regularity, up to 195 points could be awarded for a high cruise speed. Compared with 1929, the rally could convey only fifty-four percent of the maximum number of points (in 1929 it was seventy-two percent) so technical trials were more important.

The take-off on the first day was from Berlin-Tempelhof between 0900 and 0959 on Sunday, 20 July. Despite poor weather fifteen crews reached Saint-Inglevert near Calais (1,058 km/657.4 miles); among them were six British crews, four French, three Polish, and only two German, with one Spanish (CASA C-1) and one Polish (PWS-52) crew damaging their aircraft that had to withdraw, while another Pole, Tadeusz Karpinski (RWD-4), withdrew due to appendicitis.

On 21 July, poor weather prevented flying until after mid-day, but then most crews flew over the English Channel, with the fastest twenty-three able to return to France. Three British and three French crews reached Paris that day, flying 843.5 km (524 miles). One French PM XI was destroyed during a forced landing and several other aircraft were damaged on that or the previous day but were repaired.

On 22 July, the fastest pilots arrived at Madrid (3,019 km/1,875.9 miles) from the Berlin start. They were five British crews: Hubert Broad, Alan Butler (both flying DH-60Gs), Sidney Thorn (Avro Avian), John Carberry (Monocoupe 110), and H. Andrews; three German crews: Fritz Morzik and Willy Polte, both flying BFW M.23cs, and Reinhold Poss (Klemm L.25E); and two Frenchmen: Francois Arrachart and Maurice Finat (both flying C.193s). Four other aircraft, including Prince de Habsburgo-Borbon and Georg Pasewaldt, were able to fly over the Pyrenees to Zaragoza, but the French crews of Cornez (C.193) and MacMahon (C.232) crashed while trying to fly farther. The remainder were spread out on the whole route, with the slowest pilots flying only 800–1000 km (497–621 miles) from Berlin. Five more crews withdrew and one German and Spanish crew damaged their aircraft during flight to Pau. German pilot von Oertzen withdrew in London when his passenger was killed by the propeller of their Albatros L.100.

On 23–24 July, only the fastest crews arrived in Spain, because the other crews were grounded in Pau due to bad weather over the Pyrenees. Lady Bailey, the last pilot to attempt to fly to Zaragoza over the Pyrenees, was forced to return to Pau. Due to flight circumstances there were no penalties for not flying farther and the return time limit was extended by twenty-four or forty-eight hours, depending on the time when the crew arrived at Pau. Five crews reached Barcelona on the twenty-third and Lausanne the next day. On 25 July, the weather improved and the remainder of crews flew to Zaragoza. Meanwhile, the four fastest pilots—Hubert Broad, Sidney Thorn, Alan Butler, and Reinhold Poss—arrived at Breslau, and Fritz Morzik at Prague. That day four crews withdrew, including the best Polish pilot, Franciszek Zwirko (RWD-4), due to engine failure, two German crews, and Jacques Maus (St. Hubert G.1), the only Belgian entry. On 26 July, four crews reached Warsaw: Poss, Broad, Thorn, and Prince de Habsburgo-Borbon. Pole Jerzy Bajan and Germans Aichele and Dinort, who were the fastest of the crews that had been stopped by weather, reached Bern, but were 700 km (434 miles) behind the last crews of the first group, which stopped in Vienna. That day two German crewmen (Erich Offermann and E. Jerzembski, BFW M.23c) were killed in a crash landing in Lyon, hitting an aerial mast, while the other German crew of Rudolf Neininger (Darmstadt D-18) ditched in the Gulf of Lyon, but were rescued by a nearby ship.

On 27 July, the first pilots finished in Berlin—Hubert Broad and then Sidney Thorn, who was closely trailed by Reinhold Poss. Within the next hour Fritz Morzik, Maurice Finat, Prince Antonio de Habsburgo-Borbon, Georg Pasewaldt, H. Andrews, and A. S. Butler arrived . That day thirty-five crews continued in the competition. The fastest was Alan Butler (DH-60G), with an average speed of 179 km/h (111 mph), but due to a propeller exchange in Poznan he was disqualified; unofficially he would fly on to finish the rally. The fastest of the qualified crews and the only one to gain full points was Hubert Broad (176 km/h/109 mph).

On 28 July, seven crews reached Berlin: Willy Polte, Oskar Dinort, Winifred Spooner, Mary Bailey, John Carberry, François Arrachart, and Stanisław Plonczynski. On 29 July, nine more arrived, including Theo Osterkamp, Jerzy Bajan, Johann Risztics, Robert Lusser, and Oskar Notz. The remaining crews arrived during the next days, with the last crew finishing on 1 August. During these last days several crews withdrew or were disqualified.

Only thirty-six crews out of sixty finished in time from this difficult rally, but an additional six completed the circuit despite being disqualified due to time infringement or propeller repairs (did not carry a replacement propeller). Among those who withdrew were nine German crews (three of which completed the circuit), eight Polish (three completed the circuit), four French, two Spanish, and one Brit (who completed the circuit). Going into the technical trials, the leader in the general classification was Hubert Broad (DH-60G, 270 points), and behind him John Carberry (Monocoupe, 268 pts), Reinhold Poss (Klemm L.25E, 264 pts), and Fritz Morzik was fourth (BFW M.23c, 263 pts). There were eight Germans in the top fifteen finishers and two each from the UK and Switzerland. The fastest German pilot was Dietrich von Massenbach (151 km/h), but he lost ten points for regularity.

1930 RALLY FINAL RESULTS*
TOTAL POINTS (REGULARITY POINTS)

Pilot	Country/Aircraft	Points
1) Hubert Broad	UK/ DH-60G	270 points (75)*
2) John Carberry	UK (Canada)/Monocoupe 110	268 points (75)
3) Reinhold Poss	Germany/ Klemm L.25E	264 points (75)
4) Fritz Morzik	Germany/BFW M.23c	263 points (75)
5) Willy Polte	Germany/BFW M.23c	262 points (75)
6) Oskar Notz	Germany/ Klemm L.25E	261 points (75)
7) Winifred Spooner	UK/ DH-60G	260 points (75)
8) Dietrich von Massenbach	Germany/BFW M.23c	256 points (65)
9) Ernst Kruger	Germany/BFW M.23c	254 points (75)
10) Joachim von Koppen	Germany/BFW M.23c	253 points (75)

Hubert Broad

During 1915, Broad received flying instructions at the Hall School of Flying in Hendon and received his pilot certificate, after which he joined the Royal Naval Air Service at Eastchurch. After training he was posted to combat with No. 3 Squadron RNAS based at Dunkirk, France, flying the Sopwith Pup. During a bomber escort mission he received a neck wound and returned to England; while recovering he became an instructor. After recuperating, Broad was assigned to No. 46 Squadron of the Royal Flying Corps, flying the Sopwith Camel, and ended his wartime service as an instructor at the Fighter Pilots Flying School, Fairlop. After the war Broad flew demonstration flights for Avro in the UK, then flew Avro seaplanes while touring America. In 1921, flying a Sopwith Camel, he finished first in the Aerial Derby air race around London. The race drew the attention of the De Havilland Company, which employed him as chief test pilot at Stag Lane in October 1921, flying a wide variety of De Havilland aircraft, in addition to Handley Page and Gloster aircraft. At de Havilland, Broad flew many demonstration flights and was allowed to enter air races and competitions to boast De Havilland aircraft. At the 1925 Schneider Trophy seaplane and flying boat race Broad, flying a Gloster III seaplane, became the lone British entrant and finished second to an American Army test pilot, James Doolittle. In 1926, he won the King's Cup Air Race in a De Havilland Moth. In 1928, he flew in the International Light Aircraft Contest in France, finishing third. The next year, he finished second in the FAI Challenge International de Tourisme. In the subsequent Challenge International de Tourisme in 1930 he was eighth overall, but he completed the rally section in first place.

In 1935, he left De Havilland to work with the Royal Aircraft Establishment as a test pilot. He published a book in 1939 about flying, *Flying Wisdom; A Book of Practical Experiences and Their Lessons*. In 1940, he became chief production test pilot for Hawker Aircraft, where he tested Hawker's single-seat fighters as they left the production line. He was appointed MBE in 1944 for his work as a Hawker test pilot. During his career he completed 7,500 flying hours in 200 different aircraft types. Broad appears to have had an affair with Beryl Markham, the first woman to fly solo across the Atlantic from east to west (see Markham text), and was named by her second husband Mansfield Markham as a co-respondent in his 1937 divorce from Beryl.

Hubert Broad (R) being congratulated by de Havilland Chairman Alan Butler (C) for 1930 Rally win at Berlin.

Technical Trials

On 3 August, the first trial was quick wings folding, which was won by Hubert Broad's crew, who folded and unfolded the wings of their DH-60s in only forty-eight seconds. The next trial was the quick engine starting test won by Theo Osterkamp's Klemm L.25Ia, powered by a Salmson AD.9 engine. On 3 August, the fuel consumption trial was held over 304 km (189 miles) and was won by the light RWD-2s, followed by the German Klemms and BFWs. On 4 August, there was a technical evaluation of aircraft construction (described earlier) worth a maximum of 104 points of a total of 230 Technical Trial points. John Carberry's American Monocoupe was awarded the most points (74), then to three German Junkers A50s (67–69), then a Breda Ba.15S and Arado L IIa (65). Finishing last was the winning type of the 1929 challenge, a BFW M.23b. From the evening of 5 August until 7 August, short take-off and landing trials were held, with German pilot Ernst Kruger winning with a distance of 125.5 m (414 ft.), followed by Fritz Morzik with 126.4 m (417 ft,), both flying the BFW M.23c. The short landing trial was won by German Theo Osterkamp (127.3 m/420 ft.) flying an older model Klemm L.25 Ia, followed by Friedrich Siebel (Klemm L.26).

1930 Challenge International de Tourisme Final Results

The winner of the 1930 Challenge International de Tourisme was German Fritz Morzik flying a BFW M.23c (427 points to win 100,000 French francs); second and third places were taken by Germans Reinhold Poss (423 points/50,000 FRF) and Oskar Notz (419 points/25,000 FRF)—both flying Klemm L.25Es, respectively—with Brit Winifred Spooner (DH 60G) in fourth (416 points/15,000 FRF). Only thirty-five crews of sixty completed the contest, among them twenty German, six British, four Polish, two Swiss, two French, and one Spanish. Thirteen of the top twenty places were won by German aircraft: six Klemm L.25E/L.26s and five BFW M.23cs. Due to the German victory, the next challenge (1932) was also organized in Germany.

TOP 10 FINAL RESULTS

Pilot	Country/Aircraft	Points
1) Fritz Morzik	Germany/ BFW M.23c	427 points (263 + 164)*
2) Reinhold Poss	Germany/ Klemm L.25E	423 points (264 + 159)
3) Oskar Notz	Germany/ Klemm L.25E	419 points (261 + 158)
4) Winifred Spooner	UK/ DH-60G	416 points (260 + 156)
5) Willy Polte	Germany/ BFW M.23c	409 points (262 + 147)
6) John Carberry	UK/ Monocoupe 110	405 points (268 + 137)
7) Dietrich von Massenbach	Germany/ BFW M.23c	398 points (256 + 142)
8) Hubert Broad	UK/ DH-60G	395 points (270 + 125)
9) Ernst Krüger	Germany/ BFW M.23c	394 points (254 + 140)
10) Oskar Dinort	Germany/ Klemm L.25E	385 points (250 + 135)

(Rally + Technical points)

Morzik (L) and Poss with their Klemm KL26

CHALLENGE INTERNATIONAL DE TOURISME 1932

Germany organized the contest held 12–28 August, again in Berlin. The number of aircraft that took part was smaller (forty-three compared to sixty), because the contest was becoming much more difficult, demanding increased piloting expertise and more advanced aircraft. Most competing nations developed new advanced sport aircraft with high technical performance specifically for the challenge. Initially, there were sixty-seven entries, but twenty-four aircraft did not arrive for the competition, as many were unfinished or crashed during tests. Teams from six countries entered the challenge in 1932: Germany (sixteen crews), France (eight crews), Italy (eight crews), Poland (five crews), Czechoslovakia (four crews), and Switzerland (two crews). English aviator Winifred Spooner entered the contest with the Italian team as the only woman among the pilots. One Canadian (John Carberry) and one Romanian pilot (Alexander Papana) entered the contest with the German team. This challenge consisted of three parts: technical trials, a rally around Europe, and a new maximum speed test. The opening ceremony was held on 12 August 1932 at Berlin-Staaken airfield.

Aircraft

Germany, Poland, Czechoslovakia, and Italy each developed modern sports aircraft specifically to win the challenge. Germany's new highest-performance Messerschmitt BFW M.29 was a pre-challenge favorite, but was withdrawn due to two crashes during training. The six fast Heinkel He 64s became the German challenge favorite and were complimented by eight three-seat Klemm Kl 32s (plus one on the Swiss team). Both the Heinkels and Klemms were wooden low-wing monoplanes. Italy's Breda Ba.33 and Czechoslovakia's Praga BH-111were similar strutted low-wing monoplanes. Poland developed a high-wing RWD-6 and an all-metal low-wing monoplane PZL.19. All these aircraft had enclosed crew cockpits, fixed landing gear, and advanced modern wing flaps and slats. The other aircraft, especially French, were modified from serial designs and were less modern, decreasing their chances in the technical trials.

The participating aircraft were: Klemm Kl 32 (8), Breda Ba.33 (8), Heinkel He 64 (6), Praga BH-111 (3), PZL.19 (3), RWD-6 (2), Potez 43 (2), Farman 234 (2), Farman 353 (1), Darmstadt D-22a (1), Raab-Katzenstein RK-25/32 (1), Breda Ba.15S (1), Monocoupe 110 (1), Guerchais T.9 (1), Caudron C.278 (1), Mauboussin M.12 (1), and Comte AC-12 (1). The German aircraft had starting numbers from a range: A4–A9, B1–B9, C2–C8, and E1–E2; French: K1–K8; Italian: M1–M8; Polish: O1–O6; Swiss: S1–S2; and Czechoslovak: T1–T4. The numbers were placed on fuselages in a black square frame.

RWD-6

The Poles designed the RWD-6 especially for competing in the 1932 International Tourist Aircraft Challenge, which RWD had entered in 1930, without notable success. It was designed and constructed by the RWD team Stanislaw Rogalski, Stanislaw Wigura, and Jerzy Drzewiecki in the workshops of Students Mechanical Club of Warsaw University of Technology (RWD was named after each of their last names' first letters).

The RWD-6 was a two-seater sports and touring strutted high-wing monoplane of mixed metal and wooden construction: the metal frame fuselage was covered with canvas, the engine was covered in aluminum sheets, and the rectangular single-spar wing was of wooden construction, covered with canvas and plywood. The wings folded rearward, and were equipped with automatic slats and flaps and thirty-four gallon fuel tanks. The closed cabin had two entry doors, two side-by-side seats, and dual controls. The aircraft was powered by a 140 hp, seven-cylinder Armstrong Siddeley Genet Major radial engine and a two-blade metal propeller. The landing gear was conventional with a rear skid. Only three RWD-6s were built: the first was flown on 3 June 1932 by designer Jerzy Drzewiecki. The aircraft were given civilian registrations SP-AHL, SP-AHM, and SP-AHN, but during trials SP-AHM crashed and Drzewiecki was injured. The two remaining RWD-6s were sent to the challenge after their tails were modified.

RWD-6 in the short take-off portion of the Technical Trials

The 1932 Challenge was won by Franciszek Zwirko (pilot) and Stanisław Wigura (mechanic) in their RWD-6. The other RWD-6, flown by Tadeusz Karpinski, took ninth place out of forty-three competitors. During the contest, the RWD-6 was given the highest scores for technical evaluation of all participating aircraft. Not long after being feted as national heroes for their challenge victory, the RWD-6 with Zwirko and Wigura aboard crashed on 11 September 1932, during a storm while flying to an air meet in Czechoslovakia, killing both men. The cause was found to be weak wing mountings that caused wing warping at higher speeds. The last remaining RWD-6 was modified after this accident, receiving a strengthened wing with V-shaped struts and the new designation RWD-6bis. The RWD-6bis was completed and flown during September 1933, but in 1935, its fuselage was used to create the RWD-13 touring prototype. A direct development of the RWD-6 as a sport plane was a four-seater RWD-9, a winner of the 1934 Challenge.

Breda Ba.33

The Breda Ba.33 excelled in the 1932 Technical Trials due to Breda company engineer Ing Cesare Pallavicino, who led the design and development of the aircraft. The first version, the Ba.33 Serie 1, was a two-seat low-wing monoplane with external bracing between the wings and the fuselage, powered by a 120 hp de Havilland Gipsy III four-cylinder air-cooled inline engine. Later, two versions of the Ba.33 Serie 2 were built: one with the de Havilland Gipsy engine and another with a Colombo engine. Breda also developed a single-seat version of the aircraft, the Ba.33S; it differed from the Ba.33, being a single-seater and having an enclosed cockpit and a more powerful Colombo S63 engine. After the Ba.33 first flew in 1930, the aircraft and its variants proved to be a very successful series of touring and racing aircraft during the 1930s. During 1931, a Ba.33 won the *Giro Aereo d'Italia* (Air Tour of Italy). Ba.33s equipped the Italian team for the International Touring Competition in 1932, with which Winifred Spooner also entered the contest. Ambrogio Colombo was a leader of the challenge after the technical trials. Two Bredas crashed during the rally portion on 23 August 1932, due to weak wing construction (one mechanic died after bailing out), and Italy decided to withdraw all the Italian teams from the contest.

Breda BA.33

Technical Trials

Starting 13 August, the technical evaluation aircraft construction was held. The Polish designs were awarded the most points, with 86 points to the RWD-6 and 84 points to the PZL.19, giving them a 14–20 point advantage over the favored German designs: the Kl 32 (72 points) and He 64c (66 points). The Italian Breda Ba.33 (83 points) and Praga BH-111 (80 points) were third and fourth, while the Caudron C.278 biplane and Mauboussin M.12 scored the lowest (44 points).

The first flying trial was a minimal speed trial to evaluate aircraft safety, which was new in challenge contests. Flying on the edge of stalling, Pole Franciszek Zwirko was the slowest at 57.6 km/h (35 mph) speed; second was another Pole flying an RWD-6, Tadeusz Karpiński. Such low speeds were not expected and all seven contestants below 63 km/h were awarded 50 points.

Next trials were short take-off and landing, which was conducted in groups until 17 August 1932. German Wolfram Hirth (Kl 32) was first (40 points) in the short take-off phase, but two Italians (Ambrogio Colombo and Francesco Lombardi, Ba.33s) were also awarded 40 points. In the short landing trial— landing behind an 8 m high gate—Winifred Spooner (UK/Ba.33) was first with 40 points, but second place finisher Reinhold Poss (Germany/KL 32) was also awarded 40 points. The folding of wings trials were held on 16 August, followed by the quick engine starting trial. A fuel consumption trial over 300 km (186 miles) was held on 19 August, which the German aircraft won to conclude the Technical Trials. After all technical trials Italian Ambrogio Colombo (BA.33) led the general classification with 247 points, with Pole Franciszek Zwirko (RWD-6) second (245 points), Italy's Francesco Lombardi third (242 points), and Winifred Spooner (UK/Ba.33) and Renato Donati (Italy/Ba.33) tying for fourth with 241 points. Before the rally phase Winifred Spooner was forced to land near Berlin due to sabotage of her fuel and she decided to withdraw.

Rally over Europe

The second part of the challenge was a 7,363 km (4,575 mile) rally over Europe, starting with thirty-nine aircraft from Berlin and coursing via Warsaw, Krakow, Prague, Brno, Vienna, Zagreb, Postumia (checkpoint), Vicenza, Rimini, Rome, Florence, Bellinzona, Torino, Albenga (checkpoint), Imperia (checkpoint), Cannes, Lyon, St. Gallen, Stuttgart, Bonn, Paris, Deauville, Rotterdam, Dortmund, Hamburg, Copenhagen, Laholm (checkpoint), Gothenburg, Laholm (checkpoint), Copenhagen, Hamburg, and finishing in Berlin. The main waypoints were Rome and Paris; the longest section was Berlin to Warsaw (518 km/321 miles) and the shortest was Brno to Vienna (106.4 km/66 miles).

The Rally began on 21 August, and from the beginning, the German crews tried to take advantage of their faster aircraft to make up for points lost in the technical trials, while the Italians tried to maintain their lead on their way to Rome. Meanwhile, the Poles, flying their slower aircraft, tried to maintain a good cruise speed and flight regularity, which were awarded points in the rally. On the first day most crews reached Vienna or Zagreb, while the Italians reached Vicenza. Ambrogio Colombo and three Germans (von Massenbach, Seidemann, and Marienfeld) flew as far as Rimini. Three crews withdrew on the way due to breakdowns. On 22 August, German pilot Hans Seidemann was first of thirty-three crews to land in Rome, as three had forced crash landings. On 23 August, the contestants took off from Rome, but two Italian Breda Ba.33s crashed due to weak wing construction and Italy decided to withdraw all the Italian teams from the challenge, even though Ambrogio Colombo was the leader. On 24 August, the twenty-five remaining crews reached Paris, and on 27 August, the rally finished in Berlin led by German Hans Seidemann with a cruise speed of 213 km/h (135.5 mph) flying the Heinkel He 64b for 220 points. The next seven results were also Germans, including second (Wolfgang Stein, He 64c), third (Dietrich von Massenbach, He 64c), fourth (Walter Marienfeld, Da.22a), fifth (Wolf Hirth, Kl 32), and sixth (Fritz Morzik, He 64c)—all awarded with 220 points. Pole Franciszek Zwirko (RWD-6) arrived in eleventh place, but held first place in the general classification with 456 points, with Reinhold Poss in second with 451 points, Wolf Hirth in third with 450 points, and Robert Fretz (Suiss) in fourth with 448 points. Fritz Morzik was fifth with 444 points.

1932 RALLY RESULTS

1) Hans Seidemann	Germany/He 64b	220 points (213 km/h)
2) Wolfgang Stein	Germany/He 64b	220 points (208 km/h)
3) Dietrich von Massenbach	Germany/He 64b	220 points (206 km/h)
4) Walter Marienfeld	Germany/D-22a	220 points (205 km/h)
5) Wolf Hirth	Germany/Kl 32	220 points (203 km/h)
6) Fritz Morzik	Germany/He 64b	220 points (200 km/h)
7) Otto Cuno	Germany/Kl 32	218 points (198 km/h)
8/9) Reinhold Poss	Germany/Kl 32	217 points (197 km/h)
8/9) Robert Fretz	Switzerland/KL 32	217 points (197 km/h)
10) Robert Lusser	Germany/Kl 32	213 points (193 km/h)

Maximum Speed Trial

The last part of the challenge was a maximum speed trial on 28 August over a 300 km (186 mile) triangular course, beginning and landing at Berlin-Staaken airfield. Due to a handicapping system, contestants took off in order of their position in the general classification with proper intervals, and an amount of points awarded in the speed trial meant the first to the finish line would be the winner of the race. Zwirko took off first with Morzik following twelve minutes after, but landed eighty-three seconds after Zwirko; if Morzik had been able to pass Zwirko he would have won this race phase. Poss, starting five minutes after the leader, finished 2:30 minutes behind. The fastest racer was Fritz Morzik (He 64c) at 241.3 km/h (149 mph), for which he was given 14 points. The next four places were also occupied by Heinkels. Zwirko's closest rival—Reinhold Poss flying a Klemm Kl 32—was in seventh position (220.7 km/h/137.1 mph). The fastest Pole was Tadeusz Karpinski (RWD-6) in eighth place at 216.2 km/h (132.4 mph), while Franciszek Zwirko took the thirteenth with 214.1 km/h (133 mph), for which he earned five points—just enough to give him victory in the overall 1932 Challenge.

1932 Final Results

A closing ceremony was held after the maximum speed test on 28 August. The challenge was completed by only twenty-four crews out of forty-three (twelve German, four Polish, four French, three Czechoslovak, and one Swiss). Seven Klemm 32s and five Heinkel He 64bs (both German) were the top finishers among aircraft. The first prize in the challenge was 100,000 French francs, second prize was 50,000 FRF, third was 25,000 FRF, fourth was 13,000 FRF, and the sixteen other crews received 7,000 FRF. The winners were the Polish crew pilot Franciszek Zwirko and mechanic Stanisław Wigura, with 461 points flying their RWD-6 (which Wigura co-designed). Second and third place were held by Germans: Fritz Morzik (Heinkel He 64c, winner of the 1930 Challenge) and Reinhold Poss (Klemm Kl 32V), both with 458 points. Fifth place was taken by Switzerland's Robert Frenz flying a German Klemm Kl 32.

TOP 10 FINAL RESULTS

1) Franciszek Zwirko	Poland/RWD-6	461 points (245 + 211 + 5)*
2) Fritz Morzik	Germany/He 64c	458 points (224 + 220 + 14)
3) Reinhold Poss	Germany/ Kl 32	458 points (234 + 217 + 7)
4) Wolfgang Stein	Germany/He 64c	453 points (221 + 220 + 12)
5) Robert Fretz	Switzerland/Kl 32	452 points (231 + 217 + 4)
6) Wolf Hirth	Germany/ Kl 32	450 points (230 + 220 + 0)
7/8) Otto Cuno	Germany/ Kl 32	447 points (224 + 218 + 5)
9) Tadeusz Karpinski	Poland/RWD-6	443 points (238 + 200 + 5)
10) Robert Lusser	Germany/ Kl 32	437 points (219 + 213 + 5)

**(Technical+Rally+Speed points)*

Less than a month after the challenge Franciszek Zwirko and Stanislaw Wigura died in an accident while flying their RWD-6 to Czechoslovakia in a storm on 11 September 1932. Reinhold Poss and Winifred Spooner also died in 1933.

Franciszek Zwirko

During WWI Zwirko volunteered for the Russian Army and fought as an officer against the Germans. After the war he fought the Bolsheviks in the Russian Civil War, during which he completed an air observer course. After the Bolshevik victory in 1921, he returned to Poland, where he graduated from aviation school in Bydgoszcz in November 1923, then completed an advanced piloting course in Grudziądz, after which Porucznik Pilot (Flying Lieutenant) Zwirko became a fighter pilot with the 18th Fighter Squadron of the 1st Air Regiment. He also became active in sports aviation, and during August 1927, flying a military Breguet 19, he placed second in the 1st Air Contest of the Little Entente held in Yugoslavia and Poland, and then placed first in its rally portion. During 1929, he was assigned as a liaison officer to the Warsaw University Aeroclub, which allowed him to increase his sport flying. In this post he met a young engineer named Stanislaw Wigura, one of the RWD Company designers of sports aircraft, and soon the two flew together with Wigura as a mechanic and second pilot. Between 9 August and 6 September 1929, Zwirko and Wigura flew the RWD-2 prototype across Europe on the Warsaw-Paris-Barcelona-Milano-Warsaw 5,000 km (3,200 mile) route, and on 6 October, they won the 1st Rally of South-Eastern Poland. On 16 October 1929, Zwirko and Antoni Kocjan set an international FAI altitude record of 4,004 m (13,136 ft.) in the light tourist plane class (under 280 kg/616 lbs. empty weight). In July 1930, Zwirko and Wigura participated in the International Tourist Plane Competition Challenge 1930, flying the RWD-4, but they had to withdraw on July 25, due to engine failure after an emergency landing in Spain. In September and October 1930, they won the 2nd Rally of South-Eastern Poland flying an RWD-2, and then won the 3rd Light Aircraft Contest flying an RWD-4. In October 1931, they won the 4th Touring Planes Contest flying the prototype RWD-5. On 7 August 1931, Zwirko and Stanisław Prauss attempted to break another altitude record flying an RWD-7, climbing to 5,996 m (19,672 ft.), but their effort was not recognized by the FAI due to a non-standard recording device. In December 1931, Zwirko became a training escadre commander at a Deblin aviation school. During April 1932, he was selected for the Polish team for the International Tourist Plane Competition Challenge 1932 and named Wigura as his mechanic and second pilot. They won the competition over the favored German teams, flying the new RWD-6. On 11 September 1932, while flying to Prague for an air meet, Zwirko and Wigura crashed and died in their RWD-6 in the forest near Cieszyn, Czechoslovakia, when the wing broke in a heavy storm. The two men were buried as heroes on the Avenue of the Meritorious in Powązki Cemetery, Warsaw.

Franciszek Zwirko, mechanic Stanislaw Wigura, and their RWD-6.

Challenge International de Tourisme 1934

The Challenge 1934 was the fourth and last FAI International Tourist Plane Contest and took place between 28 August and 16 September 1934 in Warsaw, Poland, as Polish pilot Franciszek Zwirko had won the previous 1932 Challenge, with Poland and the Polish Aero Club organizing the event. The challenge rules were announced in June 1933, and like the previous contest, it consisted of three parts: technical trials, a rally over Europe, and a maximum speed trial—but there were changes in details. Since one of the objectives of the challenges was to stimulate the development of tourist aircraft; aircraft performance and quality were emphasized, but pilot skills remained decisive.

Opening ceremony of the 1934 Challenge in Warsaw. Left: Polish team (high-wing RWD-9 and low-wing PZL.26), Center: Czechoslovakian team (one RWD-9 and two low-wing Aero A.200), Right: German team (Bf 108, Klemm Kl 36, Fieseler Fi 97). The Italian team had not arrived yet.

The opening ceremony was held at noon on 28 August 1934, at Mokotowskie Field, Warsaw. The Italian team arrived two hours late during the ceremony due to weather. During a previous air show a Polish PZL P.7a fighter crashed while performing aerobatics, with the pilot escaping with injuries. Because the challenge was to be more challenging only thirty-four aircraft (vs. forty-three in 1932) would eventually take part in 1934. Only four countries entered teams: Poland (twelve crews), now-Nazi Germany (thirteen crews), Italy (six crews), and Czechoslovakia (three crews). British aviator Walter MacPherson entered the contest with the Polish team. The French team of eight crews resigned from the contest because a development of a new aircraft, the Caudron C.500, had not finished in time, and its weight was too great.

Aircraft

The challenge was to be a tourist aircraft contest, so the competing aircraft had to be capable of carrying at least two persons aboard (pilot and mechanic), take off and land on a short field, and cover a distance with a good cruise speed. For this challenge all countries designed new aircraft especially to meet the contest's demands, the only exception being a single modified de Havilland Puss Moth flown by MacPherson. All the aircraft were monoplanes with three or four seats in an enclosed cabin, advanced flaps and slats wing design, and of mixed or metal construction.

Most aircraft were fast cantilever low-wing monoplanes: the German Fieseler Fi 97 (5), Messerschmitt Bf 108 (4), and Klemm Kl 36 (4); the Polish PZL.26 (5); and the Italian Pallavicino PS-1 (2); or braced low-wing monoplanes, such as the Czechoslovak Aero A.200 (2) and the Italian Breda Ba.39 (2) and Ba.42 (2). An exception were the basic seven high-wing braced monoplane RWD-9 aircraft of the Polish team, one of which was also flown by the Czech crew, and the Puss Moth. Of those, the Bf 108 and PS-1 had retractable landing gear. All the German aircraft, two Italian, and the Puss Moth exceeded the empty weight limit of 560.56 kg (1,235.8 lbs.) and had to have some unnecessary components removed.

The German aircraft had starting numbers from a range 12–26, the Italian 41–46, the Czechoslovak 51–54, and the Polish 61–81. The numbers were placed on the fuselage in a black square frame.

Fieseler Fi 97

After developing the F5 two-seat tourer/trainer, Fieseler was encouraged by the German Reichsluftfahrtministerium (RLM) to develop a special four-seat version (pilot and three passengers in an enclosed cabin) to participate in the 1934 Challenge International de Tourisme. The result, the Fi 97, designed by Kurt Arnolt, was a mixed-construction low-wing cantilever monoplane with a conventional tail unit. The fuselage had a fabric-covered steel tubing frame, while the wing structure was wood and was covered with fabric and plywood. The wings could be folded aft for storage or ground transport. The undercarriage and tailskid were fixed. Five Fi 97s were built; three aircraft were powered by the 250 hp air-cooled Hirth HM 8U inverted V8 engine and two by the 225 hp air-cooled Argus As 17A inverted six-cylinder inline engine. The plane had STOL capabilities attributable to the important design aspect of the wing's high-lift devices, enabling the aircraft to be flown at low speeds. The wing leading edge had Handley Page-type automatic slats covering more than half the span. The trailing edge had Fieseler-designed Ausrollflugel, a Fowler-type trailing edge flap that increased the wing area by approximately twenty

Fieseler Fi 97

percent. These high-lift structures allowed the aircraft to be controlled down to 58 km/h (36 mph), and were later utilized in construction of the famous Fieseler Fi 156 Storch. Five Fi 97s took part in the 1934 Challenge, during which Hans Seidemann took third place overall in an Argus-powered Fi 97, outdone only by two Polish RWD-9s. More meaningful was that all the Fieselers completed the challenge, placing third, ninth, twelfth, thirteenth, and sixteenth.

BF 108

The Messerschmitt Bf 108 Taifun is arguably one of the most influential touring aircraft designs of the 1930s, and set the era's standard which has not yet been bypassed in performance by most contemporary aircraft in its class. In 1933, the RLM requested Bayerische Flugzeug Werke (future Messerschmitt AG), Fieseler, and Klemm to develop a four-seat sports/recreation aircraft to expressly compete in the fourth Challenge International de Tourisme in 1934. After only seven months, the Messerschmitt design team was ready to present the M37, forerunner of the later Bf 108. The M37 (D-IBUM) made its first flight on 13 June 1934, powered by a 247 hp Hirth HM 8U inverted-V engine driving a three-blade propeller. It was then transferred to Rechlin for tests, but once it was returned to the Augsburg plant D-IBUM crashed during test flights, killing pilot Freiherr (Baron) von Dungern, and the project was about to be canceled. Four Bf 108s participated in the challenge but were not particularly successful, finishing fifth (Theo Osterkamp), sixth (Werner Junck), ninth (Fritz Morzik), and tenth (Carl Francke). Although it was outperformed by several other aircraft in the competition, its overall performance, very low fuel consumption rate, good handling, and superb take-off and landing characteristics would make it a popular choice for record flights. Soon after the first production aircraft began to come off the Augsburg assembly line several Bf 108s had set endurance records. The Bf 108A first flew in 1934, followed by the Bf 108B in 1935. The Bf 108B used the Argus As 10 air-cooled inverted V8 engine. On 13 August 1935, Elly Beinhorn, who gave the aircraft its nickname Taifun (Typhoon), flew a modified Bf 108B-0 3,750 km (2,330 miles) from Berlin to Istanbul in only 13.5 hours. The Bf 108 was too expensive for flying schools and clubs, but during 1936, it became a success for Messerschmitt when the Luftwaffe selected it as a liaison aircraft. Seven were produced in 1936, and then 175 during 1938. The popular woman flyer Elly Beinhorn further enhanced the aircraft's reputation when she finished second in an international competition in Egypt. Between 1934 and 1942, 529 Bf 108s were manufactured in Germany. The Bf 108 was used during WWII as a liaison and staff transport aircraft. In February 1942, its manufacture was moved to SNCAN facilities in France, which then produced 115 Nord 1000 models (modified Bf 108D-2) before France was freed by the Allies. SNCAN continued to manufacture the Nord Bf 108 versions until 1962, by which time 885 of all variants were probably built.

Klemm Kl 36

Following the success of the three-seat, well-glazed enclosed cabin touring plane Klemm Kl 32 in the 1932 Challenge International de Tourisme, the company was ordered by the RLM to develop another aircraft to take part in the 1934 Challenge. Due to changes of contest rules, designer Friedrich Fechher had to devise a more modern four-seat version of the Kl 32 with better performance and better STOL capabilities. Fechner's new streamlined four-seat Kl 36 met these goals and was the fastest of all Klemm aircraft. Four of the first series (Kl 36A) were built (two powered with 225 hp air-cooled Argus As 17A inverted six-cylinder in-line engines and two with 250 hp air-cooled Hirth HM8U inverted V8 engines). It was a mixed-

Theo Ostercamp's Bf 108

Klemm Kl36 with Wolf Hirth and his invented engine

construction low-wing cantilever monoplane with a conventional tail unit. Its fuselage steel frame was canvas covered, while its three-part wing (that folded rearward and was fitted with slats and flaps), outer parts of the wings, and tail surfaces were wooden and plywood covered. The plane had a fixed tailskid landing gear. Later, eight additional Kl 36Bs were built powered with several different engines. Four Kl 36As competed in the 1934 Challenge, but none completed the rally over Europe phase. Fritz Morzik, a winner of two challenges, had to withdraw due to a fuel pump breakdown, but unofficially continued and finished the rally. During the technical portion they obtained good results, but they generally proved inferior to the Fieseler Fi 97. During WWII Klemm Kl 36s served as liaison aircraft in the Luftwaffe.

PZL.26

In 1934, the Polish Ministry of Defense ordered the PZL works to specifically design an aircraft for the upcoming 1934 Challenge International de Tourisme. The PZL.26 was a development of the PZL.19 built for the 1932 Challenge. Like its predecessor, the PZL.26 was designed by Jerzy Dąbrowski and Franciszek Misztal as an all-metal cantilever, low-wing monoplane with a fixed landing gear and a closed canopy of conventional layout. It retained the PZL.19's wings and tail with minor changes. Wings were equipped with automatic slats and split flaps and folded rearward. The fuselage, wings, and landing gear were more streamlined and strengthened. The major change was to be the more advanced and more powerful US-made 265 hp Menasco Buccaneer engine, which would prove to be a disappointment. Five aircraft were built in 1934 and one prototype for static trials. All five PZL.26s participated in the challenge, but the 9,538 km (5,236 mile) Rally over Europe seemed to overtax their engines, as three aircraft failed to finish the rally due to engine breakdowns, one placed eleventh, and the other seventeenth place (by coincidence, these results were similar to those of PZL.19s two years earlier). Then one had an engine fail during a maximum speed trial and the aircraft showed itself to have large fuel consumption resulting from their high power output. Because of unreliable engines most PZL.26s were not used in Polish sports aviation after the challenge.

PZL 26

Technical Trials

The technical evaluation of aircraft construction began on 29 August, and was comprised of the evaluation details of the 1932 tourist aircraft trials. Technical evaluation continued until 4 September, with the Bf 108s receiving the most points (450–452),followed by the Pallavicino PS-1 (438 points), the Fi 97s (428–431 points), the Aero A.200 (429 points), and the RWD-9 (427 points). The other scores were the Klemm Kl 36 with 394–407 points, the PZL.26 with 383 points, the Puss Moth with 373 points, and the Bredas with 323–346 points.

On 3–4 September, the short take-off trials were held, with the best participant being Czech Vojtech Zacek, taking off from the closest distance of 74.5 m (244 ft.) in an Aero A.200, then Jerzy Bajan (RWD-9) and Jan Ambrus flying another A.200. The Polish RWD-9s and PZL.26s and the German Fi 97s also performed well, while the Italians and most other German aircraft had mediocre performances. The winning 74.5 m (244 ft.) was much improved over the 1932 mark of 91.6 m (301 ft.).

On 4–5 September, the short landing trial followed, with 75 m (246 ft.) achieved by German Hans Seidemann (Fi 97). The best result from the previous challenge was 92.4 m (303 ft.).

On 5 September, the fuel consumption trial was flown on a 594 km (369 mile) closed circuit, with three Bf 108s scoring 86–95 points, then five Poles with 73–79 points.

A minimal speed trial began on 31 August, but it had to be continued on 2 September due to weather. Pole Jerzy Bajan, flying the RWD-9, was the slowest with a speed of 54.14 km/h (33.64 mph).

From 1–7 September, the quick folding of wings trials were held and the first seven results were RWD-9s with 36 points, followed by four Italians.

One German and one Italian crew damaged their aircraft during technical trials (Bf 108 and PS-1) and had to withdraw, which was the best ratio of crews to complete the technical trials of the previous three challenges. Generally, the top places were taken by RWD-9s (six of the top ten: first, second, third, sixth, seventh, and tied for ninth) and Fi 97s (three of the top ten: fourth, fifth, and eighth), while Bf 108s, Kl 36s, and PZL.26s were average, with the Italian aircraft finishing at the end of the technical trials results list. Three Poles, all flying RWD-9s, finished in the top three places: Jerzy Bajan (994 points), Tadeusz Karpinski (954 points), and Stanisław Płonczynski (953 points).

1934 Rally over Europe

The second part of the challenge was a route that was far longer and more difficult than in previous contests at 9,537.4 km (5,926 miles) over Europe and northern Africa, for the first time flying from Warsaw, Konigsberg, Berlin, Cologne, Brussels, Paris, Bordeaux, Pau, Madrid, Seville, Casablanca, Meknes, Sidi Bel Abbes, Algiers (stage waypoint), Biskra, Tunis, Palermo, Naples, Rome, Rimini, Zagreb, Vienna, Brno, Prague, Katowice, Lwow, Wilno, and back to Warsaw. There were also eight checkpoints. Point awards were made first for a cruise speed on a whole route, and then regularity of flight. Three nights, not including the appointed airfields, or a cruise speed below 130 km/h (80.8 mph) would demand disqualification.

The rally began on a rainy 7 September, between 0500 and 0530. The Bf 108s, using their speed advantage, were first to arrive in Berlin. That day, the twenty-four fastest crews (ten Poles, eight Germans, three Czechs, and three Italians) arrived in Paris, flying 1,752.4 km (1,088 miles). German Wolfgang Stein (Kl 36) and the Italian team's captain Ambrogio Colombo (Ba-42) had to land and withdraw due to engine malfunctions. Several other crews had similar problems but were able to repair them.

During the next day, many crews who started early, especially the fast-flying Bf 108s, had problems locating Bordeaux airfield due to heavy fog and had forced landings, lowering their cruise speed. Ernst Kruger's Klemm Kl 36 was damaged during a forced landing and had to withdraw. Fourteen crews reached Seville and nine remained in Madrid, while the last two crews remained in Bordeaux. Two Poles (Andrzej Wlodarkiewicz and Szczepan Grzeszczyk, PZL.26s) flew as far as Casablanca (3,715.2 km/2,308.5 miles).

On 9 September, all remaining crews reached Africa, with Andrzej Wlodarkiewicz and three Bf 108s in the lead. Also that day eighteen crews reached Algiers (nine Poles, six Germans, and three Czechs), flying 4,774 km (2,966.4 miles). The last two crews reached Meknes and several crews withdrew that day. Fritz Morzik (the winner of the 1929 and 1930 Challenges flying Kl 36) made three forced landings before Algiers due to a faulty fuel pump and Szczepan Grzeszczyk's PZL.26's engine failed, and he made a forced landing before Sidi Bel Abbes. German Kraft Eberhard (Kl 36) withdrew in Spain due to wing damage, Pole Tadeusz Karpinski (RWD-9) withdrew in Seville because of low cruise speed, and Italian Pierro de Angeli left because of illness.

On 10 September, the remaining pilots reached Algiers, marking twenty-four crews that completed the first part of the rally. Pole Stefan Florjanowicz (RWD-9) had to withdraw there due to engine problems.

After a short rest twenty-three crews left Algiers on 11 September and arrived in Tunis that day.

On 12 September, the crews flew over the Mediterranean for Palermo, with the over water flight safeguarded by the Italian Navy and French floatplanes. After one Italian pilot withdrew due to engine damage twenty-two crews arrived in Rome that day.

On 13 September, the weather was bad and all but two crews reached Prague (7,924 km/4,923.8 miles). The fastest pilot that day was German Theo Osterkamp (Bf 108), but the other two Bf 108 pilots had forced landings near Trieste due to weather and spent the night in Zagreb, which lowered their cruise speed.

On 14 September, sixteen crews led by Pole Ignacy Giedgowd (PZL-26) finished the rally at the Warsaw start and were greeted by large crowds. Besides Giedgowd there were four other Poles, six Germans, three Czechs, and two Italians. That day two pilots had bad luck just before finishing: the fastest Polish pilot, Andrzej Wlodarkiewicz (PZL-26), suffered engine problems and had to land before Lwow and withdrew; Walter MacPherson (Puss Moth) also withdrew due to the same cause before Lwow.

On 15 September, the last three crews (Werner Junck and Karl Francke flying Bf 108s and Piotr Dudzinski flying a PZL.26) reached Warsaw. The last pilot to withdraw was Jan Balcer (PZL.26), due to compressor damage before Wilno. Fritz Morzik (Kl 36), Tadeusz Karpinski (RWD-9), and Andrzej Wlodarkiewicz (PZL.26) finished in Warsaw that day after repairing their aircraft, flying off the contest.

Only nineteen crews out of thirty-two completed the rally. All Fieseler Fi 97s completed the rally. In spite of their highest maximum cruise speeds, the Bf 108s were hindered in placing higher by low cruise speeds in other stages of the rally. Best results were obtained by pilots, who managed to maintain a good cruise speed during the whole rally. All participants who completed the rally scored a maximum amount of 160 points for regularity, spending nights only on appointed airfields. The results of the Rally were:

Georg Pasewaldt	Germany/Fi-97	215.55 km/h	880 pts
Ignacy Giedgowd	Poland/PZL.26	213.33 km/h	880 pts
Jan Ambrus	Czech/Aero A.200	211.12 km/h	880 pts
Piotr Dudzinski	Poland/PZL.26	211.05 km/h	880 pts
Theo Osterkamp	Germany/Bf 108	208.74 km/h	875 pts
Hans Seidemann	Germany/Fi 97	208.28 km/h	874 pts
Stanisław Płonczynski	Poland/RWD-9	206.89 km/h	868 pts
Jerzy Bajan	Poland/RWD-9	205.15 km/h	861 pts
Jan Anderle	Czech/RWD-9	203.69 km/h	855 pts
Kurt Bayer	Germany/Fi 97	203.47 km/h	854 pts

Maximum Speed Trial

On 16 September, the last trial of the challenge was a maximum speed trial covering a 297 km (184.5 mile) triangular course at Mokotowskie airfield in Warsaw. Due to the handicapping system contestants took off in order of their general classification with proper intervals, and the number of points given in the speed trial meant the first pilot over the finish line would be the winner of the trial. Each km/h above 210 km/h (130.5 mph) was to be awarded one point. The fastest pilots flew three German Bf 108As, with Theo Osterkamp in the lead (81 points) at 291 km/h (180.8 mph), followed by Karl Francke with 77 points (287 km/h/178.3 mph) and Werner Junck with 73 points (283 km/h/175.9 mph). The next four places were taken by Polish RWD-9s: Stanisław Plonczynski, Jan Buczynski, Jerzy Bajan, and Henryk Skrzypinski

Final Results and Closing

A closing ceremony was held soon after the maximum speed test on 16 September. The first prize in the challenge was to be 100,000 French francs, the second 40,000 FF, the third 20,000 FF, and the fourth 10,000 FF; fifteen other crews would get 6,000 FF. Of the nineteen finishers, six were Poles (placing first, second, seventh, eleventh, fifteenth, and seventeenth), seven were German (placing third, fifth, sixth, ninth, tenth, twelfth, and sixteenth), two were Czechs (placing fourth and ninth), and two were Italian (placing eighteenth and nineteenth). Of the nineteen finishing aircraft, five were RWD-9S, five were Fi 97s, three were Bf 108As, and two were Aero A.200s. The winners were the Polish crew of pilot Jerzy Bajan and mechanic Gustaw Pokrzywka, flying the new RWD-6 and winning the competition over favored German and other teams. Their success was not only a result of their aviation skills, but also of the new technical features of their Polish-designed RWD-9.

1934 overall winner Jersy Bajan (L) with his mechanic standing behind him pose with Marshal Jozef Pilsudski (C), the military dictator of Poland.

1934 FINAL RESULTS

Jerzy Bajan	Poland/RDW-9S	1,896 points (994+861+41)*
Stanisław Płonczynski	Poland/RDW-9S	1,866 points (953+868+45)
Hans Seidemann	Nazi/Fi 97	1,846 points (939+874+33)
Jan Ambrus	Czech/Aero A.200	1,822 points (915+880+27)
Theo Osterkamp	Nazi/Bf 108A	1,810 points (854+875+81)
Werner Junck	Nazi/Bf 108A	1,806 points (895+838+73)
Jan Buczynski	Poland/RWD-9S	1,800 points (920+836+44)
Jan Anderle	Czech/RWD-9S	1,797 points (915+855+27)
Georg Pasewaldt	Nazi/Fi 97	1,704 points (885+880+29)
Karl Francke	Nazi/Bf 108A	1,792 points (899+816+77)

**Points: Technical+Rally+Speed*

EPILOGUE

Due to their victory, Poland had a right to organize the next challenge in 1936, but decided not to because of financial reasons. The FAI proposed that other countries organize the contest, but Germany, Italy, and France declined. The 1934 Challenge remained the last and the Polish Aero Club was given a right to retain a transitory cup.

PART 2:
BRITISH LONG-RANGE AIRCRAFT

1
BRITISH WORLD WAR I LONG-RANGE AIRCRAFT

BRITISH HANDLEY PAGE GIANTS

In the four years of war aircraft design and technology leapt forward, with planes becoming larger, more sophisticated, and more lethal. During the war biplane bombers with two large wings became bigger, able to carry more bombs over a longer distance. Initially bombs were dropped from an aircraft by hand and aimed by eye, but by the end of the war bombsights had been developed, and the bomber became more accurate and more feared as a weapon of war. The British RAF introduced two large Handley Page bombers: the early Type O and the later V/1500 night bomber.

HANDLEY PAGE TYPE O

The Handley Page Type O biplane bomber was used by Britain during WWI; at the time it was the largest aircraft built in the UK and one of the largest in the world. The Rolls-Royce *Eagle* powered Type O was built in two major versions: the Handley Page O/100 introduced in 1916 (forty-two built) and the Handley Page O/400 introduced in late 1918 (554 built). The upgraded O/400 had a 100 ft. wing span and wing area of 1,648 sq. ft., a length of almost 63 ft., and a height of 22 ft. It could carry 1,650 lbs. of bombs up to 700 miles, the heaviest bomb load used by British services during WWI.

HANDLEY PAGE V/1500

The Rolls-Royce Eagle powered Handley Page V/1500 was the last British heavy bomber to be developed during WWI. The V/1500 resembled a larger version of Handley Page's earlier O/100 and O/400 bombers, and was designed to bomb Berlin from bases in the UK. This long-range night bomber of 1918 was the first British bomber with four engines. The biplane had a 126 ft. wing span and wing area of 2,800 sq. ft., a length of 64 ft. and a height of 23 ft., and was able to carry up to 7,500 lbs. up to 1,300 miles. Of 225 ordered in 1918, only thirty-five were built before the Armistice and sixty in all.

1919: ENGLAND TO INDIA AND TO COMBAT

On 13 December 1918, V/1500 *HMA Old Carthusian* was readied to fly the first flight from England to India. The Handley Page was to be flown by Maj. A.C.S. MacLaren and Capt. Robert Halley, accompanied by Brig.Gen. N.D.K. McEwan (later AVM McEwan), who would be the new air officer commanding in India. Also aboard were Flight Sgt. Smith and Sgt. Crockett (fitters) and Sgt. Brown (rigger). The long flight via Rome, Malta, Cairo, and Baghdad included one leg of almost 800 miles over water and another non-stop stage of 1,000 miles from Cairo to Baghdad, finally arriving

Handley Page Type O

Handley Page V/1500 Atlantic

in Karachi on 15 January 1919. This V/1500 would be the first to see combat during May 1919, when it played a key role in ending the Third Anglo-Afghan insurrection. On 24 May 1919, Halley flew *Old Carthusian* through the Khyber Pass in pre-dawn darkness with observer Lt. Ted Villiers and Sgts. Smith, Crockett, and Brown. The V/1500 was armed with a bomb load of four 112 lb. and sixteen 20-lb. bombs intended to bomb the royal palace of Amanullah Khan in Kabul. The bombs were released from an altitude of 700 ft. and did little damage, but with the resulting panic the Khan surrendered, with this single bombing raid credited with ending the war.

Maj. A.C.S. MacLaren and the V/1500, HMA *Old Carthusian*

2
BRITISH LONG-RANGE AIRCRAFT AND FLIGHTS OF THE 1920s

VICKERS VIMY

Vickers Limited Chief Designer Reginald Pierson designed a twin-engine biplane bomber (Vickers F.B.27) to meet a requirement for a night bomber capable of bombing targets in Germany. On 14 August 1917, a contract was awarded for three Vimy prototypes named after the Battle of Vimy Ridge. The rapid production of the prototypes had the first one flying on 30 November 1917. The pilot and navigator sat in an open cockpit at the front of the Vimy. The bomber had a wingspan of 68.1 ft. and a wing area of 1,330 sq. ft., a length of 43.7 ft., a height of 15.7 ft., an empty weight of 7,104 lbs., and a maximum take-off weight of 10,884 lbs. After successful flight testing 776 were ordered before the end of WWI. Due to engine supply problems, the prototype Vimys were tested with several different engines, but the 360 hp Rolls-Royce Eagle VIII engine was selected. The bomber's performance with these engines was a maximum speed of 100 mph, a ceiling of 7,000 ft., and a range of 2,134 miles.

By October 1918, only three Vimys had been delivered to the RAF before the end of the war. It only reached full service status in July 1919, with 58 Squadron in Egypt, after which it formed the main heavy bomber force of the RAF for much of the 1920s. The Vimy performed as a front line RAF bomber in the Middle East and in the United Kingdom 1919–1925, when it was replaced by the Vickers Virginia. The Vimy is best known for its use in many pioneering record setting flights.

Vickers Vimy

DAILY MAIL TRANS-ATLANTIC CHALLENGE

In 1913, the *Daily Mail* offered a then-mammoth prize of £10,000 to the first pilot to cross the Atlantic, but before anyone could make the attempt WWI interrupted and the competition was suspended. At that time it was doubtful there were any aircraft capable of making the crossing. In late 1918, the competition resumed, but specified the flight must be made in less than seventy-two hours (another caveat was that no teams of "enemy origin" could enter, meaning no Huns!). By the Armistice, aviation technology had advanced exponentially and a trans-Atlantic flight was entirely conceivable.

In Spring 1919, four contenders arrived at St. Johns, Newfoundland, to compete for the £10,000 prize:

1) Australian pilot Harry Hawker and Scottish navigator Kenneth Mackenzie-Grieve
2) British aviators Frederick Raynham (pilot) and C.W.F. Morgan (navigator)
3) British aviators John Alcock (pilot) and Arthur Whitten Brown (navigator)
4) Handley Page Company Group, led by British pilot Adm. Mark Kerr

18 May 1919: Harry Hawker and Kenneth Mackenzie-Grieve: Sopwith *Atlantic* Biplane

Harry Hawker was one of Britain's iconic aviators, and later designer/manufacturers. In 1913, he set an endurance record of 8:20 hours; set a new altitude record of 11,700 ft.; and later set an air speed record of 92 mph. Hawker is also credited with discovering the technique of recovering from a spin, which was previously always fatal. During WWI Hawker was the chief test pilot and designer for Sopwith.

On 18 May 1919, Hawker and navigator Kenneth Mackenzie-Grieve took off from Mount Pearl, Newfoundland, in their Sopwith *Atlantic* biplane. After take-off, the Sopwith's landing gear was jettisoned to decrease weight and improve airspeed. After 14-½ hours into the flight, the engine steadily overheated and Hawks changed course to fly along shipping lanes to find a ship to ditch near. They were able to find the Danish freighter *Mary* and Hawker expertly ditched safely on a rough sea; an hour and a half later they were rescued. The *Mary* was not equipped with salvage gear, so the Sopwith was left floating in the Atlantic. Since the *Mary* had no wireless communication, it was not until 25 May, when the steamer reached Scotland, that the waiting world—which presumed they had perished—was informed they were safe. The *Atlantic* was found afloat and recovered by the US steamer *Lake Charleville*. King George V announced that he would decorate both men with the Air Force Cross, the first ever personal investitures. The *Daily Mail* acknowledged Hawker as the first pilot to fly over 1,000 miles of water without touching down and awarded him a £5,000 prize.

In September 1920, Sopwith Aviation was liquidated because of fears the British government would scrutinize the wartime aircraft production contracts of companies like Sopwith and impose a ruinous retroactive tax on them. Harry Hawker, Tom Sopwith, Fred Sigrist, and Bill Eyre then formed a new company, H.G. Hawker Engineering (renamed Hawker Aircraft in 1933). Hawker was killed on 12 July 1921, when his Nieuport Goshawk crashed near Hendon Aerodrome while practicing for the Aerial Derby.

Harry Hawker (L) and Kenneth Grieve with their Sopwith Atlantic Biplane

19 May 1919: Frederick Raynham and C.W.F. Morgan: Martinsyde Biplane

Pilot Maj. Frederick Raynham and navigator Maj. C.W.F. Morgan arrived in Newfoundland on 10 May to prepare their single-engine Martinsyde Raynor biplane for the trans-Atlantic attempt. At the time negotiations between Sopwith and the post office for carrying mail on the first aerial trans-Atlantic flight were completed. When the Hawker attempt failed, Raynham and Morgan became the picks to win the prize. On 19 May, the day after Harry Hawker left, Raynham and Morgan took

Frederick Raynham (L), C.W.F. Morgan, and their Martinsyde Biplane

off from Quidi Vidi, Newfoundland, but their Raynor flew several hundred yards and crashed into the ocean with neither occupant badly injured.

After the crash, Morgan returned to England to be replaced by Lt. C.H. Biddlesbombe on 14 June. By the time the Martinsyde's repairs were completed, Alcock and Brown had already made the first successful non-stop flight and Raynham then focused on surpassing their time of 16:12 and carrying the mail bag to England. Raynham took off at 1515 on 17 July, but flew only about sixty yards before the Martinsyde's undercarriage struck a ridge and tipped over into the ground; it was totaled, but both men were only slightly injured, and on 21 July left for England by ship. Raynham returned to England with the bag of mail, which was finally posted on 7 January 1920. The two Martinsyde attempts flew only a few hundred yards, and their attempt to fly trans-Atlantic ended as a dismal failure, but provided some of the world's rarest and most expensive air mail stamps.

14 June 1919: John Alcock and Arthur Whitten Brown: Vickers Vimy

Englishmen John Alcock and Arthur Brown were military pilots in the war and both were taken prisoner. When Alcock and Brown arrived, so many competing teams had arrived earlier that they had problems finding a suitable field for their modified Vimy, which was still aboard a steamship sailing from England. By the time their Vimy arrived in Newfoundland on 26 May, two aircraft (Hawker and Raynham) had attempted the trans-Atlantic flight, but both flights ended in crashes. Alcock and Brown procured a field to assemble their Vimy that arrived in thirteen crates, but then found the field was not long enough for the aircraft and its heavy load of fuel to leave the ground. During the two weeks it took to assemble the Vimy Alcock found a field long enough, but only after many people worked to clear rocks and fill ditches to make it smooth enough for use as a runway.

After waiting a few days for good weather they decided to fuel the Vimy at its new field and make an attempt for the first non-stop crossing of the Atlantic. (Note: Two weeks before Alcock and Brown's flight, the first trans-Atlantic flight had been made by a US Navy NC-4 flying boat commanded by Lt.Cdr. Albert Read, who flew from NAS Rockaway, New York, to Plymouth, England, with a crew of five. Their flight took more than twenty-three days with six stops, thus making it ineligible for the *Daily Mail* prize, since it required more than seventy-two consecutive hours.) Alcock and Brown aborted their first attempted take-off when the landing gear failed under the added weight of 865 gallons of fuel in the extra tanks. The repair was quick and the two took off from Lester's Field during the afternoon of 14 June, powered by a pair of 360 hp 12-cylinder Rolls-Royce engines.

Soon after take-off Brown radioed, "All well and started," but this would be their first and last radio message, as the wind-powered generator then malfunctioned and the two were without radio contact throughout the duration of the flight. Being an experienced navigator, Brown was able to determine their position using a sextant and a drift-bearing plate, but soon fog covered the sea and he was unable to determine their drift; then a haze developed and he was unable to use the sextant to determine their location. At nightfall Alcock climbed above the clouds and Brown was able to use the stars to fix on their position. Soon the Vimy entered another cloud bank and the airspeed indicator malfunctioned, so Alcock did not recognize that the Vimy was slowing down to a point that it eventually stalled and went into a spin. After they spiraled 4,000 ft. toward the North Atlantic the aircraft broke out of the clouds and Alcock was

FAR LEFT / John Alcock (L) and Arthur Brown

Fueling the Alcock/ Brown Vimy in Newfoundland.

able to recover just above the waves and continue flying east toward Ireland. The weather continued to be poor, with rain turning into snow, so Brown had to stand up in the open cockpit to clear ice and snow from the instrument sensors outside the cockpit. Eventually the ice covered the air intake of one of the engines, so Alcock had to shut the engine down before it was destroyed by backfiring. Alcock descended into warmer air, where he hoped the ice would melt before they hit the water. At around 500 feet they entered warmer, clear weather, and were able to restart the engine. Less than half an hour after restarting the engine land was seen; they had reached Ireland and decided to land. Alcock mistook a bog for a smooth field, but made a soft crash landing at 0840 near Clifton, Galway County, completing the first non-stop flight across the Atlantic. They had completed the 1,880 mile trans-Atlantic flight in 15:57 hours at an average speed of 118.5 mph to complete the longest distance ever flown by man. Alcock and Brown were awarded the £10,000 prize money, plus an additional £3,000 in London by the British Secretary of State for War and Air, Winston Churchill, who hailed the flight as "a triumph of man over nature." The two pilots were later knighted by King George V. The flight is still considered one of the most significant and dramatic in aviation history, and would not be repeated in an airplane for eight years. On 2–3 July 2005, pilots Steve Fosset and Mark Rebholz repeated the Alcock-Brown flight flying a replica Vickers Vimy. (Note: John Alcock was killed six months later while flying a Vickers Viking flying boat to Paris.)

5 July 1919: R.Adm. Mark Kerr: Handley Page V/1500

R.Adm. Mark Kerr had the fourteen-ton Handley Page *Atlantic* bomber shipped from Britain to Newfoundland in 105 crates by boat, then sent to Harbour Grace by train and wheeled to its reassembly point. The reassembly lagged interminably, and once assembled the huge bomber encountered persistent mechanical problems. Finally, on 14 June 1919, Kerr was informed that Alcock and Brown had successfully completed the first trans-Atlantic flight. Once the aircraft was ready, the *Atlantic* proceeded to New York from Canada on 5 July 1919, but was forced to crash land in Parrsboro, Nova Scotia. Repair took most of the summer, after which the *Atlantic* continued to New York on 9 October 1919, carrying with it the first airmail from Canada to the United States. The *Atlantic* then flew a series of demonstration flights in Canada and the US, but crashed near Cleveland; the crew survived, but the aircraft was written off.

R.Adm. Mark Kerr's Handley Page V/1500 Atlantic

DIRIGIBLE R34

The R33 class of British rigid airships were built for the Royal Naval Air Service during WWI, but were not completed until after the end of hostilities, by which time the RNAS had become part of the Royal Air Force. The first airship (R33) served successfully for ten years. The only other airship in the R33 Class (R34) made her first flight on 14 March 1919, and then made her first endurance flight of fifty-six hours over the Baltic 17–20 June, after which the RNAS decided to attempt the first round trip Atlantic crossing under the command of Maj. George Scott. R34 was 643 ft. long, 79 ft. in diameter, had a volume of 1.95 million cu. ft., and was propelled by five 275 hp Sunbeam Maori engines to carry its normal crew of twenty-six. The gondola appeared to be a single 50 ft. long unit, but was comprised of two sections separated by a narrow gap, intended to prevent vibration from the engine affecting the radio equipment. Incorporated in the forward section were a control room with the steering and elevator wheels and the gas valve. A ladder connected the control cabin with the long keel corridor that ran almost the entire length of the ship. R34 had not been planned as a passenger carrier, and extra accommodations were made by slinging hammocks in the keel walkway; hot food was prepared using a plate welded to an engine exhaust pipe. A month after the Alcock-Brown flight, dirigible R34 departed East Fortune, Scotland, on 2 July 1919, carrying a crew of thirty experienced RAF men flying in a naval airship, plus a stowaway, and a cat. The 3,130 nautical mile route began in East Fortune and continued via Newfoundland to New York. The admiralty sent the battle cruisers HMS *Renown* and *Tiger* to provide weather forecasts along the route. The dirigible completed the flight at 0900 on 6 July 1919, in Mineola, New York, in 108:12 hours. Maj. E.M. Pritchard parachuted from the airship to the ground to supervise landing operations. Just before midnight on 10 July 1919, R34 departed New York for its return to England, arriving in Pulham after a flight of 75:03 hours that was aided by tailwinds to complete the first round-trip crossing of the Atlantic by air. Despite enthusiastic coverage by the press, the British military establishment downplayed the event. On 27 January 1921, R34 flew into a hillside during the night and lost two propellers; it flew back out to sea using its two remaining engines and was able to return to base. Strong winds made it impossible to get the airship back into her shed and she was tied down outside for the night, but by morning further damage had occurred and R34 was written off and scrapped.

Dirigible *R34*

THE 1919 AIR RACE: ENGLAND TO AUSTRALIA

In March 1919, the Australian government announced a £10,000 prize for the first successful flight from England to Australia. Only Australians were allowed to participate, and their aircraft had to be manufactured in the British Empire. At the time 1,000 or so Australian airmen were in Britain awaiting repatriation to Australia, but because of the danger involved and little interest in backing the flight only five entries were accepted by the RAC.

Ross and Keith Smith: Vickers Vimy

The winning crew comprised the Smith brothers (Ross and Keith) and their mechanics Sgt. James Bennett and Sgt. Wallace Shiers, flying a postwar Vickers Vimy powered by two 360 hp Rolls-Royce Eagle VIII engines. Ross Smith, the organizer of the venture, had piloted Lawrence of Arabia in the Middle East and was able to use his influence to obtain the superior Vimy for the race; he was also able to use his connections to set up a reliable series of fuel stops vital for its eventual success.

The Vimy embarked from Hounslow Heath Aerodrome, England, on 12 November 1919, three weeks after the Sopwith *Wallaby* contestant. The trip was not without its mechanical problems, but mechanics Bennett and Shiers did a yeoman's job in solving them. Taking off and landing proved to be a problem. Bennett tied himself by rope to the Vimy and ran alongside the aircraft, holding the tail down to help get the plane's nose up for take-off. On another instance he left the cockpit as the plane touched down and backed along the top of the fuselage to stabilize the tail section. The Vimy arrived in Darwin, on Australia's north coast, via Singapore and Batavia on 10 December, after covering 11,130 miles in just less than 28 days, of which 135:55 hours were flying time. However, it would take another eighty days to reach Melbourne due to mechanical problems that kept the Vimy grounded at one point for about six weeks. After dividing the £10,000 prize money into four equal shares both Smith brothers were immediately knighted. Ross Smith was killed as a passenger while testing a Vickers Viking amphibian aircraft that crashed in Byfleet soon after taking off from Brooklands, England, on 13 April 1922. The Vimy is on display at the Adelaide, Australia, Airport.

The Smith brothers (Ross and Keith), their two mechanics, and their Vimy

Four other aircraft taking part in the race crashed:

Sopwith *Wallaby*: On 21 October 1919, pilot Capt. George Campbell Matthews and mechanic Sgt. Thomas Kay left Hounslow Heath, and began a journey that encountered numerous weather delays, a cracked cylinder, and even imprisonment as suspected Bolshevik spies in Yugoslavia. Finally, on 17 April 1920, the *Wallaby* crashed while landing on Bali, with Matthews slightly injured; the *Wallaby* was unable to continue.

Alliance P.2 *Endeavour*: On 13 November 1919, Lts. Roger Douglas and J.S.L. Ross took off from Hounslow Heath in an Alliance named *Endeavour* that would crash only ten minutes after take-off, with Ross killed in the crash and Douglas dying soon after of his injuries.

Blackburn *Kangaroo*: On 21 November 1919, the *Kangaroo* took off from Hounslow Heath piloted by Lt. V. Rendle and a crew of three. Once over the English Channel engine problems occurred and the aircraft landed in France. After repairs were made the flight continued, but engine problems also continued. On 8 December 1919, the aircraft crash landed on Crete with the crew uninjured, but the aircraft was unable to continue.

Martinsyde *Raynor*: On 5 December 1919, Capt. Cedric Howell and Lt. George Fraser left London in a single-engine

Martinsyde *Raynor*, an aircraft very similar to the Sopwith Martinsyde. On 9 December, the aircraft disappeared near Corfu; the wreckage and Howell's body were found offshore, but Fraser's body was never found.

Airco/De Havilland DH9 Leaves Late and Requires Seven Months to Finish

A sixth aircraft, flown by Ray Parer and John McIntosh, took off after the race had already been won and arrived in Australia seven months later. Parer and McIntosh received backing from Scottish whisky magnate Peter Dawson and purchased an aging single-engine Airco/De Havilland DH9 *PD* (for Peter Dawson) biplane for the trip. They left Hounslow, England, on 8 January 1920, on their mishap-filled 237-day adventure, arriving in Darwin on 2 August, and finishing in Melbourne on 31 August. Soon after leaving England the first of their numerous forced landings was made, and then they struggled from one misadventure to another, including a multitude of insults to their Airco: broken and damaged propellers, wings, fuselages, undercarriages, and tail skids. While in Rangoon they cobbled two old automobile radiators together to replace the aircraft radiator. Their engine caught fire twice, a fierce down-draught almost forced them into the sizzling crater of Italy's Mount Vesuvius, and during a landing in the Syrian Desert they had to fight off Arab tribesmen. Finances became a major problem, so while in Calcutta they flew advertising flights, adorning their aircraft with announcements. On their way from Darwin to Sydney they overturned the *PD*, totaling it, and had to finish the flight in loaner aircraft. (The Airco was restored and is on exhibit at the Australian War Memorial.) During their epic journey they made the first single-engine flight from England to Australia, the first single-engine flight across the eastern Mediterranean Sea to Egypt, the first single-engine crossing of the Syrian Desert, and the first such flight from Europe to Calcutta.

Ray Parer (L) and John McIntosh

BRITISH LONG-RANGE AIRCRAFT AND FLIGHTS OF THE MID-1920S

By the mid-1920s, the RAF had started a series of long-range flights designed to explore routes and facilities, and to test the feasibility of rapid reinforcement in case of trouble in their far-flung colonies.

KING'S CUP

As aircraft became more diverse, handicapping was adopted by Britain exclusively to level the playing field. The King's Cup Race was an annual British handicapped cross-country air race established by King George V as an incentive for the development of light aircraft and engine design; it was organized by the Royal Aero Club Records Racing and Rally Association. Along with the Schneider Trophy, it was one of the most prized trophies of the British air racing season. The event was only open to British pilots, but did include commonwealth pilots. The length of the course ranged from 540 miles (1927) to as much as 1,608 miles (1925). It was usually held in July, but also once in August, and three times in September. It was first contested on 8 September 1922, and the 1939 Cup was suspended after the 2 July 1938 race due to WWII. There were no races during WWII (1939–45), and the race would not resume until 1949.

KING'S CUP 1922–1938

Date	Course Miles	# Starters	Winning Pilot	Aircraft type	Average Speed
1922	810	22	Frank Bernard	Airco DH.4A	123.5
1923	794	17	Frank Courtney	AW Siskin II	149
1924	950	10	Alan Cobham	DH.50	106.5
1925	1,608	14	Frank Bernard	AW Siskin II	141.7
1926	1,464	14	Hubert Broad	DH.60 Moth	90.4
1927	540	16	W.L. Hope	DH.60 Moth	92.8
1928	1,097	36	W.L. Hope	DH.60 Moth	105.5

King's Cup continued on following page

1929	1,170	41	R.L.R. Atcherley	Gloster Grebe II	150
1930	753.25	88	Ms. Winifred Brown	Avro Avian III	102.75
1931	983	40	E.C.T. Edwards	Blackburn Bluebird III	117.8
1932	1,223	42	W.L. Hope	DH Fox Moth	124.25
1933	831	42	Geoffrey de Havilland	DH Leopard Moth	139.5
1934	801	41	Harry Schofield	GAL Monospur ST-10	134.2
1935	801	43	Tommy Rose	Miles M.3B Falcon Six	176.3
1936	1,380	26	Charles Gardner	Percival Vega Gull	164.5
1937	1,443	27	Charles Gardner	Percival Mell Gull	233.7
1938	1,102	19	Alex Henshaw	Percival Mell Gull	236.25

1922 MACMILLAN ROUND-THE-WORLD ATTEMPT

On 24 May 1922, pilot Capt. Norman Macmillan and his crew departed Croydon, England, on their *Daily News* sponsored round-the-world attempt. Macmillan was a WWI ace with nine victories and a noted postwar test pilot. Maj. W.T. Blake was selected as the co-pilot and navigator, and Col. L.E. Broome as the photographer, but he was soon replaced by Geoffrey Malins in Marseilles, France. A De Havilland DH-9 (G-EBDE) biplane was chosen for the trip with a Fairey F-3 floatplane (G-EBDI) to replace the DH-9 in Calcutta, India, since that portion of the flight had to fly over long water stretches eventually to Vancouver, Canada. The flight was plagued by problems, which were largely solved with the aid of the British military spread throughout the British colonial system and Macmillan's skilled piloting. After a hard landing in Marseilles the DH-9 was replaced with another DH-9 shuttled from England. Macmillan, Blake, and Malins continued on through Europe, the Middle East, and India, where they made a forced landing in Delhi and had to change engines. When they arrived in Calcutta, Blake suffered an appendicitis and was hospitalized. They donated their DH-9 to the University of Benares, and Macmillan and Malins flew the Fairey F-3 floatplane for the rest of the trip, with Blake forced to stay behind in Calcutta. After departing Akyab, Burma, contaminated fuel forced a water landing; after floating for three days and two nights in the Bay of Bengal they were rescued by the SS *Dorothea*, but their F-3 sank in the Bay of Bengal on 25 August 1922, and their round-the-world flight attempt ended. Macmillan would subsequently write of the attempt in his 1937 book *Freelance Pilot*.

Geoffrey Malins (L) and Capt. Norman Macmillan

1924 MACLAREN ROUND-THE-WORLD ATTEMPT

Squadron Leader Stuart MacLaren, with his two-man crew F/O William Plenderleith and Sgt. W.H. Andrews, attempted the second British flight around the world. They flew a Vickers-Napier Vulture amphibian (G-EBHO) with open cockpits, a wooden hull, wheels cranked by hand, and only a map and compass as navigational aids. They left Calshot, England, on 25 March 1924, but crashed 13,100 miles and 130 days later in the Bering Sea on 3 August 1924. After landing in a dense fog in the Bering Sea they taxied to safety in Nikolski, Bering Island, in the Commander Islands. During December 1918–January 1919, MacLaren flew a Handley Page bomber from the UK to India and into combat against Afghan rebels.

Stuart MacLaren and crew

THE DE HAVILLANDS

The de Havilland Aircraft Company Ltd. was a British aviation manufacturer established in late 1920 by Geoffrey de Havilland, and was known for its innovations. Initially, de Havilland concentrated on single and two-seat biplanes, continuing with the DH series of aircraft built by Airco, but then introduced a series of smaller aircraft powered by de Havilland's own Gipsy engines. This led to the Moth series, including the Gipsy Moth and Tiger Moth biplanes that revolutionized general aviation in the 1920s. These aircraft set many aviation records, many piloted by de Havilland himself.

Geoffrey de Havilland

ARTHUR CONINGHAM

Australian Arthur Coningham began WWI in the infantry, but transferred to the Royal Flying Corps. In eleven months flying combat he was involved in 176 patrols over enemy lines, and was credited with nine victories and three shared. While posted as a staff officer in Egypt, S/L Coningham was assigned to lead a detachment of three DH.9As of 47 Squadron on a 3,000 mile flight cross country "to introduce the first aircraft to Nigeria while undertaking a training exercise on an extended scale... using ordinary service equipment." (biographer Vincent Orange) The flight took off from Helwan, near Cairo, during the morning of 27 October 1925, and crossed Africa from east to west without incident, landing in Kano, Nigeria, on 1 November, marking the first trip by air across Africa. On 12 November, the three de Havillands retraced their route and returned to Egypt after flying an estimated total of 6,500 miles in 80 hours of actual flying time, flying sixteen of the twenty-four days of the mission, all without major difficulties. Coningham received the Air Force Cross for the feat. During WWII, Coningham distinguished himself as the RAF air leader in the Desert War Campaign, advocating an airpower doctrine that was later adopted by Gen. Eisenhower over Europe that became the tactical air doctrine of the USAAF. In January 1944, he assumed command of the British Second Tactical Air Force and played a significant role in the Normandy invasion. By the end of the war, he had attained the rank of air marshal and was later knighted by the King of England.

Arthur Coningham

ALAN COBHAM

Alan Cobham became one of Britain's most well known aviation personalities and a prolific pioneer of long distance aviation of the 1920s, flying de Havilland aircraft. After serving in the Royal Flying Corps in WWI, Cobham became a test pilot for the de Havilland Aircraft Company, and then was the first pilot for the newly formed de Havilland Aeroplane Hire Service based at Stag Lane Aerodrome, London, flying passengers to destinations in Great Britain, Europe, and North Africa. In August 1921, Lucian Sharpe, a wealthy American, chartered a de Havilland DH 9c and had Cobham fly him on a 5,000 mile air tour of Europe, visiting seventeen cities in three weeks. In 1923, Cobham was awarded the first of three Britannia Trophies for a flying tour to Egypt, Palestine, and North Africa, covering 12,000 miles in 130 hours flying time in a DH 9c. The next year and a half would be a busy and eventful time for Cobham.

1926: England to India/Rangoon Return

On 20 November 1924, Cobham took off from Stag Lane Aerodrome with new engineer Arthur Elliott and passenger Sir Sefton Brancker, who made the flight to establish an airship route to India. At the time the British government was unsure about the feasibility of using airships for trans-Atlantic and trans-India routes. At the time airship R.100 was being built by Vickers and R.101 by the government, Cobham's chosen route was Berlin, Warsaw, Lvov (Poland), Bucharest, Constantinople, across Turkey to Aleppo, Baghdad, Basra, along the Persian Gulf to Karachi, across India—with a side trip to sightsee the Himalayas—and adding Rangoon on 6 February 1925. The outward journey to Rangoon spanned 79 days and more than 8,500 miles. On 8 February 1925, he left Rangoon, with the return trip retracing the outbound route, but upon approaching Germany's Black Forest area, Cobham encountered a storm front and was unable to climb over the local mountains, making a hard emergency landing and damaging the aircraft. The de Havilland was dismantled and trucked to Stuttgart, where it was repaired and reassembled. Cobham flew back to Croydon Aerodrome, South London, on 17 March, after 38 days, flying a total of 17,000 miles in 210 hours flight time. He received a great welcome and was later awarded the second of his three Britannia Trophies. Cobham continued his heavy flying schedule, and on 29 May, flew the prototype de Havilland DH.50 Moth from Croydon to Zurich and returned in 14:49 hours. Cobham also flew the Moth in the Kings Cup Air Race, though weather forced him to land short of the finish; he placed second in a follow-up race.

(L-R) Alan Cobham, Arthur Elliott (engineer), and Sir Sefton Brancker (passenger) during their trip to Burma.

1926: England to Cape Town Return

If Cobham had not flown enough for the year, Imperial Airways commissioned a survey flight to investigate the feasibility of a Cape Town air route. Before the flight could begin its logistical particulars had to be resolved. Geoffrey de Havilland supplied the de Havilland D.H.50J Moth for the flight, while Sir John Siddeley supplied the 385 hp Jaguar engine. Flight backer Sir Charles Wakefield supplied the oil, and BP donated the gasoline. But securing oil and fuel was not as much of a problem as sending it by ship, rail, or truck (or by some or all) to the variously planned stops. Spares had to be organized, and five complete sets were sent to Cairo, Khartoum, Kisumu, Johannesburg, and Cape Town. Veteran engineer Arthur Elliott and cameraman Basil Emmott accompanied Cobham on this epic journey to Cape Town. Cobham faced the dangers of flying over unknown, often uninhabited territory in uncertain weather. On 15 November, the Moth left Stag Lane Aerodrome, beginning an excursion that would span 94 days and cover 8,125 miles when he reached Cape Town. On the way the crew stopped to sightsee the pyramids outside Cairo and Victoria Falls. On 2 February 1926, Cobham arrived at Pretoria, South Africa, then flew on to Johannesburg, and finally to Cape Town on 17 February, with all three South African cities greeting him with large enthusiastic crowds. They spent a week in Cape Town, acclaimed and feted by the South Africans. While in Cape Town Cobham was challenged to race the steamship RMS *Windsor Castle* on the return journey from Cape Town to England, with both competitors leaving at the same time carrying a letter from the Governor-General of South Africa to King George V. The *Windsor Castle* had a much shorter route than Cobham, and the steamship could travel day and night, while the biplane could only fly during the day. Cobham took off for London on 26 February 1926, and despite these disadvantages and some misadventures on the return trip, the de Havilland beat the steamship to England, reaching Stag Lane Aerodrome only sixteen days later on 13 March. Cobham personally delivered the letter to King George V at Buckingham Palace. Cinematographer Basil Emmott had photographed many unique aerial scenes and produced the feature film *With Cobham to the Cape* for a very receptive British public.

(L-R) Alan Cobham, Basil Emmott (cameraman), and Arthur Elliott (engineer) on arrival in Cape Town.

1926: England to Australia

During 1926, Cobham was involved in his most famous long-distance flight, gaining him even more wide recognition and popularity. Cobham's original intention was to deliver a petition via airplane, calling for the government to take a more determined forward look at Britain's aviation policy. Already a national idol following his well-publicized epic flights to India and South Africa, Cobham thought the way to capture the public's imagination and publicize his petition would be to fly to Australia and back to England, delivering the petition in person. However, this flight also required much advance planning and faced the dangers of flying over unknown—and often uninhabited—territory in uncertain weather, but also over large expanses of open water. On 30 June 1926, he lifted the de Havilland 50 J Seaplane off from the River Medway on his way to Australia. The flight proceeded as planned until 5 July. After leaving Baghdad and while flying over Iraq, a sandstorm forced Cobham to fly low. Bedouin tribesmen, probably seeing their first airplane, shot at it and hit Arthur Elliott, forcing Cobham to make an emergency landing in Basra, Iraq, where his good friend Elliott was taken to a hospital but died the next day. Cobham took on Sgt. R.W. Ward of RAF 84 Squadron as

Elliott's replacement and carried on. The flight continued from Basra to Bushire to Karachi, across India to Rangoon to Penang to Singapore, and then by way of Sumatra, Java, Timor, and to Darwin, where the de Havilland's floats were exchanged for a wheeled undercarriage. Cobham then flew across the huge Australian Outback to Adelaide, and when they arrived in Sydney they were greeted by 60,000 supporters. An even more tumultuous crowd of 150,000 awaited them in Melbourne on 15 August, at the end of their journey. On 29 August, accompanied by Ward and Armstrong-Siddeley representative C. Capel, Cobham departed Melbourne/Point Cook headed for Adelaide and Darwin, where the floats were re-fitted, and then on to England. They arrived during the mid-afternoon on 1 October, landing on the River Thames in front of the Houses of Parliament before huge crowds cramming bridges and embankments. The outward journey that started on 30 June had spanned 47 days over 13,000 miles and reached Melbourne on 15 August 1926, while the return trip began on 29 August and landed on the River Thames 34 days later on 1 October. For his 26,000 mile round trip to Australia Cobham was knighted and awarded his third Britannia Trophy; he became the first pilot to make a return from England to Australia in the same aircraft.

Alan Cobham greeted by a crowd of 150,000 in Melbourne.

Alan Cobham's de Havilland 50 J Seaplane lands on the Thames in front of the Houses of Parliament.

On 25 November 1926, Cobham attempted but failed to be the first person to deliver mail to New York City by air from the east, planning to fly mail from the White Star ocean liner RMS *Homeric* in a de Havilland DH.60 Moth floatplane when the ship was about twelve hours from New York harbor on a westbound crossing from Southampton. After the Moth was lowered from the ship Cobham was unable to take off due to rough water and had to be towed into port by the ship. The same year Cobham was awarded the Gold Medal by the FAI.

1927–8: African Survey Expedition

Sir Alan Cobham was a celebrity, and after working for de Havilland for six years, he felt remaining there would limit his prospects. To cash in on his celebrity, Cobham starred as himself in the 1927 British war film *The Flight Commander*. He sold his beloved Moth and formed Alan Cobham Aviation Ltd., which he soon merged to form Cobham-Blackburn Air Lines, with the intention of establishing airline service into Africa. Before he could begin service he needed to scout out routes, and for this he needed a new aircraft. The Short *Singapore* flying boat powered by two Rolls-Royce engines was selected. The Short was stripped of its military accessories and high compression 700 hp Rolls-Royce Condor engines were installed. The flight was to be in a clockwise direction, beginning in Benghazi, then following the River Nile south and then on to Durban; this part of the flight was a survey for projected Imperial Airways service to South Africa.

The flight began in Rochester, England, on 17 November 1927, when large crowds gathered to see the start of the flight. Sir Alan Cobham's wife, Lady Cobham, joined him for the first time, together with assistant pilot Capt. H.V. Worrall, engineers F. Green and C.E. Conway, and cameraman S.R. Bonnett. The flight progressed without incident until strong headwinds delayed Cobham as he landed at night off the coast of Malta, where fortunately *HMS Queen Elizabeth* allowed him to tie up for the evening. The next morning strong winds damaged their flying boat as they tried to moor off the coast. The RAF at Malta saved Cobham by pulling his flying boat onto the slipway, where their *Singapore* received major repairs and new floats from England. Cobham resumed the flight 59 days later on 21 January 1928, flying from Alexandria, Egypt, and ending in Mwanza, Tanzania, landing on Lake Victoria. They arrived in Cape Town on 30 March, and began the return trip to test this air route completely, flying up the West African Coast on 3 April. Four days later Cobham successfully completed the flight, which later persuaded East African governments to support this air route. During this flight Cobham boarded his first two paying African air route customers for a combined fare of £160. After flying 18,115 miles around Africa—during which

Cobham and his companions visited forty-nine different destinations, landing only in British territory—after six months and fifteen days the *Singapore* landed in Plymouth, England, on 31 May 1928, again greeted by huge crowds.

Afterward Cobham wrote contemporary accounts of his flights and produced several films. Cobham also organized a series of flying tours of the United Kingdom, Ireland, and South Africa which became known as "Sir Alan Cobham's Flying

Alan Cobham's Singapore Seaplane during his 1927–8 African Survey Expedition.

Circus." In 1932, he inaugurated National Aviation Day displays, which were a combination of barnstorming and joyriding. The circus had assembled a dozen or more assorted aircraft, ranging from single-seaters to modern airliners, and many skilled pilots. It toured the country, performing at hundreds of sites, and was hugely popular, giving thousands of people their first experience of flying and bringing "air-mindedness" to the public. Sir Alan Cobham's Flying Circus continued until the end of the 1935 season, during which time 990,000 people were flown as passengers on flights in his fleet of aircraft and with more than 3,000,000 people visiting the display.

With the assurance of the director of civil aviation that Imperial Airways only intended to operate in Europe and North Africa, and with the information he had gathered and agreements he had made with African governments, Cobham felt he could now establish his own airline in Africa. However, the British government owned Imperial Airways and decided they should operate all African services. Despite Cobham's protests that he had done all the pioneering work and made agreements with African countries, Cobham had no choice but to sell his company to Imperial Airways, which began operating an African service on routes he had pioneered. Cobham would continue in aviation, becoming the "Father of In-flight Refueling."

FAIREY IIID

The Fairey IIID was a prolific early long distance record setter. It was a two-seat general-purpose biplane powered by a 375 hp Rolls-Royce Eagle V-12. The bomber had a wing span of 45.8 ft., a wing area of 439 sq. ft., a length of 36.8 ft., and weighed 3,855 lbs. empty and 6,041 lbs. loaded. It entered Fleet Air Arm service in 1924, operating from shore bases, aircraft carriers, and floats until replaced by the IIIF in 1930.

In 1926, RAF Fairey IIIDs flew the first Cairo to Cape Town, South Africa, flight, and that same year the RAF Cape Flight used four IIIDs to fly a long distance formation flight from Cairo to Cape Town.

Fairey IIID

1922: Gago Coutinho and Sacadura Cabral Cross the South Atlantic

Probably the most noteworthy Fairey IIID long distance flight was the crossing of the South Atlantic from Lisbon, Portugal, to Rio de Janeiro, Brazil, in early 1922, by high-ranking Portuguese Navy fliers Gago Coutinho and Sacadura Cabral using three different Portuguese Naval Aviation Fairey IIIs. Coutinho was an expert in astronomical science and the navigator of the expedition, and Cabral was the pilot. The flight was made to prove that air navigation could be just as accurately pursued as sea navigation by a revolutionary artificial horizon for aeronautical use and deploying sextants and other available astronomical devices. Heavy rainfall had to be strictly avoided because of the open structure of the aircraft, the risk of water infiltration into the instruments and fuel tanks, and also the difficulties assessing changes in wind and making gradual navigational adjustments under rainfall. The Faireys did not have enough fuel capacity to make the entire trip unaided, so various stops were made along the way, and the aviators were trailed by a support ship, *República*.

Coutinho's Fairey (named *Lusitania*) began the flight in Lisbon at 1630 on 30 March 1922, and after using three aircraft ended in Rio de Janeiro on 17 June, with stops in Las Palmas, S. Vicente (Cape Verde), Praia (Cape Verde), St. Peter & St. Paul's Rocks, Fernando Noronha, Recife, Salvador da Bahia, Porto Seguro, and Vitoria. After landing in the Canary Islands, the

Fairey's fuel consumption was noted to be higher than expected and the engine was adjusted; on 5 April, the *Lusitania* departed for Sao Vicente Island, Cape Verde, flying 850 miles. More repairs were required and the *Lusitania* would not leave until 17 April, flying to Praia, on Santiago Island, and the next day 1,100 miles across the South Atlantic to the Saint Peter and Saint Paul Archipelago, in Brazilian waters. The *Republica* was supposed to refuel the *Lusitania* at St. Peter & St. Paul's Rocks, but sea conditions changed and they were running low on fuel and were forced to ditch. One of the aircraft floats was destroyed by the crest of a wave and the hydroplane tilted and soon sank. Coutinho and Cabral were rescued by the nearby *Republica* and were taken to Fernando Noronha Island. The Portuguese government dispatched another Fairey III (the *Patria*), which arrived in Fernando Noronha on 6 May.

Gago Coutinho (R) and Sacadura Cabral in a Fairey III-D MkII seaplane

After being outfitted to continue the flight, the *Patria* departed on 11 May, flying to the Saint Peter and Saint Paul Archipelago to resume the journey at the point where the flight was interrupted. About 1:50 hours after take-off the engine stopped due to carburetor problems, leading to another forced water landing. Coutinho managed to restart the engine for about an hour, but before they could take off the engine stopped for good and the floats began to slowly sink, despite Cabral sitting on the engine to reduce the rear weight on the floats. The *Republica* sent out a distress signal for shipping in the area to look out for the *Patria*. After drifting for about an hour and a half they saw a distant light in the dark, to which they responded with two gun shots, and were saved by the British freighter *Paris City*—en route from Cardiff to Rio—which returned them to Fernando Noronha. A third Fairey III (the *Santa Cruz*) was transported by a supporting Portuguese Navy cruiser and was put in the waters off Fernando Noronha on 5 June. Coutinho and Cabral again resumed their flight, flying to Recife, then to Salvador da Bahia, then to Vitoria, and from there to Rio de Janeiro, where they arrived on 17 June 1922, landing in Guanabara Bay after 79 days (actual flight time was just 62:26 hours).

1924: W/C Stanley Goble and Flt.Lt. Ivor McIntyre: Circumnavigation of Australia

A flight was proposed to survey the northern coastline of Australia for defense planning, and to test the proficiency of the single-engined Fairey IIID floatplane. English-born Ivor McIntyre was the lead pilot, while Stanley Goble acted as aircraft commander and navigator. The floatplane lifted off from Point Cook, Victoria, on 6 April 1924, and flew 8,450 miles in 44 days, often encountering harsh conditions. Although fuel stocks and spare parts had been stashed beforehand along the intended route, the two airmen had to struggle with illness and tropical storms, along with engine problems and fuel leaks. They flew counterclockwise around the continent, along the eastern coast through Sydney, Southport, Townsville, and Thursday Island, crossing the Gulf of Carpentaria to Darwin, and then continuing along the coast through Broome, Carnarvon, Perth, Albany, and Port Lincoln, before arriving back in Victoria to land at St. Kilda Beach, where they were welcomed by a crowd of 10,000. Prime Minister Stanley Bruce named the circumnavigation "one of the most wonderful accomplishments in the history of aviation" and presented Goble with a gift of £500 (£250 to McIntyre). The British Royal Aero Club awarded them the annual Britannia Trophy. During WWII Goble wished to make the RAAF autonomous, but came in conflict with Prime Minister Robert Menzies, and was relegated to be Australia's representative to Canada. After the war Goble was more or less forced to resign due to "certain nervous characteristics" and died of a heart/vascular condition in 1948.

W/C Stanley Goble and Flt.Lt. Ivor McIntyre in their Fairey IIID

SUPERMARINE SOUTHAMPTON

On 27 September 1927, four Supermarine Southampton flying boats of the Far East Flight under the command of G/C Henry Cave-Browne-Cave set out from Felixstowe, United Kingdom, to fly a 27,000 mile combined "flag waving" and "marine base survey." The RAF pointed out to the press: "that in no sense is the cruise to be regarded as a 'stunt,' and no attempt will be made to cover the route between London and Australia in 'record' time." The flight continued via the Mediterranean to Singapore via India before flying on to Australia and Hong Kong, then returning to Singapore, where it would settle as the island/city's first resident air squadron.

Supermarine Southampton Flying Boat

HAWKER HORSLEY

The Hawker Horsley was a two-seat British single-engine medium day and torpedo biplane bomber that served the RAF 1926–1935, and was the last all-wooden Hawker aircraft built. It had a wingspan of 56.5 ft., a wing area of 693 sq. ft., a length of almost 39 ft., and was powered by a single 650 hp Rolls-Royce Condor III V-12. The Horsley was chosen to attempt a non-stop flight to India with a specially modified aircraft carrying much more fuel, giving it a take-off weight of over 14,000 lbs. (vs. 7,800 lbs. normal take-off weight). Flown by Flight Lts. Roderick Carr (later Air Marshall) and L.E.M Gillmann, the Horsley took off from RAF Cranwell on 20 May 1927, but ran out of fuel en route, ditching in the Persian Gulf near Bandar Abbas, Iran. Nonetheless, it had covered a distance of 3,420 miles, which was sufficient to set a new world distance record that was eclipsed in a few hours by Charles Lindbergh, whose solo Atlantic flight between New York and Paris covered 3,590 miles. Two later attempts at the record failed and the modified Horsley would make valuable contributions as an engine test bed, particularly for the Rolls-Royce Merlin series.

Hawker Horsley

3
BRITISH LONG-RANGE AIRCRAFT AND FLIGHTS OF THE LATE 1920s AND 1930s

FAIREY LONG-RANGE MONOPLANES

The first aircraft was designed to meet Air Ministry Specification 33/27, issued by the Directorate of Technical Development (DTD) in December 1927, to recapture the absolute distance world record set briefly by the Hawker Horsley, which then met two failures. This aircraft was to be constructed not just "for a specific record, but as a serious study into methods of increasing the range of aircraft." The Fairey long-range monoplanes of the late 1920s and early 1930s were a pair of single-engine, two-seat, high-wing British experimental aircraft. The aircraft had a length of 48.5 ft. and a wing with a span of 82 ft. and an area of 850 sq. ft. After extensive testing, the 570 hp Napier Lion Xia 12-cylinder, liquid-cooled engine with a fixed pitch propeller was chosen to power the aircraft. Wind tunnel testing of various configurations determined that a high wing allowed a gravity feed with a mechanical fuel pump in sequence from the 1,043 gallon wing fuel tanks. The aircraft was equipped with a pneumatic bed for use by the pilots.

Fairey Long-range Monoplane

Fairey Long-Range Monoplane Record Flights

The Fairey flew for the first time on 14 November 1928, and was accepted by the RAF on 7 December. It continued testing in preparation for a record flight to Bangalore, India—a Great Circle distance of about 5,000 miles, which would exceed the existing record of 4,466 miles set by a Savoia-Marchetti S.64

(Ferrarin and del Prete) in July 1928. S/L A.G. Jones-Williams and Flt.Lt. N.H. Jenkins headed off on the record attempt from RAF Cranwell on 24 April 1929. Constant headwinds slowed the aircraft, so it had to land at Karachi after 50:48 hours in the air; although the flight was the first non-stop between Britain and India, their Great Circle distance of 4,130 miles was short of the world record. Another attempt for the record was scheduled for later in the year, although the record had been raised to 4,912 miles by a Breguet 19 (Costes and Bellonte). This attempt was planned to fly from England to South Africa with the same crew as the first UK-India flight, taking off on 16 December 1929, but crashing south of Tunis, destroying the aircraft and killing the crew.

S/L Oswald Gayford and F/L Gilbert Nicholetts (uniforms center) with Lord Londonderry and Sir John Salmond and their Fairey Long Range Monoplane at Farnborough.

Despite this setback, the Air Ministry ordered the construction of a similar (but with an autopilot) second long-range monoplane in July 1930, to be ready on 30 June 1931. From 6–8 February 1933, S/L Oswald Gayford—the officer in command of the RAF Long-Range Development Unit (LDRU)—and his navigator, Flt.Lt. Gilbert Nicholetts, flew the second aircraft non-stop from Cranwell, United Kingdom, to Walvis Bay, Southwest Africa (now Nambia), for a world long distance record of 5,410 miles in 57:30 hours. En route the autopilot malfunctioned and had to be disconnected, and the two men had to fly alternate three-hour periods using their instruments for navigation, as they could not see the horizon line at night. Gayford and the LRDU would later fly long distance record flights with the Vickers *Wellesley*.

AGE OF THE CELEBRATED LONG-DISTANCE PILOT

Sir Francis Chichester

Sir Francis Chichester is most remembered as a renowned yachtsman, but his series of history-making flights have been overlooked. After being educated in the United Kingdom, he emigrated to New Zealand in 1919, where he became wealthy as a land agent. He became interested in flying and returned to Britain in 1929 to become a pilot. On 15 December 1929, he flew from Croydon, England, on a solo flight from England to Australia in a Gipsy Moth, arriving there on 25 January 1930, after flying 14,561 miles in 182.5 flying hours over 41 days. In 1931, he flew his de Havilland Gipsy Moth floatplane solo across the Tasman Sea from Auckland, New Zealand, via Norfolk and Lord Howe Islands to Jervis Bay, Australia, and was awarded the Johnston Memorial Trophy. On 3 July 1931, he continued his intended round-the-world solo flight, flying his Gipsy Moth floatplane *Elijah* from Australia to Japan via Manila and Shanghai, but his round-the-world aspirations ended on 15 August 1931 in Katsuura Harbor, Japan, when he collided with telegraph wires and almost died. He spent WWII in Britain as an air navigation instructor, and after the war started a map publishing business. In 1953, he began yacht racing and finally realized his dream of a solo circumnavigation of the world between 27 August 1966 and 28 May 1967 in the Gipsy Moth IV sailing ketch and not in the Gipsy Moth aircraft, sailing 29,600 miles in 226 days.

Sir Francis Chichester by his de Havilland DH.60 Moth

C.W.A. SCOTT

Charles William Anderson Scott joined the RAF in 1922, where he learned to fly and became an excellent aerobatic pilot. He left the RAF in 1926 and emigrated to Australia, where he became a commercial pilot for the fledgling airline company Queensland and Northern Territory Aerial Services (QANTAS). In 1929, while on leave from QANTAS following a crash in a de Havilland DH.50J, Scott met his first wife, Kathleen. In 1930, Scott broke the solo record, flying across Australia from Brisbane to Melbourne in a de Havilland DH.60 Gipsy Moth to be present at the birth of his daughter. In 1931, Scott became internationally famous when competing against pilots such as Bert Hinkler, Charles Kingsford Smith, and James Mollison, as he broke the England to Australia solo flight record, flying a de Havilland DH.60 Moth to a record of 9 days, 4:11 hours, for which he was awarded the Air Force Cross. This would be his first of three England-

C.W.A. Scott (2R) with Sir John Salmond (2L) after the 1928 Australia flight in a Qantas DH.50.

C.W.A. Scott and his DH.60 Moth *Australia*

Australia records, the next one being a record breaking flight back to England in 1931, in another DH Moth in 10 days, 23 hours. In 1932, Scott went on to break the Australia-England solo flight record with a time of 8 days 20 hours.

In 1934, Scott and Tom Campbell Black were selected to fly one of three purpose-built de Havilland DH.88 Comet Racers to compete in the MacRobertson Air Race, which to this day is deemed one of the greatest air races of all time. The duo raced 10,500 miles to Darwin in their scarlet Comet *Grosvenor House*, shattering the England-Australia flight record of 162 hours with a time of 52:33 hours (a time that remains unbeaten today by any other piston-powered aircraft), despite flying the last stage with one engine throttled back because of an oil pressure indicator giving a faulty low reading. Finally, nearly 71 hours and 11,325 miles after the start of the race (65:30 hours in the air), Scott and Black flew their engine-weary Comet to Melbourne at low speed, landing to a cheering crowd of upward of 75,000 to place first, winning the £10,000 prize money and becoming international celebrities. Following the race Scott received several medals and awards, including the Britannia Trophy, FAI Gold Air Medal for 1934, and the Harmon Trophy, the international award for best aviator of 1934, and was celebrated wherever he went. In 1936, Scott took over Sir Alan Cobham's National Air Displays Ltd. and for one season operated C.W.A. Scott Flying Display Ltd.

C.W.A. Scott in his Comet *Grosvenor House*

In September 1936, Scott entered the Schlesinger Air Race from Portsmouth, England, to Johannesburg, South Africa. Scott's co-pilot in the MacRobertson Race, Tom Campbell Black, had died in an accident while taxiing a Percival Mew Gull preparing for the race. On 1 October, Scott and new co-pilot Giles Guthrie, flying their Vega Gull, were the only one of fourteen entrants to land at Johannesburg Rand Airport after flying 52:56:48 hours and 6,154 miles, winning the £10,000 prize money and continued adulation. Once WWII broke out Scott sank into oblivion, unable to find a place for himself, and committed suicide in April 1946, shooting himself at age forty-four.

BERT HINKLER

During WWI, Australian Bert Hinkler served with the Royal Naval Air Service as a gunner/observer; after the war, he worked as a test pilot for aircraft manufacturer A.V. Roe. In 1919, the Australian government offered a £10,000 prize for the first flight to Australia; Hinkler entered, but his Sopwith *Dove* crashed in Europe during a storm. He bought a 35 hp Avro Baby and on 31 May 1920, on a flight that won him the Britannia Trophy, he flew from Croydon to Turin, Italy—over the Alps—in 9.5 hours. When he arrived in Rome he had to discontinue flying to Australia because of mechanical problems. In 1921, Hinkler shipped his Avro Baby to Sydney, Australia, where he made a series of flights, including one from Sydney to his home town Bundaberg, Queensland (850 miles non-stop), but on the return flight he made an emergency landing due to bad weather, and strong winds overturned the Baby. After returning to England he was the chief test pilot for the Avro until 1926, and also tested autogiros for Spanish designer Juan de La Cierva. In 1927, he flew his Avro Avian non-stop from London to Riga, Latvia, and then, looking for publicity to obtain a sponsorship for a flight to Australia, made an unsuccessful attempt with R. McIntosh on the London to India air record. Hinkler would fly the first solo flight between England and Australia, departing England on 7 February 1928 in an Avro Avian and arriving in Darwin on 22 February 1928, then returning to Bundaberg, Australia, on 27 February 1928. His flight reduced the England-Australia record from 28 days to just under 15½ days. It was also the longest solo flight recorded at the time. During the Depression Hinkler went to Canada in September 1930, to look for better aviation prospects, and in April 1931, he acquired a de Havilland Puss Moth on a remarkable flight from Canada to New York, then non-stop to Jamaica (1,500 miles), then to Venezuela, Guyana, Brazil, and then across the South Atlantic to West Africa in appalling weather and on to London. This was the first solo flight across the South Atlantic, and after Charles Lindbergh Hinkler was only the second pilot to solo across the Atlantic. The epic flight gained him wide public acclaim and the Segrave trophy, his second Britannia Challenge Trophy, the Gold Medal of the Royal Aero Club, and the Johnston Memorial Air Navigation Trophy. Despite the acclaim Hinkler failed to find aviation employment in Britain and again returned to America early in 1932, to find a sponsor for an anticipated around-the-world flight by a light aircraft. Failing this, he returned to England to organize another flight to Australia, intending later to cross the Pacific to Canada. He began the flight from Heathrow on 7 January 1933 in his Puss Moth and disappeared. His crashed de Havilland and body were found on the slopes of the Apennines between Florence and Arezzo, Italy, on 27 April.

Bert Hinkler with his Avro Avian

SIR CHARLES EDWARD KINGSFORD SMITH

In October 1916, Australian Charles Kingsford Smith transferred from the army to the Australian Flying Corps, and after training in England in March 1917, he was commissioned as a second lieutenant, and was then appointed as a flying officer in May; in July he joined No.23 Squadron in France. During his first month at the front he shot down four enemy aircraft and attacked ground targets, but was shot down and wounded in August; he was awarded the Military Cross and then served as a flying instructor with the RFC. After the war he returned to Australia and was employed as a salaried airline pilot, later struggling to buy and fly passenger and transport aircraft. It would not be until 1928 that he would earn global fame when he made the first trans-Pacific flight from the United States to Australia.

In 1928, Kingsford Smith and Charles Ulm arrived in America and purchased a Fokker F.VII twin-engine monoplane, which they named the *Southern Cross*. At 0854 on 31 May 1928, Kingsford Smith and his three-man crew (Charles Ulm was the relief pilot and the other crewmen were Americans James Warner, the radio operator, and Capt. Harry Lyon, the navigator and engineer) left Oakland, California, on the first of a three-stage flight across the Pacific:

Stage 1) 2,400 miles from Oakland to Wheeler Army Airfield, Hawaii, in 27:25 hours (87.54 mph).
Stage 2) 3,155 miles from Barking Sands on Mana, Kauai (the runway at Wheeler was not long enough with the heavy fuel load), to Suva, Fiji, in 34:30 hours (91.45 mph).
Stage 3) 1,683 miles from Fiji to Brisbane in 20 hours (84.15 mph), landing at 1050 on 9 June in 83:38 hours of flying time.

The total flight distance was approximately 7,187 miles. Kingsford Smith was met by a huge crowd of 26,000 at Eagle Farm Airport, and was welcomed as a national hero.

In August 1928, Kingsford Smith flew the *Southern Cross* on the first non-stop crossing of the Australian mainland from Point Cook, Victoria, to Perth. On 10 September 1928, Kingsford Smith, along with Ulm and an Australian crew, piloted the plane from Sydney to Christchurch, New Zealand, overnight to a daylight landing. The 1,600 mile, 14 hour flight confirmed the viability of regular passenger and mail services across the Tasman Sea. (Note: the first solo trans-Tasman flight was flown by Guy Menzies in an Avro Avian named *Southern Cross Junior*, who took off from Sydney on 7 January 1931 and crash-landed in a swamp near Hari Hari, New Zealand, nearly twelve hours later.)

On 1 April 1929, Kingsford Smith and Ulm left for England, but were forced down by bad weather for an emergency landing in northwest Australia; help did not arrive until 13 April. The flight to England was resumed in June and completed in the record time of 12 days, 18 hours. He then continued to Oakland, California, completing a circumnavigation of the world that began in 1928.

Kingsford Smith flew the *Southern Cross* to the Netherlands for overhaul at the Fokker Company factory for an attempt during June 1930 of an east-west crossing of the Atlantic from near Dublin, Ireland, to Newfoundland. He flew the route in 31:30 hours and was given a triumphant welcome in New York. He then returned to England to take delivery of an Avro Avian biplane (*Southern Cross Junior*) to attempt a record breaking solo flight to Darwin in October. He flew the Avian to Darwin in 9 days, 22:15 hours, beating four competitors who had left England ahead of him and breaking Hinkler's record by 5½ days.

During 1931–32, Kingsford Smith's airline suffered heavy losses from the Depression and his health also suffered from his relentless flying regimen. After being knighted in 1932, Sir Kingsford Smith was relegated to flying "joy rides" and launching a flying school that bankrupted. Toward the end of 1933, his prospects improved. After sailing to England in September 1933, he achieved a brilliant success in October, flying solo from London to Wyndham, Western Australia, in a Percival Gull (*Miss Southern Cross*) in just 7 days and 4 hours, adding to his record number of long distance flight records he held.

In 1934, with financial help from friends and sponsors, he purchased a Lockheed Altair (*Lady Southern Cross*) in anticipation of competing in the MacRobertson Air Race for its £10,000 prize. Because modifications to the aircraft could not be completed in time he was unable to arrive in England in time for the race's start. Instead, he and P.G. Taylor flew the *Lady Southern Cross* from Brisbane to San Francisco in October–November 1934 to sell it and reimburse his sponsors. This West-East trans-Pacific flight was another first in aviation history.

Kingsford Smith arranged for the still unsold *Lady Southern Cross* to be shipped to England from America, where he would attempt another record breaking flight to Australia held by C.W.A. Scott and Tom Campbell Black. With his co-pilot John "Tommy" Pethybridge, the *Lady Southern Cross* was flown overnight from Allahabad, India, to Singapore and disappeared without a trace over the Andaman Sea in the early morning of 8 November 1935.

Charles Kingsford Smith (2L) and his crew after their record trans-Pacific flight in their Fokker F.VII *Southern Cross*.

THE HON. MRS. VICTOR BRUCE NEARLY FLIES AROUND THE WORLD

After marrying auto racer Victor Bruce, Mildred Mary Petre became a well known auto racer in her own right, then went on to break a number of power boat records. She did not take her first flying lesson until 25 May 1930, but soon after she had her pilot's license she purchased a Blackburn Bluebird IV with a De Havilland Gipsy II engine, which was sent to Blackburn for modifications in preparation for her solo around-the-world flight. On 25 September 1930, she left the United Kingdom and flew east with stops in Germany, Austria, Yugoslavia, Turkey, Syria, and Iraq. She made an emergency landing on the Persian Gulf's shore due to an oil leak and was sheltered for two days by tribesmen before being found by a British rescue party. After repairs delayed her journey for several days she continued on to India, Burma, Siam (Thailand), and French Indo-China (Vietnam). A torrential monsoon forced her to land in a jungle clearing beside the Mekong River, where she contracted malaria, further delaying her flight. Feeling better, she flew on to Hanoi, Hong Kong, Shanghai, and Seoul, to become the first person to fly across the Yellow Sea. On 24 November 1930, having traveled 10,330 miles in 25 flying days, she landed in Tokyo. Mrs. Bruce then crossed the Pacific by ship to Vancouver, where began her North American transcontinental flight. The itinerary was soon interrupted by a crash landing in Medford, Oregon, that caused another week's delay, after which she continued with stops in San Francisco, San Diego, St. Louis, and Chicago. She finally arrived in New York City in early February 1931, but then met a one-week delay following another crash in Baltimore. She sailed on the Ile de France to LeHavre, France, and on 19 February, she landed at Lympne Airport, outside London, after having flown about 19,000 miles and being the first person to fly from England to Japan, the first to fly across the Yellow Sea, and the first woman to fly around the world alone (albeit by crossing the oceans by ship). After her epic flight she experimented with aerial refueling in three failed attempts to set the world flight refueled endurance record; she joined a flying circus as star flyer; got her commercial license; attempted to set the world autogiro distance record; founded an airline prewar; and was forced out of the postwar airline business and left aviation.

The Hon. Mrs. Victor Bruce arrives in Japan.

JAMES MOLLISON AND AMY JOHNSON: THE FLYING SWEETHEARTS

James Mollison was a self-styled playboy/aviator intent on setting a flight record as a means of creating a persona. During July–August 1931, Mollison set a record time of 8 days, 19 hours for a flight from Australia to England, and in March 1932, set the solo record for flying from England to South Africa in 113:22 hours. At the time Mollison was a commercial pilot for Charles Kingsford Smith's Australian National Airways, and during one of his flights he met famous

James Mollison's DH Puss Moth *Desert Cloud*

aviatrix Amy Johnson. Only eight hours after meeting her he proposed while still in the air and they married in July 1932, and were hailed as the "Flying Sweethearts."

Amy Johnson was even more renowned than her new husband, having achieved United Kingdom and international recognition in 1930, when she piloted her de Havilland Gipsy Moth *Jason* to become the first woman pilot to fly solo from England to Australia. In establishing the record she left London on 5 May and landed in Darwin on 24 May, after flying 11,000 miles, for which she received the Harmon Trophy, as well as an Order of the British Empire (CBE). In July 1931, Johnson and her co-pilot, Jack Humphreys, flying a de Havilland DH.80 Puss Moth (*Jason II*), became the first pilots to fly from London to Moscow in one day, completing the 1,760 mile flight in approximately 21 hours. The pair then left Moscow and continued across Siberia and on to Tokyo, setting a Britain to Japan record flight time.

On 18 August 1932, Mrs. Johnson-Mollison was the first pilot to fly an East-to-West solo trans-Atlantic flight from Portmarnock, Ireland, to Pennfield, New Brunswick, Canada. (A westbound trans-Atlantic flight requires more endurance, fuel, and time than the eastward flight because of prevailing Atlantic headwinds). To save weight for this flight her de Havilland Puss Moth *Heart's Content* had the wheels and air brakes removed and additional fuel tanks added: two twenty gallon fuel tanks in the wings; a large seventy-five gallon tank in the forward part of the cabin, and another forty-seven gallon tank behind the cabin for a total capacity of 162 gallons and an overload of approximately 700 lbs. Amy Johnson's Gipsy Moth *Jason* is on display at the Science Museum, London.

Meanwhile, in November 1932, Johnson-Mollison left to try and break her new husband's England-to-South Africa record flying a DH Puss Moth, named *Desert Cloud*. Johnson-Mollison followed her husband's route and landed in 102:54 hours, besting her husband's previous record of 113:22 hours by 10:28 hours. She made the return flight in December in 175:05 hours, breaking the previous record (9.5 days established by Capt. C. D. Barnard and the Duchess of Bedford) by about two days. In February 1933, Mrs. Mollison flew from England to Brazil in three days, thirteen hours, using Africa as a stop-over, establishing a record time and the first solo crossing.

Amy Johnson Mollison in her de Havilland Gipsy Moth *Jason*

Afterward, the husband/wife team began to plan a record breaking flight across the world. On 22 July 1933, they took off from Wales on the first leg of a non-stop flight to New York, but ran out of fuel and were forced to crash land near Bridgeport, Connecticut. Both were injured and their de Havilland DH.84 Dragon *Seafarer* was stripped by souvenir seekers. After recuperating, the popular couple were celebrated by New York society and received a Wall Street ticker tape parade. After returning to England, the Mollisons participated in the MacRobertson London to Melbourne Air Race in October 1934. Their de Havilland DH.88 Comet *Black Magic* was leading at Baghdad, but they were forced to withdraw after having to use non-aviation fuel that damaged their Comet's engines.

In May 1936, Johnson-Mollison made her last record breaking flight, regaining her Britain to South Africa record in a Percival Gull. The Mollisons' marriage became stressed due to their rivalry for aviation records and to Jim Mollison's alcohol problems, and they were divorced in 1938. After her friend Amelia Earhart disappeared in 1937, Johnson lost interest in flying, but during the war Mollison and Johnson flew for the Air Transport Auxiliary (ATA). On 5 January 1941, while flying an Airspeed Oxford for the ATA, Johnson flew off course in bad weather; reportedly out of fuel, she bailed out into the Thames Estuary and drowned. In 1999, a report surfaced that she was shot down by a RAF fighter after failing to radio the signal of the day. Mollison served with distinction with the ATA during the war, but continued to have alcohol problems after the war.

James Mollison and Amy Johnson, "The Flying Sweethearts"

Beryl Markham and her Vega Gull *The Messenger*

BERYL MARKHAM

The beautiful, charismatic, nearly six- ft.-tall blue-eyed blonde Markham's romantic conquests throughout the 1920s were fabled and included author/pilot Antoine de Saint Exupery and Prince Henry, Duke of Gloucester, who was third in line to the throne. Upon discovering Prince Henry's dalliance, second husband Mansfield Markham threatened to sue for divorce and name the prince as a correspondent. To keep his name out of the courts Prince Henry agreed to put £15,000 into a trust for Beryl, which would pay her an annuity for the rest of her life with the stipulation that she leave England immediately. She moved to Kenya, where she had an affair with hunter and pilot Denys Finch Hatton, the lover of her friend Karen Blixen, who wrote *Out of Africa* under the pen name Isak Dinesen. This affair ended when Hatton died in an airplane crash, and Markham then moved her romantic interests to Tom Campbell Black, with whom she had a longstanding affair and who motivated her to begin an avid interest in flying—she has often been called "Britain's Amelia Earhart." Markham was married three times, with dozens of affairs between, and during each union caused all three husbands to divorce her for infidelity. The last marriage ended when second husband Mansfield Markham named pilot Hubert Broad as a co-respondent in his 1937 divorce from Beryl.

When Markham decided to cross the Atlantic no pilot had flown non-stop from Europe to New York, and no woman had made the westward flight solo, though several had died trying. Markham hoped to claim both records. On 4 September 1936, she took off from Abingdon, England, in her single-engine Vega Gull, *The Messenger*, but headwinds reduced her speed to only 90 mph and weather caused her to fly virtually blind but westward. After flying 21:25 hours the Vega suffered fuel starvation due to icing of the fuel tank vents and she crash landed at Baleine Cove, on Cape Breton Island, Nova Scotia, Canada, fortunately suffering only a minor head injury. Like Jim Mollison in 1932, Markham was short of New York, but became the first woman to cross the Atlantic East-to-West solo. Another unpublicized reason that Markham had attempted the flight was to impress lover Tom Campbell-Black, who had stunned her by falling in love and marrying English actress Florence Desmond while in England; she hoped her trans-Atlantic exploit would win him back. Unfortunately, Campbell-Black was killed shortly afterward on 19 September, when a landing RAF bomber ran into his *Mew Gull* as he taxied out for take off. Without Campbell-Black Markham lost her interest in flying and moved to California; in 1942 she wrote her memoir *West with the Night*, for which she is now primarily remembered, but at the time received critical but little popular fanfare. In the 1950s Markham returned to Kenya and her true passion, horses, and over the next twenty years had great success training and racing horses, including six Kenya Derby winners. During her life she had little financial expertise, and by 1980, she was destitute, living alone in a small cottage and being described as "an irascible woman who was partial to a drink." The 1983 republication of *West with the Night* became a great literary and financial success, allowing her to live the last three years of her life in comfort and as an acknowledged accomplished author.

ENGLAND-AUSTRALIA/AUSTRALIA-ENGLAND RECORD FLIGHTS 1931–1938

1931: Australia-England (solo): C.W.A. Scott flying a D.H. Moth (*Gipsy II*). Left Wyndham 26 May/Arrived Lympne 5 June. Time: 10 days 13 hours

1931: Australia-England: James Mollison flying a D.H. Moth. July–August. Time: 8 days 22:35 hours

1932: England-Australia (solo): C.W.A. Scott flying a D.H. Moth (*Gypsy II*). Left Lympne 19 April/Arrived Port Darwin 28 April Time: 8 days 20:47 hours

C.W.A. Scott and his D.H. Moth Gypsy II

1933: England-Australia (solo): C.E. Kingsford Smith flying a Percival Gull (Gipsy Major). Left Lympne 4 October/Arrived Wyndham 11 October Time: 7 days 4:44 hours

1934: England-Australia: C.T.P Ulm, G. Allen, and P. Taylor flying an Avro Ten. Left Harmondsworth/ Derby Time: 6 days 17:45 hours

1934: Australia-England: O. Cathcart Jones and K.F.H. Waller. Left Melbourne 28 October/Arrived Lympne 2 November Time: 6 days 16:10 hours

Cathcart Jones (L) and K.F.H. Waller

1937: BROADBENT AND BATTEN AUSTRALIA TO ENGLAND DUEL

After receiving his private pilot's license on 20 November 1929, the next year Australian Harry (Jim) Broadbent attempted to break Kingsford Smith's England-Australia record, but was turned back early. In 1931, Broadbent bought an Avro Avian, and on 12 August, he flew solo from Brisbane to Sydney, Melbourne, and Adelaide, linking the cities for the first time by air in one day. Within a month he set a round-Australia record by flying 7,475 miles in 7 days, 8:25 hours. After winning the annual New South Wales Aerial Derby on 14 May 1932, Broadbent purchased a three-seat Puss Moth monoplane, obtained a commercial license, and started an air taxi service. On 17–20 May 1935, Broadbent flew 7,140 miles around Australia in his new Puss Moth in a remarkable time of 3 days, 9:54 hours (a record that remains unbroken). On 10 October, Broadbent left Darwin for England, but his aircraft was damaged near Basra, Iraq, and he continued to England as an Imperial Airways passenger. On 2 November, Broadbent and Charles Melrose, flying Percival Gulls, left Croydon the same day. Broadbent reached Darwin on 9 November 1935, reducing Kingsford Smith's 1933 England-Australia solo record to 6 days, 21:19 hours, and was awarded the 1935 Oswald Watt Gold Medal for, "A most brilliant performance in the air or the most notable contribution to aviation by an Australian or in Australia" by the Royal Federation of Aero Clubs of Australia.

Jim Broadbent and his Percival Gull

Meanwhile, a friendly rivalry had developed between Broadbent and New Zealand aviatrix Jean Batten. She broke his 1935 England-Australia record in October 1936 with a time of 5 days, 21:03 hours, but he regained it by lowering the time to 6 days, 8:25 hours (27 April–3 May 1937) in his DH-85 Leopard Moth (the successor to the DH.80 Puss Moth), *Windella*, taking the record from H.L. Brook. Attempting the return flight he wrecked his Leopard Moth in Baghdad. On 18–24 October, Batten reduced his record to 5 days, 18:15 hours. Broadbent had to abort two attempts to break her record, but doggedly flying a Percival Vega Gull, on 18 April 1938, he flew a Vega Gull from Darwin and landed in England on 22 April with a record of 5 days, 4:21 hours for the fastest solo time in either direction and the last of the pre-WWII record flights on the England-Australia-England routes; his time remains a record for its class.

Jean Batten

1934: CHARLES "JIMMY" MELROSE: AUSTRALIA TO ENGLAND RECORD

Charles "Jimmy" Melrose left Adelaide, Australia, on 16 September 1934, to compete in the MacRobertson Race in his DH80A Puss Moth *My Hildergarde* (after his mother). He arrived in Darwin on 19 September, setting a record flight time of 17 hours between the two cities only three days after his twenty-first birthday and being licensed for only sixteen months having only logged 200 hours flight time. He left Darwin for the United Kingdom on 20 September, and arrived in Croydon on 28 September (8 days and 9 hours), beating Jim Mollison's 1931 time of 8 days 19 hours. His time was not recognized as a record because he had no intention of attempting the record and so had not registered his flight as a record attempt.

Jimmy Melrose by his DH80A Puss Moth *My Hildergarde*

1934: MACROBERTSON TROPHY AIR RACE

The MacRobertson Trophy Air Race (also known as the London to Melbourne Air Race) took place in October 1934 as part of the Melbourne Centenary celebrations and is considered by many as one of the most important long distance air races of all time. The Lord Mayor of Melbourne created the race, and a prize of £15, 000 was supplied by Sir Macpherson Robertson, a wealthy Australian confectionery manufacturer (now Cadbury).

The Royal Aero Club organized the approximately 11,300 mile race that overflew nineteen countries and seven seas and had five compulsory stops—Baghdad, Allahabad (India), Singapore, Darwin, and Charleville, Queensland—with the competitors able to choose their own routes. There were an additional twenty-two optional stops supplied with fuel and oil stocks. The basic rules were: no limit to the size of aircraft or power; no limit to crew size; no pilot could join the aircraft after it left England; and all aircraft were to carry three days' rations per crew member, floats, smoke signals, and efficient instruments. Prizes were to be awarded for the fastest aircraft and for the best performance on a handicap basis by any aircraft finishing within sixteen days. The racers were to take off at dawn (0630) on 20 October 1934. By take-off time a crowd of 60,000 was on hand, as only twenty of the original sixty-four entrants from thirteen countries were ready (the US had the most original entrants with twenty-seven aircraft). Included in the field were three purpose-built, beautifully streamlined twin-engine monoplane de Havilland DH.88 Comet racers, two of the new generation of American Boeing and Douglas all-metal passenger transports, and a mixture of earlier racers, light transports, and old bombers. The race was on and would be characterized by mishaps of all kinds.

The first mishap was Melbourne native Ray Parer and Geoff Hemsworth, whose Fairey Fox I had to land in Paris due to mechanical problems, but would eventually resume the flight to Australia, only arriving on 13 February 1935! (This was fast compared to his seven-month time with John McIntosch while competing in the 1919 England to Australia Air Race.) Englishmen N. Stack's Airspeed AS.8 Viceroy experienced faulty brakes in Athens that could not be repaired. The Granville R-6H Q.E.D flown by Americans Jackie Cochran and Wesley Smith Pratt was damaged due to malfunctioning flaps in Bucharest, Romania. An English Fairey Fox I flown by H.D. Gilman and J.K. Baines crashed near Palazzo San Gervasio, Italy, with both killed—the race's only casualties. As the race proceeded to the Middle East and southwest Asia contestants continued to drop out. A Lockheed Vega (*Puck*) flown by Australians J. Woods and D.C. Bennett overturned in Aleppo, Syria, and left the race. A B.A. Eagle (*The Spirit of Wm. Shaw & Co Ltd*) flown by F/Lt. G. Shaw of Britain withdrew in Bushehr, Iran, after unspecified problems. The Indian subcontinent also became a challenge. American J. H. Wright's Lambert Monocoupe 145 *Baby Ruth* left the race in Calcutta, India. The DH.88 Comets had surged ahead, but DH.88 *Black Magic*, piloted by Jim Mollison with wife Amy Johnson as his co-pilot, became lost after leaving Karachi and finally landed in Jabalpur, India, where no high octane fuel was available. Mollison decided to refuel with regular gasoline for the short flight to Allahabad, northern India. Soon after take-off the engines burned out and the "Flying Sweethearts" were out of the race. On a night take-off from Allahabad Dutch aircraft Pander S4 *Panderjager*, flown by G.J. Geysendorffer, clipped a high-standing searchlight with a wing and hundreds of gallons of aviation fuel in the wing tanks gushed out and were ignited by sparks from the engine exhaust. The *Pander* crashed, trailing burning fuel, but the three crew members escaped with help from bystanders, although Geijsendorffer and his co-pilot were badly burned and the aircraft was completely destroyed. As the race reached its final stages over Australia the weather deteriorated. The KLM Douglas DC-2 *Uiver*, flown by Capt. K.D. Parmentier and co-pilot J.J. Moll, became lost flying through extensive storms and by nightfall they were hopelessly off course over New South Wales, without a place to land. Their emergency call was received by the small town of Albury, New South Wales, which organized an emergency landing field. The citizens gathered their cars on the local racecourse and turned their headlights on to illuminate an improvised landing field. Meanwhile, the local power plant flashed the town electricity on and off to signal the Morse code letters "A-L-B-U-R-Y" and the KLM crew successfully landed on the racecourse. The Douglas airliner became stuck in the mud, but the following morning, the townspeople helped pull it out and it took off to continue the race.

Eventually nine of the twenty entrants arrived in Melbourne inside the sixteen-day deadline to complete the race. Three more arrived after the deadline and were not counted as official finishers. Five withdrew due to various problems and three were damaged or destroyed in crashes, with two fatalities and four people (including two bystanders) seriously injured. The race would be won in less than three days when the DH.88 Comet nicknamed *Grosvenor House* flown by Flt./Lt. C.W.A. Scott and Capt. Tom Campbell Black of Britain arrived in Melbourne at 1534 in 71:01:03 hours—just under three days—despite having one of the two engines throttled back due to a malfunctioning engine temperature gauge. The pilots thought the engine was suffering oil circulation problems and flew the last leg hoping the engine would not seize up. After landing, it was realized the engine was fine and it was really a malfunctioning indicator. Toward the end of the race both pilots were so tired that they tried to take half hour turns at the controls while the other slept, but had to take ten minute turns to stay awake. Coming in second place despite having been put back a day after the near-disaster in Albury, the KLM DC-2 *Uiver* (Stork) came in with a total time of 90:13 hours, even though KLM insisted on running the race as a commercial flight with three paying passengers. The DC-2 finished second in the elapsed time category and first on handicap, and the pilot was allowed to only accept one of the prizes. Since the first place prize for a handicap win was £2,000, while the second place prize on elapsed time was £1,500, Capt. Parmentier chose the handicap prize. The Boeing 247D *Warner Bros. Comet* flown by Roscoe Turner and Clyde Pangborn arrived with a total time of 92:55 hours to take third place. The 247 was leased from United Airlines by Turner for the race and had all its passenger seats and other unnecessary cabin accessories removed to make room for eight additional fuel tanks.

Of the eleven finishers, the third DH Comet (Britain), flown by O. Cathcart Jones and K.F. Waller, finished fourth with an elapsed time of 108:13 hours.

A Miles Hawk Major flown by S/Ldr. M. McGregor and H.C. Walker finished fifth with an elapsed time of 7 days, 14 hours, which was the fastest single-engine aircraft.

Sixth place went to an Airspeed AS.5 Courier (Britain) flown by S/Ldr. D. Stodart and Sgt. Pilot K. Stodart over an elapsed time of 9 days, 18 hours.

Seventh place was won by DH.80 Puss Moth *My Hildergarde* (Australia) by C.J. Jimmy Melrose, the youngest entrant at twenty-one, over an elapsed time of 10 days, 16 hours, which was second on handicap, despite an emergency landing in Darwin; he was the only solo flyer to finish and was awarded second prize of £500.

Eighth place was awarded to Danish pilots Lt. M. Hansen and D. Jensen flying a Desoutter Mk.II that arrived on 31 October.

Ninth place went to a DH.89 Dragon Rapide called *Tainui* (New Zealand) flown by J.D. Hewitt, C.E. Kay, and F. Stewart, arriving on 3 November.

Also finishing were: Miles M.3 Falcon (Britain) flown by H.L. Brook and Miss E. Lay (passenger), arriving on 20 November; and a Fairey IIIF (Britain) flown by F/O C.G. Davies and Lt.Cdr. C.N. Hill arriving on 24 November.

The MacRobertson Air Race denoted the beginning of a new chapter in aviation, as it established the performance over long distances of the newly introduced stressed metal aircraft was superior to the established wooden-bodied types. Even more significant was the second and third place finishes by passenger/transports, with the KLM Douglas DC-2 narrowly taking second place over Roscoe Turner's Boeing 247, both finishing less than a day behind the Comet winner, and thus proving that air travel was a viable alternative for international passenger transport. Flying was no longer a dangerous and demanding sport for reckless and irresponsible speed addicts and thrill seekers, but a safe, practical, and very fast means of passenger travel. Meanwhile, the *Melbourne Daily Mail* thought the Comets were "marvels," but added that, "the unfortunate fact, however, is that the aeroplanes of the Royal Air Force are a whole generation behind them in design and speed." The Comets would become the basis for de Havilland's superlative Mosquito design. The *Saturday Review* also bemoaned Britain's performance in the air race: "This is another air race, one in which Britain is very definitely lagging: the race for airpower. Britain's air force is shown to be behind those of Germany, the Soviet Union, France, Italy, the United States, and Japan."

MACROBERTSON GALLERY

H.L. BROOK: AUSTRALIA TO ENGLAND RECORD AND CAPE TOWN TO ENGLAND

H.L. (Howard Leslie) Brook first became recognized when he competed in the MacRobertson Air Race of 1934, flying a Miles M.3 *Falcon* prototype equipped with extra fuel tanks. He flew from Mildenhall, and 27 days later he reached Darwin, but his return flight was flown in a record time of 7 days, 19:15 hours, including one stage of 1,800 miles non-stop from Jodhpur to Basra. Brook next attempted to break Amy Mollison's United Kingdom to Cape Town record. On 5 April 1937, he left Gravesend in a Percival *Gull*, but after being delayed by bad weather over the Sudan and then damaging a tail wheel when taking off from Juba for Kisumu, Brook was unable to beat Amy Mollison's record. The return from Cape Town to the United Kingdom and round trip records were still within his reach. He left Cape Town on 2 May, and continued without incident until he damaged a flap in Rome due to heavy rainfall, which was quickly replaced, and he flew on without incident, finally landing at Heston on 5 May after 4 days, 0:20 hours, and 9 days, 9:30 hours over the 13,000 mile round trip—records for the return and round trip flights.

H.L. Brook and his Miles M.3 Falcon prototype.

ENGLAND TO SOUTH AFRICA FLIGHTS

The "All British" air route between Cairo and Cape Town was first opened for movement in 1920 due to the efforts of Cecil Rhodes and other "empire builders." The route was first surveyed in 1918, when three military parties were instructed to explore and, as far as possible, prepare the route. They worked with the local authorities and cut many of the aerodromes out of the dense jungle, clear cutting thousands of trees and moving tens of thousands of tons of earth to create forty-four aerodromes.

1920 FIRST ENGLAND TO SOUTH AFRICA FLIGHT: VAN RYNEVELD AND BRAND

In January 1920, *The Times* of London offered a £10,000 purse, and less than a month later, a British team sponsored by *The Times* flying a Vickers Vimy Commercial powered by two 375 hp Rolls-Royce Eagle engines set out from England on 24 January 1920 for Cape Town. It was piloted by Capts. Stanley Cockerell and Frank Broome, and included Secretary of the Zoological Society Dr. Chalmers Mitchell, two mechanics, and a *Times* reporter. On 27 February, the right engine failed on take-off from Tabora, Tanganyika, Central Africa, and the Vimy crashed and almost overturned, with the undercarriage being forced through the lower wing. The crew escaped without notable injuries, but the Vimy's fuselage was wrecked and unflyable. The fuselage was claimed by the Tabora Sporting Club to be used as a "pavilion" and the almost new engines were sent back to England.

Prime Minister Jan Smuts wanted a South African to be the first to fly the England-Cape Town, so he quickly authorized the purchase of a Vickers Vimy at a great cost of £4,500. On 4 February 1920, Lt.Col. Pierre van Ryneveld and Flt.Lt. Quintin Brand took

Capts. Stanley Cockerell and Frank Broome (under the fuselage, center) and their Vickers Vimy *Commercial*

TOP ROW / LEFT TO RIGHT

Sir Macpherson Robertson supplied a £15,000 prize and trophy for the race.

Akyab Burma was one of the twenty-two optional stops that had been supplied with fuel and oil stocks.

C(harles). W. A. Scott and Tom Campbell Black and their DH.88 Comet *Grosvenor House* finished first.

MIDDLE ROW / LEFT TO RIGHT

Capt. K.D. Parmentier (R) and co-pilot J.J. Moll flew the Dutch KLM DC-2 *Uiver* into second place.

Roscoe Turner (R) and Clyde Pangborn (2L) and their Boeing 247D arrived in third place.

O. Cathcart Jones (L) and K.F. Waller and their DH. Comet finished fourth.

BOTTOM LEFT / A Miles Hawk Major flown by M. McGregor (L) and H.C. Walker finished fifth.

BOTTOM RIGHT / TOP TO BOTTOM

The DH.88 *Black Magic*, piloted by Jim Mollison and co-pilot/wife Amy Johnson, had engine problems and dropped out.

C. W. A. Scott and Capt. Tom Campbell Black's DH.88 Comet *Grosvenor House* in Melbourne after winning the race.

off from Brooklands Aerodrome in Surrey in a Vimy named *Silver Queen*, eleven days behind the Vimy sponsored by *The Times*. Van Ryneveld and Brand had to do some night flying over Europe to catch up with the *Times* Vimy, but then encountered bad weather over the Mediterranean; the crossing took approximately 11 hours, causing more night flights. Then a leaking radiator and an overheating engine caused them to make a forced landing at night in Wadi Halfa, Egypt (present-day Sudan); although they were unhurt, the Vimy could not be repaired. The RAF loaned a second Vimy (*Silver Queen II*) to the pair in Heliopolis, Egypt, and they continued to Bulawayo, in Southern Rhodesia. On 6 March, the overloaded Vimy was badly damaged as it struggled to take off in hot conditions from the high-altitude Bulawayo airfield. Ryneveld and Brand then used a South African Air Force Airco DH.9 (*Silver Queen III*) which flew 4,000 miles before crashing. Undaunted, the South African government provided a third aircraft—a de Havilland DH9 named *Voortrekker*—and the two pilots took off for Cape Town on 14 March. After 45 days, with a flight time of 109:30 hours of nerve wracking flying, they landed in Cape Town, where the South African government awarded them £5,000 each; both men were knighted on their return to England for their achievement. Col. van Ryneveld established the South African Air Force (SAAF) in 1920 and directed it until 1933, when he was promoted to chief of the general staff (CGS), in command of the Union Defense Forces. For the next four years, the SAAF remained under van Ryneveld's direct control, as no one was appointed as the Air Force's next director until 1937. He served as CGS for sixteen years, including all of WWII. Meanwhile, during WWII Brand rose to the rank of air vice-marshal and commanded the RAF's 10 Fighter Battle Group.

1925–6: COBHAM'S LONDON-CAPE TOWN-LONDON IMPERIAL AIRWAYS SURVEY FLIGHT

Alan Cobham (pilot), Arthur Elliott (engineer), and B.W.G. Emmott (cinematographer) left Croydon, United Kingdom, in a D.H. 50J on 16 November 1925, arrived in Cape Town on 17 February, and returned to London on 20 March 1926 (see previous).

1926: The First RAF Cape Flight: Leaving on 6 November, W/C C.W.H. Pulford (flight commander), with Flt.Lts. P.H. Mackworth, E.J. Linton Hope, and L.E.M. Gillman (navigator); F/Os A.A. Jones (technical), W.L. Payne, and Sgts. Hartley (fitter); and Gardener (rigger) flew a 14,000 mile round-trip Cairo to Cape Town in Fairey III biplanes without change of personnel, aircraft, or engines.

1927: The Second RAF Cape Flight: The Second Cairo-Cape Town flight ended on 21 April, when Air Commodore C.R. Samson, leading four Fairey III biplanes, arrived at Cape Town 22 days after leaving Cairo. Samson published an account of this flight in his book aptly titled *A Flight from Cairo to Cape Town and Back*. Before transferring to the RAF after WWI Samson was a British naval aviation pioneer, was one of the first four officers selected for pilot training by the Royal Navy, and was the first person to fly an aircraft from a moving ship.

1927–28: Cobham African Survey Expedition: Sir Alan Cobham, in a Short S.5 Singapore flying boat, started from the United Kingdom on 17 November, and completed the outward journey to Cape Town on March 30, returning to England on 31 May 1928 (see previous).

1927: Richard Bentley: First Solo in a Light Aircraft to Cape Town and Return: Lt. Richard Reid (R.R.) Bentley began

Pierre van Ryneveld (L) and Quintin Brand and their Vimy *Silver Queen*

Richard Reid (R.R.) Bentley and his de Havilland 60x Moth

his 7,250 mile flight that was partially sponsored by the *Johannesburg Star* newspaper from Stag Lane Airdrome, England, on 1 September 1927 in his de Havilland 60x Moth powered by an 85 hp Cirrus II engine. The Moth was a standard production model, with the only change being an extra twenty-five gallon fuel tank installed instead of the passenger's seat. Famed South African aviatrix Lady Bailey christened Bentley's Moth with the name *Dorys*, after his then South African fiancée. Bentley landed in Cape Town 28 days later, flying the longest solo flight in a single engine aircraft to date. He left Cape Town for London on 3 March with his new wife, Dorys, as a passenger and arrived on his honeymoon trip on 12 May. He was awarded the Britannia Trophy for the most meritorious performance of the year.

1928: LADY MARY HEATH FIRST SOLO LIGHT PLANE FLIGHT FROM CAPE TOWN TO ENGLAND

Irish aviator Lady Mary Heath began life as Sophie Catherine Theresa Mary Peirce-Evans, and as a young woman Sophie was Britain's first woman javelin champion and set a disputed world record for the high jump in 1925. During an early, short, unhappy marriage to Capt. Eliot-Lynn (twenty years her senior) she became the first woman to hold a commercial flying license in Britain. Determined to earn her living by flying and to substantiate her flying abilities, she competed in handicap races and gave rides at air shows, set records for altitude flying in a small aircraft while flying a Shorts seaplane. For self promotion, she flew newspapers to Paris during the general newspaper strike there and became the first woman to parachute from an aircraft in the United Kingdom. In 1927, she seemed to have charmed the Avro Company to loan her an Avian to make a 1,250-mile flight around England to demonstrate the viability of travel by small aircraft. When her estranged first husband died, thirty-year-old Sophie began a search for a new wealthy husband to finance her fondness for flying and seventy-five-year-old Sir James Heath filled the bill; she became Lady Mary Heath in October 1927. Her marriage afforded her the funds to acquire an Avro Avian III and to fly to Cape Town, arriving on 6 December 1927. On the flight, when she requested the British Air Ministry for a plane to lead her across the Mediterranean, she was denied and asked Benito Mussolini for an escort plane; he agreed on the condition that she share her experiences with him. Once in Cape Town she used her newfound celebrity to lecture and gave flying displays. For the return journey she took off from Pretoria on 25 February 1928 on a planned three-week flight which took nearly three months, arriving in Croydon on 17 May. Her epic 9,000 mile journey made her the first pilot, male or female, to fly a small private aircraft solo from Cape Town to London, and she was labeled on worldwide front page news as "Britain's Lady Lindy" and "Lady Icarus." She later co-wrote a book about the experience, *Woman and Flying*. (Note: In late 2013, Tracey Curtis-Taylor recreated Lady Heath's Cape Town to Cairo flight in a 1942 Boeing Stearman.) The Avian was subsequently sold to Amelia Earhart. In July 1928, she became the first woman civil airline co-pilot when KLM hired her, but soon she was let go, as the public was not ready to see a woman in the cockpit. However, the actual reason was according to the all-male club (the International Commission for Aviation), a women's menstrual cycle was a disability which made them unfit to serve as commercial pilots. Lady Mary's female swagger, entertainer persona, and often outdoing her male competitors also rubbed the male establishment the wrong way, as did her appearing with her aircraft in chic clothing, her fur coat, and pearls. Lady Mary left Europe and accepted an invitation from the prestigious Chautauqua lecture circuit to lecture and promote flying in America. She qualified as America's first woman aircraft mechanic, and Cirrus Aero-Engines Limited hired her to demonstrate and sell their Cirrus engines to American aircraft manufacturers. By using her British title and fame she successfully attracted public and press attention wherever she went. Unfortunately, at the time publisher George Putnam was ruthlessly promoting Amelia Earhart as the "female face of aviation" and used his influence to have Lady Mary's and other women pilots' lecture tours and their sponsorships canceled in favor of Amelia Earhart. Of all the successful female pilots of the late 1920s (Elinor Smith, Louise Thaden, Amy Johnson, and others), only the self-serving Earhart is

The chic Lady Mary Heath with her Avro Avian III after her 1928 flight

remembered due to the efforts of George Putnam. The 1929 National Air Show in Cleveland was the biggest air show of its type and was to feature the first ever Women's Air Derby. During practice flights several women pilots' aircraft were suspiciously tampered with, and while sabotage was suspected, it was never proven. During practice Lady Mary's aircraft stalled and crashed through a factory roof; she was gravely injured and for days was near death. After months of medical treatment she never recovered her health, nor her passion for flying. She divorced Heath in 1930 and returned to Ireland with her third husband, G.A.R. Williams, a handsome black Trinidadian jockey whose race caused her sponsorships, advertising endorsements, and any chance at employment in aviation to stop. By 1939, her health was failing due to her accident and she also developed a serious alcohol problem. In May 1939, the forty-three-year-old died as a result of injuries received from a fall from a tramcar in London.

1928–9: THE HONORABLE LADY BAILEY

Lady Bailey was born Mary Westenra, daughter of the Fifth Baron Rossmore. In 1910, at the age of twenty, she became the second wife of South African diamond tycoon Sir Abe Bailey. In 1927, with five children ranging in age from six to fourteen, she became a licensed pilot and Sir Abe bought her a de Havilland DH.60 Cirrus II Moth, which she took delivery of in the United Kingdom. She soon became the first woman to fly across the Irish Sea, and on 5 July 1927, she set a world's altitude record of 17,283 ft. in a light aircraft category.

On 9 March 1928, Lady Bailey took off from Croydon Aerodrome, London, headed for Cape Town. The flight did not begin well, as over the English Channel she encountered severe weather, gale force winds, and then fog, and had to land short of Le Bourget; she then continued there in a snowstorm. The next day she flew to Lyons, again encountering snowstorms. The next legs of the flight were the over-water crossing of the Mediterranean to Tripoli and an eastward flight to Cairo. Once she arrived in Egypt, officials there impounded her Moth for "safety" (really gender) reasons, but a RAF pilot stationed in Egypt agreed to escort her, and she was allowed to continue south along the Nile, arriving in Luxor on 28 March. From there she encountered sandstorms with high winds and reduced visibility, but on 10 April, she landed in Tabora, German East Africa (Tanganyika), where her Moth flipped over, breaking a wing spar and heavily damaging the fuselage. Wealthy Sir Abe came to her rescue and purchased a de Havilland demonstrator DH.60 Moth in Johannesburg, which was flown to Tabora on 19 April. Lady Bailey departed Tabora on 21 April, and continued to Broken Hill, Northern Rhodesia, where she became ill. After four days she had recuperated enough to continue to Livingstone, then Bulawayo, and finally arrived in Cape Town on 30 March, after 52 days and 8,000 miles. After spending several months in Cape Town, Lady Bailey continued her round trip solo flight by returning to London via the western "French route"—the Belgian Congo, Angola, and the French Congo—and finally arrived back in Croydon on 16 January 1929, 18,000 miles and 10 months after flying the longest solo flight by a woman up to that time. Lady Bailey was awarded the Harmon Trophy in 1927 and 1928. In 1930, she was created Dame Commander of the Order of the British Empire. During WWII, the Hon. Dame Mary Bailey, DBE, served with the Women's Auxiliary Air Force with the rank section officer. She died 29 July 1960 at age seventy.

The Honorable Lady Bailey and her de Havilland DH.60 Cirrus II Moth

WINIFRED SPOONER

The daughter of a British Army major, Winifred received a pilot's license from the London Aeroplane Club in September 1927—only the sixteenth British woman to receive a license. She later also received an American Aviator's Certificate on 21 August 1931, signed by Orville Wright. Once she received her license she purchased a DH.60 Cirrus Moth, which she could fly and store on her family's farm. She gave flying lessons and began an air taxi service, charging £4 an hour or one shilling a mile for transport in Britain and France. During September 1927, her first long flight abroad was to Venice, to support the British team in the Schneider Cup. She soon became interested in air racing and air meets. In her first race in April 1928, she won the Suffolk Handicap (21 miles at 78 mph) ahead of five male contestants. In July 1928, she placed third in the seventh annual handicapped King's Cup Race, flying 1,097 miles cross-country north and then south over the United Kingdom, which as a woman was considered a major accomplishment. She then won the Aeroplane Club Siddeley Trophy that year. In 1929, she finished

Winifred Spooner

fifth in the King's Cup Race and then placed tenth in the Challenge International de Tourisme. That year she was awarded the Harmon Trophy as the world's outstanding female aviator, which was awarded previously to Lady Mary Bailey, the recipient of the first two aviatrix Harmon Trophies. The London newspapers regarded her as "one of the few women who matter in the air world." She was awarded the International League of Aviation's Trophy for women aviators in 1929. In 1930, Capt. C.D. Barnard, Lady Bailey's "co-pilot" (see Lady Bailey text), described Spooner as "the finest woman pilot in the world," continuing to state that Lady Bailey was regarded as the "second finest airwoman in the world." In 1930, she was a member of the British Challenge International de Tourisme team in Berlin, finishing seventh in the rally portion in her De Havilland Gipsy Moth and finishing the challenge in an impressive fourth place. In late August she finished fourth in the handicapped Italian Giro Aereo d'Italia. On 5 December 1930, accompanied by Capt. Edwards, she left England for South Africa, intending to arrive within a record five days by flying day and night. After sixteen hours in flight, and with Edwards at the controls and Spooner napping, the plane crash landed into the sea off the southern Italian coast in total darkness. Edwards could not swim, so Spooner left him sitting on the floating wooden fuselage, swam about two miles to shore, and contacted local fishermen who rescued Edwards and the de Havilland. In 1931, she took fifth place in the King's Cup Race and became the first British woman to earn her living as a private personal pilot, flying air racer and MP Sir William Lindsay Everard throughout Britain, Europe, Turkey, and the Middle East. In 1932, she was in fourth place after technical trials, but she decided to withdraw after a forced landing caused by sabotage on her fuel. She participated in three out of four Challenge International de Tourismes, and was one of only two women to be one of the top contestants, taking tenth place in 1929 and fourth place in 1930. During her career she had suffered a number of misfortunes during the contests that kept her from finishing higher and earned her the nickname "Bad Luck Wimpey." During January 1933, Spooner caught a cold which rapidly worsened into pneumonia. A specialist was summoned, but arrived late due to fog, and she suffered a heart attack. "Bad Luck Wimpey" died on Friday the thirteenth.

1930: THE DUCHESS OF BEDFORD

Born as Mary Du Caurroy Tribe, she was the daughter of Walter Harry Tribe, Anglican Archdeacon of Lahore, India. While in India she met her husband, Lord Hebrand Russell, who became fabulously wealthy when he unexpectedly inherited the Dukedom of Bedford when his father and brother died. Using her wealth, Mary became an expert hunter and fisherwoman, and mountain climber and sailor in the world's remote and inaccessible places. She also became an accomplished photographer and painter, and was a very capable mechanic and built her own radios. At sixty-one she began her love of flying and soon hired a professional pilot, Capt. C.D. Barnard, and navigator/mechanic, Robert Little, and purchased a single-engined Fokker F.VII she named *Spider*. From 1926–1937, she flew all over the world, first as a passenger, and then at sixty-five she became a fully qualified pilot, earning the sobriquet, "The Flying Duchess." On 8 April 1930, she made her first solo flight in her DH.60G Moth. The trio succeeded in establishing world record times for flights from England to India and from England to Cape Town.

On 2 August 1929, the Fokker piloted by Capt. Barnard departed on a record breaking flight from Lympne Aerodrome (United Kingdom) to Karachi (then India) and return to Croydon Airport (United Kingdom). From Lympne he proceeded to Sofia, Bulgaria, on a non-stop flight covering 1,400 miles. The following day, the Fokker covered 900 miles to reach Aleppo (Syria) and then covered another 1,000 miles over the desert to Bushire (Iran). The last leg flew south (1,050 non-stop miles) along the Persian Gulf to reach Karachi on 5 August. The next day the Fokker took off for the return flight, retracing the same route and arriving in Croydon on 10 August, completing the 10,000 mile round trip in just under eight days.

On 10 April 1930, *Spider*—flown by Barnard and sometimes by the Duchess—embarked on a record-breaking flight from Lympne to Cape Town, flying 9,000 miles in 100 flying hours over 10 days to land at Cape Town on 19 April. The return flight was made 21–30 April, but on 29 April, they had to make a forced landing in Dragoman, Bulgaria. The next day, after repairs, they returned to Croydon, completing a total flight of 19,000 miles in 21 days.

On 22 March 1937, while flying her Gipsy Moth and trying to accumulate 200 hours of solo flying time for her license renewal, seventy-one-year-old Duchess disappeared into the North Sea, with her body never being recovered.

The Duchess of Bedford, Capt. C.D. Barnard (L), navigator/mechanic Robert Little, and their Fokker F.VII Spider

1930: RHINIE FREDERICK CASPARENTHUS

Ex-RAF South African Rhinie Casparenthus left Croydon in a D.H. Puss Moth on 5 October and arrived at Maitland Aerodrome, Cape Town, on 13 October, completing the trip in the record time of 9½ days with a total flying time of 78 hours.

1931: GLEN KIDSTON

Glen Kidston's father died when he was a small boy, leaving him immensely wealthy; he grew up as a fashionable and handsome playboy who apparently was a driven thrill seeker. During WWI he served in the Royal Navy, distinguishing himself in the great naval Battle of Jutland. After the war he continued in the RN and then commanded British submarines; away from his duties as a submariner he was an early pioneer of naval flight. After leaving the RN he joined the well-known Bentley Boys, a group of wealthy British automobile racers who drove Bentley sports cars in the late 1920s and early 1930s. In 1930, he won Le Mans with Boys leader Woolf Barnato, who had three previous wins in 1928, 1929, and 1930. He also competed in the motorcycle and speedboat races, and to round out his adventurous lifestyle he was a prominent big game hunter and participated in pioneering safaris in Kenya.

On 31 March, Glen Kidston, accompanied by Lt. Owen Cathcart Jones and L.A. Valletti (the wireless operator who was replaced by L. Johnson for the second half of the flight), took off from Netheravon in his specially adapted Lockheed Vega and headed for Cape Town. The flight was promoted as a fast method to deliver the *London Times* to South Africa and to expose Imperial Airways' yet-to-be-delivered Handley Page 42 biplanes obsolete compared to fast monoplanes such as his Vega. Predictably, Imperial regarded the flight as a "stunt, bearing no relation to a proper commercial operation." Despite a delay due to a forced landing near Lichtenburg (Pretoria), they arrived in Cape Town in the late afternoon of 6 April, averaging 131 mph during 57:10 hours flying time over a record 6 days, 10 hours (154 hours). Kidston was never to make the return trip, as on 5 May, only a year after his Le Mans victory, he was killed in the Drakensburg Mountains when the de Havilland Puss Moth he had borrowed while the Vega was being overhauled broke up in mid-air during a storm.

Glen Kidston (2R), Owen Cathcart Jones (2R), and L.A. Valletti (R)

1931: MISS PEGGY SALAMAN

Miss Peggy Salaman and Mr. Gordon Store and their de Havilland 80A Puss Moth *Good Hope*

Having lived in luxury, nineteen-year-old and probably bored Peggy Salaman purchased a de Havilland 80A Puss Moth she named *Good Hope* which had previously won the King's Cup Race with the fastest time in its history. She hired Gordon Store as a "co-pilot" and in pre-flight publicity, Miss Salaman stated: "Mr. Store will sometimes take over the controls. We have two revolvers, an alarm clock, and chewing gum to stop leakages in the petrol tanks. We also have sun helmets and shorts; I am taking an evening gown to make whoopee in Cape Town, although I don't like dancing, smoking, and other modern feminine crazes. I do not regard the flight as extraordinary. Women have done far more courageous things. I am determined to do or die, but I am going to do." She and Gordon Store left Croydon 31 October, headed for Cape Town; somewhere and somehow en route she acquired two lion cubs who were bottle-fed on board. In the week they flew their journey was reported worldwide, and afterward was featured in a double-page spread in *Time* magazine. On 4 October, after five days, 6:40 hours (126:40 hours), she landed in Cape Town, breaking Kidstons' record by about twenty-eight hours. Reportedly, after hearing she had broken the record she demured, "How perfectly lovely!" adding, "We could have got here much earlier, but we slowed to 90 mph over gorgeous mountains and admired the magnificent scenery." After the flight questions arose as to the extent of her participation and the unheralded Store's part in the flight. In a post-flight interview she stated she was "not the person to whom tribute should be paid, as was only a minor part of the crew of the *Good Hope*. Mr. Store was responsible for the navigation, for the chief part of the piloting, for effecting the forced landing, and for landing and taking off at the majority of the aerodromes, particularly those where the rarified air made getting away conditions difficult; he also was responsible for the maintenance and good running of the engine. Her part was to relieve Mr. Store when the flying was straightforward (in order that he might get some rest) and to look after the general organization, such as customs, log book, sending telegrams, and dealing with the ground side generally." Eventually the lions were adopted by a private zoo and Miss Salaman became a footnote in aviation history. She served her country in the WRAAF and the WRNS during WWII. After his flight with Salaman, Store remained in South Africa as a director of Aero Services and later joined Imperial Airways, serving on the airline's African and Empire routes. In 1939, he commanded one of the three crews operating the first regular trans-Atlantic services.

Jim Mollison

1932: JIM MOLLISON

On 1 April 1932, Mollison flew from London to Cape Town in 113:22 hours, but this record and his entire career would be overshadowed by his wife Amy Johnson-Mollison's accomplishments and celebrity (see previous reference).

1932: MRS. AMY JOHNSON-MOLLISON

After Amy married Jim Mollison she continued to fly, and set out to break her husband's England-Cape Town record set that year. Mollison-Johnson took off in her new de Havilland DH.80A Puss Moth *Desert Cloud* from Lympne Aerodrome, London, on 14 November, and after a refueling stop in Barcelona arrived in Oran after 1,100 miles. After four hours in Oran she took off, flying at night across the Sahara Desert with no landmarks toward Gao, where she landed at noon after flying 1,300 miles. After a short refueling stop Mollison left for Duala, but after flying for about an hour she noticed her tanks were almost empty. When she returned to Gao she discovered that only ten gallons of fuel instead of forty-two gallons had been pumped. She then arrived safely in Duala in the evening and quickly continued during the night toward Loanda. On this leg the Moth's oil circulation became troublesome and she landed the next morning in Benguela, where she was delayed for nine hours while the problem was fixed. She then left for a refueling stop in Mossamedes the evening of November 17, after which she flew the final leg of the flight to Cape Town. Mrs. Mollison landed later than anticipated at 1500 and was greeted by a small crowd after flying approximately 6,300 miles in a total elapsed time of 4 days, 6:54 hours, breaking her husband's previous record by 10:28 hours. On her return flight Amy's time was 175:05 hours, leaving Cape Town at 0500 on 11 December, landing in Croydon on 18 December, and breaking the previous record of 9.5 days established by Capt. C. D. Barnard and the Duchess of Bedford by about two days (see previous reference). Newspapers of the day read: "She has also shown, by the splendid effort on this last flight, in which she had to fight against most unfavourable weather conditions throughout, that she undoubtedly ranks foremost amongst long-distance pilots."

Mrs. Amy Johnson-Mollison and her de Havilland DH.80A Puss Moth *Desert Cloud*

1936: TOMMY ROSE

Tommy Rose and his Miles M38 Falcon 6

Phillips & Powis Aircraft Ltd. built some of the most extraordinary private aircraft in Britain during the 1930s, and one of those was the three-passenger Miles M.3A Falcon Major as a cabin version of the successful M.2F Hawk Major. Power was initially provided by a 130 hp DH Gipsy Major 4-cylinder engine, but the racing and record breaking version had the installation of the bigger 200 hp Gipsy 6. WWI eleven victory ace Flt./Lt. Tommy Rose won the 1935 King's Cup Air Race in his Miles M38 Falcon 6 at a record average speed of 176 mph over the 801 mile cross-country course. Leaving the United Kingdom in his Miles M38 Falcon 6 on 3 March 1936, Rose broke Amy Johnson-Mollison's London to Cape Town record, flying it in 6 days, 6:57 hours, then went on to set the return to England record. From 1939–45 Rose was chief test pilot with Phillips & Powis Aircraft Ltd., which was renamed Miles Aircraft Ltd in 1943.

1936: DAVID LLEWELLYN

F/O David Llewellyn—a RAF pilot on leave—and Mrs. Jill Wyndham, flying a tiny 40 hp Aeronca C3 side-by-side two passenger coupe, left Johannesburg for England. To expedite the flight an additional fuel tank was installed in the right hand seat, extending flight time by ten hours. During the flight Llewellyn faced flooded airfields in Italy that necessitated the plane be carried to a nearby road to take off; sandstorms over Libya; and tropical storms over central Africa. When he tried to take off from elevated Tanganyika he found the small engine just could not lift him off at 6,500 ft. above sea level. After an attempt to launch the C3 off a soil ramp failed, the anxious Llewellyn tried to install a pair of high compression pistons he was carrying for aerobatic displays. Using only basic tools, he was almost finished with the second piston when he lost a vital small part in the grass and spent the next several hours on his hands searching, eventually finding the part and then flying over the surrounding hills. After three weeks and 130 hours of flying 1,900 miles, the little plane landed in London; not a record setter, but it was defined by its engine's economy. Llewellyn was killed on 21 September 1938, in an accident in a BA Swallow.

David Llewellyn and his tiny 40 hp Aeronca C3

1936: AMY JOHNSON-MOLLISON

On 4 May 1936, Johnson made her last record breaking flight, leaving Gravesend Aerodrome, Kent, England, at 0802 and regaining her Britain to South Africa record in a Percival Gull Six. In July 1932, she had set a record for flying this route solo, breaking the existing record set by her husband, James Mollison. The current record was held by Flt./Lt. Tommy Rose of 6 days, 6:57 hours. During the next three days Johnson flew approximately 6,700 miles, making several refueling stops and catching only six hours of naps on the way. She arrived at Wingfield Aerodrome, Cape Town, at 1431 on 7 May, for an elapsed time of 3 days, 6:29 hours, barely beating Rose's record by twenty-eight minutes. She then broke Rose's Cape Town-London return record time by 11:09 hours.

Amy Johnson-Mollison's *Percival Gull Six*

1936: THE SCHLESINGER AIR RACE: ENGLAND-JOHANNESBURG

Inspired by the very successful 1934 MacRobertson Air Race that celebrated the centenary of the Australian state of Victoria, multi-millionaire South African industrialist I. W. Schlesinger sponsored an air race from England to Johannesburg to promote the 1936 Johannesburg Empire Exhibition. The Schlesinger Race—also known as the Rand Race, the Portsmouth-Johannesburg Race, and contemporarily as the African Air Race—took place in September 1936, with Schlesinger offering £10,000 in prize money to be divided into two sections: a speed race and a handicap race to be flown concurrently, but no competitor could win both first prizes. Schlesinger made a major error by restricting entry to British Empire crews and aircraft only, limiting the number of contestants.

Tom Campbell Black, who won the 1934 MacRobertson Race co-piloting the DH Comet Racer *Grosvenor House*, was an entrant flying a Percival Mew Gull, but ten days before the start of the race a No. 611 Squadron Hawker Hart taxied into Black's aircraft, which was also taxiing on the runway. Black's fuselage was almost cut in two when the Hart's propeller cut into it, mortally injuring Black. Two aircraft—a Miles Peregrine and M. Chand's Percival Vega Gull—were not ready, while John

Carberry's Vega Gull was damaged when Beryl Markham crash landed in a peat bog on Cape Breton Island after flying it across the Atlantic Ocean on 4–5 September, leaving nine entrants on race day.

The start (originally scheduled to be Hatfield) was from Portsmouth, and the competitors took off in semi-darkness starting at 0630 on 29 September 1936. During the 6,154 mile race the participants dropped out one by one along the way. Cyril Alington's and P.A. Booth's B.A. *Eagle* was forced down near Regensburg, Germany, and damaged its undercarriage. Allister Miller, flying Percival Mew Gull *The Golden City*, had fuel problems and made a forced landing in Belgrade and withdrew. Next, Tommy Rose's and Jack Bagshaw's B.A.4 *Double Eagle IV* damaged its undercarriage while taxiing on an airfield in Cairo. Victor Smith's Miles *Sparrowhawk* experienced continual oil problems and withdrew in Khartoum. On 30 September, Stanley Halse's Percival Mew Gull made a forced landing in a ploughed field and overturned outside of Salisbury, Rhodesia. David Llewellyn and Charles Hughesdon landed on a shore of Lake Tanganyika due to bad weather in their Percival Vega Gull. Pilot Maxwell Findlay's Airspeed Envoy crashed during take-off from Abercorn, killing him and radio operator A.H. Morgan, while two others escaped with injuries. With only two competitors remaining, A.E. Clouston made a forced crash landing 150 miles south of Salisbury in his Miles Hawk Six. Charles W. A. Scott and Giles Guthrie in Percival Vega Gull were the only competitors remaining, and after 2 days, 4:56 hours landed in Cape Town to a small crowd, as most of the waiting spectators left by the time they arrived. The Aeroplane and Flight deemed their victory a "hollow one," and the unclaimed prize money (£6,000 out of the £10,000) was donated to the grieving Findlay and Morgan families.

C.W. A. Scott (L) and Giles Guthrie and their *Percival Vega Gull*

A.E. CLOUSTON

In 1930, after the Royal New Zealand Air Force rejected his application to join, native New Zealander A.E. (Arthur Edmond) Clouston moved to England and joined the RAF, where he stayed until 1935, when he became a civilian test pilot at RAE Farnborough. While at the RAE Clouston became interested in civil aviation, air racing, and breaking air records. In June 1937, after his forced landing near the end of the Schlesinger Race to Johannesburg, he found that Tom Campbell Black's DH.88 Comet—which won the 1934 MacRobertson Race—was for sale by a scrap dealer after it was damaged during Air Ministry testing. He persuaded architect Fred Tasker to purchase the Comet and then arranged for it to be repaired with upgraded engines and propellers. He entered the Comet in the planned 1937 New York to Paris air race, but the US Department of Commerce refused permission for the race to start on US soil, causing the French government to restructure the race to run from Istres Airfield near Marseille, in the south of France, via Damascus, Syria, and back to Paris. The 3,850 mile race was scheduled for 20–21 August, with twenty-four entries, of which thirteen started and seven finished. The competitors included eight Italians, four Frenchmen, and Clouston. On 20 August 1937, Clouston, accompanied by co-pilot Flt./Lt. George Nelson, took off from Istres against twelve aircraft, all of which were more powerful and sponsored by European governments (Clouston's Comet was nicknamed *Orphan* due to its lack of sponsors). Italians took the first three places: Cupini and Baradsi in 17:32 hours with an average speed of 219 mph; Fiori and Luccini finished second at 17:57 hours; and Stista and Bruno Mussolini (Il Duce's son) were third in 18:03 hours, all flying Italian Air Force Savoia-Marchetti SM.79 tri-motored bombers.

In 1937, Clouston became interested in breaking the record for a flight from England to Cape Town and return. Betty Kirby-Green was a novice pilot who was eager to break records and agreed to help raise money for an attempt on the Cape Town record. The Tom Campbell Black DH.88 Comet was hired from Fred Tasker, then sponsored by Burberry Clothing and named *The Burberry*; the red Comet was repainted Burberry beige. On 14 November 1937, Clouston and Kirby-Green took off from Croydon Aerodrome, and on 16 November, reached Cape Town via Cairo, Khartoum, Broken Hill, and Johannesburg. They broke the London-Cairo record in 11:04 hours (beating the previous record by thirty minutes). They continued on to Cape Town, arriving there in a total time of 45:02 hours, averaging 155.5 mph and breaking the previous record by more than thirty-three hours! On 20 November, they arrived back in Croydon in dense fog, having broken several records and covered about 14,690 miles in less than six days. As a result Clouston was awarded the Britannia Trophy and the Segrave Trophy, and Kirby-Green was awarded the Segrave Medal.

A.E. Clouston (L) and Mrs Betty Kirby-Green and the former Tom Campbell Black DH.88 Comet

A.E. Clouston's DH.88 Comet *Australian Anniversary*

Victor Ricketts, aviation correspondent for the *Daily Express*, encouraged Clouston to make an attempt on the England-Australia record flying the Comet. The aircraft was renamed *Australian Anniversary* for the Australian Sesquicentennial and the first attempt began on 6 February 1938, when Clouston and Ricketts took off from Gravesend Aerodrome. The first scheduled stop was to be Aleppo, Syria, but bad storms forced Clouston to land at a flooded airfield in Adana, Turkey. His permits were rejected by Turkish officials, but the next day he surreptitiously refueled with unofficial help and took off from a roadway, damaging the undercarriage. He flew to an unmarked airfield on Cyprus, having abandoned the record attempt. Engineer Jack Cross, plus some repair equipment, was flown to Cyprus by Alex Henshaw in his Vega Gull. After repairs to the Comet Clouston flew it back to Gravesend, accompanied by Jack Cross. On 15 March 1938, Clouston once again departed from Gravesend with Victor Ricketts in the DH.88 Comet. They flew via Cairo, Basra, Allahabad, Penang, and Singapore to Darwin, but without beating the 1934 record set by C.W. A. Scott and Tom Campbell Black in the same aircraft. He flew on to Sydney via Charleville, unaware of the London to Sydney record, until huge crowds were on hand to signal their three-day, 9:00 hour flight was a record breaker. The next day Clouston and Ricketts continued on to New Zealand, making the Tasman Sea crossing in a record 7:27 hours and arriving in Blenheim on 20 March. The following day the return flight back to Australia took 8:31 hours. The total England-New Zealand leg had taken 4 days, 8:37 hours. The return trip to England on 26 March had taken 10 days, 21:22 hours. Eleven records had been established at the end of a round trip of about 26,000 miles. The Tasman record stood until 1945, when it was reset by a B-25 Mitchell. The England-New Zealand record stood until 25 August 1946, when an Empire Air Navigation School Avro Lancastrian I made the journey in 59:50 hours. The Comet has been restored to flying condition and is in the Shuttleworth Collection at Old Warden Aerodrome, Bedfordshire, England.

PERCIVAL GULL, VEGA GULL, AND MEW GULL
EDGAR PERCIVAL

Australian Capt. Edgar Percival joined the Royal Flying Corps in 1918, and after the war returned to Australia to barnstorm and pursue commercial flying and air racing. Percival had a continuing interest in aircraft design and collaborated in building competition winning light aircraft, as well as trying to improve aircraft design and test fly others. He returned to England in 1929 and became an Air Ministry test pilot, concentrating on amphibians, seaplanes, and Schneider Trophy racers. During this time he flew a series of proving flights in carrier-borne aircraft. His interest in aircraft technology increased and he became involved in collaborative projects with Saunders Roe Limited, such as the Saro Percival Mail Carrier in 1930. In 1932, Percival and E. W. B. Leake formed Percival Aircraft Company to build his own designs; initially, the company operated from Percival's London home, contracting manufacturing to George Parnell & Sons. Percival aircraft, flown by some of the most renown pilots of the day, recorded a series of record breaking flights, cementing Percival's reputation. In 1934, after an order for twenty-four aircraft which had to be manufactured by Parnell, Percival established his own manufacturing facility in Gravesend, and two years later they consolidated operations to a larger facility under the new name Percival Aircraft Limited. Percival concentrated on his *Gull* series civilian racing aircraft. In 1933, Sir Charles Kingsford Smith flew a *Gull* on his record breaking London to

Edgar Percival with his Mew Gull

Australia flight. Percival became the first person to fly from England to Morocco to England (230 miles) in one day in 1935 and won the Oswald Watt Gold Medal. The highlight for Percival's designs was during the Schlesinger England-South Africa Race in 1936, in which almost half the entrants were Percival designs, including the *Vega Gull* Charles W. A. Scott and Giles Guthrie winner. In 1938, with a war pending, Percival Aircraft Limited developed military communications aircraft, such as the Percival *Vega Gull* and Percival *Proctor.* Percival became dissatisfied with life in England and resigned from the company in March 1940 before moving to America. The company continued independently as Percival Aircraft Limited until 1944, when it was purchased as part of the Hunting Group, who, after allowing the name to continue for another ten years, changed it to Hunting Percival in 1954, and then Hunting Aircraft in 1957.

Percival Gull

The Percival Gull was a British single-engined, low-wing cantilever monoplane constructed of wood with fabric covering. First flown in 1932, it was successful as a fast company transport, racing aircraft, and long-range record breaker. It was developed into the Vega Gull, Mew Gull, and the Proctor. All Gulls were of a similar generic structure, with the general dimensions of all Gulls being: wingspan of 36.2 ft. and wing area of 169 sq. ft., a length of 24.8 ft., a height of 7.4 ft., an empty weight of 1,170 lbs., and 2,050 lbs. gross weight. The glazed cabin merged smoothly into a raised dorsal fairing and placed the pilot forward, with two passenger seats behind. Structurally, other than a few minor components, there was very little commonality of parts between the Gulls IV and VI, the Vega Gull, and the Mew Gull. Proprietary equipment, such as engines, propellers, spinners, instruments, undercarriage legs, wheels, and tires, were used in all Gulls. The Gulls used a fixed, conventional oleo main undercarriage and a fully castoring tailskid. Small manually operated split trailing-edge wing flaps were incorporated into the main planes. Although Gull variants were powered by five different engines, those were all inverted inline air-cooled types driving two-bladed propellers, making for a neatly faired installation.

Percival Vega Gull

The main changes from the earlier Gull design, due to new Percival aircraft designer Arthur Bage, were a widened fuselage and increased wingspan, the provision of an additional fourth seat, dual controls, and flaps. Payload, range, and utility were all much improved. The enlarged Vega Gull was almost as fast as the trimmer Gull Six. During the later years of aviation's "Golden Age" the Vega Gull was widely used by record setting British and commonwealth aviators, and as described earlier was flown by Jim Mollison, Amy Johnson-Mollison, Beryl Markham, C.W.A. Scott, and others; it won races and broke speed and distance records to South Africa, South America, Australia, and New Zealand.

Percival Mew Gull

Beautifully restored Percival Mew Gull originally flown by Alex Henshaw.

The original Mew Gull was the first civil aircraft to exceed a speed of 200 mph; the fastest speed was recorded by the famous G-AEXF in its 1938 Kings Cup configuration and was in excess of 270 mph—at sea level it was faster than a Hawker Hurricane. After Alex Henshaw purchased his Mew Gull he re-registered it as G-AEXF and extensively modified it for the 1938 King's Cup, which he won at a record speed of 236.25 mph. After the King's Cup race Henshaw further modified it for the much longer UK-Cape Town-UK Race by adding extensive navigation instrumentation and increasing its fuel capacity. Henshaw installed a critical stable gyro compass, a large magnetic compass mounted just in front of the pilot, and a chronometer with three stopwatches to be used for dead reckoning. Additional fuel tanks were installed to extend range to over 1,200 miles, but when full they shifted the center of gravity so far aft that a special certificate of airworthiness had to be issued and was void after the flight. As far as pilot comfort for a long distance record flight the Mew Gull was not ideal, as its cockpit was extremely confined (only about two feet wide) and just high enough not to touch the pilot's head. The forward view was so poor on the ground that Henshaw had to concoct a taxiing scheme involving walking alongside the aircraft with the canopy open with his hand on the throttle!

Percival Gull Record Flights

Charles Kingsford Smith

On 4 October 1933, Smith took off in a Gull Four (*Miss Southern Cross*) from Lympne Aerodrome, United Kingdom, via Brindisi,

Baghdad, Gwadar, Karachi, Jhodpur, Akyab, Alur Setar, Surabaya, and Wyndham, Australia, to Darwin, Australia, arriving on 11 October 1933 in a record 7 days, 4:44 hours.

Edgar Percival

On 17 June 1935, company president Edgar Percival piloted a Gull Six from Gravesend to Oran (Algeria), returning to Croydon Airport the same day.

Amy Johnson-Mollison: UK-Cape Town Return Record

On 4 May 1936, Johnson-Mollison's Percival Gull Six with a de Havilland Gipsy Six engine took off from Gravesend, and during the next three days Johnson flew approximately 6,700 miles, making several refueling stops and napping for only about six hours. While Rose flew the East Coast route down Africa, Mollison flew along the West Coast, cutting about 700 miles from the trip but crossing 2,000 miles of the Sahara Desert, flying blind and by night. She arrived at Wingfield Aerodrome, Cape Town, on 7 May, for an elapsed time of 3 days, 6:29 hours, breaking Tommy Rose's time by 11:09 hours. Her plan was to then make the return flight and beat Rose's two-way record, which she accomplished by returning to England in 7 days 22:43 hours, despite being prevented from keeping to her schedule, as aerodromes with short and inadequate runways made it impossible for the Gull to take off with full tanks.

1937/1938 King's Cup Races

In the 1937 King's Cup Race, the rebuilt G-AEKL finished first piloted by Charles Gardner, averaging 234 mph over the 1,442-mile course. Percival flew his latest Super Mew—the sixth and last Mew Gull built—to a third place finish.

The 1,012 mile 1938 King's Cup Race was won by Alex Henshaw's much modified Mew Gull (AEKL) at 236 mph. Henshaw's AEKL was a Mew Gull that was almost cut in half when Tom Campbell Black was killed before the Schlesinger Race. Giles Guthrie in his "standard" Mew Gull placed second, while Edgar Percival flew a third Mew Gull to sixth place.

JEAN BATTEN: NEW ZEALAND'S GREATEST FLIER SETS RECORDS

New Zealand's foremost pilot—man or woman—was the beautiful Jean Batten, called the "Greta Garbo of Flying." Batten made two unsuccessful attempts to break Amy Johnson's record time to Australia flying a second-hand de Havilland Gypsy Moth that the enamored son of a prosperous English linen merchant bought for her. On her first attempt in April 1933, after encountering two sandstorms that forced her to land, her engine failed, causing her to crash land and demolish her aircraft near Karachi. Returning to London, she used her feminine charms to have Lord Wakefield, the CEO of Castrol Oil, lend her the money to buy another used Gipsy Moth. Wakefield would become her patron and help direct her career. In April 1934, she left a new fiancée stockbroker behind to make another attempt on Johnson's record, but ran out of fuel at night outside Rome and crash landed without any major injury. After the de Havilland was repaired she flew it back to London, and on 8 May 1934, Batten successfully flew solo from England to Australia in 14 days and 22:30 hours, surpassing Amy Johnson's record by more than four days and making her a celebrity.

Although the route had been flown in one direction or another more than thirty times, Batten's charisma and beauty captured huge media attention. She sailed to Australia and New Zealand, where she embarked on extensive tours and public appearances that made her suddenly affluent. Batten's book describing her trip, *Solo Flight*, was published in 1934, and was a financial success. While in Sydney, Batten fell in love with an Australian airline pilot and she broke off her engagement to her United Kingdom fiancée. She flew the Moth back to England in 17 days and 15 hours, becoming the first woman pilot to fly from England to Australia and back. In London her successes were lauded by the media, she was feted by the upper levels of English society, and she was acknowledged by the international aviation community as legitimate, even though she was a woman.

After her Australia flight and seeking new challenges and continued fame, Batten bought a new Percival Gull 6 monoplane with the generous help of £1000 from Lord Wakefield. The Gull had a lightweight metal propeller, hydraulic brakes (her previous Moth had no brakes), an automatic fuel pump, landing flaps, a 200 hp engine, and an extra fuel tank. Batten realized she had captivated England, Australia, and New Zealand with her flights and prepared for another long distance flight across the South Atlantic between West Africa and Brazil, attempting to break the record time for the route (85:20 hours) held by James Mollison. On 11 November 1935, she departed the United Kingdom and flew the France-Casablanca leg in 9:30 hours, setting an unintentional record, then flew on to Senegal to begin the 1,900 mile crossing over the Atlantic on 13 November. Storms over the Equator caused the Gull's instruments and the compass to malfunction, and after 12:30 hours in what was described as "a brilliant feat of navigation" she arrived directly at Port Natal, Brazil, using only a watch and compass. Batten established world absolute records for the ocean crossing and the overall flight, and was the first woman to fly solo across the South Atlantic. In Brazil, Argentina, and Uruguay Batten, called the "flower of the sky" by newspapers, was venerated by large crowds, honored by presidents, and rewarded with gifts. More tributes followed: Batten was awarded the Royal Aero Club's Britannia Trophy and was jointly awarded the Harmon

Trophy for the most outstanding flight by a woman in 1935 (she was to win it outright in 1936 and 1937) with Amelia Earhart. After her South American flight Batten went into seclusion with her mother, who Batten adored and was her almost constant companion throughout her life.

In October 1936, Batten emerged from seclusion to fly her longest flight, the first ever direct flight from England to New Zealand. On 5 October 1936, Batten flew from England to Darwin in the record time of 5 days, 21:03 hours, and continued flying across the Tasman Sea to Auckland to set another total record time of 11 days, 45 minutes over 14,255 miles from England. The record flight totally depleted her, as during an arduous lecture tour she suffered a nervous breakdown and spent time recuperating with her mother. In February 1937, she returned to Sydney to be reunited with her fiancée, to whom she was to be married later that year. The day she arrived he was killed in an air crash and she again went into seclusion with her mother, remaining in Sydney for many months.

Jean Batten and her Percival Gull 6

Finally, in October 1938, Batten flew the Gull from Australia to England in 5 days, 18 hours, establishing a solo record (for pilots of either sex) and becoming the first person to simultaneously hold England-Australia solo records in both directions. In 1938, she was the first woman to be awarded the FAI's Medal, one of aviation's highest awards. That year she completed her second book, *My Life*, but at age twenty-eight Batten had reached the pinnacle of her career and had flown her last long distance flight. During the war she gave lectures in England to raise money for the war effort, but the social and outgoing Jean Batten of the 1930s faded from public view after the war. Batten and her mother moved to Jamaica in 1946, where she reputedly became good friends with Ian Fleming and Noel Coward. After the novelists moved on and her mother died in 1977, she moved to Majorca and became a recluse, living in virtual poverty. In 1983, she was bitten by a dog, and after refusing treatment, died and was buried in a mass paupers' grave on Majorca.

ALEX HENSHAW: UK-CAPE TOWN-UK RECORD

In 1939, Alex Henshaw made an attempt to surpass the record for a flight from London to Cape Town and return in a Mew Gull. Henshaw took off from Gravesend at 0335 on 5 February 1939 in heavy fog and had to fly as far as Marseilles before he could see the ground to get an accurate navigational fix. Over the Mediterranean he had to descend through clouds before finding his first stop in Oran, Algeria. In Gao, Mali, he napped for an hour and took off at night, and for the next few hours he had no navigational aids on the ground. He then flew through the towering clouds and torrential rain of a tropical weather front and descended over the Atlantic, landing in Libreville, Gabon, on the west central African coast, to refuel. After a comparatively easy leg down the Atlantic coast he landed in Mossamedes, Angola, refueled, and took off for the final leg to Cape Town, where he landed at 1858 on 6 February after flying 6,377 miles in an elapsed time of 39:23 hours, beating the de Havilland Comet's record by six hours.

After spending twenty-seven hours in Cape Town dealing with the press and readying the Mew Gull for its return trip, Henshaw took off at 2215 on 7 February, and retraced his route back to the United Kingdom. On the way back he became ill due to the hot sun shining into the cockpit and an onset of a malaria attack. He felt better after landing in Libreville, but once airborne again the sickness returned, with bouts of vomiting and stomach cramps. Soon he discovered he was lost and deliriously turned east; fortunately he soon saw the Niger River, which led him to Goa. After a quick nap and some "mysterious" medication he continued across the endless and featureless Sahara, climbed over the Atlas Mountains, and landed in Oran. The flight over the Mediterranean was sunny and clear, but over France he flew into a snowstorm and ice began to form on the wings and the windscreen froze over. He was hit in the face by something and suddenly his nose and mouth filled with blood, covering the front of his flying suit and the maps on his lap. The bleeding stopped and he flew over an undercast over France and the Channel until he managed to find Gravesend, United Kingdom, landing on 9 February. After landing, he was so exhausted he had to be lifted out of the cockpit. He had completed the return leg in 39:36 hours, completing the whole 12,754 mile round trip in 4 days, 10:16 hours, breaking the record for each leg and setting a solo record for the round trip, reducing the existing solo record by 66:42 hours. Not only were all Cape Town-and-return records broken, but also for every stage en route, and remain so in the solo classification to this day. The Royal Aero Club awarded Henshaw the Britannia Trophy for his record flight. Henshaw's account of his epic flight is recounted in his book, *Flight of the Mew Gull* (1980). The Mew Gull he used (G-AEXF) was restored to its Cape flight configuration in the 1980s and was placed in the Shuttleworth Collection in 1996; as of 2015 it continues to be in flying condition. The Cape record remained for more than seventy years, but on 11 May 2009, Charles Stobart, flying a home-built Osprey GP-4, set a new record ratified by the FAI for the reverse route, Cape Town-London-Cape Town. Subsequently, on 3 September 2010, Steve Noujaim, flying a home-built Vans RV-7, landed in the United Kingdom after completing a round trip to Cape Town in 3 days, 11:16 hours, bettering Henshaw's time by just over four hours.

During WWII Henshaw was a test pilot for Vickers Armstrong and after the war he became a director of Miles Aircraft in South Africa, but after the company bankrupted he returned to England in 1948. Although only in his mid-thirties, he never again flew as a pilot, instead taking over his family's farming and holiday business interests in the United Kingdom.

Alex Henshaw in his Mew Gull

VICKERS WELLESLEYS SET A LONG-STANDING DISTANCE RECORD

Although relatively unknown, the Vickers Wellesley was actually the only RAF warplane to operate during the eighteen-month East African Campaign against Italy. The Wellesley briefly gained fame in 1938, because of an epic non-stop long distance flight of 7,158.5 miles. The Wellesley was developed from a private venture monoplane for a general purpose land plane, being first flown on 4 March 1937. The Wellesley was a single-engine monoplane with a very high aspect ratio wing and a manually operated, retractable undercarriage. It had a 74.5 ft. wingspan with a wing area of 630 sq. ft. and a length of 39.25 ft. Wellesleys introduced Barnes Wallis geodetic construction into the RAF, which was later used on the Wellington bomber. Because it was not known how to interrupt the geodetic fuselage structure with a bomb bay, the Wellesley's bomb load was carried in two streamlined panniers under the wings.

Because the Wellesley was the first RAF aircraft capable of lifting over one and a half times its own weight, five were chosen for modification for use by the Long-Range Development unit. In the preparation of the Wellesley for the flight several modifications were made to the standard service aircraft, the most noticeable being the provision of another crew position between the pilot's canopy and the raised canopy position for the observer/navigator, made visible by a triangular window showing the geodetic framework on the side of the fuselage. Additional modifications included the installation of Pegasus XXII engines and extra fuel tanks. Unlike production Wellesleys, the engine cowling was blended with the fuselage profile.

The three Wellesleys were to be flown in formation by flight commander S/L Richard Kellett, F/Lt. Andrew Combe, and F/Lt. Henry Hogan, with each aircraft having a co-pilot and radio operator/navigator. On 5 November 1938, the three Wellesleys staggered off the 3,600 ft. runway at Ismailia, Egypt, weighed down by their 18,400 lb. fuel load. Flying an optimal fuel saving altitude of 10,000 ft., after twelve hours the Wellesleys encountered unfavorable weather over the Bay of Bengal that would continue to deteriorate over the South China Sea and toward the Dutch East Indies. The aircraft piloted by Hogan was running low on fuel and landed in West Timor, 500 miles short of Darwin, and refueled. Kellett and Combe landed at Ross Smith Field, Darwin, Australia, after setting a world distance record of 7,162 miles over 48:10 hours at an average speed of 149 mph. Hogan's refueled Wellesley continued to Darwin, landing that same day and also breaking the existing record. After the record flight the three Wellesleys left Darwin on 13 November 1928 for a round Australia tour.

The previous record (non-closed circuit) of 6,306 miles had been set by Mikhail Gromov in a Tupolev ANT-25 flying from Moscow to San Jacinto, California, 12–14 July 1937. The Wellesley's record remained unbroken until November 1945, when a Boeing B-29 surpassed it on its third attempt. This flight remains today as the longest by a single-engine aircraft.

Three Vickers Wellesleys under command of S/L Richard Kellett.

Kellett's and Combe's Wellesleys at Darwin

Record setting Wellesley crews celebrating their triumph at Darwin.

4

BRITISH WWII LONG-RANGE BOMBER DEVELOPMENT

Less than a year after the Wellesley set its record war broke out in Europe, and British air forces had to concentrate on winning the war—not with intercontinental bombers, but with bombers with enough range for round trip missions to Berlin with as heavy bomb loads as possible. The Wellington and Sterling were the bombers du jour in 1939, with the longer range Lancaster—which could carry heavier loads—in the production pipeline and poised to become Bomber Command's work horse heavy bomber. Toward the end of the war the RAF had increased the bomb load, altitude, and speed of existing and new bombers, but their range remained 2,000–2,500 miles, enough for a round trip deep into Germany and back. These new designs included the Vickers Warwick and Windsor, Short Super Sterling, and the Avro Lincoln. The Lincoln was developed into prototype stage in mid-1944 and proved to be successful. By the beginning of 1945, the well established Lancaster seemed to be quite adequate to contend with the situation over Europe, while the US B-29 was better overall and had increased range capabilities for use in the air war in the Pacific, which the USAAF then dominated.

Avro Lancaster

The Vickers Company proposed a high-altitude, six-engine giant bomber to carry Barnes Wallace's huge 22,000 lb. *Tallboy* bomb and 10,000 lb. *Grand-slam* bombs, but the design never went beyond the drawing board. In early 1943, the RAF proposed the 75 Ton Bomber Project to replace the Avro Lancaster. The proposed huge bomber was to have six engines to carry a bomb load of between fifteen and twenty tons at 300 mph at between 20,000 and 30,000 ft., but still its operational range was only just sufficient for the purpose at 2,500 miles. Avro, Bristol, Shorts, Handley-Page, and Vickers showed interest in the project, but ultimately the specifications were too ambitious for all concerned, as they would result in a bomber weighing 250,000–300,000 lbs., which was just too big a leap from the previous four-engine heavy bomber designs.

5
BRITISH POSTWAR LONG-RANGE BOMBER DEVELOPMENT

As WWII ended, it became immediately apparent to Britain and its western allies that the new enemy was the Soviet Union, which had erected Churchill's "Iron Curtain." Also, it became apparent to RAF strategic planners that ultra-long-range bombers would not be necessary to bomb targets in Russia from the United Kingdom.

AVRO LINCOLN

The Avro Lincoln was renowned designer Roy Chadwick's continued development of his exceptional Lancaster, having stronger, longer span wings; powered by four two-stage supercharged Rolls-Royce Merlin 85 piston engines; and a larger fuselage with increased fuel and bomb loads. As a result, the Lincoln had a higher operational ceiling and longer range than the Lancaster—1,470 miles with a maximum bomb load (up to 14,000 lbs.)—making it a threat to the Soviet Union when operating from bases in West Germany until the RAF could develop, test, and manufacture the V-series jet bombers.

Avro Lincoln

V BOMBERS

The V Bombers were the result of Air Ministry Specification B.35/46, which proposed a "medium-range bomber landplane capable of carrying one 10,000 lb. bomb to a target 1,725 miles from a base which may be anywhere in the world." The specification also designated the fully loaded weight should not exceed 100,000 lbs. (in practice this would be adjusted upward); that the bomber have a cruise speed of 575 mph; and that it have a service ceiling of 50,000 ft. The RAF's then-current jet bomber, the English Electric Canberra introduced in May 1951, was designed during WWII and was only capable of reaching the Soviet border.

The RAF V Bomber force was used during the 1950s and 1960s as Britain's strategic nuclear strike force, known officially as V-force or Bomber Command Main Force. The V Bomber Force was comprised of the Vickers Valiant, which entered service in August 1954, the Avro Vulcan in July 1956, and the Handley Page Victor in April 1958. The development of three V bombers during the Cold War was to give the United Kingdom more autonomy from US foreign policy, which in effect was the policy of the west and controlled NATO. While the United Kingdom supported the US during the Cold War, its V Bomber force gave it independence to serve its own military requirements. The Valiant was used in the 1956 Suez Crisis, when America refused any support to Anthony Eden's government. The Vulcan served the same role during the Falklands War.

Vickers Valiant

Vickers Valiant

The Vickers Valiant was designed to the same specifications (B35/46) as the later Vulcan and Victor. The planned prototype was initially rejected as not as advanced as the Victor and Vulcan. Vickers Chief Designer George Edwards convinced the Air Ministry that it would be available much earlier than the two competitors, assuring delivery of a prototype in 1951 and production in 1953. The prototype Valiant first flew in May 1951, and was delivered to the RAF in August 1954.

The Valiant had a crew of five: two pilots, two navigators (one navigator plotter and one navigator bomber), and an air electronics officer. The Valiant was a plain, clean, conservative design with a shoulder-mounted wing and four Rolls-Royce Avon turbojets—two in each wing root—that propelled it to a maximum speed of 567 mph at high altitude. It had a wingspan of 114.3 ft. and a wing area of 2,362 sq. ft., a length of 108.25 ft., and a height of 32.2 ft. The Valiant had a maximum range of 4,500 miles with underwing tanks and a maximum ceiling of 54,000 ft. It could carry up to 21,000 lbs. of conventional or nuclear bombs.

By late 1964, it was found that all variants of the Valiant showed premature fatiguing and corrosion in wing spar attachments; rather than undertaking expensive renovation the Valiant was retired in 1965. Its duties were continued by the other V-Bombers, which remained in service until the 1980s.

Avro Vulcan

Also in response to the 1947 B35/46 specification, Avro's Chief Designer Roy Chadwick immediately began an unusual delta wing design that was to become the Vulcan, probably the most famous V Bomber. This first delta-wing bomber prototype

Avro Vulcan

originally flew on 30 August 1952, and was delivered to the RAF in July 1956.

The Vulcan had a crew of five: pilot, co-pilot, electronics officer, navigator radar, and navigator plotter. It was powered by four Rolls-Royce Olympus turbojet engines that gave it a maximum speed of 645 mph (approaching the speed of sound, Mach 0.96), a maximum ceiling of 65,000 ft., and a maximum range of 2,600–4,600 miles depending on the bomb load. The Vulcan had a wingspan of 99.4 ft. and a wing area of 3,554 sq. ft.; a length of 97.1 ft., and a height of 26.5 ft. Each bomber had the ability to carry 21,000 lbs. of conventional bombs and an assortment of nuclear bombs. Developments in weapons systems made the Vulcan effectively obsolete as a bomber and the succeeding versions were used for reconnaissance and in-flight refueling. After the delivery of 136 bombers the RAF withdrew the Vulcan from service in March 1984.

Handley Page Victor

Handley Page Victor

The Handley Page Victor was the last of the V Bombers to go into service. The bomber's crescent-shaped wings were based on research by German Arado and Blohm & Voss companies during WWII that determined the shape of these wings maximized cruising speed and range. The Victor had a crew of a pilot, co-pilot, two navigators, and an electronics systems officer. It had a wingspan of 110 ft. and a wing area of 2,406 sq. ft.; a length of 114.9 ft.; and a height of 28.3 ft. The Victor was powered by four Rolls-Royce Conway turbofan engines that gave it a top speed of 640 mph, a maximum ceiling of 60,000 ft., and a maximum range of 4,600 miles. The Victor could carry up to 35,000 lbs. of conventional bombs or one Yellow Sun free-fall nuclear bomb.

Operation Black Buck

Operation Black Buck was a series of RAF air attacks on Port Stanley, Falkland Islands, during the 1982 Falklands War between Britain and Argentina. The attacks were carried out using Vulcan bombers supported by Victor tankers, all based out of Ascension Island—in the mid-Atlantic between Brazil and the African central coast—and at that time were the longest range air attacks in history. A total of five Black Buck missions were successfully carried out (seven planned) during the war. The missions were successful, forcing Argentina to withdraw fast jets (including Mirage IIIs) from the Falkland Islands back to the mainland. Additionally, a number of Argentine radar installations and facilities were destroyed during the missions.

Each of the Black Buck missions required two Avro Vulcans and eleven Handley Page Victor tankers in three waves. In all, 220,000 gallons of jet fuel were required for the single operational attack. Each Vulcan could deliver twenty-one 1,000 lb. bombs on a target. The raids, at almost 6,800 nautical miles and 16 hours for the round trip, were the longest range bombing raids in history at that time (surpassed in the Gulf War of 1991 by USAF Boeing B-52G Stratofortresses flying from the continental United States but using forward positioned tankers).

Operation Black Buck was not only the longest range aerial bombing mission ever flown as of that date, it was also the most impractical. The long missions put extensive hours on airframes, particularly the Victor tanker fleet, putting the fleet into an early retirement. Without replacements available for at least another two years, the RAF would not have enough tankers, as the Vulcans were scheduled to retire after the war ended that year. The solution was easy: rather than retire all of the Vulcans, six would be converted to tankers to augment the Victors.

The Demise of the V Bomber

During the 1991 Gulf War eight Victor K.2s were deployed to Bahrain to provide in-flight refueling support to RAF and other coalition aircraft. Shortly after the Gulf War, the remaining Victor fleet was quickly retired in 1993, at which point it was the last of the three V-bombers in operational service, retiring nine years after the last Vulcan, although the Vulcan had survived longer in its original role as a bomber.

The cost of maintaining the V Bomber force was massive, and the RAF was faced with limited and unreliable budgets and changing requirements. Thus, the RAF devoted its funding to fighter-bombers such as the Canberra, Jaguar, and Buccaneer, and into developing the vertical take off Harrier jump jet. The end of the Cold War and the use of smaller, faster fighter-bombers, such as the Jaguar and Phantom, ended the days of the large bomber in the RAF. Nonetheless, with Britain demoted to a second-rate military power with diminishing resources, Britain and NATO felt they could rely on wealthy America's nuclear ICBMs and bomber force to keep the peace.

PART 3:
SOVIET LONG-RANGE AIRCRAFT

1
SIKORSKY SOVIET POSTWAR GIANTS

SIKORSKY S-21 RUSSKY VITYAZ: WORLD'S FIRST FOUR-ENGINE AIRCRAFT

The Sikorsky S-21 *Russky Vityaz* (Russian Knight), the first four-engine aircraft in the world, was built at the Russian Baltic Railroad Car Works (RBVZ) in Saint Petersburg and was designed by company Chief Engineer Igor Sikorsky in early 1913. The Russky Vityaz was immense for the time, with an upper wingspan of 88.6 ft. and a lower wingspan of 65.7 ft., for a total wing area of 1,300 sq. ft. The ailerons on the upper wings provided stability. The S-21 was 65.7 ft. long, 13.1 ft. high, weighed 7,496 lbs. empty, and had a maximum take-off weight of 10,891 lbs.; it was powered by four 100 hp Argus As I four-cylinder, water-cooled, in-line piston engines. The original *Bolshoi Baltisky* (Grand Baltic) design had four tractor engines installed in push-pull tandem pairs on the lower wing, while the later Russky Vityaz had four separate tractor engines on the leading edge of the lower wing outboard of the original inner tractor configuration engines. The four engines gave the aircraft a maximum speed of 56 mph, a range of 106 miles, and a service ceiling of almost 2,000 ft. Its rectangular fuselage was a girder design covered with plywood sheets. The aircraft had a three-man crew cabin with a dual control column, two passenger cabins accommodating seven to eight passengers, and a storage room for spare parts. A passenger was able to move around in the cabins without causing any stability problems in flight. In later militarized versions there was also an area in the pilot's cabin for a searchlight and machine gun. The Russky Vityaz's first test flights took place 10–27 May 1913, but on 23 June 1913, while parked on the runway, the aircraft was crushed by an engine that fell off a single-seat Morane that was landing. Sikorsky decided not to repair the seriously damaged Russky Vityaz and began working on his next giant aircraft, the *Ilya Muromets*.

A young Igor Sikorsky

Russky Vityaz, the world's first four-engine aircraft

SIKORSKY S-22 ILYA MUROMETS: WORLD'S FIRST SUCCESSFUL PASSENGER AND BOMBER AIRCRAFT

The Sikorsky S-22 Ilya Muromets was designed by Igor Sikorsky based on his S-21 Russky Vityaz and constructed at the Russo-Baltic Railcar Factory in Riga. Sikorsky first conceived and built the Ilya Muromets as the world's first multi-passenger and multi-engine airliner, which later would become the world's first mass produced bomber. The giant Ilya Muromets biplane had a top wing span of 97.8 ft. and a bottom wing span of 68.9 ft., with a total wing area of 1,350 sq. ft., a height of 13.1 ft., and a length of 57.1 ft. It had an empty weight of 6,930 lbs. and a loaded weight of 12,000 lbs. Four 148 hp Sunbeam Crusader V8 engines powered the S-22 to a maximum speed of 68 mph and a service ceiling of about 10,000 ft. The cockpit was large, with hatches through both sides of the fuselage permitting mechanics to climb out on the wings to service the engines in flight. A hatch on the left side provided an exit to the front bridge. Behind the cockpit was a large, isolated, heated, and electrically lighted passenger salon with comfortable wicker chairs and four large windows on each side. Lighting was supplied by a wind-driven generator and heating was provided by two long engine exhaust pipes passing through the corners of the cabin. In the salon's rear was a stairway to the upper bridge and a washroom. In the rear was a private cabin including a berth, small table, and a cabinet. On 10 December 1913, the Ilya Muromets was flight tested for the first time, and on 25 February 1914, took off for its first demonstration flight with sixteen passengers aboard. From 21–23 June, it set a world record by making a return flight from St. Petersburg to Kiev—a distance of about 750 miles—and return. The first leg took 14:38 hours with one fueling stop, while the return flight took only 13 hours with a fueling stop.

The outbreak of WWI prevented the Ilya Muromets from beginning passenger service, causing Sikorsky to change the aircraft's design to become the world's first purposely designed bomber. Sikorsky added internal bomb racks that carried up to 1,700 lbs. of bombs and defensive positions for up to nine machine guns in various locations, including the extreme tail. In August 1914, the S-22 was accepted by the Imperial Russian Air Service and formed the first bomber squadrons, which were so heavily defended that German fighters were reluctant to attack them—only one of the seventy-three produced 1913–1918 was lost to enemy fire. During this period the Russian Air Service was the first to bomb with heavy bombers, use bomber group raids on enemy targets, bomb at night, assess bomb damage photographically, and the first to develop defensive tactics for a single bomber engaged an air combat with a number of enemy fighters. By the end of 1916 the design had become obsolete, and subsequent modifications added too much weight. With further upgrading deemed pointless the S-22s were relegated to training. After WWI Sikorsky realized he had few prospects as an aircraft designer in war-ravaged Europe, particularly in Russia, which was devastated by the October Revolution and Civil War. Sikorsky immigrated to America in March 1919, where he would continue his brilliant aviation career, first manufacturing flying boats such as the S-42 Clipper, used by Pan Am for trans-Atlantic flights, and then becoming best known as the "Father of the Helicopter."

S-22 Ilya Muromets, the world's first successful passenger and bomber aircraft

2
TUPOLEV AND OTHER SOVIET GIANTS

Surprisingly, from the mid-1920s into the 1930s, the most important work on big bombers was not done by the victorious Allies, but by Andrei Tupolev in Russia, one of the least industrially progressive nations of the major powers.

ANDREI NIKOLAYEVICH TUPOLEV

In 1909, at age twenty-one, brilliant young Tupolev entered Moscow Higher Technical College, where he studied under Nikolai Egorovich Zhukovskii, considered the "Father of Russian Aviation." After graduation Tupolev assisted Zhukovskii in organizing the Central Aerohydrodynamics Institute (TsAGI), which would become the Soviet equivalent of America's NACA. Here he would serve as assistant director from 1918–1935, and headed its design bureau beginning in 1922.

In 1924, Tupolev designed the two-seat ANT-2 (the ANT prefix was derived from his initials), a Duralumin all-metal monoplane style that replaced the fabric and wood biplanes of WWI (the Duralumin was provided surreptitiously by Germany's Hugo Junkers). His next project was the ANT-3 biplane, first flown in August 1925, which became the Red Army's R-3 reconnaissance type, but the aircraft could not be produced in numbers due to lack of Duralumin.

Andrei Tupolev, Russia's most prolific and illustrious aircraft designer, designed and oversaw the design of more than one hundred types of aircraft, some of which set seventy-eight world records.

TUPOLEV ANT-4 (TB-1) AND ANT-6 (TB-3)

Tupolev's first bomber was the ANT-4 (TB-1), a twin-engine low-wing monoplane design first flown in November 1925. It was considered one of the most advanced designs of the time, as it was a huge divergence from American and British fabric-covered biplane bombers. Tupolev's ANT-4 evolved into the highly successful two-seat, four-engine biplane heavy bomber ANT-6 (TB-3), the first four-engine bomber to enter mass production (the ANT-5 was a biplane fighter). The ANT-4 was essentially a TB-1 powered by four imported 600 hp Curtiss Conqueror engines and had a 129.5 ft. wing span, weighed 38,360 lbs. gross, and was designed to carry 4,410 lbs. of bombs 840 miles with a top speed of 122 mph. The bomber was first flown on 22 December 1930, and production began in January 1932, continuing until 1937, when 818 had been completed (then the most numerous night bomber in the world).

Tupolev ANT-4

Tupolev ANT-6

TUPOLEV ANT-16

In April 1930, Tupolev was authorized to build the world's largest bomber (ANT-16), having a wing span of 177.2 ft. and a wing area of 4,542 sq. ft. The bomber weighed 47,000 lbs. empty, almost 74,000 lbs. loaded, and 81,500 lbs. with overload. It carried 1,750 gallons of fuel and up to twenty 1,100 lb. bombs. Its range with a 4,410 lb. payload was to be 1,242 miles, and with 17,600 lbs. the range was over 584 miles. It was powered by six 750 hp M-34 engines: four engines on the wing's leading edge and two more in tandem above the fuselage.

It had a twelve-man crew with four open cockpits in the nose, waist, and tail, each provided with twin hand-held machine guns. Because speed and altitude were not considered important for night bombing, top speed was only 124 mph and the ceiling was only 9,025 ft. On 3 July 1933, Russia's Chief Test Pilot Mikhail Gromov piloted the bomber's first flight, but after the flight test program concluded Gromov gave an unfavorable opinion of its flying qualities. The two dorsal-mounted engines performed poorly, and much of the thrust of the wing-mounted engines was absorbed by the 6.7 ft. thickness of the wing. The suggestion to re-engine the bomber with more powerful 1,250 hp engines was rejected and the ANT-16 remained a prototype.

Tupolev ANT-16

Mikhail Gromov

KALININ K-7

While Andrei Tupolev was designing his giant ANT-16, former WWI pilot Konstantin Kalinin, while working at the Aviation Design Bureau in Kharkov, was designing a large rival experimental aircraft with an unusual configuration of twin booms and large underwing pods housing machine gun turrets and fixed landing gear. The unusual landing gear pods had two sets of duo wheels in tandem. The airframe was of welded chrome-molybdenum steel. The biplane tail was held by twin tail booms. The original design called for six tractor M-34F engines in the wing leading edge, but when the projected loaded weight was exceeded a single engine in pusher configuration was added in the rear of the center fuselage. Flight crew quarters and bomb racks were in the center fuselage. The huge K-7 was 91.8 ft. long, while its wingspan was 173.1 ft.—equal to two of the newly introduced Douglas DC airliners. The most notable aspect of the K-7's size was its wing area of 4,887 sq. ft., which was the largest elliptical wing ever built, double that of a Boeing 314 Clipper or B-29, and even larger in area than the wings of a B-52! The K-7 weighed 53,680 lbs. empty and 83,600 lbs. loaded. In civil transport configuration it was projected to carry 120 passengers and 15,000 lbs. of payload, while as a troop transport it was to have capacity to carry 112 fully equipped paratroops. In its bomber arrangement it would have been armed with eight 20 mm auto-cannons, eight 7.62 mm machine guns, and up to 21,200 lbs. of bombs.

After two years of construction a brief first flight was flown in Kiev on 11 August 1933, which showed instability and serious vibration. On 21 November, after seven more test flights, the left tail boom failed in flight, destroying the K-7 and killing fifteen people (one on the ground). There was some speculation (by Britain's *Flight Magazine*) that sabotage could have been involved, as the Soviet State Security Organization was called in to investigate the crash. In recent years the Soviet aviation press has also speculated on the possibility of sabotage. Despite the crash two more prototypes were ordered in 1933, but the project was canceled in 1935, before they were completed.

Kalinin K-7

Tupolev ANT-20 Gorky (Vasily Kuptsov's painting of the I-5 fighter collision with the Gorky)

TUPOLEV ANT-20 MAXIM GORKY

The ANT-20 was constructed 4 July 1933–3 April 1934 as one of two aircraft of its type. The bomber used the Hugo Junkers design philosophy of corrugated sheet metal for many of the airframe's key components, especially the skinning of the airframe. The aircraft could be dismantled and transported by railroad if needed. Essentially, it was an enlarged ANT-16 with a 206.7 ft. wing span, with 5,231 sq. ft. of wing area, a length of 108 ft., and a gross weight of 92,593 lbs. It was powered by six M-34F engines on the wing and two in tandem above the fuselage that drove the aircraft at a maximum speed of 155 mph over 750 miles (a 1,550 mile maximum range was claimed) and to a maximum altitude of 14,750 ft. The thick wing contained tanks for 2,483 gallons of fuel and a flight engineer's station on each side. For the first time in aviation history, this aircraft used not only direct current, but also 120 volt alternating current supplied by two gasoline generators that also drove air compressors supplying compressed air.

Entrance was made through a door cut in the left side of the fuselage and by a trap door on the fuselage belly. For the first time in aviation history this aircraft was equipped with an entry ladder, which would fold on itself and become part of the floor. The fuselage arrangement in sequence from forward to aft was: saloon, pilot's cockpit, passenger cabin, radio transmitter room called "Voice from the Sky," an editorial office with a rotatory press, passenger compartment and buffet, another passenger compartment, cinema room for showing in-flight movies, microphone room and radio receiving room, other passenger cabins, baggage compartment, and lavatory. There was a photographic lab in the wing. The under surface of the wing was on the same level as the fuselage floor, making passenger access easy from the cabins in the wing to the fuselage. The passenger cabins were all over six feet high and had four bunks each. A steam heating and ventilating system was incorporated with a thermostat that provided temperatures of 70°F. A vent in the fuselage nose transmitted heat or ventilation to the cockpit, cabins, and other areas in the wing and fuselage.

The ANT-20 could carry an eight-man crew and up to seventy-two passengers, and was built to lead a propaganda squadron formed to promote Stalinist propaganda and communist philosophy across an enormous country populated by mostly illiterate farm inhabitants. The aircraft was named after iconic Soviet author Maxim Gorky, and was dedicated to the fortieth anniversary of his literary and pro-Bolshevik activities. The idea for this propaganda machine was first advanced by Michael Koltsov, a well known journalist who encouraged donations from his news readers—workers, peasants, students, Red Army men, and others who subscribed millions of rubles to build it. Besides its recognition as being the largest aircraft in the world, the Gorky also set several carrying capacity world records. The nose contained a 2.8 million candle power searchlight to light up a wide area from 3,000 ft. A loudspeaker system was also installed in the nose to broadcast "lectures, music, and news bulletins" from 3,000 ft. The ANT-20 was first flown to great fanfare by Mikhail Gromov in Moscow on 17 June 1934.

On 18 May 1935, the Maxim Gorky took off for a demonstration flight over Moscow accompanied by three other aircraft whose purpose was to fly close by to demonstrate the pronounced comparative size of the Gorky. As a result of a poorly executed loop maneuver by accompanying fighter pilot Nikolai Blagin, his I-5 collided with the Gorky, which then crashed into a residential Moscow neighborhood, killing forty-five people: ten on the ground, both pilots, and their thirty-three passengers, many of whom had built the aircraft.

TUPOLEV ANT-20BIS

The loss of the Maxim Gorky was reported to have caused "overwhelming public despair" that probably came even as a surprise to Stalin. The Soviet populace donated millions of rubles to build not only a replacement Gorky, but a whole fleet of replacements. The Soviet government committed to build another sixteen of these giants designated the ANT-20bis, each to be named after a communist leader, but without any reference to Andrei Tupolev. It would not be officially designated the ANT-20bis, but the PS-124, so that its disgraced and banished ANT designer would be forgotten.

The replacement aircraft was largely identical in design to the Maxim Gorky, but with six (rather than eight) more powerful engines. Plans to build a fleet of ANT-20bis aircraft were abandoned in 1939, as Stalin's purges of the Soviet aviation industry resulted in a shortage of qualified engineers, cutting the program back to one example which was not ready to fly until 15 May 1939. The aircraft would retain Russia's claim to the world's largest aircraft with a 206.7 ft. wing span, 111.8 ft. length, and almost 28 ft. height. Along with the Luftwaffe's Junkers Ju-52 transport, it was one of the last airliners to retain corrugated metal fuselage skin and non-retractable wheels. Its six 1,000 hp M-34FRNV engines lifted 70,650 lbs. empty and 97,000 lbs. loaded with sixty passengers and seven crewmen.

Tupolev ANT-20bis

The PS-124 served with Aeroflot (registered as CCCP-L760) on civil transport routes in Russia and Uzbekistan. After the German invasion in June 1941, it was equipped with new engines and heavily used until it crashed on 14 December 1942, near Tashkent. Investigation revealed the pilot had allowed a passenger to momentarily take his seat and the passenger apparently disengaged the automatic pilot, sending the aircraft into a nosedive from an altitude of 1,500 ft. and killing all thirty-six on board.

1937 RUSSIAN NORTH POLE EXPEDITION

On 13 February 1936, the Central Committee Political Bureau decided to mount the first Soviet expedition to the North Pole. During March 1937, four ANT-6 four-engine bombers and one twin-engine ANT-7 departed Moscow under the command of eminent polar explorer Otto Schmidt and with Michael Vodopyanov, a renowned Arctic aviator, commanding the air contingent. Vodopyanov was charged with preparing the operational plan for placing the first Soviet polar expedition (North Pole-1), led by Ivan Papanin, on an ice floe near the North Pole to be used as a drifting station. On 5 May, the weather cleared and the ANT-7 flown by Pavel Golovin left on a survey flight to locate an ice floe suitable for use as a drifting scientific station. Golovin was most probably the first to fly an airplane over the North Pole, but thick cloud cover prevented him from investigating the pack ice. Following further weather delays, on 21 May, Vodopyanov decided to fly Schmidt, Papanin's group, and their essential equipment and supplies to the Pole in an ANT-6 N specially modified to carry 1,980 gallons of fuel for the eighteen-hour round trip to the Pole. After ten hours flying over the geographic North Pole, a satisfactory floe measuring 2.5 miles by 1.2 miles was found thirty-five miles from the North Pole. Vodopyanov landed safely on the floe and left the Papanin team, and over the next two weeks the three other ANT-6s flew to the station, delivering the 10.5 tons of supplies needed for a lengthy sojourn on the ice. On 6 June, the four ANT-6s departed from the floe, leaving the four-man station party to conduct their scientific research. Papanin and three scientists spent 274 days on the ice floe as it drifted slowly southwestward toward the east coast of Greenland. During their 1,273 miles of drifting the four scientists performed numerous valuable scientific tasks, and on 17 February 1938, an ice breaker rescued them from their deteriorating ice floe drifting in the Greenland Sea. The North Pole-1 station investigation collected particularly valuable information on Arctic weather and magnetic observations, but also opened the possibility for routine air routes across the Arctic, which would soon be verified by an ANT-25 flown by Valery Chkalov.

Michael Vodopyanov (C) with his ANT-7 crew after landing on an ice floe near the North Pole.

TUPOLEV ANT-25

The ANT-25 (known as the TsAGI-25 in politically correct Stalinist Russia, but today as the ANT-25) was designed by the Experimental Aircraft Design Department of TsAGI, led by Pavel Sukhoi under the overall supervision of Andrei Tupolev. The first prototype, designated Experimental Airplane RD-1 (RD meaning *Rekord Dalnosty*, "Range Record"), the aircraft's bright red wings had a span of 111.7 ft. and an area of 938 sq. ft., a length of 44 ft., an empty weight of 8,157 lbs., and a gross weight of 17,637 lbs.

A single 750 hp Mikulin M-34 V-12 liquid-cooled piston engine powered the original ANT-25's three-blade propeller, while the second prototype (RD-2) used a geared M-34R engine with a modified rudder, which substantially increased its range. The ANT-25's reported fuel capacity was 12,963 lbs., with an oil capacity of 772 lbs. The aircraft carried a crew of three: a pilot in front, a navigator/radio man amidships, and a backup pilot seated aft with no forward vision and only capable of intermittent instrumented flight. The ANT-25 was successful due to the design of its long, narrow wing, having an area of only 938 sq. ft. and giving the aircraft good range and fuel efficiency, as the proportion of the wingspan to the chord was more than a factor of thirteen. Fuel was fifty-two percent of take-off weight, with the fuel tanks relocated from the fuselage to the wings, allowing the wings to tension as fuel weight opposed aerodynamic forces. Two crews of three were trained to fly the aircraft: one crew comprised of Mikhail Gromov and crew A. Filin and I. Spirin, and the other crew composed of pilot A. Yumashev and P. Stefanosky and S. Danilin.

The first prototype's maiden flight was on 22 June 1933, piloted by famed veteran Soviet test pilot Mikhail Gromov and his crew. The second prototype (RD-2) was also flown by the Gromov crew on a long-range test flight in September 1934, spending 75 continuous hours in the air and traveling a total of 7,712 miles in a single trip (Moscow-Ryazan-Tula-Dnepropetrovsk-Kharkov); it was unable to return to Moscow due to a fuel shortage. The flight was not recognized as a closed-circuit world record as it did not complete the circuit back to Moscow, and the direct distance between Moscow and Kharkov was too short to be considered for a straight-line record. For the well-publicized flight Gromov was made a Hero of the Soviet Union and his crew was awarded the Order of Lenin in a well-publicized ceremony.

SOVIET LONG-RANGE AN-25 PILOTS

The 1930s were a time of Soviet history, when aviation's standing as a cultural symbol was second only to that of Stalin himself, with the Soviet government glorifying its pilots in general and concentrating on particular personalities. By purposely lionizing pilots to popularize them with the Soviet people created no political risk to the paranoid Stalin, nor his government, and raised the population's morale.

Sigismund Levanevsky

After an attempt at the straight-line record along the traditional long-range route from Moscow via Africa and the Atlantic Ocean to South America was canceled in Spring 1935, the next record long-range flight planned was from Moscow to America via the North Pole, with famed Polar pilot Sigismund Levanevsky in command.

In 1925, Levanevsky graduated from the Sevastopol Naval Aviation School and became a military pilot dedicated to flying long distance flights. On 13 July 1933, Levanevsky rescued American pilot James Mattern, who was forced to land near Anadyr during his attempt at a flight around the world. In April 1934, Levanevsky took off from an improvised airfield on the Arctic ice of the Chukchi Sea, taking part in the successful aerial rescue operation to save people from the sinking steamship *Cheliuskin*, and was awarded the title Hero of the Soviet Union.

To accommodate the long take-off run of the heavily loaded ANT-25, a 2.5 mile sloping concrete (the first Soviet) runway was built at Schelkovo Airbase, near Moscow. During the early morning of 3 August 1935, veteran Polar pilot Sigismund Levanevsky, co-pilot Georgy Baidukov, and navigator Viktor Levchenko took off, and for the first thirty-one miles the RD ascended to only 1,600 ft., maintaining an average speed of 103 mph, and then steadily increased altitude to 16,000 ft. as fuel was used and the aircraft became lighter. After flying approximately 1,200 miles an oil leak caused an emergency landing near Novgorod, ending the flight. Levanevsky was called before a Politburo meeting to discuss the failure. Under Soviet-style inquisition of the time Levanevsky blamed Tupolev for the failure, stating that the single-engine ANT-25 was underpowered and the four engine Tupolev ANT-6 (TB3) was a safer choice. Co-pilot Baidukov, who was also an aero-engineer, disagreed with Levanevsky and proposed a second attempt to the Russian Far East.

Propaganda photo of Stalin proclaiming Sigizmund Levanevsky a Hero of the Soviet Union.

Valery Chkalov

In 1934, a non-stop transpolar flight to the US was proposed and Valery Chkalov, a skilled and popular former fighter pilot with little navigational experience, was chosen as the pilot to join co-pilot Georgy Baydukov and Aleksander Belyakov—an Air Force Academy chief instructor—to be the pilot navigator. The Soviet government only approved a non-stop flight from Moscow to the Far East. In the early morning of 20 July 1936, Levanevsky's former ANT-25 flew along the so-called Stalin's Route from Moscow, across Siberia, to the Far East in 56:20 hours over a distance of 5,858 miles to land on a beach at Udd Island (now named Chkalov Island to honor pilot Chkalov), near the Amur River. The next day *Pravda* published a lead article, "Glory to Stalin's *Sokols* [Falcons]!" A wooden runway was constructed on Udd Island, and on 2 August, the ANT-25 left for Moscow on a week-long return trip, making stops at which they were greeted as national heroes. The ANT-25's trio became Heroes of the Soviet Union and were awarded the Order of Lenin. However, the flight was not recognized by the FAI as breaking the March 1932 long distance record of 5,657 miles in 56 hours from New York to Syria set by French fliers Paul Codos and Maurice Rossi flying their Bleriot 110.

Although Chkalov's supposed record flight had become world famous, the Soviet Politburo desired the publicity of a direct flight, and on 14 August 1936, ordered Gromov to fly to Brazil in the second ANT-25. On 25 September, Brazilian officials denied access to the Soviet aircraft and the flight was canceled. The Soviets then looked to a Moscow-to-San Francisco flight over the North Pole and preparation for the Polar flight began. As was usual, Soviet bureaucracy concocted a detailed itinerary and plan prepared by a multitude of experts which then required approval, sometimes from as high as the Kremlin. For some reason the detailed planning included a month's food supply to be carried for the three-day flight, but finally it was deleted, as its 250 lb. weight was calculated to add 185 miles to the flight. The crew considered parachutes as useless, as either the flight was flown at too low an altitude to use them or a successful bail out would be over icy seas or tundra, where rescue would be doubtful. Finally, at 0405 on 18 June 1937, the favored ANT-25 crew of pilot Valery Chkalov, co-pilot Georgy Baidukov, and navigator Alexandre Blyakov took off from Moscow to San Francisco via the North Pole flight with the words "Trail of Stalin" painted on its side. Soon after take-off the aircraft's magnetic compass became inoperable and navigation was solely on dead reckoning and a solar heading indicator. Headwinds and storms slowed the ANT-25's progress and caused fuel to be consumed at a distressing rate. While flying through a cold weather front, the plane was in constant danger of icing and only the ANT's propeller was capable of de-icing. The ANT-25 reached the North Pole after about twenty-four hours of flying, then reached the coast of Canada just after midnight. When they reached the Rocky Mountains they had to ascend through clouds and suffered from extreme -20°F cold in the cockpit, then finally ran out of oxygen. At the sixty-hour point they passed Seattle and after two more hours they passed the Portland Lighthouse on the Columbia River. As they headed farther south along the US West Coast they calculated they were running low on fuel and turned back toward the military airbase at Vancouver, Washington, just across the Columbia River from Portland, landing at Pearson Airfield at 1640 on 20 June. The 5,475 mile trip took 63:16 hours, but had not flown far enough to establish a new record, falling just short of the Codos-Rossi Bleriot 110 New York to Rayak, Syria, 5,657 mile record set August 1933.

During fall 1938, Chkalov was assigned to test Polikarpov's I-180 fighter. On 15 December, in the middle of the test flight, the fighter's engine stopped and Chkalov chose to save the aircraft, but it caught fire, and he is said to have steered it away from some apartment buildings. Chkalov's death, like that of many prominent figures of the Stalin era, remains a mystery. Chkalov had refused to accept the post of People's Commissar of the Interior and is speculated to have been assassinated by aircraft malfunction. Chkalov was venerated with a statue in Red Square and his remains were consigned in a place of honor in the Kremlin Wall. Stalin and his Foreign Minister Molotov served as pallbearers, although rumors persisted that the Soviet dictator might have played a role in the aviator's death.

(L-R) Valery Chkalov (pilot), Alexandre Blyakov (navigator), and Georgy Baidukov (co-pilot)

Mikhail Gromov

Mikhail Gromov vied with Chkalov and Lavanesky as the preeminent prewar Soviet pilot, and his 12–14 July 1937 record trans-polar added to his claim. The Gromov, Yumashev, and

Danilin crew flew for 62:17 hours from Moscow ovcr thc North Pole to San Jacinto, California, covering 7,100 miles. After landing, it was found the aircraft still had sufficient fuel for approximately 930 miles, enough to reach Panama. The crew had actually flown as far south as San Diego, circling for two hours looking to land at San Diego's Lindbergh Field, but had to double back and circle for another four hours because they were unable to find an opening in the thick fog obscuring the coastline. They flew inland, which was clear, and were finally able to land in a pasture in San Jacinto, a tiny rural town between San Diego and Los Angeles. After landing the three exhausted fliers struggled out of their cramped cockpit and were greeted by surprised ranchers. The crew showed small white cards with the English words "bath," "eat," 'and "sleep." They were taken to nearby March Field for rest and recuperation, and afterward they received a ticker tape parade in Los Angeles, and were feted in Hollywood by Shirley Temple and Eddie Cantor. Later in New York they were received by Mayor Fiorello La Guardia and met with President Roosevelt at the White House. All three were welcomed back in Russia as heroes in the Soviet Union, and all eventually became generals in the Soviet military during WWII. Their ANT-25 was dismantled and returned to the USSR by ship, where it was put on display in a museum, but this historic aircraft was eventually destroyed in a fire. In 1989, the Tupolev Design Bureau built a replica of an ANT-25 which resides at the Monino Aviation Museum outside Moscow. Their trans-polar route would become an important commercial airline route postwar.

Tupolev ANT-25A

ANT-25 flown by the Gromov, Yumashev, and Danilin crew in San Jacinto, California.

Gromov's new record was to be short-lived, as it was broken by two British Vickers Wellesley bombers which flew a distance of 7,160.6 miles from Egypt to Australia in November 1938. The record breaking flight and pilots (Gromov and Chkalov) were celebrated throughout Russia, just as Charles Lindbergh had been in America, but the celebration would soon be marred when Levanevsky and his crew would disappear on the same route in a new 4-engined DR-A in August. Then the Soviets would discontinuc thc distancc racc duc to Stalin's political and military "repression" (purges) as the work of the Aviation Design Bureau stalled; Tupolev was jailed; and Gromov was a persona non grata and on the verge of arrest. Chkalov mysteriously crashed while testing a new fighter on 13 December 1938. Both Tupolev—as a renowned aircraft designer—and Gromov—as a test pilot, and then as commander of various Soviet Air armies—would regain their status. Baidukov and Belyalkov would serve as air generals during their long military careers.

1937: SIGIZMUND LEVANEVSKY AND THE DB-A DISAPPEAR

During summer 1937, Soviet aviators made history with back-to-back non-stop flights from Russia over the North Pole to America in Tupolev ANT-25s—single-engine aircraft that famed Russian pilot Sigizmund Levanevsky deemed were nothing more than glorified powered gliders. Levanevsky, who had Stalin's ear, convinced the Soviet leader to allow him to fly the much larger and heavier four-engine Bolkhovitinov DB-A bomber converted into a N-209 civilian aircraft. Levanevsky planned to fly 4,150 miles (the DB-A's range) from Moscow to Fairbanks, Alaska, via the North Pole, then continue on to Chicago and New York to pioneer a new route for passenger and cargo flights. Possessing an advanced clean, sleek design for the time, the DB-A bomber was to be a replacement for the Tupolev TB-3 heavy bomber. It was constructed with stressed skin aluminum alloy, aerodynamic cowls, and fully retracting main wheels and tail wheel. It was powered by four 900 hp turbo-charged M-34FRN engines and included the recent innovation of in-wing gas tanks, providing a 6,000 gallon fuel capacity sufficient to fly over 4,000 miles. It had a wingspan of 129.8 ft. (which was twenty-six feet more than the B-17) and a wing area of 2,476 sq. ft., a length of 129.78 ft., an empty weight of 35,600 lbs., and a gross weight of 48,500 lbs. Flight trials began on 2 May 1935, factory tests were completed by April 1934, and testing was performed during May and June 1935.

Although Levanevsky's civilian N-209 conversion could carry twenty-five passengers or tons of cargo, its true purpose was to carry bombs as the DB-A bomber, and Stalin wished to demonstrate its intercontinental potential to the world (Germany). To fly as soon as possible, Levanevsky's testing and training time was reduced to only three months. In this time only several short training flights (none in poor visibility conditions) and only a 1,200 mile round-trip flight from Moscow to Melitopol, in the Ukraine, were made in preparation for the proposed thirty-plus hour Moscow-Fairbanks route. Propaganda value trumped any concerns. Meanwhile, once the decision was made to fly non-stop from Moscow to Alaska, the DB-A prototype was modified to fly at an overload weight of 76,500 lbs. and carry enough fuel to fly 5,244 miles. After attempting the route once previously but aborting due to a broken oil line, Levanevsky left Moscow in the red DB-A on 12 August 1937. A radio message reported that the DB-A had uneventfully crossed the North Pole, but after 14:32 hours another radio message stated that one engine was out and they were encountering heavy winds and losing altitude, then giving a revised ETA for Fairbanks. A final message indicated an emergency landing was imminent. After no more messages were received an unprecedented air search to find Levanevsky was initiated by pilots from Alaska and Canada. Jimmy Mattern, the American whom the Russian had rescued during his around-the-world flight attempt, flew from California to join the search. Famed Arctic explorer Vilhjalmur Stefansson was contacted to lead the search, which included the noted Australian Polar explorer Hubert Wilkins and numerous volunteer pilots. The search continued, covering an area the size of Montana in a grid pattern. After extended search attempts were unsuccessful Levanevsky and his crew were presumed dead.

Bolkhovitinov DB-A

Sigizmund Levanevsky

Sixteen DB-A production aircraft were ordered in 1937, but only twelve were completed, as they were succeeded by the Petlyakov Pe-8, the only four-engine Russian heavy bomber built during the war (only ninety-three examples). Though Levanevsky never attained his objective, the efforts to find him contributed considerably to aviation over northern and Polar areas. Today countless passengers and tons of cargo fly across the North Pole each year, fulfilling Levanevsky's vision.

TUPOLEV ANT-26

In layout and structure, the ANT-26 was a further development of the ANT-16 (TB-4), but it was larger (311.7 ft. wing span and 128 ft. length), heavier (110,000 lbs. empty/167,500 lbs. maximum), and had more powerful engines, with twelve M-34FRN engines: eight installed in the wing leading edge and four above the fuselage in two tandem pairs. There was also a project to install six M-44 engines, each of which would have had twice the output of the M-34FRN.

In 1935, a two-seat glider representing a quarter-scale model of the ANT-26 was built for aerodynamic research, with the flight tests to log the characteristics being made by test pilot B. N. Koodrin. All work on the civil version was temporarily suspended to concentrate on the military version. Construction of the TB-6 6M-44 prototype began with completion scheduled initially for December 1935, then postponed to August 1936. All further work on the project was terminated in July 1934,

Tupolev ANT-26 (display model)

when the airframe was seventy-five percent complete and the entire aircraft had reached only sixteen percent completion.

The cancellation was at a time of limited resources and Soviet leaders were having doubts about their very heavy bomber program. They considered one hundred slow, heavy bombers would be less effective and much more vulnerable to anti-aircraft fire and enemy interceptors than 300 smaller SB (high-speed bomber) that could be manufactured more inexpensively, quicker, and in greater numbers. The ANT-40, also known by its service name Tupolev SB, was an advanced twin-engine, three-place monoplane with retractable wheels and the first modern bomber with smooth stressed skin, instead of the corrugated surface of older types. Numerically it was the most important and formidable bomber in the world in the late 1930s. It was produced in quantity in the Soviet Union, with many versions seeing extensive action in the Spanish Civil War, China, Mongolia, and Finland. By June 1941, more than ninety percent of the bombers in the Red Army Air Force were SBs. When Germany invaded Russia in June, the SB could not compete against Luftwaffe fighters and was declared obsolete, being replaced by the inimitable Petlyakov Pe-2.

ANDREI TUPOLEV AND THE GREAT SOVIET ARMED FORCES PURGE

On 21 October 1937, along with more than 36,000 Soviet officers and Soviet Air Force chiefs, Tupolev was arrested, together with fellow aircraft designer Vladimir Petlyakov, and the entire directorate and 150 engineers of the Central Aerohydrodynamics Institute (TsAGI) on trumped up charges of sabotage, espionage, and aiding the Russian Fascist Party. Although many of Tupolev's colleagues were executed, the valuable designer was moved from prison in 1939 to a *Sharashka* near Moscow. (A Sharashka was a special secret NKVD prison for aircraft designers which was soon dubbed "Tupolevka" after its most eminent inmate.) In 1940, Tupolev was officially tried and convicted to a ten-year sentence, during which time he developed the Tupolev Tu-2, the Soviet's second most important twin-engine bomber after the Pe-2. He was released in July 1941, "to conduct important defense work" (under supervision), but was considered not fully "rehabilitated" until two years after Stalin's death in 1953. As part of the purges, all ANT/Tu designated aircraft were hastily given new designations that did not reveal their Tupolev origins. The effect of the purges on Soviet aviation was enormous, as the creative design leadership of previous years ceased to exist and it prolonged the service life of older combat types that were long past their prime. Worried manufacturers merely expanded the production of older types, trusting that obsolescent quantity would compensate for more contemporary quality. Consequently, thousands of obsolete Soviet warplanes were destroyed on the ground and in the air by superior Luftwaffe designs during the first weeks of the Nazi invasion of Russia in June 1941.

LAST SOVIET LONG-DISTANCE FLIGHT: VLADIMIR KOKKINAKI WITH MIKHAIL GORDIENKO

The last Soviet long distance record flight occurred on 28 April 1939, when renowned Soviet test pilot Vladimir Kokkinaki, with Mikhail Gordienko as co-pilot, attempted to fly an Ilyushin DB-3 bomber from Moscow to New York. Previously, on 27–28 June 1938, Kokkinaki had flown a modified TsKB-30 *Moskva* from Moscow to Spassk-Dalny, in the Soviet Far East, covering a distance of 4,710 miles in 24:36 hours for a Soviet record, for which he was made a Hero of the Soviet Union. The proposed Moscow to New York flight was intended to pioneer a new northern Great Circle route and to complete the first East-West non-stop trans-Atlantic flight that was to coincide with the opening of New York's "Land of Tomorrow" World's Fair. About twenty hours after leaving Moscow the weather deteriorated over northern Canada and their radio compass malfunctioned. The Russians spent hours searching for a safe landing place and finally crash landed on Miscou Island, New Brunswick, 700 miles north of New York. Even though he failed to reach his original destination, Kokkinaki still covered a distance of about 5,000 miles in 22:56 hours. In spite of the flight's failure, Kikkonaki returned to Moscow a national hero, greeted by Stalin. Kokkinaki remained with the Ilyushin Design Bureau (OKB) as its chief test pilot until 1964, after setting a total of twenty-two world and Soviet flying records. The Great Circle route Kikkonaki pioneered has been used for regular commercial airline flights between New York and Moscow since 1959. Coming not long after the death of Valery Chkalov, the Stalin purges, and with the approaching war, this well-publicized flight was the last of the Soviet long-range aviation exploits of the 1930s.

Vladimir Kikkonaki

3
TOWARDS A SOVIET POSTWAR INTERCONTINENTAL BOMBER

TU 4 (BULL) B-29 KNOCK-OFF

During WWII, the Soviet Union relied on its immense tactical air forces to drive Nazi ground forces from Mother Russia, but left the strategic bombing of Germany to the British and Americans. By the end of the war the Soviet's only heavy long-range bomber were the ninety-eight four-engine Petlyakov Pe-8 bombers developed from a 1934 design to replace the obsolete Tupolev TB-3 heavy bomber. The Soviet Union had requested B-17s and B-24s from the US under Lend Lease, but their requests were rejected, instead receiving thousands of other American aircraft, particularly the Douglas A-20 light bomber, which aided the Soviets greatly as a tactical bomber. As the war neared its end Soviet Union air planners realized they would need strategic air bombing capability similar to that of the American Army Air Forces, whose B-29 Superfortresses were regularly bombing Japanese cities into oblivion from distant Pacific bases. Stalin became absorbed with the B-29 Superfortress, the embodiment of US bomber aircraft technology and a veritable treasure trove of American aviation manufacturing expertise. The Soviets requested the coveted B-29s under Lend Lease, but as expected were twice rejected.

During 1944, four intact B-29s made emergency landings in Soviet territory and another crashed but was not destroyed after its crew bailed out. Under the Soviet-Japanese Neutrality Pact, the Soviets were considered a neutral nation and the bombers of "belligerent" America were therefore "interned" by the Soviets. This practice began with the Doolittle "30 Seconds over Tokyo" mission, when some B-25s landed in Vladivostok in April 1942. Despite Soviet neutrality, being a European war ally, and a Lend Lease "partner," the US demanded the return of their prized, technologically advanced B-29s, but the Soviets declined.

On 22 June 1945, Stalin appointed a reluctant Andrei Tupolev—who had no choice but to accept—as the lead designer to reverse engineer a prototype Tu 4 Superfortress clone "as soon as possible." In doing so Stalin canceled Tupolev's own comparable ANT-64 postwar long-range, four-engine bomber project developed from the Tu 2 bomber. The three flyable B-29s were flown to Tupolev OKB in Moscow, where one B-29 was dismantled, the second was used for flight tests and training, and the third served as a standard for cross-reference in the reverse engineering process. After Japan surrendered, the fourth intact B-29 was returned to the US, along with its crew. The three usable interned AAF B-29s were:

Ramp Tramp (42-6256) was unable to return to its base after a raid in Manchuria and landed in Vladivostok on July 29, 1944

The *General H.H. Arnold Special* (42-636) was damaged during a raid against Omura, on Kyushu, and was forced to divert to Vladivostok on 11 November 1944

Ding How (42-6358) landed in Vladivostok on 21 November 1944

From the onset of the replication process, Tupolev was confronted with the mammoth ASAP undertaking which ordinarily would require many years to complete. Stalin deemed the replication as urgent, and so it became. The *General Hap Arnold Special* was completely disassembled by teams of engineers and technicians who measured, numbered, labeled, photographed, and documented each of the 105,000 parts and subassemblies due for replication. Over 1,000 draftsmen produced 40,000 detailed drawings. Each component was then thoroughly analyzed, sometimes under protracted and meddling government scrutiny, before it was to be reproduced.

The extensive re-engineering required was made much more difficult since the Soviet Union used the metric system, and everything from rivets to large metal fuselage aluminum sheets had to be converted from English to metric units. Tupolev replicated the basic airframe, but sheet aluminum in thicknesses matching the B-29's English measurements were unavailable and equivalent quality metric-gauge aluminum was of different thicknesses. Official Soviet strength margins had to be decreased to avoid further redesign. The B-29 was also made up of unfamiliar lightweight metallic alloys (including magnesium alloys) and other materials that had to be replicated. Despite all of these challenges, the completed prototype Tu 4 copy weighed only less than one percent more (about 750 lbs.) than the USAAF B-29 original. Another problem due to the use of the metric system occurred during flight testing, when Russian pilots had difficulty reading the English-labeled instruments and every instrument had to be re-labeled in Russian and recalibrated in metric units.

The only changes allowed were limited to the engines, armament, radio, and the Identification Friend or Foe (IFF) equipment. The existing Soviet engine (Shvetsov ASh-73) was a poor facsimile of the B-29's Wright R-3350, and most of the required changes and problems in the Tu 4 copy mainly related to engine and propeller failures. The B-29's sophisticated remote-controlled gun turrets were redesigned to accommodate the more powerful and longer-range Soviet Nudelman NS-23 23 mm cannon. The Soviets deemed their communications and IFF equipment adequate when considering the time and complexity of replicating the AAF versions.

The Soviets were ultimately unable to adequately remanufacture the wing fuel tanks, the curved Plexiglas nose, fabricate the oversized tires for the landing gear (agents were sent to the west to purchase them), or replicate the pressurization system and the huge landing gear, all of which would be major contributors to future problems. The placement of the miles of wires and tubing was a major undertaking that had to be constantly checked against the untouched interned B-29 cross-reference bomber. Equipment modifications would be required throughout the Tu 4's troubled service life.

The Tu 4 first flew on 19 May 1947, piloted by test pilot Nikolai Rybko, and serial production began immediately. Tupolev was able to produce twenty copies of the aircraft for acceptance trials in a relatively short two years. The Tu 4 was first displayed during a flyover for the Aviation Day parade on 3 August 1947, at Moscow's Tushino Airport. As three large bombers flew overhead, western observers assumed that these were the three B-29 bombers known to have been interned by the Soviets. When a fourth aircraft appeared several minutes later it was realized the Soviets now had a bomber capable of bombing any target in the US, but only on a one-way mission.

Dubbed by NATO as the Bull and tongue-in-cheek as the "Superfortresski," the Tu 4's performance was inferior to the later American B-29/B-50: maximum speed 347 mph vs. 357; maximum range 3,355 miles vs. 5,600 miles; and service ceiling 32,000 ft. vs. 36,745 ft. In service, the Bull experienced constant engine overheating and short engine life, runaway props, frequent propeller failures, continuing landing gear failures, and problems with the pressurization system and the advanced avionics of the central fire control gunnery system. Most problems were caused by poor quality control in the manufacturing plants, but this was eventually upgraded and the more severe defects were corrected. It was not until mid-1949 that Tu 4s with sufficient range to attack the United States became fully operational, with about 300 in service.

Soviet Tu 4 production ended in 1952, after 847 had been built; they were subsequently replaced by jet aircraft. Although the Tu 4 never saw combat, its mere presence had a major effect on America's Cold War defensive policy. On 18 October 1951, a Tu 4 dropped an atomic bomb, causing the United States to develop a costly system of ground radar installations, radar picket aircraft, surface-to-air missiles, and jet interceptor fighters. While Stalin's questionable decision to copy the B-29 did give Russia a credible strategic bomber, it also caused the modernization of the Soviet aviation industry in an effort to achieve aerial parity with NATO air forces, which they approached but never realized.

LEFT / An interned American B-29 undergoing dismantling at the Tupolev factory to reverse engineer the Russian Tu 4 Superfortress knockoff.

BELOW / Tupolev Tu 4 (Bull)

TUPOLEV TU 80

Tupolev began design work on the Tu 80 in February 1948, as an updated and enlarged Tu 4 with much greater range (3,350 to 5,100 miles) and a higher maximum speed of 390 mph by installing revised, more fuel efficient engines (2,600 hp, 18-cylinder, two-row, radial Shvetsov ASh-73 TKFN). The Tu 4 design also offered additional fuel tanks, improved aerodynamics, and redesigned engine nacelles with smaller cross sections. The wing span was slightly increased sixteen inches from 141.3 ft. to 142.6 ft., increasing the wing area from 1,741 sq. ft. to 1,798 sq. ft. To increase its bomb bay size, its length was increased from 99 ft. to 112.6 ft., while its height increased from 27.8 ft. to 29.3 ft., its empty weight increased from 81,240 lbs. to 83,444 lbs., and its maximum take-off weight increased from 122,577 lbs. to 133,598 lbs. It was to carry a maximum bomb load of 26,000 lbs. On 12 June 1948, the Council of Ministers ordered the prototype to be ready for state acceptance trials in July 1949. Construction began in November 1948, using as many Tu 4 components as possible to accelerate construction, but by the time the first flight occurred on 1 December 1949, the Council of Ministers had already canceled the program on 16 September 1949, in favor of the Tu 85, which was expected to have much better performance. The lone Tu 4 was relegated to serve as a research aircraft, testing reversible pitch propellers and structural deformation in heavy aircraft. The prototype eventually succumbed as a bombing and gunnery range target.

Tupolev Tu 80

TUPOLEV TU 85 (BARGE)

Neither the Tu 4 nor the Tupolev Tu 80 was a true intercontinental strategic bomber, as each lacked the range to attack the United States from bases in the Soviet Union and return.

The Tupolev Tu 85 was the ultimate development of the Soviet B-29 series, being much larger: length: 129 ft. vs. 99 ft.; wingspan: 183.6 ft. vs. 141.3 ft.; height: 37.3 ft. vs. 27.8 ft.; wing area: 2,945 sq. ft. vs. 1,741 sq. ft.; empty weight: 120,364 lbs. vs. 81,240 lbs.; and maximum take-off weight: 236,534 lbs. vs. 122,577 lbs. Much of the armament and equipment was derived from the late-model Tu 4, except the tail turret was an Argon ranging radar and each of the two bomb bays was enlarged to carry a 20,000 lb. FAB-9000 bomb. To achieve the necessary range, the Tu 85 was equipped with more powerful and fuel efficient engines using additional fuel (16,800 gallons in forty-eight flexible tanks) and a redesigned wing that increased lift/drag ratio. Tupolev considered a large number of engines and preferred the new but undeveloped 4,500 hp Shvetsov ASh-2K, which was essentially two air-cooled ASh-82 radial engines paired together; he had to settle on the liquid-cooled 4,300 hp Dobrynin VD-4K radial. Both engines were equipped with turbochargers and power recovery turbines which converted them into turbo-compound engines.

Design work began in August 1949, and a directive from the Council of Ministers dated 16 September required the first prototype to be ready for manufacturer's tests in December 1950. Construction of the first aircraft began in July 1950, and was completed in September. The first Tu 85 flew on 9 January 1951, with the manufacturer's tests completed in October 1951. On 12 September, the first prototype flew 5,600 miles with an 11,000 lb. bomb load and landed with enough fuel remaining to have covered an equivalent intercontinental round trip range of 7,468 miles. The second prototype included the revision and reinforcement of the airframe and an assortment of changes to its equipment and systems. It was first flown on 28 June 1951, with trials lasting until November 1951. Series production was approved on 23 March 1951, to succeed the Tu 4 on the production line, but the Tu 85 program was canceled, as during the ongoing Korean War Soviet MiG-15s shot down many USAF B-29 bombers. The days of the piston engine combat bomber were over and the Soviets gave priority to the higher performing turboprop Tu 95 Bear.

Tupolev Tu 85 (Barge)

TUPOLEV TU 95 BEAR

A new requirement was issued to Tupolev and the newly formed Myasishchev Experimental Design Bureau (OKB-23) for a proposed bomber with an un-refueled range of 4,970 miles (8,000 km) with a 22,000 lb. (10,000 kg) payload, which would give the bomber sufficient range to threaten strategic targets in the United States. The critical factor in meeting the criteria of this proposal was the power plant to be used. The Tu 4 had already revealed that piston engines were not powerful enough to fulfill that requirement, while the fuel-guzzling AM-3 jet engines of the proposed T-4 intercontinental jet bomber would not provide sufficient range. Turboprops were more powerful than available piston engines, had better range than the available jet engines, and had a maximum speed that fell between these two engine options.

Tupolev's Tu 95 design proposal was selected, and its development was officially approved on 11 July 1951. The Tu 95 used four 12,000 eshp* Kuznetsov coupled turboprop engines driving eight-bladed, contra-rotating propellers. The fuselage was a conventional mid-wing cantilever monoplane with thirty-five degrees of sweep, an angle which ensured the main wing spar passed through the fuselage in front of the bomb bay. It was equipped with a retractable tricycle landing gear, with all three gear struts retracting rearward and the main gear retracting rearward into extensions of the inner engine nacelles. After successful flight testing, series production of the Tu 95 was initiated in January 1956, and it became Russia's counterpart to America's Boeing B-52 Stratofortress; like the B-52, it has become an enduring icon of the Cold War era and a symbol of Soviet national prestige.

Tupolev Tu 95 (Bear)

*Turboprop aircraft produce power and thrust. The amount of thrust they produce is converted into horsepower units and added to the shaft horsepower for the equivalent shaft horsepower, or eshp.

PART 4: AMERICA'S PIONEERING PILOTS AND THE REALIZATION OF THE INTERCONTINENTAL BOMBER

1

QUEST FOR DISTANCE AND ENDURANCE: THE FLYING FUEL TANKS: 1911–1927

During the years immediately following WWI, the fledgling Army Air Service had to confirm its very existence, as many politicians and the American public regarded aviation as an unnecessary and expensive luxury. Air Service pilots realized their livelihood depended on their ability to showcase their competence with record-setting flights and various exploits that many regarded as stunts.

Meanwhile, after WWI, there were many military pilots who became unemployed and faced further postwar unemployment, especially in aviation. Some became so enamored with flying that they bought one of the cheap surplus Jennys and tried to eke out a living giving weekend rides; the more entrepreneurial types started barnstorming companies, performing outrageous flying stunts. A few others flew for recognition, questing after records of various types—anything to earn a dollar to make a living doing something they loved and to afford their aircraft and its maintenance, fuel, and oil (no insurance in those days).

1919: FIRST ARMY AIR SERVICE US TRANSCONTINENTAL FLIGHT

After Calbraith Rodgers completed the first transcontinental flight (East to West) across America and Robert Fowler the second transcontinental flight (first West to East), it would not be until after the war that another significant attempt would be made. The Army Air Service had recently accepted the first American-designed twin-engine MB-1 Glenn Martin Bomber (GMB) into inventory, and to test its long-range capabilities chose to fly the GMB completely around America's periphery. The GMB had a 71.5 ft. wingspan, a length of 44.8 ft., and a weight of 10,300 lbs. It was powered by two 400 hp Liberty 12A engines that propelled the large bomber at 100 mph over a range of 390 miles. The GMT (Glenn Martin Transcontinental) was a long-range GMB version with a 1,500 mile range. Since time and speed were not considered, the leisurely AAS flight began in a counterclockwise direction, leaving from Bolling Field, Washington, DC, on 23 July 1919. The flight proceeded westward across the northern tier of states, south down the Pacific Coast, and then eastward along the Mexican border and across the southern tier of states, returning to Bolling on 9 November after flying approximately 10,000 miles in 114:45 hours of flying time.

GMT (Glenn Martin Transcontinental) MB-1

1919: CURTISS NCS: FIRST US TRANS-ATLANTIC FLIGHT

Near the end of WWI, the Navy and Curtiss Company designed and constructed four large flying boats (NC-1, -2, -3, and -4)—called the NANCYs (NCs)—that were intended to cross the Atlantic to fly combat against German U-boats. The war ended before the trans-Atlantic flight could be made and then was postponed, as NC-2 was damaged in a hangar fire and was salvaged to repair NC-1's wing, which was damaged in a storm.

On 8 May 1919, NC-1, -3, and -4 took off from NAS Rockaway, Long Island, headed for Trepassey, Newfoundland, the intermediate stop before crossing the Atlantic. The flight was under the command of John Towers, who was also commanding officer and navigator of NC-3. NC-4 was commanded by Lt.Cdr. Albert Read and NC-1 by Lt.Cdr. Patrick Bellinger, with Lt.Cdr. Marc Mitscher as pilot. After bad weather and NC-4 engine problem delays all three NCs finally left Trepassey the evening of 16 May, with the crews flying at 90 mph maximum speed in exposed open, unheated cockpits. There were twenty-one US Navy destroyers stationed at approximately fifty-mile intervals between Cape Race, Newfoundland, and Corvo, the westernmost island of the Azores, to serve as visual and radio navigation aids and communication links, and to provide weather information and rescue service if necessary.

After seventeen hours, the flight neared its scheduled fuel stop in the Azores in foggy weather. NC-4 landed safely in Horta Harbor, but NC-1 and NC-3 landed in the high seas well off the Azores and were unable to take off again. NC-1 landed in rough seas and snapped a control cable; the crew climbed to the top wing until they were rescued by a Greek freighter that took NC-1 in tow, but it sank three days later. NC-3 had previously discarded its emergency radio transmitter to reduce weight for take-off and could receive radio calls, but could not transmit, and so was unable to relay its position when it landed in high seas. Commander John Towers used his Navy seamanship experience and sailed/drifted the flying boat, which was now only a boat, for three days; the pummeled NC-3 sailed 200 miles into Ponta Delgada Harbor on 19 May.

After weather delays, engine repairs, and other problems, at 0818 on 27 May, NC-4 finally took off with its six-man crew comprised of Lt.Cdr. Albert Read, USN, commander/navigator; Lt. Walter Hinton, USNR, pilot; Lt. Elmer Stone, USCG, pilot; Lt. James Breese, USNR, flight engineer; Chief Eugene Rhoads, USN, flight engineer; and Ens. Herbert Rodd, USNR, radio operator. Read followed another sequence of destroyers that extended between the Azores and Lisbon, and at 20:01 hours that day landed in Lisbon to complete the first trans-Atlantic flight. Less than three weeks later, on 14–15 June 1919, John Alcock and Arthur Brown flew from Newfoundland to Ireland non-stop in 16:27 hours in their Vickers Vimy. As of 2017, the reassembled NC-4 is on loan from the Smithsonian to the National Museum of Naval Aviation in Pensacola, Florida.

Curtiss NC-4 taxiing in Lisbon Harbor.

Crew of the NC-4 (L-R Read, Byrd, and Hinton) after their landing in Lisbon Harbor.

NOTE: Future US Navy admiral and pioneer naval aviator John Towers made valuable contributions to the piloting, technical, and organizational development of naval aviation from its beginning in WWI. Towers (Naval Aviator #3) and Marc Mitscher (Naval Aviator #33), who crewed on NC-1, were the only early Naval aviation visionaries to survive the dangers of early flight and remain in naval aviation throughout their careers. Towers was the first naval aviator to achieve flag rank and was the most senior advocate for naval aviation during a time when the Navy was dominated by "battleship admirals." Towers eventually served as chief of the Bureau of Aeronautics (1939–1942) and commanded carrier task forces during WWII, retiring in December 1947. Before flying with the NCs Towers set a distance record in October 1911, flying a Curtiss A-1—the Navy's first seaplane—over 112 miles from Annapolis to Old Point Comfort, Virginia, in 122 minutes. On 6 October 1912, Towers set an American endurance record by flying for 6:10:35 hours by equipping extra fuel tanks in a Curtiss A-2 seaplane. On 8 May 1913, Lt. Towers flew 169 miles in a Curtiss flying boat from the Washington Navy Yard down the Potomac River and then up the Chesapeake Bay to the US Naval Academy in 3:05 hours.

Future Admiral John Tower with aviation's movers and shakers of the 1920s: Standing (L-R): Capt. E.S. Gorrell, Jerome Hunsaker, Lt. John Towers, and Capt. Virginius Clark. Sitting: Lt.Cdr. A.K. Atkins (L) and Maj. Benjamin Foulois.

1920: FIRST US TO ALASKA FLIGHT

In early 1920, St. Clair Streett led a five-week, 4,000 mile survey flight to assess airfield conditions in eleven northern tier states. Streett next commanded the Alaskan Flying Expedition, an exploratory flight made by the Air Service at the suggestion of Gen. Billy Mitchell, who wished to strengthen American air presence in Alaska Territory. The first flight from the US to Alaska was made by four De Havilland DH4Bs of Black Wolf Squadron which departed Mitchel Field, Long Island, New York, on 15 July 1920, and arrived in Nome, Alaska, on 24 August. They had flown 8,690 miles in 110 hours flying time, dividing the route into fifteen legs across the northern United States and the western provinces of Canada, then north to Fairbanks, Alaska, via Dawson City, Yukon. An advance party had scouted weather conditions, cut landing strips out of virgin forest in the flight legs north of Jasper, Alberta, and stocked fuel and provisions to replenish the flyers and their aircraft. Part of their mission was to deliver the first airmail to Alaska with an air-dropped copy of the *New York Times* delivered to the roof of the Brunswick Hotel in Juneau. The four D.H.4Bs and crews returned to Mitchel Field on 20 October, completing a 9,000 mile round trip. For this pioneering flight that established Alaska could be linked by air to the United States, Streett was awarded the Distinguished Flying Cross and the Mackay Trophy for the "most meritorious flight of the year" made by a US military airman. In an interview after the flight Streett ventured, "Someday this trip may be made overnight, who knows?"

DH 4B crew under the command of St. Clair Streett

1922–1934: WORLD ENDURANCE RECORDS AND IN-FLIGHT REFUELING

1922: LTS. MACREADY AND KELLY SET THE WORLD ENDURANCE RECORD

In late 1921, 1Lts. Oakley Kelly and Muir Fairchild began evaluating aircraft in Army inventory for flying the first non-stop transcontinental flight and decided the Fokker F-IV (Army designation T-2) had the characteristics they were considering. The Army had recently acquired two to be used as testbeds for the Liberty 12 engine and the AAS, eager to publicize the service, made one available. The T-2 was a large, eight-passenger plane with a large, cantilevered, wood-covered wing with a span of 81.3 ft. and a wing area of 372 sq. ft., a length of 49.3 ft., and a height of 11 ft.. It had an enclosed metal tubing and fabric-covered fuselage that seated one pilot in an exposed cockpit in front of the wing. It was powered by a 400 hp Packard-built Liberty L12 piston engine that gave it a maximum speed of 93 mph, a normal range of 2,550 miles, and a service ceiling of 10,500 ft. The Fokker Company had built only two in the Netherlands and no others were built, as the aircraft was considered too large for use by contemporary airlines.

To increase the T-2's range, 1Lt. Earnest Dichman, the flight's chief engineer, modified it by increasing its fuel load to 725 gallons, with the standard 130 gallon fuel tank in the wing being augmented by a 410 gallon tank placed in the wing center section and a 185 gallon tank in the passenger cabin. Other essential modifications included additional water and oil tanks in the cabin, larger and stronger wheels, auxiliary water and oil radiators, a door between the open cockpit and the cabin, and a second set of flight controls in the cabin.

Fairchild, who was recovering from an unrelated accident, was replaced by 1Lt. John Macready, who was awarded a MacKay Trophy in 1921. Pilots 1Lts. Oakley Kelly and John Macready had to decide from which coast to start their planned non-stop, cross-country flight. The Weather Bureau strongly recommended flying from west to east, to take advantage of the prevailing twenty-plus mile per hour westerly wind during August and September, and the California-to-New York route was again selected. The Fokker arrived at Rockwell Field on North Island, California, on 24 September 1922, and final preparations were made, including the installation of an overhauled Liberty 12 engine; adding hinges to the back of the pilot's seat for easier access between cockpit and cabin; and a continuous-cord message system was installed, enabling the pilots to communicate in flight.

On 22 October, after flipping a coin to determine who would pilot first, Kelly barely lifted the heavily laden Fokker off the 10,000 ft. San Diego Rockwell runway. About fifty miles into the flight the pilots encountered unforecasted light fog. Since the Weather Bureau had not indicated bad weather in the mountains the aviators disregarded the fog and flew on. When the pilots reached Banning, California, they found the tops of the mountains covered in fog. After wasting several hours looking for a break in the fog they decided to turn back, as even if they could find their way through the fog, they had by now used up too much fuel to complete the trip to New York.

The pilots returned to Rockwell Field, and as they flew over the field they dropped a note saying they had decided to abort the transcontinental flight and instead would attempt to break the world endurance record. The duo circled Rockwell Field, and when they landed the Fokker to the cheers of a thousand supporters they had set a new endurance record of 35:18:30 hours in the air. The record was declared unofficial by the Aero Club of America because appropriate measures had not been made prior to the flight. Nonetheless, they were awarded the Mackay Trophy—Macready's second Mackay—and he and Kelly would win it again the following year. Because fuel carrying capacity of aircraft was nearing its limits, it became apparent that to extend the endurance record a method of in-flight refueling would be necessary.

The flight proved that the T-2 and its pilots could stay aloft long enough to make a non-stop transcontinental flight. All they needed was favorable weather. Buoyed by their new endurance record, on 3 November 1922, the two pilots waited for adequate daylight before Kelly once again took the controls for take-off and headed east toward New York. With no fog and good weather the T-2 easily climbed over the mountains in California, and once they crossed the Colorado River Macready took the controls. When they approached the Continental Divide Kelly doubted his ability to fly over it, but with each gallon of fuel burned the plane became lighter. With Kelly now at the controls, he coaxed the laboring Fokker across, avoiding disaster from a sudden downdraft. After crossing the Divide at dusk, the Fokker flew eastward in total darkness, with no visible landmarks for direction. As the plane headed east clouds forced Kelly to fly close to the ground so he could follow his "iron compass," the Southern Pacific Railroad tracks. Once they reached Pratt, Kansas, they left the railroad tracks and Macready took over and followed a compass course. At the Kansas-Missouri border Kelly took over and they reached St. Louis at sunrise, thinking they would have smooth flying to New York. As they approached Indiana they discovered a cracked cylinder jacket, but since the engine was not yet losing cooling water they continued. As they flew over Terre Haute, Indiana, they were rapidly losing coolant and about fifty miles from Indianapolis the engine temperature was rising rapidly; pilot Macready prepared to land while Kelly was pouring coffee, broth, and any other liquid he could find into the water tank. This remedy lowered the water temperature enough to allow the stricken T-2 to land safely on the Indianapolis Speedway. Macready later wrote in *National Geographic* about another transcontinental attempt: "We were through. Any man who was foolish enough to want our job was welcome to it. Never, never again for us! Neither one said much, but we did a lot of thinking, and decided in our own minds that transcontinental non-stop flights were good things to keep away from. We were entirely willing for someone to take our place. We wanted to forget it."

Lts. John Macready (L), Oakley Kelly, and their Fokker T-2

1922: 1LT. JAMES DOOLITTLE: FIRST US TRANSCONTINENTAL FLIGHT DURING ONE DAY

Since the end of the war the Air Service had been flying missions with the intent to set endurance, distance, altitude, and speed records to promote favorable PR and gain public support for the funding of the Army War Department's Major Project Number 4 (the *Lassiter Plan*) for the expansion of the Air Service. The first transcontinental flight across the US in a single day (twenty-four hour period) was set by Lt. James "Jimmy" Doolittle on 2 September 1922, flying a DH 4B-1-S single-engine biplane adorned with a pair of "Lucky 7" dice on the side of the fuselage. Doolittle took off from Pablo Beach, Florida, and landed at Rockwell Field, near San Diego, covering a distance of 2,163 miles in 21:20 hours with one refueling stop at Kelly Field near San Antonio, Texas, that lasted 1:16 hours. For his feat Doolittle received the Distinguished Flying Cross, with the citation crediting him with demonstrating "the possibility of moving Air Corps units to any portion of the United States in less than 24 hours." The DH 4 was a very successful fighter of WWI designed by Geoffrey de Havilland and was produced by several manufacturers in Europe and the United States. Army Air Service DH 4s were powered by water-cooled 400 hp Liberty engines and had an increased fuel capacity of 110 gallons. It had a maximum speed of 128 mph and a service ceiling of 19,600 ft. Another DH 4B-1-S was flown from the Gulf of Mexico to the Canadian border by Lt. H. G. Crocker on 26 May 1923. Unlike most "seat-of-their pants" aviators of the time, after setting this transcontinental flight record the scholarly Doolittle enrolled in the Massachusetts Institute of Technology (MIT) in 1923, and would continue to earn a master's degree and then a PhD in the new field of aeronautical engineering.

The first US transcontinental flight in a single day (twenty-four hour period) was made by Lt. James "Jimmy" Doolittle and his DH 4B-1-S.

1923: FIRST NON-STOP US TRANSCONTINENTAL FLIGHT: 1LTS. JOHN MACREADY AND OAKLEY KELLY

Despite Macready's "never again vow" after their two west-to-east transcontinental failures, Macready and Kelly re-evaluated their route, then decided to fly east-to-west, as they could immediately throttle back after take-off and remain at lower altitudes until they reached the Continental Divide, by which time they would have burned enough fuel to allow an easy climb over the mountains. The Weather Bureau determined that during the last two weeks in April there was usually a shift in the continental weather pattern, producing two or three strong east-to-west wind streams that they could utilize.

During the evening of 30 April 1923, a weather report showed favorable conditions developing and Macready and Kelly took off from Roosevelt Field, Long Island, New York, early the next morning. The Fokker T-2, heavily loaded with fuel, climbed very slowly, and was just able to climb and maintain level flight, scarcely clearing poles and trees. Over Pennsylvania Kelly detected that the voltage regulator was discharging and they were flying on the battery. Turning the controls over to Macready, Kelly spent the next half hour removing the voltage regulator and was able to repair it. They flew through clouds and the darkness of night by compass from St. Louis to New Mexico, exchanging piloting chores. As they approached the Continental Divide San Diego was seven hours away with nine hours of fuel remaining. They were again unable to cross and had to fly south and look for a gap between the peaks. Fortunately Macready soon found a gap and flew on toward California. Since Macready was a San Diego native he took the controls and landed the T-2 at Rockwell Field 26:50 hours after leaving New York. For their successful non-stop flight across the US Macready and Kelly were again awarded the Mackay Trophy for 1923. Macready became the only pilot in history to win the Mackay three times. After their grueling flight Kelly and Macready hoped the grateful Army would grant them an extended leave, especially since Macready had gotten married a few days after they landed. The honeymoon would have to wait, as the fliers were ordered to report to Washington, DC, with the T-2, where the plane was donated to the Smithsonian; it is now on display at the National Air and Space Museum.

John Macready (L) and Oakley Kelly pose with drums of gasoline before their Fokker T-2.

1Lts. Oakley Kelly (R) and John Macready, seen here with Orville Wright (C).

1924: 1LT. RUSSELL MAUGHAN: US TRANSCONTINENTAL FLIGHT DURING DAYLIGHT

In 1923, the Air Service's Assistant Chief Brig.Gen. Billy Mitchell wanted to not only improve on both Doolittle's transcontinental time and distance, but to have the achievement highly publicized by having it take off and land during daylight at major US cities New York and San Francisco. Mitchell's military rationale for the flight would be to validate the possibility of rapidly moving air units from one border to the other, an ability that the ground Army and Navy did not possess.

Mitchell's planners determined that during early summer—including twilight—twenty hours of daylight were available for a westbound flight, and by averaging 160 mph, the 2,670 miles between New York and San Francisco could be flown in 16:40 hours. Mitchell had previously purchased twenty-five new PW-8 fighters from Curtiss Aircraft that were modeled after the R-6 Racer, and Mitchell cajoled Curtiss to help modify one of the XPW prototypes for use on his transcontinental mission. The XPW-8's D-12 engine produced 435 hp, and with the intended modifications the flight could be made at full throttle. Armament and unnecessary equipment were removed and additional fuel tanks were installed to extend its range, as were larger oil tanks for engine cooling. The flight plan followed a recently established airmail route with four thirty-minute refueling stops: McCook Field, Dayton, Ohio; Saint Joseph, Missouri; Cheyenne, Wyoming; and remote Salduro Siding, Utah. 1Lt. Russell Maughan was chosen as the flight's pilot because he was an experienced test pilot and a four aerial victory combat veteran who had established speed records in 1922 and 1923.

In 1922, the Air Service entered the Pulitzer Trophy Race and Maughan, flying a Curtiss R-6 racer—a precursor of the PW-8 design—won the Pulitzer race with an average speed of 205.8 mph. The following year Maughan officially set a new international speed record of 236.5 mph in the R-6.

During 1923, Maughan had made two unsuccessful attempts at the transcontinental record. On 10 July 1923, Maughan took off from Mitchel Field, Long Island, at 0456 and proceeded over the Allegheny Mountains, which were concealed by a thick undercast. Unable to navigate by landmarks, Maughan flew the 570 mile first leg by dead reckoning, arriving at McCook Field ninety minutes behind schedule; the repair of a broken tail fin rib caused a further delay. A clogged fuel line over Illinois caused Maughan to make a forced landing in a farmer's field, damaging the landing gear and ending the flight. On July 19, the PW-8 was ready for a second attempt to set the record and after a 0508 departure Maughan landed at McCook Field at 0835, refueling and taking off again at 0853. He arrived at Saint Joseph, but experienced severe nausea from oil fumes on the next leg. When he reached Cheyenne a broken oil line was found and quickly soldered. About an hour and a half after leaving Cheyenne the oil line ruptured again and nausea forced him to land at the airmail field in Rock Springs, Wyoming, ending the flight. These first two attempts revealed that flying the PW-8 at maximum performance was over-stressing its engine, and with available daylight already reduced no further flights were made that year.

The next year Curtiss modified the fourth PW-8 production aircraft at its Long Island plant, removing its armament and increasing the seventy-seven gallon fuel capacity by an additional one hundred gallons. Maughan took off from Mitchel Field at 0358 EST on 23 June 1924, and flew through intermittent rain and fog, arriving at McCook Field at 0810 EST. While there one of the field's mechanics over-torqued the fuel filler cap and broke off the fuel intake valve, which required an hour to solder. After the repair Maughan reached Saint Joseph without incident, but the grass field there was soft from heavy rain, limiting his load of fuel on take-off and causing Maughan to detour to North Platte, Nebraska, where he completely filled the fuel tank, causing an additional twenty-minute delay. This detour then resulted in Maughan encountering strong headwinds on his way to Utah, landing at 1830 local time. While there he calculated that he could still reach San Francisco by dusk. The last leg of the flight over Nevada and the Sierra Nevada Mountains was familiar to him and he landed in San Francisco to be greeted by an estimated 50,000 spectators at 2146 PST, reportedly a minute before dusk. Maughan's total transit time was 20:48 hours, and his actual flight time was 18:20 hours at an average groundspeed of 156 mph. In addition to the public relations value of being the first transcontinental flight within daylight hours, the flight established new records for time, distance, and average speed (128.37 mph). Maughan's record would stand until 20 August 1928, when Hollywood stunt flier Arthur Goebel flew the first non-stop flight across the continent from west to east, flying from Los Angeles to Curtiss Field, New York, in a Lockheed Vega in 18:58 hours averaging 142 mph.

Lt. Russell Maughan in a Curtiss PW-8

1924: FIRST ROUND-THE-WORLD FLIGHT: DOUGLAS WORLD CRUISERS (DWC)

In 1924, four Douglas World Cruisers (DWC) and eight American crewmen set out from Seattle, Washington, to attempt the first around-the-world airplane flight. After 175 days three of the aircraft and crews would become the first to circumnavigate the earth by air.

In the early 1920s, the aviation world was enticed by the completion of the first around-the-world flight. In 1922, the British had made an unsuccessful around-the-world attempt and the following year the French also failed. Soon the British, Italians, and Portuguese announced plans for world-circumnavigating flights. In Spring 1923, the US Army Air Service began planning the mission and sought a suitable aircraft and crews. The Air Service considered the Fokker T-2 transport and the Davis-Douglas Cloudster, and although both aircraft were satisfactory, the USAAS planning group considered a more suitable dedicated design that could be equipped with interchangeable landing gear (wheels or pontoons for water landings). When head of the Davis-Douglas Company Donald Douglas was asked for information on the Davis-Douglas Cloudster, he instead submitted data on a modified DT-2, a torpedo bomber that Douglas had built for the Navy in 1921 and 1922. The DT-2 had demonstrated itself to be a rugged aircraft that could accommodate interchangeable wheeled and pontoon landing gear and had folding wings for easy storage. Since the aircraft was an existing model, Douglas stated that a new aircraft, which he named the Douglas World Cruiser (DWC), could be delivered in forty-five days after a contract was awarded. The Air Service agreed and sent Lt. Erik Nelson (later the pilot of the *New Orleans*)—a member of the planning group—to California to finalize the particulars with Douglas.

Donald Douglas (L) and David Davis

Douglas, assisted by Jack Northrop, began to modify a DT-2 to suit the Army's circumnavigation requirements. The major modification was to increase the fuel capacity, so all internal bomb carrying structures were removed, additional fuel tanks were added, and the wing and fuselage fuel tanks were enlarged, increasing the total fuel capacity from 115 gallons to 644 gallons. Lt. Nelson presented the Douglas DWC proposal to the Washington Air Service brass, where Chief of the Air Service Maj.Gen. Mason Patrick approved it on 1 August 1923, and the War Department let a contract to Douglas for the construction of a single prototype. The completed prototype met all expectations and a contract was awarded for four more production aircraft and spare parts; the last of the five DWCs was delivered on 11 March 1924. The spare parts included fifteen extra Liberty engines, fourteen extra sets of pontoons, and enough replacement airframe parts to complete two aircraft. These parts would be a very important facet of the success of the trip, as they were sent ahead along the route the around-the-world aircraft would follow. With the cooperation of the Royal Air Force and the US Navy, twenty-eight nations supplied thousands of gallons of fuel and oil along the flight path. At prearranged way points the DWCs would have their engines changed five times and new wings fitted twice.

After prototype testing at Langley Field, Virginia, four additional DWCs were accepted for production. Meanwhile, the four pilots trained in meteorology and navigation at Langley, where they also practiced flying the prototype. Once the production aircraft left the factory the crews were sent to Los Angeles to begin flying them. Each of the aircraft was named after a US city representing a compass point: *Seattle*, crewed by Maj. Frederick Martin (pilot and flight commander) and SSgt. Alva Harvey (the only fully qualified mechanic on the flight); *Chicago*, crewed by Lt. Lowell H. Smith (pilot) and 1Lt. Leslie Arnold; *Boston*, with 1Lt. Leigh P. Wade (pilot) and SSgt. Henry H. Ogden aboard; and *New Orleans*, with Lt. Erik Nelson (pilot) and Lt. Jack Harding in the cockpits.

On 4 April 1924, the *Seattle*, *Chicago*, *Boston*, and *New Orleans* left Santa Monica, headed for Sand Point, Washington, near Seattle, which was to be the official start of the voyage. On 6 April 1924, they left for Alaska, but after arriving at Prince Rupert Island lead aircraft *Seattle* needed repairs and remained behind. When it was repaired the crew attempted to catch up, but on 30 April, the *Seattle* crashed in dense fog into a mountainside near Port Moller, Alaska, on the Alaska Peninsula. The crew survived and were rescued on 10 May, but the aircraft was destroyed.

The three remaining aircraft continued, with *Chicago* assuming the lead. Taking off from the Aleutian Islands, the flight traveled across the North Pacific Archipelago, avoiding the Soviet Union, which had not given permission for the expedition to cross into their airspace. The three DWCs crossed Japan, Korea, the coast of China, Hong Kong, French Indochina, Thailand, Burma, and India, and proceeded into the Middle East and then Europe. During the flight *Chicago* was forced to land in a lagoon off the Gulf of Tonkin, in French Indochina (now Vietnam), due to a broken connecting rod. Missionaries supplied the pilots with food and engaged three sampans paddled by local crews to tow *Chicago* for ten hours and twenty-five miles to Hue, where repairs were made.

The flight arrived in Paris on Bastille Day (14 July) and flew to London, then onto the north of England to prepare for the

Atlantic Ocean crossing. On 3 August 1924, while flying across the Atlantic, *Boston* was forced down. *Chicago* was able to contact a Navy destroyer and dropped a note about the troubled *Boston* tied to *Chicago's* only life preserver. While being towed by the Navy light cruiser USS *Richmond* that picked up the crew, *Boston* capsized and sank. Still in the lead, *Chicago* and *New Orleans* continued and crossed the Atlantic via Iceland and Greenland, reaching Canada. The original prototype, now renamed *Boston II*, met the remaining two DWCs in Pictou, Nova Scotia, and the three aircraft flew on to Washington, DC, where they were accorded a hero's welcome. The three Douglas World Cruisers then flew to the West Coast on a multi-city tour, stopping briefly at "home", Clover Field, Santa Monica, on 23 September, and were welcomed by a huge estimated crowd of 200,000. On the twenty-eighth, the three aircraft left for Seattle via San Francisco, completing the epic 28,945 mile journey.

TRIP ITINERARY

Preparation and Testing (17 March to 5 April 1924)
Division 1: Seattle, WA, to Attu, Aleutian Islands
(6 April–14 May 1924)
Division 2: Attu, Aleutian Islands,–Kagoshima, Japan
(15 May–3 June 1924)
Division 3: Kagoshima, Japan,–Calcutta, India
(4-30 June 1924)
Division 4: Calcutta, India,–Constantinople, Turkey
(1-11 July 1924)
Division 5: Constantinople, Turkey,–London, England
(12-16 July 1924)
Division 6: London, England,–Boston, Mass.
(17 July 7–September 1924)
Division 7: Across the United States
(8-28 September 1924)

The trip totalled 175 days covering 27,553 miles, with stops in sixty-one cities for a total flying time of 371:11 hours. Celebrated radio commentator Lowell Thomas eloquently described the DWC flight as a "new voyage of Magellan." Until that time the Douglas Company was a relatively unknown West Coast aircraft company, known to the Navy because of the DT torpedo plane, but not well known to the Air Corps. The DWC flights firmly established Douglas as the leading designer and manufacturer of long-range aircraft. The Douglas Aircraft Company adopted the motto, "First Around-the-world—First the World Around." (Note: The Douglas World Cruiser [DWC] *Chicago* is on display in the *Pioneers of Flight* Gallery at the Smithsonian.)

The prototype Douglas World Cruiser seaplane *Boston II* was substituted for DWC *Boston* late during the round-the-world journey.

The DWC *Chicago* crew in Seattle after completing their around-the-world trip.

1925: CDR. JOHN RODGERS EPIC TRANS-PACIFIC ATTEMPT

After commanding Aircraft Squadrons, Battle Fleet in Langley in 1925, Cdr. John Rodgers was assigned to organize a trans-Pacific flight to Hawaii. Three Naval Aircraft Factory PN-9s were selected for the 2,100 mile journey. The planners calculated that the PN-9's range was barely sufficient to reach Honolulu, but assumed that northeast trade (tail) winds would give a fifteen percent increase in range, providing the necessary safety margin. To reduce the risk, the Navy positioned ten ships at 200-mile intervals (an hour of flying time) along the Great Circle Route between California and Hawaii. The ships were to provide visual navigational aids—black smoke by day and searchlights at night—with the two ships nearest Hawaii capable of refueling the PN-9s if necessary.

During the early afternoon of 31 August, only two PN-9s left San Francisco, as on the day of the flight PB-9 No. 2, which was a new design, was not ready in time. In addition to Rodgers, who served as navigator of PN-9 No. 1, the four other crewmen were Lt. B.J. Connell as senior pilot, two enlisted pilots Kiles Pope and W. H. Bowlin, and Radioman 1st Class Otis Stanz. After about five hours and 300 miles into the flight Lt. Allen Snody's PN-9 had an engine failure and was forced to land in the ocean; he was towed safely back to port. Rodgers' aircraft proceeded with few difficulties for more than the halfway point (over 1,200 miles). Calculations showed higher than expected fuel consumption and lower ground speed due to a weaker than predicted tailwind, requiring Rodgers to land on the ocean and refuel at some time. As they neared the Hawaiian Islands their speed improved and Rodgers bypassed the nearby station ship, deciding to fly nearer to Hawaii. As they flew onward the fuel situation grew more critical and Rodgers headed for a refueling ship, but the navigation technology of the time and then erroneous navigation information provided by the refueling ship caused Rodgers to not find the ship. The PN-9 was forced to land in the ocean intact when it ran out of fuel on 1 September.

Since the PN-9's position was not known while it was in the air and the plane's radio could not transmit when the plane was floating on the water, Rodgers and his crew were not found by an extensive, multi-day search by aircraft and a large number of ships. The plane's radio operator jury-rigged an antenna on the wings and was able to hear messages from the ships, but was unable to transmit. After a few hours it became apparent the ships were indeed searching for them, but it was also clear they were looking in the wrong place, and Hawaii was hundreds of miles to the west. A miscalculation by the search team placed Rodgers' actual position far to the east of the search. After passing a night without rescue, Rodgers and his crew used fabric from a wing to rig a makeshift sail and sailed toward Hawaii. Finally, nine days later, after sailing the plane 450 miles without food and with limited water, they were within fifteen miles of Kauai, where they were found by submarine USS *R-4* on routine patrol. *R-4* towed them near the reef outside the port and the harbor master helped Rodgers and his crew surf over the reef and into the safety of the harbor. The seaworthiness of the PN-9's new all-metal hull and the seamanship and courage of the crew had saved them. After their return Rodgers and his crew were feted as heroes. Despite not reaching Hawaii by air, their flight established a new non-stop air distance record for seaplanes of 1,992 miles and Cmdr. Rodgers also delivered Hawaii Governor Farrington the first letter to arrive in Hawaii by air. After this experience Rodgers served as assistant chief of the Bureau of Aeronautics until the plane he was piloting suddenly and fatally nose-dived into the Delaware River on 27 August 1926.

Although Rodgers' flight did not meet its objective, it pointed out the poor state of naval aviation, and in June 1926, resulted in legislation to increase the Navy's air arm to 1,000 planes over the next five years. Meanwhile, further trials and tribulations over the next decade would result in a flying boat capable of reaching Hawaii from the West Coast and later produce the superlative PBY Catalina that would patrol the Caribbean and Pacific Rim in masses.

Rodgers' Naval Aircraft Factory PN-9 and fuel supply before flight

Cdr. John Rodgers (C) with his crew in Hawaii after their epic flight

1926–1927: PAN AMERICAN GOOD WILL FLIGHT

In late 1926, the Army Air Corps prepared five Loening OA-1A Amphibians—named after American cities—to take part in the Pan American Good Will Flight, whose stated mission was to "take messages of friendship from the United States to the governments and people of Central and South America, promote US commercial aviation, and forge aerial navigation routes through the Americas." For the mission ten volunteers were chosen, with each being an accomplished pilot and a skilled mechanic, because there were very few airfields or repair facilities along the route.

Among the fliers were a few of the future leaders of the AAC:

Crew of *New York*: Maj. Herbert Dargue, Lt. Ennis Whitehead
Crew of *San Francisco*: Capt. Ira Eaker, Lt. Muir Fairchild
Crew of *San Antonio*: Capt. Arthur McDaniel, Lt. Charles Robinson
Crew of *Detroit*: Capt. Clinton Woolsey, Lt. John Benton
Crew of *St. Louis*: Lt. Bernard Thompson, Lt. Leonard Weddington

Pilots of *San Francisco*: Capt. Ira Eaker (L) and Lt. Muir Fairchild stand with the Pan Am Flight insignia.

By combining the fuselage and hull into a single structure, the Loening OA-1A Amphibians could act as a seaplane and land plane. The OA-1A was a large high-performance single-hull amphibian with stabilizing floats underneath each lower wing. The retractable landing gear was operated by a hand crank in the cockpit, and the aircraft was equipped with a tailskid for operations on land. The crew of two was situated in a tandem open cockpit and could fly the aircraft from either cockpit, with a wheel control in the forward cockpit and a removable stick control in the rear. Navigation and engine instruments were in the forward cockpit.

The first Distinguished Flying Cross (DFC) was awarded on 2 May 1927 by President Coolidge to the crews of the Pan Am Flight.

Before the flight, 50,000 gallons of aviation fuel and 5,000 gallons of oil were pre-placed along the route and official good will events were coordinated each country. On 21 December 1926, the five Loenings took off from Kelly Field, San Antonio, Texas, and progressed somewhat slowly, as the flyers paused for a few days in each country. The 22,000 mile flight took 59 flying days, interposed with 74 days for scheduled maintenance and diplomatic meetings and ceremonies in twenty-one Central and South American countries. The flight terminated at Bolling Field, Washington, DC, on 2 May 1927, where the pilots were greeted by President Coolidge, who presented each pilot with the first Distinguished Service Crosses, which had been authorized by Congress only a few months before. Within three weeks their impressive achievement was overshadowed by Lindbergh's solo trans-Atlantic flight. (Note: The *San Francisco* was the only aircraft to complete the journey without interruption from mechanical breakdown and is now on display at the Smithsonian Air and Space Museum.)

2
LINDBERGH AND THE GOLDEN AGE OF LONG-DISTANCE FLIGHTS: 1927–1932

Charles Augustus Lindbergh was born in Detroit on 4 February 1902, to Evangeline and Charles August (C. D.) Lindbergh. The Lindbergh marriage experienced constant disruption and his parents separated in 1909, while his father was a US Congressman (R-MN) 1907–1917 (C. D. was one of the few congressmen to oppose the entry of the US into WWI). During his childhood and teenage years Lindbergh attended more than a dozen schools from Washington, DC, to California (none for more than a year or two), resulting in Lindbergh never forming lasting friendships as a child and becoming quiet and shy as an adult. During WWI, Lindbergh was too young to enlist, and when he turned eighteen the war was already over; he enrolled in the University of Wisconsin-Madison's College of Engineering in late 1920. During March 1922, in the middle of his sophomore year and lacking interest in academics, Lindbergh dropped out to begin flight training at the Nebraska Aircraft Corporation's flying school in Lincoln. At the school Lindbergh, the student pilot, was never allowed to solo because he could not afford to post the bond that the school insisted on to indemnify the neophyte flyer if he were to damage the school's only trainer. Lindbergh left the school in June to gain flight experience and earn money for additional flying instruction. He spent the next months barnstorming as a wing walker and parachutist, and spent winter 1921–23 back in the Minnesota home. He did not fly solo until May 1923, at Souther Field, Americus, Georgia—a former Army flight training field—where he purchased surplus WWI Curtiss JN-4 Jenny biplane for $500. About a week later Lindbergh took off on his first solo cross-country flight from Americus to Montgomery, Alabama, followed by his first night flight. In the course of flying Lindbergh damaged his Jenny several times.

On 19 March 1924, Lindbergh received orders to report to Brooks Field, Texas, to begin a year of military flight training with the US Army Air Service—both there and later at nearby Kelly Field. On 5 March 1925, near the end of his training, Lindbergh suffered his most serious flying accident when he was involved in a midair collision with another Army S.E.5 while practicing aerial combat maneuvers and was forced to bail out. In March 1925, Lindbergh graduated first overall in his class of eighteen of the 104 cadets who began flight training, earning his Army pilot's wings and a second lieutenant commission in the Air Service Reserve Corps. At that time the Army did not need any active duty pilots and immediately after graduation he returned to civilian aviation as a barnstormer and flight instructor. As a reserve officer he continued to fly part time by joining the Missouri National Guard during November 1925, and was soon promoted to first lieutenant.

During October 1925, Lindbergh was hired by the Robertson Aircraft Corporation (RAC) at Lambert-St. Louis Flying Field first to plan routes and logistics, then serve as chief pilot for the newly designated 278-mile Contract Air Mail Route #2 (CAM-2), which was to provide service between St. Louis and Chicago with two intermediate stops in Springfield and Peoria, Illinois. Lindbergh and three other RAC pilots flew mail over CAM-2 in four modified war surplus de Havilland DH-4 biplanes. Lindbergh continued as chief pilot of CAM-2 until mid-February 1927, when he left for San Diego to organize, fund, and oversee the design and construction of an aircraft which was to be the first aircraft to be flown solo non-stop across the Atlantic to win the Orteig Prize.

The Orteig Prize of $25,000 ($351,000 in 2017) was offered on 19 May 1919 by millionaire New York hotelier French-born Raymond Orteig to the first Allied aviator(s) to fly non-stop from New York to Paris, or vice versa. Orteig offered the prize for five years at a time when aviation technology had not advanced to a point that an aircraft could complete a non-stop trans-Atlantic flight. When the five-year stipulation expired in 1924, Orteig extended it for another five years, encouraging technological improvements, and aviators like Lindbergh were determined to claim the prize. The enticement of the Orteig Prize changed the face of aviation from one of daredevils and barnstormers to one of pilots/engineers and innovative aircraft. Some estimates determined that for every dollar Orteig offered $16 of investments in new technologies were expended.

Unlike the other prominent aviators competing for the prize, Lindbergh was an unknown young Contract Air Mail pilot who would find that obtaining financing to acquire and modify an aircraft and cover other expenses would be a major challenge. He ultimately obtained local funding for the purchase of an aircraft through a $15,000 loan from the State National Bank of St. Louis, made on 18 February 1927, to St. Louis businessmen Harry Knight and Harold Bixby, the project's two principal backers and trustees. Another $1,000 was donated by Frank Robertson of RAC, while Lindbergh was able to add

$2,000 from his savings earned flying air mail, giving Lindbergh's group a relatively small sum of $18,000 to work with when compared to his more highly funded competitors.

For the flight Lindbergh reasoned that an advanced and aerodynamically streamlined single-seat monoplane design powered by a reliable engine would provide him with greater range and the best chance of success. The Lindbergh group tried to buy a production line single or multi-engine monoplane from Wright Aeronautical (Wright-Bellanca) of Paterson, New Jersey; then Travel Air of Wichita, Kansas; and finally an aircraft from Charles Levine's and Giuseppi Bellanca's newly formed Columbia Aircraft Corporation of Hempstead, New York. These manufacturers would not agree to a sale unless they were allowed to select the pilot. The group then contacted B. F. Mahoney's much smaller Ryan Aircraft Company in San Diego, which agreed to design and build the requested monoplane, dubbed the *Spirit of St. Louis*, for $10,580, and on 25 February a contract was signed. A fabric-covered, single-seat, single-engine Ryan NYP high-wing monoplane (CAB registration N-X-211) was custom designed by the Ryan Company Chief Engineer Donald Hall under Lindbergh's direction. The *Spirit of St. Louis* was based on a standard Ryan M-2 high-wing, strut-braced monoplane design with the wingspan lengthened by ten feet for greater range and the fuselage slightly enlarged and lengthened by two feet; its structural members and wing cellule were redesigned to accommodate the size and weight of the greater fuel load. The cockpit was moved somewhat aft and the dependable 223 hp air-cooled 9-cylinder Wright J-5C Whirlwind radial Wright engine was moved forward. The engine was equipped with a special apparatus designed to keep it greased during the entire flight. Fuel load and efficiency were the key to the flight's success, and the *Spirit of St. Louis* had a total fuel capacity of 450 gallons (2,710 lbs.), which was the calculated load to have the necessary range to complete the anticipated trans-Atlantic non-stop flight. The fuel was stored in five fuel tanks: a forward tank (eighty-eight gallons), the main (209 gallons), and three wing tanks for a total of 153 gallons, making the *Spirit* the epitome of a flying fuel tank. Lindbergh requested the large main and forward fuel tanks be placed in the forward section of the fuselage, in front of the pilot, with the oil tank acting as a firewall. This scheme not only improved the center of gravity, but gave the pilot some protection from being crushed by the engine in case of a crash. This arrangement necessitated that there was no front windshield installed and that forward visibility would be limited through the side window. As a former airmail pilot Lindbergh was accustomed to flying in the rear cockpit of mail planes with mail bags stored in the front compartment; to look forward he would slightly yaw the aircraft and look out the side window. Upon its completion on 28 April 1927, the *Spirit of St. Louis*, painted in its famous silver motif, was 9.67 ft. high, 27.67 ft. long, had a 46 ft. wingspan, and weighed 2,150 lbs. empty.

On 28 April 1927, just two months after the start of construction, the *Spirit* flew for the first time. After completing a series of test flights, on 10 May, Lindbergh flew the aircraft from San Diego to Roosevelt Field, on Long Island , New York, stopping in St. Louis and landing after 21:40 hours to set a new transcontinental record. On 20 May 1927, after a night of heavy rain the weather cleared and Lindbergh took off from Long Island at 0752, while a crowd of 500 spectators cheered him on. During the well-documented 3,610 miles and 33:30 hours of the epic flight, Lindbergh flew through several storms in the North Atlantic; when darkness fell and initial fatigue set in he climbed above the clouds so he could see the stars to keep himself oriented, and as exhaustion was about to overcome him he stamped his feet, sang aloud, and even slapped his own face. After flying through the night and the following day, Lindbergh finally spotted fishing boats off the rugged Irish coastline. In exhausted elation he headed south, and at 2224 on 21 May 1927, landed safely at Le Bourget Field, near Paris, where he was greeted by a frenzied crowd of 150,000. Lindbergh climbed out of the plane and was immediately swept up by the crowd and carried away. He was soon rescued and his plane was secured, but only after spectators had torn pieces from the fuselage for souvenirs. The records set by Lindbergh's flight were officially certified by Secretary of the National Aeronautic Association Carl Schory based on the readings from a sealed barograph Schory had placed in Lindbergh's aircraft, and were subsequently verified by the FAI. On 31 August 1927, the flight was certified as the Class-C World Record for non-stop flight for the distance of 5,809 km (3,610 miles).

Lindbergh was celebrated and honored throughout Europe during a series of briefs to Belgium and Great Britain. He sailed home aboard the United States Navy cruiser USS *Memphis* in June, arriving in Washington, DC, on 11 June, and was then escorted up the Potomac River by a fleet of warships and multiple flights of pursuit, bombers, and the rigid airship USS *Los Angeles*. Lindbergh was honored with a parade and awarded the Distinguished Flying Cross by President Coolidge. He was also promoted to colonel in the Officer's Reserve Corps.

Lindbergh then flew from Washington to New York City on 13 June, arriving at the Battery, in lower Manhattan, to then travel up the Canyon of Heroes to City Hall, where he was received at a ceremony hosted by Mayor Jimmy Walker. A massive ticker-tape parade followed, ending at Central Park Mall, where he was honored at another ceremony hosted by New York Governor Al Smith that was attended by a crowd of 200,000 (it was estimated that upwards of four million saw Lindbergh that day). The next day Lindbergh met Raymond Ortieg and was presented with his $25,000 check. The media then followed Lindbergh everywhere; uncomfortable in the limelight, Lindbergh retreated to the only place he could be alone and toured the US in the solitude of the *Spirit of St. Louis'* cockpit. At the request of the Guggenheim Fund for the Promotion of Aeronautics Lindbergh toured the United States in the *Spirit of St. Louis* during Summer and Fall 1927. Traveling a total of 22,350 miles, he visited seventy-five cities, landing in each of the forty-eight continental states, and dropped messages on towns where he could not stop .On his stop in Madison, Wisconsin, Senator Robert M. La Follette stated: "This tour which Colonel Lindbergh is making of all the states in the Union will go far to transform and direct the awakened energy of a hundred and fifteen million people into coordinated activity that will build airports and bring to our doors the practical advantages of aviation within the next decade." Within a year of his flight, a quarter of Americans (an estimated 30 million) personally saw Lindbergh and the *Spirit of St. Louis*. On 14 December 1927, a special act of Congress awarded Lindbergh the Medal of Honor—almost always awarded for heroism in combat—which was presented to Lindbergh by President Coolidge at the White House on 21 March 1928. (Other non-combat awards of the Medal of Honor made to aviators went to Richard Byrd and Floyd Bennett for their 1926 North Pole flight, as well as arctic explorer Adolphus Greely in 1935—the year of his death at ninety-one—for lifetime achievement.) Lindbergh's influence on American and world aviation was profound. Over the remainder of 1927, applications for pilot's licenses in the US tripled, the number of licensed aircraft quadrupled, and the number of US airline passengers grew 1926–1929 from 5,782 to 173,405. Charles Lindbergh joined or perhaps surpassed movie star Mary Pickford or Babe Ruth—who hit sixty home runs that same year—as America's most illustrious celebrity.

Lindbergh then extended his air tour into Latin America, where he met American Ambassador Dwight Morrow in Mexico City. He spent Christmas 1927 with Morrow's family, becoming acquainted with twenty-one-year-old daughter, Anne. The two became close, spending time together over the next year as Lindbergh taught Anne how to fly. After they married on 27 May 1929, the Lindberghs, with Anne as co-pilot, navigator, and radio operator, made several important flights, collecting important information that would help plot international flight routes. In 1931, the Lindberghs charted international air routes for new commercial airlines flying across Canada to Asia. Two years later they flew 30,000 miles, mapping out commercial routes across the Atlantic. They set a record for flying across the US in just over fourteen hours and were the first aviators to fly from America to China. The Lindberghs became parents on 22 June 1930, with the birth of Charles Jr. During the evening of 28 February 1932, twenty-month-old Charles was kidnapped from his crib at the Lindbergh's secluded Hopewell, New Jersey, home. Police found a ladder outside the nursery window and a $50,000 ransom note in the child's room. The ransom was paid, but the Lindbergh child was not returned to his parents. In May 1932, Charles Jr's body was found a few miles from the family home and investigators concluded the kidnapper had dropped the baby while descending the ladder the night of the abduction, killing him. After more than two years of investigation German immigrant Bruno Richard Hauptmann was arrested, tried, convicted, and executed in April 1936 for what was called "the crime of the century." The Lindbergh's second son, Jon, was born in August 1932. (The Lindbergh family later grew to include two daughters and two more sons.) Lindbergh became exasperated with the unremitting attention the press and public placed on them after the kidnapping and sensational Hauptmann trial. Concerned for the physical safety of their then three-year-old Jon, the Lindberghs secretly moved to England in 1935, where they secluded themselves. They continued to live and travel extensively in Europe for more than three years, including notable visits to Nazi Germany.

In 1936, Lindbergh was invited by Hermann Goering to inspect the emerging German aviation industry and its aircraft. Lindbergh was the first American permitted to examine the Luftwaffe's newest bomber, the Junkers Ju 88, and to fly Germany's front line Messerschmitt Bf 109 fighter. Goering convinced Lindbergh that the Luftwaffe was far more powerful than it actually was. Impressed by what he saw, Lindbergh reported that Germany's air power was far superior to that of other European nations, and that Germany was leading in "metal construction, low-wing designs, dirigibles, and diesel engines." On a return visit to Germany in 1938, Lindbergh received the German Service Cross from Goering and was photographed wearing it with resulting public outrage. At the urging of US Ambassador to England Joseph Kennedy, Lindbergh wrote a secret memo to the British, warning that if Britain and France responded militarily to German dictator Adolf Hitler's violation of the Munich Agreement in 1938 it would be suicide for them. Lindbergh stated that France's military strength was inadequate, and that Britain had an outdated military overly reliant on naval power. He recommended the two nations immediately strengthen their air arsenal to force Hitler to turn his ambitions eastward to a war against "Asiatic Communism" (i.e., the Soviets). During this time Anne wrote several well-received and awarded books; her first book, *North to the Orient* (1935), won one of the inaugural National Book Awards (Most Distinguished General Nonfiction of 1935), while her second book, *Listen! The Wind* (1938), won the same award.

In April 1939, the Lindberghs finally decided to return and reside in America. The reason for their return was mainly the

Charles Lindbergh and his Ryan *Spirit of St. Louis*

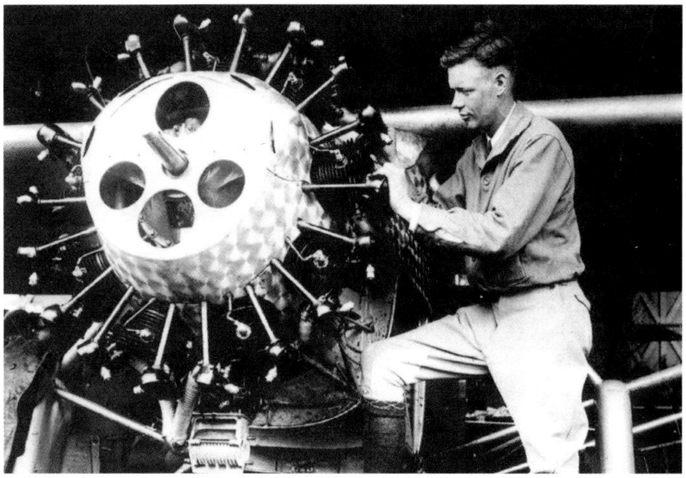

Lindbergh moved the Wright J-5C Whirlwind engine forward to accommodate a fuel tank forward of the pilot's compartment and had to look out the side window during the flight.

Lindbergh's *Spirit of St. Louis* in Paris Le Bourget

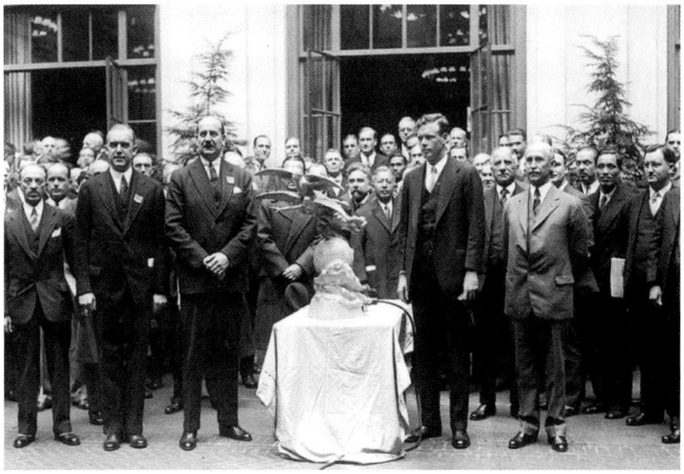

Charles Lindbergh (2R) accepts the second Harmon Trophy with Raymond Ortieg (R), Wilbur Wright (2L), and President Calvin Coolidge (L) looking on.

Millionaire New York hotelier Raymond Ortieg presents Charles Lindbergh with the $25,000 check for being the first Allied aviator to fly non-stop from New York to Paris.

Charles and Anne Morrow Lindbergh

result of a personal appeal by then-AAC Chief Gen. Hap Arnold, in which Lindbergh was a colonel in the Reserves. Arnold requested that Lindbergh accept a temporary call up to active duty to help evaluate the AAC's readiness for a potential war by evaluating new aircraft types in development, recruitment procedures, and finding a site for a new air force research institute and other potential air bases. Flying a Curtiss P-36 fighter, Lindbergh toured various facilities for four months and made his report. Back home Lindbergh continued his provocative views in a controversial 1939 *Reader's Digest* article, in which Lindbergh stated, "Our civilization depends on peace among Western nations" and deplored the rivalry between Germany and Britain, but favored a war between Germany and Russia. The article was shaded by anti-Semitism and his views on white supremacy. Lindbergh's speeches and writings continued to reflect his adoption of Nazi views on race and religion. He wrote in his memoirs that all of the Germans he met thought their country would be better off without its Jews. In late 1940, he became spokesman of the anti-war America First Committee and soon became its most prominent public spokesman, speaking to overflowing crowds in Madison Square Garden in New York City and Soldier Field in Chicago. In speeches heard by millions, Lindbergh argued that America "did not have any business attacking Germany" and believed in upholding the Monroe Doctrine, which his interventionist rivals felt was outdated. His speeches were widely criticized as anti-Semitic and racist, and Lindbergh's popularity was in steep decline.

When the Japanese bombed Pearl Harbor Lindbergh was forced to concede that America had no choice but to enter the war. Perhaps guilt-ridden, Col. Lindbergh requested to be recommissioned in the USAAF, but Secretary of War Henry L. Stimson declined the request on instruction from President Roosevelt. Denied an active military role, Lindbergh approached several US aviation companies to serve as a consultant. As a technical adviser with Ford in 1942, he became very involved in troubleshooting early problems on their giant Willow Run Consolidated B-24 Liberator bomber production line. Afterward, he joined United Aircraft in 1943, as an engineering consultant to its Chance-Vought division. During 1944, UA designated him a technical representative in the Pacific to study aircraft performance under combat conditions for their F4U fighter, including decreasing fuel consumption and to show Marine pilots how to take off safely with a bomb load double the Corsair fighter-bomber's rated capacity. While in the Pacific Lindbergh introduced engine leaning techniques to P-38 pilots, greatly improving fuel consumption at cruise speeds and enabling the long-range fighter to fly longer range missions.

After the war Lindbergh went into virtual seclusion, working variously as a consultant, but it was his wife Anne's books that helped to rebuild the reputation the Lindberghs had gained and lost before WWII. The publication of Anne's *Gift from the Sea* in 1955 earned her a place as one of the leading advocates of the emerging environmental movement and became a national bestseller. Lindbergh's reputation was slowly reestablished after the war and was greatly enhanced in 1954, when President Dwight Eisenhower honored the former hero by appointing him as a Reserve brigadier general. That same year he won the Pulitzer Prize for his memoir *The Spirit of St. Louis*. In 1957, actor James Stewart portrayed Lindbergh in the movie *The Spirit of St. Louis*, but the movie was a commercial failure. Following wife Anne's lead Lindbergh spent the final decade of his life involved in environmental causes and became the spokesman for the World Wildlife Fund and the Nature Conservancy. After being diagnosed with lymphatic cancer in 1972, Lindbergh spent his remaining days at his Maui home. He died on 26 August 1974, and was buried in Hawaii during a simple ceremony. (Wife Anne died in 2001 at age ninety-four.)

1927: LTS. ALBERT HEGENBERGER AND LESTER MAITLAND: FIRST TRANS-PACIFIC FLIGHT

For the California to Hawaii route the AAC carefully selected pilot Lester Maitland, who had piloted one of the Billy Mitchell MB-1 bombers that bombed captured German battleships in 1921 and became the first man to fly faster than 200 mph, setting a world speed record at 236 mph four years earlier. His navigator, Albert Hegenberger, was a graduate of MIT, former chief of the Instrument Branch at McCook Field, and helped develop navigational instruments used by pilots of that era. During 1926, Maitland and Hegenberger lobbied Chief of the Air Service Gen. Mason Patrick to organize a flight from California to Hawaii. The easier route from Hawaii to California could have been selected, but this flight was to be about navigation—reaching a small island in the vast ocean—rather than about speed. On 15 June 1927, Lts. Maitland and Hegenberger flew an Atlantic-Fokker C-2 Tri-motor monoplane transport *Bird of Paradise* and a team of aeronautical engineers on a cross-country check flight to assess fuel consumption and the reliability of the aircraft and its navigational instruments. On 24 June, Secretary of War Dwight Davis approved the flight to Hawaii.

The *Bird of Paradise* was one of three Atlantic-Fokker C-2 tri-motor transports developed for the Air Corps from the civilian Fokker F.VIIa/3m airliner. With its 4,000 lb. load capacity it was able to carry sufficient fuel for the 2,500 mile flight and its three 220 hp air-cooled Wright J-5 engines provided a safety factor; in the event one engine failed an additional seventy gallon fuel tank was installed before the flight. The *Bird of Paradise* carried 1,134 gallons of fuel and forty gallons of oil, and was equipped with an inflatable rubber raft, rations, and five gallons of water stowed on board for survival in case of the not-unlikely event they were forced down at sea (no parachutes were provided).

Lindbergh's recent flight and the $25,000 prize offered by James Dole to the first aviator(s) to make a similar trans-Pacific flight between California and Hawaii motivated great interest in San Francisco. Civilians Ernest Smith and Charles Carter, across the Bay in Oakland, were nearly ready for a flight to Hawaii, and Hollywood stunt flyer Richard Grace was in Hawaii preparing a solo flight to the West Coast. Enthusiasm became so great that War Department Secretary Davis and the two pilots avowed no interest in a "race," maintaining that the scheduling of the flight was a "coincidence" and that the purpose of its flight was testing the radio beacon navigational aids at Crissy Field, San Francisco, and Paia, Maui, Hawaii. The Air Service declared airmen Hegenberger and Maitland were ineligible for the Dole Prize and they also had to decline $10,000 for the publication of their story.

The newly opened Oakland Municipal Airport's 7,000 ft. runway was used to accommodate the long take off-roll with a full fuel load. Five weeks after Charles Lindbergh flew non-stop from New York to Paris, Maitland and Hegenberger took off at 0709 on 28 June to the cheers of thousands. Unable to climb due to their heavy fuel load, Maitland and Hegenberger flew at 300 ft. during the first hours of the flight. The C-2's earth inductor compass failed just after take-off. The directional radio receiver that was to use the Signal Corps beacon on Maui operated only intermittently before failing. Despite increasing clouds, Hegenberger navigated most of the charted Great Circle Route by dead reckoning, using a magnetic compass and driftmeter supplemented by celestial navigation observations. That evening they climbed to 10,200 ft. to get above the clouds for celestial navigation, but had to descend to 7,000 ft. when the Fokker's carburetor iced up. Several ships at sea were contacted to verify their position and adjust the original flight plan. At about the halfway point the crew began searching for food that was supposed to have been stowed aboard, but none could be found by either flyer. During the night Hegenberger used a pocket flashlight to read instruments and charts to compute the route.

At 0320 on June 2, due to Hegenberger's brilliant navigation, Kauai's lighthouse beacon was spotted, but they decided to circle the ocean until daybreak in rain and complete darkness one hundred miles from Wheeler Field so Maitland could visually fly over Oahu's mountainous terrain in daylight. As Maitland approached Wheeler he observed thousands of spectators and flew a low pass over the field to acknowledge the crowd before landing at 0629 on 29 June, ending the flight in 25:49 hours after covering 2,425 miles over water.

Although the recognition bestowed on Maitland and Hegenberger was far less than the idolization given to Lindbergh, their feat was arguably more significant from a navigational perspective, as if Hegenberger was even three to four degrees off course they would have passed Kauai and vanished, while Lindbergh had the large British Isles and then the whole European continent to make landfall. The two were awarded Distinguished Flying Crosses (the third award) and were awarded the Mackay Trophy. In 1928, Maitland and Charles Lindbergh were invited to the White House to meet President Calvin Coolidge.

During WWII, Lt.Col. Maitland was the 28th Bomb Squadron Commanding Officer at Clark Field, in the Philippines, when it fell to the Japanese in 1942. He flew forty-four medium bomber combat missions over Europe. He rose to the rank of brigadier general and retired from the Army in 1943. He became an Episcopal priest in 1955, and remained active until 1985. He passed in 1990 at age ninety-one. Albert Hegenberger flew the first solo "instruments only" flight at Wright Field in 1932, and played a prominent role in developing blind flying instruments and techniques. Maj.Gen. Hegenberger passed in 1983 at age eighty-eight. The *Bird of Paradise* flew as an inter-island transport until the late '30s, when it was dismantled and shipped to Dayton, Ohio, to be included in the Air Corps Museum, but was scrapped in 1944 because of a "lack of space."

Hegenberger-Maitland Fokker C-2 Tri-motor Monoplane fuel tank is ready to be installed.

Lts. Lester Maitland (R) and Albert Hegenberger

1927: ERNIE SMITH AND C.H. CARTER: SECOND TRANS-PACIFIC FLIGHT

Ernie Smith and Capt. C. H. Carter had arrived in Oakland earlier for the Dole Prize attempt, but due to mechanical difficulties their small Travel Air 5000 civilian monoplane took off two hours after Maitland and Hegenberger, and then had to return with a broken windshield and with no hope of catching the Army lieutenants. Carter quit after the record was lost; Smith hired Emory Bronte as his navigator and the *City of Oakland* was ready to take off again on July 14. Maitland and Hegenberger, who had just returned from Hawaii by ship, came to the airport to wish the two flyers luck and to give advice. Smith attempted to taxi for take-off but found the overloaded Travel Air would not move, so some of the 10,000 spectators were enlisted to push it along. The *City of Oakland* began to slowly move down the dirt runway until it ran into a hole and ground-looped. No damage was done and the Travel Air lifted off toward Hawaii and flew flawlessly until they were about five hours from Oahu, when Bronte calculated they only had an hour's fuel remaining. Bronte sent out SOS signals, but recalculations determined that with prudent fuel management they could possibly reach the more eastern island of Molokai. Upon reaching the rugged Molokai coast and nearly out of fuel, at 0847 on 15 July, Smith expertly set the plane down into a large clump of trees after 26:36 hours in the air with only scratches from the Molokai—not Honolulu—thorn trees and thus received no prize money.

Ernie Smith and Capt. C. H. Carter inspect their crashed Travel Air 5000.

1927: DOLE TRANS-PACIFIC RACE

On 25 May 1927, shortly after Lindbergh's successful trans-Atlantic flight, Hawaii pineapple magnate James Dole offered a $25,000 prize for the first fixed-wing aircraft to fly the 2,400 miles from Oakland, California, to Honolulu, Hawaii, and $10,000 for second place. Before the Dole Race the Pacific had been crossed twice (on 28 June, by AAC Lts. Maitland and Hegenberger, and next by Smith and Carter), but Dole disqualified both because they did not land on Honolulu. Soon Dole changed the rules, declaring the prize money would be awarded in a race and set a starting date.

On the 8 August entry deadline fifteen aircraft had signed on and the official drawing for starting positions followed. Soon the race seemed to be dogged by portents of disaster. Two days after drawing unlucky #13, USN Lts. George Covell and R. S. Waggener were killed after taking off from San Diego for Oakland in their Tremaine Humming Bird, flying into a fog-shrouded cliff. On 11 August, as J. L. Giffin and Theodore Lundgren, sponsored by cowboy movie star Hoot Gibson, approached Oakland airfield, their International CF-10 Triplane *Pride of Los Angeles* ditched into San Francisco Bay instead; the two men were unhurt, but the *Pride* was out of the race. On the thirteenth, Lafayette Escadrille veteran Arthur Rogers took off on a test flight in the twin-engine *Angel of Los Angeles*, and when circling to land the plane suddenly plunged into the ground with Rogers leaping free, but his parachute failed to open. Meanwhile, *Miss Doran*, the Buhl Air Sedan aircraft of Mildred Doran, pilot Augy Pedlar, and navigator Manley Lawling, experienced spark plug problems while flying into Oakland, but landed successfully in San Joaquin Valley and was repaired. The day before the race six aircraft and crews were disqualified in the interest of safety. To give disqualified contestants an opportunity to remedy their safety issues and get back into competition the race was postponed until 16 August.

The race began on 16 August, and was attended by a crowd estimated at 75,000–100,000, but there were only eight aircraft on the starting line:

Oklahoma, a Travel Air 5000 sister ship of *Woolaroc* piloted by Bennett Griffin and navigated by Al Henley.

El Encanto, a Goddard Special metal monoplane and heavy favorite flown by Norman Goddard and Kenneth Hawkins.

Pabco Flyer, a Breese-Wilde Monoplane flown alone by Livingston Gilson Irving, with no navigator.

Golden Eagle, the prototype Lockheed Vega 1 monoplane flown by Jack Frost, navigated by Gordon Scott, and sponsored by George Hearst, publisher of the *San Francisco Examiner*.

Miss Doran, a Buhl CA-5 Air Sedan flown by Auggy Pedlar, navigated by Vilas R. Knope, and carrying passenger Mildred Doran.

Aloha, a Breese-Wilde 5 Monoplane flown by Martin Jensen and navigated by Paul Schluter.

Dallas Spirit, a Swallow Monoplane flown by nine-victory WWI ace William Erwin and navigated by Alvin Eichwaldt.

Woolaroc, one of two modified Travel Air 5000 aircraft, flown by Arthur Goebel and navigated by Navy Lt. William Davis, who was an active duty Navy pilot on thirty days leave from his North Island, San Diego, station. Phillips Petroleum loaned Goebel $4,500 he needed to take delivery of the Travel Air and in return Goebel promised to use a new aviation fuel developed by Phillips during the cross Pacific flight. Goebel named the Travel Air *Woolaroc*, which was the name of Frank Phillips' Oklahoma ranch (after the woods, lakes, and rocks of the scenic Osage Hills near the ranch).

The Race was plagued from its start, as at 12:01 the *Oklahoma* was the first aircraft airborne, but as it passed the Golden Gate it returned with mechanical difficulties. The second starter, *El Encanto*, was thrown off course by a side wind; the pilot managed to get about four feet into the air but then crashed to the ground, completely demolishing the left wing and was out of competition.

The third aircraft off was *Pabco Flyer*, which after reaching ten feet into the air suddenly fell back into a soft watery marsh, badly damaging its tail wheel. Irving pulled off for repairs and another start at the end of the line, intent not to let down fellow employees of the San Francisco firm who were his backers.

The *Golden Eagle* was the first aircraft to successfully take off and fly on. *Miss Doran* took off, but circled back with a malfunctioning engine and landed less than ten minutes later. The *Aloha* and *Woolaroc* then took off uneventfully. Then *Dallas Spirit* returned to Oakland with fabric ripping off the fuselage. On its second attempt, *Miss Doran* succeeded to get airborne. *Pabco Flyer* had its damaged tail wheel repaired and attempted another take off, but the overloaded aircraft crashed, smashing one wing; its pilot and navigator were unhurt. Only four competitors were left in the race: *Golden Eagle*, *Aloha*, *Woolaroc*, and *Miss Doran*.

Goebel and Davis (*Woolaroc*) made good headway, reporting their position to ships along the route for marking and emergency purposes. Davis had four compasses and a bubble sextant for sun and star observations, and laid out the Great Circle Route from San Francisco to Maui as flown weeks before by Smith and Bronte and Maitland and Hegenberger. Davis had been briefed by B. J. Connell from the 1925 John Rodgers almost-to-Hawaii crew about his experience over the route. The radio worked well, with the radio beam an invaluable aid to navigation, but Davis did most of his very accurate navigation using the radio only as a check. Davis sent out a radio message 200 miles from Wheeler Field, Honolulu, and thousands of sightseers and officials converged there. The Travel Air's radio transmitter suddenly went dead, but the competent Davis repaired it and sent out a position report. Soon Davis sighted Maui's faint outline, confirming he had been right on course, and then headed toward Oahu. As the *Woolaroc* passed Diamond Head toward Honolulu, Davis shot off flares from the Very pistol and dropped smoke bombs. At a point the engine sputtered as if low on fuel, but continued to turn smoothly. Soon swarms of Army and Navy aircraft joined them and Goebel circled Wheeler once before landing. Landing to a cheering crowd of 25,000–30,000 after a flight of 26:17:33 hours, Goebel and Davis were surrounded by officials and spectators and were presented the $25,000 prize. The *Aloha* arrived in 28:16 hours, earning Jensen and Schluter the $10,000 second prize. The finish was a personal triumph, as Jensen and navigator Schulter did not have an airplane to fly until five days before race start since he could not find financial backers. The *Aloha* originally had only a 130 gallon fuel capacity, which was insufficient for the flight, so for additional fuel Jensen intended to store forty-nine five gallon gasoline containers in the airplane. Their in-flight plan was for Schulter to pour gasoline into a central tank, and using a hand pump transfer it to the fifty gallon tank in use when the supply got low. Messages were to be transferred between the men by means of a pulley and line system. This makeshift fuel arrangement was sufficient to have the judges not disqualify the *Aloha*.

When it became obvious the *Golden Eagle* and *Miss Doran* were lost, Dole put up a $10,000 reward for anyone finding the missing planes, while sponsors of the two missing aircraft also put up an equal amount for their planes. A huge search party was formed of forty-two ships and aircraft. Amazingly, Jensen took off in the *Aloha* for a five-hour search over Oahu, Molokai, and Maui. The search would also turn tragic. After Erwin and Eichwaldt repaired *Dallas Spirit's* tail, they took off three days after the race's start to help search for the two lost aircraft, but they also vanished. One of the Army's search planes crashed into the sea, killing its two occupants. The search was to no avail. The *Woolaroc* survived and is on display at the Frank Phillips' Woolaroc Ranch Museum in Oklahoma.

Pilot Arthur Goebel (L) and navigator William Davis

1927: EDWARD SCHLEE AND BILLY BROCK CROSS THE ATLANTIC ON AN AROUND-THE-WORLD ATTEMPT

On 23 August 1927, Edward Schlee and William (Billy) Brock took off from Detroit to begin their attempt to fly around the world. Schlee, a Detroit gasoline station millionaire and flying enthusiast, had purchased a Stinson Detroiter monoplane that he had sponsored in the Ford Air Reliability Tour and named it *Pride of Detroit*. Schlee contacted airmail and barnstorming pilot Billy Brock to be his co-pilot to cross the Atlantic, hoping to circle the globe in fifteen days to become the first non-military aviators to do so.

Schlee and Brock arrived in Harbour Grace, Newfoundland, which would play an important role in future trans-Atlantic and circumnavigation attempts. Fred Koehler of Stinson Aircraft Corporation had recognized Harbour Grace as a potential refueling point and the community and Newfoundland government built an airport. The *Pride of Detroit* left Newfoundland on 27 August 1927, and landed at London's Croydon Airport without any problems. The Stinson then made fourteen stops across Europe and Asia: the first was Munich, then Belgrade, Yugoslavia, and on to Constantinople (Istanbul), Turkey, where they were held up for two days by bad weather and red tape. Baghdad was their next stop, then Bender Abbas, Persia (Iran); Karachi, India; and Rangoon, Burma, on 7 September, where a revolt was threatening. Over the past days of flying and delays they had fallen behind schedule and wished to make up lost time flying from Hanoi to Hong Kong to Shanghai, but encountered head winds. On their way to Japan a thunderstorm forced them down on Kyushu Island, still 600 miles from Tokyo, and then a typhoon and tidal wave struck Kyushu, killing hundreds of people and grounding the *Pride of Detroit* until 14 September. When Schlee and Brock finally arrived in Tokyo they were hopelessly behind schedule. They had flown 12,275 miles in nineteen days, averaging 646 miles a day, and needed to nearly double that pace over the next nine days if they were to break the record, which was not possible. Then Tokyo became the target of a typhoon and their families sent telegrams, imploring them to give up, as they had just heard about the Dole Derby race from California to Hawaii in August 1927, during which ten lives were lost, six aircraft were total losses, and only two of the eight planes successfully landed in Hawaii. Schlee and Brock then decided to return home by ship. When they arrived back in Detroit they were accorded a heroes' welcome. It would not be until October 1931 before Clyde Pangborn completed a trans-Pacific flight from Japan.

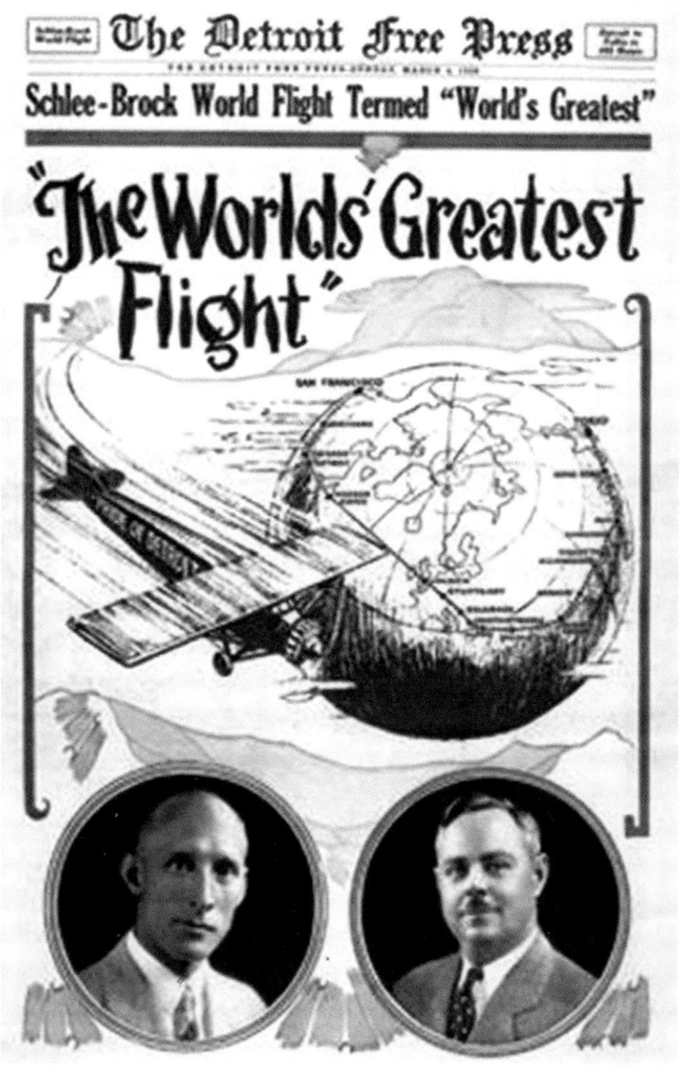

Headlines proclaim Schlee (L) and Brock's "World's Greatest Flight."

1927: RUTH ELDER AND GEORGE HALDEMAN TRANS-ATLANTIC FLIGHT ATTEMPT

"Flamboyant beauty" and aspiring silent film actress Ruth Elder and her instructor/co-pilot, George Haldeman, took off on 11 October 1927 from Roosevelt Field in her attempt to become the first woman to duplicate Lindbergh's trans-Atlantic crossing to Paris. During the flight their Stinson Detroiter *American Girl* first encountered a storm and then oil line problems, and was forced to ditch on the ocean

Ruth Elder and her "instructor/co-pilot," George Haldeman

after a flight of 2,623 miles. Fortunately, they were rescued by a Dutch oil tanker which they flew over as Haldeman ditched the aircraft. As their Stinson was being hoisted on deck it caught fire and was totally destroyed. News of their air adventure and rescue spread rapidly over the globe and their return was closely followed, from their debarkation in Portugal to their glorious reception in Paris and their return to the US and ticker tape parade in New York City; they also had a luncheon at the White House. The flight crowned her as the "Miss America of Aviation," and she starred in a number of silent movies afterward. Soon the even more self-serving Amelia Earhart would replace her as America's favorite aviatrix.

1928: CHARLES COLLYER AND JOHN MEARS (ALMOST) CIRCLE THE GLOBE

From 28 June–22 July 1928, John Mears, Charles Collyer, and their white terrier mascot aptly named Tail Wind flew in their Fairchild C-2 *The City of New York* for the second around-the-world trip from New York and back in 23 days, 15:21 hours to establish an FAI record. The first around-the-world flight was the 1924 Douglas World Cruiser adventure that took 175 days, covering more than 27,553 miles. Although Collyer and Mears did not fly all the way around the world (they crossed the Atlantic and Pacific by ship), their circumnavigation was completed faster than a lunar cycle (27 days, 7 hours), which the newspapers touted as their "race with the moon." They departed New York on 28 June 1928, in a seaplane piloted by Capt. Harry Rogers and intercepted the steamer *Olympic*, with their plane carried on deck to cross the Atlantic. The *Olympic* unloaded their aircraft at the port of Cherbourg, France, and

John Mears (L), Charles Collyer, their white terrier mascot *Tail Wind*, and their Fairchild C-2

they then proceeded by plane to Paris; Cologne and Berlin, Germany; Koenigsburg, East Prussia; and then over Russia: Smolensk, Moscow, Kagan, Kourgan Siberia, Novosibirsk, Krasnoyarsk, and Chita; Mukden, China; Pyongyang, North Korea; and Osaka and Tokyo, Japan. They crossed the Pacific via the steamer *Empress of Russia* with the plane carried on deck. Disembarking at Victoria (British Columbia), Canada, they flew across the US via Spokane, Washington; Minneapolis, Minnesota; Chicago, Illinois; Cleveland, Ohio; Middletown, Pennsylvania; and Staten Island, New York.

Finally, on 22 July 1928, they arrived in Manhattan by the Staten Island Ferry almost four days ahead of the moon.

1928: ARTHUR GOEBEL: FIRST NON-STOP WEST-TO-EAST TRANSCONTINENTAL FLIGHT

After winning the tragic Dole Race the previous year, in March 1928, Goebel and Ernest Robertson of the Fairchild Aviation Company flew a well-publicized goodwill tour of Japan in a Fairchild monoplane. They began from Curtis Field, Long Island, stopping along the way in Los Angeles to demonstrate the Fairchild, sailed to Tokyo, and barnstormed around Japan, giving rides, performing stunts, and generally selling aviation to the Japanese.

After returning from Japan Goebel decided his next challenge would be to fly across America from West to East non-stop to break Russell Maughan's 1924 record. Harry Tucker's Lockheed Vega *Yankee Doodle* was to be the aircraft, but only if Tucker was a passenger. The Vega's 450 gallon fuel capacity was insufficient to complete the cross-country flight and there was not enough time to modify the Vega as the *Woolaroc* had been. Collyer solved the fuel problem by storing seventy-five 5-gallon cans of gasoline and a hand pump inside the aircraft, and Tucker would pump the gasoline into the wing tanks in flight, then open the passenger door to chuck the empty cans, being careful not to be sucked out of the plane or losing the door in the slipstream.

After an unsuccessful first attempt Goebel and Tucker took off from Mines Field, Los Angeles, on 19 August, flying east over the Rockies in the afternoon, the plains at night, and landing on the East Coast (Curtis Field, Garden City, New York) in the early morning 18:58 hours later. Goebel became the national figure he had expected to become after the Dole Race in 1927. He was the first pilot to fly non-stop across America from west to east, the first flier to cross the continent in less than twenty-four hours non-stop, and the record holder for least elapsed non-stop time crossing North America.

1928: GOEBEL FLIES EAST-TO-WEST TRANSCONTINENTAL

The National Air Races, which began in 1924, were next on Harry Tucker's flying agenda, intending to fly America east-to-west non-stop. On 13 September 1928, the nine planes that entered the race were assembled at Roosevelt Field on Long Island. There was no starting order; when planes and crews were ready they could take off, but they only had a twenty-four hour window for starting, with the pilot who landed in Los Angeles in the least elapsed time without stopping winning. At dusk, Goebel and passenger Tucker were the eighth to take off. Climbing in the fully loaded *Yankee Doodle* over the Allegheny Mountains was much easier than climbing over the Rocky Mountains had been flying in the opposite direction the month before. Flying in daylight cross-country, Tucker left a trail of empty gasoline cans across the plains while Goebel struggled to maintain 140 mph headway into strong head winds. But as they approached the Rockies the remaining racers encountered a solid storm front. Over Arizona, the *Yankee Doodle's* carburetor began icing and oil pressure was falling quickly, so Goebel was forced to land at Prescott. After adding oil and topping off the gas tanks the storm began to break and Goebel and Tucker headed toward Los Angeles. After 23:20 hours after leaving New York, Goebel and Tucker landed at Mines Field. Goebel has to confess that they had landed at Prescott and were ineligible for the non-stop prize. No other contestants finished the race, but Richfield Oil Company awarded Goebel and Tucker $10,000 in recognition of their having finished the race, even though they made a stop.

Arthur Goebel (L) and Roscoe Turner

After the race Goebel decided to take time off racing and began an association with the Guiberson-Diesel Engine Company in Dallas, helping them to develop a diesel powered airplane. Goebel's plan was to fly the finished plane around the world. In May 1932, the experimental aircraft crashed near McKinney, Texas, with the mechanic flying with him being killed in the accident and Goebel suffering a broken leg. After recuperating he became a skywriter and flew promotional tours for Phillips Petroleum, which had sponsored his Dole Race flight. During the war he served in the Army Air Corps Reserves, participated in training, and continued to serve in the Reserves until after the Korean War.

1928: CHARLES COLLYER: NEW NON-STOP EAST TO WEST TRANSCONTINENTAL RECORD

After flying to the transcontinental west-to-east non-stop record with Goebel, Tucker wanted to break the transcontinental non-stop record from east to west. Goebel wanted to take a break from flying and turned Tucker's proposal down. Tucker then contacted barnstormer and former mail pilot Capt. Charles Collyer, and on 24–25 October 1928, he and passenger Harry Tucker flew Tucker's Lockheed Vega, *Yankee Doodle*, covering approximately the same course flown by Goebel. After 24:51 hours Collyer flew to a non-stop east to west record set in 1923 by the Army Air Service (MacReady/Kelly). Passenger Tucker became the first person to fly non-stop round trip across the continent. On 3 November, after breaking Goebel's new west-to-east record, Collyer crashed near Prescott, Arizona, killing him and aircraft owner Harry Tucker.

Arthur Goebel (L) and Charles Collyer

THE LOCKHEED VEGA, AMELIA EARHART, WILEY POST, AND OTHERS

The Lockheed Vega high-wing monoplane was one of America's first important and successful aircraft that became famous for its use by a number of record breaking pilots, including Amelia Earhart and Wiley Post, who were drawn to its tough and very long-range design. It was also one of

America's first successful commercial transports and marked the beginning of Lockheed as one of the world's most important aircraft manufacturers. The aircraft was originally designed to serve on Lockheed's own airline by Jack Northrop and Gerard Vultee (both would later form their own companies). The design, which incorporated a monocoque fuselage, cantilever wings, and the best available engine, placed the Vega among the world's sleekest, most rugged, long-ranged, and fastest aircraft. The Vega 1 had a wingspan of 41 ft. and a wing area of 275 sq. ft., a length of 27.5 ft., a height of 8.5 ft., and weighed 2,900 lbs. fully loaded and fueled. It was powered by a single 225 hp air-cooled nine-cylinder Wright Whirlwind J-5 engine that gave it a cruising speed of 118 mph and a range of 900 miles. The Vega, named for the fifth brightest star visible from the Earth, began the Lockheed practice of naming aircraft after stars and other astronomical features.

The inaugural Vega flight occurred on 4 July 1927, just months after Lindbergh's flight. The *Golden Eagle* prototype Vega 1 flown by Jack Frost and Gordon Scott was lost in the ill-famed Dole Derby race from California to Hawaii in August 1927. Despite the loss, the Vega attracted great interest from pilots intent on endurance flights. The Vega's many records for speed and endurance inspired Allan Lockheed to coin the Lockheed motto, "It takes a Lockheed to beat a Lockheed." Later commercial airlines expressed an interest, although the Vega could never carry enough passengers to be a viable airliner (the Vega I carried four passengers, while the Vega Model 5 series accommodated seven). Private concerns eagerly placed orders for the Vega, which won every speed trophy at the National Air Races in Cleveland in 1928.

Lockheed Vega

The original Vega 1 would evolve into the much more capable Lockheed Model 5, which had the same dimensions as the Vega 1, but had increased power and speed. It was powered by a single 450 hp air cooled Pratt & Whitney R-1340 Wasp engine that gave it a cruising speed of 155 mph, a maximum speed of 170 mph, and a service ceiling of 15,000 ft. It had a fuel capacity of ninety-six gallons, which gave the Vega a range of 725 miles that could be greatly extended with fuel tank additions. Lockheed built only 132 Vegas of all models 1927–1934. Both Wiley Post's *Winnie Mae* and Amelia Earhart's Vega are on display at the National Air and Space Museum original building in Washington, DC.

AMELIA EARHART

Born in Atchison, Kansas, on 24 July 1897, Earhart's childhood was marked by her father's alcoholism, by watching her parents separate and her mother struggle financially, and then living with her grandparents much of the time. During Fall 1919, Earhart enrolled in pre-med at Columbia University, but left after a year to rejoin her reconciled parents in Los Angeles. In Los Angeles, Earhart saw her first airshow and had her first plane ride, and became smitten with flying. During January 1921, she took flying lessons at Bert Kinner's airfield from female pioneer aviator Anita "Neta" Snook, who flew a rebuilt Canuk, the Canadian version of the Curtiss JN4 Jenny. To help finance her flying lessons and to buy a plane of her own Erhart worked in a photography studio and as a filing clerk at the Los Angeles Telephone Company. That summer she purchased a secondhand bright yellow Kinner Airstar she named *The Canary*. She also bought a leather aviator's jacket and cropped her hair short in the style of other female flyers of the day, which would become her signature look. Soon she began participating in aerial demonstrations and air rodeos. During Fall 1922, she set an unofficial altitude record for women, flying to 14,000 ft. On 17 March 1923, her flying abilities gained her top billing for the air rodeo and the opening event at Glendale Airport in Glendale, California. On 15 May 1923, Earhart became the sixteenth woman to be issued a pilot's license (#6017) by the FAI. Unfortunately, the Earhart family again had marital and financial problems and Earhart was forced to sell the Airstar in June 1923. In 1924, her parents divorced and Earhart moved to Boston with her mother and sister, where she worked at Denison House, teaching English to immigrant families until 1928. During this time Earhart continued her interest in aviation, becoming a member and then vice president of the American Aeronautical Society's Boston chapter. She flew out of Dennison Airport and was a Kinner aircraft sales representative for the Boston area.

In 1928, pilot Wilmer "Bill" Stultz and co-pilot/mechanic Louis "Slim" Gordon invited her to join them as a passenger on their trans-Atlantic flight to become the first woman to fly across the Atlantic. On 17 June 1928, they left Newfoundland in a Fokker F7 equipped with pontoons named *Friendship*. Upon taking off the aircraft twice failed to lift from the water and the crew reluctantly dumped fuel, reducing the load from 830 gallons to 700 gallons, which even with advantageous tail winds was a narrow margin. When they landed at Burry Port, Wales, on 18 June 1928, only about fifty gallons of fuel remained after the 20:40 hour flight. The successful flight made world headlines, mainly due to publisher and publicist George Putnam, who was involved in the project. Putnam would become Earhart's manager and eventually her husband. Putnam arranged a New York City ticker-tape parade and a White House reception by President

Calvin Coolidge that placed the crew and, particularly, Earhart in the public eye. By the end of the year Putnam had published her first book, *20 Hours, 40 Minutes, Our Flight in the Friendship: The American Girl, First Across the Atlantic by Air, Tells Her Story*. During this time Putnam used Earhart's physical resemblance to "Lucky Lindy" Lindbergh to influence newspapers and magazines to refer to her as "Lady Lindy."

In August 1929, the trans-continental Cleveland Air Race was opened to women as a nine-stage race that began in Santa Monica, California, and ended in Cleveland, Ohio. The Women's Air Derby, labelled the "Powder Puff Derby" by humorist Will Rogers, included many of the top America female pilots. Four of the twenty starting pilots, including one fatality, failed to complete the race. Louise Thaden won the Class D race flying a Beechcraft Travel Air Speedwing, Gladys O'Donnell was second flying a Waco ATO, and Earhart finished third—two hours behind the winner—in her new Lockheed Vega-1, the heaviest of the aircraft flown in her class. Because of the fellowship during the race Thaden, O'Donnell, Earhart, Ruth Nichols, Blanche Noyes, and Phoebe Omlie discussed forming an organization for female pilots. All 117 of the women pilots licensed at the time were invited to join, and on 2 November 1929, twenty-six women, including Earhart, met and formed "The Ninety-Nines," named for the ninety-nine charter members, with Earhart as its first president (see The Ninety-Nines and the 1929 Powder Puff Derby in text for a more detailed account).

Following Putnam's divorce in 1929, his professional relationship and friendship with Earhart developed into numerous marriage proposals, which Earhart finally accepted, and they were married on 7 February 1931. Putnam continued to manage Earhart's career, arranging her flying commitments, which were often followed by lecture tours, to maximize the opportunity for publicity. On 8 April 1931, Earhart set an altitude record (18,415 ft.) in a Pitcairn autogiro that would stand for years. Putnam arranged for Amelia a sponsorship by the Beech-Nut Company to become the first pilot to fly an autogiro from coast to coast, but discovered on her arrival that another pilot had achieved the feat a week before. She then attempted to be the first to complete a trans-continental round trip flight in an autogiro, but crashed after taking off in Abilene, Texas, on the return leg of the trip, for which she received a reprimand for negligence from Assistant Secretary of Commerce for Aviation Clarence Young. She completed the autogiro trip, but abandoned the rotorcraft after several other mishaps.

Soon rumors circulated that Earhart was not a skilled pilot, but only a celebrity created by Putnam. To dispel these rumors the two began planning a solo trans-Atlantic flight from Harbor Grace, Newfoundland, to Paris, which would make her the first female and second person to fly solo across the Atlantic—a major piloting achievement. Earhart lifted her Lockheed DL-1 off on 20 May 1932, a Putnam-arranged five years to the day after Lindbergh began his historic flight. Her technical advisor for the flight was famed Norwegian-American aviator Bernt Balchen, who helped prepare her aircraft and flight. After a flight lasting 14:56 hours, during which she contended with strong northerly winds, icy conditions, and mechanical problems, Earhart landed in a pasture in Culmore, north of Derry, Northern Ireland. Earhart was seen as "Lady Lindy," and was considered the world's premiere female pilot. The National Geographic Society awarded her a gold medal presented by President Herbert Hoover, and Congress awarded her a Distinguished Flying Cross, both awarded to a woman for the first time.

Earhart continued to set records and achieve firsts for women in aviation. In August 1932, she became the first woman to fly nonstop coast-to-coast in her Lockheed Vega. In 1933, she was one of two women to enter the Cleveland to Los Angeles Bendix Race, which had opened to women, allowing them to compete against men in the same race for the first time. Although she crossed the finish line six hours behind the men, on her return flight she bettered the non-stop trans-continental flight record she set the previous year by two hours.

On 11 January 1935, Earhart became the first aviator to fly solo from Honolulu to Oakland. This trans-oceanic flight had been attempted by many others, especially by the ill-fated participants in the 1927 Dole Air Race (see text) that had flown the reverse route (California to Hawaii). Despite the dangers, previous outcomes, and opinion that the flight was dangerous and pointless, Earhart's Vega was shipped to Honolulu in late December. On 11 January 1935, Earhart took off from Wheeler Army Airfield, near Honolulu, and little more than eighteen hours later she landed in Oakland after an uneventful flight. On 19 April, she flew her Vega solo from Los Angeles to Mexico City. This flight was intended to be non-stop, but she became lost sixty miles from Mexico City and had to land for directions, settling to be a solo flight from Los Angeles to Mexico City. While in Mexico, her next record attempt was a nonstop flight from Mexico City to New York beginning on 8 May, which was an uneventful flight met by large crowds in Newark, New Jersey. Earhart participated in long-distance air racing, placing fifth (195 mph) in the 1935 Bendix Trophy Race despite racing purpose-built air racers that could fly at more than 300 mph. Between 1930 and 1935, Earhart had set seven women's speed and distance aviation records in a variety of aircraft, including the Kinner Airster, Lockheed Vega, and Pitcairn Autogiro. Earhart received many awards and accolades for her record setting achievements. She won the Harmon Trophy as America's Outstanding Airwoman for 1932, 1933, and 1934. She was given honorary membership in the National Aeronautic Association and was awarded the Cross of Knight of the Legion of Honor by the French government. In 1935, the Putnam/Earhart New York home burned down and Earhart convinced Putnam to move to California, where she became a friend and business partner of West Coast aviation guru Paul Mantz.

Circumnavigation of the Globe

By 1935, she recognized the limitations of her Vega for long, trans-oceanic flights, especially a planned circumnavigation of the globe and, with the financial aid of her sponsors, purchased a Lockheed Electra 10E. Lockheed built the aircraft to her specifications, which included extensive modifications to the fuselage to incorporate a large fuel tank. Although the Electra was publicized as a "flying laboratory," Earhart had planned little science and the flight was arranged around Earhart's sole intention to circumnavigate the globe to gather material and draw attention to her next Putnam book. For her trip Earhart initially decided to use two navigators to navigate from Oakland to Hawaii and on to Howland Island, in the South Pacific, an especially difficult portion of the flight, then continue to Australia, where Earhart would proceed solo for the remainder of the trip, which had been frequently flown and was easy to navigate with multiple stops. Fred Noonan was chosen as a navigator, as he had extensive experience in marine (as a licensed ship's captain) and celestial flight navigation. Noonan had recently left Pan Am, where he established most of the company's China Clipper seaplane routes across the Pacific and was also responsible for training Pan American's navigators for the San Francisco-

TOP TO BOTTOM
Amelia Earhart and her Lockheed Vega

Earhart, Fred Noonan (L), and Paul Mantz posing in front of Earhart's Vega in Oakland before their first, ill-fated attempt to fly around the world

Earhart and husband, George Putnam pose in Miami before her second circumnavigation attempt leaving on 1 June 1937

Manila route. Capt. Harry Manning, who was the captain of the *President Roosevelt*, the ship that brought Earhart back from Europe in 1928, was to be the second navigator.

On 17 March 1937, Earhart and her crew (Noonan, Manning, and Paul Mantz, Earhart's technical advisor) flew the Oakland to Honolulu portion. On arrival the Electra required repairs to rectify lubrication problems and servicing of the propeller hubs' variable pitch mechanisms. The flight resumed three days later, with Earhart, Noonan, and Manning on board. During the take-off run Earhart ground-looped due to debated circumstances, including a blown tire (Earhart and witnesses) and pilot error (Mantz and other witnesses). Nonetheless, the Lockheed was severely damaged, the flight was canceled, and the aircraft was shipped by sea to the Lockheed Burbank factory for repairs and the installation of a new radio direction finding unit.

While the Electra was being repaired Earhart and Putnam solicited additional funds and prepared for a second attempt, now flying the circumnavigation in the opposite (west to east) direction. The flight's new route was partly due to changes in global wind and weather patterns along the earlier planned route since that attempt. The second attempt began with an unpublicized first leg flight from Oakland to Miami, and after arriving there Earhart very publicly announced her plans to circumnavigate the globe. On this second attempt on 1 June, Earhart and Fred Noonan as navigator departed Miami, and after numerous stops in South America, Africa, the Indian subcontinent, and Southeast Asia, arrived in Lae, New Guinea, on 29 June, after flying 22,000 miles and with the remaining 7,000 miles over the Pacific.

At midnight on 2 July 1937, Earhart and Noonan took off from Lae Airfield in their heavily loaded Electra, headed northeast 2,556 miles for Howland Island, a small island only 1.25 miles long. Their last known reported position was near the Nukumanu Islands, about 800 miles from Lae into the flight. The USCGC *Itasca* was on station at Howland, assigned to communicate with Earhart's Electra and guide them by RDF to the island once they arrived in the vicinity. The final approach to Howland Island was not successful due to a number of possibly controversial causes, mostly blaming the new radio direction finding system and communications problems with the *Itasca*, whose RDF system could not tune in the Vega's frequency. Earhart continued to ask the *Itasca* for bearings and she thought she seemed to be within one hundred miles of Howland Island at 0645. Her 0742 transmission stated: "We must be on you, but cannot see you, but gas is running low. Have been unable to reach you by radio...." In her last known transmission at 0843 Earhart broadcast Noonan's (mis) calculated line of position several times on different frequencies.

The *Itasca* began an eventually unsuccessful search beginning approximately one hour after Earhart's last recorded message using erroneous guesstimated plots. President Roosevelt authorized a massive naval, air, and land search. The US Navy soon joined the search, committing all available ships to the area, including the battleship *Colorado*, which coordinated the search, and the aircraft carrier USS *Lexington*. The two vessels searched for six and seven days, respectively, and were joined by US Coast Guard ships. The $4 million (official) 150,000 square mile air and sea search by the Navy and Coast Guard continued until 19 July 1937, and was the most costly and intensive search in US history. Immediately after the end of the official search Putnam financed a private search by local establishments of nearby Pacific islands, concentrating on the Gilbert Islands and then expanding even farther. No trace of the Electra, Earhart, or Noonan was found. Putnam became the trustee of Earhart's estate and had the seven-year death waiting period waived so he could pay for the searches (Earhart was declared legally dead on 5 January 1939).

Earhart, the independent, charismatic, accomplished woman aviatrix, was a widely known international celebrity and feminist icon during her lifetime, and continues so to this day, with only Lindbergh surpassing "Lady Lindy" as an American aviation superstar. Her mysterious disappearance continues to this day to fuel speculation and searches, and has become one of the greatest mysteries of the twentieth century.

WILEY POST

Wiley Post, Earhart, and Lindbergh were the most celebrated personalities of aviation's "Golden Age," with Post known for having flown around the world on two different occasions. In 1930, the record for flying around the world was not held by a fixed-wing aircraft, but by the *Graf Zeppelin* dirigible, piloted by Hugo Eckener in 1929 in 21 days.

On 23 June 1931, Post and his navigator, Harold Gatty, took off from Roosevelt Field, Long Island, New York, in his Lockheed Vega—the white and purple *Winnie Mae*—on their way around the world, stopping at Harbour Grace, Newfoundland; Flintshire, Wales; Hanover and Berlin, Germany; the Soviet cities Moscow, Novosibirsk, Irkutsk, Blagoveshchensk, and Khabarovsk; across the Bering Sea to Nome, Alaska, where his propeller was repaired and Fairbanks where the propeller was replaced; Edmonton, Canada; and Cleveland before returning to Roosevelt Field on 1 July, after flying 15,474 miles in the record time of 8 days, 15:51 hours, which was twelve days faster than the previous record set by the *Graf Zeppelin* in 1929.

On 15 July 1933, Post departed from Floyd Bennett Field, intending to circle the globe in six days with only five stops, but bad weather and a problem with the autopilot kept Post from achieving his goal. His first stop was Berlin, where repairs were attempted on his autopilot; then he stopped in Konigsberg to replace some forgotten maps; Moscow for more repairs to his autopilot; Novosibirsk, Irkutsk, for final repairs to the autopilot; Rukhlovo, Khabarovsk; on to Flat, where his propeller had to be replaced; Fairbanks; Edmonton; and back to Floyd Bennett Field, where 50,000 people greeted him on his return on 22 July, after 7 days, 18:49 hours—twenty-one hours less than his previous record. Post's solo flight would not be duplicated until 1947, when William Odom circled the globe solo, flying 19,645 miles in 3 days, 1:05 hours (73:05 hours) in a Douglas A-26 twin-engine medium bomber 7–10 August 1947.

In 1934, Post flew the *Winnie Mae* to a record altitude of 40,000 ft., and then to another record-breaking altitude of approximately 50,000 ft., which was not confirmed due to a faulty barograph. In preparation for the high-altitude flight, Post realized the *Winnie Mae* could not be equipped with a pressurized cabin, so he flew wearing the world's first high-altitude aircraft pressure suit that he modified from a deep-sea diver's suit. While flying at that altitude Post discovered the Jet Stream (the fast-moving currents of air that streamed in a westerly direction). Post postulated that if an aircraft could fly in the Jet Stream, it would fly faster and use less fuel than an aircraft at a lower altitude. In 1935, Post confirmed this by cruising at more than 30,000 ft. at an average speed of 279 mph, which was more than 100 mph above the Vega's normal cruising speed.

On 15 August 1935, Post and American humorist Will Rogers were killed when Post's hybrid aircraft (Lockheed Orion fuselage and Lockheed Explorer long wings) crashed on take-off from a lagoon near Point Barrow, Alaska.

Wiley Post and his Lockheed Vega

1926–29: SIR HUBERT WILKINS AND CARL BEN EIELSEN: ARCTIC AND ANTARCTIC FLIGHTS

Lockheed's third Vega was used by Australian Arctic explorer Sir Hubert Wilkins and Alaskan bush pilot Carl Ben Eielsen for a series of Arctic flights. Wilkins' first Arctic Expedition of 1926 was unsuccessful, although Eielson became the first aviator to cross the Arctic Ocean and land a plane on the Arctic slope. In 1927, Eielson joined Wilkins again on another unsuccessful Arctic-North Pole Expedition. On the 1928 Expedition, in April, Wilkins and Eielsen flew their Vega on a 2,200 mile route over the Polar ice cap from Point Barrow, on the North Slope of Alaska, to Spitzbergen Island, Norway. This was the first flight from North America over the Polar Region (not the North Pole) to Europe, although Richard Byrd and Floyd Bennett claimed to have flown over the Pole in 1926. For their flight Eielson was decorated with the Distinguished Flying Cross and won the 1928 Harmon Trophy, while Wilkins was knighted.

Eielson accompanied Wilkins on an Antarctic Expedition later in 1928, arriving at Deception Island, on the Graham Land Peninsula, in November. On 20 December 1928, Wilkins and a team of pilots flew two Vegas to Antarctica to conduct aerial mapping of 100,000 square miles of the continent. Their exploration flights of the Graham Land Peninsula were the first time anyone had flown a plane in Antarctica, and they became the first to fly over both Polar regions. Wilkins had planned to fly to the South Pole, but he was unable to find an area on Deception Island to build a runway long enough to get the Vega into the air with sufficient fuel to complete the distance. Nevertheless, it was the first time in history undiscovered land was mapped from a plane, as Adm. Richard Byrd's Ford and Fokkers were still heading south aboard ships. Note: In 1931, Wilkins led the failed expedition to reach the North Pole by taking a surplus United States Navy submarine renamed *Nautilus* under the pack ice!

Sir Hubert Wilkins (R) and Carl Eielsen pose by their Lockheed Vega.

RICHARD BYRD FLIES OVER THE ARCTIC (?) AND ANTARCTIC

1926 Arctic Expedition

In 1925, Lt.Cdr. Richard Byrd's naval aviation group was attached to D. B. MacMillan's expedition to Greenland. During that expedition Byrd met pilot Floyd Bennett, and the two planned an Arctic expedition to fly over the North Pole in

1926. On 9 May, with Byrd acting as navigator and Bennett as pilot, the two claimed to have flown their Fokker tri-motor *Josephine Ford* on the first airplane flight over the North Pole, flying from King's Bay, Spitsbergen, Norway, to the Pole and return in a flight lasting 15:44 hours. For their achievement both were awarded the Congressional Medal of Honor and were acclaimed as national heroes. Over the years there has been a running controversy as to whether Byrd actually flew over the Pole. Almost immediately the controversy largely hinged on whether Byrd's Fokker could have flown the distance to the Pole in their recorded time of 15:44 hours, when the flight should have taken about eighteen hours, considering the aircraft's ground speed. Then the controversy flared again with the 1996 discovery of a Byrd diary describing his celebrated flight that "suggests" he was about 150 miles from the Pole when Byrd decided to turn back because of an oil leak. If these assertions are true, then credit for the first flight over the North Pole actually belongs to Norway's Roald Amundsen, American Lincoln Ellsworth, and Italian Umberto Nobile, who completed a well-documented flight over the Pole in the airship *Norge* three days after Byrd's flight. If Byrd's flight is discredited, then the first airplane flight over the North Pole actually belongs to Soviet pilot Pavel Golovin, who on 5 May 1937, flew an ANT-7 on a survey flight from the Russian Polar expedition *North Pole-1* to locate an ice floe suitable for use as a scientific drifting station and would be the first to fly over the North Pole in an airplane. Between 18–20 June 1937, Soviet pilot Valery Chkalov was the first to fly non-stop from Europe (Moscow) to the American West Coast (Vancouver, Washington) via the North Pole, flying a single-engine Tupolev ANT-25 for 63 hours and covering 5,475 miles.

In early 1927, Byrd and Bennett began planning to be the first to cross the Atlantic flying their Fokker *America* to win the Orteig Prize, but Bennett suffered serious injuries when the *America* crashed on a test flight that also slightly injured Byrd and another pilot. In May Charles Lindbergh won the prize.

1928 Antarctic

Although Bennett had not completely recovered from his injuries, Byrd, now an admiral, appointed him as his second in command and planner of his 1928–1930 South Pole Expedition. Before the expedition departed by ship, Bennett and Bernt Balchen flew a Ford Tri-motor to aid in the rescue of the crew of the Ju W33 *Bremen*, the first aircraft to cross the Atlantic from west to east. While flying to the crash site off the coast of Labrador, Bennett, debilitated from the crash of the *America*, contracted pneumonia and was taken to a hospital in Quebec. Charles Lindbergh volunteered to fly medication to Bennett, but arrived too late, as Bennett died on 25 April. After Bennett's death Byrd continued with his expedition "to explore the unknown regions of the Antarctic from the air." Byrd's polar expedition was to be the largest and best-equipped ever, being backed by the Fords, Rockefellers, and even donations from the American public suffering in the midst of the Depression. An extensive and well-supplied base called Little America was built on the Ross Ice Shelf, and was manned by more than eighty men and equipped with four ships and three individual aircraft: a Ford Tri-motor honoring and named *Floyd Bennett*, a Fokker, and a Fairchild. Although Wilkins and Eielson were mainly interested in surveying Antarctica by aircraft, Byrd was obsessed with being the first to fly over the South Pole. On 29 November 1929, the weather cleared and Byrd was ready to fulfil his goal to fly over the South Pole. Byrd, pilot Bernt Balchen, co-pilot Harold June, and photographer and aerial cartographer Ashley McKinely took off in the *Floyd Bennett*, planning to fly directly to the Pole and then, on their return trip, refuel and resupply at a remote ground base. During the flight, as they approached the Queen Maud mountain range, they had to quickly drop several bags of food and supplies to lighten the Ford enough to climb over the mountains. Once over the mountains they flew directly over the Pole, and after a round trip flight of approximately 1,600 miles that took 17:26 hours, Byrd was feted as the first person to have flown over both poles.

Lt.Cdr. Richard Byrd (L) and Floyd Bennett

BELOW / Adm. Byrd and Balchen Ford Trimotor

RICHARD HALLIBURTON AND MOYE STEPHENS

Richard Halliburton was a famous American traveler, adventurer, and author whose adventures thrilled readers around the world. In 1930, Halliburton employed pioneer aviator, one of TWA's original pilots, and Hollywood stunt pilot Moye Stephens on a handshake with no pay but unlimited expenses to fly him around the world in an open cockpit modified Stearman C-3B biplane named *Flying Carpet*, after the magic carpet of fairy tales; it was also the title of Halliburton's 1932 best seller. In this book he enthuses to pilot Stephens: "I've just given myself an airplane and I want you to fly us to all the outlandish places in the world, Turkey, Persia, Paris and Pasadena. We're going to fly across deserts, over mountains, rescue imprisoned princesses and fight dragons. We must have the world. We can have the world!" The duo left on Christmas Day 1930 from Los Angeles to New York City, making two emergency landings en route, plus a delay for an unscheduled engine overhaul. In New York they crated *Flying Carpet* and sailed to England, where they flew to France, then Spain, Gibraltar, and on to Africa in Fez, Morocco, crossing the Atlas Mountains and the Sahara to Timbuktu using the fuel caches of Shell Oil Company. They then continued eastward, spending several weeks in Algeria with the French Foreign Legion, and continued via Cairo and Damascus, with a side trip to Petra. In Persia (Iran) they met German aviator Elly Beinhorn, who was grounded by mechanical problems, and assisted her and then flew with her. Later, Halliburton wrote a foreword to her book, *Flying Girl,* about these and other of her adventures in the air. Halliburton was exhausted and *Flying Carpet* was becoming worn out, but they continued their eastward journey. In India, Halliburton and Beinhorn visited the Taj Mahal and in Nepal, the two aircraft flew over Mount Everest; Halliburton stood up in *Flying Carpet's* open cockpit and took the first aerial photograph of the mountain. The Maharajah of Nepal was thrilled by their daring aerobatics. They were the first Americans to fly to the Philippines, and in Manila *Flying Carpet* was again loaded onto a ship to cross the ocean. In San Francisco the landing wheels were again installed for the final leg of their flight back to Los Angeles. The air journey took 18 months to circumnavigate the globe, covering 33,660 miles and visiting 34 countries. The around-the-world trip cost Halliburton more than $50,000, plus a $14,000 fuel bill from Shell Oil Company, but the book, *The Flying Carpet,* earned him huge Depression royalties of $100,000 its first year. Soon after finishing his fifth book Halliburton's insatiable readers demanded ever more death defying adventures. Nearing forty, exhausted, and in financial trouble, Halliburton set sail on a replica Chinese junk *Sea Dragon* crewed by Cornell undergraduates and skippered by an Australian alcoholic. He was last heard from via radio after he left Hong Kong on 23 March 1939, saying he was encountering heavy weather near the International Dateline. After the *Flying Carpet* adventure Moye Stephens was unable to resume a career as an airline pilot during the Depression and took several sales positions in the depressed Los Angeles aviation market. In 1939, he was influential in the promotion and organization of Northrop Aircraft, Inc., for which he was awarded stock interest, and was appointed to the Northrop board as secretary and was chief of the flight division and chief test pilot. He tested the experimental and innovative Northrop Flying Wing bomber series: the twin-engine NIM, first flown in 1940; the four-engine XB-35 in 1946; and the eight (jet) engine XB-49 in 1947—prototypes of today's B-2 bomber. At the close of WWII Stephens and Northrop Sales Manager Ted Coleman left Northrop to start a franchise air cargo business in the interior of Brazil, but the climate severely affected his young son's health and Stephens returned to the United States.

Richard Halliburton (R) and Moye Stephens in their Stearman C-3B biplane, *The Flying Carpet*

CHARLES HEALY DAY

Charles Healy Day built his first aircraft in 1909, working with Glenn L. Martin, and is credited with developing the technique of using laminated wood to make propellers, thus increasing their strength. (See my book *The Martin B-26 Marauder: The Ultimate Look from Drawing Board to Widow Maker Vindicated*, Schiffer, PA, 2014.) In 1910, he built and flew the first tractor biplane—an aircraft of his own design. He became vice president and chief design engineer of the Sloane Airplane Company, which became the Standard Aircraft Corporation. There, he designed and built several aircraft leading to the famous Standard J-1 used for pilot training in WWI, flying the mail, and for barnstorming in the 1920s, with its large forward cockpit profitably carrying two passengers instead of one. In 1926, he joined Ivan Gates, of the Famous Gates Flying Circus, to form the Gates-Day Aircraft Company in Paterson, New

Jersey. It was reorganized in 1928 as the New Standard Aircraft Corporation. During that time Day designed his most famous and enduring aircraft, the GD-24, which evolved into the D-25 and many variants, all of which had a huge front cockpit capable of carrying up to five passengers. In 1931, Day resigned as Standard Aircraft's president, and in Spring 1931 built the Day Model A in his Paterson, New Jersey, work shop, then tested it at the Teteboro, New Jersey, airport. The small trainer, with an open side-by-side seating cockpit, was designed for safety and comfort. Its bi-wing construction had the upper wing forward of the lower and its Martin engine gave it a cruising speed of 85 mph and a landing speed of 30 mph. The Model A, named *Errant*, was shipped to England by steamer on 8 May 1931, where it was reassembled for flight on 18 May. Day and his wife, Gladys, departed Heston Airport on 28 May, making stops in France (Abbeville and Paris), landing in a German potato field, and continuing across Germany with stops in Cologne, Frankfurt, and Berlin; then on to Prague, Vienna, Budapest, and Istanbul. They made stops in the Middle East: Syria (7 July), Iraq, Iran, and on to Pakistan (26 July); and five stops in India (with a month's stay in Calcutta due to illness). They arrived in Shanghai, where they boarded a ship and landed in San Francisco, then back in Newark on 20 December. After consulting for several years in the US, in 1934 Day accepted an offer from Chiang Kai-Shek, head of the Canton government in China, to organize and operate an aircraft factory. The factory was quickly constructed and producing Fushin trainers, Curtiss Hawks, and Russian I-15 pursuits under license until 1937, when the Japanese began to bomb it. By 1940, the factory, which was dispersed into the surrounding area, was cut off from materials needed for continued operation. The Days left China, and back in New York he was in great demand for the lecture circuit. After Pearl Harbor he was commissioned a major in the Army Air Corps, stationed at Wellston Air Depot, Georgia (now Robins AFB). In November 1942, he was allowed to resign his commission to head the Glenn L. Martin Modification Center in Omaha, where he remained until 1945. By that time he was having some health problems, but continued working as an aviation consultant until his death at his home on 26 May 1955.

Charles and Gladys Day and their Day Model A, the *Errant*

JAMES "JIMMIE" MATTERN: INTERRUPTED CIRCUMNAVIGATION

On 5 July 1932, James Mattern and Bennett Griffin began an around-the-world flight, flying their Lockheed Vega *The Century of Progress* from Floyd Bennett Field, New York, to Harbor Grace, Newfoundland, and then non-stop to Berlin. They landed in Berlin after 18:41 hours in the air, during which they set a new record of 10:50 hours for crossing the Atlantic Ocean. Continuing on, they made an emergency crash landing in Belarus, USSR, on 7 July 1932, ending their flight. On 3 June 1933, Mattern flew a reconstructed and much altered *Century of Progress* solo from Floyd Bennett Field on another around-the-world attempt. He crossed the Atlantic without incident, but on 14 June 1933, he made a forced landing in Siberia, where he had to abandon the *Century* and was eventually rescued by Eskimos and flown to Nome, Alaska, by noted Soviet pilot Sigizmund Levanevsky, then flew back to New York, completing an interrupted global circumnavigation.

James Mattern's colorfully painted Lockheed Vega *The Century of Progress*

RUTH NICHOLS

The daughter of wealthy parents, Ruth Nichols was known as the "Flying Debutante," and was the only female pilot to hold simultaneous world records for speed, altitude, and distance while flying Lockheed Vegas. In 1930, she broke Charles Lindbergh's record time for a cross-country flight, completing the trip in 13:21 hours. In March 1931, she set the women's world altitude record of 28,743 ft. In April 1931, she set the women's world speed record of 210.7 mph. In June 1931, she attempted to become the first woman to fly solo across the Atlantic Ocean, but crashed in New Brunswick, Canada, and was severely injured. After she recovered in October 1931, she set the women's distance record (1,977 miles) with a flight from Oakland, California,

Ruth Nichols, the "Flying Debutante," and her Lockheed Vega

to Louisville, Kentucky. On 14 February 1932, Nichols set a new world altitude record of 19,928 ft. for diesel-powered aircraft at Floyd Bennett Field, New York, while flying in a Lockheed Vega. On 29 December, Nichols became the first woman to pilot a commercial passenger airline, flying for New York and New England Airways Company.

THE BELLANCA'S AIRCRAFT SET ENDURANCE AND DISTANCE RECORDS

Giuseppe Bellanca immigrated to America in 1911, and built his first successful aircraft in Brooklyn in 1913. His design became the standard for aircraft design, incorporating a tractor design with a front propeller, wing in the middle, and a tail in the rear, which was just the opposite of aircraft design at that time (i.e., the Wright Flyers). Bellanca worked for several aircraft companies as their chief designer, and in 1926, became a consultant for the Wright Aeronautical Company to design a five to six passenger aircraft for installation of their new Wright Whirlwind J-4 engine. Bellanca built the all-wood WB-1, which crashed at Curtiss Field during an attempt for the world non-refueled endurance record. The WB-2 successor was constructed of fabric-covered steel tubing and was already in development to test the updated Wright Whirlwind J-5. The WB-2 first flew at the 1926 National Air Races, where it set both efficiency records. Wright Aeronautical elected to continue to develop the Whirlwind engine, but would discontinue aircraft manufacture and operations to sidestep competition in lucrative engine sales with rival aircraft manufacturers. Bellanca left Wright Aeronautical with the rights to the WB-2 design and the prototype and formed the Columbia Aircraft Company with flamboyant millionaire investor Charles Levine.

Giuseppe Bellanca

1927: CLARENCE CHAMBERLIN AND CHARLES LEVINE: TRANS-ATLANTIC FLIGHT

Bellanca and Levine felt the WB-2—renamed *Columbia*—could surpass the current world endurance record set by Maurice Drouhin and Landry Jules in France. On 12 April 1927, Clarence Chamberlin and Bert Acosta stayed aloft over Roosevelt Field, outside New York City, for 51:11:25 hours over an estimated distance flown of 4,100 miles, which was 500 more than needed for the Orteig Prize trans-Atlantic attempt between New York and Paris. The Bellanca WB-2 was actually Lindbergh's first choice for his proposed New York to Paris flight, but he was snubbed by Levine, who also desired to personally win the $25,000 Orteig prize money. Instead, Lindbergh had Ryan build his specially designed *Spirit of St. Louis*. Meanwhile Levine, in choosing the crew for his flight, somehow assured three people of having the aircraft's two available seats, so *Columbia* was grounded by a court order to resolve the seating situation. Meanwhile, Lindbergh took off on his successful flight to Paris, and two weeks after Lindbergh won the Orteig Prize, the *Columbia's* litigation was resolved and Clarence Chamberlin and Charles Levine took off on its successful trans-Atlantic flight on 4 June 1927, with Berlin as their destination. The *Columbia* did not reach Berlin, landing one hundred miles short on a field in Eisleben, Germany. The flight covered 3,905 miles in 42:45 hours, which was 315 miles and 9:06 hours longer than Lindbergh's flight; and Levine became the first passenger to cross the Atlantic.

Bellanca's WB-2, renamed *Columbia*.

Clarence Chamberlin (R), Charles Levine, and their WB-2 *Columbia*

THE TRANS-ATLANTIC ESCAPADES OF CHARLES LEVINE AND THE "QUEEN OF DIAMONDS"

While Charles Levine was in Europe, the attractive and flamboyant socialite Mabel Boll, the "Queen of Diamonds," asked him to let her fly to America in the *Columbia*, which was in France following the record flight from New York. After an earlier marriage Boll married Colombian coffee king Hernando Rocha in 1922, who gifted her with more than a million dollars in jewels, earning her nickname. Boll desired the publicity of being the first woman to cross the Atlantic and acquire the new nickname, "Queen of the Air." Levine had contracted with French pilot Maurice Drouhin to fly the *Columbia* back to America, but when the flight was canceled, Drouhin was owed a $4,000 cancellation fee and had the *Columbia* guarded from leaving. Although an inexperienced pilot, Levine took off for England, telling the guards he was just going to test the engine. Boll followed Levine to England by boat to fly to America from London, but just before the flight Levine's new pilot, Capt. Walter Hinchcliffe, publicly refused to let Boll be a passenger, and she set out for New York by boat in January 1928, after being promised an east to west crossing from New York.

In 1928, the same teams that attempted to win the Orteig Prize were competing to be the first to fly a woman across the Atlantic (as a passenger). Levine chose Boll, while Amelia Earhart was chosen by sponsors George Palmer Putnam and Amy Phipps Guest. On 26 June 1928, with great fanfare Boll left Roosevelt Field in the *Columbia*, owned by Columbia Aircraft Corp. Chairman Charles Levine and piloted by Oliver LeBoutillier and Arthur Argles. When Boll arrived in Harbour Grace, Newfoundland, Amelia Earhart and German Thea Rasche were also there waiting to leave to cross the Atlantic. After several failed attempts days earlier, on 17 June, Wilmer Stultz and Louis Gordon, piloting the Fokker *Friendship* with Earhart aboard, crossed the Atlantic while the crew of the *Columbia* were grounded for five days due to weather. Upon learning of the successful flight by Earhart and crew Boll returned to America. Boll still desired the nickname, "The Queen of the Air," and for her last serious record attempt Levine purchased a customized long-range Junkers W33 for his mistress with "Queen of the Air" emblazoned across the sides. By this time Levine's wife had enough of her husband's mistress and divorced him. Bert Acosta was to fly Boll and Levine from Paris to New York for a new record, which was changed to a London to New York attempt. By the time the aircraft arrived in the United Kingdom in late August 1928, the flying season had ended and Levine was preoccupied with chronic legal matters in America. The Junkers *The Queen of the Air* was transported back to America, damaged, and sold to William Rody, who renamed it *de Espírito Santo Agostinho* and attempted a three-man trans-Atlantic record crossing from Lisbon on 13 September 1931. The aircraft landed in the Atlantic Ocean and the aircraft's empty tanks kept the crew afloat for several days before they were rescued. Boll avoided the hazards of record setting flights until 1936, when she announced she had been "cured of her flying obsession."

After a series of bad business investments and losses in the 1929 stock market crash Levine was sued by the federal government for a half million dollars in back taxes. In 1930, Levine was arrested in the company of Mabel Boll for attempting to purchase dies to produce counterfeit 2 Franc coins. Levine was arrested in 1932 on a charge of violating the Workmen's Compensation Law and he received a suspended sentence, but was arrested again in 1933 on a counterfeiting charge. In 1934, after his release, he was charged with illegally smuggling a German-Jewish refugee from a Nazi concentration camp into America and spent five months in prison. After his release in 1934, he attempted suicide with a gas range. In 1937, he was charged with smuggling 2,000 lbs. of tungsten powder from Canada and he served two years in federal prison. Levine subsequently lived to be ninety-four.

Passengers Charles Levine and Mabel Boll with pilot Oliver LeBoutillier

GIUSEPPE BELLANCA BEGINS BELLANCA AIRCRAFT CORPORATION

Bellanca was disappointed because the *Columbia* was not the first to Paris and probably had enough of the flamboyant, insufferable Levine, so he took the rights to the WB-2 and started his own company, the Bellanca Aircraft Corporation of America, renting facilities on Staten Island, New York. Bellanca remained president and chairman of the board from the corporation's inception on 31 December 1927 until he sold the company to L. Albert and Sons in 1954, when it became AviaBellanca Aircraft. In the late 1920s and 1930s, Bellanca's aircraft (the J and CH series) were known for their efficiency and low operating costs, and would set a number of world endurance and distance records. Among these records were:

1928: Royal Thomas, flying a Bellanca J named *Reliance*, established a new Solo World Endurance Record of 35:25 hours.

1929: Martin Jensen, flying a Bellanca J *Green Flash*, set a new Solo Endurance Record of 35:33 hours.

THE CONTEST FOR THE WOMEN'S ENDURANCE RECORD

Viola Gentry's employment as a cashier at home state North Carolina and New York restaurants while trying to make ends meet as a pilot earned her the nickname, "The Flying Cashier," in the newspaper articles after she flew under the Brooklyn and Manhattan Bridges. Evelyn Trout was known as "Bobbie" and the "Flying Tom Boy" because of her short "bobbed" hairdo. Elinor Smith's father was an actor and her mother a singer performing in New York and England; she lived in Freeport and was known as "The Flying Flapper of Freeport." On 20 December 1928, Viola Gentry flew 8:06:37 hours, which set the first non-refueling endurance record for women. This record was broken three weeks later when Bobbie Trout took off from Van Nuys Airport at 0625 on 2 January 1929 and landed after being in the air for 12:11 hours, beating Gentry's endurance record. Trout's record was only to last until 31 January 1929, when Elinor Smith was ready for a try at the record, as was Gentry. In the New York winter Roosevelt Field was passable for a heavily loaded take-off, but Smith was able to obtain permission to use the Army's nearby Mitchel Field. On 30 January, flying an open cockpit Bruner Winkle biplane during a frigid 0°F day, Smith set a women's solo endurance record of 13:16 hours. She had planned to fly through the night and land in daylight, but the effect of the cold forced her down early before dawn with a heavy remaining load of fuel. She had never tried a nighttime landing and fired a flare to warn the field to turn on the landing lights, but the lights did not go on. Jimmy Doolittle saw her flare and led her to a safe landing. The next day Gentry crashed on take-off while attempting to better Smith's new record. Gentry was unharmed, but her plane was damaged. Bobbie Trout took back the FAI endurance record flight on 10–11 February 1929 at Mines Field, Los Angeles, as the first woman to fly an overnight endurance record of 17:05 hours flying approximately 860 miles at 50.3 mph in the prototype 60 hp R.O. Bone Co. *Golden Eagle* monoplane. Meanwhile, Louise Thaden exceeded Smith's record, flying 22:03 hours over Oakland, California, in March. In April Smith smashed that record, soloing 26:23 hours in a Bellanca CH-300 at the age of only seventeen and a half. Because of her youth and good looks Smith became the pilot darling of the national press. In an attempt to regain the endurance record from Smith, Gentry set out on 27 July 1929, but her aircraft, *The Answer*, crashed in Old Westbury, killing co-pilot Jack Ashcraft. Gentry survived with a fractured skull and crushed shoulders and was rushed to a hospital, where she spent more than six months recovering. In 1931, Gentry quit professional flying and returned to her previous job as a cashier at a North Carolina restaurant. Nonetheless, she continued to fly, and on 10 December 1933, Gentry and co-pilot Frances Marsalis took off from Miami, Florida, attempting to reset the endurance record while supported by a refueling aircraft operated by Jack Loesing and Fred Fetterman. Gentry intended to remain aloft for 9 days, 22 hours, and surpassed the then-current record of 9 days, 4:06 hours set by Marsalis and Louise Thaden.

TOP LEFT / Viola Gentry, the "Flying Cashier"
TOP RIGHT / Elinor Smith, the "Flying Flapper of Freeport"
BOTTOM / Evelyn "Bobbie" Trout, the "Flying Tom Boy"

SMITH AND TROUT: WOMEN'S REFUELED ENDURANCE RECORD

In November 1929, Elinor Smith and Bobbie Trout collaborated to set a new women's refueled endurance record flying a Sunbeam biplane powered by a 300 hp J-6 Wright engine. Smith did the flying while Trout handled the fueling hoses from their Curtiss Pigeon refueling aircraft, piloted by Paul Whittier, with Peter Reinhart managing the hose. The women were hoping for a record of at least one hundred hours and hopefully for a week (164 hours). The two aircraft were not well matched for their duties and relative speeds as the Pigeon, selected for its large capacity to carry fuel, was an obsolete aircraft with an undependable engine for which spare parts were not easily obtained. In refueling position the Pigeon's pilot could not see the Sunbeam at all, so there was no way to signal about any engine problems that would mean sudden loss of altitude. The Sunbeam was not considered a particularly stable aircraft and had to be constantly flown at all times, especially during refueling. The Pigeon had to fly near its top speed while the Sunbeam slowed down to just above its stalling speed.

Elinor Smith, Bobbie Trout, and their Sunbeam biplane

On 16–17 November, they attempted to reset the women's refueling endurance record at LA Metropolitan Airport, Van Nuys, California, but were forced down after 18:26 hours during refueling near Catalina Island. A sudden turbulence tore the hose from Trout's grasp, covering her and the Sunbeam with gasoline, while at the other end of the hose Reinhart was cut and bleeding; the Sunbeam had to return to California.

On 25–26 November they took off at 0829 and were forced down at 1445 after a disappointing flight of 6:16 hours with two refueling contacts.

Finally, on 27–29 November and with the rainy season approaching, the team flew for 42:03:30 with three and a half refueling contacts. The half refueling contact occurred when the Pigeon's engine failed and forced an emergency landing after only half the fuel was transferred. Smith coaxed the Sunbeam onward, stretching their flight out to a world's record 42:5 hours.

1929: POWDER PUFF DERBY: AVIATION WOMEN'S ELITE MEET

The first Women's Air Derby of 13–20 August 1929 was a transcontinental race as part of the National Air Races in Cleveland that humorist Will Rogers dubbed the 'Powder Puff Derby"—the most common name. Air race promoter Cliff Henderson was the founder of the first Women's Air Derby, which he modeled after the men's transcontinental air races. (Paradoxically, Henderson would ban women from competing in the 1934 Bendix Trophy and National Air Races after Florence Klingensmith's fatal crash flying a Gee Bee Y during the 1933 Phillips Race in Chicago.) At a time when there were only seventy women pilots licensed in the US, only forty met the race requirements, having one hundred hours of solo flight—including twenty-five hours of solo cross-country—a license from the FAI, and an annual sporting license issued by the National Aeronautics Association (NAA). Of that group, there were twenty competitors in the derby, with eighteen from America, fourteen in the heavy aircraft class, and six in the lighter class. The derby was to begin in Santa Monica, California, and to keep all competing aircraft safely separated as they climbed to altitude during the start of the daily race legs they were lined up in rows and took off at timed intervals.

The competitors navigated the challenging route using only dead reckoning and road maps, and there were many inevitable problems, especially the first day, when the pilots did not get off until 1400 because of the crowds and press hoopla. Mary Haizlip damaged her airplane the day of the race and was forced to start a day late with a replacement that had a smaller fuel tank, causing her to make more stops. Soon after take-off Phoebe Omlie was forced down in a field near Santa Monica and was briefly arrested on suspicion that she was a drug smuggler. Amelia Earhart had a mechanical problem which briefly delayed her.

Fortunately, the first leg was a short hop from Santa Monica to San Bernardino, but when arriving at San Bernardino, the pilots discovered the organizers had failed to constrain the crowds and the airfield was covered by spectators and parked cars. The pilots landed on a rough, dusty adjacent field instead. Opal Kunz' aircraft suffered damage to its landing gear which was repaired for the next leg. Amelia Earhart's landing overran the small runway and passed through the assembled crowds, who were able to flee unharmed. After this bad start the problems continued. Claire Fahy's Travel Air was forced out of the race in Calexico due to suspected sabotage, as there were men who did not wish to see the women race. Thea Rasche's engine quit and she dead-sticked to a safe landing (suspicious contaminants were found clogging the fuel lines). Pancho Barnes lost her way and landed in Mexico, but her Spanish language skills from her previous flying vocation of running guns and smuggling alcohol across the border helped her ask directions. Mary Haizlip also landed in Mexico, but was soon directed north. Ruth Elder had her maps blown out of her cockpit and she became lost and landed in a pasture to ask directions. Unfortunately, the pasture was inhabited by a bull that would not let her out of the cockpit. Marvel Crosson was overcome by an exhaust leak that flooded her cockpit on the way to Phoenix and she passed out, crashing in the Gila River Valley, and was killed. There was a public protest demanding the race be canceled, but the pilots decided the most fitting tribute would be to finish the derby. Blanche Noyes had a fire in-flight, but was able to quickly land in the desert and extinguish the fire with sand and her bare hands. A sandstorm delayed all remaining contestants in El Paso. Pancho Barnes was forced from the race when her plane hit a car that crossed into the runway in Pecos, Texas. Margaret Perry contracted typhoid fever and was hospitalized in Abilene, Kansas. During the last leg Ruth Nichols crashed into some construction equipment in Columbus, Ohio, and had to drop out.

An estimated 18,000 people gathered in Cleveland to greet the pilots at the end of the race. The ten finishers of the heavy class were:

1. Louise Thaden
2. Gladys O'Donnell
3. Amelia Earhart
4. Blanche Noyes
5. Ruth Elder
6. Neva Paris
7. Mary Haizlip
8. Opal Kunz
9. Mary von Mach
10. Vera Dawn Walker

Four women completed the race in the light class, which was won by Phoebe Omlie, the first woman to receive a transport pilot's certificate and also the first to earn a mechanic's license.

Powder Puff winner Louise Thaden (L), Gladys O'Donnell (2nd place), and Ruth Nichols (R)

THE NINETY-NINES

After the race, on 2 November 1929, at Curtiss Airport, Valley Stream, New York, Neva Paris and Opal Kunz organized many of the competitors, as well as other women pilots, into the "86s." At the time there were eighty-six women pilots certified in the US, and when their number grew to ninety-nine the organization's was renamed the Ninety-Nines—a women's flying association that continues to this day.

THE POWDER PUFF DERBY CONTINUES

After WWII, the All Women's Transcontinental Air Race (AWTAR), better known as the Powder Puff Derby, was renewed with an $8,550 purse for the top ten crews and additional leg prizes for those finishing outside the selected group of ten. In 1977, rising costs, insurance premiums, and reduced corporate sponsorship caused AWTAR to come to an end after thirty years. In 2002, the Air Race Classic was reincorporated with a top ten purse of $15,000. The current race routes are approximately 2,400 miles, and the contestants are usually allowed four days—flying VFR in daylight hours—to reach the finish line. Each plane is allocated a handicap speed, and the objective is to have the actual ground speed be as far over the handicap speed as possible. The pilots are thus given the latitude to play the elements, waiting for better weather, winds, etc., with the intent being to fly the "perfect" cross-country. In this race, the official standings are not released until the final participant has crossed the finish line, meaning the last arrival can actually be the winner.

1930–1935: BELLANCAS CONTINUE TO DOMINATE

1930: A Bellanca CH won the *Detroit Daily News* Efficiency Award at the National Air Races for the third consecutive time, giving Bellanca permanent possession of the trophy.

1931: RUSSELL BOARDMAN AND JOHN POLANDO: WORLD LONG-DISTANCE RECORD

On 24 July 1931, two friends and pilots, Russell Boardman and John Polando, took off from Floyd Bennett Field on their attempt to fly non-stop to Turkey. Boardman's Bellanca Special J-6 monoplane *Cape Cod* had been sent back to the Bellanca factory to be refurbished at a costly $25,000. Soon after take-off the plane's weight was found to be unbalanced and the pilots were forced to jettison most of their 728 gallons of fuel over the Atlantic off New York City and return to Floyd Bennett.

The weight/balance situation was remedied, and the two pilots were ready for their second attempt the morning of 28 July. The same day Clyde Pangborn and Hugh Herndon were to leave Floyd Bennett in their Bellanca to break the around-the-world flight record time set just two weeks earlier by Wiley Post and Harold Gatty. After paying Lindbergh $25,000 for his story the *New York Times* paid these two fliers $2,500 for their exclusive story and to drop sixteen copies of the paper at various points on the trip. They also had a mailbag containing 10,000 postcards they had sold for $2 apiece that were to be mailed from Istanbul. After take-off they flew from New York over Long Island north to Newfoundland through a huge cloud bank where they dropped a *New York Times* to the Harbour Grace Island Lighthouse. They flew uneventfully across the Atlantic to Ireland; proceeded to Paris and Munich; detoured around the Alps at night; and when they landed in Istanbul the early afternoon of 30 July, they only had about fifteen minutes of fuel left in the tank, but now held a new world's record for a distance of 5,011.8 miles over 49:08 hours. Coincidentally, the previous record holders, Costes and Bellonte, happened to be in Istanbul with a French aviation delegation to sell the Turks new military aircraft and briefly met with the new record holders.

Russell Boardman, John Polando, and their Bellanca

While Boardman and Polando's flight was the fourteenth successful crossing of the Atlantic, theirs was the first trans-Atlantic flight in four years—since Lindbergh's New York to Paris flight—to reach the pre-determined destination announced to the press. Upon landing their barograph, which recorded their flight information and was sealed before the flight by an FAI official to prevent tampering, was immediately removed from the aircraft and sent to Paris in a diplomatic pouch to determine whether they broke the record. Their new record remained intact for about eighteen months, when it was broken by Englishmen O.R. Gayford and Gilbert Nicholetts, who flew 5,300 miles from England to South Africa in January 1933. Then Frenchmen Maurice Rossi and Paul Codos recaptured the record when they flew 5,657 miles from New York to Ravak, Syria, in July 1933. In July 1933, two years after his record breaking flight, Boardman died as a result of injuries sustained on take-off in the GeeBee during the cross-country Bendix Cup air race. Polando flew in the 11,123 mile England to Australia 1934 MacRobertson Race, during which Polando and his co-pilot landed in the Persian Desert, where Polando was briefly held captive by Arabs and after flying on had to abandon the race in Calcutta.

1933: STEPHEN DARIUS AND STANLEY GIRENAS TRANS-ATLANTIC FLIGHT

On 15 July 1933, Lithuanian-American pilots Stephen Darius and Stanley Girenas flew their Bellanca CH-300 Pacemaker *Lituanica* from Floyd Bennett Field, intending to fly non-stop to Kaunas, Lithuania. After having successfully made the seventh successful crossing of the Atlantic, the *Lituanica* crashed in Pomerania, Germany, due to undetermined causes on 17 July, killing both pilots.

1934: George Pond and Cesare Sabelli flew their Bellanca J on the eighth trans-Atlantic flight from New York to Lahinch, Ireland.

1934: Benjamin and Joseph Adamowicz flew their Bellanca J *White Falcon* on the ninth trans-Atlantic flight, flying from Newfoundland to Caen, France.

1934: DR. RICHARD LIGHT: AROUND-THE-WORLD FLIER AND PHOTOGRAPHER

Richard Light took flying lessons at Ypsilanti Air Field while attending medical school at the University of Michigan, then postponed his residency to enlist in the Army Air Corps for a year, qualifying as a pilot in 1929. Afterward, he bought a small plane and flew over Central America, becoming known as the "Flying Doctor." By 1934, Dr. Light decided to fly a unique around-the-world flight, and with State Department help he obtained permission to fly over twenty-eight foreign countries. On 20 August 1934, with college friend Robert Wilson, they took off from New Haven, Connecticut, in their Bellanca Skyrocket floatplane. Their flight covered more than 29,000 miles, taking five months, and ended at Long Island on 24 January 1935. They had flown to Iceland, across the North Atlantic to Great Britain, the Netherlands, Denmark, Sweden, Germany, Italy, Greece, Cyprus, Iraq, Iran, India, Thailand, Malaya, Java, Borneo, and the Philippines. Because of distance they shipped the Bellanca across the Pacific to Vancouver, Canada, and flew back to Long Island. In 1937, emulating Charles and Anne Morrow Lindbergh, the newlywed Lights bought a new Bellanca for a planned 35,000 mile, four-month flight to photograph Central America, South America, and Africa,

Dr. Richard Light (L), wife Mary, and their Bellanca Skyrocket floatplane

with wife Mary acting as co-pilot, radio operator, and photographer. They flew along the coasts of Mexico and Central and South America, over the Andes to Rio de Janeiro, and then sailed to Cape Town, South Africa. While in Africa they took an extensive library of photos that were published by the American Geographical Society as a highly regarded book entitled *Focus on Africa*.

FLYING HUTCHINSONS

During 1931, American family Col. George Blanche and daughters Kathryn and Janet Hutchinson became nationwide celebrities as the "Flying Hutchinsons," when they flew to the capitals of all forty-eight United States. The next year the Hutchinsons gained further fame when the newly feted "America's First Flying Family" attempted an around-the-world flight in their Sikorsky S-38, which was decorated with numerous sponsor ads, much like the cars of today's NASCAR drivers. The Sikorsky crash-landed off Greenland and the family was stranded for several days before being rescued by a fishing trawler and transported to the United Kingdom. Their adventures earned them an appearance on the front of a Wheaties box, vaudeville appearances at Loew's State Theater on Broadway, and a year's engagement on the NBC Radio Red Network, where they dramatized their travels. So great was their popularity that more than four million copies of a jigsaw puzzle featuring the Hutchinsons in front of a map showing their route from New York to Europe were distributed by their sponsor Cocomalt. George and Blanche wrote two books about their adventures, *The Flying Family in Greenland* (1935) and *Flying the States* (1937). In the tension-ridden world of Fall 1939, the family attempted another around-the-world flight in a Lockheed Electra; the purpose of their goodwill flight was to carry a scroll with a message of peace to the sixty-eight nations of the world, but this flight only reached Mexico before it was canceled when Germany invaded Poland in September. Despite the early cancellation of the flight an NBC radio dramatization was subsequently produced, starring the family.

The Flying Hutchinsons and their Sikorsky S-38

RICHARD ARCHBOLD

Richard Archbold was a wealthy American zoologist and philanthropist who used his wealth to sponsor, finance, and personally lead three major biological expeditions to New Guinea. During the first New Guinea expedition logistical problems and limitations caused Archbold to consider the use of aircraft for future expeditions, as well as radio for communications. The second 1936–37 Archbold New Guinea expedition used radio, as well as a Fairchild 91 amphibian flying boat; however, the loss of the aircraft at anchor at Port Moresby during a tropical storm limited its use. The third (April 1938–May 1939) and most ambitious Archbold New Guinea expedition used a PBY-2 Catalina flying boat *Guba II*, piloted by Russell Rogers. The Catalina could land on suitable lakes and rivers, providing supplies to the expedition, as well as performing other duties, such as aerial reconnaissance and photography. Toward the end of the expedition in 1939, with Archbold intending to return to the US across the Pacific, Australian representative Capt. P.G. Taylor approached him, wanting him to determine the practicality of an air route with war impending from Australia to Europe over the Indian Ocean and via Africa rather than Asia. At the time *Guba II* was the only available suitable aircraft and Archbold agreed to the project, with Taylor as navigator. The intended route was to cross the Indian Ocean from Western Australia to the Cocos Islands, Diego Garcia, the Seychelles, and Mombasa, Kenya. The flight was made without any significant problems except during the initial leg, when the amphibian was forced to detour via Batavia (now Jakarta) because of bad weather. Taylor left the crew in Mombasa to return to Australia while Archbold continued the flight westward, landing in New York City in July 1939.

Richard Archbold and his PBY-2 Catalina flying boat, *Guba II*

MORE ENDURANCE RECORDS

1928: EDWARD STINSON AND GEORGE HALDEMAN: ENDURANCE RECORD

Edward Stinson was born into a flying family, having two sisters who were also skilled pilots and aviation pioneers. In 1912, sister Kate became the fourth female licensed pilot and set several air records, becoming known as the "Flying Schoolgirl," performing exhibitions in the United States and overseas and becoming the first woman pilot authorized by the Post Office to fly airmail. Katherine and her mother, Emma, founded the Stinson Aviation Company in Hot Springs, Arkansas, in 1913, where they built, sold, and rented aircraft. Stinson's sister Marjorie was the ninth licensed US female pilot and flew as a stunt pilot until 1928, and trained Canadian Air Force cadets during the war.

In 1920, Stinson formed the Stinson Aircraft Company in Dayton, Ohio, and began designing and building aircraft. In 1925, Stinson headed a consortium of Detroit investors forming the Stinson Aircraft Syndicate, which would manufacture a new commercial aircraft, with the prototype SB-1 Detroiter first flying on 21 February 1926. Stinson and George Haldeman flew non-refueled for 53:35 hours over the Jacksonville, Florida, area in a Stinson Detroiter in late March 1928. Thirty-eight-year-old Stinson died in 1932, while attempting an early evening emergency landing on a Chicago golf course after a career of flying 16,000 hours since 1911, which is ostensibly the most air hours by any pilot to that date. During his relatively brief career in aviation Stinson earned the sobriquet "Dean of American Airmen" from his peers, having served in WWI as an instructor and then following his love for flight to become a barnstormer, stunt pilot, instructor, test pilot, airline operator, aircraft inventor and builder, salesman, and manufacturing executive. Stinson's legacy is the L-5 Sentinal built for the US military, with 530 sold in 1939 and 1940 before WWII, when it would be redesigned, with 3,950 L-5s delivered to the military. Stinson's SR-1 to SR-10 Reliant saw service in WWII with 1,327 built 1933–1941.

Edward Stinson and George Haldeman's Stinson Detroiter

1928: WILLIAM BROCK AND EDWARD SCHLEE: ENDURANCE RECORD

Following their successful Atlantic crossing and failed around-the-world attempt in August–September the year before, William Brock and Edward Schlee flew their Bellanca J Pathfinder *Rosemarie* 29 September–1 October 1928 to a non-refueled endurance record of 59:30:01, despite being forced down by a fuel leak while flying over Rockwell Field, San Diego.

During the years after setting this record their small aircraft company went bankrupt during the Depression, and in 1931, their beloved *Pride of Detroit* was sold at auction to satisfy a debt. The following year Brock died of cancer at thirty-six and Schlee drifted into obscurity. The *Pride of Detroit* was saved and is now exhibited at the Henry Ford Museum, Dearborn, Michigan.

William Brock (R) and Edward Schlee flew their Bellanca J to a non-refueled endurance record over San Diego in 1928.

1931: WALTER LEES AND FREDERIC BROSSY ENDURANCE RECORD

From 25–28 May 1931, Walter Lees and Frederic Brossy—two Packard test pilots—flew their Bellanca Pacemaker to a new endurance record on their third attempt. Their Pacemaker was a six-place monoplane with the seats and passenger furnishings removed to provide space for fuel storage. It was powered by a 225 hp Packard DR-980 standard Diesel aircraft engine. The first diesel powered engine was developed by the American Packard Motor Company of Detroit in 1928, in collaboration with German aircraft engineer Hermann Dorner, who was to be a key figure in the development of Nazi Germany's air force. The first flight of the test plane took place in September 1928, and was so successful that Packard rushed the engine into production, building a plant during the first half of 1929 solely for production of its diesel engine, with 500 engines a month manufactured in July 1929. Their record breaking flight marked a significant achievement for the aero-diesel engine, which was designed to compete with the Wright J-5 Whirlwind that powered Lindbergh's *Spirit of St. Louis*. The fuel on this flight was carried in two wing tanks, with five gallon cans placed in the cabin and a detachable belly tank that hung below the fuselage. Fuel was first used from the belly tank, which was dropped when empty. The five gallon cans in the cabin were used next, and as they were emptied they were also dropped overboard, finally leaving the full fuel tanks in the wings. The flight took place over Jacksonville, Florida, for 84:32 hours, breaking Boussoutrot and Rossi's non-refueling record of 75:23:07 set the year before in Oran, Algeria, by 9:10 hours. Rather than risk a hazardous night landing the pilots landed the Bellanca-Diesel at dusk with sufficient fuel in the tanks to have continued at least 8.5 hours longer, or a total endurance of more than 93 hours. Despite breaking the record, the Packard Diesel was unpopular, despite its economy and reliability, due to the unpleasant diesel exhaust fumes and significant vibration when running. A noticeable aspect of the DR-980 was its oil cooler, which was a spiral of metal tubing placed around the propeller shaft. Lees and Brossy's piston-powered aircraft record would officially stand for more than fifty-five years until 14–23 December 1986, when Dick Rutan and Jeana Yeager flew for 216:03:44 in their Rutan *Voyager*.

Walter Lees, Frederic Brossy, and their Bellanca Pacemaker

Walter Lees and Frederic Brossy pose with their Collier Trophy.

1931: CLYDE PANGBORN AND HUGH HERNDON COMPLETE THE FIRST TRANS-PACIFIC FLIGHT

Clyde Pangborn became a pilot in the Army during WWI, and after the war became one of the foremost barnstormers of the 1920s. By the end of the 1920s, growing flight restrictions began to put aviation stunt shows out of business, so the colorful "Upside Down" Pangborn decided to get recognition by breaking records. The first record was to beat the around-the-world speed record held by the German airship *Graf Zeppelin* in 1929, with a time of 20 days, four hours. However, Pangborn needed backing, and he sought help from his wealthy friend Hugh Herndon, who would become his co-pilot. For the flight Pangborn chose a bright red 1931 Bellanca J-300 Long-Distance Special he named *Miss Veedol*, which could carry 696 gallons of fuel. In June 1931, a month before Pangborn and Herndon's planned take-off, Wiley Post and Harold Gatty flew around the world in 8 days, 15:21 hours for a new world record. Nonetheless, Pangborn and Herndon set out to break this new record, leaving Roosevelt Field, Long Island, New York, on 28 July 1931, then flew via northern Europe, Moscow, Siberia, and Japan. Time consuming weather, navigation, and hard landing problems on crude Siberian and Mongolian runways caused Pangborn to abandon their around-the-world effort and he looked for an alternative world record to set. They decided to attempt the first trans-Pacific flight between Japan and the US, which had never been accomplished in an airplane, although the *Graf Zeppelin* had completed the flight in 1929. To add to the flight's attraction Japan was offering the $25,000 "foreigner's prize" offered by *Asahi Shimbun* for the first successful trans-Pacific airplane flight. When *Miss Veedol* was flying to Tokyo the Japanese government accused the two pilots of spying along the route and detained them, but after paying fines and US Embassy negotiations, they were released to fly across the Pacific. During their detainment Pangborn decided the aircraft would be too heavy for the amount of fuel (915 gallons) it could carry and set up a mechanism that would jettison the landing gear after take-off, as he was confident he could belly land safely. The loss of the gear would also reduce drag and extend the Bellanca's range, a concept that Australian Harry Hawker had previously used in 1919, in an unsuccessful attempt to cross the Atlantic.

On 4 October 1931, *Miss Veedol* took off from Sabishiro Beach using a specially prepared wooden runway with a ski run-type launching ramp at the end. The aircraft was loaded much beyond the Bellanca Company's specified maximum operating weight and only barely managed to lift off. Three hours after take-off the landing gear was jettisoned as planned, but two supporting struts remained attached, making a safe belly landing impossible. Pangborn had to crawl out on the wing to manually remove them 14,000 ft. above the Pacific and traveling at 100 mph in freezing weather. After hours of flying over the ocean Pangborn saw an Aleutian volcano that was his first real position check. Through most of the trip Pangborn remained at the controls, with Herndon responsible for transferring fuel via a hand-operated wobble pump from the large auxiliary cabin tank to keep the main wing tanks topped. Herndon forgot twice, but the first time he was able to pump fuel fast enough to keep the engine running. The second time the propeller stopped, and because the Bellanca did not have an electric starter Herndon started to pump furiously as Pangborn steepened the dive, frantically trying to windmill the propeller to start it in the thin air. After losing 13,000 ft. and only 1,500 ft. above the ocean the prop began to windmill in the denser air and the engine started. Although they had intended to land in Spokane, the weather was bad throughout the Northwest, and they belly landed safely at an airfield outside Wenatchee, Washington, after flying 4,500 miles in 41:13 hours and completing the first airplane flight across the Pacific Ocean.

Clyde Pangborn (R) with co-pilot and financial backer Hugh Herndon and their Bellanca J-300 Long-Distance Special *Miss Veedol*

Because Herndon and his mother had been the main financial backers of the flight they kept most of the prize money and the proceeds of sale of *Miss Veedol*. Pangborn only received $2,500, but won the 1931 Harmon Trophy, symbolizing the greatest achievement in flight for that year; he then continued, much as before, as an airmail pilot, air racer, and a test and demonstration pilot. During WWII he used his long distance flying expertise to assist in organizing the RAF Ferry Command, during which time he flew approximately 170 trans-ocean flights. After his discharge from the RAF he continued his career as a commercial pilot, pioneering commercial routes, and logged more than 24,000 flight hours over his forty years of piloting.

FLYING FUEL TANKS: COMMON DENOMINATOR OF RECORD-SETTING FLIGHTS

The common denominator of these record setting flights was they were set by aircraft that were essentially flying fuel tanks. To fly commercially or militarily significant intercontinental flights required the development of very large, multi-engine (preferably four or more) aircraft capable of carrying large payloads of passengers or armament that included large quantities of fuel needed to fly the large aircraft and its heavy load over long distances. Unlike a commercial carrier, the maximum range of a bomber had to be halved (combat radius) to allow the bomber to return safely to base. The answer to extending range seemed to be in-flight refueling.

3
IN-FLIGHT REFUELING: EXTENDING RANGE AND ENDURANCE

As a method of extending the short ranges of contemporary bombers, early experiments in aerial refueling took place in the 1920s, with two slow-flying aircraft flying in formation with a hose and nozzle lowered from a hand-held fuel tank on the upper aircraft; a receiver crewman on the lower aircraft caught the dangling nozzle by hand and plugged it into the standard fuel tank filler and held it in place, hoping there was enough slack until the acrobatic procedure was completed.

12 NOVEMBER 1921: AERIAL REFUELING IS BORN?

On 12 November 1921, Wesley May, an accomplished stunt man and wing walker, was flying as a passenger in pilot Frank Hawk's Lincoln Standard biplane over Long Beach, California, to meet Earl Daugherty in his Curtiss JN-4 Jenny and attempt a stunt they had previously practiced at barnstorming airshows. At 1,000 ft., Hawks would carefully approach the Lincoln while May, with a five gallon can of gasoline strapped to his back, climbed to the top of the right wing and worked his way out to the wingtip. Meanwhile, Daugherty would ease his Jenny close enough above the Lincoln for May to grip the bottom port wing strut on the Jenny. May then pulled himself up onto the top of the lower wing as the two aircraft banked away from each other. May then made his way to the Jenny's front passenger cockpit, where he would have access to the fuel tank behind the engine. May unscrewed the fuel tank cap and carefully poured the fuel into the Jenny's tank before sitting down in the cockpit. The stunt—or first aerial refueling—was documented by a chase aircraft.

27 JUNE 1923: LTS. SMITH AND RICHTER FLY THE FIRST SUCCESSFUL AERIAL REFUELING

The first successful aerial refueling took place on 27 June 1923, when a DH-4B crewed by Lts. Virgil Hine and Frank Seifert dropped a fifty foot hose with manually operated quick-acting valves at each end to refuel another DH-4B crewed by Lts. Lowell Smith and John Richter. During the refueling seventy-five gallons of gasoline was passed from the tanker to the receiver. After only one refueling Smith and Richter landed after 6:38 hours when their aircraft developed engine trouble, but the flight demonstrated the feasibility of in-flight refueling.

Lts. Lowell Smith (L) and John Richter

Wesley May performs the first air-to-air refueling.

DH-4B tanker and receiver biplanes of Lts. Lowell Smith and John Richter

27–28 AUGUST 1923: LTS. SMITH AND RICHTER SET THE WORLD REFUELED ENDURANCE RECORD

On 27–28 August 1923, an endurance record was set by three single-engine DH-4B biplanes: a receiver aircraft flown by Lts. Lowell Smith and John Richter; tanker #1 flown by Capt. Robert Erwin and 1Lt. Oliver McNeel; and tanker #2 flown by 1Lts. Frank Seifert and Virgil Hine. The flight took off at 0504 on 27 August, and ended at 1830 the next day, remaining aloft for 37:15 hours and flying about 3,200 miles using nine mid-air fuel transfers of 687 gallons (about seventy-five gallons each time) of aviation gasoline and thirty-eight gallons of engine oil, plus food and water

25 OCTOBER 1923: LTS. SMITH AND RICHTER FLY TRANSCONTINENTAL USING AERIAL REFUELING

On 25 October 1923, Lts. Lowell Smith and John Richter flew their DH-4B from Sumas, Washington, on the Canadian border, to Tijuana, Mexico, then landing in San Diego after 12 hours (a distance of 1,250 miles) after being refueled over Eugene, Oregon, and Sacramento, California, by their August refueling teams. An accident the next month put an end to their refueling trials. (Note: Lowell Smith also piloted the Douglas World Cruiser *Chicago*, which, along with one other DWC, made the first aerial circumnavigation in 1924. Smith held sixteen records for military aircraft in speed, endurance, and distance, and was awarded the Mackay Trophy twice for best annual achievement in flight.)

1–4 JUNE 1928: BELGIANS SET A NEW ENDURANCE AERIAL REFUELED RECORD

From 2–4 June 1928, Adjutant Louis Crooj and Sgt. Victor Groenen established a new endurance record of 2 days, 12:07 hours (60:07 hours) while flying their De Havilland DH-9 over Tirlemont, Belgium.

1929: A YEAR OF RECORD AERIAL REFUELED ENDURANCE FLIGHTS

JANUARY 1929: FUTURE AAF VIPS FLY TO A NEW WORLD REFUELED ENDURANCE RECORD

From 1–7 January 1929, the Fokker C-2 tri-motor transport *Question Mark*, whose iconic crew, including Maj. Carl Spaatz, Capt. Ira Eaker, Lt. Elwood Quesada, 1Lt. Harry Halverson, and Sgt. Roy Hooe, would establish a world record for an endurance flight while flying a 110 mile loop over Southern California. The Douglas C-1-C Refueling Airplane No. 1 (at Rockwell) was crewed by pilots Capt. Ross Hoyt and 1Lt. Auby Strickland, with 2Lt. Irwin Woodring manning the hose reel. Refueling Airplane No. 2 (at Van Nuys) was crewed by pilots 1Lt. Odas Moon and 2Lt. Joseph Hopkins, with 2Lt. Andrew Solter at the hose. The Fokker was named *Question Mark*, as when crew members were asked how long they intended to stay aloft they would answer that was the question, so a large question mark was painted on both sides of the fuselage, piquing the interest of the press even more and promising much needed publicity for the still fledging air force.

The two Douglas C-1s alternated refueling by lowering a hose through a trapdoor in the top of *Question Mark*, transferring 5,660 gallons of fuel and 245 gallons of oil during the thirty-seven refuelings and furnishing food and water six other times (twelve of the forty-three hook ups occurred at night). Hoyt, piloting Refueling Airplane No. 1 from Rockwell and a backup airport in Imperial, California, resupplied *Question Mark* twenty-seven times (ten at night), while Moon's refueler from Van Nuys flew sixteen sorties (two at night). Because of the undependability and additional weight of air-to-air radios none of the three aircraft carried them. The aircrews communicated with hand and flashlight signals, notes dropped to the ground, and by messages written on blackboards carried in the planes, while ground panels helped to relay signals to the aircraft above.

The addition of two 150 gallon tanks increased the Fokker's total fuel capacity to 580 gallons. The refueling technique necessitated both aircraft fly a straight course at 80 mph, with the refueling aircraft approaching from the rear, flying slightly above and ahead of *Question Mark,* and sustaining a separation of about thirty feet. The Douglas C-1C extended the hose to Spaatz, who was dressed in a raincoat, face mask, goggles, and gloves to protect him from any spilled gasoline and the slipstream. He would seize the end of the hose, ground the copper wire against the copper plate, and then insert the hose nozzle into the receptacle. On his signal the tanker crew would open the valve, allowing fuel to flow at the rate of seventy-five gallons per minute. During one nighttime refueling, while not wearing his raincoat, the hose separated from the tank and Spaatz was covered with gasoline. The quick thinking Spaatz hastily stripped off his flight clothes and wiped off the toxic liquid before it harmed his skin, which would have required him to bail out to seek medical care.

Although the Fokker was flown at low cruising speeds to conserve its engines, eventually they became strained from extended use, with the port engine losing power early on the third day. To lubricate the straining engines Hooe taped his flapping trouser cuffs, strapped on a parachute, fixed a lifeline to himself, and serviced the engines from the makeshift catwalks. Nonetheless, after a while the cylinders began missing, and Eaker shortened the flying circuits to remain within gliding distance of Van Nuys in case the engines shut down. During the afternoon of 7 January, the port engine seized and Hooe ventured out on the catwalk to attempt repairs, immobilizing

Fokker C-2 tri-motor transport *Question Mark* refueled by a Douglas C-1.

the windmilling propeller with a rubber hook. The aircraft continued to lose power and descended, and Hooe returned inside. *Question Mark* landed under power at Metropolitan Airport at 1406, after spending 150:40:14 hours and more than 11,000 miles in the air. In all, the flight broke existing world records for sustained flight (heavier-than-air), refueled flight, sustained flight (lighter-than-air), and distance. America had regained the endurance record from the Belgians.

In his report to Chief of Air Corps James Fechet, Spaatz stated that aerial refueling was "both safe and practical, and that for bombardment operations made potential radius of action almost unlimited while allowing heavier bomb loads to be carried because the weight of fuel at take-off could be reduced." Despite *Question Mark's* unquestionable success and the palpable military potential of in-flight refueling, somehow the Army, and even some of its future leaders, could not find any reason for continuing aerial refueling tests. After the publicity value had been wrung out of the feat the War Department, which regarded the flight as little more than a stunt, deemed that little could be gained by breaking the Army's own endurance record. Thus, aerial refueling trials were abandoned until mid-1943, when a half-hearted trial was resurrected using a B-24D Tanker and a B-17E Receiver at Eglin Field, Florida.

Crew of the *Question Mark*: (L-R) Sgt. Roy Hooe, Lt. Elwood Quesada, 1Lt. Harry Halverson, Capt. Ira Eaker, and Maj. Carl Spaatz

MAY 1929: ROBBINS AND KELLY SET A NEW REFUELED ENDURANCE RECORD

Beginning on 19 May and ending on 26 May 1929, Reginald Robbins and co-pilot James Kelly landed their Ryan Brougham monoplane *Fort Worth* at Meacham Field—Fort Worth, Texas', municipal field—after an endurance flight of 172:31 hours and 12,900 miles, surpassing the record of the Army-sponsored *Question Mark* by nearly a day. They were finally forced to land by a cracked propeller after seventeen fuel contacts by Jimmie Mattern (refueling pilot), who transferred 1,510 gallons. During the flight Kelly lubricated the engine rocker arms by climbing out the left hand window, using a safety belt and edging his way along a catwalk welded to the fuselage. The pilots were greeted by a crowd of 40,000 people at the airport and an additional 75,000 along the roads and highways around Meacham Field.

Reginald Robbins (L) and co-pilot James Kelly

JULY–SEPTEMBER 1929: THE ENDURANCE RECORD BROKEN THREE TIMES IN TWO MONTHS

Mitchell and Newcomb

After taking off on 30 June 1929, Roy Mitchell and Byron Newcomb landed their single-engine Stinson Detroiter monoplane, *The City of Cleveland,* at Cleveland Airport on 6 July, having been aloft for 174:00 hours, but this record was not recognized as an official record by FAI because it did not exceed the previous record by at least one percent.

Mendell and Reinhart

Also during 2–12 July, pilot Loren Mendell and co-pilot Roland "Pete" Reinhart closed out a 246:43 hour flight in their old Buhl Airsedan *Angeleno* in Culver City, California. The duo was "forced down" when trash they had thrown out became entangled in the empennage and caused the *Angeleno* to have control problems preventing the precise formation flight required with their refueling aircraft. After their record was broken the two attempted to regain it beginning in September 1930, flying a Zenith high-wing monoplane named *Pride of Hollywood.* They took off on four different occasions to attempt to set the record, but each of the attempts ended early due to engine problems, with the longest flight lasting only sixty-six hours. Mendell later served with the US Treasury Department as a patrol pilot to detect liquor smuggling, but later he was arrested for smuggling illegal aliens into the US from Mexico and served a year in a Los Angeles jail. He was killed on 17 January 1935, while flying in fog, and crashed into a mountainside north of Los Angeles. Reinhart flew for Delta Airlines, retiring as a Convair 880 captain in 1962, then joined Convair as a B-58 Hustler test pilot; he also flew the F-111.

Jackson and O'Brine

During 13–30 July 1929, a Curtiss Robin piloted by Dale Jackson and Forest O'Brine stayed aloft in the St. Louis area for 420:21 hours. Supposedly they only landed because they had to attend the funeral of a good friend.

Hunter Brothers

On 30 September 1929, brothers John and Kenneth Hunter attempted to surpass the Jackson-O'Brine endurance record flying a Stinson SM-1 Detroiter named *Chicago We Will*. After eleven days they had to discontinue their flight when a heavy fog made it impossible to refuel their Stinson.

TOP TO BOTTOM /

Roy Mitchell (L) and Byron Newcomb
Loren Mendell and Roland Reinhart's Buhl Airsedan *Angeleno* being refueled.
Dale Jackson (L) and Forest O'Brine

FIRST ROUND-TRIP TRANSCONTINENTAL NON-STOP REFUELED FLIGHT: MAMER AND WALKER

Between 15–21 August 1929, a Buhl Airsedan named *Spokane Sun God* was the first aircraft to complete a non-stop US transcontinental round-trip flight when Nick Mamer (pilot) and Art Walker (mechanic) flew it more than 7,200 miles from Spokane, Washington, to New York City and returned, taking 120:01:40 hours and eleven in-flight refuelings.

Mamer and Walker ran a Spokane-Portland-Seattle passenger airline and obtained the backing of Buhl and Texaco for their proposed journey. Mamer found that the logistics for the coast-to-coast deployment of the refueling aircraft difficult and somewhat ambiguous, as none of the scheduled refueling aircraft had radios, and their pilots would have to communicate by notes dropped in flight, by messages chalked on blackboards and held up in cockpit windows, or by plain arm waving and gestures. Refueling schedules set up previously could become unreliable and difficult due to weather, overcast, bad timing, and the inability of the refueler to find them. The *Sun God* would have to completely rely on the refuelers' punctuality.

The *Sun God* left Spokane the evening of 15 April, and headed west along the Columbia River to the Pacific, then south down the coast to San Francisco, where they refueled the next morning, then turned east across country. At their next scheduled refueling the refueler was contacted only after prolonged searching and circling. Fuel deliveries improved the next day over Cleveland, and when the Buhl arrived in Armonk, New York, it was convoyed to Roosevelt Field, Long Island, where it took on more fuel and dropped an air mail letter from San Francisco's Mayor, "Sunny Jim" Rolph, to New York's Jimmie Walker. Afterward, the Buhl headed west with renowned Texaco representative Frank Hawks leading the way across the Alleghenies to Cleveland. During the flight the crew used the restroom, consisting of a round, life-preserver shaped cushion laid over a trap door in the cabin floor. The flight went well until the Buhl was over South Dakota, when the engine began to vibrate, the scheduled refueler was lost, and visibility was near zero due to heavy smoke from forest fires in the mountains ahead of them. The engine calmed down as they continued through the night, and at dawn on the final day, Mamer's old cowboy friend from Miles City flew alongside with his front cockpit packed with five gallon milk cans filled with gasoline, which were lowered safely to be emptied into the Buhl for the final leg home. Once over Spokane Mamer and Walker circled in the Buhl while they shaved, changed clothes, and watched their own company Ford Tri-Motor bring twelve sight-seers to greet them at $5 per trip. The *Sun God* landed just as the sun went down with a new transcontinental round trip record.

Pilot Nick Mamer (L), mechanic Art Walker, and their Buhl Airsedan *Spokane Sun-God*

AMERICANS CONTINUE TO SET ENDURANCE RECORDS

1930: Hunter Brothers

The next year, the four Hunter brothers (John, Kenneth, Albert, and Walter) purchased a Stinson SM-1 Detroiter and named it *City of Chicago*. On 11 June 1930, John and Kenneth Hunter took off from Sky Harbor Airport in Northbrook, Illinois, for another attempt on the endurance record using the experience gained from the 1929 attempt. Albert and Walter were to fly *Big Ben*, the refueling Stinson that initially made refueling about every six hours, but after a week refueling contacts were increased to every three hours due to a leak in one of the fuel tanks in the "endurance plane." On 29 June, the *City of Chicago* surpassed the O'Brine-Jackson endurance record with John flying low over Sky Harbor Airport and Kenneth standing on the catwalk, waving to a crowd estimated to be about 75,000 people. On 4 July, John and Kenneth had experienced problems all day, as an oil screen in the motor clogged and the engine began to heat due to lack of oil. After having been airborne for 553:41:30 hours they landed, establishing a new record.

The four Hunter brothers (John, Kenneth, Albert, and Walter) purchased the Stinson SM-1 Detroiter *City of Chicago*.

1930: Jackson and O'Brine

On 21 July 1930, after their record was broken, Jackson and O'Brine flew from St. Louis' Lambert Field in a new Curtiss Robin named *The Greater St. Louis* and remained in the air for 647:26 hours (almost twenty-seven days), with their Robin refueled forty-eight times. The National Aeronautic Association denied their record claim, as Jackson and O'Brine failed to complete their logs and other official procedures.

Jackson and O'Brine's Curtiss Robin *The Greater St. Louis* being refueled.

1935: Key Brothers

It was not until 1935, when the Key brothers (Fred and Al) demonstrated a spill-free refueling nozzle designed by A. D. Hunter. Flying over Meridian, Michigan, 4 June–1 July 1935, the two brothers flew a Curtiss Robin monoplane named *The Ole Miss* to surpass the Hunter brothers' record by nearly one hundred hours. The Key brothers endured many trials and tribulations during their more than twenty-seven days of flight.

The brothers flew the Robin over the field hourly in a predetermined orbit, and when enough fuel remained for two orbits (to give a second chance at refueling if the first failed), the refueling aircraft would take off to rendezvous with the Keys at an altitude (usually 3,000 ft.) predetermined by VHF radio before take-off. James Keeton, the refueling pilot, orbited inside the wider orbit of the Keys' Robin and then closed to ten to fifteen feet above and ahead of *Ole Miss*. At this point refueler William Ward would lower the hose for attachment. If the hose pulled out, which frequently occurred, the Keys' new mechanical cut-off valve connecter halted all fuel flow instantly. Usually there were four or five daily aerial refueling operations, including drops of food and drink packed by the Keys' wives and replacement oil. On 22 June, brother Al radioed he had a bad toothache and a dentist was consulted to gather dental supplies to be lowered to Fred, who was to administer to Al midair. Fortunately an abscess appeared and Fred trimmed the Robin for straight and level flight, then Fred was able to easily lance Al's abscess and the duo continued their flight. Maintenance and oil changes were required while the flight continued. To change oil, Fred would move out on to a catwalk welded on the aircraft's nose to drain and fill with replacement oil as the engine turned nearby. After almost three weeks in the air they surpassed the record and were cheered by thousands as they made a low fly-by to celebrate. The brothers gained more press attention over the next days and Meridian airfield was renamed Key Field. On 29 June, the flight almost came to a tragic end when one of the metal oil cans came in contact with some exposed electrical wiring during the time it was being lowered during refueling, causing a short circuit. A fire flared and threatened to explode the newly filled fuel tanks, so pilot Al cut the engine and Fred barely managed to extinguish the flames as Al pulled out of a dive, restarting the engine at less than one hundred feet from the ground. On 1 July, a storm damaged the stabilizer, forcing the brothers to end their record flight after 653:34 hours in the air flying 52,000 miles. *Ole Miss* had been refueled more than one hundred times, transferring more than 6,000 gallons of fuel and oil and 400 containers of supplies, food, water, toiletries, and fresh clothing.

Fred and Al Key and their Curtiss Robin *The Ole Miss*

1939: Carroll and Schlieper

The last prewar endurance record was set in 1939, during 1–30 October, when Wes Carroll and Clyde Schlieper flew their Piper Cub seaplane *Spirit of Kay* for 726 hours over Long Beach, California. The plane was refueled in an unusual manner, as a convertible drove along the runway and a man holding a five gallon can of gasoline (and also bags of food and water) would attach it to a line with a hook that was dropped from the aircraft to be pulled up into the plane.

Wes Carroll, Clyde Schlieper, and their Piper Cub *Spirit of Kay*

BRITISH PREWAR REFUELING TRIALS

The American success in aerial refueling inspired Europeans to perform similar trials. In France during December 1925, Capt. Pierre Weiss and Adj. Van Caudenburg of Aviation Militaire conducted numerous successful trials and demonstrations of aerial refueling that seem to have been discontinued for unspecified reasons. During June 1925, the Royal Air Force directed the Royal Aircraft Establishment (RAE) at Farnborough to explore the potential of aerial refueling, but it would not be until February 1926 that two Bristol fighter aircraft were modified for trials. During these trials only water was transferred between the two aircraft, and although considered successful, no further trials were planned.

Despite all of the manic American activity of the time, aerial refueling technology had not advanced significantly past the unwieldy and dangerous hose-dangling technique. In the early

1930s, the RAF was again interested in aerial refueling, not as a means to extend an aircraft's range, but to reduce take-off weights, especially since the League of Nations was considering bomber size restrictions and less fuel on take-off meant more bombs could be carried by aircraft. Britain's Royal Aircraft Establishment (RAE) was also experimenting with in-flight refueling, intending to use the technique to extend the range of the long-distance flying boats servicing the British Empire.

In 1930, RAF Squadron Leader (later Air Marshal) Richard Atcherley was attending the US National Air Races, where he observed aerial refueling and appreciated its potential for military and civil users. Once he returned to England and the RAE in 1931, he began to develop a safer and more reliable method using two Vickers Virginias by eliminating the role of the observer in the receiver, substituting as the Cross-Over-Contact Method. Using this method involved trailing a horizontal line that ended in a grapnel from the tail of the receiver. Then the tanker, trailing a weighted line, would fly side-to-side above and astern of the receiving aircraft below. Once contact was made between the two lines the refueling hose would be passed from tanker to receiver by hauling in the receiver's line. Atcherley submitted this refueling proposal to the Air Ministry, which considered it not an improvement over existing methods. In 1934, while deployed to the Middle East, he developed and patented the Looped Hose Method. In this method, the receiving aircraft trailed a long horizontal line with a grapnel at the end. The tanker trailed a weighted line and approached the receiver from behind and to one side. It then crossed to the other side, causing the two lines to cross and touch. The receiver aircraft then hauled in the lines and hose from the tanker. The RAF continued to refine this system, including adding a drogue to the hose that created drag and assisted in unspooling the hose in flight. (A drogue is a special type of parachute that was used to ensure the hose trailed behind the tanker and did not thrash about.) In March 1935, Atcherley's technique was successfully tested using a Westland Wallace and Hawker Hart, and was to be incorporated in the design specification of future aircraft, but again, no further action was taken.

In 1932, Sir Alan Cobham, an experienced long-distance aviator, realized that long distance flights necessitated stocks of fuel be placed along the route, requiring months of planning. Aerial refueling during long distance flights could drastically reduce the time to complete them by the positioning of tankers in suitably based locations, making non-stop flights a likelihood. During take-offs for long distance flights the aircraft was always heavily loaded with fuel, and considering the unreliability of engines of the time, a catastrophic, fiery crash was always a distinct possibility. Cobham maintained that taking off carrying minimum fuel and then refueling when safely airborne could greatly reduce this risk. Cobham began trails using two de Havilland DH.9s.

Sir Alan Cobham, the "Father of Modern Aerial Refueling"

Meanwhile, Mrs. Victor Bruce, record breaking auto and speedboat racer and around-the-world aviator, had plans to attempt to set the world's in-flight refueled endurance record. In July 1932, she purchased a Saro Windhover amphibious aircraft to be the receiver aircraft and named it *City of Portsmouth*, and also purchased a Bristol F.2 and had it converted as a refueling tanker. During August 1932, Bruce and her co-pilot, FLt. John Pugh, flew the two aircraft over the Solent in three failed attempts to break the world flight-refueled endurance record, but the longest flight was terminated short of the record after 54:13 hours due to engine lubrication problems.

Cobham continued his experiments into 1934, when he purchased Atcherley's in-flight refueling system and founded Flight Refueling Ltd. (FRL) on 29 October 1934, carrying out air-to-air refueling experiments from Portsmouth. With some modifications and continuous improvement of technique Cobham developed the first practical refueling system. In his system a receiver aircraft trailed a steel cable which was then grappled by a line dropped from the Handley Page W10 tanker flying in tandem, and the line was then drawn back into the tanker, where the receiver's cable was connected to the refueling hose. The receiver could then haul back its cable, bringing the hose to it. Once the hose was connected, the tanker climbed sufficiently above the receiver aircraft to allow fuel to flow by gravity feed. On 22 September 1934, Cobham and observer S/L William Helmore attempted to fly non-stop from Portsmouth, England, to Karachi, India, in his modified Airspeed Courier to be refueled by a Handley Page W10 that Cobham purchased from Imperial Airways. Initially carrying one hundred gallons of fuel, the Courier was to be refueled en route, collecting a further eighty gallons from the Handley Page on the approach to Malta and then proceeding to the next refueling point. The throttle linkage of the Courier failed, causing the flight to be abandoned with Cobham gliding to an almost powerless, but safe, wheels-up landing.

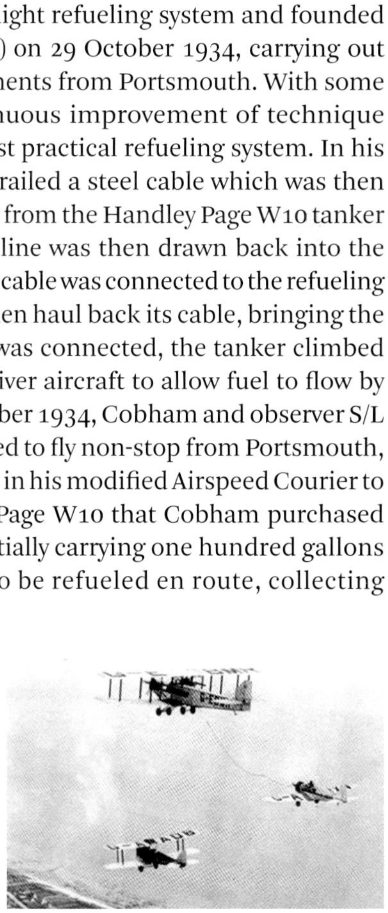

Cobham's Airspeed Courier being refueled by a Handley Page W-10.

In 1934, Flight Refueling Ltd. (FRL) was incorporated as a company for experimental development work on in-flight refueling sponsored by Imperial Airways and Shell Oil, with Cobham to remain as its director. Flight Refueling Ltd. moved to Ford Aerodrome, Sussex, where it assumed Atcherley's work on the cross-over contact system at the Royal Aircraft Establishment in Farnborough. This partnership was successful, as it resulted in the implementation of their ideas into the Looped Hose Method, in which the receiver trailed a hauling line terminating in a sinker weight and pawl, while the tanker flew to the side of, and below, the receiver, with the tanker then firing a line with a contactor hook that optimistically crossed over the receiver's hauling line and engaged the pawl grapnel. The tanker then hauled in the receiver's hauling line and climbed above the receiver; while the remaining contactor hook was fully hauled in the hook and the sinker weight were removed from the hauling line and the refueling hose was connected to it. Once this was accomplished, the receiver hauled in the refueling hose until the nozzle engaged the receiver's coupling. The tanker and receiver would then fly in formation during the fuel transfer. On completion, the receiver would again trail the released hauling line and refueling hose. After a certain length had been trailed the tanker would then climb and turn away from the receiver, causing a weak link in the hauling line to break and achieving the refueling and disconnection. A number of trials were carried out on behalf of Imperial Airways and the Air Ministry, including various experiments with Vickers B19/17 tankers and Boulton Paul Overstrand aircraft as receivers.

In 1935, Imperial Airways became increasingly interested in in-flight refueling, and discussions were held on the possibility of using the system on some of the Empire routes and projected trans-Atlantic crossings. Imperial Airways entered into an agreement with the company for further development of the methods and equipment while the Air Ministry continued to support developmental work in good faith by providing two Virginias. During Summer 1936, the progress made with the two Virginia aircraft was sufficient to accomplish a "most convincing" demonstration of flight refueling for the benefit of Imperial Airways directors.

It was anticipated that early trans-Atlantic flights would be conducted by flying boats, but this was not to be. Pan American Airways' Clipper Ships had been flying Latin American and Pacific routes for several years, but it was not until July 1937 that Imperial Airways was ready with two flying boats (the *Caledonia* and *Cambria*) to cross the Atlantic. These two Short C-Class Empire-type flying boats could only fly 760 miles with a full payload—nowhere near the 3,300 miles of an Atlantic crossing. Nevertheless, the two flying boats were delivered unfurnished to save weight and had six extra fuel tanks installed in the wings and hull to enable the required range. The *Caledonia* made her first experimental crossing from Foynes, Ireland, to Botwood, Newfoundland, on 5 July 1937, and before the beginning of October, the *Caledonia* had completed six crossings and the *Cambria* four. While these flights demonstrated the Atlantic could be crossed non-stop, the Short Flying Boats had no payload or passenger carrying capability, so further research and experiments were necessary.

In January 1938, trials were conducted at Hamble using the discarded (by the RAF) single prototype Armstrong Whitworth AW 23 transport (later to become known as the Whitley bomber) as the tanker and an Empire Flying Boat as the receiver. The data collected in all weather conditions concluded that refueling could be used to operate air transport service, and in 1939 Atlantic service began.

At the time Imperial Airways Empire Flying Boats were able to fly a trans-Atlantic service via Ireland and Newfoundland only with increased fuel capacities, and thus with reduced payloads. To increase payloads, experimental fuel transfer from Handley Page Harrows (Handley Page 51s, prototype Harrow bombers) to an Empire Flying Boat receiver aircraft were conducted. Flight Refueling Ltd. bought three Harrow bombers in February and March 1939, and modified them as tankers by adding an extra 1,000 Imperial gallons in internal fuel tanks and the necessary valves and nozzles for controlling rapid fuel transfer through long hoses which could be reeled out and back by powered winches. The function of these tankers was not to increase the range of the receiver, but instead to increase the payload. Because the tanker flew above, ahead, and slightly starboard of the receiver, it was difficult to observe the procedure, so large windows were added to the port side of the tanker's fuselage fabric. In the meantime, the flying boats were modified and their crews were given about four hours flying experience of the process. During this part of the program seventeen flights were conducted—many in extremely bad weather conditions—during January 1938, and were totally successful.

As the trans-Atlantic operation would require two refuelings on the westward crossing it was necessary to provide refueling stations and extra tanker aircraft: the two stations were to be Foynes, Ireland, and Botwood, Newfoundland. Three tanker aircraft were required to complete the operation and the Handley Page Harrow bomber was selected. In early 1939, Hugh Johnson gathered the three aircraft from Handley Page Ltd. for conversion into tankers. During the Harrow conversion attempts were made to improve the refueling technique by installing two horns on the nose of one aircraft, enabling the pilot to catch the receiver's hauling cable. This new method, called the Cobham Trip System, was flown in trials, but was eventually replaced when Cobham suggested a line-throwing gun to fire the tanker's contact line across the receiver's hauling line, making the revised looped hose system more foolproof and practically ensuring a safe contact during each attempt. The Harrow conversion consisted of three cargo fuel tanks mounted amidships in the fuselage with a capacity of 125 Imperial gallons of fuel in each tank. These were connected to the aircraft's inboard wing tanks, which could then be fed via a main fuel valve through the rear cargo tank to the hose drum unit. The hose drum unit was toward the forward end of the fuselage on the aircraft's center line and beneath the forward cargo tank; forward of this were the hose guide roller, a manually operated winch, and the hauling line reel; above the hose drum unit and forward of the front cargo tank was the hose drum driving winch, which was also manually operated when winding in the refueling hose on the completion of an operation. The hose drum winch also controlled the trailing speed of the refueling hose via a manually operated brake. To the rear of the aircraft was the line throwing gun, mounted on the port side of the fuselage. To enable the contact line to be attached to the contact winch, the line ran from the winch to the line throwing gun externally beneath the fuselage, and was held in position via contact line catches. When the hose was not in use, though ready for operation, it ran forward from the hose drum on to the hose guide roller, thence externally of the fuselage, the nozzle of which was then secured in a locking vice beneath the hauling line winch. Besides the capacity of the 375 (Imp.) gallon cargo fuel tanks, the aircraft's inboard wing tanks contained another 968 (Imp.) gallons, thus providing a total of 1,343 (Imp.) gallons; of this total 960 (Imp.) gallons were available for transfer to a receiver, and 150 (Imp.) gallons were available from the cargo fuel tanks to supply the aircraft's engines. One Harrow tanker was based in Rineanna (now Shannon), Ireland, and the two other Harrows were shipped as deck cargo to Montreal and were then uncrated and reassembled by Fairchild Aircraft, then flown to Hattie's Camp (later Gander), along with personnel and spare parts. After extensive testing, the first success occurred on 5 August 1939, when a weekly service from Southampton to New York was begun, with the two Imperial Airways Short S-30 Empire flying boats *Cabot* and *Caribou* relying on the Harrow tankers. The two flying boats flew westbound on the Southampton-Foynes-Botwood-Montreal-New York route, refueling in the air twice: once over Ireland and once over Newfoundland.

The service was terminated at the end of September 1939 by WWII after sixteen—once weekly in each direction—completed trans-Atlantic flights. Fifteen refueling operations were successful, with the other crossing having refueling unnecessary because there was a very strong westerly wind. The average time between tanker/receiver contact—the dropping and connecting of the refueling hose—was five minutes, while the transfer of 800 (Imp.) gallons of fuel was usually completed in seven to eight minutes. The conclusions of these flights were:

1) The refueling equipment was adequate and required no major modification, although the addition of a flow meter was "very desirable." Mechanization of the units would save manpower.
2) The tankers required adequate "wireless" and "must be fitted with homing and blind landing sets."
3) The Harrows were adequate for refueling the Empire Boats, but for larger and faster airliners it would be necessary to have more advanced tankers.

After the outbreak of the war the Empire Flying Boats were pressed into service by the RAF and were destroyed in Norway on 1 May 1940. Two Harrows remained at Gander, while the other, along with the Armstrong Whitworth 23, were destroyed at home base in Sussex in June 1940, during a Nazi bombing attack.

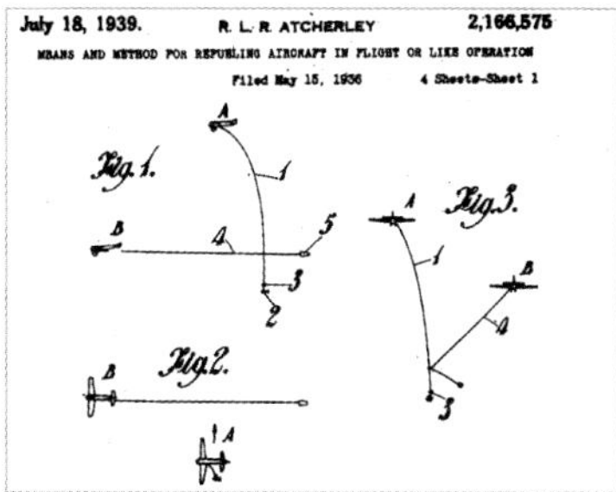

TOP / Handley Page Harrow tanker

BOTTOM LEFT / Imperial Airways Short S-30 Empire flying boat *Cabot* being refueled by a Handley Page Harrow tanker.

BOTTOM RIGHT / Richard Atcherley's patent for his inflight refueling system

IN-FLIGHT REFUELING FADES AS WAR BREAKS OUT

By 1939, the AAC considered aerial refueling a fad or stunt akin to flag pole sitting that lasted a decade after their 1929 *Question Mark* aerial refueling trials without resulting in any significant advancements that could be utilized by military aircraft. The development of improved engines and all-metal monoplane bombers like the B-17 and B-24, which were capable of longer and sufficient range for their intended mission, postponed further military interest in aerial refueling.

What these refueled flights using small aircraft had accomplished, beyond confirming pilot stamina and skill, was validate the innovative concept of in-flight fueling teams. Also, in-flight refueling proved the ability of aircraft engines, particularly radial air-cooled engines coming online, to be able to operate continuously and reliably for very long periods. Not only were pilots and engines being tested and proven, the low-wing, all-metal airframes offered a new era of aircraft design. This decade of almost frantic in-flight refueling trials would fade during WWII, but would be resurrected afterward to become a vital part of Cold War strategic bombing strategy.

MAYO-COMPOSITE PICK-A-BACK: AN ALTERNATIVE TO IN-FLIGHT REFUELING

As discussed, Short Brothers had built Empire Flying Boats able to operate over the long-range routes across the extensive British Empire, but could only attempt the trans-Atlantic route by replacing passenger and mail carrying space with extra fuel. A Short C-Class Empire S.21 Flying Boat was to be adapted to be the lower carrier *Maia*, while the smaller, high-winged, four-engined Short S.20 floatplane *Mercury* was designed to be mounted pick-a-back on and above *Maia*. When they were in the pick-a-back configuration they were known as the Mayo-Composite, for its originator, General Manager of Imperial Airways Maj. R. H. Mayo, and Short's Chief Designer Arthur Gouge. The idea of the composite was to use the combined power of both aircraft to bring the smaller top aircraft to operational altitude, at which time the two aircraft would separate, with the carrier aircraft returning to base, while the other flew on to its destination. The British Air Ministry issued Specification 13/33 to this project.

Although generally similar to the Empire Flying Boat, *Maia* differed considerably in detail: the hull sides were flared rather than being vertical as on the Empire to increase the planing surface (necessary for higher take-off weights); larger control surfaces; an increase in total wing area from 1,500 sq. ft. to 1,750 sq. ft.; four 920 hp Bristol Pegasus XC radial engines were mounted further from the wing root to clear Mercury's floats; and the rear fuselage was swept up to raise the tailplane relative to the wing. Like the Empire boats, *Maia* could be equipped to carry eighteen passengers. *Maia* first flew (without *Mercury*) on 27 July 1937, piloted by Shorts' Chief Test Pilot John Parker.

The upper component *Mercury* was a twin-float, four-engine seaplane crewed by a single pilot and navigator who sat in tandem in an enclosed cockpit. It could carry 1,000 lbs. of mail and 1,200 (Imp.) gallons of fuel. Flight controls, except for elevator and rudder trim tabs, were locked in neutral until separation. *Mercury's* first flight, also piloted by Parker, occurred on 5 September 1937.

The *Mercury* was designed to be placed on four supports mounted on the upper surface of *Maia's* central fuselage—two to each float—with the location being a ball and cup, with two further ball and cups in a structural box beam in *Mercury's* lower fuselage. Both the upper and lower aircraft of the composite were initially flown separately to determine handling and performance characteristics, all of which were proven satisfactory. On 1 January 1938, the two aircraft were positioned in the composite configuration and completed their first water taxiing trial. By February, the experimental trials were successful and flight trials were ready to begin. The first successful in-flight separation was conducted from the Shorts works in Borstal on 6 February 1938, with *Maia* flown by test pilot John Parker and *Mercury* by Harold Piper. A public demonstration was held to great fanfare on 23 February 1938, with the separation occurring at a height of 700 ft.

However, it was still necessary to demonstrate the composite's capability of crossing the Atlantic non-stop with a sufficient payload. During the trials the *Mercury's* engines showed a high fuel consumption rate that would not meet the necessary absolute range requirement of 3,000 nautical miles and the engines were changed to four 365 hp Napier Rapier VI 16-cylinder engines. *Mercury*, flown by Capt. Donald Bennett, was launched from *Maia*, flown by Capt. A.S. Wilcockson, over Foynes (now Shannon), Ireland, on 1 July 1938, carrying 600 lbs. of mail and landing in Montreal, having flown 2,900 miles in 20:22 hours. As well as carrying *Mercury*, *Maia* also carried ten passengers and luggage. *Mercury's* flight was the first commercial non-stop east-to-west trans-Atlantic flight by a heavier-than-air aircraft. The Mayo-Composite continued in use with Imperial Airways, including *Mercury* flying to Alexandria, Egypt, in December 1938. After modifications to extend *Mercury's* range it subsequently established a record flight for a seaplane on 6–8 October 1938, when *Mercury* was launched over Dundee, Scotland, headed to Alexander Bay, South Africa, establishing an as yet (2015) unbroken non-stop international seaplane distance record of 6,045 miles.

Though the 1938 trials disclosed the composite configuration could fly non-stop across the Atlantic, it was also found to be unprofitable, due to *Mercury's* time-consuming empty return flight that also necessitated landing in Foynes, Ireland.

No matter the outcome of the program, it was canceled due to the outbreak of the war. *Maia* was severely damaged by the German bombing on Poole Harbour on 11 May 1941, and subsequently sank. *Mercury* was transferred to 320 (Netherlands) RAF Squadron, and when this squadron was re-equipped with Lockheed Hudsons during August 1941, *Mercury* was scrapped for its aluminum.

Short Empire S.21 Flying Boat *Maia* carrying the upper component *Mercury* that was a S.20 Short Seaplane.

NOTE: GERMAN MISTEL PICK-A-BACK COMPOSITES

During the latter stages of WWII, the Luftwaffe developed a composite aircraft configuration, with the Mistel (German for mistletoe, a parasitic plant) being the larger, unmanned explosives carrying drone, while a small piloted control aircraft was mounted pick-a-back above the Mistel. The most successful of these composites employed a modified Junkers Ju 88 bomber as the Mistel with the entire nose/crew compartment replaced by a specially designed nose filled with a 4,000 lb. load of shaped-charge explosives. The upper component was a fighter aircraft—an FW 190 or Me 109—joined to the Mistel by struts and wired to the bomber's throttles and flight controls. The fighter pilot took off with the composite, flew it to the target area, then aimed it directly at the target, releasing his fighter from the bomber and returning to base while the bomber flew into the target on autopilot. The first composite combination was flown in July 1943, and the Luftwaffe KG 200 Test Unit then tested it as Beethoven. Mistels eventually became operational in June 1944, when a few were used against Allied D-Day invasion shipping at the end of the month, but none hit a ship. As part of the proposed Operation Iron Hammer in late 1943 and early 1944, Mistels based in Germany were selected to conduct strategic missions against Soviet weapons manufacturing facilities and electricity generating plants around Moscow and Gorky. Though more than 250 Mistels were built Iron Hammer never took place, as before the plan could be implemented the Red Army was already advancing into Germany, and it was decided to use the Mistels against the Soviet bridgehead at Kuestrin. The Mistels were expended in piecemeal attacks, mostly against bridges in hopes of stemming the massive advance of Allied forces toward Germany. Other composite combinations included the Ta 154/FW 190, Ar 234/Fi 103, Do 217K/DFS 288, and Si 204/Lippisch D-1, while projected composites included the Ju 287/Me 262 and AR 234C/Arado E.377.

Me-109 (top)/Ju 88 (bottom) Mistel composite

4
AMERICAN TRANSCONTINENTAL AND OTHER RECORDS: 1929–1934

From February 1929–September 1934, a spate of US transcontinental flight records were set by small, powerful aircraft mostly piloted by Frank Hawks and Roscoe Turner.

Date	Duration (H/M)	Pilot(s)	Aircraft	Location
2/4/29	18:22	Frank Hawks	Lockheed Air Express	LA to NYC
6/27/29	19:10	Frank Hawks	Lockheed Air Express	NYC to LA
6/28/29	17:36	Frank Hawks	Lockheed Air Express	LA to NYC
4/20/30	14:45	Charles Lindbergh	Lockheed Sirius	LA to NYC
5/27/30	18:43	Roscoe Turner	Lockheed Air Express	NYC to LA with 3 passengers
8/13/30	12:25	Frank Hawks	Travel Air Mystery S	LA to NYC
9/4/31	11:16	Jimmy Doolittle	Laird Super Solution	Completed for a bonus prize after winning the inaugural Bendix Trophy race, LA to Newark
8/29/32	10:19	Jimmy Haizlip	Wedell-Williams Model 44	Completed after winning the 2nd annual Bendix Trophy race
11/14/32	12:33	Roscoe Turner	Wedell-Williams Model 44	NYC to Burbank, CA
7/1/33	11:30	Roscoe Turner	Wedell-Williams Model 44	NYC to Burbank, CA
9/2/34	10:03	Roscoe Turner	Wedell-Williams Model 44	Burbank, CA to NYC

FRANK HAWKS

Frank Hawks was one of the aviation legends of the Golden Age of Flight, but he is little remembered today. After serving in the war as a flight instructor and a captain in the Army Air Service, after WWI, like many other pilots, he appeared on the barnstorming circuit and took part in the first in-flight refueling with Wesley May in 1921. In early 1928, Texas Oil Company (Texaco) hired Hawks to pilot Texaco One, a custom-built Ford Tri-motor that Texaco's Aviation Department purchased to promote aviation across the country. Hawks visited 175 cities, carried 7,200 passengers, and flew cross-country 56,000 miles before the Tri-motor was destroyed in December 1928. Texaco bought a Lockheed Air Express named *Texaco Five* in February 1929 that Hawks flew from the Burbank factory to New York in 18:22 hours, a new transcontinental record. Four months later Hawks flew the *Texaco Five* to a new transcontinental record that was forty-three minutes faster. In 1930, Hawks flew the first transcontinental glider flight when he piloted a towed glider for 2,860 miles across the country on an eight-day trip that included forty-four hours of flight time.

In the late 1920s, the Travel Air Company built several Mystery Ships that were air racers whose construction details were closely kept secret by the company. The reason for the secrecy was the military's complete dominance of air racing at the time and Travel Air's wish to introduce it at the 1929 Cleveland Air Races. Two Travel Air designers (Herb Rawdon and Walter Burnham) decided to show they could design a scratch-built civilian racing aircraft that was superior to any military racer. Instead of the biplane design common at the time they used the streamlined monoplane planform, thin wings braced with wires, and introduced the NACA engine cowl and large drag reducing wheel pants to commercial aviation. The sleek, polished fuselage continued the shape and width of the cowl throughout, with the fully enclosed cockpit with a small windscreen forming a flush turtle deck that extended to the vertical tail. The racing design was a complete success, as a Wright Whirlwind-powered Travel Air piloted by Douglas Davis reached a winning speed of 194.90 mph, with Davis winning the first Thompson Trophy and the Mystery Ship becoming the first commercial aircraft to outclass the Army and Navy's best entrants.

In 1930, Texaco bought the fourth Mystery Ship, *Texaco 13*, from the Travel Air for Hawks to fly in the National Air Races. *Texaco 13* was identical to the other Mystery Ships, except it included many special instruments for long distance flights. *Texaco 13* was vividly painted a Stearman vermilion and white, with a blue stripe separating the red and white. Hawks never fared well in races, as the aircraft was not set up for pylon-type racing, crashing twice, with Hawks being injured seriously once. During his 20,000 mile goodwill tour of Europe in 1931, Hawks established fifty-five intercity records in twelve countries; after returning from Europe in late 1931, he set more than 130 US point-to-point records in *Texaco 13* until 16 April 1932, when the aircraft was seriously damaged in a crash. *Texaco 13* is now displayed at the Museum of Science and Industry in Chicago.

One of the first aircraft the new Northrop Corporation produced was the purpose-built mail carrying Gamma. The first two Gamma 2As were specially built for Frank Hawks as the replacement for *Texaco 13*, and the Gamma 2B specially built for the Lincoln Ellsworth Trans-Antarctic Expedition. Hawks' sleek, all metal high-speed mail and cargo aircraft was powered by a 785 hp 14-cylinder Wright Whirlwind twin-row, air-cooled radial engine and was initially named *Texaco 11*, but later changed to *Sky Chief*, when Hawks was honored by the Sioux Indian Nation as a chief. *Texaco Sky Chief* became linked to all Northrop Gammas and was adopted as the name for Texaco's premium gasoline. Hawks continued to set records in his new aircraft, and on 2 June 1933, he set the west-to-east transcontinental airspeed record, flying from Los Angeles to Floyd Bennett Field, New York, in 13:25:15 hours at an average speed of 181 mph. A popular saying coined at the time was "Don't send it by mail, send it by Hawks."

After setting many new intercity marks, Hawks resigned from Texaco in 1935, remaining active as an aviation consultant and a test and demonstration pilot. Northrop hired him to fly the Gamma 2E attack bomber, a conversion of the original Gamma 2A. He demonstrated the aircraft to the Argentine Navy, effectively demonstrating its long distance capabilities by flying 8,090 miles from Buenos Aires to Los Angeles in three days. On 3 May 1935, with Northrop's chief test pilot Gage Irving in the gunner's seat, Hawks broke ten intercity speed records on the way to Los Angeles, with the resultant publicity ultimately responsible for orders of fifty-one Gamma 2E attack aircraft.

In 1936, Hawks approached Howell "Pete" Miller, chief engineer for the Granville Brothers and their famous Gee Bee racers, to build a racing aircraft to his own design. Hawks obtained sponsorship from the Gruen Watch Company and named the aircraft *Time Flies*. The Hawks-Miller HM-1 design featured a streamlined fuselage, including the unusual feature of burying the cockpit with a curved windshield contoured to fit the fuselage top extended in take-off and landing but retracted in flight, with the pilot's seat lowered and the windshield flush with the fuselage. After its first flight 18 October 1936, Hawks flew *Time Flies* from Hartford, Connecticut, on 13 April 1937, to Miami, Florida, in 4:55 hours; about an hour later he took off and flew to Newark Airport, New Jersey, in 4:21 hours, but on landing he damaged the aircraft. Hawks did not rebuild *Time Flies* due to financial problems and sold it.

Hawks retired from air racing in 1937, and was hired by the Gwinn Aircar Company as vice president of sales, touring the US and giving flying demonstrations in Gwinn's new "safety" aircraft, the Gwinn Aircar. On 23 August 1938, Hawks was to demonstrate the aircraft to Sportsman J. Hazard Campbell and kept his appointment by landing on the estate's polo field. Soon after take-off the aircraft crashed, killing Campbell and forty-one-year-old Hawks.

Even more than Roscoe Turner, Hawks exploited his image as an "ace" pilot with numerous promotional schemes, such as innumerable posters that highlighted an idealized Hawks photo titled "Captain Frank Hawks." Hawks was a well-known spokesman for Post Cereals, and featured in newspaper comic strips and in children's adventure books, with his "Air Hawks" and "Sky Patrol" fan clubs being children's favorites.

Frank Hawks and the Lockheed Air Express *Texaco 11*

ROSCOE TURNER

Roscoe Turner was probably the greatest air racing pilot of the Golden Age, and perhaps the most colorful. Turner was born to poor parents and quit school in the tenth grade to become an auto mechanic. During WWI he tried to enlist in the Army's Aviation Section, but was rejected because of his lack of education; he transferred into the Army Signal Corps Aviation Section as a balloon pilot/observer trainee, where he learned to fly, but the war ended too soon for him to fly combat. After leaving the ASCAS he and former Army pilot Harry Runser bought a surplus Curtiss JN4D Jenny and barnstormed over the US, with Turner performing most of the wing walking and parachute jumping. Part of Turner's charisma was not only his neatly waxed mustache, but also his flying apparel, as he and Runser wore crowd-pleasing military uniforms while performing. When Turner's uniform deteriorated he fashioned his colorful trademark uniform: a sky blue jacket, tan whipcord breeches, and black riding boots, topped off with a military officer's cap.

When barnstorming began to decline at the end of the 1920s, Turner moved to Hollywood in 1928 and worked as a movie stunt pilot, performing in Howard Hughes' film *Hell's Angels*. By 1929, Turner had honed his flying abilities and used his charisma to obtain corporate sponsorships. Turner persuaded Gilmore Oil Company to sponsor him, and since Gilmore had a lion on its corporate logo, the perceptive Turner acquired a lion cub he named "Gilmore" and began flying with him. Thus, Turner began his remarkable racing career with a new and distinctive partner, Gilmore, an African lion! They both became well-known national figures and photos of Gilmore and the colorfully attired Turner often appeared in newspapers and newsreels over America. Gilmore was onboard when Turner set two transcontinental speed records in May 1930, flying eastbound (Los Angeles to New York in 15:37) on one and westbound (back to Los Angeles in 18:42 hours) on the other. Turner and Gilmore soon flew across three countries non-stop from Vancouver, Canada, to Auga Caliente, Mexico, in a record 9:14 hours. Soon Gilmore became too big for the cockpit and was retired from flying, with Roscoe Turner becoming forever known as the peculiar pilot with the lion.

In 1932, Turner acquired a new aircraft, a Wedell-Williams Model 44 Racer designed and built by one of the era's leading pilots, veteran air racer Jimmy Wedell, who had formed a business partnership in 1929 with millionaire Harry Williams. The little Racer had a 26 ft. wingspan, 24.5 ft. length, 8 ft. height, and 2,500 lb. weight. It was powered by a 1,020 hp Pratt & Whitney R-1690 engine that drove the Racer to a maximum speed of 316 mph and a range of 900 miles. The aircraft gave Turner the edge he needed to become competitive in aviation's most prestigious races. That year Turner finished third in the Bendix and Thompson races and in the Shell Speed Dash, which was an important component of the National Air Races in Cleveland. He also set a new transcontinental record from New York to Los Angeles and received the Harmon Trophy for being the best American aviator of 1932.

On 1 July 1933, Turner flew the Racer in the Bendix Trophy Race from New York to Los Angeles to a first place finish, ahead of Jimmy Wedell in his Model 44 in 11:30 hours, which also broke his own east to west transcontinental airspeed record. Wedell went on to win the Thompson Trophy Circuit Race despite finishing behind Turner, who was disqualified after a strict pylon rules infringement. In Fall 1933, Turner upgraded his Model 44 again with a 1,000 hp supercharged Pratt & Whitney R-1690 Hornet engine. On 2 September 1933, he flew the all gold painted Racer from Los Angeles to New York in 10:04:30 hours to break the west to east transcontinental airspeed record, complementing his existing east to west record.

In 1934, Turner finally won the Thompson Trophy Race and was second in the Shell Speed Dashes. In October, he joined Clyde Pangborn and Reeder Nichols and competed in the prestigious MacRobertson London to Melbourne Race, flying a specially modified passenger/transport Boeing 247D airliner and placing third overall behind famous C.W.A Scott's and Tom Campbell Black's de Havilland Comet, with the KLM Douglas DC-2 narrowly taking second place over Turner's Boeing 247 and both airliners finishing less than a day behind the Comet winner, thus proving that air travel was a viable alternative for international passenger transport.

In 1935's Bendix Trophy Race, flying from Los Angeles to Cleveland, he finished only 23.5 seconds behind the winner and led the Thompson Trophy Race until the last half lap, when his Pratt & Whitney blew. When he neared the field Turner climbed for altitude; at first he thought about bailing out, but then considered the Wedell-Williams might crash into the spectator stands and chose to make a safe, skillful, high-speed dead-stick landing.

In 1936, Turner designed his own racing plane, the Laird-Turner Meteor, a mid-wing monoplane that incorporated all of the latest aerodynamic developments and accommodated the 1,000 hp Pratt & Whitney R-1830 Twin Wasp intended to keep Turner competitive in cross-country races and closed circuit pylon races; he would realize some of his greatest racing accomplishments while flying the Meteor. In August 1937, Turner test flew his new aircraft, but on 3 September 1937, fuel leaks and subsequent repairs caused Turner to miss the start of the Bendix Trophy race from Burbank to Cleveland. On 6 September, Turner flew the racer in the Thompson Trophy race and led the race, but then made another pylon mistake and finished third.

In 1938, he won the Thompson Trophy Race a second time, becoming the first pilot to win it twice, and was also awarded the Harmon Trophy for being America's foremost aviator. In 1939, he won the Thompson for a yet unmatched third time and then stunned the aviation world by announcing his retirement. Turner established his own flight school in Indianapolis and trained more than 3,300 pilots during WWII. During his colorful and impressive career Turner won numerous races and established seven transcontinental speed records.

Roscoe Turner, the Lockheed Air Express aircraft, and lion mascot Gilmore dropped in a harness.

BEN HOWARD: 1935: THE YEAR OF MR. MUILLIGAN

At eighteen, Ben Howard used his savings to buy a Standard biplane, and in the process of learning to fly it he was unable to pull out of a spin, breaking his leg in the crash and totaling the plane. The crash did not dim Howard's passion for aviation, as he then went to work at Curtiss Aircraft, where he absorbed the art of aircraft design and fabrication. At the request of a Houston bootlegger his first big project was to design and build a "rum-runner" aircraft using spare parts. When the buyer saw the aircraft he declared it a "Damn Good Airplane," which led to future Howard aircraft being trademarked with the initials DGA. While flying his first hand-built racing plane *Pete* he won five air races, and as he entered more competitive races he and his partner, Gordon Israel, built two larger, low-wing, wire-braced monoplanes *Mike* and *Ike*, which completed their sponsor's name, *Miss Chevrolet*.

His sixth plane, the four-seat *Mr. Muilligan*, was designed spefically to win the Bendix Trophy by introducing a new technique in transcontinental racing: to fly the course non-stop at high altitude using fewer refueling stops. While en route to the 1934 air races, oxygen and fuel system problems led to an off-field emergency landing that damaged the landing gear and propeller. The aircraft could not be repaired in time and missed the 1934 season. The winner of the previous three seasons was the superb and faster Wedell-Williams Model 44 Racer powered by a 1,000 hp Pratt & Whitney Hornet vs. *Mr. Muilligan's* 850 hp Pratt & Whitney Wasp. Howard's engineering advantage was his low-drag airframe and increased fuel capacity, leading to fewer refueling stops in the race from Burbank to Cleveland. For the 1935 Bendix Race *Mr. Muilligan* was loaded with 300 gallons of gasoline, thirty gallons of oil, and oxygen equipment for two, giving the airplane the ability to fly for seven hours at 22,000 ft. On 30 August 1935, Howard, engineer Gordon Israel, and their DGA-6 were one of eight entrants who took off from Burbank in the 1935 Bendix. After their single re-fueling stop in Kansas City, they sped on to Cleveland in an elapsed time of 8:33:16.3 hours and an average speed of 238.7 mph, which was the best speed made in a Bendix Race since Jimmy Haizlip won it in a Wedell-Williams Racer in 1932. Roscoe Turner, flying a gold Wedell-Williams #57 with almost double the horsepower, had taken off much later than Howard, but the race was decided on elapsed time. After an endless wait Turner flew across the finish line in 8:33:39.8 hours, only 23.5 seconds later and .2 mph slower than Howard. Howard's DGA-6 and the Wedell-Williams were so superior that they beat the third place finisher, a Northrop Gamma flown by Russell Thaw, by 1:33 hours, and Amelia Earhart's Lockheed Vega, the fifth and final finisher, by 5:14 hours.

On 2 September, Howard made a last minute decision to enter *Mr. Muilligan*, piloted by Harold Neumann, in the Thompson Trophy Race at the 1935 National Air Races, as its Pratt & Whitney Wasp engine had run near or at maximum power for more than eight hours in the Bendix Race. Due to a prolonged wait at the starting line *Mr. Muilligan's* spark plugs began to foul, causing the engine to run rough. When the starter's flag finally went down *Mr. Muilligan* got off to a very slow start, but Neumann began to close on Roscoe Turner's Wedell-Williams. However, at the eighth lap Turner's engine blew and Neumann won the race with a speed of 220.2 mph (vs. 218.7 mph for the runner-up). No other aircraft had ever won the Bendix and Thompson races. Neumann had also won the 1935 Greve Trophy Race flying Howard's Mike Racer. Howard's DGA-6 also had the distinction of being the only racer to evolve into a successful commercial production aircraft, first as the DGA-8 and DGA-9, and later the DGA-11 and DGA-12. During 1936, it placed in competition for several pilots, but was destroyed in an accident during the 1936 New York-Los Angeles Bendix Transcontinental Race. The loss of a propeller blade over New Mexico caused Howard and his co-pilot wife, Maxine "Mike," to crash land, costing Howard his aircraft and his leg and injuring his wife. Roscoe Turner ground-looped on a rough Texas field, ending his race, which was won by aviatrix Helen Thayer's Beechcraft *Staggerwing*. After the accident Howard flew airmail and passenger transports and became an outstanding test pilot and engineer for Douglas Aircraft.

With the salvaged parts from the crash site as patterns Robert Reichardt was able to recreate *Mister Muilligan*, but was killed in 1977 while doing a timed run over the Tonopah, Nevada, Dry Lake. A second replica DGA-6 was built by James Younkin and Bud Dake.

ABOVE / Ben Howard and his DGA *Mr. Muilligan*

LEFT / The 1935 Thompson Trophy being presented to Harold Neumann (L) by Fred Crawford and Ruth Chatterton, with Roscoe Turner (R).

THE TWO TRANSCONTINENTAL BENDIX TROPHY RACES

Bendix competitors typically flew from Burbank to Cleveland, Ohio, except for 1933 and 1936, when the contest began in New York and ended in Los Angeles.

1933 Bendix

The East-West Bendix Transcontinental Race attracted ten entries, including two radical GeeBee racers and two women pilots, Amelia Earhart and Ruth Nichols. In 1933, Jimmie Wedell began testing a new design (the *45*), but mechanical problems forced him to leave the aircraft in New Jersey for the 1933 New York to Los Angeles National Air Races. Instead, the *45's* Pratt and Whitney Wasp 985 engine was mounted on Roscoe Turner's *44*, which was painted in a combined Gilmore and 20th Century Fox Pictures scheme. The Wedell-Williams *92* was flown by famous racer Lee Gelbach, but was forced down with mechanical troubles near Indianapolis. Of the ten starters Turner's and Wedell's racers were the only two to finish. Roscoe Turner's Wedell-Williams *44* set a new record of 11:30 hours (214.78 mph) and Jimmie Wedell's *44* at 11:58 also beat Turner's own 1932 record of 12:33 hours, which had surpassed Frank Hawks'1930 record of 14:50 hours in his *Texaco No.13* Travel Air. The two GeeBees (R-1 and R-2) were entered, but Russell Boardman's R-1 had a fatal crash in Indianapolis, while Russell Thaw's R-2 ground-looped there. Amelia Earhart in her Lockheed Vega and Ruth Nichols in her Orion both dropped out.

1936 Bendix

The finish line of the 1936 race was moved to Los Angeles' Mines Field due to the Cleveland Airport expansion, and was to be started at Floyd Bennett Field, New York. The starting lineup included an impressive initial list of aircraft/pilot combinations, including Benny Howard's *Mr. Muilligan* that won the 1935 Bendix; Roscoe Turner's Wedell-Williams *44* entry; Joe Jacobson entered a Northrop Gamma; Lee Miles the *QED*; Amelia Earhart flying her new Lockheed Electra; Louise Thaden and co-pilot Blanche Noyes flying a Beechcraft Staggerwing; Laura Ingalls in a Lockheed Orion; and William Gulick in a Vultee. Unexpected events changed the complexion of the race, as favorites Benny and Maxine Howard crashed in New Mexico and Roscoe Turner ground-looped his Wedell in Texas. During the race a large toll was taken on its contestants, resulting in the slowest Bendix ever won by Louise Thaden and Blanche Noyes, to become the first women to win a national air trophy.

Jimmy Wedell and his superb Wedell-Williams Racer

LOUISE THADEN

Louise McPhetridge left college in 1927 to join the Travel Air Corporation, where Olive Beech, wife of Walter Beech (craft), found her a position in California in which she could learn to fly.

Louise soloed in 1927, and in 1928, she married Herbert Thaden, a former US Army pilot and engineer. That year she set her first world record for the women's altitude mark of 20,260 ft. and in March 1929, she set a new women's endurance record of 22:03 hours flying a Travel Air. She then became the fourth US woman to earn a transport license. In August 1929, she became the first woman to win a national air race when she won the 2,500 mile Women's Air Derby flying from Santa Monica to Cleveland.

In 1932, Thaden, along with Francis Marsalis, set a new endurance record by flying a Curtiss Thrush biplane for 196 hours over Long Island, New York. During their eight days in the air Thaden made seventy-eight air-to-air refueling contacts and made live radio broadcasts to a national listening audience. Meanwhile, Blanche Noyes, wife of US Airmail pilot Dewey Noyes, gave up an acting career to learn to fly. She took flight instructions from Noyes and soloed with less than four hours of dual instruction to become Ohio's first licensed woman pilot. In 1934, Thaden and Noyes gained flight experience employed by the US Bureau of Air Commerce, establishing air route landmarks and "providing related services essential to the development of US commercial aviation." Thayer also worked as factory representative and demonstration pilot for Beech Aircraft.

In 1936, Thaden returned to private flying, and in July she set a new woman's speed record. In September 1936, long-time friend Olive Beech recommended that her husband, Walter Beech, enter his Beech Staggerwing in the Bendix Transcontinental Speed Dash with Louise Thaden as pilot and Blanch Noyes as co-pilot and navigator. The two women welcomed the opportunity to compete with the men, but did not think they would win with the Staggerwing because it was a biplane, whereas racers or twin-engine planes especially built for transcontinental flights were favored. But then pre-race favorites Howard and Turner were out of the race. When the women landed they thought the turmoil surrounding their Beech was because they crossed the finish line backward, not that they were the first women to win the Bendix race (Laura Ingalls was second flying a Lockheed Orion). Thaden's victory was a rather slow 14:54 hours, but they were awarded the $4,500 first place money and the $2,500 prize for the first female team to cross the finish line, and Thayer received the Harmon Trophy as the "outstanding woman pilot in the US in 1936."

After winning the Bendix Thaden returned to the Bureau of Air Commerce for a short time, but then returned to the Beechcraft Company, demonstrating their planes from coast to coast. After 1937, Thaden decided to spend time with her family and write her memoir, *High, Wide and Frightened* (1938). During WWII Thaden became active in the Civil Air Patrol and served with Ruth Nichols in Relief Wings, a humanitarian air service.

Louise Thaden, Vincent Bendix, and Blanche Noyes at the 1936 Bendix Race

LAURA INGALLS

Laura Ingalls and her Lockheed Air Express

Laura Ingalls was a highly successful female pilot of the 1930s, but is largely unknown today. The daughter of a wealthy New York City family, Ingalls learned to fly in 1928, and quickly set several unusual records. In 1930, she performed 344 consecutive loops, setting a women's record; then she shortly broke her own record with 930 loops and added 714 barrel rolls, breaking both women's and men's records. Ingalls held more US transcontinental air records during the 1930s than any other woman, including a transcontinental record of 30 hours east to west and 25 hours west to east (round trip New York and Los Angeles), both in 1930. In 1934, she became the first woman to fly non-stop from the East coast to the West coast, and then immediately broke Amelia Earhart's 1933 non-stop transcontinental west-to-east record of 13:07 hours with a flight from Los Angeles to New York in 10:05 hours. Ingalls' most well-known flights were made in 1934 and earned her a Harmon Trophy as the most outstanding female aviator of the year. Ingalls flew in a Lockheed Air Express from Mexico to Chile, over the Andes Mountains to Rio, to Cuba, and then to New York, marking the first flight over the Andes by an American woman, the first solo flight around South America in a land plane, the first flight by a woman from North America to South America, and setting a women's distance record of 17,000 total miles. In 1936, she placed second behind Louise Thaden in the prestigious Bendix Trophy Race. Ingalls' popularity began to fade after September 1939, when she "bombed" the White House with fliers endorsing the peace appeals of the America First Committee. In December 1941, she was arrested and charged for accepting unknown payments from the German Embassy since March of that year, and with being an unregistered agent of the Nazi German government. She was found guilty, was sentenced on 20 February 1942, and was imprisoned for twenty months.

1939: LAST PREWAR TRANSCONTINENTAL RECORD: BEN KELSEY AND THE XP-38

On 11 February 1939, after the prototype Lockheed XP-38 Lightning (37-457) had just flown for the first time two weeks earlier, 1Lt. Benjamin Kelsey departed March Field, California, at 0632 PST (0932 EST) and flew to Amarillo, Texas, landing at 1222 EST for the first of two refueling stops. He flew on to Wright Field, Dayton, Ohio, and landed at 1510 EST to be refueled, leaving at 1528 EST on the final leg of his transcontinental flight. He was overhead Mitchel Field, New York, at 1655 EST, but his landing was delayed by other aircraft in the traffic pattern. On Kelsey's approach the XP-38 was behind several slower training planes so he throttled back the engines. When he tried to throttle up the engines would not accelerate, but remained at idle, and he was forced to bring the XP-38 down on a golf course short of the airport, totaling the aircraft. At this time the P-38's future was on the line and an investigation was immediately opened to determine the cause of the crash. The cause was blamed on either vapor lock or possibly icing of the engines, which satisfied the AAC that nothing major had occurred. The total elapsed time of the flight was 7:45 hours (7:02 hours in the air), a performance so impressive that the ACC ordered thirteen additional YP-38s from Lockheed.

Lt. Ben Kelsey examining the wreckage of his XP-38.

1938: DOUGLAS CORRIGAN: "WRONG WAY" TO IRELAND

While working for Claude Ryan in 1926, Douglas Corrigan was responsible for the wing assembly, the installation of the gas tanks, and the instrument panel on Lindbergh's *Spirit of St. Louis*. After Lindbergh flew across the Atlantic in 1927, Corrigan became obsessed with emulating his idol. During the 1930s, Corrigan worked as a pilot, mechanic, flight instructor, passenger, barnstormer, and airport manager, using his earnings to buy a series of small used aircraft. Corrigan bought a secondhand OX5 Curtiss Robin for $325 and began to modify it for long distance flights, and as early as 1935, after having installed a not-new engine and extra fuel tanks, Corrigan applied to the Bureau of Air Commerce, asking permission to make a non-stop flight from New York to Ireland, but his application was rejected, citing his Robin as being unsound for a non-stop trans-Atlantic flight. Corrigan began flying long distance flights in August 1936, when he flew the Robin non-stop from San Diego to New York by way of St. Louis, but engine problems forced him to make several stops. In October 1936, he flew 1,900 miles non-stop from Floyd Bennett Field, New York, to San Antonio, Texas, in nineteen hours. Corrigan returned to San Diego, working as a flight instructor while he overhauled the Robin, and installed additional fuel tanks to extend its range. In 1937, he flew to the East Coast twice (not non-stop), specifically to obtain permission from several New York airfields to fly to the British Isles. He was turned down because neither he nor his plane was licensed for over-ocean flight. Then, even after these extensive modifications, his aircraft was refused renewal of its license because it was again deemed unsound for any safe flight. On his next bi-coastal flights in his "unsound" aircraft Corrigan had to use remote airfields for his illegal take-offs and landings. After Amelia Earhart disappeared over the South Pacific that summer the government suspended the issuance of licenses for ocean flying. In late Fall 1937, broke and exasperated, Corrigan returned to work at Northrop in California, but during the following winter and spring he continued to prepare his Robin for another try at a long distance flight, but it still had no radio and its compass was twenty years old. Like Lindbergh's *Spirit of St. Louis*, with the fuel tanks mounted in the front of the aircraft, Corrigan could only see out the side windows.

During July 1938, Corrigan acquired a so-called experimental (temporary) license for a non-stop cross-country flight and took off from Long Beach, California, on 8 July, his flight plan stating he was taking a "test hop" to El Paso, Texas, but he arrived unannounced at Floyd Bennett Field, New York, non-stop, in less than 27 hours and 2,700 miles later—enough for a trans-Atlantic flight. Fuel efficiency became critical toward the end of the flight due to a gasoline leak that filled the cockpit with fumes. Because Howard Hughes' impending round-the-world flight was garnering most of the media attention Corrigan received no recognition for his flight, and when he applied for permission to make a trans-Atlantic flight he was refused again. The disgruntled Corrigan then logged a flight plan stating he was going to return to California and took off in the Robin with the still-leaking fuel tank during the early morning of 17 July 1938 from Floyd Bennett Field. After flying for about twenty-six hours Corrigan claimed to have noticed a navigational "error." In his autobiography, *That's My Story*, Corrigan maintains that after ten hours his feet got cold because the cockpit floor was drenched with gasoline leaking from the unrepaired tank. He used a screwdriver to punch a hole through the cockpit floor so the fuel would drain away on the side opposite the hot exhaust pipe, reducing the risk of a midair explosion. But had he actually been oblivious of being over the ocean and not solid land as claimed, it seems as though with the leaking gasoline emergency he would have descended, looking for a place to land in an emergency. His autobiography states he instead speeded up on the notion that the faster he flew, the sooner he would reach "California" and the less time there would be for gasoline to trickle out. Nonetheless, on 18 July, after 28:13 hours in the air, he landed at Baldonnel Aerodrome, County Dublin, and after introducing himself to airport authorities he reportedly said, "Just got in from New York. Where am I? I intended to fly to California."

Whether or not Corrigan intended to fly to Ireland has long been debated, but Corrigan always rigorously maintained that California had been his destination and that he had somehow misread his marginal instruments. After his arrival Irish aviation authorities had a laundry list of infractions, but he received a minimal punishment; his pilot's license was suspended for fourteen days, and his plane was impounded as unsafe. Corrigan had achieved the celebrity he had dreamed of and was promptly dubbed "Wrong Way Corrigan" by the media, which kept him in the public eye for weeks. On 4 August, Corrigan and his crated Robin returned to New York, sailing on the liner *Manhattan*. His ticker-tape parade along Broadway was reported to have been even greater than Lindbergh's in 1927. He then embarked on a nationwide tour, including another well-attended ticker-tape parade in Chicago. His autobiography was published before the end of the year and soon he played himself in the film version of his life called *The Flying Irishman*. Due to the deteriorating political situation in Europe and the now rather ordinary feat of flying over the Atlantic, Corrigan failed to achieve the same long-lived standing of his hero, Lindbergh. The remainder of thirty-one-year-old Corrigan's life was commonplace, with brief newspaper features appearing on the anniversary of his famous flight. His lasting memorial is his famous epithet "Wrong Way Corrigan." In 1988, his Robin was reassembled from storage and put on display for the fiftieth anniversary of his flight, but in a dispute it was taken back by Corrigan and to date remains intact in storage. Corrigan passed on 9 December 1995, at age eighty-eight.

Douglas "Wrong Way" Corrigan and his old Curtiss Robin.

1938: HOWARD HUGHES RECORD AROUND-THE-WORLD FLIGHT

Howard Hughes was one of the world's wealthiest men, whose resumé included businessman and industrialist, investor and financier, engineer and inventor, filmmaker, philanthropist, and aviation interests that included aircraft design and manufacture, airlines, and later the aerospace and defense industries. Hughes was a lifelong aircraft enthusiast and pilot who set world records and commissioned the construction of custom aircraft. On 13 September 1935, Hughes flew his custom H-1 Racer to the land plane speed record of 352 mph, which was the final time the world airspeed record was set in an aircraft built by a private individual. On 13 January 1936, Hughes flew a Northrop Gamma from Burbank, California, to Newark, New Jersey, setting a new cross-country record of 9:27:10 hours and besting Roscoe Turner's Wedell-Williams Model *44* record of 2 September 1934 mark by thirty-six minutes, for which he was awarded the Harmon Trophy. On 19 January 1937, flying the same H-1 Racer with longer wings, Hughes set a new transcontinental airspeed record by flying non-stop from Los Angeles to Newark in 7:28: 25 hours (beating his own previous record of 9:27 hours), with an average ground speed over the flight of 322 mph.

By 1938, the around-the-world flight record remained a grand aviation objective, with no one flying the circumnavigation since Wiley Post five years earlier. Howard Hughes had set several transcontinental speed records over the past two years and had the resources and inclination to pursue that goal. Hughes gathered his flight crew of Harry Connor (co-pilot), Thomas Thurlow (navigator), Edward Lund (flight engineer), and Richard Stoddard (radio operator), while Al Lodwick, vice president of Curtiss-Wright, managed on ground operations and clearances, landing permits, and en route refueling. The flight was sponsored by the New York World's Fair, for which Hughes was an aeronautical advisor; the flight was to promote "the triumph of American aviation technology, illustrating that safe, long-distance air travel was possible."

As Hughes was known for his love of the minutia, seven months were required to ready the crew and to equip the Lockheed Super Electra with the latest and most sophisticated equipment ever to be installed on a private aircraft. The navigational equipment included four specially designed compasses for multiple checks of course and position, a homing radio compass to maintain the aircraft's course by taking bearings from ships at sea, a new periscopic drift indicator, and a new Sperry automatic gyro-pilot, which would perform most of the flying. Radio operators along the route were contacted to monitor the flight and aid Hughes' navigators in establishing radio lines of bearing. The radio equipment included the most advanced and powerful radio transceiver available, connecting the Super Electra to the antenna at the World's Fair to inform the world and also current girlfriend, actress Katherine Hepburn, of each leg of Hughes' journey. Hughes consulted leading meteorologists and planned a flight path around the world, and to arrange for a system of weather codes to be transmitted to the aircraft in flight. Further logistics insured the availability of food and mechanical support at each projected stopover en route.

On 10 July 1938, Hughes' Super Electra took off from Floyd Bennett Field and continued to Paris (3,641 miles in 16:38 hours, which was a new trans-Atlantic record); then over Russia to Moscow (1,640 miles in 7:51 hours), Omsk (1,400 miles in 7:27 hours), and Yakutsk (2,158 miles in 10:31 hours); on to Fairbanks, Alaska (2,457 miles in 12:17 hours); Minneapolis, Minnesota (2,441 miles in 12:02 hours); and then returning to Floyd Bennett (1,054 miles in 4:26 hours) for a total of 91:19 hours to totally eclipse Wiley Post's July 1933 solo record of 186:44 hours by four days. For his feat Hughes was given a ticker-tape welcome in New York City and received the 1938 Harmon Trophy, the Collier Trophy, and the FAI Bibesco Cup. Hughes was planning a second circumnavigation the next year, but WWII ended his plans.

Howard Hughes' Lockheed Super Electra on its arrival at Floyd Bennett Field after its around-the-world flight.

5

FLYING BOATS: QUEST FOR SIZE AND DISTANCE: 1930–1946

PAN AM BECOMES THE FIRST INTERCONTINENTAL AIRLINE

By the early 1930s, Pan Am President Juan Trippe wanted to establish regular mail, cargo, and passenger service to Hawaii and on to more outlying locations in the Pacific, initially from San Francisco to China. During 1935, Pan Am flew the first survey flights and gained experience for operating the trans-Pacific route, and by October 1935, mail and cargo service was initiated. The first passenger flight followed on 21 October 1936, and was expanded to weekly flights, with the first services stopping in Manila, capital of the US territory of the Philippines, for political reasons. Service continued to expand and eventually reached Hong Kong and Singapore. Pan Am was interested in the more lucrative America-Europe market, but poor weather conditions made year-round Atlantic service very chancy. Finally, Pan Am began service to Europe in 1939, but as expected, poor weather canceled forty percent of the flights, and many that completed the flight had been delayed for several days before take-off. The most well-known Pan Am flights were to Central and South America, where distances were long, airports few, and facilities mostly nonexistent. Although Pan Am used airports when available, there were many more bays and harbors than airports, and the airline operated flying boats and float planes extensively. The opening of Latin American operations forced Pan Am to develop long-distance navigation, radio communication, and the creation of fully functional air support and hotel facilities where none existed.

Although aircraft companies were ready to develop large four-engine aircraft, there were few airports that could accommodate them outside the continental US, and four-engine flying boats were the solution. To cross the Pacific, Pan Am required far larger flying boats than available to carry economic payloads. The first Pan Am Clipper, the Sikorsky S-42, was really designed for the Americas, although S-42s surveyed some Pacific routes and flew the short hop between Manila and Hong Kong. Next came three larger Martin M-130s, providing the first regular service, followed by the definitive Boeing 314s and 314As.

Sikorsky S-42

MARTIN CLIPPERS (MARTIN M-130)

The most well-known long distance commercial flights of the late 1920s through the 1930s were flown by American air carrier Pan American Airways, which began to fly in Central and South America in 1927.

By the mid-1930s, Pan American Airways, operating multi-engine flying boats with highly trained crews, was carrying passengers, mail, and cargo to Latin America, showing an operating profit and an impressive safety record. Pan American Airways President Juan Trippe issued a directive to American aircraft manufacturers to develop and build trans-Atlantic planes to carry mail non-stop with midair refueling, but this concept was thought to be too audacious for the time. A trans-Pacific flying boat carrying passengers was specified by Charles Lindbergh, who was the chairman of Pan Am's Technical Committee. Three Martin M-130s were ordered to meet Pan Am's specifications for range and payload at $417,000 (fully-equipped) per aircraft, which was nearly double the $242,000 price tag for a Sikorsky S-42 Flying Boat and more than five times the $78,000 price of the leading airliner of the day, the Douglas DC-2.

In November 1932, construction began on the largest aircraft ever built in America at the Middle River Plant under project engineer L. D. McCarthy. The M-130's first flight was on 30 December 1934, when the giant flying boat was rolled down the factory ramp into the Middle River. Test pilot Ken Ebel and L. D. McCarthy as co-pilot were at the controls, with Benny Zelubowsky, the foreman of the experimental department, as the flight engineer. A large crowd consisting of Martin employees and officials, along with news reporters and spectators, lined the river's shores and crowded boats. Ebel taxied into the river and eased the throttles forward, and the giant flying boat was soon "on the step"; then its four Pratt & Whitney R-1830 Twin Wasp engines lifted it into the air.

On 9 October 1935, Pan Am took delivery of the *China Clipper* a year behind schedule. Martin had designated the flying boat the Martin Ocean Transport, but to the public they were all referred to as the *China Clipper*, a name which evolved into a generic term, Clipper, for Pan Am's entire fleet of large flying boats, including the Martin M-130, Sikorsky S-42, and Boeing 314. On 22 November 1935, the *China Clipper*, piloted by Capt. Edwin Musick and First Officer R.O.D. Sullivan, flew the first trans-Pacific airmail route from San Francisco to Manila with a blue ribbon passenger list and 111,000 air mail letters. The flight received national publicity and President Roosevelt proclaimed, "I thrill to the wonder of it all!" Radio broadcasts and newspaper headlines followed its progress to Manila.

The *China Clipper* was truly a magnificent and luxurious aircraft, with six flying officers and three cabin stewards. The *Clipper* measured almost 91 ft. long, 24.5 ft. high, had a wingspan of 130 ft., and weighed 52,250 lbs. It had a maximum speed of 180 mph and cruised at 130 mph for a range of 3,200 miles at a service ceiling of 10,000 ft. The M-130 could carry forty-six passengers in its daytime configuration, but in its more typical overnight service it provided sleeping accommodations for up to thirty passengers in three ten-berth compartments (one forward and three aft), with a sixteen-seat dining room/lounge compartment amidships.

Only three M-130s were built: the *China Clipper*, the *Philippine Clipper*, and the *Hawaii Clipper*. The *Philippine Clipper* inaugurated passenger service between the US and Hong Kong on 14 October 1936, while a week later, the *Hawaii Clipper* inaugurated scheduled trans-Pacific passenger service between California and the Philippines. The *Hawaii Clipper* flight departed the US on 21 October 1936, and the round trip to and from Manila required two weeks to complete.

In July 1938, the *Hawaii Clipper* disappeared over the Pacific on a flight between Guam and Manila, with the loss of nine crew and six passengers; no cause for the loss was determined. The *Philippine Clipper* was lost on 21 January 1943, en route from Hawaii to San Francisco, with the loss of all nineteen on board. The *China Clipper* was sold to the Navy in 1942, and crashed at Port of Spain, Trinidad, on 8 January 1945.

A fourth flying boat (designated M-156) called the *Russian Clipper* was built for the Soviet Union that was essentially identical to the three Pan Am models, except it had a larger wing (giving it a longer range), twin vertical stabilizers, and weighed 63,000 lbs. (11,000 lbs. more than the earlier *Clippers*), and could carry seventy passengers. *Russian Clipper* flew for the first time on 27 November 1937, under Ken Ebel. Three months later the airplane was delivered in New York, dismantled, and packed in crates to sail for Europe on the deck of a freighter. The lone M-156/PS-30 was put into regular service by Aeroflot in 1940, along the Soviet Far East Pacific Coast, where it was flown until it was scrapped in 1944.

In 1936, Pan Am decided to expand its fleet of *Clippers* and Glenn Martin was so confident he would receive the contract he built a large new addition at the Middle River plant. To his dismay, in June 1936, Pan Am chose Boeing's B-314 *Yankee Clipper* instead, as the Martin Clippers were too expensive to operate. Martin had suffered serious losses it could not afford on the three *Clippers* ($230,000 in 1934 and $270,000 in 1935) which Martin had planned to amortize over the life of the contracts, but there were no more *Clippers* to be built. Martin would not build another commercial flying boat or a passenger plane until after WWII.

Martin M-130 *China Clipper*

Boeing 314 and 314A Clippers

In early 1936, Pan American sent out proposals requesting a four-engine flying boat with unparalleled range that would enhance the airline's fleet of only three trans-Pacific Martin M-130s. Sikorsky responded with a design that would eventually be developed as the S-44; it met Pan Am's requirements for speed and range, but was rejected because it carried too few passengers. Consolidated Aircraft proposed a four-engine design based on its PBY Catalina flying boat, but was also rejected as too small. Martin proposed the M-156 *Russian Clipper* design, but Pan Am also rejected it, which infuriated Glenn Martin, who had sustained a loss on the small M-130 production run and anticipated reimbursement by the acceptance of his M-156 proposal. Boeing's bid—a combination of Wellwood Beall's design and the Boeing XB-15 bomber (the installation of new Wright 1,500 hp Double Cyclone engines eliminated the lack of power that had handicapped the XB-15)—was accepted, and on 21 July 1936, Pan American signed a contract for six Boeing 314 *Clippers*.

Beall used a series of heavy ribs and spars that produced a strong fuselage and cantilevered wing, making external drag-inducing struts to brace the wings unnecessary. In place of the traditional floating stabilizers at the wingtips Boeing integrated Dornier Do X-type sponsons into the hull. The sponsons were broad lateral extensions at the waterline on both sides of the hull, shaped to add additional lift in flight. Sponsons performed several functions: they provided a wide platform to stabilize the craft while floating on the water; served as an entryway for boarding passengers; and contained fuel tanks which, with those in the wings, totaled 4,246 gallons for the -314 and 5,450 gallons for the -314A. Among the technical innovations forged by the B-314 were Hamilton Standard fully-feathering propellers that made it possible for a mechanic to perform repairs in flight, as the -314's wing was thick enough to allow access via a walkway to the engines in flight.

The enormous, whale-shaped flying boat was manufactured at Boeing Plant 1, on the Duwamish River, and then towed to Elliott Bay for taxiing and flight tests. Renowned Boeing test pilot Edmund "Eddie" Allen piloted the -314 on its first flight on 7 June 1938. Allen found he had inadequate directional control with the single vertical tail and the aircraft was returned to the factory; endplates were mounted on the ends of the horizontal tail, replacing the single vertical fin. This tail configuration was also found to be wanting and finally the centerline vertical fin was reinstated, giving the flying boat acceptable flying characteristics.

These enormous 84,000 lb. (maximum gross weight) aircraft had large areas for passengers and cargo, and would be the widest passenger aircraft until the Boeing 747 years later. The prevailing passenger airliner at the time was the twin-engine Douglas DC-2, which carried fourteen passengers (vs. seventy-four passengers for the -314) over routes nearing 1,000 miles (vs. the -314's 3,500 miles) and cost much less at about $80,000 (vs. $620,000). The *Clippers* were built for "one class" luxury air travel, a necessity given the long duration of trans-oceanic flights. Since first class was the only class, the fares could be afforded by only the very wealthy, but the journey was only about one-third of the time required to travel these distances by ship. The seats were couches that could be converted into thirty-six bunks for overnight accommodation. The passenger space was divided into five compartments, along with a roomy main lounge, separate men's and women's restrooms and changing rooms, and even a bridal suite in the tail. Five- and six-course gourmet meals were served on China dining and silver service by white-coated stewards. For most of the rather slow 188 mph journey, passengers only flew during the day and slept at comfortable hotels at night. Pan Am only assigned the very best and most experienced flight crews to Boeing 314 flying boat duty, with all Pan Am captains and first and second officers logging thousands of hours of flight time in other seaplanes and flying boats. They were also well-trained in dead reckoning, timed turns, judging drift from sea current, astral navigation, and radio navigation. Pan Am used nautical terminology during the flights and called its cabin attendants Stewards and later Stewardesses, terminology that survived until the politically correct age of "Flight Attendants."

The six-day, 8,200 mile, sixty-hour (flying time) flight from San Francisco to Manila was made in six hops, with the longest—between San Francisco and Honolulu (2,400 miles)—about 1,000 miles longer than any of the routes. Overnight flying was hazardous, because aircraft could fly into unforeseen storms; consequently, only the Honolulu-San Francisco leg included unavoidable overnight flying. Beyond Hawaii, Midway Island was 1,400 miles away, Wake Island was 1,300 miles farther, and Guam was an additional 1,600 miles; all could be flown in daylight. On barren Midway and Wake Islands, Pan Am had to construct service facilities and comfortable hotels. Since these facilities were used only once or twice a week and operating costs were huge, later Pan Am introduced *Clipper* service to New Zealand and other southern points. The Model 314 was drafted into service at the outbreak of WWII to ferry materials and personnel.

After the success of the six initial *Clippers* Pan Am placed an order for six improved 314A models to be delivered in 1941, doubling their service on the Atlantic and Pacific routes.

The 314A could carry seventy-seven daytime passengers, had increased engine power supplied by four 1,600 hp 14-cylinder air-cooled Wright GR-2600 Twin Cyclone radial engines, and had about 1,000 gallons more fuel capacity than the -314. The prototype Boeing 314A first flew on 20 March, but the fall of France in 1940 made Pan Am uncertain about whether the Atlantic service would continue and passenger numbers were already reduced due to the war. Three models were then bought by the British government and allotted to BOAC for use as transport aircraft.

After the war seaplanes became archaic, as non-stop, over-ocean aircraft such as the Lockheed Constellation would supersede them. The twelve large flying boats were destroyed (three were lost to accidents), sold off to start-up airlines (seven to World Airways), or were cannibalized for parts. In 1946, the *California Clipper* was the last Pan Am -314 to be retired after it had logged more than a million flight miles, ending the "Golden Age of Flying Boats."

Boeing 314 *Atlantic Clipper*

FIRST COMMERCIAL FLYING BOAT AROUND-THE-WORLD SERVICE

The First Round-the-World Commercial Service Flown

On 30 April 1940, Tasman Empire Airways Limited (TEAL), flying their Short S-30 Empire flying boat, initiated flight service between New Zealand and Sydney, Australia. This inaugural Auckland-Sydney flight was flown in Short S-30 (ZK-AMA) *Aotearoa* (Maori name for New Zealand), commanded by Capt. J. W. Burgess with ten passengers. Then the westward leg was flown via Imperial Airways to London (18 May), then connected with Pan American's trans-Atlantic flight service to New York (18 May), then westward via Pan Am transcontinental US service

Short S-30 Empire Flying Boat

from New York, New York (27 May), Denver (28 May), San Francisco (28 May), and finally left San Francisco on Pan Am's Trans-Pacific service back to New Zealand on 4 June, stopping in Hong Kong and then leaving for Australia on 12 June, and arriving in Auckland on 4 July, completing the not-so-fast round-the-world service.

FIRST (UNSCHEDULED) COMMERCIAL PAN AM ROUND-THE WORLD FLIGHT

On 7 December 1941, the Pan Am *Pacific Clipper* was en route to Auckland, New Zealand, when Capt. Robert Ford received a coded message that Pearl Harbor had been attacked by the Japanese and to land at the next destination and await instructions. The luxurious Boeing 314 Flying Boat was stranded six days from its San Francisco home port and its route back to the US cut off. After a week in the US Embassy in Auckland, Ford was finally instructed by Pan Am that they were to return to the US by flying westward over unfamiliar territory—much over water—without the assurance of gasoline and supplies. On 16 December, Ford, three passengers, and ten crew, including John Henry Mack (co-pilot), Rod Brown (navigator), and John Poindexter (radio operator), took off backtracking to Noumea, New Caledonia, to collect the Pan Am staff left there and headed west for Australia, landing north of Brisbane on the Coral Sea. The next day, the *Pacific Clipper* headed northwest to Darwin, then 1,400 miles over open ocean to Surabaya, in the Dutch East Indies (Indonesia). After refueling with automobile grade gasoline since no 100 octane fuel was available, the *Pacific Clipper* headed for Trincomalee, Ceylon (Sri Lanka), without any charts, but by navigator Roderick Brown's skillful navigation alighted safely and refueled. The Boeing 314 left Trincomalee on Christmas Eve, but soon had to return after losing an engine. After repairs they left for Karachi, India (Pakistan), and after an uneventful flight, Capt. Ford continued safely on to Bahrain and then across the vast Arabian Desert to Khartoum, Sudan, where they alighted on the Nile. The *Clipper* crossed the African continent to Leopoldville, Belgian Congo (now Kinshasa), and landed on the Congo River. It then flew 3,583 miles westward across the South Atlantic to Natal, Brazil, then up the coast to Port of Spain, Trinidad, and finally, on 6 January 1942, reached the Marine terminal at La Guardia, Long Island, New York. Total flight time was 209 hours and covered 31,500 miles, touching down on five continents, crossing three oceans, making eighteen stops, and crossed the equator six times to complete the first around-the-world flight by a commercial airliner. After this historic flight, the *Pacific Clipper* was assigned to the US Navy for the remainder of the war. When the war ended, the aircraft was sold to Universal Airlines, which salvaged it after it was damaged in a storm. (Note: The tale of this epic round-the-world journey is documented in *The Long Way Home* by Ed Dover.)

Pan Am Pacific Clipper

LARGE WARTIME FLYING BOATS

PBM Mariner Series

In 1937, the Martin Company was asked to develop a replacement to the very successful Consolidated PBY Catalina patrol flying boat. The Navy wished to supplant the PBY with a larger and longer-ranged aircraft, and the result was the PBM Mariner series (Mariner in keeping with Martin's custom of giving their aircraft names starting with M.) The Mariner had a wing span of 118 ft. and wing area of 1,408 sq. ft., a length of 79.8 ft., a height of 27 ft., an empty weight of 33,175 lbs., and a loaded weight of 58,000 lbs. The Mariner stressed crew comfort for long-range patrols, featuring soundproofing, heating, ventilation, fold-down bunks, and a galley that included a refrigerator, water heater, and an electrical stove. The Mariner carried the equipment it needed for routine maintenance. Many Mariners (1,364) were built, but its Wright 2600 engines were always considered under-powered and needed to be continually upgraded. With a range of only 2,250 miles, the Mariner was deemed only an adequate supplement and not a replacement for the venerable PBY Catalina.

PBM Mariner

JRM Mars

The US Navy had an interest in a very large patrol boat and awarded a contract to Martin on 23 August 1938 for the XPB2M-1 Mars, which would not be completed until September 1941.

Martin JRM Mars

The Mars was a scaled-up, extensively redesigned Mariner and was a bona fide "flying dreadnought," rivaling its BV 238 German Blohm & Voss competitor with a wingspan of 200 ft. (wing area 3,683 sq. ft.), a length of 117.3 ft., a height of 38.4 ft., an empty weight of 75,573 lbs., and a loaded weight of 165,000 lbs. The aircraft was powered by four 2,000 hp Wright 18-cylinder R-3350-18 Duplex Cyclone radial engines that gave it a range of almost 5,000 miles. The prototype first flew on 23 June 1942, and Martin continued test flights and upgrades until November 1943, when the Navy decided that large, lumbering patrol bombers were too vulnerable and the first Mars was converted to a cargo aircraft. The Navy then ordered twenty purpose-built JRM-1 transport versions for the sole intent of proving transport service (35,000 lbs. or up to 133 troops) between San Francisco and Honolulu. The first JRM-1, the *Hawaii Mars*, was completed in June 1945, but was destroyed in an accident in Chesapeake Bay on 5 August 1945. After the atomic bomb ended the war a few days later the Navy canceled all but five Mars flying boats. The remaining reliable and economical JRM-3s operated regularly on the San Francisco-Honolulu route, setting a number of records for freight hauling. The four remaining (one crashed) examples were retired in 1956 and were stored at NAS Alameda. In Spring 1959, the US Navy sold the four to British Columbia, where they were equipped with 6,000 gallon water tanks and used as water bombers for fighting Canadian forest fires.

HUGHES H-4 HERCULES SPRUCE GOOSE

Although Donald Douglas invested $2.5 million in the XB-19, the most notable self funding of an experimental aircraft was the Hughes H-4 Hercules *Spruce Goose*, which cost Howard Hughes three times more. The original design was the creation of Henry J. Kaiser, the leading builder of Liberty ships, who collaborated with aircraft designer Hughes to build what would become the largest aircraft up to that time. The original HK-1 designation reflected the Hughes and Kaiser collaboration. Its fully loaded cargo capacity was 150,000 lbs., which made the aircraft capable of carrying 750 fully equipped troops or two thirty-ton M4 Sherman tanks. The HK-1 contract was issued in 1942 as a developmental contract, requiring three aircraft be constructed within a two-year deadline. Seven configurations were considered, including twin-hull and single-hull designs with combinations of four, six, and eight wing-mounted engines. The final design chosen eclipsed any large transport then built. It would be constructed mostly of wood to conserve metal (its elevators and rudder were fabric covered), giving it the *Spruce Goose* label by the media. Kaiser did not have an aeronautical background and deferred to Hughes and his designer, Glenn Odekirk, to develop the aircraft. Development stretched out, frustrating Kaiser, who partially attributed the delays on the limitations placed on the acquisition of strategic materials like aluminum, but also placed much of the blame on Hughes' well-known insistence on "perfection." Although construction of the first HK-1 took place only sixteen months after the receipt of the development contract, Kaiser withdrew from the project in mid-1944. Hughes continued the program on his own under the designation H-4 *Hercules*, signing a new government contract that limited production to one aircraft. Work proceeded very slowly, and the H-4 was not completed until well after the war was over. The completed aircraft was truly impressive, with a wing span of 320.9 ft., a length of 218.8 ft., a height of the empennage of 79.3 ft., 30 ft. of the fuselage, and an empty weight of 250,000 lbs. and a loaded weight of 400,000 lbs. The aircraft was powered by a record eight 3,000 hp Pratt & Whitney R-4360 Wasp Major radial engines. In 1947, Hughes was called to testify before the Senate War Investigating Committee concerning the use of $25 million of government funds for this aircraft (Hughes had invested $7 million of his own money on the project to keep it going) and the $22 million spent for only two F-11 photo-reconnaissance prototypes, one of which crashed while Hughes was at the controls, nearly killing him. On 2 November 1947, during a break in the Senate hearings, Hughes returned to California to conduct H-4 taxi tests. The taxi tests began with Hughes at the controls and thirty-five others on board, including a co-pilot, two flight engineers, sixteen mechanics, two other flight crew, seven invited newspaper reporters, and an additional seven industry representatives. After the first two taxi runs, the final test run of the day was begun and the now famous newsreel showed the *Goose* picking up speed and lifting off to seventy feet above Long Beach Harbor at a speed of 135 mph, then "flying" for about a mile, "vindicating" Hughes, but the *Spruce Goose* never flew again. With the *Spruce Goose's* embarrassing exhibit the age of large flying boats ended.

Hughes' H-4 Hercules *Spruce Goose*

6
THE MILITARY BOMBER: QUEST FOR DISTANCE AND SIZE: 1920–1932

THE POSTWAR AMERICAN AIRCRAFT INDUSTRY

Soon after the 1918 Armistice, the American aircraft industry lapsed back into a prewar malaise, with the government cancelling contracts worth $100 million. US aircraft production plummeted from 4,345 aircraft in the last quarter of 1918 to just twenty-six during the last quarter a year later, with total US investment in the aircraft industry being about $5 million. More than ninety percent of the wartime aircraft production facilities were liquidated during 1919, and major investors lost interest, especially in light of the 1920 stock market mini-crash and worldwide economic downturn.

MB-1 AND MB-2 (NSB-1): THE STANDARD AAC BOMBER

The original MB-1 was a three-seat aircraft, with a gunner in the front who was to support troops on the ground. Donald Douglas used his engineering skills to adapt foreign technology, particularly that of the British de Havilland bomber designs, to increase the MB-1's power and size so the Army would consider it a bomber. The three-man, 45 ft. long MB-1 was an impressive aerial weapon, boasting a 71 ft. wing span and weighing more than 6,000 lbs. empty. It was powered by two 400 hp Liberty engines that propelled it to maximum speeds of 105 mph at 10,000 ft. The armament was an impressive five machine guns and 1,000 lb. bomb load. Only ten MB-1s were produced before the war ended: the first four "gunner aircraft" were used for observation and training; the next three were extensively redesigned by Douglas et al to the "bomber" configuration (only one was completed); and the last three were again extensively redesigned (one each) as the so-called GMT (Glenn Martin Transcontinental) long distance version—GMC (Glenn Martin Cannon) nose cannon armed and the GMP (Glenn Martin Passenger) carrying ten passengers in a cabin with windows. During the redesigns the cost of the MB-1 ballooned from $50,000 to $84,000.

The MB-2's first flight took place on 3 September 1920, as a wood and canvas twin-engined biplane (without staggered wings) bomber powered by two 420 hp Liberty 12A liquid-cooled V-12 engines which gave the bomber a then-remarkable speed of 100 mph and a range of 560 miles. Unlike the MB-1, whose engines were mounted between the wings, the engines of the MB-2 were fixed to the lower wing over the four main landing wheels on a single shaft. The twin vertical tails carried twin rudders. It was crewed by four men housed in open cockpits: a gunner/bombardier in the nose, pilot and co-pilot seated side-by-side in the control cockpit, and a rear gunner aft of the wings. The 48.7 ft. biplane with a 74 ft. wingspan could carry 1,800 lbs. of bombs in its enclosed bomb bay and a ton of external ordnance. It was heavily armed with four or five Lewis .30-caliber machine guns. Interestingly, the crew members of the bomber were protected with armor plate and Martin was experimenting with bullet-proof fuel tanks. Additionally, the MB-2 also had a unique folding wings system hinged outside the engine nacelles to fold backward for storage in small hangars. The basic MB-2 design was the criterion against which prospective US Army bomber designs were compared until the production of the Martin B-10 in 1933. Billy Mitchell used the bomber in his 1921 demonstration of the potential of air

Glenn Martin MB-1 bomber

Billy Mitchell's MB-2 bomber sinks the German battleship *Ostfriesland*.

power when he sunk German battleship *Ostfriesland* and established the MB-2 as the standard bomber serving the US Air Corps until the late 1920s, when they were replaced by the Keystone series of bombers.

BARLING BOMBER: AMERICA'S FIRST GIANT

After WWI, the US Army Air Service investigated the technical advances made by German Imperial Air Service, and Gen. William "Billy" Mitchell became intrigued with the German giants. The engineering division hired Walter Barling, a recent British immigrant who had worked at the Royal Aircraft Factory, to create a design to be designated XNBL-1 (Experimental Night Bombardment, Long distance), which was to be able to carry a 5,000 lb. bomb load at 10,000 ft. at speeds no less than 100 mph. Barling's design was similar to, but an improvement on (better engine placement), his unsuccessful RAF Tarrant Tabor (it nosed over in a fatal crash) design. On 23 June 1920, a contract for two prototypes was let to the lowest bidder, the Witteman-Lewis Company, Teterboro, New Jersey. The company manufactured all the parts, which had to be crated and shipped for assembly at Wilbur Wright Field, Dayton, Ohio, because it was one of only six US airfields that could accommodate the huge bomber.

To lift the desired load 4,200 sq. ft. of wing area was required, distributed over three wooden, fabric-covered wings with an overall span of 120 ft. Because the parts would have to be shipped by rail, a survey of tunnels and flatcars determined that the wings could not be more than 13.4 ft. wide for shipment. Although the aircraft used three wings it was not a tri-wing, but a two and a half wing, as the middle wing had no control surfaces and was shorter and narrower than the two primary wings. The fin and rudder resembled a box kite, with four vertical fins and rudders joining the horizontal surfaces. The all-spruce barrel-shaped fuselage was 10 ft. in its largest diameter and 65 ft. in length. At 27 ft., the Barling was taller than the Staaken Giants. Weight was 27,132 lbs. empty, 32,203 lbs. with normal load, and 42,569 lbs. with the full fuel load. The main landing gear had four wheels on each side, and the oleo struts allowed the forward pairs to be adjusted by the pilots for "eight point" landings and take-offs. A pair of safety wheels under the nose were added to prevent nose overs, but were deleted after flight tests. The engineering division was obligated to use four 420 hp Liberty 12A water-cooled engines because of its overabundance/availability. Four engines were placed between the lower and middle wings in a tractor arrangement with two-bladed tractor propellers, and an additional two in a pusher position turning four-bladed pusher propellers. Its two pilots sat in separate cockpits on either side of the fuselage, while the bombardier sat in the nose. One or two flight engineers sat behind the cockpits to supervise the engines (a first) and a radio operator and navigator were seated next to them. The Barling was armed with seven .30-caliber Lewis machine guns operated from five stations, protecting the bomber from every quadrant. Bomb racks were mounted in the enclosed bomb bay under the 2,000 gallon capacity fuel tanks. It was one of the first bombers to incorporate bomb bays on the bottom of the fuselage. The aircraft could carry 12,000 lbs., or up to 5,000 lbs. of bombs could be substituted for some of the fuel. Since Billy Mitchell championed this aircraft it was to be able to carry 2,000 or 4,000 lb. bombs designed specifically to sink a battleship.

The second prototype was canceled on 31 January 1922, and while parts for the first prototype arrived in Dayton in July, its final assembly had to await construction of a building large enough to cover the NBL-1. The original $375,000 estimate for two prototypes eventually increased to $525,000 for one. The Witteman-Lewis Company had to absorb the cost overruns and went out of business a few months later. Lt. Harold Harris, accompanied by co-pilot Lt. Muir Fairchild (later USAF chief of staff), a mechanic, and passenger/designer Walter Barling made the first flight (twenty-eight minutes) to Fairfield on 22 August 1923. Harris described the NBL-1 as not difficult to fly, but slow to respond to the controls. The aircraft required thirteen seconds and 960 ft. to take off; critics claimed it appeared as though it would roll all the way to Fairfield before it took off. By October 1924, Harris had made record flights to 6,722 ft. with a 4,410 lb. load and 4,472 ft. with 8,820 lbs., but this modest altitude capability prevented a flight over the mountains to either coast. Performance proved quite disappointing, with a range of 335 miles with maximum fuel, or only 170 miles when bombs replaced half of the fuel. Cruising speed was 61 mph, with a top speed of 96 mph at sea level. It took nearly twenty minutes to reach 5,000 ft., where 93 mph was possible. The service ceiling was only 7,725 ft., although an absolute ceiling of 10,200 ft. was thought possible.

Barling XNBL-1 bomber

Walter Barling shown much later with Consolidated's B-36.

The *Barling Bomber* encountered several embarrassing situations during testing caused by being seriously underpowered. The complex structure of the three wings caused so much drag that the six engines were just barely adequate. Performance was disappointing, as a fully loaded long-range XNBL-1 only had a range of 170 miles with a maximum speed of 96 mph, while the short-range Martin NBS-1 had a range of about 450 miles and could carry a one ton payload at the same speed. During a scheduled appearance at an airshow in Washington, DC, the bomber was unable to cross over the Appalachian Mountains! Then a $700,000 special hangar had to be constructed in 1925 at nearby Fairfield Air Depot to house the aircraft, whose wings collected water when outside in rainy weather.

Though often referred to as "Mitchell's Folly," Gen. Mitchell defended the project as "entirely successful from an experimental standpoint," but the *Barling* was never placed into production. The aircraft made its last flight in 1925, was disassembled in 1927, and placed in storage at Fairfield. In 1929, then-Maj. Hap Arnold submitted a Report of Survey to the office of the chief of the Air Corps (a position he would later hold) requesting permission to salvage the aircraft for parts and then burn the rest. Since several members of Congress had continued interest in the bomber Arnold's "to burn" request was denied, but a similar request was approved later, and the bomber was burned at Fairfield in 1930. The *Barling Bomber* would remain the largest American-built aircraft until 1935, when the Boeing XB-15 appeared.

An interesting sidelight to the *Barling Bomber* story was that a young Army Air Corps engineer named Isaac Laddon was signed on to several *Barling* test flights. Laddon would join Consolidated Aircraft Company in 1927, where he would design a series of seaplanes that would culminate in the renowned PBY Catalina, followed by his B-24 Liberator, the most produced WWII bomber. During 1941–42, when Laddon was the chief engineer on the XB-36 project in San Diego, Walter Barling would be working there.

In his 1949 biography, *Global Mission*, Hap Arnold justified the expensive development of the X-aircraft:

> "People generally do not understand that a plane (the *Barling Bomber*) like that cannot be classed as a one hundred per cent failure. It is true, the *Barling* itself failed to fly as planned, but many aeronautical engineering problems were solved by it. Records from wind-tunnel tests, theoretical analyses of details of assemblies, and newly devised parts on paper are all right, but there are times when the full-scale article must be built to get the pattern for the future. The B-19 and B-15 are other examples of this method of securing data. The big wooden airplane of Howard Hughes is still another. The positive progress gained from such 'abortive' experiments is always more important than the negative lessons learned from paper drawings. The *Barling*, if we look back on it without bias, certainly had some influence on the development of the B-17s that bombed Germany and the B-29s that bombed Japan."

MID-1920S HEAVY BOMBER COMPETITION

In 1926, funds were available to re-equip Army bomber squadrons with large five-place biplane heavy bombers and a number of aircraft companies were eager to be awarded a contract to remain viable. The Keystone Aircraft Corporation and the Curtiss Aeronautical Company were the two participants in the competition.

Huff-Daland/Keystone XB-1

Huff-Daland/Keystone

The Huff-Daland XB-1 *Super-Cyclops* prototype bomber was the first US aircraft using a B designation. Prior to 1926, the US Army used LB- and HB- prefixes (Light Bomber and Heavy Bomber). In 1927, the corporation was taken over and merged to become the Huff-Daland Division of the Keystone Aircraft Corporation. After the Army Air Corps decided that single-engined bombers such as the XHB-1 performed more poorly and with less safety than the more traditional twin-engined bomber, the only example of the single-engine Huff-Daland XB-1 bomber became the Keystone XB-1B, after its original 510 hp Packard 2A-1500 engine was replaced with two 600 hp Curtiss V-1570-5 Conqueror engines in 1928. The Keystone bomber, while not outstanding, was inexpensive, economical, and had good flying qualities, but still did not compare favorably to the other aircraft of the period and never entered production. Keystone merged with the Loening Company in 1928. By 1931, Keystone had become the Keystone Aircraft Division of Curtiss-Wright Corporation.

Atlantic-Fokker XLB-2

The Atlantic Aircraft Corporation of Teterboro, New Jersey, was the American subsidiary of Holland-based Fokker aircraft manufacturing company, and manufactured some Fokker-designed pioneering high-winged monoplane commercial airliners. Atlantic submitted a monoplane design developed from the Fokker monoplane C-2 transport under the designation XLB-2 in response to a 1926 USAAC competition for a successor to the Martin-designed NBS-1 bomber. A single prototype (s/n 26-210) was ordered on 28 May 1926, and was first flown 5 August 1927, having the distinction of being the first USAAC bomber designed as a monoplane. It was powered by a pair of 410hp Pratt & Whitney R-1340 Wasp radials suspended underneath the high cantilever wing. A crew of five manned the bomber, with the bombardier housed inside a glazed area in the lower nose. A pair of 0.5-inch machine guns were mounted in each of two open defensive gunner positions: one situated in the extreme nose and the other in a dorsal position on the upper rear fuselage. A single gun could be fired through a position in the lower rear fuselage. A 2,050 lb. bomb load could be carried. The aircraft was later fitted with a pair of 525 hp R-1690-1 radials, raising the maximum speed from 116 mph to 123 mph. The performance of the XLB-2 was not much better than that of existing Army biplane bombers. In addition, the Army was quite reluctant to consider such radical innovations as cantilever monoplane designs, and the XLB-2 was not ordered into production.

Atlantic-Fokker

Sikorsky S-37

In April 1927, Igor Sikorsky had a contract with Consolidated Aircraft to finance his Sikorsky S-37B Guardian biplane bomber that was completed on 9 December 1927, in College Point, New York. It was powered by two 525 hp air-cooled Pratt & Whitney Hornets. The biplane had a 100 ft. span upper wing overhanging a 58 ft. lower wing with obsolescent twin tail and rudders. Consolidated was to manufacture the production version had the S-37B won a contract, but the duralumin, fabric-covered airframe weight was nearly 1,000 lbs. over the design estimate, and it revealed major structural flaws in initial testing. The project was canceled when Consolidated refused to pay for the failed project, so Sikorsky remodeled it into a civil transport, that operated until 1934.

Sikorsky S 37

Curtiss XB-2

The Curtiss XB-2 was a direct development of the Curtiss-built Martin MB-2 (NBS-1) through the two Curtiss XNBS-4s, the primary difference being steel tubing was used instead of wood fuselage construction. Two new 600 hp Curtiss Conqueror liquid-cooled engines housed inside nacelles mounted on top of the lower wing were used in place of war surplus Liberty engines. A single Curtiss XB-2 Condor prototype (26-211) was ordered on 2 June 1926, and was tested first in July 1927, at Mitchel Field. The B-2 was a large fabric-covered biplane with two engines in nacelles between the wings. Like the NBS, the XB-2 had twin rudders with twin horizontal stabilizers on a twin tail, which was becoming obsolete by that time. In 1928, a production run of twelve B-2s was ordered and they were delivered May 1929–January 1930. Notable B-2 differences from the XB-2 included the use of three-bladed propellers and somewhat shorter and wider radiators mounted on top of the engine nacelles. During the early 1930s, advances in bomber design were so rapid that canvas-covered biplanes such as the B-2 rapidly became obsolete. Consequently, the B-2 served only briefly with the Army, being taken out of service in 1934. The last B-2 was surveyed in July 1936. Following production of the B-2 Curtiss Aircraft left the bomber business and concentrated on the Hawk series of pursuit aircraft in the 1930s.

Curtiss XB-2K Condor

Keystone XLB

The Wright-powered LB-6 was in competition with the Curtiss XB-2 for production in early 1928, and will be described next.

ARMY SELECTION BOARD

When the seven-officer Army Board met in February 1928 to select a bomber for production, it immediately rejected the

Huff-Daland/Keystone XB-1B, Atlantic-Fokker XLB-2, and Sikorsky S-37, but disagreed on the merits of the Curtiss XB-2 and Keystone XLB. Although Curtiss certainly had better performance, the XLB only cost $24,750 per unit, while the per unit cost of the B-2 was $76,373. Besides, the Curtiss was too big for existing hangars. By a four-to-three decision the board gave the Keystone XLB a production contract, but on 23 June 1928, Curtiss was granted a $1,050,473 contract for two B-2s (28-398/399) with a further ten ordered in 1929 (serials were 29-28/37). The B-2s were delivered 10 August 1929–16 January 1930, and remained in service with the 11th Bomb Squadron in California until 1934.

KEYSTONE BOMBERS

Between 1927 and 1932, the Air Corps took delivery of 210 Keystones of nineteen different models. All were twin-engine, five-place biplanes constructed of steel tubing covered by fabric, but continued to have open cockpits, struts, wires, and exposed wheels, appearing and performing much the same as the bombers they had replaced and giving military analysts and funding politicians cause to feel they had not gotten their money's worth. The bomber was called the *Panther* by the company, but the Army rejected the name.

The first Keystone was the LB-5 (Light Bomber-5), a twin-engine bomber of which thirty-six were built. These bombers had a wingspan of 74.7 ft. and a wing area of 1,145 sq. ft., a length of 48.8 ft., a height of 15.7 ft., an empty weight of 7,705 lbs., and a loaded weight of 12,952 lbs. Its two 525 hp Wright R-1750-3 radial engines gave a maximum speed of 111 mph, a cruising speed of 98 mph, and a range of 815 miles. It was armed with three .30-caliber machine guns and could carry a normal bomb load of 2,500 lbs., and up to 4,000 lbs. on short missions.

The LB-5 was followed by eighteen similar LB-6s and twenty LB-7s. The LB-10 was next to be ordered in large numbers, but before it could enter production the LB (Light Bomber) designation was canceled, and the aircraft was redesignated the Keystone Bomber-3A (B-3A). Of the sixty-three aircraft ordered, thirty-six were produced as B-3As and twenty-seven as re-engined B-5As. The final Keystone bombers were the B-4A and B-6A, of which thirty and forty-four were produced. All of these aircraft were actually only minor variations on the original LB-5, using different engines and in some cases different tail planes.

Keystone bomber

Keystone biplane bombers made up almost the entire US Army bombardment strength during the early 1930s, but their striking power, range, and ability to defend themselves were little greater than those of their predecessors, and their top speed reflected only that improvement offered by installing engines with more horsepower. These fabric-covered biplanes could not fly as fast or as far as required for strategic bombing, but a generation of new monoplane bombers would change that situation.

BOEING B-9

In the mid-1930s, AAC bomber squadrons were primarily equipped with slow, mediocre Keystone B-6 biplanes, and Boeing decided to design and build a twin-engine bomber based on its Monomail design as a private venture to re-equip the Air Corps. The Boeing YB-9, an enlarged version of the company's Model 200 Monomail Commercial Transport, was the first all-metal monoplane bomber aircraft designed for the Army Air Corps. The YB-9's innovative design emulated the Monomail's all-metal, semi-monocoque fuselage with stressed-skin construction, semi-retractable landing gear and a retractable tailwheel undercarriage, a cantilever mono-wing, and flight control servo tabs. The bomber had a wingspan of 76.8 ft. and a wing area of 954 sq. ft., a length of 52 ft., a height of 12 ft., an empty weight of 8,941 lbs., and a maximum take-off weight of 14,320 lbs. Its two 600 hp Pratt & Whitney R-1860-11 Hornet radial engines powered it to a maximum speed of 188 mph and a cruising speed of 165 mph over a range of 540 miles. So, while the YB-9 was much faster than the Keystone bombers, there was no improvement in range or bomb load. It was armed with two .30-caliber machine guns and could carry 2,360 lbs. of bombs.

The first of the two prototypes to fly was the Hornet radial-powered Model 215, which first flew on 13 April 1931, and was then leased to the Air Corps for testing under the designation XB-901. Testing was successful, and the XB-901 and incomplete Model 214 were purchased as the YB-9 and Y1B-9, respectively, on 13 August 1931, with an order for a further five for service testing following shortly afterward. The Y1B-9 (the Y1 indicating funding outside normal fiscal year procurement), powered by two liquid-cooled Curtiss V-1570-29 Conqueror engines, first flew on 5 November 1931. Meanwhile, the YB-9 was re-engined with more powerful air-cooled Hornet Bs that yielded slightly better performance than the Y1B-9; therefore, it was also re-

Boeing B-9

engined with Hornet Bs. Although the B-9s equaled the speed of all existing American fighter aircraft and it was a great advance over previous AAC bombers, only seven aircraft were built, as the Glenn L. Martin Company had flown a prototype of a more advanced bomber (XB-907) that was ordered into production as the outstanding Martin B-10, and later as the B-12.

Martin B-10

MARTIN B-10

The Martin B-10 was a groundbreaking bomber design, rendering all contemporary bombers wholly obsolete. At the time of its creation, the B-10 was so advanced that Ge. Henry Arnold declared it the "airpower wonder of its day." It featured an all-metal monoplane airframe, retractable landing gear, closed cockpits, Sperry automatic pilot rotating gun turrets, internal bomb bay, 600–775 hp Wright R-1820 Cyclone engines, full engine cowlings, constant-speed propellers, the addition of wing flaps, de-icers, and numerous structural and maintenance improvements. In 1932, Martin received the Collier Trophy for designing the XB-10.

The B-10B had a crew of four: pilot, co-pilot/radio operator, bombardier/gunner, and gunner. It had a wingspan of 70.5 ft. and a wing area of 678 sq. ft.; a length of 44.8 ft.; a height of 15.4 ft.; an empty weight of 9,681 lbs.; a loaded weight of 14,700 lbs.; and a maximum take-off weight of 16,400 lbs. Its Wright 1820s propelled the B-10B to a maximum speed of 213 mph; a cruising speed of 193 mph over a range of 1,240 miles; and a service ceiling of 24,200 ft. It was armed with three .30-caliber machine guns in the nose, dorsal, and ventral positions and carried a 2,260 lb. bomb load.

The B-10's advanced design made the bomber twice as fast as the current Keystone biplane bombers and as fast as many fighters, which convinced the AAC that bombers could successfully attack strategic targets without long-range fighter escort. From 1933–1936, the Air Corps ordered 121 B-10s, their largest bomber procurement since WWI. The Air Corps then ordered an additional thirty-two of these aircraft with 700 hp Pratt & Whitney R-1690 Hornet engines, designating them B-12s. By the late 1930s, B-17s and B-18s had replaced B-10s and B-12s, but once the AAC's orders had been filled in 1936, Martin received permission to export Model 139s. Martin delivered Model 139 versions to several air forces; the Chinese and Dutch air forces flew them in combat against Japan at the beginning of WWII. In a bungled attempt to modernize the design as the Model 146, Martin entered it into the AAC long distance bomber design competition of 1934–1935, but lost to the Douglas B-18 and the much larger Boeing B-17.

1934: Hap Arnold Flies the B-10 to Alaska

In 1934, the Martin B-10 was considered the most advanced bomber in the world. To demonstrate its capability the Air Corps sent a flight of ten bombers 4,000 miles to Alaska, which would "not only prove the feasibility of sending an aerial force to Alaska in an emergency, but it would be excellent training for personnel flying across isolated and uninhabited areas." The B-10s, under the command of an up-and-coming AAC officer, Lt.Col. H. H. Arnold—known as "Hap"—left Bolling Field, near Washington, DC, on 19 July. The route took the B-10s over the northern Midwest and Winnipeg and Edmonton, Canada, and on 24 July they arrived safely, circling Anchorage in formation and then, one by one, landing at Merrill Field, in Fairbanks, Alaska. For the next month they flew numerous exploratory flights over Alaska, including missions for the aerial photography of 23,000 square miles of isolated and desolate territory in only three days. Arnold and his executive officer, Maj. Hugh Knerr, also interviewed local pilots to collect information on air routes, weather, equipment, instruments, charts and navigation aids, and valuable information for winterizing the aircraft and their engines. The Martins left Fairbanks on 16 August and returned to Washington, DC, via Seattle and Omaha, landing at Bolling on 20 August, where they were welcomed by Secretary of War George Dern and Chief of the Army Air Corps Maj.Gen. Benjamin Foulois. On 9 April 1935, the recently promoted to Brig. Gen. Hap Arnold was awarded the Mackay Trophy for the mission.

Lt.Col. H. H. Arnold and the Martin B-10

7
QUEST FOR LONG-RANGE BOMBERS BEGINS

THE AIR MATERIEL COMMAND AND LONG-RANGE BOMBER REQUIREMENTS

By the mid-1930s, the global situation had begun to change, with the rise of Hitler and Mussolini in Europe and Japanese militarism in the Far East. In 1933, the disciples of Billy Mitchell's strategic air power theories had been promoted to levels of some importance in the Army Air Corps, particularly its research and development branch, the Air Materiel Command at Wright Field, Dayton, Ohio.

In the early 1930s, the Army Air Corps realized they needed a bomber with speed and range. However, range was contingent on aircraft size: the more fuel carried for longer range meant a bigger aircraft and larger wing to carry the increased fuel supply. Large aircraft were dependent on the availability of sufficient power plants (four). In 1933, the requirements of a long-range bomber were discussed at Wright Field by chief engineer James Howard, his assistant Al Lyons, aircraft branch chief James Taylor, Hugh Kneer of the field service section, and Leonard "Jake" Harman, the Air Materiel Command representative. The group decided to categorize the future bomber types that would be required:

Wingspan, 75 feet; gross weight 15,000 lbs. (that was already contemporary in the B-9 and B-10)

100 ft. span; 40,000 lbs. gross weight
150 ft. span; 60,000 lbs. gross weight
200 ft. span; 150,000 lbs. gross weight
250 ft. span; 200,000 lbs. gross weight
Etc.

In Fall 1933, it was decided to disregard the No.2 category, while category No.3 was considered a feasible choice and was to be identified as "Project A." Jake Harman drew up the requirement and Gen. Conger Pratt of Air Materiel Command authorized the funds for engineering designs and sent the request to Washington for approval. At the time strategic air power had few advocates, but long-range defensive patrol aircraft did have their proponents in Air Chief Benjamin Foulois and the Army General Staff. In 1933, Foulois directed his assistant, Brig.Gen. Oscar Westover, to fly missions testing the defense of the West Coast. Westover's report to the General Staff found the observation and patrol aircraft that flew these missions to be "woefully obsolete." He suggested that modern bombers flying in formation with increased speed and range could frustrate any "known agency." Pratt was able to sell the idea of the 5,000 mile bomber, as it could protect Alaska and Hawaii, and was a step in establishing a mobile General Headquarters Air Force (GHQ).

TOP / AAC hierarchy: Assistant Chief of the AAC Benjamin Foulois (L), Chief of the AAC James Fechet (C), and Chief of the Materials Division Conger Pratt (R)

BOTTOM LEFT / Chief of the AAC Oliver Westover

BOTTOM RIGHT / CO of the General Headquarters (GHQ) Air Force Frank Andrews

In the early 1930s, there was a dichotomy in the War Department. The conflict engaged the traditionalists, led by Army Chief of Staff Gen. John J. Pershing, who believed the infantry ruled the battlefield, while the Army Air Arm, led by the defrocked Gen. Billy Mitchell, espoused the future role of air power in warfare. The government organized a number of boards and committees to study air doctrine and its role in future warfare. The most influential of these groups was the Baker Board Report of July 1934, which recommended America's national defense policy was not based on aggression and its purpose was to defend the homeland and overseas possessions, with the Army fending off any invader until civilian forces could be mobilized. The Baker Report stated:

> The idea that aviation can replace any of the other elements of our armed forces is found on analysis, to be erroneous. Since ground forces alone are capable of occupying territory, the Army with its own air forces remains the ultimate decisive factor in war.

Baker Board member Jimmy Doolittle voiced the minority dissent, supporting the separation of the Army and its air forces and advocating the development of an air doctrine for its employment.

Although the Baker Board rejected an independent strategic air force, it did support the creation in March 1935 of a General Headquarters Air Force that would be under the control of the Army commander in the field. However, there were conflicting opinions of the role of the GHQ Air Force. One was that it would be allocated and attached to field armies and utilized under their direct control. Another view had the GHQ Air Force engaged as an integrated force acting to further the mission of the Army. The view held by most airmen was to have it act as a unified force not only to support the Army, but also to act beyond the realm of the Army with missions of its own. Maj. Gen. Frank Andrews was CO of the GHQ Air Force and forcefully advocated the airmen's point of view. As the possibility of a war in Europe approached the War Department was in a state of flux and the GHQ Air Force and its concepts were replaced by ideas formulated by the Joint Army-Navy Board that culminated in the First Strategic Air Plan (AWPD-1). AWPD-1 was submitted to the Army General Staff War Plans Division on 12 August 1941. The responsibility of the AWPD was to formulate a general plan for the employment of air power to defeat the Axis that would utilize air power to its fullest capability. The AWPD was to determine the size of the air forces required to defeat Germany first and then defeat Japan. Generally, it called for 24,500 combat aircraft, of which approximately 10,000 were to be four- and six-engine bombers. On 11 September 1941, Gen. Marshall accepted AWPD-1.

PROJECT A

On 14 April 1934, the top echelon of the Army General Staff (former cavalry officers) grudgingly approved top secret Project A, which was endorsed by young Billy Mitchell devotees who had risen to decisive positions in the AAC. The bomber was to be used not as an "offensive" weapon, but one for "hemispheric defense," intended to carry out defensive operations to Alaska, Hawaii, and Panama from CONtinental US (CONUS) bases.

Gen. Conger Pratt, head of Air Materiel Command, mailed out four requests for proposals for a bomber design that could fly 5,000 miles (four to five times the range of the B-10) at 200 mph carrying a one-ton bomb load. No production was to be actualized, as Project A was more of a proof-of-concept than a production military bomber. The submissions of the Glenn Martin Company of Baltimore and the Boeing Company of Seattle were chosen. On 12 May 1934, Pratt was authorized to begin negotiations for initial designs. On the fourteenth, he met with Boeing President Clair Egtvedt and Martin Works Manager C. A. Van Dusen (before Consolidated's Reuben Fleet hired him away from Martin the next year) at Wright Field. Pratt's aide, Leonard "Jake" Harman, explained the importance of Project A and presented the ambitious proposal, outlined design and cost estimate procedures, and told the two company representatives that he would like to have their proposals by 15 June. Back in Seattle, Boeing began a flurry of activity by drawing up the preliminary design for its Model 294 that the AAC designated XBLR-1 (eXperimental Bomber, Long-Range, Number-1). On 28 June, Boeing was awarded a $600,000 contract to build its Project A design, which was then designated the XB-15, and Martin was given another $600,000 contract for its Model 145, to be called the XB-16 (but no XBLR designation was assigned). The Boeing and Martin original designs were not similar in general configuration, with the Boeing design being more conventional.

EARLY PROJECT A BOMBER CONCEPTS

Martin XB-16 (Model 145A)

In late 1934, the Martin Company presented the AAC with a proposal for a large, fast, long-range heavy bomber twin-tail design with a wing span of 140 ft. and wing area of 2,600 sq. ft., a length of 84 ft., and a height of 19.6 ft. It was to weigh 32,000 lbs. empty (65,000 lbs. gross), and had a useful load of 33,000 lbs. that was to include a bomb load of 2,500 lbs. It was to have a normal range of 5,000 miles and a maximum range without bombs of 6,200 miles. The XB-16 was to be powered by four Allison V-1710 inline liquid-cooled engines instead of the large air-cooled radial engines in common use in bombers of the 1930s (Boeing's XB-15 design used Pratt & Whitney radials). The four 1,000 hp Allisons were buried entirely in the wings, driving 12.25 ft. propellers via extension shafts. The inboard nacelles were enlarged to accommodate the dual five foot tires of the landing gear. Estimated top speed with supercharging at 20,000 ft. was to be 237 mph, while cruising speed was to be 120 mph. The service ceiling was estimated at 22,500 ft., with a rate of climb of 740 ft. per minute. A landing speed of 60 mph was anticipated via the use of large Fowler-type flaps measuring 360 sq. ft. that spanned 80 ft. The defensive armament was to be in the Plexiglas nose and tail enclosures and retractable dorsal and ventral turrets. A bomb load of 12,180 lbs. was to be carried 3,200 miles with a flight endurance of 42 hours with 4,238 gallons of fuel. A crew of ten was to have operated the aircraft.

XB-16 (Revised)

In 1935, Martin revised the XB-16 design with two thin P-38-like tail booms attached to the wings and a curious P-38-like central pod-type fuselage housing the 10/11 man crew cockpit and payload as part of the wing. The wing span was increased from 140 ft. to 173 ft. (twenty percent greater than the B-29 Superfortress), giving it a 4,256 sq. ft. wing area. The bomber was 114.8 ft. long, ending in a twin tail. Its empty weight was 50,660 lbs. and its gross weight was 104,880 lbs. It was powered by six buried 1,000 hp V-1710-3s: four tractors on the leading edge of the wing and another pair of V-1710 pusher engines added to the trailing edge, each driving their propellers through extension shafts. A fuel tank capacity of 7,435 gallons gave the aircraft an estimated range of 3,300 miles carrying 2,500 lbs. of bombs. It had a maximum speed of 265 mph, a cruising speed of 140 mph, and an estimated landing speed of 77 mph. The bizarre proposal included one of the first tricycle landing gears, with large diameter main tires partially exposed when the gear retracted into the wing.

Martin XB-16 (Model 145A)

Martin designers failed to understand that their advanced design would not be chosen, as the economics at the time would not support the costs of developing such a complex and ambitious project. Also, the Allison V-1720 was not available until mid-1937, and then for established fighter aircraft ready for production. The Martin XB-16 project was canceled by the AAC while on the drawing board, while Boeing's immense XB-15 was built and flown, giving Boeing valuable data on constructing large aircraft.

Martin XB-16 (Revised)

Boeing XB-15 (Model 294)

By mid-1934, Boeing was coming to the end of manufacturing a long line of biplane fighters based on the same design: the P-12 for the Air Corps and the F4B for the Navy. The company had orders for the P-26 all-metal monoplane pursuit, but most were to be delivered by Summer 1934, and the Navy had already rejected Boeing's offer for a successor to the F4B. Boeing had plans to develop the smaller Model 299 four-engine bomber (the future B-17), but had no assurances that the design would be successful, or that the AAC would then purchase it.

Once the Martin XB-16 proposal was rejected, on 29 June 1935, a new Boeing aircraft was officially designated the XB-15 (AAC serial number 35-277). A Boeing press release heralded the XB-15: "Engineering work began on this Boeing design in January 1934 and the result is a single remarkable research model that is the largest aircraft ever built." The XB-15 was an all-metal 70,700 lb. giant with a 149 ft. wingspan, an 87.7 ft. length, and a 19.4 ft. height. The aircraft was very similar in appearance to the B-17, except for its much tapered wing.

The Boeing design team, headed by Jack Klystra, initially intended the aircraft to use 2,600 hp Allison V-3420 liquid-cooled W engines (coupled V-1720s), but since these were not ready, 850 hp Pratt & Whitney R-1830 air-cooled radial engines were to be used instead. Developmental problems delayed its first flight until 15 August 1937, when the XB-15 was equipped with four more powerful 1,000 hp (rated) Pratt & Whitney

R-1830-11 engines. But even these more powerful engines were found to be insufficient, thus the XB-15 was underpowered and its performance was mediocre; a problem that would be faced by all would-be super bombers. The ACC specified speed of 200 mph was not quite attained even when the aircraft was empty, as its best speed attained in level flight was 197 mph; with the specified 2,000 lb. load, the maximum speed was a disappointing 145 mph, which was considered too slow for a combat aircraft. The Boeing engineers did project one advantage: the prototype would be capable of carrying the heaviest air cargo to date—a load of 8,000 lbs. Although the under-powered XB-15 did not fulfil AAC specs, in depressed 1935, the government could only afford to buy one ex-super bomber from Boeing as a flying laboratory (much like the Douglas XB-19).

In the meantime, the prototype B-17 (designated Model 299) had been developed and built at Boeing's own expense, combining features of the experimental XB-15 with the Boeing 247 transport aircraft. The Model 299 made its first flight on 28 July 1935—two years earlier than the XB-15—and was officially designated the Y1B-17, with thirteen already completed, so the well-known B-17 Flying Fortress saga began.

Nonetheless, with the time and money already invested and with a design that was unique in many ways, Boeing continued design and testing under the XBLR Project D program. The XB-15 would provide its engineers with beneficial experience toward future development of the B-29 and used an adapted XB-15 wing for its Model 314 Flying Boat that would give the company an advantage over Sikorsky and Martin for Pan American Clipper orders.

The XB-15 was—at the time, until the XB-19—the most heavily armed bomber ever built, as it was defended by three .30-caliber and three .50-caliber machine guns supplied with 7,200 rounds in six turrets. It had the first 110 volt AC electrical system, with generators driven by two auxiliary power plants (independent of the main engines). The XB-15 also pioneered autopilot and deicing equipment. It had a "comfort conditioned" living and sleeping quarter, including a kitchenette and lavatory for its crew of ten, which included for the first time a flight engineer. There was a passageway leading through the thick wing for in-flight servicing of the engines.

On 2 December 1937, the XB-15 flew from Seattle to Wright Field, Ohio, to be accepted by the AAC for testing and reevaluation. The XB-15 project was to be continued as the Model 316 in March 1938, as a proposed service test type (the Y1B-20) in June, and would bear a striking resemblance to the future B-29. The high (157 ft./2,920 sq. ft.) winged Y1B-20 was to have pressurized crew quarters, four 1,400 hp Pratt & Whitney GR-2600-A73 engines, and a tricycle landing gear carrying its 109 ft. fuselage. Secretary of War Harry Woodring canceled the proposed project before construction began in favor of the continuation of the Douglas XB-19, which was already under (slow) development. Boeing persisted with an internal redesign of the XB-15, and thus the progression of design work beginning with the XB-15 finally resulted in the Model 345 in May 1940, the very heavy bomber which led to the Boeing B-29 Superfortress.

Boeing's Model 314 Clipper Flying Boat, one of the largest aircraft of the time, benefitted from the XB-15 program, especially the intact transfer of its wing, which helped the aircraft achieve the range necessary for transoceanic flights. Boeing Chief Salesman Wellwood Beall, who had worked on the XB-15 original design, was instrumental in the sale of the Flying Boat to Pan Am. Twelve *Clippers* were built; nine for Pan Am that were later transferred to the military, while the remaining three were sold to British Overseas Airways Corporation (BOAC) and delivered in early 1941.

In 1939, Boeing had developed a large flying boat proposal for the Navy (the Model 320) based on XB-15 technology. It was to have two thin hulls, with a central fuselage nacelle that was partially enclosed in the thick section of the leading edge of an up-scaled wing that resembled that of the XB-15. Its wing span was 200 ft. and area was 4,415 sq. ft., as compared to the XB-15's 149 ft. and 2,780 sq. ft., respectively. It was powered by six 1,650 hp Wright GR-2000 Double Cyclones, which would carry the proposed bomber 7,000 miles while carrying twenty-four 1,000 lb. bombs, plus six 3,300 lb. torpedoes. The proposed bomber, while impressive on paper, remained on paper.

Later, after its use as a test bed and flying laboratory was terminated, the original XB-15 had a large door cut into its fuselage and continued its days as the XC-105 transport, based in Panama with the 6th Air Force. It would set several payload and load-to-altitude records and flew relief supplies to earthquake victims in Chile before it was scrapped in 1945.

Boeing XB-15 (Model 294)

Boeing Y1B-20/XB-20 (Boeing 316)

After a comprehensive reassessment of the underpowered XB-15, the Model 316 was presented to the Army by Boeing in March 1938 as a design improvement on the XB-15. The Model 316 was offered in several variations, including one with four 1,350 hp Wright GR-2600-A73 14-cylinder Cyclones and another powered by 1,400 hp Pratt & Whitney R-2180-5s. The 109.2 ft. long, 23.3 ft. high Model 316D version featured a high-wing design of 152 ft. span with an area of 2,920 sq. ft. It had a tricycle landing gear, a standard single tail, and a pressurized crew quarter for nine to ten crew members in the fuselage. This Wright-powered Model 316 was to have an estimated maximum speed of 258 mph, a cruising speed of 242 mph, a service ceiling of 31,200 ft., and a range of 4,000 miles. In this configuration it weighed 50,680 lbs. empty and 87,600 lbs. gross, including a 17,600 lb. bomb load ranged from sixteen 1,100 lb. bombs to forty-two 100 lb. bombs and a fuel capacity for 4,450 gallons. Proposed armament included four .50-caliber and three .30-caliber machine guns singly in teardrop turrets. The AAC ordered two examples of this version in June 1938 under the designation Y1B-20, and is sometimes referred to as the XB-20. However, the reversal of the super bomber concept soon caused the cancellation of both Y1B-20 prototypes, while the order was still in the model/drawing board stage. The Army concluded the Y1B-20 was just too expensive, and that it did not require a new bomber with range or carrying ability over that of the B-17. Boeing continued to develop and refine the original design, which would culminate in the B-29 Superfortress.

Boeing Y1B/XB-20 (Boeing 316)

Boeing Model 299 and the YB-17

In a memorandum of 14 July 1934, Air Materiel Command had changed its thinking and decided that a second bomber that was not as grand as the Project A bomber could more easily be realized and put into production. The new AAC bomber was to have the same 2,000 lb. bomb load, but its speed was to be 200 mph and its range was to be at least 1,020 miles, although 2,200 miles was much preferred. The AAC proposal was for "multi-engines," which to the AAC meant two, but to Boeing meant four. On 26 September 1934, the board of directors of the newly independent Boeing Airplane Company met for the first time after parent United Aircraft & Transport was finally dissolved. The new board boldly voted $275,000 to design and build a bomber to meet the new AAC specification. Boeing President Claire Egtvedt assigned Project Engineer E. G. "Giff" Emery, with Edward Wells as his assistant and Frederick Laudan as construction supervisor to work on the Model 299. The bomber was to be a low-wing monoplane that would have four engines powering it and was essentially an up-scaled version of Boeing's streamlined Model 247 twin-engine airliner first flown in February 1934. Concurrently, Egtvedt ordered Emery to develop a four-engine airliner based on the Model 299 design that was to become the Model 307 Stratoliner. With Emery running the Model 307 project, Egtvedt placed twenty-four-year-old Edward Wells as project manager of the Model 299, which had been unofficially designated the "XB-17" by Boeing before it was approved by the AAC. The Model 299 made its first flight on 28 July 1935, and the media was impressed by its size, dubbing it the "Flying Fortress." On 20 August, project test pilot Leslie "Les" Tower flew it cross-country 2,100 miles to Wright Field for evaluation at an average speed of 232 mph.

During testing at Wright Field, the four-engine Boeing Model 299 was to challenge Douglas Aircraft's twin-engine DB-1 bomber—the XB-18 developed from the company's successful DC-3 airliner design. From August into October the AAC examined both bombers, and the Boeing's better range and reliability earned it the lead in gaining a contract. On 30 October 1935, Boeing test pilot Les Tower, AAC pilot Maj. P. P. "Pete" Hill, and the test crew took off in the Model 299. Once it became airborne, the bomber became uncontrollable, and as it passed over the end of the runway it crashed in a nearby pasture. Hill was killed on impact, but Tower survived with horrible burns, dying twenty days later. Lt. Donald Putt was pulled from the burning wreckage and given little chance of survival, but Putt did survive, and four years later would become the project manager of the B-29 program. Investigation showed that the ground crew had not unlocked the tail control surfaces, causing the crash that would put the Boeing program in jeopardy. The Douglas XB-18 had also done relatively well in tests, and two of these twin-engine Douglas bombers could be manufactured for the cost of one Model 299. On 17 January 1936, the Army General Staff decided to order 133 production B-18s and only thirteen Model 299s now designated the YB-17 (the "Y"

Douglas XB-18

Model 299 crash

Boeing YB-17

meant the aircraft was not experimental, but a "service test" model that could, or not, precede production aircraft). Boeing put the Y1B-17 into production. The first Y1B-17 rolled off the Seattle line on 2 December 1936, and the last of the thirteen was finished on 5 August 1937. One Y1B-17 was sent to Wright for testing and the other twelve were assigned to the Second Bombardment Group at Langley Field, Virginia, under Lt.Col. Robert Olds. The B-18 would fade into oblivion, while the B-17 was slated to become America's premier four-engine bomber.

B-17 Long-Distance Flights of the Late 1930s

As part of their effort to have their bombers and pursuits realized as a weapon of war, the AAC's High Command—especially the emerging young officers and disciples of the "Billy Mitchell doctrine"—flew and then touted their long-distance flights. After the 1927 Lindbergh trans-Atlantic flight and its accompanying hoopla the American public had an appetite for the romance of aviation and the AAC wanted to showcase its new B-17.

Joint Air Exercise No. 4

On 4 March 1937, the 2nd Bombardment Group, commanded by Lt.Col. Robert Olds, received the first of the newly developed B-17 Flying Fortress heavy bombers, with twelve delivered during Spring and Summer 1937. The B-17 was to make their first noteworthy operational impact during Joint Air Exercise No. 4, an Army-Navy summer maneuver conducted in the Pacific off San Francisco authorized by a directive of President Roosevelt on 10 July 1937. The target ship *Utah* was assigned to represent an enemy fleet of two battleships, an aircraft carrier, and nine destroyers. A patrol wing of thirty Navy aircraft commanded by R.Adm. Ernest King was assigned to locate the enemy, after which a force of forty-one Air Corps bombers (including seven B-17s and several B-18s operating from March Field) were to engage it. The War Department limited Air Corps aircraft to operating no more than 300 nautical miles offshore, even though the directive specified an exercise area out to 500 nautical miles.

The Navy patrol planes began the twenty-four hour exercise at noon on 12 August 1937, and after several hours of searching through a low fog found the *Utah* 275 nautical miles offshore and trailed it heading northwest. The Air Corps bombers were dispatched to attack the former battleship *Utah*, but were unable to locate it, because the *Utah* had actually been fifty nautical miles west of the search area due to an error in the Navy's position reports, which Admiral King later blamed on a "clerical error." The *Utah* then vanished into the widespread low fog during the night and poor weather prevented an early morning search. At 0900 on 13 August, Brig.Gen. Delos Emmons, commander of the GHQ Air Force's 1st Wing, dispatched Olds, accompanied by Maj.Gen. Frank Andrews (commanding the GHQ Air Force), to lead his bombers to search a 30,000 square mile area covered by low clouds. Olds speculated the *Utah* had feinted toward San Francisco, but headed south to attack the industrial Los Angeles area. They patrolled toward the south, where a Navy patrol plane reported the *Utah* at 1100 moving southeast 285 nautical miles off the coast. Olds' B-17s located the *Utah* shortly before the noon conclusion of the exercise and effectively dropped Navy-supplied water bombs from an altitude of 400 ft. on the *Utah*.

When the Navy disputed the low altitude attack, maintaining that evasive action could have avoided the bomb hits, both B-17s and B-18s repeated the mission the next day, with the B-17s bombing the *Utah* from 18,000 ft. After this mission the Air Corps produced photographs and bombing data that showed it achieved a better percentage of hits and near misses than before. The Navy subsequently had the exercise classified secret, while the joint report sent to the president by the secretaries of the Navy and war omitted the data showing the Air Corps' success in navigation and bombing. Despite the secrecy restriction, the success of the B-17s was leaked to radio commentator Boake Carter, who disclosed it to the public.

B-17s Fly to Latin America

Lt.Col. Robert Olds, Commander of the 2nd Bomb Group, made two record breaking non-stop transcontinental flights in January 1938 between Langley Field, Virginia, and March Field, California, completing the 2,317 miles in just over 11 hours on the return flight. The next month President Roosevelt approved a B-17 "goodwill" flight to be commanded by Olds, with a young 1Lt. named Curtis LeMay as its lead navigator. The trip stopped in Miami, Panama, and Lima, and arrived in Buenos Aires on 17 February. Three days later they conducted a flyover for the inauguration of President Roberto Artiz. The B-17s returned to Langley via Santiago, Lima, and Panama, completing a nearly 11 hour direct flight from the Canal Zone on 27 February. The 11,952 mile round trip won the 1938 Mackay Trophy, earned Olds the DFC, and the B-17 Flying Fortress and the 2BG favorable widespread attention from Latin American and US press. Secretary of War Harry Woodring

Commander of the 2BG Lt.Col. Robert Olds

stated: "This flight of over 10,000 miles was accomplished with a high degree of skill in pilotage, navigation and maintenance proficiency."

INTERCEPTING THE ITALIAN LINER REX

During May 1938, the Air Corps conducted one of the largest maneuvers in its history, comprising 468 officers, 2,380 enlisted men, and 131 aircraft from all three wings of the GHQ Air Force based at eighteen airports in the northeast United States; they were assigned as the Blue Force, defending New England from the Black Force, an attacking aircraft carrier fleet. After the Joint Air Exercise No. 4 debacle, the Navy refused to send ships for Black Force. When newspapers criticized the maneuvers for using a "mythical fleet" as a target, Chief of the Air Corps Information Division Lt.Col. Ira Eaker suggested that the Italian Line's SS *Rex*—headed for New York—be substituted. Olds then devised a "training mission" in which a flight of B-17s would intercept the *Rex* at sea to demonstrate the long-range bomber's capabilities. During the morning of 12 May 1938, three B-17s took off from Langley Field commanded by Maj. Caleb Hayes, with 1Lt. Curtis LeMay as the lead navigator for the flight. Information Officer Eaker made certain that two of the B-17s had New York newspaper reporters aboard, while the third had an NBC radio commentator aboard to give a live broadcast of the *Rex* flyover. Despite poor weather, after a four-hour flight the three B-17s successfully intercepted the *Rex*, which was cruising about 800 miles east of New York City, and made several passes over the ship to allow for still and motion picture photography. The Air Corp's low altitude photographs were featured the next day on the front pages of hundreds of newspapers, as Eaker exploited the mission to bolster the credibility of the Air Corps' claims that air power was essential in defending the western hemisphere. The US Navy protested that the flight was not for coastal defense, which was its province. (Note: On 24 August 2007, three B-52 Stratofortresses of the 2nd Bomb Wing, successor to the 2nd BG, conducted Operation Rex Redux, a training mission commemorating the interception of the *Rex* by flying from Barksdale AFB, Louisiana. Using the radio call signs Rex 51, Rex 52, and Rex 53, the B-52s intercepted the Military Sealift Command ship *MV 2nd Lt. John P. Bobo* east of Bermuda to test a new targeting system.)

B-17s intercepting the Italian liner *Rex*.

PROJECT D: BLR FOR "BOMBER, LONG-RANGE"

On 5 February 1935, the Army Air Corps initiated a top secret project for an experimental long-range bomber, that combined Project A into the new Project D, which was a proposal asking for "the maximum feasible range into the future," pushing the technological envelope when it came to building a very long-range bomber. On 21 March 1935, Project D was tentatively approved, and on 29 April 1935, Military Characteristics were submitted. Final approval of the project was given on 23 May 1935, after the submission of further supporting data. Type Specification X-203 was prepared by the Materiel Division to cover preliminary design data and mockups. Both contracts included an option to purchase complete or partial physical articles. No production expectation was envisaged, since Project D was more of a proof-of-concept instrument than a serious proposal for a production military aircraft.

The combined program was designated BLR for "Bomber, Long-Range," and much like classified bomber competitions, the manufacturers were given an XBLR designation. Under Project D, the slow-to-develop XB-15 was to continue its development as the XBLR-1, as it was considered the winner of the Project A competition against the non-starter Martin XB-16. Contract W-535-AC-8132 with the Douglas Aircraft Company and with Sikorsky Aviation Corporation was prepared to cover preliminary design data and mockups. Both contracts included an option to purchase complete or partial physical articles. Thus, the XB-15/XBLR-1 was joined under the BLR program by two other projects: one from Douglas Aircraft as the XBLR-2 and one from Sikorsky Aircraft called the XBLR-3. These three major manufacturers were competing to build what would be the most advanced bomber ever conceived by the US. The next year, the XBLR contract was canceled for the Boeing prototype, and it once again reverted to the XB-15 designation. The AAC ordered full-scale mockups of each design for evaluation.

Sikorsky XBLR-3

Little is known of the original Sikorsky XBLR-3 competitor designed in 1935–1936. The original XBLR-3 concept was thought to be an exotic, twin boom bomber design powered by four engines using pusher and tractor propellers and bristling with many gun stations. A final, more conventional design was tendered to the AAC on 29 February 1936, as the XBLR-3 (Project No. M5-35 Restricted). The 120 ft. long, 35 ft. high aircraft was to have a 205 ft. wing span and 3,614 sq. ft. wing area. Four 1,600 hp Allison XV-3420-1s were to turn four three-bladed 15 ft. diameter constant-speed propellers. A tricycle gear supported a gross weight of approximately 120,000 lbs., including a 7,000 lb. fuel load. It was to have a maximum range of 7,650 miles, a service ceiling of 18,200 ft., and a cruising speed of 130 mph. A wooden mockup was fabricated and wind tunnel tested, and was then presented to the AAC in March 1936, but after analysis the AAC rejected the design in favor of the XB-19. The XBLR-3 was to be the last land plane design prepared by Sikorsky before the company committed itself to helicopters.

Sikorsky XBLR-3

Douglas XBLR-2/XB-19

At a time when Boeing was experiencing a somewhat precarious financial situation, the company was cautious about its XB-15 contract. With his company in a prospective financial upswing, Donald Douglas was eager to garner the new prestigious XBLR-2/XB-19 contract from the AAC. In February 1935, when Douglas first began talks with the Air Corps for a second Long-Range Experimental Bomber (with no XBLR designation yet assigned) under Project D, it was anticipating initial mass orders for the first of its ground breaking new DC-3 commercial airliners, which had begun construction two months before. Its military business would also soon pick up, with substantial orders for its B-18 bomber derivative of the DC-2, and over the next three years ongoing contracts were signed or anticipated for its new SBD Navy dive bomber and the new DB-7 twin-engine attack bomber that would lead to the peerless A-20 Havoc light bomber. While Douglas' future profitability was insured, Donald Douglas would come to regret the XB-19 contract.

XBLR-2

The enormous, all-metal, low-winged XBLR-2 was an innovative design supported by an unconventional (for the time) retractable tricycle undercarriage with the largest wheels ever installed on an aircraft. The aircraft was to be powered by complex and very powerful engines, and passages were built into the lower section of the thick internal wing structure for mechanics to service the engines in flight. The original power plants were to be four experimental 1,600 hp Allison XV-3420-1 liquid-cooled, 24-cylinder engines that were basically a pair of 12-cylinder Allison inline V engines coupled together. These complex engines were not yet available, and were replaced with 2,000 hp Wright R-3350 air-cooled radial engines.

XB-19

By 1938—three years after the original Project D proposal—the AAC awarded the XBLR-2 a production contract for a single prototype re-designated XB-19 (the XB designated it as an eXperimental Bomber). Never a high AAC priority, as time passed funding for the gigantic bomber was erratic and slowed progress on its construction. Meanwhile, numerous changes increased its weight, and the XB-19 was becoming obsolete, so Donald Douglas requested the project's cancellation. The AAC refused and Douglas continued half-hearted, sporadic construction.

Because many of its technologies were no longer revolutionary enough to justify keeping the XB-19 secret, finally, in 1940, the AAC declassified the giant bomber. The media was captivated by the "top secret gigantic super bomber that could fly across oceans and attack foreign countries and return home." In May 1941, the completed XB-19 was the largest aircraft America had ever built, with a 212 ft. wingspan (about 18 ft. longer than an early Boeing 747-100's span), 132 ft. long (vs. 232 ft. for the 747-100), 42.5 ft. high (vs. 63 ft. for the 747-100), and weighed 130,000 lbs. empty and 159,000 lbs. loaded (vs. 358,000 and 735,000, respectively, for the 747-100). The aircraft was to be operated by a crew of sixteen, but could carry an additional eight more crew for extended missions, consisting of relief pilots and mechanics. Bunks and a complete galley were also an innovation, as the aircraft's relatively low cruise speed of approximately 170 mph and 11,000 gallon fuel load would mean missions could last more than twenty-four hours and fly 7,500 miles in ferry configuration. For combat, the XB-19 was bristling with guns: five .50-caliber and six .30-caliber machine guns, and a pair of 37 mm cannons unique among American bombers of the time. The XB-19 carried a very heavy bomb load in its very large bomb bay, which could accommodate an enormous load of 18,000 lbs. of bombs, while the ten underwing racks could carry bombs of up to 2,000 lbs. each. The maximum bomb load totaled an incredible 37,000 lbs., although its normal 4,200 mile range would be noticeably shortened. By comparison, the B-17 could carry a maximum load of about 8,500 lbs. of bombs on short-range missions, but typically carried half that on long-range missions.

Years behind its original schedule, the XB-19 finally flew in June 1941, amidst great media hoopla. The bomber continued test flights over California from March Field with relatively few problems throughout the remainder of 1941. When Pearl Harbor was attacked the XB-19 had its polished aluminum fuselage painted in olive camouflage, and armament was installed for its last few test flights due to fears of a Japanese strike on the West Coast. The virtually obsolete bomber was transferred to Dayton, Ohio, to serve as a "flying laboratory," and test flights continued for some time before it became obvious the massive and impressive bomber had been superseded by the smaller B-24 and B-1, which could be built more quickly, less expensively, and in greater numbers; and by then the Boeing B-29, which, owing many of its innovations to the XB-19, was on the production line. Once testing was concluded, the XB-19's Wright 3350 engines were replaced with the production version of her original intended power plant, the 24-cylinder, turbocharged, 2,600 hp Allison V-3420-11 engine, which changed the XB-19's designation to XB-19A. The four Allisons increased the aircraft's performance and dramatically increased the top speed fifty miles per hour from 225 mph. Nonetheless, the XB-19A steadily became even more of a white elephant and served the last years of the war hauling cargo, then serving in the All-Weather Unit more or less as a parked aircraft. By mid-1946, it was stored at Davis Monthan AFB, Arizona, intended for future display, but in 1950, the aircraft was mistakenly scrapped. (For a comprehensive look at the XB-19 see *An Illustrated History of the Douglas XB-19: America's Would-be Intercontinental Bomber*, Schiffer 2017.)

Douglas XB-19 with 2,000 hp Wright R-3350 engines

XB-19A with 2,600 hp Allison V-3420-11 engines

XB-19 Cockpit

XB-19 engineer and radio compartment

THE 1937–1938 "SUPER BOMBER" REQUISITES

In October 1937, AAC Chief of Staff Gen. Oscar Westover decided to initiate informal design requisites for another "super bomber" that would succeed the B-17 and stifle the development of the too-large XBLR-2/XB-19. This super bomber was to be much larger and heavier than the B-17, and also to be able to fly farther and faster with a heavier bomb load. Previously, scant attention had been paid to improving bomber operational efficiency by totally redesigning and cleaning up its airframe configuration and increasing the fuselage size to accommodate the interchangeability of fuel and bomb loads. The tricycle landing gear concept was in vogue with designers, and while it did ease ground handling, take-offs, and landings, it added weight to the design. A super bomber that was to fly faster and farther would require designing new and more powerful engines. Designers understood the means to increase range and speed was to fly at altitudes above 25,000 ft., but this presented problems of extreme cold and lack of oxygen not only for the crew, but also for the engines. The engines would have to be "supercharged" for the intake of compressed and heated air. The crew compartments were to be "pressurized" to avoid having the crew wear warm heavy clothing and to use oxygen gear for long periods at high altitudes.

Aircraft companies were reluctant to take on new designs as, unlike today's cost-plus contracts, the AAC was by law only permitted to let fixed-price contracts, with no money paid in advance. Compensation was only made when the contracted aircraft was built and had flown. Meanwhile, aircraft companies had to use their own money to buy materials and tools, and also pay the salaries of their engineers and employees, and the time from contract signing to prototype flight could range from months to years. Contracts had no "cost overruns clauses," and then there was no guarantee the prototype would be accepted for production.

Only four companies responded to Westover's request: Boeing in Seattle, Consolidated in San Diego, Douglas in Los Angeles, and the United Aircraft Sikorsky Division in Hartford. The design submissions were considered mediocre and the Douglas design was considered the best of the lot. Even though Douglas was the only profitable company of the four, its design was merely a lackluster upgrade of its new DC-4 airliner. Despite having four-engine bomber expertise, Boeing's submission was nothing more than a reworked XBLR-2/XB-15 design whose mid-1930s technology was obsolete. Despite having been awarded the B-17 contract, Boeing had yet to receive any compensation and was having problems on its early production phase, so the AAC refused to purchase more of the bombers. In fact, Boeing would take a federal loan in 1940 to keep the company from going bankrupt.

On 21 September 1938, Westover died in an aircraft accident and was succeeded by Henry "Hap" Arnold, who had risen through the ranks, starting as a fledgling lieutenant in the new Aeronautical Division of the Signal Corps in 1911. By the mid-1930s, Arnold and other disciples of Billy Mitchell's theory of airpower had gradually gained prominent positions in the Army Air Corps and were able to exert an "air" influence in the "horse soldier" dominated Army. When Arnold took over the AAC his bomber force consisted of fourteen B-17s, while the twin-engine B-18 was his most ubiquitous bomber. In January 1939, President Roosevelt, after a review of American air power at Bolling Field, requested the production of "500 bombers a month." On 30 March 1939, the AAC approved Consolidated's Model 32 design that would lead to the XB-24 and then the B-24. The Liberator would make its first flight on 29 December 1939, and join the B-17 as America's primary journeyman heavy bombers in the upcoming war.

THE B-24 IS DESIGNED, CONTRACTED, DEVELOPED, AND FLIES

By the autumn of 1938, Brig.Gen. H. H. Arnold, while confident the B-17 was a qualified success, was concerned that if war came Boeing would be unable to build sufficient numbers of the bomber. Arnold considered the possibility that Consolidated should manufacture the B-17 under license, and in December, Consolidated's Isaac Laddon and C. A. Van Dusen went to Seattle to discuss licensing with Boeing. They found Boeing actually did not have enough work at that time to share orders; moreover, the B-17 design was already four years old in a time of rapidly changing aircraft designs. The Air Corps had recently issued Type Specification C-212 for a bomber with a 3,000 mile range, 35,000 ft. ceiling, a maximum speed of 300 mph, and a bomb load of 8,000 lbs. Laddon and his engineering staff were confident they could design a new bomber that would be able to carry the same bomb load as the B-17, but at higher speeds and at a longer range. Consolidated had experimented with the Davis Wing on its Model 31 deep-hulled twin engine flying boat and found the wing improved performance by twenty percent. By the end of January 1939, Fleet sent his son, David, to accompany Laddon to Wright Field with specifications and primary data for the proposed Model 32 bomber (B-24). The Air Corps had made inquiries of Sikorsky and Martin, asking if they had any designs that could meet the C-212 specifications, and neither had anything on the drawing board, as they had only three weeks to respond to C-212. Consolidated had a wooden mockup ready for AAF assessment on 1 February 1939. On 21 February, the Air Corps declared that Consolidated was the only company that had a C-212 contender, and on 30 March, awarded Consolidated a contract for a single XB-24 prototype (USAAC s/n 39-556) with a completion date of 30 December 1939. Since the world situation was deteriorating in early 1939, seven YB-24 service test aircraft with spare parts for $2.88 million were contracted in April 1939 and thirty-eight B-24As were added in August. On 29 December 1939, the XB-24 prototype, piloted by William Wheatley and George Newman, flew from Lindbergh Field on a seventeen minute test flight.

A distinctive aircraft, the B-24 featured a twin-tail and rudder assembly, as well as a flat, slab-sided fuselage. The Liberator is often compared with the better-known Boeing B-17, but the B-24 was a more modern design with a higher top speed, greater range, and a heavier bomb load. It had an eleven-man crew (pilot, co-pilot, navigator, bombardier, radio operator, nose turret, top turret, two waist gunners, ball turret, and tail gunner); its slender, innovative Davis Wing had a span of 110 ft. and an area of 1,048 sq. ft. (the Liberator had a length of 67.7 ft. and a height of 18 ft.). The B-24's empty weight was 36,500 lbs. and maximum take-off weight was 65,000 lbs. It was powered by four 1,200 hp Pratt & Whitney R-1830-35 or -41 turbo-supercharged radial engines that gave the bomber a maximum speed of 290 mph, a cruising speed of 215 mph, a service ceiling of 28,000 ft., and a range of 2,100 miles.

Consolidated XB-24

The B-24 was employed in operations in every combat theater during WWII, and because of its great range it was particularly suited for such missions as the famous 2,100 mile round trip raid from North Africa against the oil industry in Ploesti, Rumania, on 1 August 1943. These characteristics also made the bomber particularly suitable for the long over-water missions in the Pacific and the British converted them for use in maritime patrols far out over the Atlantic.

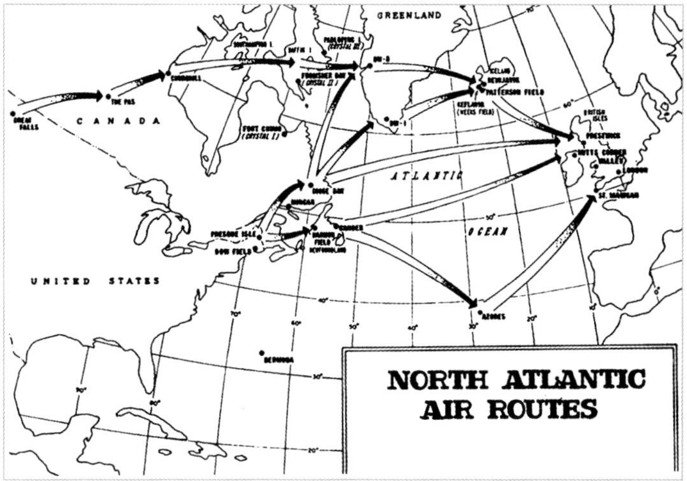

B-17S AND B-24S: BIG BUT NOT INTERCONTINENTAL

B-17S AND B-24S FLY THE TRANS-ATLANTIC FERRY ROUTES NON-STOP

During the war, four major Trans-Atlantic Ferry Routes were established between North America and Great Britain. The North Atlantic Route originated at several Army air bases in New England, which allowed short-range, single-engine aircraft to be flown to Britain using a series of intermediate airfields in Newfoundland, Labrador, Greenland, and Iceland, then mostly landing in Prestwick, Scotland. Long-range multi-engine aircraft could be flown from Newfoundland directly using Great Circle routes to airfields in Ireland and southwest England, or via the Azores Islands to the United Kingdom, or airfields in French Morocco to support Allied campaigns in the MTO. Later in the war air routes over the North Atlantic were developed from South Florida via Bermuda to the Azores. The North American jump off points were Goose Bay, Labrador, or Gander, Newfoundland, and the major drop off point was Prestwick (2,250 miles from Goose Bay and 2,150 miles from Gander). Other long distance ferry flights were between San Francisco (2,400 miles) and Los Angeles (2,570 miles) to Honolulu, and the hop between Bermuda (2,200 miles) and the Azores after originally leaving Florida. The B-17, with a combat range of 1,750 miles, had a ferry range of 2,800 miles, while the B-24 had a combat range of 2,100 miles and a ferry range of 3,700 miles. As can be seen by these actual miles to destination vs. combat range, the fuel capacity for the B-17 and B-24 had to be augmented with auxiliary bomb bay fuel tanks to be able to make non-stop flights, which would become routine. The B-24 had a longer ferry range, as two ferry fuel tanks could be carried in each of its two bomb bays, while the B-17 could only carry two tanks in its one bomb bay. On long-range combat missions the B-17 was also penalized with a reduced bomb load, as it could carry one 410 gallon tank on either side of the bomb bay with bombs on the other side. B-24s could carry two 410 gallon tanks in either of its bomb bays, leaving both sides of the other bomb bay for bombs.

On 14 December 1941, a meeting was convened, including the Army Air Corps' fledgling Ferrying Command; the Navy's Air Transport Service (NATS, established only two days earlier); Office of Production Management (OPM); the Civil Aeronautics Board and Authority; and the Air Transport Association (ATA, which represented the airlines Pan American and Transcontinental & Western Airways). In case of impending war it was realized that distant parts of the world would be (China, the Philippines, and Australia by the Japanese) and had been (Russia and England by the Nazis) cut off from men and supplies from both the United Kingdom and America. The meeting members took stock of America's meager four-engine air transport resources: eleven crudely converted Ferrying Command B-24A bombers, a Boeing *Clipper* that the War Department had purchased from Pan Am which could be supplemented by eight more, two Martin Flying Boats owned by Pan Am, and five TWA Boeing Stratoliners. America's domestic airlines were exclusively equipped with intermediate and short-range aircraft, mainly Douglas DC-3s and Lockheed Lodestars.

The Air Corps' logistical duties (1926–1942) were assigned to the Office of the Chief of the Air Corps Materiel Division, headquartered at Wright Field, Ohio, and with four major depots distributed over the United States. In the early 1930s, the AAC began investigating the systematic use of air transport for the distribution of aviation supplies. In 1932, the Materiel Division established a provisional 1st Air Transport Group with four transport squadrons—each equipped with Bellanca Aircruisers and Douglas DC-2s—assigned to one of the four major air depots to transport supplies and spare parts from one depot to another. The group was redesignated the 10th Transport Group in 1937, under the control of GHQ Headquarters. During the late 1930s, the AAC found it did not have sufficient transport aircraft to support its growing operations, with the

GHQ Air Force's 10th Transport Group remaining as the only dedicated AAC airlift unit at that time.

In May 1938, GHQ Air Force conducted maneuvers in the Northeastern United States, during which the First Wing moved forty-two aircraft and 945 men from stations in California to unfamiliar fields in New England using sixteen converted bombers as transports. Although this deployment of forces was impressive for its time, it would be totally insufficient for the impending global war.

Once war broke out in Europe in September 1939, the Allied combatants found they needed American aircraft to supplement their air forces, and initially British or contracted American pilots were engaged to ferry these aircraft to Britain. Over-water delivery of American-built aircraft to England began in November 1940, when a Canadian company began trans-Atlantic deliveries of aircraft that had been flown to Montreal by factory employed delivery pilots. In March 1941, Congress passed the Lend Lease Act, in which America affirmed its intention to provide military equipment to the countries that were already engaged in war against the Axis nations—unnamed but unabashedly the British. However, the increase in deliveries from the Lend Lease Act would cause a shortage of factory pilots. To contend with the problem, the Army Air Corps established its Ferrying Command (ACFC), under the command of Brig.Gen. Robert Olds—the former commander of the 2nd Bombardment Group. On 29 May 1941, Northeast Airlines was contracted to provide pilots to make the domestic deliveries of Lend Lease aircraft from American factories to US East Coast or Canadian embarkation points, from where British pilots flew them across the North Atlantic to England. After Pearl Harbor, the ACFC also contracted Pan American Airways to provide pilots to ferry aircraft to British forces in the Middle East via South America and Africa. The ACFC afforded Army pilots experience flying the latest combat equipment and freeing civilian factory pilots to join the British body responsible for trans-Atlantic deliveries from North America to England.

Brig.Gen. Robert Olds, Ferrying Command (ACFC) Commander

Meanwhile, because for several months of the year winter weather prohibited flights over the North Atlantic, the Ferrying Command looked to establish new routes from the US. A South Atlantic route was surveyed and established, originating in Miami, and was then routed over the Caribbean to British Guyana and Brazil, then over the Atlantic to Ascension Island, on to the west coast of Africa, then over the African continent to Cairo. The Ferrying Command also inaugurated a flying boat service to West Africa using Pan Am flying boats withdrawn from Pacific service. In addition to the Pan American ferry service, the War Department also established a military operated transport service to Cairo, again using converted B-24s.

Before Pearl Harbor, the USAAC had ordered the conversion of most of its initial order of B-24As to fill the transport role and had used them to open the first overseas routes. On 1 July 1941, famed AAC test pilot (Boeing XB-15) Lt.Col. Caleb Haynes, co-pilot Capt. James Rothrock, navigator 1Lt. John Montgomery, and five other passengers were assigned to fly one of the first B-24A bombers that Consolidated delivered to the Army on a secret flight to test a North Atlantic air route to Great Britain. The transformed B-24A was "converted" to ferry status by removing armament (except the tail gun), laying down a plywood floor, and installing basic seating in the bomb bay. During the flight the crew was extremely uncomfortable due to the bitter cold and ineffective heaters, which often became inoperative. Smoking was only allowed on the flight deck, as the rear fuselage was notorious for harboring inflammable gasoline fumes. Passengers were allowed to smoke one at a time on the flight deck, which probably became a chimney. Hayes took off from Bolling Field, Washington, DC, refueled in Montreal, and then again at Gander Lake, Newfoundland, before arriving in Prestwick, Scotland, delivering the first B-24 overseas. Prestwick, just outside Glasgow, was chosen as the terminus because of its "relatively" good weather, but the B-24 was forced to circle the field for 2½ hours and then make an almost blind landing. On the return flight the scheduled refueling stop in Newfoundland was bypassed due to bad weather. The crew was awarded DFCs for the flight in a secret ceremony. The new service, soon labeled the "Arnold Line," was flown by twenty-two converted B-24s (with the passengers seated in the bomb bays) during the next three and a half months, until forthcoming winter weather over the North Atlantic halted the flights in October. These flights were not without incident, as on the second flight the Liberator was intercepted by a roving Luftwaffe Dornier which was driven off by the Liberator tail gunner. On another flight Liberator pilot 1Lt. William Vickers let down through thick overcast, only to find himself over an Allied convoy that immediately opened fire on his aircraft.

Soon Haynes was assigned with scouting and establishing another air route, which was to cross the Southern Atlantic from the US during the winter months when bad weather precluded flights across the North Atlantic. On 31 August 1941,

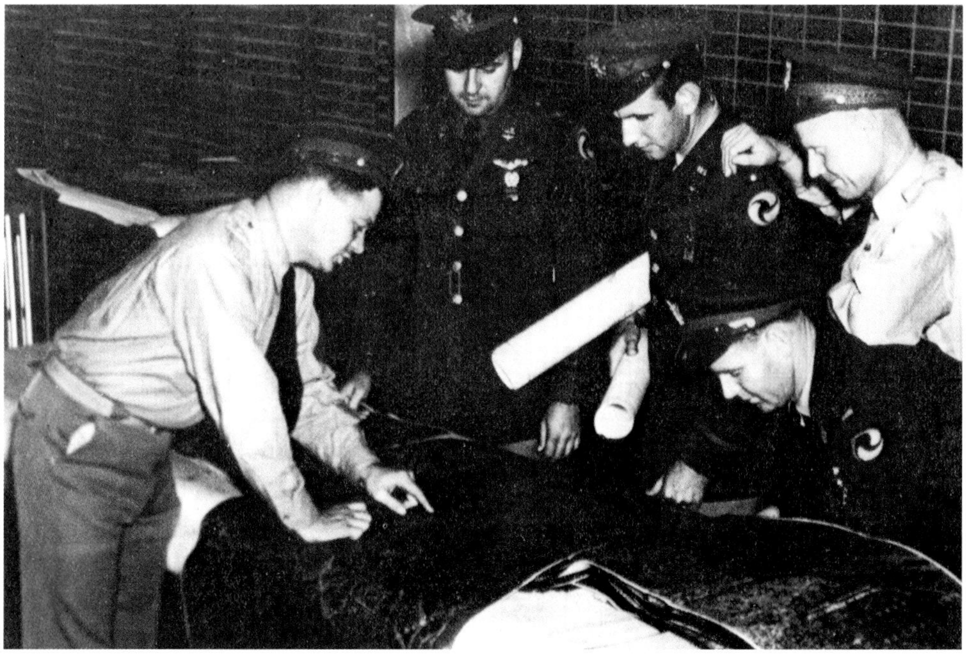

Maj. Curtis LeMay (L) and Lt.Col. Caleb Haynes (second from left) map their August 1941 26,000 mile round trip to Egypt and then beyond to Basra, Iraq, on a special mission to investigate possible Lend Lease air routes to Russia.

Previously, beginning in April 1924, Sgt. Alva Harvey was the mechanic on the *Seattle*, one of four Douglas World Cruisers under the command of Maj. Frederick Martin (the *Seattle* pilot) of the US Army Air Service that departed from Sand Point Airfield, Seattle, Washington, flying westward to circumnavigate the globe. The *Seattle* crashed into an Alaskan mountain, terminating its flight. Three Cruisers returned to Sand Point on 28 September 1924, to become the first ever to fly round-the-world.

Soviet Ambassador Constantin Oumansky, returning from the US, was to be one of the passengers, and was to act as liaison with the Russian authorities. The route for the secret mission to Moscow was carefully selected, and it was decided that the two planes would fly around Norway to Archangel, then south to Moscow, rather than flying directly over German-held territory. The chance of Luftwaffe interception, even on a high-altitude night flight, was only one consideration in this decision; equally important was that the Russians could not guarantee that any aircraft heading in from enemy Germany would not be attacked by their notoriously trigger happy AA gunners and interceptors, who were not known for their aircraft identification expertise.

with Maj. Curtis LeMay as his co-pilot and Chief of the Air Corps Maj.Gen. George Brett as a passenger, Haynes took off from Bolling Field to begin the first 26,000 mile round trip to Egypt and then beyond, carrying Brett to Basra, Iraq, on a special mission to investigate possible Lend Lease air routes to Russia. On 7 October, Haynes and LeMay retraced their flight to land back in the US, proving the Southern Route satisfactory. England then agreed to purchase sixteen LB-30s to be delivered via this route to Cairo, with four completing the trip before the remainder were redirected into American service (another was destroyed beyond repair in a crash). Haynes' 1941 flights gave America an advantage in developing viable air routes for its military forces that began in 1942, when these routes were adapted for year-round movement of aircraft, units, supplies, and materials to combat theaters.

THE RECORD B-24 HARRIMAN MISSION FLIGHTS

During September 1941, Averell Harriman was to arrive in Moscow with an Anglo-American commission to discuss Lend Lease. While Harriman was going to cross the Atlantic by ship and then accompany Winston Churchill to Moscow, it was decided to fly some of the participants there and also have an American aircraft available while the visitors were in Russia. Two Ferrying Command B-24s piloted by Maj. Alva Harvey and 1Lt. Louis Reichers, after having flown routine trips from Washington to Prestwick, were to remain there for the mission.

Harvey took off from Prestwick at 21:20 on 23 September, with Reichers following ten minutes later. Near the Shetland Islands they were intercepted by patrolling British aircraft, but were recognized after they fired the colors of the day. They continued their flight in the cold, dark night, remaining 200 miles off the coast of Norway and then crossing the Barents Sea far north of the Arctic circle. They arrived over Archangel in daylight, but as it was overcast and there was snow and sleet in the area they decided to fly on non-stop to Moscow. Nearing Moscow, although the Liberators' radios were functioning the pilots could get no response from any Russian station.

Harvey chose an airfield and landed without any directives or apparent recognition of his presence. Once on the ground Russian officers came to meet him and shortly he and his crew were feted with the preordained Russian welcome of caviar and unrestrained vodka toasts. Reichers likewise chose a landing field and was greeted in the same manner. The two Liberator pilots had successfully completed non-stop flights of 3,150 miles under trying and even dangerous circumstances, with their accomplishment ranking among the great flights in history.

After arriving in the UK by ship, US Representative Averell Harriman (C) arrives at Moscow in Winston Churchill's (R) personal B-24. Commando, accompanied by Soviet Minister of Foreign Affairs, Vyacheslav Molotov.

Maj. Alva Harvey

1 Lt. Louis Reichers

Reichers remained in Moscow for eleven days and Harvey for another week while they were entertained but kept under strict constant surveillance while their aircraft were thoroughly examined. Col. Robert Olds had foreseen the opportunity that these Moscow flights presented for further long-range flight investigation. When the Harriman mission was completed Reichers left on the second, and equally noteworthy, part of his journey. Supplied with remarkably good weather information and maps, he set his course to Baku and then to Habbaniyeh, Iraq, but discovered that the Caucasus Mountains were substantially higher than the data indicated. From Iraq he flew on to Cairo and then south, exploring the area over which Pan American Airways established a new route. In June 1941, Pan American had organized a special department to make deliveries of British-purchased Douglas DC-3 transports to Africa. Flown by Pan American Airways crews, the first transports left Florida for Africa on 21 June. At the time it was determined that Pan American, as well as other US airlines, would play a major role in the Ferrying Command and the subsequent Air Transport Command for the duration. Under an agreement reached with the War Department and the British, Pan Am assumed responsibility for establishing ferry and air transport routes to Africa, and also for operating a trans-African transport route that had been previously established by the British. Speedy aircraft delivery from the States to British combat units in Africa was the primary purpose of the new service, with air transport of cargo and personnel secondary. As it transpired, Pan Am would only deliver a dozen aircraft (all transports) prior to Pearl Harbor. The flight continued satisfactorily until he arrived in Fasher, on the edge of the Sudan, during Ramadan; the Mohammedan radio operators had celebrated the night before and were sleeping during the fast day and were unavailable. Reichers landed successfully on the strange field and searched for 2,500 gallons of fuel, which was only in four gallon tins widely scattered and buried for safety in case of attack; they were brought in over a month by one hundred camels working steadily between El Fasher and Khartoum. Five hundred tins were unearthed and lifted onto the wing, and the fuel was poured into the tanks individually. After stopping at Takoradi, on the Atlantic coast, Reichers found no weather information available for his long and arduous flight across the Atlantic to Natal, Brazil, but was advised that the weather was generally good at that time of year; on that basis he took off across the Atlantic for Brazil. When he reached the mainland at Natal, he found one runway under repair and that using the other one would involve landing in a high cross wind, so he flew on to Fortaleza, where he landed on a rough field. His next stop was Belem, where Pan American was established, and from there he continued uneventfully to Washington, gathering invaluable information about little-known, important areas.

Maj. Harvey's return flight was even more notable, as Col. Olds, acting on his own initiative, ordered Harvey to continue around the world via India, wanting him to investigate the routes in that direction. Harvey's route took him from Habbaniyeh to Karachi, at the western edge of India, and then to Calcutta, where he found the runway at Dum Dum airfield was only 2,400 ft. long—supposedly an impossible length for landing a B-24. With great skill he made his landing, but then while taxiing found the wheels of his heavy aircraft were sinking into the surface. Harvey noticed the concrete compass rose testing area and parked on it. Harvey then flew on to Rangoon, Singapore, Darwin, Port Moresby, Wake Island, Hickam Field (near Honolulu), and March Field, California, and finished by returning to Bolling Field via Fort Worth for another record setting flight. Along with Haynes' explorations, Reichers' flight was followed by regular Ferrying Command service on 14 November, and continued until the outbreak of war, when the Ferrying Command was operating eleven converted B-24s loaned by Army Air Corps Combat Command. After Pearl Harbor flight schedules were no longer regular and were controlled by urgent need.

Meanwhile, operations over the North Atlantic had to be suspended on 18 October, as winter weather made the crossing virtually impossible in the then-undeveloped state of the route. By that time the ACFC was making some progress in securing communications, weather reports, and other aids, as well as the construction of bases across the North Atlantic which would eventually make year-round crossing routine. Twenty-two round trips had been flown in three and a half months, or about one every five days.

Itinerary for Reicher's Round-the-World Flight
Departed Washington, DC (13 September 1941)
Montreal, Canada
Newfoundland
Preswick, Scotland (over the northern tip of Norway and Finland)
Moscow, Soviet Union
Habbaniyeh, Iraq
Karachi, Pakistan
Calcutta, India
Rangoon, Burma
Singapore
Port Darwin, Australia
Port Moresby, Papua New Guinea
Wake Island
Honolulu, Hawaii
March Field, California
Fort Worth, Texas
Arrived Washington, DC (30 October 1941)

WENDELL WILLKIE: AROUND-THE-WORLD FLIGHT

The best-known C-87A was *Gulliver I* (41-11608), which carried Wendell Willkie as President Roosevelt's "One World Ambassador" during a 28,487 mile trip in August 1942. The aircraft, assigned from the 10th Ferry Squadron, was flown by American Airlines pilot Maj. Richard Kight with co-pilot Alexis Klotz during the fifty-one day mission. Willkie was accompanied by publisher Gardner "Mike" Cowles (*Look* magazine), foreign correspondent Joseph Barnes (*New York Herald Tribune*), US Navy Capt. Paul Pihl, and US Army Maj. Grant Mason. In August 1942, President Roosevelt asked Willkie—his 1940 Republican opponent for the presidency—to make an around-the-world flight as his "special emissary and fact finder" to persuade world leaders that although America was engaged in an energetic isolationist political debate at the time, the country was united against fascism. The flight involved stopovers in Cairo, Palestine, Baghdad, Tehran, Moscow, and China, and then a return to the United States via a route across the Pacific. A number of firsts were made on this flight: first flight from the Soviet Union into China, from China to Alaska, and from China to the United States across the Pacific. Willkie later recounted his world travels in the *Gulliver* in his 1943 best-selling book for popular audiences, *One World*. This highly influential book made a well-supported appeal for postwar international cooperation and solidified Willkie's role as a major force in American politics, but he died of a heart attack in October 1944, at the relatively young age of fifty-two. *Gulliver I* was scrapped by RFC at Bush Field on 19 November 1945.

C-87A Gulliver I (41-11608)

Wendell Wilkie arrives in Moscow aboard the B-24 Gulliver during his 28,487 mile "One World Ambassador" trip during August 1942.

TOKYO TANKS: EXTENDING THE RANGE OF B-17S AND B-24S

So-called Tokyo tanks were internally mounted self-sealing fuel tanks used mainly in the B-17, but also in the B-24. Installed in the B-17, they consisted of eighteen removable rubberized fuel cells installed inside the main wings, nine to each side. Tokyo tanks were installed on either side of the joint where the inboard wing and outboard wing panels were connected. Five cells, totaling 270 gallons, were placed side-by-side in the outboard wing, and were joined by a fuel line to the main tank delivering fuel to the outermost engine. The sixth cell was in the space where the wing sections joined, with the remaining three cells side-by-side in the inboard wing, and these four cells supplied 270 gallons of fuel to the feeder tank for the inboard engine. The same arrangement was installed on the other wing. Tokyo tanks added 1,080 gallons of fuel to the original 1,700 gallons carried in the six regular wing tanks and the 820 gallons that could be carried in a tank that could be mounted in the bomb bay, giving a combined total of 3,600 gallons.

The 94th and 95th Bomb Groups were equipped with the first B-17s with factory-installed Tokyo tanks and were sent to the 8th Air Force in England in April 1943. From the beginning of July 1943, all replacement B-17s were so equipped. Although the tanks were removable, this could only be done by the arduous removal of the outboard wing panel. Major downsides to these tanks was that there was no method of determining the fuel quantity remaining, and although the tanks were self-sealing, vapor buildup in partially drained tanks made them vulnerable to explosion in combat.

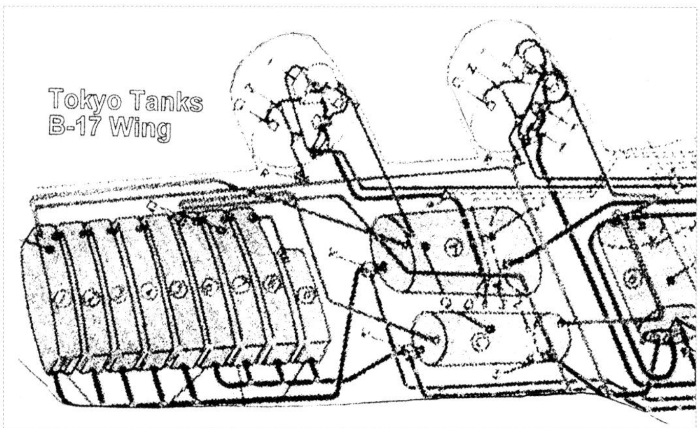

Tokyo tanks

SUPER BOMBER REVIVED

Meanwhile, the super bomber concept languished until late 1938, when Maj.Gen. Arnold called a secret meeting of AAC officers and aviation experts to discuss the future of the AAC and the heavy bomber predicament. Charles Lindbergh had visited Hitler's Germany, and was impressed and alarmed over the emphasis the Luftwaffe had put on bombardment aircraft. Arnold asked Lindbergh to serve on a board headed by Brig. Gen. Walter Kilner and aided by Col. Carl Spaatz, Col. Earl Naiden, and Maj. Alfred Lyon. The Kilner Board issued its report in June 1939, and members of the group thought that in a European war Germany would not only overrun the continent, but also conquer Great Britain and then Africa, and perhaps establish bases in South America. If the Japanese began a war in the Pacific it would have to be fought over long expanses of ocean extending from Alaska to Hawaii to the Philippines, to as far as Australia. In this scenario the B-17 would surely be inadequate and the super bomber notion was revived. The role of the super bomber was no longer thought to be as a strategic bomber, but was to be a defensive bomber able to fly long distances to strike an enemy advancing on the American continents. The board proposed a five-year research and development program for new aircraft and engines. Engine development was to be liquid-cooled and range in horsepower from 1,500 to 2,400, and eventually to 3,000 hp. The board recommended that two-engine light and medium bombers and a 2,000 mile range four-engine heavy bomber be developed, along with another heavy bomber with a large fuselage that could carry bombs and/or enough fuel to give it a range of 5,000 miles. From the latter specification the B-29 would eventually be developed for hemispheric defense. Although the Kilner recommendation was accepted by the AAC, at the time there was an isolationist sentiment in America and the AAC could do nothing until Congress appropriated funds. Meanwhile, progress on the XB-19 would continue to languish, much to Donald Douglas' $2.5 million dismay.

MCD-392: WRIGHT FIELD'S FANTASTIC PROPOSED GIANT

Like the aircraft manufacturers, the aircraft laboratory at Wright Field encouraged their engineering division to design fanciful aircraft that were never intended to reach production, primarily as a discipline for their designers to maintain proficiencies, and also to compare their design skills against what the aircraft industry was developing. At a time when the design proposals from Boeing, Consolidated, and Douglas were unquestionably imaginative and innovative, the MCD-392 design was almost outlandish.

Its wing was enormous, with its 280 ft. span (vs. 141 ft. for the B-29, 212 ft. for the XB-19, and 230 ft. for the future B-36) and 7,140 sq. ft. of area (more than double the B-29, vs. 2,648 sq. ft. for the XB-19 and 2,368 sq. ft. more area than the B-36). However, its length was not excessive at 129 ft. (vs. 162 ft. for the B-36 and 132 ft. for the XB-19), nor was the height of its single vertical stabilizer that loomed 48.5 ft. above the tail wheel (vs. 46.75 ft. for the B-36 and 42.75 ft. for the XB-19). Its relatively short length, combined with its huge tail and wing span, made the aircraft similar to Tupolev's earlier Russian giants. The design's gross weight was 500,000 lbs., and its 283,390 lb. useful load included up to 120,000 lbs. of bombs and 23,500 gallons of fuel. Maximum speed was estimated at 342 mph (20,000 feet) with a service ceiling of 36,250 ft., but it had a very long take-off distance of 9,200 ft. There was to be a provision for bunks and a lounge/galley area in the rear fuselage.

With a maximum bomb load of 120,000 lbs. its range was estimated to be 6,100 miles, increasing to 9,100 miles with

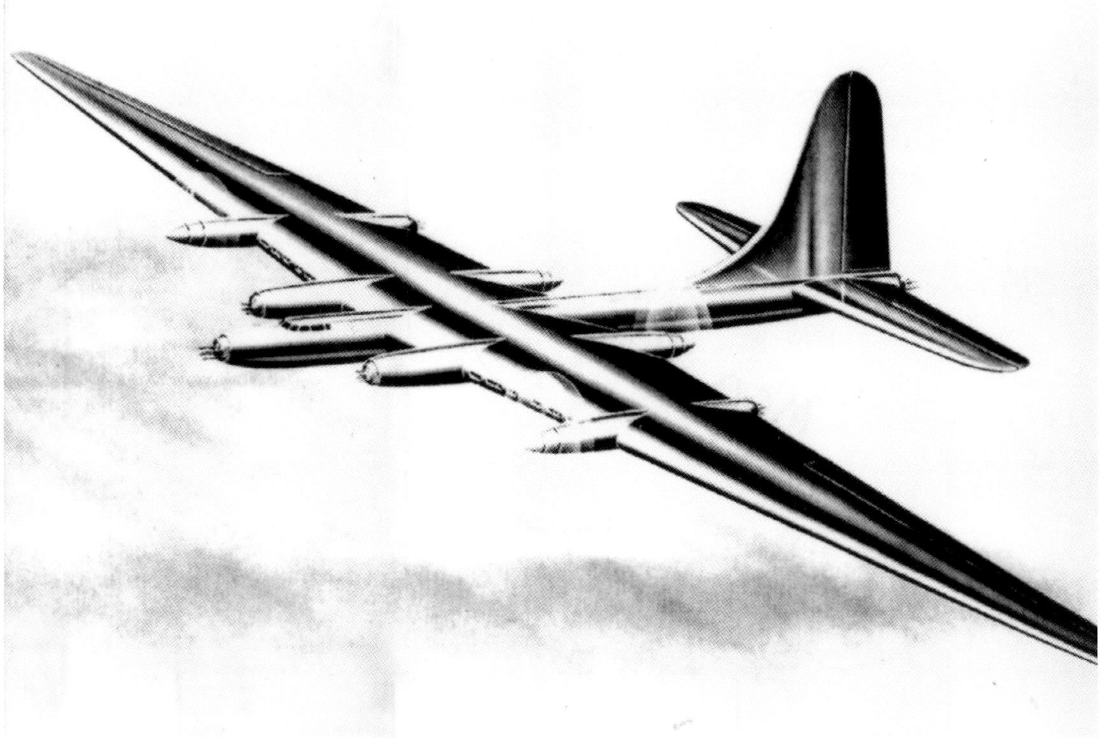

Wright Field's MCD-392

half that bomb load. Ferry range was 12,000 miles. The future B-36 could carry 72,000 lbs. of bombs over 4,700 miles, but could carry only 10,000 lbs. of bombs over 10,000 miles (its ferry range was 11,400 miles). Of the operational WWII US bombers, the B-29 could carry 20,000 lbs. of bombs over 3,500 miles (ferry range 5,800 miles), while the B-17 was limited to only 600 lbs. at its maximum range of 3,500 miles (ferry range 4,250 miles).

The wing was very thick and crew accessible, and much like the future Northrop XB-35 flying wing, the bomb load was spread span-wise, instead of being concentrated completely in the fuselage. The bomb load extended into the wing as far as the inboard nacelles, and one set of bomb racks anterior and posterior to the fuselage/wing racks. This configuration alleviated the bending moment of the wing, allowing for a lighter structure.

The MCD's engine configuration was very different from any contemporary design: a pusher engine/propeller inboard on each wing with a tractor engine/propeller outboard. A pair of unspecified 3,600 hp liquid-cooled engines (Allison V-3420s?) drove each of two four-bladed, counter-rotating propellers in each nacelle. Each nacelle contained a gun turret at one end, with two engines in the middle driving its propeller at the other end via a long propeller/engine shaft linkage. Each of the nacelle turrets housed four .50-caliber machine guns at its end (for a total of sixteen machine guns) provided with 1,000 rounds per gun, while the nose and tail turrets were armed with four 20 mm cannon (for a total of eight cannons) provided with 300 rounds per gun.

Unlike the single main wheels selected by Douglas for their XB-19 and Consolidated for their XB-36, Wright Field engineers selected two wheels in an unusual configuration for each main landing gear. The inboard gear was between the two engines and extended outward, while the second gear was outboard of the outboard engine and extended inward, so the two wheels were only feet apart when extended with a total tread of seventy-seven feet. This wide tread distance would have placed heavy landing stress far out on the wing. Unlike the XB-19 and XB-36, a tail wheel was provided in the conventional tail-dragger configuration of the time. The wheel base distance between the main wheels and tail wheel was seventy-five feet.

A further design proposed a 12-engine version with two inboard nacelles each containing two pusher engines each driving their propeller and four outboard nacelles each containing two engines each driving their propeller. This gigantic version had a proposed wingspan of 321 ft., a wing area of 9,355 sq. ft., a length of 160 ft., a design gross weight of 655,000 lbs., and a useful weight of 360,000 lbs. The outboard nacelles contained no guns.

8
R-40-B VERY LONG-RANGE BOMBER SPECIFICATION

In November 1939, due to an energetic campaign by Maj. Gen. Henry Arnold, Congress approved funding and Arnold was authorized by Gen. George Marshall to let R-40-B study contracts (R-40-B translates as Requirement number 40, Bomber) for the Very Long-Range bomber. Capt. Donald Putt of Air Materiel Command at Wright Field defined a statement of the military characteristics of the new bomber. The bomber was to have a range of 5,333 miles and be able to carry a bomb load of a ton over half that distance and have a (rather overly optimistic) speed of 400 mph. Being a high-altitude strategic bomber, it was to be pressurized. In early 1940, after the experience of five months of war in Europe, the AAF saw that there were limitations in its earlier requirements and issued another specification to supersede its R-40-B Specs in April. The AAF restructured its heavy bomber requirements, requesting self-sealing fuel tanks, increased armor protection, and multiple turrets with heavier caliber machine guns and cannons. On 29 January 1940, the AAC sent Request for Data R-40-B and Spec XC-218 to a number of aircraft companies that designed heavy bombers. The request was sent via US postal mail marked "Urgent" from Washington, DC. The companies were given thirty days to submit design proposals and were then expected to finish a full-scale engineering mockup by 5 August 1940; the first completed aircraft was to be ready by 1 July 1941, and subsequent aircraft one month later. Four West Coast companies would submit designs: Lockheed and Consolidated of San Diego, Douglas of Los Angeles, and Boeing of Seattle. Again, none of the companies was motivated to submit far-reaching designs. Whatever resources they had available were being invested in expanding their factories and workforce to build established but mediocre contemporary aircraft for the three American military services and foreign air forces that were at war and in dire need of anything that could fly and fight.

On 8 April 1940, Boeing, Lockheed, and Douglas Consolidated (and later Martin) tendered their R-40-B proposals to Air Materiel Command. The AAC Evaluation Board decided that all had met the requirements, and on 14 June, all were awarded contracts to construct wooden scale models for wind tunnel testing and evaluation, and were also requested to furnish comprehensive engineering drawings and data, along with cost estimates. Air Materiel Command initiated negotiations for price and delivery dates for a pair of prototypes with an option to purchase 200 production bombers. The Evaluation Board designated the proposals in order of preference: the Boeing proposal was designated XB-29, the Lockheed XB-30, the Martin XB-33/33A, the Douglas XB-31, and the Consolidated XB-32. The contracts were valued at only $85,652, which was a pittance compared to the $3 billion military aircraft allotment Congress had approved for 1940.

THE LONG-RANGE BOMBER CONTEST ALSO-RANS

Lockheed XB-30

Lockheed based its Model 51-81-01 XB-30 proposal on its triple-tailed Model 49 C-69 Constellation cargo/transport design that was, in turn, based on its Model 49 Airliner. The design was similar in dimension to the airliner, except for the lengthening of the nose that was covered by Plexiglas for the bombardier and the tail that contained two .50-caliber machine guns and a 20 mm cannon. The design had a wingspan of 123 ft., a length of 104.7 ft., a height of 23.8 ft. (at the vertical stabilizer), and an empty weight of 51,725 lbs. (gross 86,000 lbs.). It was powered by four 2,200 horsepower Wright R-3350-13 radial engines that were predicted to have a top speed of 450 mph (cruise at 240 mph), a service ceiling of 40,000 ft., and a range of 3,380 miles. It was to have an eight-man crew, with the pilot and co-pilot seated side-by-side under separate bubble canopies. On 6 September, the Lockheed board of directors made a policy decision and withdrew its proposal from the super bomber competition while it was on the drawing board.

Lockheed XB-30

Douglas XB-31

Douglas continued to rework its basic DC-4 transport design into the proposed XB-31, but their project never progressed beyond the drawing board. There was no XB-31 as such, but the designation denoted a series of engineering studies that created a range of shapes and sizes. The Model 423 was typical of the designs spawned from the bomber development of the commercial DC-4 airliner. The design, submitted in Fall 1941, was the largest and heaviest of all the proposals, with a wingspan of 207 ft. (five ft. less than the XB-19), a wing area of 3,300 sq. ft., a length of 117.3 ft. (only three inches less than the XB-19), and a height of 40.4 ft. (vertical stabilizer). It weighed 109,000 lbs. empty and grossed at 176,000 lbs., and could drop 25,000 lbs. of bombs through its double bomb bays. It was to be powered by four 28-cylinder 3,000 horsepower Pratt & Whitney R-4360 X-Wasps (later named the Wasp Major) radial engines to turn its huge 25 ft. three-bladed propellers. The fuel load was 13,000 gallons, and its 450 gallon oil tank capacity exceeded the fuel load of many of the bombers of the 1930s! The eight-man crew was accommodated in a beautifully streamlined pressurized fuselage, with the pilot and co-pilot stations in two small Plexiglas bubble canopies protruding from the top of the fuselage behind the nose. The six other crew were accommodated in separate stations throughout the bomber. Defensive armament was to have been twin .50-caliber machine guns mounted in remotely-controlled dorsal and ventral turrets and a pair of .37 mm cannon in the tail. The immense maximum bomb load of 25,000 lbs. was to be carried in two fuselage bomb bays. The potentially remarkable XB-31 never progressed beyond the design study phase, but some of its innovations shaped other later Douglas aircraft. The Douglas C-74 Globemaster transport and XB-42 experimental bomber utilized the twin bubble canopies, and on a smaller scale the B-26 Invader tail assembly resembled the Model 423 tail. The promising XB-31 lagged behind the accelerated Boeing XB-29 design, and the XB-31 was formally canceled in late 1941, after the AAC ordered 250 B-29s in September.

Douglas XB-31

Martin XB-33 and XB-33A

XB-33

In late 1940, when the AAC was continuing to solicit high-altitude twin-engine medium bomber designs as a possible twin-engine replacement for its B-26 Marauder, the Martin Company presented a design that was to be designated XB-33. The canted twin-tail design featured a pressurized fuselage and resembled Martin's recently developed PBM Mariner Navy Patrol bomber. It was slated to use two 1,800 hp 18-cylinder radial Wright P-3350 Cyclone engines and was to measure 71 ft. long, 22.5 ft. high, and have a 100 ft. wingspan. The continued evolution of the design caused a great increase in weight that precluded Martin from achieving the performance specifications required by the AAC. Martin then set aside the XB-33 program and expanded it to a four-engine program, the XB-33A.

Martin XB-33

XB-33A

At the time Martin was in competition with Boeing and Consolidated for a long-range heavy bomber design and felt its Model 190 showed promise. Martin was awarded a contract (AC-18645) to begin construction of two prototype XB-33A airframes. On paper the "Super Marauder" was to have a 79.8 ft. fuselage, 24 ft. height, and 134 ft. wingspan (1,646 sq. ft. area). Instead of the proposed R-3350s reserved for B-29s, it was to be powered by four 1,800 hp Wright R-2600-15 Cyclones with two-stage GE CMC-3 turbo superchargers that were to give the bomber a top speed of 345 mph at 39,000 ft. (cruise at 242 mph) over a range of 2,000 miles. The empty weight was 65,000 lbs. (gross 98,000 lbs.) with a bomb capacity of 10,130 lbs. The fuselage was to house a remote firing system that operated power turrets of twin .50-caliber machine guns in the nose, forward belly, upper rear, and tail. Three thousand rounds of ammunition fed the eight .50-caliber machine guns. The proposed performance specs were so promising the AAC ordered 400 more XB-33As on 17 January 1942—at the government-owned plant in Omaha, Nebrasksa, operated by Martin—before the prototypes were even built! By this time the course of the war pointed toward a Japanese defeat and the need for a third long-range heavy bomber was redundant, as the B-29 was proving itself over Japan and its B-32 backup had been relegated as a non-player. The XB-33A project was canceled to permit the Omaha factory to concentrate on manufacturing the B-29 and the two unfinished prototypes were dismantled.

Martin XB-33A

CONSOLIDATED AND BOEING AWARDED LONG-RANGE BOMBER CONTRACTS

Boeing and Consolidated were contracted to build the XB-29 and XB-32 not on a fixed cost basis, but on a cost plus a fixed six percent management fee basis. Once the contracted aircraft were finished the cost basis was the expense of salaries, materials, and depreciation less any advances and progress payments. Boeing and Consolidated would receive a six percent fee of the total cost for managing the project. To give the companies an incentive to keep costs down they were to be awarded a percentage of the savings under the expected cost. The six percent was essentially the company's profit.

Consolidated is Awarded the XB-32 Contract

On 6 September 1940, contract number AC 15549 ordered two XB-32 prototypes to be delivered. The first prototype (#41-141) was to be delivered in eighteen months (March 1942), while the second (#41-142) was to be delivered three months later (June 1942). That same day contract AC 15429 for two flyable XB-29s and a non-flying static test aircraft was let to Boeing. On 14 December 1941, the contract was revised to add a third flyable XB-29 and a third XB-32 prototype (#41-18336) that was to be delivered in March 1943. Consolidated designated the XB-32 its Model 33 and named R. C. "Sparky" Seabold as project engineer. Seabold used the experience gained in this project later as the project engineer for Consolidated's giant postwar intercontinental B-36 bomber.

The contract stipulated that Consolidated submit a wooden model to Air Materiel Command at Wright Field for wind tunnel tests. Consolidated submitted drawings of its initial design to Wright Field, where wind tunnel tests were completed using a 1/35 scale birch wood model that had a forty-six inch wingspan and had a very different look from the final contracted model. To facilitate the wind tunnel tests the turrets and landing gear were removable to replicate their retraction, and the controls—elevators, rudders, and stabilizer—were movable. The tests uncovered that while the twin-tailed configuration gave the bomber "satisfactory" longitudinal control, its directional stability was assessed as "insufficient." Although the wind tunnel tests led to many minor modifications that were incorporated in the contracted version, the twin-tail configuration was not changed and was to be the bane of the prototype.

By early December 1940, Consolidated had built revised mockups using new data from the previous Wright Field wind tunnel tests. On 6 January 1941, the modified mockup as suggested by the Wright wind tunnel tests was approved by AAC inspectors who had continued reservations about the twin-tail configuration. On 17 April, the engine mockups were inspected and approved. In mid-June, the AAC awarded a contract to build thirteen YB-32 service test models for $221.7 million to be developed and built along with the original three XB-32 prototypes.

The B-32 had always been considered a contingency to the B-29, but once the Superfortress' engine problems were solved the B-32's role as a Very Heavy Long-Range Bomber ended. In the late stages of the Pacific War it was considered a replacement as a heavy bomber for the aging B-17 Flying Fortress and the B-24 Liberator. However, as B-29s were being readied to drop atomic bombs on Hiroshima and Nagasaki, B-32s were deployed to the Philippines, where they flew a handful of conventional heavy bomber missions against Formosa (Taiwan). (Note: For a comprehensive look at the B-32 see my book, *The Consolidated B-32, The Ultimate Look from Drawing Board to Scrapyard*, Schiffer.)

Consolidated XB-32

Boeing is Awarded the XB-29 Contract

From early 1938, Boeing engineers had been working on various super bomber designs (Models 316, 322, 333, 333A/B, 334, 334A, and 341), trying various engines (Allison V-1710, Wright X-1800, Pratt & Whitney R-2800, and finally the Wright R-3350), fuselage configurations, and wing designs. Boeing continued to evaluate its earlier Model 341 proposal and made numerous improvements that led to the Model 345. Compared to the Model 341, the Model 345 reflected the exigencies of the European air war in its design. After working day and night for two months, on 11 May 1940, Boeing responded by sending the preliminary design for the Model 345 to Wright Field. The Model 345 was essentially a reworked Model 341 with a crew of twelve contained in a pressurized cabin. The Boeing design team worked in close association with the flight test and aerodynamics division to produce the most aerodynamic design possible. The fuselage skin joints were to be smooth and all external rivets were to be flush. All "normal" protuberances, lights, thermometers, antennas, de-icers, drains, vents, and air scoops were to be streamlined, faired or flush. The new design requirements increased the gross weight of the Model 345 to 112,300 lbs., or 27,000 lbs. more than the Model 341. The weight increase decreased its speed by 23 mph (to 382 mph) compared to the Model 341's 405 mph (at 25,000 ft.). The new remote armament system weighed 4,153 lbs. compared to the Model 341's armament of 1,646 lbs. This 2,500 lb. increase in weight required 1,680 lbs. of additional fuel to carry the bomber over a constant range, while the newly added self-sealing fuel tanks weighed 3,000 lbs. more and required another 2,000 lbs. of fuel. Generally, for each pound added to the Model 345 there were two-thirds pounds of fuel needed to carry it over the required range of 5,333 miles. To accommodate these increases the Model 345 had 17 ft. more wingspan (141.3 ft.) and was almost 16 ft. longer than the Model 341. Edward Wells and Wellwood Beall of Boeing's aerodynamics department had continued their work on high lift wings from the Model 334A in August 1939 and developed the Boeing 115 Aerofoil, which was later developed into the 117 airfoil by George Schairer and would help characterize the B-29. The bomber was supported by a tricycle landing gear with double wheels, with the main wheels retracting into the inboard engine nacelles instead of into the wing as in previous models. It was powered by four new Wright air-cooled R-3350 twin-row radial engines and more than met the one-ton bomb load over 5,333 mile requirement, as it was capable of an eight ton maximum bomb load over 6,950 miles. While the Model 341 mounted only six flexible manual .50-caliber machine guns, the Model 345 bristled with ten .50-caliber machine guns and one 20 mm cannon. The machine guns were mounted in pairs in four Sperry retractable turrets, and one pair plus a 20 mm cannon were mounted in the power operated tail turret. The previous problem of pressurizing the gun positions was solved in a new innovative way. Instead of having the gunners positioned inside each turret they controlled the guns remotely via sighting periscopes from stations in pressurized cabins inside the fuselage.

At this time the Boeing engineering department was stretched thin, as the Boeing B-17 venture was ready for mass production and the AAC was about to place an order for 250 B-17Es. Over the previous two years the preliminary design engineers and aerodynamic engineers had developed the Model 345 into the XB-29 design from the performance specifications set by Air Materiel Command and issued by its procurement division into a detailed plan with dimensional specifications. Detailed scale models were approved and fabricated for wind tunnel tests, which were very successful and led to the approval of a mockup. On 24 August 1940, before the mockup was even completed, the AAC was so impressed by wind tunnel data that it let a contract for two flyable Model 345 prototypes at a cost of $3,615,095. The first prototype was scheduled to be delivered in April 1942, and the second in June. The AAC redesignated the Model 345 the XB-29 (eXperimental Bomber 29, as it was the twenty-ninth Army bomber since the Martin B-1 of 1918). The XB-29 was to be the largest and fastest bomber ever built at 116,000 lbs. and a cruising speed of 380 mph (at 25,000 ft.). The bomber would have a wingspan of 141 ft. and a fuselage length of 99 ft. It would carry a crew of ten, with five in the nose cabin: pilot, co-pilot, engineer, navigator, and bombardier; four in the rear pressurized cabin: central fire control gunner, two more gunners, and a radio operator; and a lone gunner in the tail. The pressurized forward and rear cabins were to be connected by a crawl tunnel across the top of the bomb bay. The XB-29 was truly to be a super bomber at twice the weight and horsepower of the B-17 and half again as large dimensionally.

The war in Europe was escalating and Gen. Oliver Echols summoned Boeing President Philip Johnson and Earl Schaefer, vice president of the existing Boeing-Wichita factory, to Dayton, but because of a threatened strike Oliver West went in Johnson's place. At the meeting Echols told the two Boeing representatives that the AAC was going to contract for 512 B-17s and two XB-29s, and the Seattle plant would need to be doubled to accommodate the new B-17 production. To accommodate the B-29 orders, Plant #2 would have to be built in Wichita, as the B-29 would not be built on the West Coast. To get part of the Wichita plant built B-17 tails were to be fabricated there until B-29 production began later. With the government contract in hand, Boeing was able to obtain loans and buy material from suppliers and begin in earnest its long quest to develop the XB-29 into the preeminent bomber in WWII.

After its agonizing teething problems were solved, the B-29 was deployed to bomb Japan from bases in China, but in addition to the logistical problems associated with operations from China (i.e., flying fuel over the Hump), the B-29 was only able to reach a limited area of Japan. The solution was to capture the Mariana Islands, which would bring Tokyo to about 1,500 miles away and within the 3,250 mile round trip range of the B-29, although a large number would make emergency stops at Iwo Jima. The Superfortress devastated Japanese cities to the point of annihilation and then dropped two atomic bombs to suddenly end a war that was predicted to have gone on for at least another year or two.

The last completed B-29 was by Boeing Renton on 28 May 1946, and the bombers were phased out, with many aircraft sent to storage and ultimate scrapping as surplus to requirements. The remaining B-29s were the basis of the Strategic Air Command when it was created on 21 March 1946, and unlike many other wartime bombers, remained in service long after the war ended. The B-29 was the precursor of a series of Boeing-built bombers, transports, tankers, reconnaissance aircraft, and trainers, including the re-engined B-50 Superfortress. During its postwar tenure highly modified B-29s set a number of intercontinental distance records. (Note: For a comprehensive look at the B-29 see my book, *The Boeing B-29 Superfortress: The Ultimate Look from Drawing Board to VJ-Day*, Schiffer.)

Boeing XB-29

Boeing XB-39

In November 1943, Boeing sent a modification request to the Fisher Body Aircraft Development Section General Motors, Cleveland, for flight tests for their first YB-29 (S/N 41-36954, *The Spirit of Lincoln*) using the 3,000 hp 24-cylinder Allison V-3420-17 liquid-cooled inline W24 twin-V12 (essentially two V-1710s with a common crankcase, giving this engine its "W"-shaped frontal appearance). Fisher was chosen for the modification, as it was familiar with the engine, which was to power the P-75 Eagle that they were developing at the time. XB-39 testing began in early 1944. The basic dimensions of this conversion remained the same as the YB-29.

In early 1944, due to increased bomber losses to Luftwaffe interceptors in air combat over Europe, the AAF decided it required a long-range air superiority fighter, and Fisher was then directed to focus on the development of its P-75 at the expense of XB-39 testing. Meanwhile, flight tests of the XB-39 had been delayed by a succession of changes in the planned turbo-supercharger installation, as the originally specified GE Type CM-2 two-stage turbo-supercharger became unavailable due to demands on GE's production of its other turbo-superchargers.

Toward the end of 1944, Fisher finally resumed testing on the V-3420 powered XB-39, with the first flight made on 9 December 1944, in Cleveland. The initial flight tests of the B-39 without turbo-superchargers installed were impressive, as due to the increase in power the XB-39 had a maximum speed of 405 mph at an altitude of 25,000 ft., a cruising speed of 282 mph, and a service ceiling of 35,000 ft. Its maximum range was 6,290 miles with 3,333 gallons of fuel. Its empty weight of 75,500 lbs. was three tons more than the B-29B, but the gross weight of 105,000 lbs. was much lighter. It was to carry 20,000 lbs. of bombs.

By this time the B-39 program had been critically delayed, and despite ongoing problems with the R-3350-powered B-29s that had been rushed into combat in June 1944, its Wright engine was functioning acceptably enough in combat. Thus, the AAF decided the problems involved in setting up and then manufacturing the V-3420 engine for the B-29 were not viable and the B-39 was not ordered into production.

Boeing XB-39

Boeing XB-44 and B-50

The Wright-powered B-29 had always been considered underpowered for its weight, and Boeing designers believed the B-29 wing to be more than capable of mounting a larger engine. The XB-44 program was initiated in September 1943, when Pratt & Whitney offered to modify a B-29 by replacing its 2,500 hp Wright R-3350 Duplex Cyclones with larger 3,500 hp Pratt & Whitney R-4360-33 Wasp Majors. In July 1944, a contract was awarded for the modification of a Boeing B-29A-5-BN (S/N 42-93845) as an engine test bed. The new four-row 28-cylinder Pratt & Whitney R-4360 Wasp Major air-cooled radial engine was larger than the R-3350 and required a total redesign of the nacelles, featuring a distinctive oil cooler scoop intake on the underside and a redesign of a section of the wing around the new nacelle.

The XB-44 that first flew in May 1945 had a wing span of 141.25 ft., a wing area of 1,728 sq. ft., a length of 99 ft., and a height of 29.7 ft. Since the XB-44 was to be used exclusively for engine testing, all but the two .50-caliber guns in the tail were removed, decreasing the gross weight to only 105,000 lbs. Empty weight was 75,035 lbs. The XB-44 had an increased performance over the Wright B-29s with cruising at 282 mph, a maximum speed of 392 mph, and a service ceiling of 29,000 ft. The maximum fuel capacity was 9,300 gallons, giving the test bed a range of 4,500 miles—hardly intercontinental, but much more than Wright B-29s' range of 2,800–3,200 miles.

Although the XB-44 had superior performance to the Wright B-29, the program was nearly canceled at the end of the war, but AAF planners felt they would continue to require a very heavy long-range bomber postwar and promoted the extension of the program. An order for the production of 200 bombers under the designation B-29D was placed in July 1945, but was reduced to only fifty after V-J Day. In December 1945, the designation of the B-29D was changed to B-50A. Officially, the justification for the new B-50 designation was made on the basis that the changes introduced by the B-29D were so significant it was actually a wholly new aircraft, and the B-50 survived to become an important component of the postwar Air Force.

Boeing XB-44

Boeing B-50

FIRST NON-STOP B-29 TRANS-ATLANTIC FLIGHT

In April 1944, after it had been decided the B-29 was to be flown against the Japanese, the ninth YB-29 (41-136963) flew from Wichita to Miami under secret orders and headed north over the Atlantic to Gander, Newfoundland, for refueling and then flew non-stop to Horsham St. Faith, England. Within an hour after its arrival the bomber was discovered and photographed by a Luftwaffe photo-recon aircraft which, as the point of the mission, was to make the Germans believe the B-29 would be deployed to the ETO. Soon this YB-29 would fly from England directly to Karangpur, India, and would become the second B-29 to arrive in the CBI.

YB-29 in England

B-29 TRANS-PACIFIC FLIGHT

On 18–19 September 1945, three specially modified Boeing B-29 Superfortresses left postwar Japan, attempting a record breaking flight. They took off from the northern Japanese island Hokkaido, intending to fly to Chicago and then continue to Washington, DC. Three Guam-based B-29s with faultless mission records and no previous mechanical problems were designated for the mission. Over the previous ten days, to reduce weight and drag the bombers were stripped of unnecessary items such as heavy protective armor, gun turrets were faired over, blister-type bubble windows were replaced with flat ones, and aluminum aircraft skin was highly polished. All group markings were removed and Twentieth Air Force logos were painted on each vertical tail. Five 600 gallon fuel tanks were installed in each bomb bay, increasing total fuel capacity to 10,000 gallons. The increased fuel load gave each B-29 a weight of 144,000 lbs., which would be the greatest overload attempted by a B-29 at that time.

On 14 September, the three B-29s left Guam and over-nighted on Iwo Jima, where they were loaded with as much fuel as possible, as the intended air base on Hokkaido did not have enough fuel available to fill all three B-29s for the long-distance flight. The next day the three aircraft left Iwo Jima and landed on Hokkaido, unsure if the wheels of their heavily loaded bombers would crack the concrete runway.

For the trans-Pacific flight the three bombers were to be commanded by three of the highest ranking generals in the Pacific. The first aircraft was to be commanded by Deputy Commander of the US Strategic Air Forces in the Pacific Lt.Gen. Barney Giles, and carried the only weather officer making the long-distance flight. The commander of the second bomber was Chief of Staff of the Strategic Air Forces Maj.Gen. Curtis

LeMay. Number 3 B-29 was commanded by Brig.Gen. Emmett O'Donnell, who was finishing his service as commander of the 73rd Bombardment Wing (VH).

The planned route was to be a "Great Circle" itinerary (shortest distance on the surface of a globe), using the Jet Stream as a tailwind to aid the bombers to fly farther using less fuel. The route was to fly over the Kamchatka Peninsula, on the eastern border of the Soviet Union, then continue over the Bering Sea to Nome, Alaska, and over Fairbanks, over the Canadian Rockies and much of Canada, over the Great Lakes, and then on to Washington, DC, landing after flying 6,762 miles over a scheduled 26 hours in the air. The planners and crews realized this distance would not break the world's distance record set by the Royal Air Force on 5 November 1938, when three Wellesleys flew non-stop from Ismailia, Egypt, to Darwin, Australia, setting a world distance record of 7,162 miles over 48:10 hours. Nonetheless, the flight was ordered for its publicity value, reiterating US postwar airpower dominance.

On 18 September, a weather observation aircraft took off an hour before the first B-29 to report the latest meteorological conditions along the route ahead. Dumbo and Super Dumbo aircraft (B-17s and B-29s equipped for air-sea rescue) were flying on alert. Because of the scheduled dawn take-off time the airfield was lit by truck headlights. Number 1, commanded by Giles, was to be the first to take off from the 8,200 ft. concrete runway at 0600, LeMay's #2 at 0615, and O'Donnell's #3 was a few minutes later.

Five hours after take-off LeMay's #2 was over Kamchatka when the bomber was met by three American-built Lend Lease P-63 Kingcobras piloted by Soviet pilots. The Soviets briefly scrutinized the unarmed B-29 at close range and then flew off while performing aerobatics. After about thirteen hours the Superfortresses had flown over the Bering Sea to Nome, but nearing Fairbanks the three bombers, expecting help from tailwinds from the Jet Stream, met major headwinds instead. Navigator William Townes determined they were now behind schedule and then, while crossing into Canada, the headwinds increased, and ice began to form on the wings. Although the B-29s had been delivered to the Pacific with de-icing equipment installed, this equipment had been removed as unnecessary on arrival to reduce weight and therefore increase its combat range and speed. The ice continued to increase during the night and the crews would have to wait until it melted off in warmer daylight hours while flying at lower altitudes.

Near Regina, Saskatchewan, with fuel being consumed more rapidly than anticipated due to the headwinds and flying at lower altitudes, the first decision regarding early fuel stops were deliberated. One proposed solution was for Giles to land in Minneapolis, O'Donnell to land in Detroit, and LeMay (who had enough fuel) to continue as planned to Washington. Giles radioed this proposal to the War Department, but soon Giles determined that Chicago Municipal Airport was the only airport large enough to accommodate the B-29s. He and O'Donnell were to land there while LeMay radioed to the War Department that he had sufficient fuel and was heading on for Washington. O'Donnell landed at 1743, with Giles landing about forty-five minutes later. Just as LeMay flew past Chicago the War Department informed him weather was "marginal" in Washington and that he was to refuel in Chicago, so he landed there at 1843. The B-29s had flown a straight-line distance over the globe of about 5,840 miles. The later flight from Chicago to Washington, DC, was uneventful and the three bombers flew over National Airport (now Ronald Reagan Washington National Airport) in formation at 2130 and landed, and were then greeted by AAF senior officers, reporters, and family.

ABOVE / Three B-29s ready to fly the first Trans-Pacific flight.

RIGHT / General of the Air Force Hap Arnold (2R) greets successful trans-Pacific B29 commanders Curtis LeMay (L), Emmett O'Donnell (2L), and Barney Giles (R).

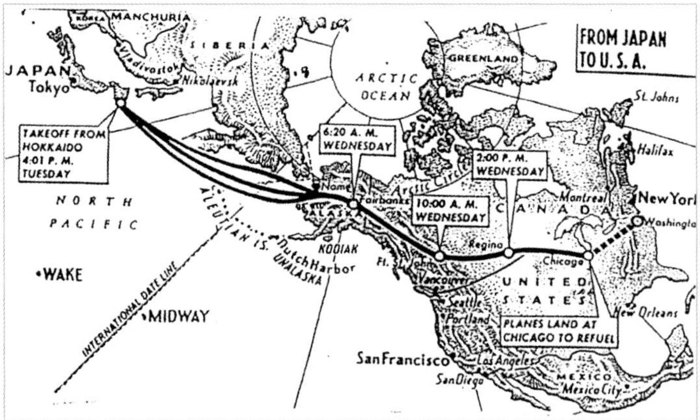

B-29 Trans-Pacific Flight From Japan to America

THE B-29 SETS NEW WORLD DISTANCE RECORDS

On 19–20 November 1945, Col. Clarence Irvine and Lt.Col. G. R. Stanley set the new world's distance record of 7,915 miles while flying non-stop and unrefueled from Guam to Washington, DC, taking 35:05 hours. Irvine was deputy chief of staff Pacific Air Command when he planned and flew a Bell B-29B-60-BA *Pacusan Dreamboat* that was redesignated as a YB-29J for its several record setting flights. The combat B-29B was a lightweight B-29 version intended for low-altitude operation, being stripped of most of its standard armor plate and its four power turrets and their .50-caliber machine guns, leaving only a radar directed 20 mm cannon and two .50-caliber machine guns in the tail for defense. The B-29B was equipped with nacelles modified for improved cooling for its four air-cooled, fuel-injected Wright R-3350-CA-2 Duplex Cyclone two-row 18-cylinder radial engines that turned specially designed propellers. For its record flights *Pacusan Dreamboat* was further lightened by 3,000 lbs. with the useless tail guns removed and its tail remodeled to give it an empty weight of 66,000 lbs. to help it carry 10,000 gallons of fuel and its twelve-man crew (151,000 lbs. gross weight).

Two months after its first long-distance record flight (Guam to Washington, DC) Col. Irvine piloted *Pacusan Dreamboat* on a 9,444 mile non-stop flight from Hickam Field, Hawaii, to Cairo via the North Pole. The bomber followed an approximate Great Circle route from Hawaii via Alaska, Iceland, London, Paris, and Foggia (Italy), and finally to Cairo in 39:36 hours. Soon after Irvine flew *Pacusan Dreamboat* to a new transcontinental record from Burbank to New York in 5:27 hours using the West-East Jetstream to average 451.9 mph.

In March 1946, Irvine continued his quest for records when he flew *Fluffy Fuz V* from Honolulu to Manila non-stop in a record 21:49 hours. While on Guam, Irvine directed ground operations for the Marathon Project during May 1946, and the following payload/altitude records were set: *The Challenger* was flown to 41,561 ft. true altitude with a 22,200 lb. load and to 39,500 ft. with a 33,000 lb. load; a B-29 named *Queen of the Niches* carried 4,400 lbs. to 46,522 ft. on May 13, then the following day took 11,000 lbs. to 45,252 ft.; and *Fluffy Fuz* climbed to 47,910 ft. carrying 2,200 lbs.

In October 1946, Irvine flew a re-modified *Pacusan Dreamboat*—grossing 149,000 lbs. and now carrying 13,400 gallons of fuel—from Honolulu 10,000 miles over the Arctic to Cairo in 39:36 hours. After its stint as a record breaking YB-29J, *Pacusan Dreamboat* was later modified for photo reconnaissance and its designation was changed to FB-29J (later RB-29J). In 1948, General Irvine took command of the 509th Strategic Bomb Wing at Walker Air Force Base, New Mexico. In 1950, he became commanding general of the B-36 Wing at Carswell AFB and during this time he led attempts at the re-engineering and modification of the B-36 Strategic Bomber to increase its combat effectiveness.

The *Pacusan Dreamboat*

The *Pacusan Dreamboat* crew with pilot Col. Clarence Irvine (second row first left)

THE P2V-1 SETS THE NON-STOP DISTANCE RECORD

The third production Lockheed P2V-1 Neptune was selected to exceed the 9,444 mile non-stop record set by the Army's B-29 *Pacusan Dreamboat* in January 1946; this was also a publicity ploy to demonstrate the Navy's new patrol bomber's ASW and reconnaissance trans-ocean capability.

The Lockheed P2V Neptune was a twin-engine, long-range patrol bomber normally operated by a crew of eight. The first production variant (P2V-1) was 75.3 ft. long, with a wingspan of 100 ft. (a wing area of 1,000 sq. ft.), and a height of 28.5 ft. Empty weight was 33,720 lbs. and gross weight was 61,153 lbs. The Neptune was powered by two 2,300 hp air-cooled supercharged Wright Duplex-Cyclone R-3350-8A two-row 18-cylinder radial engines that drove four-bladed propellers. The P2V-1 had a maximum speed of 303 mph (at 15,300 ft.), the service ceiling was 27,000 ft., and normal range was 4,110 miles. Standard armament consisted of six .50-caliber machine guns, two torpedoes carried in the internal bomb bay, and conventional bombs or up to twelve depth charges and nuclear weapons could also be carried.

The P2V, nicknamed the "Turtle," was modified by Lockheed to achieve maximum range by replacing the standard configuration Wright R-3350-8A engines with two R-3350-14 Duplex Cyclones. All armament was removed, including the nose gun turret, as was most ASW electronic and other unnecessary equipment, such as crew oxygen and de-icing equipment. Extra fuel tanks were installed in virtually every free space. In addition to a 2,200 gallon bomb bay tank, the aircraft also had tanks in the outer wing panels that contained another 1,542 gallons. The jettisonable wing tip tanks held 400 gallons; an 858 gallon tank was installed in the new lengthened streamlined nose; and an additional 2,082 gallons were carried in another tank in the rear fuselage. Even the sonobuoy chute was equipped with a tank holding 128 gallons, while an additional 140 gallons were estimated to be contained in the system of lines that connected all these fuel tanks with the engines. A total of 8,592 gallons was carried, which was 5,000 gallons more than the standard production P2V-1. In case of an emergency, the fuel system incorporated a rapid fuel dumping system: a ten-inch diameter pipe was in the fuselage on rollers and could be coupled to a three-way valve leading to the nose, bomb bay, and fuselage tanks. The pipe, which poked through the belly aft of the weapons bay, could dump 800 gallons in the first twenty seconds and 5,200 gallons in six minutes. Four jet assisted take-off (JATO) rockets were added—two on each side of the fuselage—to facilitate fuel overload take-off.

By Fall 1946, the Turtle conversion was completed and the Navy aircrews and Lockheed technicians flew it across the Pacific in hops to Perth, Australia's Pearce Aerodrome, with its long 6,000 ft. runway. In press releases immediately before the flight the Navy referred to the aircraft as the "Truculent Turtle" to give it a more aggressive nature than just plain "The Turtle." On 29 September, weather forecasts were positive, and the flight would also be aided by the prevailing tailwinds at this time of the year. Take-off was in the cooler night air and would provide more power and less turbulence. On 29 September 1946, command pilot Cdr. Thomas Davies, co-pilot Cdr. E.P. Rankin, and Cdr. W. S. Reid and Lt.Cdr. R. A. Tabeling as navigators/radio operators/relief pilots were ready to take off. A last minute addition to the crew and aircraft weight was a nine-month-old kangaroo that was to be a gift from Australia to be presented to the Washington, DC, Zoo. When the *Turtle* was ready it weighed 85,575 lbs., nearly thirteen tons over its normal take-off weight and much more than any other twin-engine aircraft had ever lifted. Davies taxied the *Truculent Turtle* to the end of the 6,000 ft. concrete runway where fueling was completed, since the full fuel load would have exceeded the strength of the aircraft's landing gear during taxiing and turning. During the twelve-second burn time each JATO bottle developed 1,000 lbs. of static thrust to supplement the 2,800 hp the engines developed at full throttle. The aircraft lifted off the runway with one thousand feet to spare.

With the intention of using less fuel during the climb to cruising altitude, the initial plan was to remain at 3,500 ft. for the first few hundred miles to burn off fuel and reduce weight for the climb. However, a wind at lower altitude caused turbulence that severely shook the overloaded aircraft and endangered its wing integrity. Sacrificing fuel, Davies climbed to 6,500 ft., where the air was calmer, but continued through some turbulence during part of the route. During the aircraft's first voice radio contact of the flight *Honolulu Radio* warned of icing and severe turbulence over Seattle, the scheduled US landfall. Davies altered his course to cross over the Northern California coast, dropping the empty 200 gallon wing tip tanks and climbing to 10,000 ft. After 44 hours and 9,000 miles the Neptune crossed the California coastline far south of Seattle thousands of pounds of fuel lighter. Davies had to climb to cross over the Sierras and then climb even higher over the Rockies. Rain, sleet, and snow pummeled the aircraft, which began to severely ice up, as de-icing equipment had not been installed. With the Rockies looming ahead, descending into warmer air to shed ice was not an option and Davies had to apply ever higher power settings to force his way over the mountains, using more fuel. At dawn of 1 October, the weather finally cleared and Davies flew eastward all morning over the Plains States, but as he neared Chicago the fuel situation was becoming critical and the intent to reach Washington, DC, ended; the crew then scrambled to find a suitable landing field. Davies and his exhausted crew landed at NAS Columbus, Ohio, after being in the air for two and a half days and covering 11,236.6 miles in 55:18 hours. The next day a *New York Times* dispatch affirmed:

> The 7,916-mile record that it shattered was that made by the Army's Boeing Superfortress Dreamboat. A plane like the P2V can carry an atomic warhead from any point on the earth's surface to a point half-way round the globe.

The *Times* article failed to recognize that carrying a bomb to a target 12,000 miles away would be a one-way mission for a P2V; the bomb would not be nuclear, but very small due to the huge fuel load required to reach the target; or that enemy air defenses would probably discover the P2V during its two to three day approach.

The *Turtle's* record was not officially recognized and the distance record would stand until 10 January 1962, when a Strategic Air Command jet-powered B-52H flew 12,519 miles non-stop and unrefueled from Kadena Air Base, Okinawa, to Madrid, Spain, in 21:52 hours. Lees and Brossy's piston-powered non-refueled aircraft record of 84:32 hours of May 1931 would stand until 14–23 December 1986, when Dick Rutan and Jeana

Yeager flew for 216:03:44 in their Rutan Voyager in the process of circumnavigating the globe. The *Truculent Turtle* is on display at the National Museum of Naval Aviation, NAS Pensacola.

Lockheed P2V-1 Neptune *Truculent Turtle*

Truculent Turtle flight crew: (L-R) Cdr. Eugene Rankin (command pilot), Cdr. Thomas Davies (co-pilot), and Cdr. Walter Reid and Lt.Cdr. Ray Tabeling as navigators/radio operators/relief pilots

9

THE POSTWAR US INTERCONTINENTAL BOMBER IS REALIZED

Near the end of WWII, the US had two potential specially designed intercontinental bombers (XB-35 and XB-36) on the drawing board, but within a year after the war only one would prove to be viable. Meanwhile, two other long range bombers (B-29 and XB-19) survived the postwar rush to scrap. The prop-driven B-29 as the B-50 continued to serve with moderate distinction in the blossoming of the jet age, while the XB-19 remained parked and went on to an ignominious end and is virtually unknown today, except as a footnote.

NORTHROP FLYING WINGS

Aviation pioneer and innovator John (Jack) Northrop dedicated much of his career to validating the all-wing, more popularly Flying Wing, concept as a practical aircraft design; trading the weight and drag of a conventional fuselage and tail for increased speed and range. The all-wing design, not requiring a conventional fuselage and tail assembly, would produce much less drag as it moved through the air and the air resistance thus saved could in turn be exchanged for the important advantages of higher speed or the ability to carry a larger load over a much increased range. Because the bomb load was carried within a narrow and heavily-stressed mid-section, its weight could be distributed evenly across most of the lifting surface, resulting in a lighter and more efficient structure. By July 1940 Northrop had flown the N-1M Flying Wing, establishing that it was possible for an aircraft to fly without the conventional fuselage and empennage configuration.

John (Jack) Northrop

N9-M and XB-35 Flying Wings

In August 1939, after years at Douglas Aircraft, Jack Northrop became president and chief engineer of Northrop Aircraft Inc., and pursued his life-long desire to develop an all-wing aircraft. Less than a year later, on 3 July 1940, the world's first pure all-wing aircraft (N-1M) made its first flight. It was not long before the AAC became aware of the impressive flight characteristics of his revolutionary research vehicle.

On 11 April 1941, the AAC issued a request for a bomber that could carry 10,000 lbs. of bombs on a round-trip mission of 10,000 miles at a maximum speed of 450 mph, a cruising speed of 275 mph, and a service ceiling of 45,000 ft. This proposal was first submitted to Boeing and Consolidated, and eventually led to the production of the Convair B-36 Peacemaker.

On 27 May 1941, the AAF requested Northrop investigate the use of the Flying Wing as it related to requirements for a bomber with a range of 8,000 miles, a minimum cruising speed of 250 mph, a service ceiling of 40,000 ft., and a bomb load of 10,000 lbs. These requirements were far less challenging than the preliminary ones of April 1941. The May requirements were revised again in August 1941, and this slightly upgraded version was again submitted to Northrop and other potential manufacturers of conventional, long-range bombers.

In September 1941, Northrop tendered the proposal of the future XB-35 to the AAF, which was immediately followed by contract negotiations. Northrop had previously determined that extensive engineering would be necessary on the project and before the initial procurement of the Flying Wing requested a purchase order for engineering data, model tests, and evaluation of reports on the N-1M, which had been flight tested since June 1940. Also included was the procurement of the N-9M, a ⅓ scale flying mockup of the XB-35 that Northrop intended to use flight data from to test the XB-35's future configuration, and would accelerate the development of the B-35 project. Secretary of War Henry Stimson approved the order on 3 October 1941, and contract W535-ac-21341 was signed on 30 October.

Chief of the AAF Maj.Gen. Arnold endorsed the procurement of the first full-scale flying wing on 9 September 1941, and on 22 November, it came under contract W535-ac-21920. At Northrop's request the contract, estimated at $2.9 million, was to be cost plus fixed fee, because the development of the large XB-35 project would require capital beyond Northrop's resources for experimental purposes and materiel, and labor costs were anticipated to increase significantly before the November 1943 scheduled XB-35 delivery. Contract W535-ac-21920 also included one XB-35 mockup and engineering data, plus an option clause covering the purchase of another XB-35 which was exercised on 2 January 1942. Northrop cited a delivery date of April 1944 for the second XB-35, also known as the "back up article," at an estimated extra cost of $1.5 million.

On 17 December 1942, cost plus fixed fee $22.7 million contract W535-ac-33920 was approved, granting the construction and testing of thirteen service test models of the XB-35 (designated the YB-35), and also spare parts and Northrop's contractor's fee. A few months later, the AAF approved the purchase of two additional N-9Ms, with a fourth and last N-9M being ordered in mid-1943.

The N-9M's first flight took place on 27 December 1942, about three months behind schedule. The 7,100 lb. N-9M research model, with its 60 ft. wing span, was very similar to the N-1M and was a scaled-down version of the future full-scale XB-35 Flying Wing. Two Menasco C654 engines powered the N-9M instead of the four Pratt & Whitney R-4360s assigned to the XB-35. Most of the N-9M's flight tests were abbreviated by mechanical failures of some type involving the Menasco engines that also equipped the next two N-9Ms. On 19 May 1943, after twenty-two hours of flying time, the initial N-9M crashed on its forty-fifth test flight, killing the Northrop test pilot. On 24 June 1943, the second N-9M's first flight followed soon after the crash and was joined by a similar third N-9M. N-9MB was the fourth N-9 and was the replacement for the lost N-9M; it differed (i.e., MB designation) from the others as it was powered by two Franklin 0-540-5 air-cooled engines. After 150 test flights the slightly different N-9Ms and the N-9MB continued to be tested into late 1945.

The Northrop N-9M

The AAF anticipated the rather new Northrop Company would have problems fulfilling its XB-35 contracts. The company also suffered from an industry-wide shortage of engineers and skilled and unskilled labor, and not benefitting from government-assisted new plant finance and construction, it lacked suitable production facilities and there was no prospect of expanding the Hawthorne facility. At the end of 1942, to remedy Northrop's problems the AAF concluded negotiations between Northrop and the Glenn L. Martin Company in which Northrop agreed it would fabricate only the experimental and prototype B-35s and Martin would receive an impending production contract for 200 B-35s and, in anticipation, Martin had happily canceled a pending production contract for 400 troubled B-33 Super Marauders on 25 November.

The N-9 flight test program was hindered by numerous mechanical problems that prevented the acquisition of reliable flight data through 21 September 1943, when the last of the N-9s (N-9MB) was ready for its first flight. The N-9MB included all up-to-date design innovations of the XB-35, except for the engines. When the N-9MB's testing concluded at the end of November, test results indicated that the XB-35's range would probably be 1,600 miles less than predicted and that the bomber's maximum speed would be at least 24 mph below earlier estimates. These rather disappointing figures of the XB-35's proposed virtues caused the AAF's upper echelons to question any plans for extensive B-35 production.

Nonetheless, contract W535-ac-24555 for the planned production for 200 B-35s beginning November 1942 was finally enacted on 30 June 1943, and Martin was asked for the delivery of the first bomber by June 1945. In mid-1943, projected B-35 delivery was reduced by fifty percent, as Martin had experienced personnel problems, particularly a shortage of engineers and men lost to the draft, and was reluctant to devote their available personnel to an uncertain project. Martin became even more cautious when Northrop requested numerous changes, and even more so when shortages of materiel for the project appeared. By March 1944, the B-35 tooling was not yet under fabrication at the Martin Middle River Baltimore Plant and an unenthusiastic Martin Company rescheduled delivery of the first B-35 to 1947. On 24 May 1944, the AAF had little choice but to cancel the Martin production contract. Nonetheless, the cancelation did not end Northrop's Flying Wing Project, as in November, the Air Technical Service Command's Engineering Division stated that the XB-35 project seemed worthy "even if the B-35 never becomes operational."

In December 1944, after the Martin production contract was canceled, the AAF decided that Northrop was to build the first six B-35 prototypes (YB-35s) based on the XB-35's design, but with specific allowances for individual aircraft. Soon afterward, Northrop was authorized to build two of those six prototypes as all-jet engine models, which would lead to the beginning of a new Flying Wing program. In 1945, two YB-35s were added to the first YB-35 consignment to replace the two allocated for jet conversion. The AAF directed Northrop to manufacture the remaining five aircraft to more advanced specifications as YB-35As.

The first XB-35 was finally ready, and was an impressive sight, with its futuristic design comprised of no fuselage or tail and two huge joined one-piece aluminum alloy, tapered, swept-back wings. The XB-35 had a wingspan of 172 ft., wing area of 4,000 sq. ft., a length of 53 ft., a height of 20.3 ft., an empty weight of 89,300 lbs., a loaded weight of 180,000 lbs., and a maximum take-off weight of 180,000 lbs. The engines were two turbo-supercharged Pratt & Whitney R-4360-17 and two R-4360-21 radial engines of 3,000 hp each, initially driving dual contra-rotating three-blade propellers by a long extension shaft connected to a complex gearbox arrangement. Because of serious and continuing problems with the propeller gear boxes the dual propeller arrangement was soon replaced by a single propeller. The three-blade propeller was replaced by a four-blade type that slightly increased the overall performance of the aircraft: the maximum speed was 393 mph, its range was an imposing 8,100 miles, and its service ceiling was 39,700 ft.

The nine man crew consisted of a pilot, co-pilot, bombardier, navigator, engineer, radio operator, and three gunners. The crew compartment and various systems bays were fully pressurized. Future B-35s would provide six beds and a small galley to permit six of the fifteen crewmen rest and relaxation during long missions. The XB-35 also had eight spacious bomb bays that could accommodate 51,000 lbs. of bombs, while the defensive armament was to include twenty .50-caliber machine guns.

On 25 June 1946, the XB-35 finally made its first flight from the Northrop Hawthorne Factory Field to Muroc Lake for flight testing; the "satisfactory, trouble-free" flight (which would be one of the aircraft's few) was piloted by Max Stanley and another factory pilot.

The first XB-35 was then flown on nineteen contractor test flights totaling only about twenty-four hours before gear box malfunctions, propeller control problems, and landing gear closure failure caused the AAF to ground the XB-35s on 11 September 1946. Meanwhile, the second XB-35 was not flown until 26 June 1947, and only eight test flights were flown by Northrop test pilots with similar results and grounding. After undergoing many time consuming extensive modifications, especially to the dual-rotation propellers and gear boxes, the testing on the first XB-35 would not resume until February 1948, with single-rotation propellers, less complex gear boxes, and modified landing gear doors installed. While gear boxes seemed to function adequately, the new single rotation props created a vibration and the doors still failed to close after gear retraction. Most importantly, test pilots immediately reported reduced aircraft performance.

The cost of the first XB-35, initially estimated at $2.9 million, soared to a considerable $14.3 million. In February 1947, Northrop reported that the two all-jet prototypes (YB-49s) and the first six YB-35s (built to XB-35 specifications) were either complete or nearing completion. The originally allocated $23 million on the contract would only be sufficient for the construction of three or four of these aircraft. Northrop stated that an additional $8 million "might" fund the completion of these eight aircraft, while for $16 million all thirteen (including the five YB-35As in the program changes of 1945) could be completed. On 28 May 1947, the AAF approved $12 million for cost overruns, which was $4 million under Northrop's estimate. At the end of January 1948, Northrop stated that an additional $4.4 million would be necessary to complete all thirteen aircraft.

By mid-1948, not unexpectedly, the prop-driven XB/RB-35s could not match the performance of jet bombers already in development and approaching production. In its mid-1948 configuration the Flying Wing was found to be less stable than a conventional wing/fuselage aircraft, which made it a mediocre bombing or camera platform. It was only because of the multi-million dollar investment in the aircraft's development, with no palpable return, that the Air Force continued with the XB-35. Wanting to find some use for its now white elephant, the Air Force decided on a reconnaissance version of the jet-equipped YB-35s originally ordered in 1945. In June 1948, the decision was enacted as an order for the production of thirty reconnaissance aircraft to be designated RB-49AS. Meanwhile, to justify their immense investment in the XB-35 project the AAF attempted to save face by initiating a study in mid-1948 to determine the feasibility of a B-35 for in-flight refueling, which seems to have come to naught.

During the second half of 1948, Northrop and the AAF Air Force continued to search for a tactical or strategic mission for the aircraft and looked into many proposals for conversions and modifications. In August, Northrop requested that if no further changes were made the company could complete the existing experimental contracts with the funds already allotted, but Air Materiel Command replied that changes were necessary to solve the XB-35's continuing problems, particularly the single rotation propeller's vibration problems. Also, by this time the XB-35's complex exhaust system began to cause dire maintenance problems and the R-4360 engine cooling fans were beginning to fail due to metal fatigue. Air Materiel Command's solution to the prop engine problem was to convert every B-35 prototype to a jet engine configuration that would have no propellers to vibrate!

So by the end of 1948, five YB-35s and four YB-35As were each projected to be equipped with six Allison J35-A-17 jet engines and camera installations and redesignated as RB-35B reconnaissance aircraft. One YB-35A was also to be allocated for static tests; a second YB-35B, with six new Allison jets, was to be the reconnaissance prototype for the B-49 program; and a third YB-35A was to be converted to the jet configuration as the EB-35B to test the advanced Northrop T-37 Turbodyne turboprop engine, each driving a pair of contra-rotating, paddle-blade propellers. When the EB-35B project was canceled, the Air Force had Northrop's Turbodyne engine name, all its patents, and technical data reassigned to General Electric. All elements of this program were projected to cost an additional $13 million.

By the end of fiscal year 1948, development costs of the experimental B-35 program had reached $66,050,506 (including $1,644,603 for the conversion of two YB-35s to the six jet-equipped B-49 prototypes). For $25,632,859 of the $66 million the Air Force had two XB-35s on the first cost plus fixed fee contract (535-ac-21920), which was $21 million more than originally estimated! The remaining $40,417,647 covered the second and last cost plus fixed fee contract (535-ac-33930) which, as supplemented by Change Order No. 11, totaled $24,417,647, excluding cost overruns of $12 and $4 million approved in April 1947 and April 1948, respectively. With the $13 million modification proposal the USAF lost interest in the B-35 conversion program, especially at a time when postwar funding was limited. During August 1949, the two XB-35s and the first two YB-35s were scrapped. In November, the Air Staff canceled plans to convert remaining YB-35s and YB-35As,

Northrop XB-35 on the ground

Northrop XB-35 in flight

stating that conventional bombers could fulfill requirements as efficiently as the Flying Wing.

The Northrop XB-35 Flying Wing program was terminated due to its overriding technical difficulties, immense cost, and the impending obsolescence of its piston/propeller engines in the jet age; besides, the program was far behind schedule and over budget. The competing prop-driven B-36 was also obsolete by that time and had encountered as many or even more development problems. The Air Force required a very long-range, postwar atomic bomber to counter the supposed Soviet threat and had more confidence that the more conventional B-36's teething problems could be overcome more quickly, compared to those of the new and radical Northrop Flying Wing.

Two XB-35s and thirteen YB-35s were paid for and also accepted, with some diverted to the B-49 program, but most others, although finally completed, immediately scrapped beginning in December 1949 and ending in March 1950, when the EB-35B test bed was disassembled.

YB-49 Flying Wing

The jet-propelled YB-49 evolved from the avant garde XB-35 Flying Wing concept of 1944. It was part of Northrop's and the AAF's continuing effort to establish some tactical or strategic use for the XB-35 Flying Wing that had yet to be flown and was already beleaguered by almost overwhelming problems. On 1 June 1945, Change Order 11 to contract W535-ac-33920, a December 1942 contract for thirteen B-35 prototypes, confirmed earlier verbal decisions and authorized Northrop to convert two future YB-35s to the YB-49 configuration by replacing the four Pratt & Whitney R-4360 radial engines driving dual contra-rotating propellers with eight Allison TG-180 (J35) turbojet engines. In addition to the installation of the jet engines other modifications were required, including the addition of four vertical stabilizers—two on each wing—installed on both sides of the jet engine exhausts. Four air dams/fences extending forward from the vertical stabilizer were installed on each wing to minimize the airflow down the swept wing (reducing lift), rather than over the wing.

The design concept of a jet-powered Flying Wing gave the aircraft increased range and speed for the same power; a more efficient airframe; significant weight lifting ability; and fewer aircrew. Its payload could be dispersed more uniformly along the entire span, eliminating the need for heavy internal bracing. Bomb bays, once limited to along the narrow center section, could be extended across the wing underside. That was the design concept, but many compromises and modifications would be necessary while converting a piston engine design to jet propulsion. The conversion of the YB-35 to the YB-49 configuration was to be completed by June 1946, but would be delayed for more than a year. The delay was caused by unforeseen design problems, especially adding fins to the wings to provide the stabilizing effect that the propellers and propeller shaft housings gave to the basic XB-35.

Northrop YB-49

Because the all-metal XB-35 airframe was used for the conversion, the YB-49 was virtually identical to the YB-35, but was powered by eight (two more than planned) 4,000 lb. thrust Allison J35 engines; had four small trailing edge fins to replace the XB-35's yaw-dampening propeller shaft housings; had four large wing fences; and had a reconfigured wing leading edge forward of and between each pair of fences that provided a low drag intake slot for each of the two sets of jet engines. The jet engines gave the YB-49 a maximum speed of 510 mph that was more than 100 mph faster than its prop-powered predecessor, but the YB-49 cruised nearly 100 mph slower than its developing future rival Boeing XB-47 jet bomber. The XB-35 never met its projected bomb load and neither would the XB-49, as its bomb bays were basically too small to carry contemporary nuclear weapons. The cockpit layout was mediocre at best, as the pilot's one-man bubble, while giving good visibility, could not be opened; to leave his position the pilot had to rotate his seat ninety degrees, lower it several feet, and walk to a hatch fifteen feet away. The co-pilot's position was submerged in the wing leading edge and he had a very poor view that prevented him from taking off or landing the aircraft.

The first flight of YB-49 (42-102367) was on 21 October 1947, when it was flown thirty-four minutes from Northrop's Hawthorne Plant to Muroc Army Airfield. Subsequent flight testing revealed stability problems which could not be resolved using prevailing technology. The Northrop designers did not anticipate the critical control requirements essential for the pilot to fly this large all-wing bomber. The YB-49's control capability at the time was inadequate and did not afford the requisite margin of flight safety. Tests showed that the bomber could not be maneuvered precisely and took too long to get into an effective bombing run. Testing of the first YB-49 had been extensive, as Northrop test flew it on 120 flights for almost 200 hours, while the Air Force completed about seventy hours in twenty flights. On 4 February 1949, the first YB-49 flew from Muroc to Andrews Air Force Base, near Washington, DC, in 4:25, after which President Truman ordered a rooftop White House flyby. During the return flight to Muroc four of the eight engines had to be shut down as no oil had been replaced in these engines during a Wright Field stop and a successful emergency landing was made at Winslow Airport, Arizona.

The second YB-49 was first flown on 13 January 1948 from Northrop to Muroc, and test flights were begun. Northrop test pilots flew the aircraft twenty-four times for about fifty hours, while the Air Force test flew the second YB-49 five times for about thirteen hours. This YB-49 made a noteworthy flight on 26 April 1948, as while testing the aircraft's range it remained aloft for nine hours, of which six were at an altitude of 40,000 ft. During this testing phase only one engine and one auxiliary power unit failure occurred.

The second YB-49 prototype was transferred to the Air Force on 28 May 1948. On 5 June 1948, pilot Maj. Daniel Forbes and co-pilot Capt. Glen Edwards were flying the second prototype northwest of the base when the aircraft "departed from controlled flight" and broke apart in the sky, killing all five crew. Crash investigations found no specific cause, but determined that a major structural failure had taken place in flight and the aircraft cartwheeled uncontrollably before hitting the ground. The loss of the aircraft and further wind tunnel tests continued doubts concerning the Flying Wing's aerodynamic stability and confirmed the need for additional flight testing. Later Forbes Air Force Base was named for pilot Maj. Daniel Forbes, while Muroc was renamed Edwards Air Force Base after co-pilot Capt. Glen Edwards.

The fatal crash of the second YB-49 motivated Northrop and the Air Force to decide whether the remaining first prototype would be flight tested an extra 125 hours, but before tests were resumed the first aircraft was to be modified and equipped with additional flight performance measuring instruments. The YB-49's stability as a bombing platform had always been in question and Deputy Commander of the Air Materiel Command Lt.Gen. Benjamin Chidlaw ordered that it be evaluated against a B-29 (with an autopilot) on comparable mission tests. The YB-49 (without an autopilot) performed poorly, as test pilots found it "extremely unstable" and "impossible to hold a steady course or a constant airspeed and altitude." The YB-49's bombing circular average error and range error were twice those of the B-29, which consistently gained bomb run stability in less than forty-five seconds, while the YB-49's best time was more than four minutes.

By 1948, progress in the range extension of jet propelled bombers had downgraded the YB-49's status to that of a medium bomber, albeit a very large one. At the time there were a number of medium jet bomber competitors: the North American B-45 (in production), and the Convair XB-46, Boeing XB-47, and Martin XB-48 (all in flight testing). Although these projects were a year away, the Aircraft and Weapons Board decided to use flight test results to evaluate the B-47 and B-49 as possible "special piloted atomic" carriers.

Between May 1948 and Spring 1949, the YB-49 prototype was involved in five "incidents," most due or linked to engine problems. However, on 15 March 1950, while an Air Force crew was testing aircraft stabilizer response during a high speed taxi run, the nose wheel began to shimmy uncontrollably and collapsed, and the first YB-49 was destroyed and several crewmen were injured. Ironically, the crash occurred the same day that the YB-49 program was canceled by the Air Force.

B-49A

On 1 October 1948, Northrop was awarded a production contract for thirty jet-powered B-49A Flying Wings. However, the Air Force also had doubts concerning Northrop's capability to operate a large production program. Initially, the Air Force proposed a merger between Convair and Northrop, but Jack Northrop utterly rejected this proposal and finally, on 13 October 1948, Convair signed a letter of intent with Northrop to produce twenty-nine of the B-49As. The first aircraft would be manufactured by Northrop Hawthorne, where the prototype XB-35s and YB-49s were built. The agreement called for Northrop to be responsible for all engineering on the B-49A, including the drawings of production tooling. Convair would manufacture the required tooling and actually produce the aircraft. The Flying Wing Convair assembly line would initially be set up in the 120 ft. bay of Building No. 4, next to the 200 ft. bay turning out the one hundred aircraft run of B-36s. The Flying Wing continued to exhibit serious stability and control problems, and this, along with its inability to carry the current generation of atomic weapons and increasing confidence in the B-36, forced the Air Force to cancel B-49A production before it began.

YRB-49A

Only one more Flying Wing bomber would fly, the six jet engine YRB-49A reconnaissance prototype modification of a YB-35A.The YRB-49A was modified from YB-35A (42-102376) by installing four 5,000 lb. thrust Allison J35 turbojet engines in the wings and adding two more in pylon-mounted nacelles that were designed to act as vertical stabilizers and expected to solve the YB-49's stability problem. The placement of two engines in nacelles allowed more space for additional fuel in the wings, which was necessary for the long-range reconnaissance mission. For the photo reconnaissance role camera equipment was installed in the center and aft fuselage. The aft lower center fuselage was also modified for a radar navigation system with an extensive external modification required for the radome. It could carry six 188 lb. T-89 photoflash bombs over a range of 2,250 miles at an altitude of 35,000–40,000 ft., a maximum speed of 380 mph, and with a cruising speed of 340 mph. The YRB-49A first flew on 4 May 1950, followed by a short test program of only thirteen flights before the aircraft was put into storage in late 1950. The aircraft was flown one more time on 26 April 1951, from short term storage facilities at Edwards AFB, California, to long term storage at Northrop's Ontario Airport facilities, California, where the YRB-49A remained until it was scrapped in November 1953.

Northrop YRB-49A

NORTHROP FLYING WING LEGACY

Although its small radar signature had been noted during tests during the late 1940s, it was for this reason that interest in the Flying Wing concept was revived in the 1980s, due to their potentially low radar reflection cross sections. Stealth technology relies on shapes that reflect radar waves only in certain directions, thus making the aircraft hard to detect unless the radar receiver is at a specific position relative to the aircraft; a position that changes continuously as the aircraft moves. The Northrop B-2 Spirit stealth bomber is the result of this revival. The B-2 has nearly identical dimensions as the XB-49, with a low radar signature capable of penetrating sophisticated and dense air defenses. It is capable of all-altitude attack missions up to 50,000 ft. with a range of more than 6,900 miles unrefueled and more than 11,500 miles with one refueling, making it able to attack targets around the world within hours.

CONSOLIDATED B-36 PEACEMAKER: WORLD'S FIRST INTERCONTINENTAL BOMBER

Wartime Development

After the Nazi's impressive blitzkrieg campaigns through Poland during September 1939, and then the Low Countries and France in 1940, culminating in the French surrender on 22 June, the fall of Britain was an impending reality. American air planners became concerned about the range of their current new heavy bombers (B-17 and B-24), as if Britain fell, further air combat would require a bomber with intercontinental capability and sufficient range to strike targets in Europe from all-weather bases in Newfoundland, a 5,800 mile round trip to Berlin. The Douglas XB-19 seemed to be the answer when it was designed in 1935, but late 1930s foot dragging by the AAC and Douglas left that bomber design in limbo and virtually obsolete, but useful as a "flying laboratory" for developing a fast, high-altitude intercontinental bomber capable of carrying a heavy bomb load over an unprecedented range. The large six-engine Model 35 bomber proposed by Consolidated in 1941 seemed to be the answer, and by 1946, the B-36 would become America's first true intercontinental bomber.

To begin their quest for the intercontinental bomber, the Air Corps' Request for Preliminary Design Proposals of 11 April 1941 was sent to Consolidated, Boeing, and Douglas. The request specified a bomber with a maximum speed of 450 mph (at 25,000 ft.), a 275 mph cruising speed, a service ceiling of 45,000 ft., and an overall range of 12,000 miles (at 25,000 ft.). The 45,000 ft. service ceiling was above the maximum effective altitude of almost all Nazi anti-aircraft Flak guns. It had to be able to carry a 10,000 lb. bomb load a distance of 5,000 miles round trip (combat radius) and had to be able to carry 72,000 lbs. of bombs over a reduced range. It also had to be able to take off and land on a 5,000 ft. runway. These requirements were far beyond aircraft capabilities at the time.

Reuben Fleet's Consolidated Aircraft Company, after concentrating for many years on seaplanes, especially the superb PBY Catalina, returned to the land plane market in early 1940, with development of the B-24 Liberator. The AAC selected Douglas as part of the long-range bomber competition, as it had been working for several years on the just recently flown XB-19 and planned to use the then-obsolete bomber as a "flying laboratory" to gather information that would aid in the design and construction of future giant long-range aircraft. Boeing was selected because its B-29 was involved in the long-range very heavy bomber project. Of the contenders, Consolidated seemed to show the most interest, as on 3 May 1941, the company submitted a preliminary proposal for the project which was their twin-tail Model 35, although at this time Consolidated designers were uncertain whether a six-engine or four-engine configuration would be employed.

Northrop was contacted later on 27 May, when it was also asked for further design studies on a Flying Wing with detailed engineering to begin in early 1942, with the first example to be delivered in November 1943, and the second in April the next year.

Solicited much later, the Glenn L. Martin Company declined the invitation due to a shortage of engineering personnel, as it had the B-26 Marauder and the Mars and Mariner Flying Boats in production and had been under contract since June 1941 on the four-engine XB-33 Super Marauder and was about to become involved in the Northrop Flying Wing program.

The Air Corps realized that these specifications were excessive, and during a 19 August conference to accelerate the bomber project attended by Assistant Secretary of War for Air Robert Lovett, Chief of the Air Corps Maj.Gen. George Brett, and ranking officers of the Air Staff, these specifications were revised downward. Nonetheless, this revision continued to be excessive in its demands, with a minimum overall range of 10,000 miles and an effective combat radius of 4,000 miles with a 10,000 lb. bomb load—about four times the combat radius of the Boeing B-17, the AAF's latest and most advanced operational bomber. The revision further specified that the prospective intercontinental bomber should have a cruising speed between 240 and 300 miles per hour and a 40,000 ft. service ceiling (5,000 ft. less than originally requested).

After a review of the preliminary data submitted by Boeing, Consolidated, and Douglas, the Air Corps' Materiel Division suggested that immediate action should be initiated on the Consolidated proposal, which included several long-range bomber designs powered by both four and six engine pusher and pusher/tractor types. Douglas Aircraft stated that it did not desire to undertake an "out and out 10,000 mile airplane project" and instead proposed the development of the Model 423, a 6,000 mile bomber, which was rejected. As for Boeing, the AAC believed as late as April 1942 that the company was "overly conservative" and had not yet "really tackled the (long-range) airplane design with the necessary degree of enthusiasm." Two Boeing bomber designs (Models 384 and 385) submitted in September were never developed.

Then Commanding Officer of the Air Corps Experimental Division and Engineering School at Wright Field, Ohio, Brig. Gen. George Kenney considered a more comprehensive Consolidated Model 35 proposal submitted on 6 October, consisting of drawings and a bid which solicited $15 million plus a fixed fee of $800,000 for research and development of mockup, tooling, and production of two experimental long-range Model 35 bomber prototypes. On 16 October, Maj.Gen. Arnold, on Kenney's recommendation, announced that the Consolidated proposal had been selected, and on 15 November 1941, a contract (W535-AC-2232) meeting Consolidated's provisions for two XB-36 experimental aircraft was issued under the designation XB-36. The two XB-36s were to be built in San Diego, with the first one to be delivered by May 1944, followed by the second six months later. On 22 November, the Wright Field Engineering Division concluded that the six-engine design rather than the four-engine design should be implemented, but that the twin fin and rudder configuration be retained. On 10 December, Consolidated redesignated the Model 35 as the Model 36, so that it would not be confused with the Northrop Flying Wing, which was then known as the B-35.

Isaac Laddon

Executive Vice President Isaac M. Laddon was in charge of the XB-36 program. Laddon had joined Consolidated as chief engineer in 1927, and his designs began with the Admiral Flying Boat in 1928, which was the first in a series of famous Consolidated seaplanes that evolved into the legendary PBY Catalina, of which 3,282 were built. Laddon's B-24 Liberator had the largest production run of any WWII bomber, with more than 18,400 manufactured. After his work on the B-36 he would be responsible for designing the postwar Convair airliners. Aiding Laddon on the B-36 project was Harry Sutton, as head of the engineering department; Ted Hall, as head of the preliminary design group; Ralph Bayless, as head of the aerodynamics group; Kenneth Ward, in charge of finalizing the external aircraft configuration; and Robert Widmer, in charge of wind tunnel testing. At this juncture the slightly swept back wing had a span that had increased to a record 230 ft. with an area of 4,772 sq. ft. The wings contained six fuel tanks with a huge capacity of 21,116 gallons. The aircraft was planned to be powered by six 28-cylinder Pratt & Whitney "X" air-cooled radial engines that were a pair of 14-cylinder R-1830 Twin Wasp engines linked together (only in the design stage at the time). Like the XB-19, the engines were to be accessible for maintenance in flight via passageways in the 7.5 ft. thick wing root. These pusher-configured engines were to drive 19 ft. three-bladed Curtiss propellers. The rarely used rearward facing pusher configuration was favored by aerodynamic theory because the unavoidable propeller turbulence did not interfere with wing lift. Four separate bomb bays holding a maximum capacity of 42,000 lbs. were under the 163 ft. long fuselage. Like in the B-29, only the forward crew compartment and the gunner's remote sighting stations were pressurized. To move back and forth between the forward crew compartment to the rear gunners' compartments a 2.1 ft. diameter, 80 ft. long pressurized tube with a wheeled trolley ran alongside the bomb bays. The fifteen man crew consisted of a pilot, co-pilot, flight engineer, radar/bombardier, navigator, two radiomen, three forward gunners, and five rear gunners. Like the XB-19, four bunks were provided for rest during long flights. The bomber had an exceptionally heavy defensive armament array, consisting of five 37 mm cannon and ten .50-caliber machine guns dispersed among four retractable turrets and a radar-directed tail turret. The guns were to be remotely sighted by gunners positioned at sighting stations dispersed throughout the fuselage.

After more than six months of honing the chosen design, controlling weight, reducing drag, and eliminating various developmental problems associated with any new design, the B-36 mockup was inspected on 20 July 1942. The mockup committee's inspection caused disagreements that nearly caused the cancellation of the experimental program. Some committee members wanted to reduce defensive armament and crew number to have the B-36 meet the 10,000 mile range requirement. Other members contended that with these changes the bomber would become "tactically useless," and would remain experimental and thus redundant, as the experimental engineering division already had the XB-19 "flying laboratory." If this were the case the committee was about to recommend that the AAF discontinue the project and transfer its substantial resources and manpower into more productive bomber programs. The mockup committee and Consolidated eventually compromised and agreed to delete "less necessary" equipment to reduce the mockup's weight and temporarily spare the program.

By August 1942, the Consolidated San Diego Plant was at capacity, filling PBY and B-24 contracts, and the company recommended that the XB-36 project be transferred to its new government leased plant in Fort Worth. Although the transfer was completed in September 1942—less than thirty days after being approved by the AAF—the move caused the project to be delayed by several months, since all of the drawings, mockup, engineers, and the tooling had to be moved from California to Texas. At Fort Worth, R. C. Seybold became chief of engineering and Herbert Hinkley became the XB-36 project engineer; they were tasked to solve the innumerable problems that remained. Progress on the B-36 at Fort Worth moved slowly because the B-24 Liberator and later the B-32 Dominator were given higher priority. Military setbacks in 1942 led the AAF to concentrate on the Boeing B-29 (under production order since September 1941) at the expense of the B-36.

Consolidated contended that development could be reduced by two years if the preliminary work on production B-36s began without waiting for completion of the prototypes, which had been the case with the B-26 and B-25 designs. Consolidated requested that the AAF place a contract for quantity production of the new aircraft, but Consolidated's request came during early 1942: a time of military setbacks, particularly in the Pacific. Because of these bleak times, in addition to the fact that even under the best circumstances the B-36 would become operational in the near future, the AAF decided not to divert its limited resources for its production.

During summer 1942 Consolidated then requested the development of an XC-99 cargo configuration of the XB-36. Consolidated's ploy was to use the XC-99 to test the engines, landing gear, and flight characteristics of the XB-36s, as the company believed the XC-99 could be ready to fly much sooner than either of the two XB-36s because armament and other military gear could be left out. The AAF agreed, but to Consolidated's disappointment, the deal provided that one of the two experimental bombers was to be produced at least three months ahead of the C-99 cargo version, and a $4.6 million contract was approved by the end of the year. The proposed C-99, also powered by six pusher engines, was projected to carry 400 fully equipped troops or more than 100,000 lbs. of cargo on its double decks. Only a single XC-99 was built and was the largest piston-engine, land-based transport aircraft ever built. Its first flight was not until 23 November 1947 in San Diego, and after testing it was delivered to the Air Force on 23 November 1949, and remained in inventory until 1957.

The military setbacks that had hindered the program in 1942 worsened during Spring 1943, as China looked as though it was near collapse, which reversed the XB-36's situation. The operational AAF heavy B-17 and B-24 bombers had insufficient range to operate over the vast distances of the Pacific Theater. The B-29, in the early stage of production, was experiencing more problems than typical of a new design, particularly with its new Wright R-3350 Cyclone engines. The parallel development of the Convair B-32 was largely considered by the AAF as "insurance" in case the B-29 failed. The B-32 also did not progress as well as anticipated due to problems with its twin tail to single tail reconfiguration. Also, the B-29's higher priorities also hindered the B-32's development. Regardless, even if their developmental and production delays could be overcome, neither of these bombers could reach Japan if the proposed bases in China were lost. Strategic planners realized it would require many battles over more than a few years before the Mariana Islands could become a base that was within the range of B-29 or B-32 operations over the Japanese homeland. Accelerated B-36 development was considered to provide a means—perhaps the only one—for attacking Japan. During the Trident Conference attended by President Roosevelt and Prime Minister Churchill in May 1943, both "China Hands" (Lt.Gen. Joseph Stilwell and Maj.Gen. Claire Chennault) corroborated that the situation in China was desperate. Subsequently, Secretary of War Henry Stimson, Assistant Secretary of War Robert Patterson, and senior AAF officers convened to discuss the matter, and led by Stimson, the usual procurement processes were waived and the AAF authorized B-36 production without awaiting completion and testing of the two contracted prototypes (like the earlier B-25 and B-26). On 19 June, Gen. Arnold ordered procurement of one hundred B-36s, and on 23 July, the AAF issued a Letter of Intent for one hundred B-36s issued to Convair on 23 July 1943. The government was not to be liable should this letter of intent be canceled, as was not the case for the more often used letter contract, which obligated funds. On 23 August 1943, much to Convair's relief, the letter of intent was supplemented by Letter Contract W33-038 ac-7. The final $160 million contract (including a $6 million fixed fee and the cost of all spare parts and engineering data) continued to cover the production of the one hundred B-36s, but no longer carried any priority rating. Delivery schedules were unchanged: the XB-36 prototype was to be ready for flight by September 1944; the first production B-36 was due in August 1945; and the last contracted B-36 was due in October 1946. Not surprisingly, these delivery dates were subsequently changed, as was the $160 million contract, which was increased by $61 million on 26 August 1946, when Change Order No. 10 was approved.

The XB-36's developmental problems continued with weight increases. Its twin tail was scrapped and replaced by a single vertical tail that reduced weight by 3,850 lbs., stabilized direction, and decreased drag. The tail modification was approved on 10 October 1943, when the initial development contract (W535 ac 22352) was amended by Change Order No. 7 (previous COs were trivial). This change order also allowed Consolidated to delay delivery by 120 days, which meant the AAF would not receive its first XB-36 until September 1944, at best.

Regardless of its new interest in the project, the B-36 program proceeded slowly, as necessary wind tunnel tests of the new design were postponed until Spring 1944, because other projects had higher priorities and there were no alternate testing facilities available. In addition to the typical engineering problems, Convair became alarmed over the increasing weight of the new Pratt & Whitney R-4360-5P Wasp Major radial piston engines selected for the prototypes. The first Wasp Major test engine was to have been delivered to Fort Worth in May 1943, but design improvements delayed it until October. Convair, not wanting to be tied to one unproven engine, had considered the low fuel consumption Lycoming BX liquid-cooled engine, but that engine had been discontinued, as its further development would require vital manpower, materiel, and facilities needed for other, more essential programs. So the AAF informed Convair to continue with the Wasp Major because the development of a new engine would only delay "expeditious prosecution of the B-36 design."

The new engine became a moot question, as the military situation in the Pacific improved significantly by mid-1944, when the Marianas Campaign had reached a successful conclusion. The airfields on Saipan, Tinian, and Guam were now available and the B-29's production troubles were nearly resolved so Convair accelerated the B-32 program. That being the case, Convair downgraded but slowly continued the XB-36 program.

By 1945, Convair's concern about the ever-increasing weight of the XB-36 continued. The six new R 4360-25 engines, Pratt & Whitney's third version of the original X Wasp, added a 2,304 lb. weight increase. A mockup of a new nose section had been approved in late 1944, and would become a prototype nose for the second XB-36. The addition of nose guns had required an extensive rearrangement of the forward crew compartment. The radio and radar equipment in the new nose would increase gross weight by at least 3,500 lbs., or more if the antenna of the AN/APQ 7 radar could not be installed in the leading edge of the wing.

The XB-36's single-wheel landing gear required the largest tires ever manufactured up to that time: 9.2 ft. in diameter, 3 ft. wide, and weighing 1,320 lbs., with enough rubber for sixty automobile tires. These tires placed so much weight per unit area on runways that the XB-36 would be restricted to the Fort Worth airfield where it was manufactured and to only two other USAF bases. The dual versus single main wheel configuration for the aircraft's landing gear was also problematical, and each had its merits. In mid-1945, Assistant Chief of Air Staff for Materiel, Maintenance, and Distribution Maj.Gen. Edward Powers recommended that a new landing gear be developed to distribute the aircraft's very heavy weight more evenly, thus reducing the necessity for specially built runways. The four wheel truck-type gear that was eventually implemented was 1,500 lbs. lighter than the one previously considered and enabled the B-36 to use any airfield suitable for the B-29. A tank-like tracked landing gear was also tested on the XB-36, but was found to be too heavy and noisy and was soon abandoned.

After the German surrender on 8 May 1945, and with the Japanese cities and war machine devastated by the B-29, US war contracts were being evaluated for cancellation or extreme cutbacks. On 25 May 1945, US aircraft production was ordered to be reduced by thirty percent (17,000 aircraft) over an eighteen-month period. The B-36 contract was left intact, as planners surmised the atomic bomb would probably not remain an American monopoly for long, and the intercontinental bomber would be the atomic delivery vehicle capable of retaliating against "an enemy" without the need for distant forward bases.

The production B-36 was projected to outperform the B-29 and the B-35 Flying Wing for long-range missions, and was to be fifty percent more economical to operate than the B-29 in cost per ton per mile. On 6 August 1945, Gen. Arnold approved the Air Staff's recommendation to preserve the one hundred B-36 production contract intact, with funds from the canceled B-32 program to be transferred to the B-36 project. On 9 August, Lt.Gen. Hoyt Vandenberg, then-assistant chief of Air Staff for operations, commitments, and requirements (OCR), supported the formation of four Very Heavy groups equipped with B-36s to constitute an "effective, mobile task force for our post-war air force."

The XB-36 under construction.

The gigantic size of the XB-36 when parked next to a B-29.

Meanwhile, AAF inspectors found a number of problems on the XB-36, including faulty workmanship (due to the use of unqualified labor), the use of substandard materials, and other discrepancies, not all of which were Convair's responsibility. The company agreed to correct these problems quickly, and progress was made until labor strikes called at the Fort Worth plant in October 1945 and February 1946 delayed the program for several months. On 25 March 1946, Maj.Gen. Edward Powers recommended a new landing gear be developed to distribute the aircraft's very heavy weight more evenly, and also indicated the structural limitations of the XB-36 might make it unusable, other than as a test vehicle for the initial flight (making it another XB-19?). Since the XB-36 was the only intercontinental bomber candidate appearing as a hard copy at the time, work continued on the project.

XB-36: THE FIRST PROTOTYPE

The first XB-36 (42-13570) left the Fort Worth factory on 8 September 1945, but like the XB-19, the XB-36 would not fly until almost six years after issue of its development contract. On 8 August 1946, the first XB-36—the heaviest and largest land plane ever to fly up to that time—finally took off from Fort Worth on its maiden flight. It was piloted by Beryl Erickson and G. S. "Gus" Green supported by seven other crewmen. The thirty-seven minute initial flight was considered successful, despite the bomber's known structural limitations. Further flight tests discovered problems with the wing flap actuating system, poor engine cooling, and turbulent airflow off the wings that caused propeller vibration which adversely affected the wing structure. But the major concern was that the aircraft's overall performance did not fulfill the original specifications: its range fell short and the speed was too slow. Because of engine cooling problems the XB-36 was unable to maintain

XB-36 maiden flight piloted by Beryl Erickson (L) and G. S. "Gus" Green.

altitudes over 30,000 ft. for any extended length of time. The first XB-36's single wheel landing gear was already obsolete, it carried only a minimum of components, and it was not equipped with the nose armament designed for the second XB-36. The aluminum wiring installed to save weight in place of the more reliable but heavier copper wire caused problems.

On 12 December 1946, Gen. Kenny—then head of Strategic Air Command—believing the B-36 to be inferior to the B-50 (modified B-29), suggested that the B-36 contract be reduced to only a few service test aircraft. The XB-36 was looking to become another XB-19, but neither the Air Staff nor Gen. Nathan Twining agreed with this assessment, arguing that the production B-36 should not be judged solely on the performance of the single XB-36, which had just begun flight testing. Gen. Carl Spaatz, commander of the USAF, agreed with Twining and the B-36 contract was spared.

After being grounded again for modifications, the XB-36 was flown for 160 hours by pilots of the USAAF Air Materiel Command. It was then returned to the contractor for further testing, during which Convair pilots made fifty-three test flights, logging 117 flying hours. In June 1948, the single-wheel main undercarriage was replaced by a four, fifty-six-inch diameter wheel bogie-type undercarriage, reducing runway thickness requirements; it was to be standard on production models. In addition, 3,500 hp R-4360-41 engines were installed and the bomber was then redesignated YB-36A, and was flown in this configuration in June 1948.

The YB-36A was then transferred to the USAF in June 1948, one week before the scheduled delivery of the first production B-36As. It had limited operational value, so it was used briefly by the Strategic Air Command primarily for training. It was soon returned to Convair-Fort Worth, where it lingered outdoors for the remainder of 1948 and most of 1949. After being tested briefly with a track-type undercarriage in 1950, the aircraft was returned on charge by the USAF at Wright Patterson AFB in August 1950. However, the Air Force determined it would be too expensive to bring it up to production standards, and the YB-36A was returned to Fort Worth and put in storage. It was officially retired on 30 January 1952, and towed to a field at the north end of the Fort Worth plant, where its engines and equipment were removed. The bomber languished in the open for the next five years and was finally towed across the runway to nearby Carswell AFB and used in the base's firefighting program.

YB-36: THE SECOND PROTOTYPE

On 27 April 1945, the second prototype, designated YB-36 (42-13571), was selected to be the production prototype. Test pilots found the XB-36's poor cockpit visibility to be a chronic problem, and during early June 1945, engineering studies began on an improved cockpit layout. The result was a new high-visibility canopy, with the raised roof and redesigned forward crew compartment that would become standard in the production version. During the war AAF bombers were particularly vulnerable to enemy interceptor frontal attacks, and the Air Force stipulated that the new crew compartment be designed so that nose armament could be installed. The new cockpit contained the pilot, co-pilot, and flight engineer, who faced aft, looking towards and checking the pusher engines now equipped with more efficient turbo-superchargers. Beryl Erickson was at the YB-36's controls on its maiden flight on 4 December 1947, and found that it easily outperformed the first XB-36/YB-36A; during its third flight it was able to climb to over 40,000 ft. The YB-36 continued to use the original single-wheel undercarriage of the XB-36, but new four-wheel main landing gear struts were retrofitted to the aircraft during testing. Since the YB-36 was primarily intended for flight testing no defensive armament was installed.

The YB-36 was transferred to the USAF on 31 May 1949, and was then returned to Convair in October 1950, to be modified for reconnaissance under the redesignation RB-36E. In Spring 1957, it was transferred to the Air Force Museum at Wright-Patterson AFB, Ohio, where it was scrapped in 1971, when the new museum facility was built.

ABOVE / New B-36 high-visibility canopy. (Note: XC-99 (L) and B-29 in background.)

LEFT / B-36 engineer's panel

Specifications of Convair XB-36:

Engines: Six 3,000 hp Pratt & Whitney R-4360-25 Wasp Major air-cooled radial engines.

Performance: Maximum speed 346 mph at 35,000 ft. Cruising speed 216 mph. Initial climb rate 1,740 ft. per minute. An altitude of 25,000 ft. could be reached in 42 minutes. Service ceiling 36,000 ft. Absolute ceiling 38,000 ft. Range 9,500 miles with 10,000 lbs. of bombs, 3,850 miles with 77,784 lbs. of bombs.

Weights: 131,740 lbs. empty, 276,506 lbs. gross. 19,976 gallons of fuel.

Dimensions: Wingspan 230 ft., Wing Area 4,772 sq. ft., Length 162.1 ft., and Height 46.7 ft.

Armament: No defensive armament.

Normal bomb load up to 72,000 lbs.

THE OPERATIONAL B-36

From the end of WWII, relations with the Soviet Union had continually deteriorated, culminating to near warfare during the Soviet blockade of West Berlin beginning in June 1948. This flagrant Soviet hostility made it obvious that America needed a long-range bomber to threaten the Soviets with nuclear annihilation. At the time the B-36 was the only bomber in inventory, and by default became the mainstay of Strategic Air Command (SAC) until the arrival of superior jet-propelled bombers then on the way.

B-36 VARIANTS, B-36A TO J

B-36A

The two B-36 prototypes were followed by twenty-two evaluation bombers designated B-36A. The B-36A designation theoretically labeled the bomber as a production aircraft, but it was specifically dedicated as an interim aircraft to be used by the 7th Bomb Group at Carswell AFB exclusively for flight testing and transitional crew training, and later for conversion. The B-36As incorporated several of the new improvements developed on the YB-36, particularly the enhanced domed canopy and the four-wheel main landing gear (as opposed to the single-wheel landing gear used by the XB-36 and the YB-36). These new features were first included on the B-36A rather than the YB-36, because the B-36A flew first on 28 August 1947, six months earlier than the second YB-36 prototype (4 December 1947). The B-36As had no defensive armament installed as the armament system was not ready.

On 8–9 April 1948, one of the first B-36As, flown by Beryl Erickson and Doc Witchell, flew 6,922 miles (with enough reserve fuel remaining for an additional 206 miles) in 33:10 hours, shuttling between Fort Worth and San Diego three times. The bomber carried a 10,000 lb. bomb load that was dropped halfway through the flight at 25,000 ft. on the bomb range in Wilcox, Arizona. The average cruising speed was 214 mph, but would have been more if two of the engines had not been down or at less than full power. In May 1948, the same aircraft, with a gross weight of nearly 300,000 lbs., was flown from Fort Worth to Hawaii by the same pilots over 8,062 miles round-trip, lasting 33:08 hours. When the newer B-36B became available all B-36As were converted to reconnaissance aircraft and redesignated RB-36E.

B-36B

The B-36B was the first full-scale production version, with seventy-three being built. Because it was manufactured largely of aluminum and magnesium it received the moniker, "Magnesium Overcast." While the two prototypes and B-36As were driven by the less powerful 3,000 hp R-4360-25 engine variant, the B-36B was powered by six 3,500 hp Pratt & Whitney R-4360-41 Wasp Major air-cooled radials with twenty-eight cylinders consisting of four banks of seven cylinders in a "corncob" spiral. The Wasp Majors turned oversized 19 ft., three-bladed pusher props through drive shafts, with a reduction gearing system reducing prop RPM to half that of the engine to prevent the propeller tips from becoming supersonic.

The scale of the B-36 could be considered by realizing that the total area of its control surfaces alone (flaps, ailerons, rudder, and elevators) measured more than the total wing area of a B-24 Liberator. The flight control surfaces were unexpectedly all manually operated, with the pilot shifting a small servo tab that drove actuators to move the control surfaces. The B-36B had four bomb bays, with a tunnel on the lower left side of the fuselage through which a prone crewman could pull himself on a trolley with an overhead rope to move between the forward and aft crew sections.

The B-36B had an optical bombsight, as well as an AN/APQ-23 bombing/navigation radar in a blister under the forward fuselage integrated with the optical bombsight, and an electromechanical analog computer in the K-1 bombing system. Hypothetically, the B-36 could conduct conventional bombing missions, carrying 132 500 lb. bombs and up to two Mark 17 Runts weighing 42,000 lbs., or 43,600 lbs. of T-12 Cloudmaker bombs (twice the size of the M110 [T-14], the previous largest US bomb), but could not carry its maximum bomb load over long distances. In 1953, when fission atomic bombs and fusion hydrogen bombs became available, the B-36 was selected to be armed with several. B-36s performed several "live drops" of nuclear weapons in test programs.

The B-36B had a substantial defensive armament array: Fixed twin M24A1 20 mm cannon installed in the nose and tail positions with an AN/APG-3 gun-laying radar in a small radome above the tail turret. Six retractable remotely-controlled turrets with twin 20 mm cannon each supplied with 600 rounds were covered in pairs under doors in normal flight, but "popped up," with one turret covering the bomber's left side and the other the right. There were three of these dual-turret installations: two upper aft turrets, two lower aft turrets, an upper left forward turret, and an upper right forward turret. The five gunners in the aft pressurized compartment operated the tail turret, the two upper aft turrets, and the two lower aft turrets. In the forward pressurized compartment the co-observer operated the nose turret; the upper right forward turret was operated by the third pilot, while the second radio operator manned the upper left forward turret. There was no provision for switching control of the turrets between gunners, as each gunnery station was devoted to the control of a particular turret. This remote armament system was reported to be extremely complicated and unreliable.

After the first B-36B was flown by Convair on 8 July 1948, the company began delivery to the Air Force on 30 November, and by the end of the year Strategic Air Command had thirty-five Peacemakers in inventory. SAC Commander Gen. Curtis LeMay was eager to demonstrate the capabilities of SAC's new B-36s and B-50s, and consigned a B-36B of the 7BG and a B-50 of the 43BG to fly from Carswell AFB to Hawaii round trip on 7–8 December 1948, to commemorate the Pearl Harbor attack. The B-36, piloted by Maj. John Bartlett and a crew of fifteen, was to fly non-stop, unrefueled, dropping a dummy 10,000 lb. bomb load off Hawaii and return. The mission took 35:30 hours of flight time, covering 8,100 miles at an average speed of 236 mph, and was undetected by Hawaiian defenses. The bomber had 2,800 gallons of fuel remaining, which could have added several hundred miles to the flight. Although this flight was a record for the B-36 and SAC at the time, it would be routine in the future. The B-50 also completed the flight, but needed to be refueled in-flight three times.

A well known B-36 flight occurred on 20 January 1949, when five B-36Bs flew from Carswell on a spectacular overfly of Washington, DC, as part of President Harry Truman's inaugural ceremony. On 15 February, Truman again was impressed by eleven Peacemakers that participated in an aerial and static demonstration at Andrews AFB. Further imposing demonstrations of the bomber's capability were conducted on 29 January 1949, when a pair of dummy 42,000 lb. bombs were dropped (one from 35,000 ft. and the other at 40,000 ft.) on Muroc AFB by a B-36B flown by Maj. Stephen Dillon.

On 10–12 March 1949, Maj. John Bartlett flew a B-36B on a remarkable 9,600 mile, non-stop flight without in-flight refueling and carrying 10,000 lbs. of bombs over 5,000 miles before dropping them into the Gulf of Mexico. The flight's itinerary carried the bomber from Carswell, Fort Worth, over Minneapolis, Minnesota, and Great Falls, Montana, and then southeast over Key West, where President Truman was vacationing, then back northwest to Great Falls and Spokane, Washington, and on to Denver. During this leg the aircraft developed engine trouble and was forced to land two hours early at Carswell after a record 43:37 hours in the air. The bomber had fuel remaining for two more hours flying time, so taking into account this excess fuel, some engine problems, and headwinds, it was estimated the B-36 would have exceeded the bomber's original 10,000 mile range specification.

VIPs ready for a demonstration flight in a B-36: (L-R) Gen. Curtis LeMay, Sen. Richard Russell (Georgia), Gen. Roger Ramey, Maj. John Bartlett, Air Force Secretary Stuart Symington, Sen. Lyndon Johnson (Texas), and Rep. Thornberry.

These demonstrations showed that the B-36 was truly an intercontinental bomber, and SAC was able to fly missions from bases in Alaska, Labrador, or Maine to bomb any potential enemy target in Europe and return safely to a recovery base in Greenland, the Azores, or Okinawa.

However, problems with the armaments and other complex systems, combined with parts shortages, meant some B-36Bs were cannibalized to keep others in the air. Full operational status was not achieved until 1952. Sixty-four of the seventy-three B-36Bs built were redesignated B-36Ds when turbo jet engines were added.

B-36C

While the B-36B met all the 1941 requirements, it had serious problems with some performance factors, engine reliability, armaments reliability, and the availability of spare parts. Because of criticisms about the B-36B's performance, Convair engineers developed various models. The B-36C was to be equipped with improved R-4360-51 engines, which had an auxiliary "jet exhaust" to increase speed. These new engines would have required moving the engine configuration from pusher to conventional tractor, and investigation revealed that the increase in performance was negligible and the B-36C was never built.

Consolidated B-36D

B-36D

The more practical solution to increase performance was to augment the six existing piston engines by adding four jet engines installed in pairs in pods, with a single pod outboard on each wing. The ten engines were the most ever for a mass-produced aircraft. The D-model prototype, using Allison J35 engines in Boeing B-47 Stratojet pods, flew its first "mixed power" flight on 26 March 1949. Production B-36Ds used more powerful General Electric J47-GE-19 turbojets, but only on take-off for a significantly shorter take-off run and to gain increased speed and ceiling performance in enemy airspace. The turbojet intakes were covered with an "iris" that closed the engines off to reduce drag from windmilling when the turbojets were not in use. During long-range cruise it was not unusual to shut down two or even three of the piston engines, as well. If all ten engines were functioning normally at full power during pre-take-off warmup, the lead flight engineer would inform the pilots: "six (piston) turning and four (jet) burning." Erratic reliability could lead to the report: "four turning, two burning, two joking, and two smoking," or variations thereof.

The B-36D also had a distinctive astrodome blister on top of the canopy and "snap action" bomb bay doors: four hinged panels that folded up on themselves, replacing the roll-open B-24 type bomb bay doors of earlier models. Early B-36Ds used the K-1 bombing system, which was later replaced with the more sophisticated and reliable K-3A bombing system. The optical bombsight was viewed as redundant and was removed, with the nose bombsight panel faired over with a metal plate. B-36Ds originally carrying AN/APG-3 tail radar were upgraded later to AN/APG-32 tail radar, featuring the so-called "Chiclet-style" radome.

The first B-36s to fly out of US territory were six B-36Ds that flew to RAF Lakenheath, United Kingdom, in January 1951. In late Summer 1953, the 92nd Heavy Bombardment Wing made a mass flight to the Far East, primarily to demonstrate that the US was prepared to continue operations after the end of the Korean War. The 92BW was the first wing to be fully deployed overseas, departing October 1953 for a ninety-day stay on Guam.

There were twenty-six newly-built B-36Ds and fifty-nine B-36Bs modified to the B-36D standard, with initial service delivery on 17 August 1950 to Carswell. The turbojet-assisted D model had the following characteristics and performance:

Wingspan: 230 ft.
Wing area: 4,772 sq. ft.
Length: 162.1 ft.
Height: 46.75 ft.
Empty weight: 166,165 lbs.
Maximum take-off weight: 410,000 lbs.
Maximum speed: 418 mph
Cruise speed: 230 mph
Service ceiling: 43,600 ft.
Combat radius: 3,985 miles
Ferry range: 10,000 miles

RB-36D

The RB-36D strategic reconnaissance version of the B-36D featured a manned pressurized module with fourteen cameras in the forward bomb bay; up to eighty photoflash bombs in the second bomb bay; a fuel tank in the third bomb bay; and electronic intelligence (ELINT) gear, which was revealed by an additional antenna fairing under the nose and three fairings under the rear bomb bay. There was some variation in these bomb bays, and they were also able, in principle, to carry bomb loads. There were twenty-four new-production RB-36Ds, with initial delivery on 3 June 1950.

RB-36E

Twenty-one B-36As and the YB-36A were upgraded to a standard similar to that of the RB-36D and given the designation RB-36E, the first being flown on 18 December 1949. These reconnaissance variants tended to carry large crews of up to twenty-two to operate the photographic and ELINT equipment.

Featherweight

From the mid-1950s, a "Featherweight" program was conducted to strip gear from selected B-36s to improve their ceiling. There were three configurations:

Featherweight I removed all defensive hardware, including the six gun turrets, with the gunners' blisters either faired over or replaced with flush windows.

Featherweight II removed the rear compartment crew comfort features and all hardware accommodating the McDonnell XF-85 Goblin parasite fighter, but retained their armament.

Featherweight III incorporated configurations I and II, except for the tail armament.

B-36F and RB-36F

The B-36F was similar to the B-36D, but with uprated 3,800 hp P&W R-4360-53 piston engines and improved radar and countermeasures. The K-3A bombing system and AN/APG-32 tail radar was standard, and a chaff dispenser system was later added. The initial flight was on 28 November 1950, and the last of thirty-four was delivered early in 1953. An additional twenty-four RB-36F reconnaissance aircraft with increased fuel load were also produced.

Ficon-equipped Consolidated B-36F

JRB-36

During this time a JRB-36 bomber was being used for a range extension project called Fighter Conveyer (FICON). The bomber carried the reconnaissance version of the F-84F Thunderflash (RF-84F) on a trapeze-like cradle mounted on the B-36's belly that was to release and seize the fighter midair. FICON was followed in 1955 by Project Tom-Tom, in which two RF-84F jet reconnaissance fighters were attached to the end of the wings of the JRB-36F as a way of increasing their range. Tom-Tom was intended to evaluate the difficulty of approaching the wing tip of the B-36, which was equipped with a jaw capture mechanism on its right wing tip and a retractable scissors unit on its left wing tip. The concept of range extending parasite aircraft was abandoned because of the development of fighter in-flight aerial refueling and the arrival of the long-range U-2 reconnaissance aircraft.

B-36H & RB-36H

The B-36H continued the refinement of the B-36, improving the flight deck, adding AN/APG-41A tail gun radar with twin side-by-side radomes, and other small changes, but was very similar to the B-36F. Initial flight was on 5 April 1952 and eighty-three were built, as well as seventy-three RB-36H reconnaissance versions, giving a production run of 156 H aircraft, the most of any B-36 model.

B-36J

The last of the 383 B-36s to be built was the B-36J (there was no B-36I, as the Air Force did not use "I" as a suffix, since it could be confused with a "1.") This model had additional wing tanks to extend range and a reinforced landing gear to handle the higher gross weights. The initial flight was on 3 September 1953. Thirty-three were built, with the final fourteen becoming the Featherweight configuration.

B-36G/YB-60

By 1950, the B-36 design was more than ready to be replaced by an all-jet bomber. Convair responded with the B-36G (soon renamed YB-60) all-jet bomber based on the B-36. However, it had a much more swept wing, longer fuselage, and was taller. It was first flown on 18 April 1952. Because it shared much of its design and parts with the B-36, it was relatively more economical compared to its competitor, the Boeing B-52. However, the B-52 was a much superior design and was awarded the contract. The desperate Convair Company offered to build their remaining allocation of B-36s as B-60s without additional charge, but the Air Force rejected the proposition.

Consolidated All-Jet YB-60

FIRST FLIGHTS

XB-36	8 August	1946
B-36A	28 August	1947
B-36B	8 July	1948
B-36D	26 March	1949
RB-36E	18 December	1949
B-36F	28 November	1950
B-36H	5 April	1952
B-36J	3 September	1953
XC-99	23 November	1947
XB-36G	18 April	1952

THE INTERCONTINENTAL B-36 SUCCUMBS TO THE B-52 AND THE SCRAPYARD

The B-36 was the largest mass-produced piston engine aircraft ever built. With a range of 9,900 miles and a maximum payload of 73,000 lbs., the B-36 was the world's first manned bomber with an unrefueled intercontinental range. Its 230 ft. wingspan was the longest of any combat aircraft ever built: two-thirds longer than the B-29 Superfortress (230 vs. 141.3 ft.) and 18 ft. longer than the XB-19 (230 vs. 212 ft.). Its wingspan and tail height exceeded those of the Soviet Antonov An-22 (211.3 feet/41.2 ft.), which was the largest ever mass-produced propeller-driven aircraft and was capable of the heaviest ever 551,160 lb. maximum take-off weight. The B-36's maximum payload was more than ten times the load carried by the B-17; was more than four times that of the B-29; and was similar to that of its B-52 successor. In all respects except speed, the B-36 could match what was arguably its approximate Soviet counterpart, the Tupolev Tu-95 Bear, a large, four-engine turboprop-powered strategic bomber first flown in 1952 and entering Soviet service in 1956, remaining in service today.

The B-36B was America's last true piston-engine strategic bomber, and in retrospect, it seems obvious this large late-war bomber should have been jet powered from the onset. Although the turbojet was developed during WWII, it was for short-range, fast-climbing, high-flying interceptors that used fuel at an extraordinary rate, which was unacceptable for bomber operations. The piston-powered B-36 was slow and unable to refuel in midair, and found itself in a new air combat realm of jet interceptors. The B-36 was not designed to carry a large nuclear weapon because the existence of such weapons was top secret during the period when the B-36 was conceived and designed (1941–46). Nevertheless, the B-36 was the first bomber capable of carrying any of the US nuclear weapons in its four bomb bays without modification. The B-36's jet challenger, the Boeing B-47 Stratojet, which did not become fully operational until 1953, lacked sufficient range to attack the Soviet Union from North American airbases and could not carry the huge first-generation hydrogen bomb. (Neither could the other American piston bombers of the day, the B-29 and B-50.) Intercontinental ballistic missiles (ICBMs) did not become operational until the 1960s. Until the Boeing B-52 Stratofortress became operational in the late 1950s, the B-36, as the only truly intercontinental bomber, was the mainstay of SAC and would set the standard for range and payload for subsequent US intercontinental bombers. From February 1956, B-36s were being flown to Davis-Monthan AFB, Arizona, where they were scrapped. Defense cutbacks led to a slowdown in B-52 procurement and some updating of the B-36 by Convair, extending its operational life by a few years.

During its eight years of service the Peacemaker lived up to its name, as it was America's major air deterrent and never had to fire a shot or drop a bomb in anger, as they arrived in service too late for the Korean War and were out of service by Vietnam. A total of 383 B-36s were accepted by the Air Force (eleven were lost in accidents) at a cost of $3.6 million. The last B-36J (52-2827) was built in August 1954, and was flown to Amon Carter Field in February 1959, where it was left on permanent display.

EPILOGUE

LONG DISTANCE CIVILIAN AND MILITARY AIRCRAFT FROM THE COLD WAR AND BEYOND

1
POST WORLD WAR II CIVILIAN AIRCRAFT AND MILITARY FIGHTERS

POSTWAR TRANS-ATLANTIC JET AIRCRAFT FIRSTS

1948: First Trans-Atlantic Jet Flight Eastward

During WWII, David Schilling scored 22.5 aerial victories flying a P-47 Thunderbolt with the 56th Fighter Group in the ETO. After the war he again commanded the 56FG and pioneered long-distance jet operations in the P-80 Shooting Star. In early 1948, Col. Schilling conceived an operation called Fox Able One (phonetic for Fighter Atlantic-1), in which jet aircraft that at the time were ferried to Europe by ship would be flown across the Atlantic. Fox Able One was to be flown during that summer to Germany, both as a show-of-force response to the Berlin Blockade that began three weeks previously and as a proof of concept.

While at Selfridge Field, Michigan, Schilling and Lt.Col. William Ritchie formulated Fox Able One, which was simple in concept: the flight from Selfridge to Germany was to be segmented into 900-mile sections within the range of the F-80. Refueling stops were to be made in Bangor, Maine; Goose Bay, Labrador; Bluie West 1, Greenland; Meeks Field, Iceland; RAF Stornaway, the Hebrides; and finally to the airfield in Furstenfeldbruck, American Zone, Germany. Bypassing the usual bureaucracy, Fox Able One was directly forwarded to Air Force Chief of Staff Gen. Carl Spaatz, who gave his approval for Schilling to lead sixteen Shooting Stars to Germany on 14 July. At the same time a similar flight of six British de Havilland Vampires began, flying Fox Able One in reverse. The two groups met in Iceland and held a brief ceremony on the tarmac to mark the occasion. Because of stops and weather it took ten days for all sixteen fighters to reach Germany. In 1949, Fox Able Two made the trip from Selfridge to Europe, again led by Schilling.

P-80 Shooting Star of Fox Able One

1948: First Trans-Atlantic Jet Flight Westward

The first jet aircraft to cross the Atlantic Ocean from east to west occurred on 14 July 1948, when six de Havilland Vampire F3s of No.54 RAF Squadron, commanded by W/C D. S. Wilson-MacDonald, flew via Stornoway (United Kingdom), Iceland, and Labrador to Montreal on the first leg of a goodwill tour of the US and Canada. The flight was a simultaneous reverse of the USAF's Fox Able One.

De Havilland Vampire led by W/C D. S. Wilson-MacDonald (2L).

1950: First Non-Stop Refueled Trans-Atlantic Jet Flight

On 22 September 1950, Col. David Schilling flew from RAF Manston, United Kingdom, to Maine in the first non-stop trans-Atlantic flight by a jet fighter. Using probe-and-drogue flight refueling, Schilling and Col. William Ritchie, flying F-84E Thunderjets, were first refueled by a Cobham Flight Refueling Ltd (FRL) Lancaster tanker near Prestwick, Scotland, followed by a refueling from a FRL Lincoln tanker near Iceland. During the third and final tanker rendezvous offshore of Labrador by a USAF KB-29 tanker, Ritchie's nose probe, which had been damaged in the refueling with the Lincoln, was unable to transfer fuel. He was forced to eject over Labrador when he ran out of fuel, but was rescued safely shortly afterward. Schilling's refueling was uneventful and he landed in Limestone, Maine, after a 10:08 hour, 3,300 mile flight, for which he received the Harmon Trophy. On 14 August 1956, Schilling, a rising star in the newly independent USAF, was killed in England while driving an Allard sports car.

WWII fighter ace Col. David Schilling

1951: First Non-Stop Jet Trans-Atlantic Flight

The first jet aircraft to make a non-stop trans-Atlantic flight occurred on 21 February 1951, when an RAF English Electric Canberra B Mk 2 flown by S/L A Callard flew from Aldergrove, Northern Ireland, directly to Gander, Newfoundland, in 4:37 hours over 2,063 miles. The aircraft was being flown to the US to act as a pattern aircraft for the Martin B-57 program.

RAF English Electric Canberra

1952: First Mass Movement and Refueling of Jet Fighter Aircraft

On 26 June 1952, the 31st Fighter Escort Wing, stationed at Turner AFB, Albany, Georgia, was assigned to Operation Fox Peter One—the mass movement of an entire fighter wing to the Korean Theater. Three squadrons of F-84G Thunderjets and key administrative and maintenance personnel were to be conveyed in four transport aircraft. 31st Wing Commander Col. David Schilling had only eight days to prepare for the mission, which was to be:

First mass movement of jet fighters across the Pacific.
First mass midair refueling movement of jet fighters.
Longest mass movement of a complete jet fighter wing by air.
Longest mass non-stop over-water flight by jet fighters (California–Hawaii).

In a rehearsal for Fox Peter One on 4 July 1952, fifty-seven F-84Gs left Turner AFB and flew 2,071 miles to Travis AFB, California, non-stop, being refueled en route by twenty-four KB-29Ps over Texas. Fox Peter One officially began on 6 July, when the first of the 31FW's three F-84G squadrons flew 2,140 miles from Travis AFB to Hickam AFB, Hawaii, relying on in-flight refueling with no alternate landing sites or divert fields. All Thunderjets made successful landings in Hawaii after flying the longest segment of the trans-Pacific flight and then island-hopped the rest of the way to Yokota Air Base, Japan, via Midway Island, Wake Island, Eniwetok, Guam, and Iwo Jima. The last aircraft arrived in Japan on 16 July, less than two weeks after leaving Georgia, and Fox Peter One was considered an unqualified success.

The following October, the 27th FEW, commanded by Col. Donald Blakeslee (another famous WWII leader and ace with 15½ victories in the ETO), flew from Bergstrom AFB, Texas, replicating the route and in-flight refuelings, and relieved the 31st FEW. During the war Blakeslee led the first "shuttle" mission, escorting B-17s from England to Russia on 21 June 1944, flying 1,470 miles in a P-51 during a mission lasting more than seven hours.

Operation Fox Peter One: F-84G Thunderjets being refueled in-flight by KB-29Ps.

1952: First Round Trip Trans-Atlantic Jet Flight in the Same Day

On 26 August 1952, the first trans-Atlantic round trip within twenty-four hours in the same day (with fuel stops) was flown by renowned British test pilot W/Cdr. Roland Beaumont and crewed by Flt./Lt. Peter Hillwood and S/L Dennis Watson. Their English Electric Canberra flew from Belfast, Northern Ireland, to Gander, Newfoundland, and back (4,144 miles) in 10:03 hours round trip. The westward portion took 7:59 hours and the return eastward to Belfast, aided by the Jet Stream, took 3:24 hours. Most of the flight was flown at more than 600 mph at over 40,000 ft., with tests conducted over 50,000 ft., which was 5,000 ft. above the interception altitude of any fighter in the world at the time. Upon landing at Gander, special English

(L-R) Dennis Watson, Roland Beaumont, and Peter Hillman receive the Britannia Trophy.

Electric crews were on hand to perform a quick turn-around for the flight back to Belfast. This Canberra was flown as a demonstration aircraft prior to USAF acceptance of a huge 400 aircraft Canberra contract let to the Martin Company to be manufactured and modified to meet USAF standards. Beaumont and his crew were awarded the Britannia Trophy for their flight.

1957: F-100F Spirit of St. Louis II Flies Thirtieth Anniversary of Lindbergh's Flight

On 21 May 1957, to celebrate the thirtieth anniversary of Lindbergh's first trans-Atlantic flight, Maj. Robinson Risner established a record when he flew a North American F-100F Super Sabre *Spirit of St. Louis II* across the Atlantic to Paris over the same Lindbergh route. Maj. Risner flew the 3,680 mile flight in 6:37 hours, while Lindbergh required 33:30 hours. Riser's flight originated at McGuire AFB, New Jersey, but was officially timed from a flyover of Floyd Bennett Field, New York, to Le Bourget Field, Paris, France. Risner had flown 108 missions over Korea and was credited with the destruction of eight MiG-15s. Risner would be assigned to Vietnam as a combat pilot and was shot down and became a POW with John McCain for 7½ years in the infamous Hanoi Hilton.

Maj. Robinson Risner and his F-100F *Spirit of St. Louis II*

LAST US PISTON-ENGINE RECORD TRANSCONTINENTAL AND TRANS-ATLANTIC FLIGHTS

1945: The C-97 Sets a West to East Transcontinental Record

Toward the end of WWII, Boeing developed the Model 367, a military transport based on the B-29 bomber. (Its civilian counterpart was the Model 377 Stratocruiser.) Designated C-97, it had a double-lobe fuselage consisting of two intersecting circular sections, with the 74 ft. long upper deck having a larger diameter. Cargo was loaded through large clamshell-type doors in the belly of the aircraft using a built in ramp and a hoist. Its wings, engine gear, and other parts were similar to the B-29. On 9 January 1945, the first of three prototype XC-97 Stratofreighters (43-2747), piloted by Maj. Curtin Reinhardt, flew from Seattle to Washington, DC, in 6:04 hours at an average speed of 383 mph with 20,000 lbs. of cargo. The production version that flew in June 1949 had outboard wing fuel tanks to increase its range. Since this aircraft was pressurized it flew at 30,000 ft.

Maj. Curtin Reinhardt (L)

Prototype XC-97 Stratofreighter

1945: The Unusual XB-42 Mixmaster Sets a Transcontinental Record

On 8 December 1945, Lt.Col. Henry Warden and Capt. Glen Edwards flew the second prototype Douglas XB-42 Mixmaster (43-50225) from Long Beach, California, to Washington, DC, in 5:17:34 hours, averaging 433.6 mph and setting a new transcontinental speed record. The Mixmaster was an unusual design, using two engines installed inside the fuselage to drive counter-rotating three-bladed propellers in a pusher configuration at the tail that produced a very low drag aircraft that was much faster than similar sized and powered aircraft. The XB-42 was 53.8 ft. long and 18.9 ft. high, with a wingspan of 70.5 ft. (wing area of 555 sq. ft.), an empty weight of 20,888 lbs., and a maximum gross weight of 35,702 lbs. The prototype's cruising speed was 310 mph and its maximum speed was 410 mph, with a service ceiling of 29,400 ft. and a normal range of 1,840 miles. A pilot and co-pilot sat side-by-side under separate bubble canopies (later changed to a single canopy to improve communication between the crew), while the third crewman (navigator/bombardier) occupied the nose. The co-pilot was also a gunner, operating four remotely-controlled .50-caliber machine guns in two retractable power turrets inside the trailing edge of the wings. Another two .50-caliber machine guns were fixed, aiming forward. The bomber was intended to carry an 8,000 lb. bomb load. The XB-42 was powered by two 1,325 hp liquid-cooled supercharged Allison V-1710-129 V-12 engines. The port engine rotated clockwise and drove the 13.3 ft. diameter forward propeller. The starboard engine turned counterclockwise and drove the 13 ft. diameter rear propeller. Five Bell P-39 Airacobra drive shafts connected the engines to a gear drive assembly in the tail, which in turn drove the Curtiss Electric propellers. There was a two-inch difference in propeller diameter to prevent interference of the blade tip vortices. The XB-42 prototype (43-50224) first flew on 1 August 1944. On 16 December 1945, it was on a routine flight from Bolling Field, Washington, DC, with Lt.Col. Fred Ascani in command, when a series of failures caused the crew to bail out, after which it crashed in Oxon Hill, Maryland. The second record setting prototype is in storage at the National Museum of the United States Air Force, Wright Patterson AFB, Ohio. Later, Warden went to work for North American Aviation on the B-70 Valkyrie program. Edwards was killed on 5 June 1948, testing a YB-49 Flying Wing.

(R-L) Brig.Gen. Reuben Hood congratulates Capt. Glen Edwards and Lt. Col. Harold Warden.

Douglas XB-42 Mixmaster

1945: B-29 Sets West to East Transcontinental Record

In December 1945, Col C. S. Irvine flew the B-29 *Pacusan Dreamboat* from Burbank, California, overhead Floyd Bennett Field, New York, averaging 450 mph over 5:27:08 (see previous).

Paul Mantz: Three Bendix Trophies and Other Long-Distance Records

Albert Paul Mantz was considered by his contemporaries a "one of kind" pilot who succeeded at long-distance air racing, aerobatics, and would have a virtual monopoly on movie stunt flying. After finishing third in the 1938 and 1939 Bendix Trophy Races flying an old Lockheed Orion, the race was suspended at the outbreak of WWII. When the races resumed, Mantz fashioned his legend with an unprecedented three consecutive Bendix wins. Hoping to re-enter the Bendix, Mantz had purchased a P-51C-10-NT (44-10947)—a stateside training aircraft—from the Reconstruction Finance Corporation (RFC) in 1946. He modified the Mustang for racing and painted it bright red, naming it *Blazing Noon*. To increase the Mustang's range for these long-distance flights Mantz removed the small and heavy standard ninety-gallon pressure-molded Firestone self-sealing tanks from each wing and converted the entire wing into a fuel tank (wet wing). In 1946, he began his unprecedented run of three consecutive Bendix victories over the 2,400 mile California-to-Cleveland speed run by flying at 435.5 mph in 4:42 hours; the next year he flew the same aircraft in 4:27 hours at an average speed of 460.42 mph; and then in 1948, Mantz flew a different war surplus Mustang, winning in 4:34 hours at an average speed of 447.98 mph. He did not win the 1949 Bendix because he did not enter. Between Bendix flights he set other records. On 28 February 1947, Mantz set a new west-east record for a piston-engined aircraft by flying the P-51 from Burbank to LaGuardia Field in 6:07 hours. In 1948, he returned to California via LaGuardia, setting a new east-west record for this class, reaching Burbank in 7:00 hours. Renamed *The Houstonian*, *Blazing Noon* was flown by Linton Carney and placed second in the 1948 Bendix to Mantz flying another Mustang. Mantz sold his Mustang to Charles Blair, who also set several records flying it (see next). During WWII, Mantz enlisted and was commissioned a major (later promoted to colonel), serving with the First Motion Picture Unit in California. Following his discharge in August 1944, Mantz purchased a fleet of 475 wartime surplus bombers and fighters for $55,000 to use in film work. Mantz is said to have had the sixth-largest air force in the world. Mantz was killed in 1965, while flying an experimental airplane for the film *Flight of the Phoenix*.

Paul Mantz

1951: Capt. Charles Blair: Trans-Atlantic Record

During WWII, Charles Blair flew transports and was a test pilot for Grumman Aircraft, testing fast fighter aircraft such as the F6F Hellcat, F7F Tigercat, and F8F Bearcat. Following the war, Blair commanded testing and the first scheduled flights of the Lockheed Constellation and Boeing Stratocruiser, and in 1950, Blair became a Pan Am pilot. In 1950, Paul Mantz sold his champion P-51 to Blair for his attempt to set a new round-the-world speed record. He originally named the plane *Stormy Petrel* but soon changed it to *Excalibur III*. On 31 January 1951, Blair flew 3,478 miles from New York to London in 7:48 hours at an average speed of 450 mph, assisted by strong tailwinds. This record broke the old New York-London record by 1:07 hours; a record that still stands for piston-engined aircraft. On 29 May 1951, Capt. Blair set off from London to Bremen, Oslo, and Bardufoss, Norway, and then over the North Pole to Fairbanks, Alaska; upon landing Blair had flown 3,260 miles non-stop in 10:27 hours. Blair navigated by using a system of pre-plotted sun lines on an astro-compass, as a magnetic compass was useless near the Pole and there were no radio navigation aids available. On 18 September 1952, President Harry Truman presented Blair with the Harmon International Trophy for this flight. Following Blair's flights, in 1953, he donated *Excalibur III* to the Smithsonian, while its sister ship, the 1948 winner, was donated to the International Flight and Space Museum in Santa Ana, California, by Paul Mantz. Blair died flying a Grumman Goose in the Virgin Islands in 1978. He had married his fourth wife, beautiful and well-known actress Maureen O'Hara, in 1968.

Capt. Charles Blair (L) checks out his astro-compass on the wing of his P-51 Mustang.

1954: Joseph DeBona: P-51 Mustang Sets Transcontinental Record

On 30 March 1954, Joseph DeBona flew a North American P-51C from Los Angeles (LAX) non-stop to New York (Idlewild) for a west-to-east record of 4:24:17 hours, which remains a prop record today (2015). The Mustang was owned by movie actor James Stewart, and about this time N5528N was repainted in a yellow and black scheme and was renamed *Mr. Alex* in honor of Jimmy Stewart's father, Alexander Stewart.

Joseph DeBona with sponsor/actor Jimmy Stewart on the wing of their P-51 Mustang

US JET-ENGINE RECORD TRANSCONTINENTAL FLIGHTS

1946: William Councill: P-80 Non-stop Transcontinental Record

On 26 January 1946, Col. William Councill, USAF test pilot at the Flight Test Division, Wright Field, piloted a Lockheed P-80A-1-LO Shooting Star (44-85123) on a record-breaking flight from Daugherty Field (Long Beach Airport), California, to overhead LaGuardia Airport, New York, in 4:13:26 hours, setting a new transcontinental non-stop record for the 2,457 miles by averaging 584.82 mph. Councill's P-80A had been modified with the installation of a one-hundred-gallon fuel tank in the nose, along with 300-gallon wing tip tanks, increasing the Shooting Star's maximum fuel load to 1,165 gallons. Councill was accompanied by two other P-80s flown by Capts. John Babel and L. Smith, whose jets also had the nose fuel tank installed, but carried 150 gallon wing tip tanks; they had to stop in Topeka, Kansas, to refuel. Ground crews met them with four fuel trucks and they were airborne in four minutes and six minutes, respectively. Col. William Councill disappeared on 5 April 1954 while flying a Lockheed T-33A Shooting Star trainer from New York to Virginia.

William Councill in his P-80 Shooting Star

1949: B-47 Transcontinental Record

On 8 February 1949, the B-47 prototype Stratojet flew west to east from Larson AFB, Moses Lake, Washington, to Andrews AFB, Washington, DC, in an unofficial record of 3:46 hours at an average speed of 607.8 mph. The unstated purpose of the flight was to demonstrate the Stratojet's long-range capabilities, and while in Washington the aircraft was shown to members of the House Armed Services Committee in the hope of Boeing obtaining sizable production orders.

1954: Willard Millikan: P-84 Transcontinental Record

On 2 January 1954, WWII triple fighter ace Col. Willard Millikan flew a North American F-86F-25-NH Sabre (51-13393) *Minuteman* from Los Angeles (LAX) to New York (Idlewild) in 4:06:16 hours, averaging 595.91 mph. Col. Millikan took off from Los Angeles at 10:11 EST and climbed to 40,000 ft. for most of the flight. He dropped his two emptied 670 gallon wing tanks over the southwest desert and then made a refueling stop at Offutt AFB, Omaha, Nebraska, where a waiting twenty-man crew attached two full wing tanks; he was airborne in only 6:28 minutes. Millikan dropped the second set of tanks over Lake Michigan, but as he approached the finish line at Floyd Bennett Field at 14:19 EST his engine flamed out as the Sabre ran out of fuel at 5,000 ft. Colonel Millikan made a successful "dead stick" landing at Idlewild Airport, New York City.

Willard Millikan in his P-84 Thunderstreak

1955: Robert Scott: F-84 Non-Stop, Refueled Transcontinental Record

On 9 October 1955, WWII, Korea, and Vietnam Air Force veteran Lt.Col. Robert Scott led eight Republic F-84F Thunderstreaks from LAX to overhead New York Floyd Bennett in 3:46:34 hours, requiring two aerial refuelings by Boeing KB-29 tankers. Scott, the commanding officer of the 510th Fighter Bomber Squadron, 405th Fighter Bomber Wing, Langley AFB, Virginia, was accompanied by the Thunderstreaks of Maj. Robert Ruby and Capt. Charles Hudson and five other F-84s that would not finish. Hudson and Ruby carried extra gas tanks and made one in-flight refueling each, while Scott carried no extra fuel and had two in-flight refuelings. Ruby finished just one minute behind at 3:47:33 hours, while Hudson also broke the record, landing with a time of 3:49:53. The three Thunderstreak pilots were the first to cross the continent in less than four hours. 1Lt. James Colson attempted to finish without refueling, but was low on fuel near Pittsburgh, Pennsylvania. Of the other four that did not finish one withdrew in California, two in Kansas, and one in Missouri. The three finishing pilots reported that they could have made faster times except for the slow and obsolete in-flight refueling tankers. Although setting a Los Angeles-New York record, Scott failed to beat the Navy's East Coast-West Coast time from San Diego to New York (2,438 miles, or seven miles shorter). Lt.Cdr. Francis Brady flew from San Diego in 3:45:30 on 1 April 1954, flying a Grumman F9F Cougar.

Robert Scott in his F-84 Thunderstreak

1955: Hackett and Moneypenny: Canberra Trans-Atlantic Record Round Trip

Pilot Capt. John Hackett and navigator Peter Moneypenny were awarded the Britannia Trophy while flying an English Electric Canberra, setting point-to-point records London-New York in 7:30 hours, landing at Floyd Bennett, and after waiting thirty-five minutes for refueling, took off for London and arrived in 6:17 hours. The round-trip of 14:22 hours was the first ever to breakfast in London, lunch in New York, and get back to London for dinner. In 1958, Hackett and Moneypenny, with Lt. Antonio Leyba of the Venezuelan Air Force, established the official point-to-point record from Washington, DC, to Caracas.

Pilot Capt. John Hackett, navigator Peter Moneypenny, and their English Electric Canberra

1957: Douglas A3 Skywarrior Has Its Day in the Sun

Before the nuclear capability of the US Navy's Polaris-armed submarines was proven, the twin-jet A-3 Skywarrior was the Navy's primary nuclear deterrent. Significant development problems, largely due to the original engines, delayed the introduction of the Skywarrior until spring 1956. The A-3 was by far the largest and heaviest aircraft ever designed for routine use on an aircraft carrier. It was initially to be operated as a nuclear capable bomber, and to justify this nuclear claim the Navy scheduled a number of long-distance flights.

On 21 March 1957, Cdr. Dale Cox and his crew broke the westbound US transcontinental record with a time of 5:12 hours and the Los Angeles-New York-Los Angeles record with a time of 9:31 hours.

Dale Cox' Douglas A3 Skywarrior

On 6 June 1957, Skywarriors made the first carrier to carrier transcontinental flight, landing aboard the USS *Saratoga* off the east coast of Florida and flying 4:01 hours after having been launched from the USS *Bon Homme Richard* off the California coast.

Record flights between the San Francisco Bay area and Hawaii were made twice during 1957: two A3D-2s of VAH-2 covered the distance in 4:45 hours on 16 July, while on 11 October, a VAH-4 Skywarrior covered the same distance in 4:30 hours.

1957: F-100 Sets the New Transcontinental Record

On 19 May 1957, a North American F-100F flew west to east from Palmdale, California, to McGuire AFB, New Jersey, in 3:38 hours.

1957: First Transcontinental Carrier-to-Carrier Jet Flight: Vought F8U Crusader

In 1956, the US Navy had a hot, new carrier-borne fighter (Vought F8U Crusader) it was impatient to display. During August, the Crusader set several speed records, flying more than 1,100 mph and winning the Thompson Trophy that year.

On 6 June 1957, two F8U-1s piloted by Capt. Robert Dose and Lt.Cdr. Paul Miller took off from USS *Bon Homme Richard* (CVA-31), cruising off the California coast, and flew to the USS *Saratoga* (CVA-60) waiting off the Florida coast. With one midair refueling by a North American AJ-2 Savage tanker near Dallas, Texas, the Crusaders made the trip in 3:28 hours and were greeted by President Eisenhower, who happened to be aboard as they landed. The two aircraft set an unofficial speed record and performed the first carrier-to-carrier transcontinental flight in history.

Robert Dose and Paul Miller land their F8U Crusader on the *Saratoga*.

1957: Project Bullet: Maj. John Glenn Sets Transcontinental Record

The purpose of Project Bullet was to prove that the Pratt & Whitney J-57 engine could endure an extended period at combat power and full afterburner without damage using in-flight refueling. On 16 July 1957, two USMC Vought F8U-1P Crusaders piloted by USMC Maj. John Glenn and USN Lt.Cdr. Charles Demmler took off for a non-stop flight from NAS Los Alamitos, California, to Floyd Bennett Field, New York, led by a pathfinder jet to keep them alerted to weather ahead. In 1955, the US Navy mandated that all carrier-based aircraft were to be capable of in-flight refueling. The F8U-1 had its refueling probe on the starboard side of the fuselage, aft of the cockpit, which made refueling somewhat problematic. During the first refueling Demmler's Crusader was damaged, forcing him to withdraw from the project. Glenn's Crusader had no search radar, so for each refueling he had to find the AJ Savage tankers by using a direction finder to home on the tankers' beacons. The AJ Savage was North American's converted carrier-based, twin-piston R-2800 engine bomber and they were sent up in pairs for redundancy. During his three in-flight refills Glenn decreased his speed to approximately 350 mph, and after each 1,300 gallon refueling Glenn applied full afterburner and climbed to about 30,000 ft., drifting up to 50,000 ft. for maximum range as fuel burned off. Glenn landed after 3:23 hours at a record speed of 725.55 mph (Mach 1.1), despite three refuelings, surpassing the previous record set on 19 May by an F-100F Super Sabre by fifteen minutes. Glenn was the first to traverse the continent at a speed faster than sound. During the flight on-board reconnaissance cameras on Glenn's Crusader operated continuously for the entire flight to record the first continuous transcontinental panoramic photograph of the United States. After the flight Pratt & Whitney engineers disassembled the J-57 and, based on their examination, determined the engine could perform in extended combat situations. Maj. John Glenn had established himself as a premier test pilot that day, but would go on to greater accomplishments, becoming an astronaut and an Ohio senator.

Future astronaut John Glenn in his F8U Crusader

1957: F-101 Voodoos of Operation Sun Run Set New Transcontinental Records

Operation Sun Run was planned for six RF-101C Voodoo fighter aircraft: two to fly round-trip from Los Angeles to New York and back again; two for the one-way flight from Los Angeles to New York; and two for backups if the four primary aircraft had problems. Sun Run required considerable coordination of aircraft crews and radar and weather stations from coast to coast. Six experienced photo reconnaissance pilots from the 17th and 18th Tactical Reconnaissance Squadrons (363rd Tactical Reconnaissance Wing) prepared for the round-trip flight, since they would not know to which flight they were to be assigned until a few days before the operation. The success of Sun Run depended on the refueling capability (twenty-six refuelings) of the KC-135 Stratotanker, the USAF's newly available first jet tanker. The jet-powered KC-135's speed allowed the RF-101s to refuel at 35,000 ft. and a speed of Mach 0.8. At 0659 on 27 November 1957, Capt. Ray Schrecengost took off from Ontario International Airport, near Los Angeles, on the first RF-101 round-trip flight of Operation Sun Run. Next into the air were Capt. Robert Kilpatrick on his one-way flight and Capt. Donald Hawkins flying backup. Capt. Hawkins followed until the first refueling was complete and then flew back west to March AFB,

California. At 0750, Capt. Robert Sweet took off on the second round-trip flight and 1Lt. Gustav Klatt followed, beginning his one-way trip. Their backup, Capt. Robert Burkhart, also flew to March AFB after the first successful refueling. All four Voodoo pilots easily surpassed the previous speed records and established new ones. The new Los Angeles to New York record was established by 1Lt. Klatt at 3:07:44 hours, Capt. Sweet set the round-trip record at a time of 6:46:36 hours, and the New York to Los Angeles record at a time of 3:36:32 hours.

F-101 Voodoo of Operation Sun Run

During 1958, the F-101s flew several other notable long-distance flights:

22 May: Two F-101Cs flew a 5,600 mile circuit starting and ending at Bergstrom AFB, Texas, in 11:35 hours (air refueled).
10 August: Seven F-101Cs were ferried non-stop from Bergstrom AFB to RAF Bentwaters, Suffolk, United Kingdom, in 11:02 hours
25 September: Operation Long Leap: An F-101A flew 1,896 miles between Carswell AFB, Texas, and Bermuda for the longest non-stop/un-refueled flight for any century series fighter.

1961:F4H Phantoms of Operation LANA Set New Trans-continental Records

Operation LANA, to celebrate the fiftieth anniversary of Naval Aviation (L = the Roman numeral 50, while ANA = Anniversary of Naval Aviation), was to be part of a Transcontinental Bendix Trophy Race speed dash from California to New York. The F4Hs made four supersonic dashes separated by three subsonic midair refuelings by tanker-configured Douglas A3D-2 Skywarriors of VAH-1. Three of the USN Phantoms finished, abolishing the record set in November 1957 by a USAF McDonnell RF-101C Voodoo during Operation Sun Run. Phantom 148270, piloted by Lt. Richard Gordon (future NASA astronaut) and Lt.(jg) Bobbie Young, averaged 869.73 mph and completed the trip in 2:47 hours, for which the two were awarded the 1961 Bendix Trophy.

F4H Phantoms of Operation LANA being refueled by an A3D-2 Skywarrior.

1955: First Transcontinental Round Trip Flight During the Same Day

Operation Boomerang, the first transcontinental round-trip flight during the same day ("dawn to dusk"), was flown by 1Lt. John Conroy on 21 May 1955. Prewar teen movie actor and WWII B-17 pilot and POW Jack Conroy returned from the war and continued to fly with non-scheduled airlines, and also joined the California Air National Guard at Van Nuys Air Base, California, as a 1st lieutenant attached to the 115th Fighter Interceptor Squadron. During 1955, Conroy was selected to be Boomerang's Sabrejet pilot and took part in several weeks of planning and groundwork. The six-year-old F-86A (49-1046), nicknamed *California Boomerang*, had its overall natural aluminum finish polished to ensure that all rivet heads were smooth, and seams in the fuselage and wing skin panels were tweaked for precise fit and were then sealed. The gun ports for the six .50-caliber machine guns in the nose were plugged, then covered with doped fabric and painted. Its General Electric J47-GE-13 turbojet was overhauled, then tested and fine tuned for maximum efficiency. Five refueling stops were setup across America by Air National Guard personnel. In a divergence from peacetime procedures, the Sabre was permitted to be fueled with its engine turning (the F-86 was not capable of in-flight refueling). Arrangements for official timing of the round trip were arranged by Sabre manufacturer North American Aviation, whose personnel also provided technical support to the Air National Guard.

At 0600 PST, 21 May 1955, Conroy took off from the California ANG base at San Fernando Valley Airport and climbed to approximately 40,000 ft. toward his first refueling stop in Denver. He landed at 0748 PST, where the aircraft was refueled, and took off again in only six minutes. From Denver he continued eastward to Springfield, Illinois, arriving at 0932 PST, and was refueled in five minutes. He reached the East Coast at Mitchel Field, Long Island, New York, at 1119 PST, refueling and remaining on the ground for thirty-nine minutes. Conroy headed westward from Mitchel Field at 1158 PST and arrived at Lockburne AFB, Ohio, at 1258 PST, refueling in seven minutes. The jet landed in Tulsa, Oklahoma, at 14:26 PST, where it was refueled and airborne again in six minutes. Conroy landed in Albuquerque, New Mexico—his last refueling stop—at 15:58 PST for a seven-minute pause. *California Boomerang* took off on the final leg of the round-trip journey, finally landing back at Van Nuys in the dusk at 17:26:18 PST. John Conroy's Coast-to-Coast-to-Coast "dawn to dusk" flight had covered 5,058 miles with a total elapsed time of 11:26:33 hours at an average speed of 445 mph. Weather across the country caused some delays, as Conroy had to make instrument approaches to three of the refueling stops. In 1965, Conroy and co-pilot Clay Lacy duplicated his *Boomerang* daylight, coast-to-coast round-trip flight in a Lear jet during Operation Sunrise Sunset, the first time a business jet completed the trip. Postwar Conroy formed the Aero Spacelines Company, which developed the Pregnant and Mini Guppy and then the Super Guppy in 1965, carrying the Saturn V rockets

John Conroy's F-86 Sabrejet being refueled.

SR-71 BLACKBIRD: IN A LEAGUE OF ITS OWN

The SR-71 Blackbird was a long-range, Mach 3+, advanced, strategic reconnaissance aircraft developed from A-12 and YF-12A aircraft as a "black project" by Lockheed's Skunk Works Division and its renowned designer, Clarence "Kelly" Johnson. The SR-71 was designed to have basic stealth characteristics and was a forerunner of future stealth aircraft. The SR-71's first flight took place on 22 December 1964, and it entered service with the 4200th Strategic Reconnaissance Wing at Beale AFB, California, in January 1966. During aerial reconnaissance missions the SR-71 operated at such high speeds and high altitudes that it could out-accelerate and out-fly surface-to-air missiles. The faster the Blackbird flew the more efficient it became due to the ramjet effect (the compression of air and fuel at supersonic speeds). The aircraft had to refuel about every ninety minutes or every 2,500 miles. The fifty-six KC-135Q tankers were a greatly modified version of the standard KC135 tanker that could only be used to refuel the SR-71. Thirty-two SR-71s served with the USAF 1964–1998, with twelve lost in accidents, but none lost to enemy action. The USAF retired its SR-71 fleet on 26 January 1990, due to dwindling defense budgets and high operation costs. Several SR-71s were reinstated into service in 1995, so it could be used for NASA research projects, but by 1999, the final NASA Blackbirds were grounded permanently.

The SR-71 was the world's fastest and highest flying operational air-breathing manned aircraft throughout its tenure. On 28 July 1976, SR-71 61-7962 broke the world absolute altitude record of 85,069 ft. in sustained flight. That same day SR-71 61-7958 set an absolute speed record of 2,193.2 mph—approximately Mach 3.3. On 1 September 1974, a SR-71 flown by pilot Maj. James Sullivan and reconnaissance systems officer (RSO) Maj. Noel Widdifield set the Speed Over a Recognized Course record for flying from New York to London (3,461.53 miles) at 1,806.96 mph, an elapsed time of 1:54:56 hours (an average velocity of Mach 2.72, including deceleration for in-flight refueling). By comparison, the best commercial Concorde flight time was 2:52 hours, while the Boeing 747 averages 6:15 hours. On 26 April 1971, SR-71 61-7968, flown by Majs. Thomas Estes and Dewain Vick, flew over 15,000 miles in 10:30 hours, for which it was awarded the 1971 Mackay Trophy and the 1972 Harmon Trophy. On 6 March 1990, Lt.Col. Raymond Yielding and Lt.Col. Joseph Vida piloted SR-71 61-7972 on its final flight and set four new speed records:

Los Angeles to Washington, DC (2,299.7 miles), at an average speed of 2,144.8 mph and an elapsed time of 64:20 minutes.

West Coast to East Coast (2,404 miles) at an average speed of 2,124.5 mph and an elapsed time of 67:54 minutes.

Kansas City, Missouri, to Washington, DC (942 miles), at an average speed of 2,176 mph and an elapsed time of 25:59 minutes.

St. Louis, Missouri, to Cincinnati, Ohio (311.4 miles), at an average speed of 2,189.9 mph and an elapsed time of 8:32 minutes.

These records remain unbroken after thirty-five years, and it seems the SR-71 will remain the fastest manned air-breathing aircraft until the SR-72.

Lockheed SR-71 Blackbird

Lockheed Martin SR-72

Joseph Vida (L), Raymond Yielding, and their SR-71 on its final flight.

The Mach 6 Lockheed Martin SR-72 is projected to fill a coverage gap between surveillance satellites, subsonic manned aircraft, and unmanned aerial vehicles for intelligence, surveillance, and reconnaissance (ISR), and strike missions. The company plans on having an optionally piloted, scaled down (about the size of the current F-22 fighter) demonstrator of the SR-72 technology flying by 2023, with the SR-72 possibly entering service by 2030. However, the Northrop Grumman RQ-180 stealth UAV may be accepted by the Air Force, as it is less complex to design and manufacture, less susceptible to problems with acquisition, and could enter service at an earlier date than the SR-72.

Northrop Grumman RQ-180

1927–PRESENT: LONG-DISTANCE COMMERCIAL FLIGHTS: A BRIEF OVERVIEW

Throughout the 1920s and 1930s, because land-based planes lacked sufficient range and as necessary runway infrastructure was not common and would be too expensive to construct for the relatively small number of flights, the only viable means to operate long-range, trans-ocean civilian commercial flights was by flying boat. Thus, trans-Atlantic or trans-Pacific air travel was flown by large seaplanes, from the Do X to the Shorts Empires and Pan Am Clippers, usually with many intermediate stops along the way. From 1931 onward, long-distance commercial air travel took a detour when the *Graf Zeppelin* operated the world's first scheduled trans-Atlantic passenger flights, mainly between Germany and Brazil and sometimes stopping in Spain, Miami, London, and Berlin.

Once Lindbergh successfully crossed the Atlantic in May 1927, closely followed in June 1927, by the first trans-Atlantic air passenger Charles Levine, when he accompanied Clarence Chamberlin, the race to cross the Atlantic began in earnest, with passenger flights as the ultimate objective. In 1935, trans-Atlantic commercial air travel took a step forward with an agreement between America, Britain, Canada, and the Irish Free State, which was to be the European terminus for trans-Atlantic air services at the most westerly town of Foynes. Airfields in Eastern Canada, Newfoundland, Nova Scotia, and Labrador had already been established as western bases.

Shorts entered the flying boat market and produced a series of designs (the first was known as the Singapore), and then Shorts began design work on one of their most famous designs, the Calcutta, based on the Singapore layout, but larger and more powerful. The Calcutta first flew in 1928, and began active service with Imperial Airways in August. Two more were added to the fleet by April 1929, and flew passenger preferred coastal routes from Genoa, Italy, to Alexandria, Egypt, by way of Rome, Naples, Corfu, and Athens. A number of Calcuttas were used on shorter routes, and were instrumental in permitting long-range airline services between outposts of the British Empire. Calcutta production was followed by the larger Kent, which in turn was followed by a series of even larger aircraft designs, such as the Short Empire, the first of which was launched on 2 July 1936. Imperial Airways' Short Empire seaplanes were primarily used along the empire routes in Africa and Asia, but they began to explore the possibility of using it for trans-Atlantic flights from 1937. The type was used by British Overseas Airways Corporation (BOAC) to operate the first trans-Atlantic westbound service from Foynes to Newfoundland on 5 July 1937. The Short S.26, intended as the mainstay of Imperial Airways' Empire services, was built in 1939 as an enlarged Short Empire, powered by four 1,400 hp Bristol Hercules radial engines and designed to have the capability of crossing the Atlantic without refueling. On 21 July 1939, the first S.26 (*Golden Hind*) was flown by Shorts, but by the time Imperial Airways received their Empires and trained their crews war broke out and the aircraft were impressed by the RAF. During the war Shorts produced some of their best-known aircraft, including the Sunderland Flying Boat and the Stirling bomber.

Shorts Calcutta

February 1934–August 1939, Deutsche Lufthansa operated a regular airmail service between Natal, Brazil, and Bathurst, Gambia, continuing via the Canary Islands and Spain to Stuttgart, Germany. From December 1935, Air France opened a regular weekly airmail route between South America and Africa. In 1938, a Lufthansa Focke-Wulf FW200 Condor long-range airliner flew non-stop from Berlin to New York and returned non-stop with their crews as a proving flight for the development of passenger carrying services. This was the first land plane to fulfil this function and marked a departure from British and American reliance on seaplanes for long over-water routes. A regular Lufthansa trans-Atlantic service was planned but did not start before WWII.

Lufthansa FW 200 Condor

The Boeing seaplane B-314 *Yankee Clipper's* inaugural trip across the Atlantic occurred on 24 June 1939, flying from Southampton to Port Washington, New York, with intermediate stops in Foynes, Botwood, Newfoundland, and Shediac, New Brunswick. On 20 May 1939, Pan Am's *Dixie Clipper* flew the first regularly scheduled airmail flight to Europe, and a month later, after its return, the *Dixie Clipper* inaugurated the first regular trans-Atlantic passenger service on 28 June. Soon the B-314 Clippers were flying to destinations around the world. On 8 July 1939, a service began between New York and Southampton, and trans-Atlantic service continued until the beginning of the war. The Clipper fleet was then pressed into military service and the flying boats were used for ferrying personnel and equipment to the European and Pacific fronts.

Pan Am B-314 *Dixie Clipper*

Meanwhile, in the late 1920s, Pan American began flying large seaplanes in the Caribbean between Key West and Havana, and then to South America, with the flying boats "bringing their runways with them." At a time when trans-Atlantic flights were stalled by disputes—mostly political—over landing rights, the Pacific became the objective, with the first commercial Pacific flight taking place four years before a commercial flight crossed the Atlantic. Pan Am had experience with seaplanes, had rigorous training standards for crews, and conducted survey flights. Once the company received an air mail contract it ordered three Martin M-130s to fly commercial trans-Pacific flights. The first regularly scheduled trans-Pacific flight occurred when a Pan American Martin 130 seaplane took off on 22 November 1935, from San Francisco; one week and four stops later the *China Clipper* landed in Manila. It was the beginning of a new era. The voyage would have taken fifteen to sixteen days by fast steamship. The Pan Am seaplanes flew until WWII, logging 2.4 million miles and carrying 3,500 wealthy passengers and 750,000 lbs. of mail and air freight. When postwar service resumed advances in aviation had ended the flying boat era.

World War II

It was from the demands of WWII that the crossing of the Atlantic by land plane became practical and commonplace. With the fall of France in June 1940 and the loss of much war materiel during the retreat from the continent, the need for the British to purchase replacement materiel from the United States was urgent. The first American aircraft purchased by Britain were flown to airports in Nova Scotia and Newfoundland, partially disassembled, and loaded on ships and transported to England, where they were unloaded and reassembled; a process that could take several weeks, not considering repairing the damage to aircraft during transit. Furthermore, German U-boats operating in the North Atlantic were sinking the shipping transporting these aircraft. While larger aircraft could be flown directly to the United Kingdom, early in the war various ferry routes for aircraft with lesser range were organized, linking America and the United Kingdom, particularly along the North Atlantic Ferry Route and then the South Atlantic Route, making trans-Atlantic flight commonplace and paving the way for postwar long distance flying.

Seventy-three-year-old Orville Wright climbing aboard a Lockheed Constellation.

Postwar

Howard Hughes realized the postwar commercial potential of the Lockheed Constellation and flew a well-publicized transcontinental flight from Burbank, California, to Washington, DC, on 17 April 1944. Hughes and TWA president Jack Frye piloted the Connie to an average speed of 331 mph, flying non-stop in 6:57:51 hours over about 2,300 miles and setting the transcontinental record. On the return trip Hughes landed at Wright Field, and in a brilliant PR move gave seventy-three-year-old Orville Wright his last aircraft flight more than forty years after his historic first flight. Wright is said to have commented that the Constellation's wingspan (123 ft.) was longer than his first flight (by three feet).

During June 1947, Pan Am initiated the first scheduled round-the-world airline flight with a weekly DC-4 scheduled to leave San Francisco at 2200 Thursday as Flight 1, stopping in Honolulu, Midway, Wake, Guam, Manila, and Bangkok, and arriving in Calcutta on Monday at 1245, where it met Flight 2, a Constellation that had left New York at 2330 Friday. The DC-4 returned to San Francisco as Flight 2, while the Constellation left Calcutta 1330 Tuesday, stopping in Karachi, Istanbul, London, Shannon, and Gander, and arriving at LaGuardia Thursday at 1455.

The first jetliner service was inaugurated by BOAC on 2 May 1952, between London and Johannesburg, South Africa, flying their ill-fated de Havilland Comet on a flight that took 23:38 hours, including stops. In August 1953, BOAC scheduled non-stop London to Tokyo flights by Comet for thirty-six hours, compared to 86:35 hours using their Argonaut piston airliner. (Pan Am's DC-6B was scheduled for 46:15 hours.) The Comet offered a relatively quiet and comfortable flight with good range and speed, but a year after entering commercial service three Comets broke up mid-flight in well-publicized accidents due to catastrophic airframe metal fatigue. The Comet was withdrawn from service and extensively tested and redesigned, and although sales never fully recovered, the Comet 4 series that debuted in 1958 had a productive thirty-year career.

Lockheed Constellation

De Havilland Comet

Because of TWA's impending introduction of its faster, pressurized Lockheed Constellations, Pan Am ordered its own Constellation fleet and began trans-Atlantic Constellation flights on 14 January 1946, three weeks before TWA. On 5 February 1946, TWA began its trans-Atlantic service, with the Constellation flying the New York-Gander-Shannon-Paris route. On 21 May 1946, KLM was the first continental European airline to begin trans-Atlantic scheduled flights between Amsterdam and New York City using Douglas DC-4s.

On 19 October 1953, TWA began the first non-stop eastbound scheduled transcontinental service with Super Constellations. The non-stop flight from Los Angeles to New York took eight hours, but because of prevailing head winds westbound transcontinental service continued to stop in Chicago to refuel.

The Boeing 707 vs. the Douglas DC-8

In 1952, Douglas continued as the most successful of the commercial aircraft manufacturers, having almost 300 orders for its piston-engined DC-6 and its successor, the DC-7. Douglas' decision to stay with piston engine aircraft seemed to be vindicated by the Comet tragedies and the airline industry's general lack of interest in jet aircraft. Meanwhile Boeing, believing that a requirement for a jet-powered tanker was inevitable, began work on a new jet tanker aircraft that could be modified into an airliner. In the airliner configuration it would have similar seating capacity to the Comet, while its swept wing would give it higher cruising speed and better range. On its introduction in 1950 as the Model 473-60C, there was no interest by the airlines, but Boeing remained committed that the project was worthwhile and continued with a prototype 367-80 "Dash-80," spending $16 million of its own money. The Dash-80 first flew in June 1954, and on 16 October 1955, the prototype Boeing 707 jet crossed America twice in one day, from Seattle to Washington, DC, and back in 16:08 hours, with the eastbound flight averaging 592 mph and the westbound flight 567 mph.

The Boeing 707's main competition was the Douglas DC-8, but both companies found the major airlines were reluctant to commit themselves to the large financial and technical requirements of jet aircraft, but none could afford not to buy jets if their competitors placed orders. Unexpectedly, in October 1955, Pan American placed orders for both aircraft, which led other airlines to rush to place orders. By the beginning of 1958, Douglas had only sold 133 DC-8s, compared to Boeing's 150 707s. Douglas attempted to close the gap between the DC-8 and 707, but their reluctance to change the DC-8 fuselage in various models caused a further market loss and 707 orders moved farther ahead.

On 11 March 1957, a company test Boeing 707 set a transcontinental speed record for passenger flight, flying from Seattle to Washington, DC, in 3:48 hours, carrying forty-two passengers and a crew of ten. Boeing delivered the first of 1,010 707s and 732 KC-135 Stratotankers on 15 August 1958. The aircraft's first commercial flight was from Idlewild, New York, to Le Bourget, Paris, on 26 October 1958, with a fuel stop in Gander, Newfoundland. In December, National Airlines operated the first US domestic jet airline flights, flying between New York/Idlewild and Miami using 707s leased from PanAm. American Airlines was the first domestic airline to fly its own jets on 25 January 1959. TWA began domestic 707-131 flights in March and Continental Airlines started 707-124 flights in June; meanwhile, airlines that had ordered only the Douglas DC-8, such as United, Delta, and Eastern, were left without jets until September and lost market share on transcontinental flights. Qantas was the first non-US airline to use 707s, beginning in 1959.

By the mid-1960s, the future of the Douglas DC-8 was in jeopardy, but it then released the three Super Sixties models in April 1965. With a longer fuselage, the Super Sixties were able to seat 269 passengers and were the largest airliners on the market until Boeing introduced the 747 in 1970. Continuing to lag behind the 707 in sales, in the late 1960s, the DC-8 evolved from the Super Sixties to the Super Seventies, the world's quietest four-engine airliner, which improved sales somewhat. Nonetheless, throughout the years the DC-8 was considered a copy of the 707, which greatly outsold it (1,010 707s and 732 KC-135s vs. 556 DC-8s).

Boeing 707

Douglas DC-8

On 29 September 1957 a TWA L-1649A Starliner flew from Los Angeles to London in 18:32 hours over 5,420 miles. In December 1957, an El Al four (piston) engine Bristol Britannia flew the longest flight by any commercial airline on the New York/Tel Aviv route (5,680 miles), flying 14:46 hours.

In January 1958, the Boeing 377 Stratocruiser/B-29 derivative flew the California to Tokyo flight daily (31:45 hours from San Francisco or 32:15 hours from Los Angeles).

On 7 August 1958, a de Havilland Comet 4 set a west-east transatlantic record, flying from New York to Hatfield, England, in 6:27 hours.

The first scheduled trans-Atlantic jet passenger service took place on 4 October 1958, when BOAC flew their de Havilland Comet from London to New York with a stopover in Gander. Pan American began daily jet service from New York to Paris on 26 October 1958.

In 1961, an El Al Boeing 707 flying from New York to Tel Aviv set three world records: the fastest flight, the first non-stop service on that route, and the world's longest non-stop commercial flight, covering 5,760 miles in 9:33 hours.

In April 1963, American Airlines pilot Wylie Drummond set a national record for commercial jets by flying 2,474 miles from Los Angeles to New York in 3:38 hours at a speed of 680.9 mph.

In August 1967, Aerolineas Argentinas' new Boeing 707 non-stop service between Madrid and Buenos Aires flew 6,300 miles in 12 hours for the longest-ever scheduled flight (by distance) until the Boeing 747 entered service in 1976.

Once Boeing 747s and Douglas DC-10s entered service long-haul non-stop flights of more than 6:30 hours came into wide use and were continually increased in range with the introduction of enhanced variants. In April 1976, Pan Am set a new record for the longest non-stop scheduled flight with its Boeing 747SP, flying the New York-Tokyo route of 6,744 miles. In December a Pan Am 747 set a new record (Sydney-San Francisco), covering 7,417 miles. In May 1988, El Al began its 747 long-haul passenger flight from Tel Aviv to Los Angeles, completing its journey in 13:40 hours over 7,574 miles. In August 1989, the first Qantas Boeing 747-438 set a new distance record for a commercial aircraft by flying non-stop between London and Sydney, flying the distance of 11,185 miles in 20:09 hours while delivering the aircraft to Qantas Airlines without passengers.

With the introduction of the Boeing 777LR and the Airbus A380-500 and A340-500, ultra long-haul flights were introduced, characterized by having no scheduled intermediate stop of any kind; a route length over 7,500 miles; and usually flying a Great Circle Route, often passing over Polar regions. Currently Boeing is the dominant manufacturer in the ultra long-haul aircraft segment, with twenty-five of the thirty longest non-stop flights being operated by Boeing airliners, such as the 777-300ER, 777-200LR, and the 747-400ER, with the Airbus A380 used on the others.

On 3 February 2004, Singapore Airlines long-range Airbus 340-500 flew passengers from Singapore to Los Angeles for a new passenger record mileage of 8,770 miles in 18:05 hours. On 28–29 June 2004, Singapore Airlines Airbus 340-500 established a new distance record when it launched a non-stop 18:50 hour, 9,535-mile flight between Singapore and Newark, New Jersey. These two flights held the record for the longest commercial passenger non-stop flights in the world based on time and

Boeing 747

Airbus

Boeing 777

distance until both routes were canceled in October and November 2013, respectively. On 9 November 2005, a Pakistan International Airlines Boeing 777-200LR, the *Worldliner*, completed the world's longest non-stop passenger aircraft flight, flying 13,423 miles eastward (westward is 5,994 miles) from Hong Kong to London in roughly 22:43 hours. This broke a distance record set in 1962 by an unrefueled B-52 bomber during Operation Persian Rug, flying a 21:52 hour flight that covered 12,532 miles, but it was a ferry and not a passenger flight.

Airline Time Aloft Record: Double Sunrise Service

The time aloft record for an airliner is a controversial record first claimed by the 1939 Berlin-New York non-stop flight of a specially built piston-powered Deutsche Lufthansa Focke-Wulf Fw 200 for a flight time of 24:56 hours. On 1–2 October 1957, a Trans World Airlines Lockheed L-1649 Starliner on the inaugural London-San Francisco Polar route had a flight time of 23:19 hours over 5,550 miles. This L-1649A was the last of the Constellation series and the ultimate piston-engine airliner in terms of range and endurance.

The record for longest time aloft for an airliner can also be claimed by Qantas, which 1943–1945 operated a weekly return flight called the *Double Sunrise Service* from Western Australia to Sri Lanka flying Consolidated PBY Catalinas. In 1943, Royal Australian Air Force personnel were transferred to Qantas Airlines to conduct flights between Western Australia and across the Indian Ocean to southern Ceylon (Sri Lanka), navigating without the aid of radio and depending only on compass and celestial navigation during the flight. The Catalinas were stripped of all non-essential equipment so they could carry 1,988 gallons of fuel, giving them a range of 4,100 miles at a maximum take-off weight of 35,400 lbs. The flights took between twenty-seven and thirty-three hours, with the departure scheduled so that the flight crossed Japanese occupied territory during darkness. The crews would observe sunrise twice, which led to the service being known as the "Double Sunrise Service." The service made 271 crossings, delivering more than 10,000 lbs. of mail and 860 passengers.

Qantas PBY Catalina of Double Sunrise Service

THE CONCORDE: AN AIRLINER IN A LEAGUE OF ITS OWN

British and French aerospace companies collaborated to design and build twenty Concorde commercial supersonic transport aircraft (SST) between 1966 and 1979. It was one of only two SSTs to enter commercial service, the other being the Tupolev Tu-144. Of the twenty, six were prototypes and development aircraft and seven each were delivered to Air France and British Airways. Flying with Air France and British Airways, the supersonic jets offered a luxurious and swift trip across the Atlantic for twenty-seven years. Flown by a crew of three (two pilots and a flight engineer) with 92–120 passengers, it was capable of speeds more than twice the speed of sound, and at altitudes as high as 60,000 ft. the Concorde could fly from London to New York and return in the time it took a conventional aircraft to fly one way. The Concorde had a wing span of 84 ft. and wing area of 3,856 sq. ft., a length of 202.3 ft., a height of 40 ft., and an empty weight of 173,500 lbs. The internal passenger area was quite cramped at 8.7 ft. wide and 6.5 ft. high.

1973: 26 September: Concorde 02 (F-WTSA) set a new Paris to Washington record of 3:33 hours.
1974: 7 November: G-AXDN flew from Fairford, England to Bangor, ME to set a new record time for an East to West Atlantic crossing by a commercial aircraft of 2:56 hours. This was the first leg of a trip to Moses Lake in Washington where the aircraft would undergo de-icing trials. The flight from Bangor to Moses Lake required 4:43 hours and set a new record for an East to West crossing of the USA.
1975: 1 September: Concorde G-BOAC becomes the first commercial aircraft to make four Atlantic crossings in one day, flying twice from London to Gander, Newfoundland, and return.
1979: 16 December: A British Airways Concorde sets a new record of 2:59:36 hours on the New York to London flight.
1983: 1 January: A British Airways Concorde set a new New York to London record of 2:56 hours.
1984: 11 September: Concorde G-BOAB set a new airliner distance record of 4,565 miles flying from Washington to Nice.
1985: 13 February: A chartered Concorde set a new London to Sydney record of 17:03 hours.
1985: 28 March: A chartered Concorde set a new London to Cape Town record of 8:08 hours.
1985: 19 December: Concorde G-BOAC records a speed of 1,488 mph, a new record for a commercial aircraft.
1987: 6 September: Concorde sets a new coast-to-coast trans-Atlantic record of 1:35 hours flying between Newfoundland and Ireland.
1987: 22 November: Richard Noble sets a new passenger record by being the first to cross the Atlantic three times in one day.

Concorde

1988: 7 February: Concorde G-BOAA sets a new New York to London record of 2:55:15 hours.

1990: 14 April: Concorde sets New York to London record at 2:54:30 hours.

1992: 12–13 October: F-BTSD sets the current record for a westbound round-the-world flight at 32:49:03 hours. This flight was in commemoration of the 500th anniversary of Columbus' first New World landing. The route was Lisbon to Santo Domingo to Acapulco to Honolulu to Guam to Bangkok to Bahrain and back to Lisbon.

1995: 15–16 August : F-BTSD set the current record for an eastbound round-the-world flight: 31:27:47 hours. The route was New York (JFK) to Toulouse to Dubai to Bangkok to Guam to Honolulu to Acapulco and back to New York (JFK).

1996: 7 February: Concorde G-BOAD, piloted by Capt. Leslie Scott, with Senior First Officer Tim Orchard, set the current New York to London record of 2:52:59 hours.

1999: 2 March: 30th Flight Anniversary: The Concordes had recorded 920,000 flight hours with more than 600,000 supersonic.

1999: 21 September: The flight time of 3:06 hours was a record for a flight between London and Boston.

2003: 5 November: Concorde G-BOAG, flown by Capts. Mike Bannister and Les Brodie, was given clearance to fly supersonically over northern Canada and completed the trip from New York on the east coast to Seattle on the west coast in a new record time of 3:55:12 hours. The aircraft was being taken to its retirement home at the Seattle Museum of Flight.

2003: 8 October: Concorde G-BOAD, piloted by Chief Concorde Pilot Capt. Mike Bannister, set the east to west Atlantic crossing record with a time of 3:05:34 hours.

On 10 April 2003, British Airways and Air France simultaneously pronounced they would retire their Concordes, citing low passenger figures following the 25 July 2000 crash, the decline in air travel following the 11 September 2001 terrorist attacks, and increasing maintenance costs. Although Concorde was technologically advanced when introduced in the 1970s, thirty years later its analogue cockpit was dated. There had been little commercial pressure to upgrade the Concorde due to a lack of competing aircraft, unlike other airliners of the same era, such as the Boeing 747.

TUPOLEV TU-144: THE RUSSIAN CONCORDE

The Tupolev Tu-144 (NATO: Charger) was the world's first commercial supersonic transport aircraft (SST). The prototype first flew on 31 December 1968, two months before the first Concorde flight. The Tu-144 first went supersonic on 5 June 1969, and on 26 May 1970, became the first commercial transport to exceed Mach 2. A Tu-144 crashed in 1973 at the Paris Air Show, delaying its further development. The aircraft was placed into passenger service on 1 November 1977, almost two years after the Concorde. In May 1978, another Tu-144 (an improved version, the Tu-144D) crashed during a test flight while being delivered and the passenger fleet was permanently grounded after only fifty-five scheduled flights. The aircraft remained in use as a cargo aircraft until 1983, by which point a total of 102 commercial flights had been completed. Although its last commercial passenger flight was in 1978, after sixteen aircraft were built, production terminated in 1983.

Tupolev Tu-144

THE HELICOPTER

Early Helicopters: An Overview

The original helicopter design can be accredited to the Chinese, who still use the children's toy bamboo flying top first seen in 400 BC and depicted in a 1463 European painting. *Pao Phu Tau* is a fourth century Chinese book that describes some of the essential ideas found in rotary wing aircraft. About 1490, Leonardo da Vinci first conceived the semi-practical, manned helicopter that could be described as an "aerial screw." His notes indicate he built small flying models, but there were no indications for any provision to stop the rotor from making the whole craft rotate.

Mikhail Lomonosov demonstrated a small coaxial rotor powered by a spring to the Russian Academy of Sciences in July 1754.

Christian de Launoy and his mechanic, Bienvenu, constructed a model with a pair of counter-rotating rotors using turkey's flight feathers as rotor blades in 1783 and demonstrated it to the French Academy of Sciences.

In 1843, Sir George Cayley, the father of British aviation, designed his "Aerial Carriage," which had four rotors arranged coaxially in pairs, but he was unsuccessful finding an engine, so the design continued on the drawing board. Later its wide fanlike rotors resembled those used on the 1922 de Bothezat machine and the lateral side-by-side arrangement of its rotors were similar to the Focke helicopters built in Germany in the late 1930s.

Alphonse Penaud, "The Father of Flying Models," was the first person to build and successfully fly heavier-than-air rubber band powered model flying machines, including coaxial rotor model helicopter toys in 1870. It was one of Penaud's rubber band powered helicopters which first interested two of Bishop

Gustave de Ponton d'Amecourt

Milton Wright's sons, Orville and Wilbur, of Dayton, Ohio, in the possibility of flight.

Gustave de Ponton d'Amecourt, a French writer and inventor, set up an association to collaborate the many helicopter designs of the time. In 1863, d'Amecourt constructed a model using established counter-rotating rotors, initially powered by steam, which failed—but a clockwork version did fly. D'Amecourt was the first person to coin the term "helicopter" from the two words "helicon" for spiral and "pter" meaning wings.

Other designs covering a wide variety of forms included Pomes and De la Pauze (1871); Penaud, Achenbach (1874); Dieuaide (1887); Melikoff (1877); Forlanini (1877); Castel (1878); and Dandrieux (1878–79). Enrico Forlanini's unmanned helicopter was powered by a steam engine and was reported to rise to a height of 39 ft., where it remained for about twenty seconds, after a vertical take-off in Milan. Engineer Maurice Stanislas Ledger's helicopter lifted a person vertically into the air in 1905 in Monaco.

In 1906, French brothers Jacques and Louis Breguet began experimenting with airfoils for helicopters, which during the next year resulted in the Breguet-Richet Gyroplane No.1, possibly the earliest known example of a quadcopter. On 14 August (?) 1907, the Gyroplane No. 1 lifted its pilot, a Monsieur Volumard, into the air about two feet for a minute. Gyroplane No. 1 was shown to be extremely unstable

Breguet-Richet Gyroplane No.1

and required a man at each corner of the airframe as tethers to hold it securely in place. Therefore, the flights of Gyroplane No. 1 are considered to be the first manned flight of a helicopter, but not as a free or untethered flight; eventually testing was discontinued in favor of building a completely new aircraft. The following year Breguet produced his second helicopter powered by a 55 hp Renault engine spinning twin 25 ft. rotors, but it was also equipped with a set of biplane wings. On 22 July 1908, it lifted vertically to almost 15 ft. and flew for a short period of time, apparently under control, but it was destroyed on landing.

In 1885, Thomas Edison was granted $1,000 by newspaper tycoon James Gordon Bennett to conduct experiments toward developing flight. Edison built a helicopter using guncotton to power an internal combustion engine which was damaged by explosions and badly burned one of his workers. Edison's calculations demonstrated it would require a motor with a ratio of three to four pounds per horsepower produced to be successful. Based on Edison's experiments Slovak inventor Jan Bahy'a adapted the internal combustion engine to power his helicopter model that reached a height of 1.6 ft. in 1901. On 5 May 1905, his helicopter rose to 13 ft. and flew for more than 4,900 ft. In 1908, Edison patented his own design for a helicopter powered by a gasoline engine with box kites attached to a mast by cables for a rotor, but it never flew.

French inventor Paul Cornu designed and built the Cornu Helicopter, consisting of a V-shaped frame that used two 20 ft. counter-rotating rotors driven by a 24 hp Antoinette engine. The transmission was provided by a large 73 ft. belt linking the engine to two big pulleys on either side of the structure that supported twin-blade propellers. Inclinable planes for steering were installed just beneath the propellers. On 13 November 1907, in Lisenux, France, it lifted its inventor to one foot and remained aloft for 20 seconds. Even though this flight did not surpass the flight of the Gyroplane No. 1, it was reported to be the first truly free flight with a pilot. Cornu's helicopter completed a few more flights and achieved a height of nearly 6.5 ft., but was abandoned and proved to be unstable, as it was found to have insufficient engine power to lift the 575 lb. load, including a pilot; had a lack of transmission belt adhesion; and incorrect propeller sections.

Paul Cornu

American railroad mechanics William Purvis and Charles Wilson designed a 20 ft. high cast iron aircraft intended to take off and land vertically. They filed an application for a patent in March 1910. While the model flew, the cast iron full-sized product remained stationary. By the time the patent was issued in 1912, Purvis and Wilson had abandoned their project and returned to the railway.

William Purvis and Charles Wilson

Danish inventor Jacob Ellehammer built the Ellehammer Compound Helicopter in 1912. It consisted of a frame equipped with a 6 hp engine that drove both the two counter-rotating discs and a conventional propeller. At regular intervals around the perimeter of the wings were six vanes pivoting about its circumference. After indoor tests, the aircraft was demonstrated outdoors and made several free take-offs. Experiments with the helicopter continued until September 1916, when it turned over during take-off, destroying its rotors.

Argentine Raul Pateras Pescara, while working in Europe in the early 1920s, found one of the first successful applications of cyclic pitch, allowing an aircraft lateral movement without a separate propeller to push or pull it. Pescara also demonstrated the principle of autorotation, by which helicopters safely land after engine failure. By January 1924, Pescara's Helicopter No. 1 was found to be underpowered when tested, as it could not lift its own weight. His second attempt was much improved and set a record, flying 2,429 ft. in 4:11 minutes at about 8 mph, maintaining a height of six feet. The British government funded further research by Pescara which resulted in Helicopter No. 3, powered by a 250 hp radial engine and which could fly for up to ten minutes.

Raul Pescara

Etienne Oehmichen

Frenchman Etienne Oehmichen's first successful flight in a helicopter took place on 18 February 1921, and by 11 November 1922, he first flew Oehmichen No.2, an improved helicopter with small vertically mounted rotors that rotated in the opposite direction of the large lifting rotors, introducing the first reliable flying helicopter capable of carrying a person. Oehmichen set the first helicopter world record recognized by the FAI while flying his quadrotor helicopter 1,188 ft. and then 1,733 ft. on 14 April 1924. On 18 April 1924, Pescara surpassed Oehmichen's record, but on 4 May, Oehmichen set the first 1 km closed-circuit helicopter flight in 7:40 minutes with his No. 2 machine, winning a prize of 90,000 Francs. Oehmichen then reclaimed the world record when he flew his No. 2 machine again for a 14-minute flight covering 5,550 ft. (while climbing to a height of 50 ft.). Later that year he made a flight with two passengers.

George de Bothezat completed his helicopter for the US Army Air Service in December 1922, and the first flight was made by Maj. T. H. Bane of the engineering division on 18 December 1922. The helicopter had four six-bladed rotors at the end of enormous, bridge-like girders braced with piano wire; the craft had two vertical propellers called "steering airscrews" for lateral control and two additional three-bladed propellers mounted horizontally above the Le Rhône engine to provide airflow for cooling. Over the next year more than one hundred flights were completed, carrying up to four passengers in addition to its pilot and setting records for duration (2:25 minutes) at an altitude (30 ft.). Thomas Edison proclaimed it the first successful helicopter, but full control of the aircraft in flight was never really successful, requiring a "favorable" wind for forward flight, but it was "remarkably stable." De Bothezat wanted to build an improved version, but in 1924, the Army decided to terminate further work, canceling the contract and scrapping it.

George de Bothezat

Albert von Baumhauer, a Dutch aeronautical engineer, saw his first prototype being flown by Dutch Army Air Arm Capt. Floris Albert van Heijst on 24 September 1925. Von Baumhauer's cyclic and collective patents were granted by the British Ministry of Aviation on 31 January 1927.

American inventor Arthur Young began investigating model helicopters in 1928, and in 1941, he took his calculations and models to Bell Aircraft, and the company agreed to sign over his patents and build full-scale prototypes. His budget was US$250,000 to build two working helicopters in secret due to the war. In just six months he completed the first Bell Model 1, which led to the Bell 30 in July 1943, and on 8 March 1946, Bell received Helicopter Type Certificate H-1 for the world's first commercial helicopter, the Bell Model 47. This helicopter featured in the *M*A*S*H* movie and television series, and was so successful that it continued to be manufactured through 1974. A design as well as a utilitarian success, it was added to the permanent collection of the Museum of Modern Art of New York in 1984.

Arthur Young's Bell Model 47 *M*A*S*H* helicopter

Hungarian aviation engineer Oszkar Asboth developed a helicopter prototype in 1928 that took off and landed at least 182 times, with a maximum single flight duration of 53 minutes. Over two years of testing the two large wooden propellers positioned one above the other and rotating in opposite directions, Asboth was able to have the aircraft and pilot lift off more than 250 times and for periods of almost one hour. Because of their rigid propellers Asboth's "helicopters" became unstable in forward flight or when exposed to a strong side wind.

Italian engineer Corradino D'Ascanio built his D'AT3 (a coaxial helicopter) in 1930. It was relatively large, having two, two-bladed, counter-rotating rotors. Control was accomplished by using auxiliary wings or servo-tabs on the trailing edges of the blades, which was later implemented by other helicopter designers. Three small propellers mounted to the airframe were used for additional pitch, roll, and yaw control. The D'AT3 set FAI speed and altitude records for the time, including altitude (59 ft.), duration (8:45 minutes), and distance flown (3,540 ft.).

Soviet aeronautical engineers Boris Yuriev and Alexei Cheremukhin, working at the Central Aerohydrodynamic Institute (TsAGI), constructed and flew the TsAGI 1-EA single rotor helicopter, which used an open tubing framework, a four-blade main rotor, and twin sets of six foot diameter, two-bladed anti-torque rotors: one set of two at the nose and one set of two at the tail. By 14 August 1932, Cheremukhin flew to an unofficial altitude of 1,985 ft., smashing d'Ascanio's records, but as the Soviet Union was not yet a member of the FAI Cheremukhin's record remained unrecognized.

Nicolas Florine, a Russian engineer, built the first twin tandem rotor machine to complete a free flight at the Laboratoire Aerotechnique de Belgique in April 1933, flying at an altitude of 20 ft. and an endurance of 8:00 minutes. The co-rotating configuration was because the gyroscopic stability of the rotors would not cancel and the rotors had to be tilted slightly in opposite directions to counter torque, making it at the time one of the most stable helicopters in existence.

The Breguet-Dorand Gyroplane Laboratoire, a coaxial, contra-rotating helicopter, was built in 1933, and after many ground tests and an accident it first flew on 26 June 1935. Within a short time the aircraft was setting records with pilot Maurice Claisse at the controls, becoming the first successful helicopter to fly in Europe and perhaps in the world. On 14 December 1935, Claisse set a record for closed-circuit flight in a 1,600 ft. diameter circuit. On 26 September 1936, Claisse set a height record of 520 ft., while on 24 November, he set a flight duration record of 1:03 minutes over a twenty-seven mile closed circuit at 27.8 mph.

Breguet-Dorand Gyroplane

NAZI GERMANY HELICOPTER RECORDS

On 25 October 1937, famed woman aviator Hanna Reitsch flew the prototype Focke-Wulf FW61—considered the first practical, functional helicopter—approximately sixty-eight miles without landing at Stendal-Berlin. The Focke Wulf FW 61 subsequently set several records for altitude, speed, and flight duration, culminating in June 1938 with an altitude record of 11,243 ft. and a straight line flight record of 143 miles.

On 25 February 1945, the Focke-Achgelis Company had one of their Fa 223 Drache helicopters available at Berlin-Tempelhof, which Hitler ordered to fly to Danzig. Based on the FW 61 design, the Fa 223 is considered to be the largest and most efficient helicopter of the war, with the eleven manufactured being recognized particularly by their value as a transport and resupply helicopter. On 26 February 1945, the Fa 223 was flown by Hulmut Gerstenhauer and two copilots from Tempelhof toward Wurzburg, but soon became lost in bad weather and was forced to land early and overnight in Crailsheim. Once the bad weather began tapering off they took off and landed in Würzburg to refuel, then continued to Meiningen. The next day they flew (a record) 196 miles to Werder; on the third day they continued toward Stettin-Altdamm, but bad weather again forced them to land in Prenzlau. The next day, the weather remained poor and they had to stop in Stolp, west of Danzig, for the night. The next day they left Stolp just before Russian troops arrived and flew directly to Danzig, which was being besieged by the Soviets, and had to land west of the city. The next day, with Danzig about to fall, Gerstenhauer was ordered to return to Werder by a long flight along the Baltic coast and arrived in Werder on 11 March. The entire flight had covered a record 1,041 miles with an in-flight time of 16:25 hours. In September 1945, the Fa 223, piloted by Gerstenhauer, became the first helicopter to cross the English Channel to England. During flight trials the following month it was destroyed, having had a flying life of 170 hours, when the rotor failed.

Focke-Achgelis Fa 223 Drache

In America, Russian-born engineer Igor Sikorsky and W. Lawrence LePage competed to construct the US military's first helicopter. LePage received the patent rights to develop helicopters patterned after the German FW 61 and built the XR-1. Meanwhile, Sikorsky chose a simpler, single rotor design (VS-300), which became the first practical single lifting rotor helicopter design and potentially the best flying one since the Soviet TsAGI 1-EA, which had flown nearly a decade before. After experimenting with configurations to counteract the torque produced by the single main rotor Sikorsky decided on a single, smaller rotor mounted on the tail boom.

Igor Sikorsky flies his VS-300.

Sikorsky R-4

Developed from the VS-300, Sikorsky's R-4 was the first large-scale mass-produced helicopter, with an initial production order for one hundred aircraft. The R-4 was the only Allied helicopter to serve in WWII, when it was used primarily for rescue in areas of harsh terrain. Total production reached 131 helicopters before the R-4 was replaced by other Sikorsky helicopters, such as the R-5 and R-6. In all, Sikorsky produced more than 400 helicopters before the end of WWII, all of which set many records, as they were the best and only helicopters available.

In 1951, Charles Kaman modified his K-225 Synchropter, which was a design for a twin-rotor helicopter concept first pioneered by German Anton Flettner in 1939. The K-225 was equipped with a turbo-shaft engine, a new type of engine that was an adaptation of the turbine engine. The engine provided a large amount of power to Kaman's helicopter with a lower weight penalty than piston engines that had heavy engine blocks and auxiliary components. On 11 December 1951, the Kaman K-225 became the first turbine-powered helicopter in the world and two years later, on 26 March 1954, a modified Navy HTK-1—another Kaman helicopter—became the first twin-turbine helicopter to fly.

Charles Kaman in his Kaman K-225

MODERN HELICOPTER RECORD FLIGHTS: 1945–PRESENT

1949: First Transcontinental Helicopter Flight

A commercial Hiller 360 flew from San Francisco to New York City with numerous stops.

Stewart Graham

1949: First Unescorted Transcontinental Helicopter Flight

On 6 April 1949, US Coast Guard Lt. Stewart Graham and crewman AM2 Robert McAuliffe completed the longest unescorted helicopter transcontinental flight to date when they flew a Sikorsky HO3S-1G (51-234) from Coast Guard Air Station Elizabeth City, New Jersey, to Coast Guard Air Station Port Angeles, Washington, via San Diego, California, flying 3,750 miles in 57:36 hours over eleven days. Graham was a Navy and Coast Guard helicopter pioneer. On 16 January 1944, Lt. Graham was the first pilot to fly a helicopter from a ship when he flew a Sikorsky YR4B (46445) from the deck of British freighter SS *Daghestan* while in convoy from New York to Liverpool. After thirty minutes he returned to the freighter.

1952: First Trans-Atlantic Helicopter Flight

Between 15–31 July 1952, two Sikorsky H-19s flew 3,410 miles from Westover, Massachusetts, to Prestwick, Scotland, to complete the first trans-Atlantic helicopter flight. The lead ship *Hop-A-Long* was flown by Capt. Vincent McGovern, mission commander, WWII bomber pilot, and Korean War veteran with ninety-six helicopter rescue missions and his co-pilot, Capt. Harry Jeffers. The second helicopter, *Whirl-O-Way*, was flown by 1Lt. Harold Moore, who had flown 112 helicopter missions in Korea, and his co-pilot was Capt. George Hambrick. The helicopters had their pontoons, rescue hoists, sound proofing, cabin heaters, and other unnecessary equipment removed. Each aircraft had three extra one hundred gallon fuel tanks installed in the cargo hold, increasing the fuel capacity to 480 gallons. The helicopters were escorted by a converted B-17 (SB-17) rescue aircraft equipped with rescue gear that provided advance weather information and navigational guidance for the helicopters over water. A SC-54 transport carrying spare parts, mechanics, and observers also accompanied the mission. The itinerary included:

15 July: Presque Isle, Maine (380 miles), then grounded for one day.
17 July: Goose Bay, Labrador (570 miles).
28 July: Bluie West One (770 miles): after five airborne attempts and five weather delays the two Sikorskys left for Bluie West, which was socked in due to weather. They made a dangerous landing on a small island forty-two miles short of BW, but continued to land safely the next day.
29 July: Keflavik, Iceland (850 miles/9:50 hours).
31 July: Prestwick, Scotland (947 miles/10:10 hours) after a day's delay in Keflavik.

Sikorsky H-19 Hop-A-Long

The two H-19s continued the next day to join the 9th Air Rescue Squadron in Wiesbaden, Germany.

The 3,984 statute mile trip took twenty days and accounted for 51:55 hours flying time at cruising speeds of 80–85 mph at altitudes varying between fifty and 3,500 ft., as determined by the weather, with the usual altitude about 500 ft. *Whirl-O-Way* is on display at the Strategic Air & Space Museum, Ashland, Nebraska.

1952: Bell 47D Sets a New Distance Record

On 17 September 1952, the iconic Bell 47 D was flown by Elton Smith 1,217 miles from Fort Worth, Texas, to Niagara Falls, New York, without landing.

1962: Closed-Course Distance

On 13 June 1962, Capt. Richard Coan set a world-class closed-course distance record of 655.64 miles for type flying a Kaman

H-43B Huskie. Then, on 5 July 1962, the same Kaman H-43B, piloted by Capt. Chester Radcliffe, surpassed its own distance record with a flight of 888.4 miles.

1964: Bell UH-1D Sets a New Distance Record

On 27 September 1964, the Bell UH-1D Huey, probably the world's most recognizable and famous helicopter, flew 1,357 miles without landing, flying from Edwards AFB, California, to Rogers, Arkansas.

1965: Sikorsky SH-31 Flies the First Helicopter Transcontinental Non-stop Flight

On 6 March 1965, the *Dawdling Dromedary,* a US Navy Sikorsky SH-3A Sea King helicopter crewed by pilot Cdr. James Williford, co-pilot Lt. David Beil, and crew chief AMM 1C Paul Bert, took off from aircraft carrier USS *Hornet* (CVS-12) docked at NAS North Island, San Diego, California, at 0418 PST and flew non-stop, without refueling, to land aboard aircraft carrier USS *Franklin D. Roosevelt* (CVA-42) off Jacksonville, Florida, at 23:10 EST. The Sea King flew 2,105.6 miles over an elapsed time of 15:52 hours, surpassing the previous record distance by almost 750 miles. On take-off, *Dawdling Dromedary* was about 4,000 lbs. over its gross weight of 23,000 lbs. with a fuel load of 1,690 gallons, but only had sixty gallons remaining on landing. To reduce fuel consumption, after climbing over Guadalupe Pass, Texas, one of the Sikorsky's two turbo-shaft engines was shut down and Williford flew on a single engine for 9.5 hours, only restarting the second engine as they descended through 5,000 ft. over Jacksonville.

Dawdling Dromedary crew: Paul Bert (L), David Beil (C), and James Williford

1966: Jack Schwiebold: Distance Without Landing

Shortly after its introduction in 1966, the teardrop-shaped Hughes OH-6 Cayuse began operations that would set twenty-three world records for helicopters that year for speed, endurance, and time to climb. On 26 March 1966, Jack Schwiebold set the closed circuit distance record in a YOH-6A at Edwards AFB, California, staying in the air without landing for 1,740 miles. Along with Robert Ferry, Jack Schwiebold was probably one of the foremost helicopter pilots and engineers of the 1960s, having engineering degrees and graduated from the USAF Officers and Flight Training schools. He served as Allison Gas Turbine Engine Division's chief test pilot and held FAA pilot ratings in airline transport, land and sea planes, helicopters, and as a flight instructor. He logged nearly 20,000 flight hours, primarily in experimental aircraft, and has been credited with more than thirty-five records in turbine-powered aircraft, seaplanes, STOLs, and helicopters.

Jack Schwiebold

1966: Robert Ferry: Maximum World Long-Distance and Transcontinental Record

On 6 April 1966, Robert Ferry set notable records in a helicopter that still stand today. After earning his fighter pilot's wings in 1945, Ferry applied for helicopter school and was sent to Panama, later serving in the Korean War, where he evacuated wounded troops and flew rescue missions behind enemy lines. After the war Ferry spent nearly six years at the test pilot school at Edwards AFB. He was project pilot on the XV-3 tilt-rotor helicopter developed by Bell Helicopter for the USAF. After twenty years in the USAF, Ferry retired as a lieutenant colonel and joined the Hughes Tool Company as a helicopter test pilot.

Ferry's greatest achievement occurred on 6 April 1966, when he piloted a stripped down Hughes OH-6 on a long-distance world record (and transcontinental record) for helicopters. The flight was sponsored by the Hughes Tool Company Aircraft Division, which hoped to beat a record set in 1965 by a twin-engine Sikorsky SH-3A, an aircraft ten times heavier than the OH-6A. The helicopter carried three times its empty weight, with more than a ton of its weight being fuel. The rear seat and copilot seat were replaced with auxiliary fuel tanks. A CV-7 Buffalo served as the chase plane, carrying an official of the National Aeronautic Association—which documents all record attempts—and two of Ferry's ground crew. Ferry lifted off from Hughes' Culver City, California, pad and headed for Miami, Florida, aided by a strong tailwind and averaging nearly 150 mph as he headed east. With no autopilot, Ferry had to remain alert and keep his hands on the cyclic and collective control sticks for the entire flight. From about the seventh hour of the flight until just before landing Ferry flew above 10,000 ft. and wore an oxygen mask. As he burned off fuel and the weight went down he climbed, and for the final two or three hours he was at a record of about 24,000 ft. As he passed St. Augustine, Florida, the low fuel warning light glowed and Ferry set down on a deserted beach near Ormond Beach, hundreds of miles north of the media waiting at Miami. For the record 15:08 hour, 2,213.1 mile flight Ferry was awarded the Sikorsky International Trophy. These records still stand as of 2017. In 1975, he made the first flight of the Apache attack helicopter at Hughes. Before retiriing from Hughes Ferry logged more than 10,000 hours in 125 aircraft.

Robert Ferry (pilot)

1974: Distance without Landing

On 20 April 1974, Siegfried Hoffman (pilot) and Adam Teleki (flight engineer, both German) flew their BO 105-C powered by two 640 shp Allison 250-C-20 engines over 1,065.55 miles from Ottobrun, near Munich, Germany, to Hinojosa del Duque, southern Spain. This established a new distance record for Class Id rotorcraft which still stands today. Hoffmann was killed in 1989 in the US while performing helicopter aerobatics for a movie.

Siegfried Hoffman (L-pilot), Adam Teleki (R-flight engineer), and their BO 105-C

1982: H. Ross Perot Jr.: Around-the-World Record

On 6 August 1982, Australian Richard Smith had started, but not completed, an around-the-world solo attempt in a JetRanger from Dallas, Texas. H. Ross Perot Jr., the twenty-three-year-old son of wealthy Texas real estate developer H. Ross Perot Sr., was determined to fly the first helicopter to circumnavigate the earth. Perot immediately purchased a single-engine Bell 206L-1 LongRanger II for $750,000 specifically for this flight, and within three weeks modified it with an additional 151 gallon fuel tank, giving the helicopter approximately eight hours' endurance. He also added "pop-out floats" (inflatable pontoons that could be deployed for emergency water landings); a life raft and other emergency equipment and supplies; and additional communication, navigation equipment, and radar. For the flight the LongRanger, named *Spirit of Texas*, was supported by a military transport-sized Hercules with an eleven-member crew to service the chopper at most of its fifty-six stops. Despite the support Perot and Jay Coburn, a friend who had flown helicopters in Vietnam, encountered a few problems along the way. Near Quebec a fuel pump malfunction forced an emergency landing in an Eskimo village, where Perot purchased a tank of jet fuel from a local leader with his Shell credit card. There were two unauthorized landing "incidents" in India and Burma where angry army troops demanded a written apology. Because the Soviet Union would not authorize refueling stops, Perot Sr. arranged for a container ship to be available for a refueling stop that happened in fifteen-foot seas, with forty knot winds. There were no major mechanical problems in flight. On 30 September 1982, Perot and Coburn completed their around-the-world helicopter flight when they landed at their starting point in Dallas, Texas. They had flown the LongRanger II more than 26,000 miles in 246.5 flight hours (8.5 hours per average) over 29 days, 3:08 hours. During the circumnavigation over twenty-six countries the helicopter burned 56,000 lbs. of jet fuel and made fifty-six fueling stops. Perot and Coburn were the 1983 recipients of the Langley Gold Medal from the Smithsonian Institution. On 15 November 1982, the *Spirit of Texas* was flown to Andrews AFB and donated to the National Air and Space Museum.

H. Ross Perot Jr. (L), Jay Coburn, and their Bell 206L-1 *LongRanger II*

1993: Distance without Landing

On 22 April 1995, Ron Williamson (USA) flew his 1,350 shp Bell UH-1H 1,976.05 miles from Oxnard, California, to Marietta, Georgia.

1994: Speed Around the World, Eastbound

Between 28 June and 22 July 1994, pilot Joe Ronald Bower (US), in a Bell JetRanger III powered by one 317 shp Allison 250-C20J engine, flew 23,800 miles in 24 days, 4:36 hours at an average speed of 40.99 mph.

1996: Speed Around the World, Westbound

Between 17 August and 3 September 1996, pilot Joe Ronald Bower (US) and co-pilot John Williams (US), in a Bell 430 powered by two 811 shp Allison 250-C40 engines, flew 23,600 miles at an average speed of 57.01 mph after 83 take-offs and landings requiring 17 days, 6:29 hours.

Joe Ronald Bower's Bell 430

2004: Speed Around the World, Eastbound

Between 4–21 June 2004, Simon Oliphant-Hope (UK) flew a Hughes HU50/MD 500E powered by a 412 shp Rolls-Royce from Shoreham, England, around the world in 17 days, 0:14 hours.

2006: Transcontinental Speed

On 9 August 2006, James Rodgers and Carl Nurmi (US) flew their Bell OH-58 Kiowa powered by a 317 shp Allison T 63 engine from San Diego, California, to Savannah, Georgia, at an average speed of 72.21 mph, covering 2,092 miles and setting a record for one-way at 28.47 hours.

2008: Kasprowicz and Sheik: Transcontinental Record

On 16 February 2008, Scott Kasprowicz and Steve Sheik (US) flew from New York to Los Angeles in 15:09:10 hours to set a new transcontinental helicopter speed record, averaging 161.8 mph. The pair left LaGuardia, New York, at 0412 EST and flew 2,462.3 statute miles, crossing the US and making six fuel stops before arriving at Los Angeles International Airport (LAX) at 1921 EST. The previous record set in 1985 was 19:00:15 hours.

2008: Kasprowicz and Sheik: Speed Around the World

Leaving on 7 August 2008, Scott Kasprowicz and Steve Sheik began their "Grand Adventure '08" to set an around-the-world speed record flying a factory standard Agusta Westland A109S Grand powered by two Pratt & Whitney PW207C Turboshaft engines from New York eastward via Europe, Russia, Alaska, and Canada, covering 23,068 miles at an average speed of 84.9 mph during a record 11 days, 7:02 hours, and breaking the previous record by four days during a trip that took them through eighteen countries, twenty-four time zones, and thirty states. From New York, the pilots flew across the far North Atlantic, over Greenland, Iceland, the Faeroe Islands, and then across Britain. Their flight from New York to London covered 3,969 miles and took 40:41 hours, breaking the trans-Atlantic helicopter record. Much of the route was flown through uncontrolled airspace, making navigation and weather monitoring particularly difficult for the seventy-eight stops for refueling and required maintenance checks and rest. After crossing Western and Central Europe they had to cross Russia's twelve time zones, encompassing one-sixth of the earth's land mass, much of which is sparsely populated and with little ground support available. After successfully crossing the most arduous and complicated portion of the flight, they finally crossed the Bering Strait into Alaska before flying over more helicopter-friendly North America.

Scott Kasprowicz (L) and Steve Sheik pose with their Agusta Westland A109S Grand.

THE PISTON RUTAN AND THE JET FOSSETT COMPOSITE AIRCRAFT SET DISTANCE RECORDS

Rutan: Model 76 Voyager

The Voyager, a unique, two-pilot aircraft, was constructed almost entirely of lightweight (¼ in.) sandwich graphite honeycomb and graphite fiber composite materials (ninety-eight percent of the aircraft). It had a wingspan of 110.8 ft. with a wing area of 363 sq. ft., was 29.2 ft. long, 10.3 ft. high, and weighed only 2,250 lbs. empty and had a gross weight of 9,695 lbs., most of which was fuel (72.3 percent of its gross take-off weight), plus the pilot's weight. Voyager was virtually a flying fuel tank, equipped with seventeen tanks: eight fuel storage tanks on each side of the aircraft and a fuel tank in the center. The pilot transferred fuel from tank to tank during the flight to maintain balance. Two engines, one at each end of the fuselage, powered the aircraft to a maximum speed of 122 mph over an unbelievable range of 25,000 miles and an endurance of 216 hours. The extremely efficient 110 hp liquid-cooled rear engine, a Teledyne Continental IOL-200, ran during the entire flight, except for four minutes when a fuel problem caused a temporary shutdown. The 130 hp air-cooled front engine, a Teledyne Continental o-240, was used for a total of 70:08 hours during the initial heavyweight stage of the flight, and while climbing over weather and at other critical times. These engines drove Hartzell constant-speed, variable-pitch aluminum propellers that were instrumental in giving the Voyager the range to set the record.

Rutan Model 76 Voyager

Fully loaded with fuel, the sleek white aircraft piloted by Dick Rutan and Jeana Yeager lifted from the 15,000 ft. runway at Edwards AFB, California, at 0801:44 on 14 December 1986, and returned nine days later at 0805:28 (216;03:44 hours) on 23 December, after flying 24,986 miles at an average speed of 116 mph. During the flight the pilot in the cockpit flew the aircraft, navigated, maintained ground communication, and transferred fuel to balance the Voyager. The other pilot in the cabin area rested, handled logistics support, and provided navigation and flight monitoring assistance. The flight broke Walter Lees' and Frederic Brossy's very long-standing piston-powered record of 84:32 hours set 25–28 May 1931. For their record breaking, unrefueled, non-stop piston-powered flight pilots Dick Rutan and Jeana Yeager, designer Burt Rutan, and crew chief Bruce Evans were awarded the Collier Trophy. The Voyager is now on display at the Smithsonian National Air and Space Museum.

Fossett: GlobalFlyer

Millionaire adventurers Steve Fossett and Richard Branson pooled their resources to design and build the jet-powered composite Virgin Atlantic GlobalFlyer designed by Burt Rutan. The aircraft had a wingspan of 114 ft., a length of 44.1 ft., a height of 13.3 ft., an empty weight of 3,700 lbs., and a gross weight of 22,100 lbs. Its skin was constructed of carbon fiber reinforced epoxy and Aramid honeycomb, permitting the storage of fuel in thirteen tanks comprising eighty-three precent of the take-off weight. The twin outboard tail booms mounted outboard of a shorter central fuselage nacelle contained large fuel tanks and ended in tail surfaces which were not cross-connected. The aircraft's main structural member was its high-aspect ratio single-spar 114 ft. span wing with an area of 400 sq. ft. The wings were constructed of high-strength composite materials. The single 2,300 lb. Williams FJ44-2 turbofan engine was mounted in an unusual position above the fuselage at a point several feet behind the cockpit, much like the Luftwaffe's Heinkel He 162 *Volksjager*. The single jet engine design was selected for its better reliability over piston engines driving propellers and for a quicker circumnavigation for the solo pilot. The turbofan was to carry the aircraft to a maximum speed of 296 mph over an enormous range of 25,766 miles at a service ceiling of 51,000 ft.

First Solo Circumnavigation

After solo test flights in Mojave, California, in January 2005 by Chief Engineer Jon Karkow and pilot Steve Fossett, the Virgin Atlantic GlobalFlyer was moved to Salina Municipal Airport, Kansas. Salina had recently lengthened its runway to 12,300 ft. to accommodate the fuel-ladened aircraft's anticipated long take-off roll on its attempt to be the world's first solo circumnavigation of the globe. The attempt had to be delayed until 28 February, to wait for a global weather forecast with good tailwinds and low turbulence for the delicate GlobalFlyer. A tailwind was crucial to complete the 36,787.559 km/22,858.729 mile (the length of the Tropic of Cancer) FAI requirement needed for the circumnavigation. Sitting in the small seven-foot pressurized cockpit, Fossett lifted the GlobalFlyer off the runway and headed east. The GlobalFlyer plan was to carry only enough fuel to complete the flight, but a design fault in the fuel venting system caused the loss of about 2,600 lbs. of fuel early in the flight. Fossett and his mission control had to decide whether to terminate the flight and land when it approached Japan. Fossett decided to postpone the final decision until he neared Hawaii, by which time favorable winds appeared and the decision to complete the circumnavigation was made. The GlobalFlyer landed in Salina mid-afternoon on 3 March 2005, having completed its circumnavigation in two days, 19:01:46 hours (67:01:46 hours) for the fastest around-the-world trip in its class at a speed of 344 mph. The distance flown was calculated at 36,912 km/22,936 miles and barely surpassed the minimum distance required by 125 km/78 miles.

Second Solo Circumnavigation

The next year Steve Fossett planned a second circumnavigation to break the Absolute Distance without Landing Record for airplanes, and to exceed the longest distance by any kind of aircraft, which was set by the round-the-world balloon flight of Bertrand Piccard and Brian Jones in 1999. At noon on 8 February 2006, Fossett flew eastbound from Kennedy Space Center and had a relatively uneventful flight until he was about to land at his record-setting destination, Bournemouth Airport, England. Fossett declared an emergency and diverted because the GlobalFlyer suffered generator failure at 40,000 ft., giving him only about twenty-five minutes until his batteries were exhausted and causing the loss of all electrical power. The GlobalFlyer was also running low on fuel. As Fossett descended to land ice formed on the inside of the canopy, obstructing his view. Then "touching" down, he discovered that one tire was flat from the take-off roll and the remaining main tire burst due to frozen brakes. Despite these problems Fossett was able to land safely with little damage, but with only 200 lbs. of fuel remaining. The flight had a duration of 76:45 hours and an official distance of 25,766 miles (41,467 km) that set a new record for the longest aircraft flight in history, breaking the old records of 24,987 miles (40,212 km) in an airplane and 25,360 miles (40,814 km) in a balloon.

Absolute Distance Over a Closed Circuit Record

The Absolute Distance Over a Closed Circuit was the last record Fossett and the GlobalFlyer would attempt to break. The definition for a Closed Circuit record is the aircraft is required to take off and land at the same location and the distance has to be measured over verifiable waypoints. Dick Rutan and Jeana Yeager had previously flown the Voyager around the world in 1986, so Fossett needed a longer closed circuit course to break their record. Fossett took off from Salina, Kansas, on 14 March 2006, and flew eastward; once over Japan he diverted south and then flew along the Equator, maximizing his distance while crossing the Pacific Ocean. He landed back in Salina on 17 March after flying 25,294 miles (40,707 km) to set a new Absolute Distance Over a Closed Circuit Record. The GlobalFlyer is now on permanent display at the Smithsonian Institution National Air and Space Museum Steven F. Udvar-Hazy Center.

Virgin Atlantic *GlobalFlyer*

SOLAR-POWERED AIRCRAFT

Gossamer Penguin

Gossamer Penguin

The Gossamer Penguin was a solar-powered experimental ¾ scale version of Paul MacCready's AeroVironment Gossamer Albatross II (see Human-Powered Aircraft) and was sponsored by DuPont in exchange for the advertising value of using its lightweight materials with very high strength to weight ratios, including Kevlar, Nomex, Delrin, Teflon, and Mylar. It had a 71 ft. wingspan and a weight without pilot of only 68 lbs. The power plant was an AstroFlight Astro-40 electric motor designed by Robert Boucher and driven by a 541 watt solar panel consisting of 3,920 solar cells. The Penguin was so fragile and difficult to control that flight was limited to the calmest of conditions, usually occurring just after dawn. Unfortunately, the low angle of the morning sun limited the amount of energy falling on the flat wing surface solar cells, which had to be mounted upright on a tilting panel to keep the cells perpendicular to the sun. The test pilot for initial flights was MacCready's thirteen-year-old son Marshall, who weighed 80 lbs. The official pilot for the project was Janice Brown, a charter pilot with commercial, instrument, and glider ratings who weighed slightly less than 100 lbs. and flew the Penguin approximately forty times before flying it 1.95 miles in 14:21 minutes during its public demonstration at NASA's Dryden Flight Research Center, California, on 7 August 1980.

Solar Challenger

The Solar Challenger, also designed by Paul MacCready and sponsored by DuPont, was to be a more robust, powerful, and more maneuverable improvement on the Gossamer Penguin, and was to be able to endure sustained high altitude flight (as much as 12,000 ft.) and normal turbulence. It was more than three times as heavy as the Penguin at 198 lbs. (without pilot) and had a shorter wingspan (47 ft.), but was proportionately more powerful. The electricity was supplied by 16,128 PV solar cells providing 2,600 watts of power that were installed directly to the wing and large horizontal stabilizer, both of which had to be flat on top to accommodate them. The solar cells turned two 3 hp AstroFlight motors, each three inches wide and seventeen inches long, operating in tandem on a common shaft to drive a single, controllable-pitch propeller. On 7 July 1981, the aircraft, piloted by Steve Ptacek, flew 163 miles from Pontoise-Cormeilles Aerodrome, north of Paris, to RAF Manston, United Kingdom, remaining aloft 5:23 hours. The Challenger is currently owned by the Smithsonian Institution's Air and Space Museum.

Solar Challenger

Solar Impulse

The first flights of Solar Impulse I took place in mid-2009; on 5 June 2012, it successfully completed its first intercontinental flight, a nineteen-hour trip from Madrid, Spain, to Rabat, Morocco. On 3 May 2013, the aircraft began its cross-US flight with a journey from Moffett Field, California, to John F. Kennedy International Airport, New York, on 6 July. Each flight leg was flown between nineteen and twenty-five hours, with multi-day stops in each city between flights.

Construction of the second Solar Impulse aircraft began in 2011 with completion initially planned for 2013 and a twenty-five-day circumnavigation of the earth planned for 2014. A structural failure of the aircraft's main spar occurred during static tests in July 2012, causing delays in the flight testing schedule for repairs. Solar Impulse 2's first flight occurred at Payerne, Switzerland, aerodrome on 2 June 2014; the first night flight was completed on 26 October 2014; and the aircraft reached its maximum altitude during a flight on 28 October 2014. The solar-powered, carbon fiber aircraft "has the wingspan of a Boeing 747 (236 ft.) but weighs as much as the family car (5,070 lbs. empty)," and is propelled by lithium batteries recharged by 17,000 solar cells placed on top of the wing and tail that drive the aircraft at 28 mph cruise and 56 mph maximum speed. It features a larger, non-pressurized cockpit and advanced avionics, including an autopilot to allow for multi-day transcontinental and trans-oceanic flights. Supplemental oxygen and various other environmental support systems allow the pilot to cruise at an altitude of 39,000 ft.

Solar Impulse 2: Successful Solar Around-the-World Flight

The repair work to the aircraft's main spar delayed Solar Impulse 2's circumnavigation of the globe from 2012 until March 2015. The aircraft was delivered to Masdar, in Abu Dhabi, for the World Future Energy Summit in late January 2015, and it began the journey from Al Bateen Executive Airport on 9 March 2015, and was scheduled to return to the same location August 2015, via a route entirely over the Northern Hemisphere. A mission control center for the circumnavigation was established in Monaco using satellite links to gather real-time flight telemetry and remaining in constant contact with the aircraft and the support team.

Twelve stops were originally planned along the route, with pilots Swiss aeronaut Bertrand Piccard—who co-piloted the first balloon to circle the world non-stop—and Swiss businessman Andre Borschberg alternating; at each stop, the crew awaited good weather conditions along the next leg of the route. For most of its time airborne Solar Impulse 2 cruised at a ground speed of between 31 and 62 mph, usually at the slower end of that range at night to save power. Legs of the flight crossing the Pacific and Atlantic Oceans were the longest stages of the circumnavigation, requiring as many as five days and nights. On multi-day flights the pilots took twenty-minute naps and used yoga or other exercises to promote blood flow and maintain alertness.

By the end of May 2015, the aircraft had traversed Asia, but made an unscheduled stop in Japan to await favorable weather over the Pacific, adding an additional thirteenth leg to the journey. With Borschberg in the cockpit, the aircraft began the flight from Japan to Hawaii on 28 June 2015, and arrived in Hawaii on 3 July, setting new records for the world's longest solar-powered flight by time (117 hours, 52 minutes) and distance (4,481 miles). The flight's duration was also a record for longest solo flight by time for any aircraft. During that leg the batteries were damaged by overheating, as they were packed in too much insulation. New batteries were ordered, but it was late in the year when days became shorter in the Northern Hemisphere, grounding the Impulse 2 in Hawaii. The US Department of Transportation stored the aircraft in a hangar at Kalaeloa Airport on Oahu.

New batteries were installed and test flights began in February 2016, to prepare for resumption of the circumnavigation once days in the Northern Hemisphere lengthened enough to permit multi-day solar-powered flights. A favorable weather window

Solar Impulse 2

opened in April 2016, and the journey was resumed, landing at Moffett Field, California, on 23 April. During that flight Piccard, via a live video link, spoke with the United Nations general assembly, commenting on that day's historic signing of the Paris Agreement and discussing how using clean technologies can create jobs and fight global warming. Additional legs of the flight were added in the US, flying to Phoenix, Arizona; Tulsa, Oklahoma; aviation-historic Dayton, Ohio; Lehigh Valley, Pennsylvania; and New York City, arriving there on 11 June 2016.

Piccard piloted the aircraft across the Atlantic Ocean, arriving in Seville, Spain, on 23 June, with the next stop in Cairo, Egypt, on 13 July, and landed in Abu Dhabi on 26 July, completing the around-the-world trip in seventeen stages and 16½ months; it was the first circumnavigation of the Earth by a piloted fixed-wing aircraft using only solar power.

HUMAN-POWERED AIRCRAFT

Gossamer Condor

The Gossamer Condor, created by noted American aeronautics engineer, designer, and world soaring champion Paul MacCready and Peter Lissaman of AeroVironment, was the first human-powered aircraft capable of controlled and sustained flight. At the time MacCready was $100,000 in debt after guaranteeing a loan in 1970 to his brother-in-law, who had developed a scheme for manufacturing fiberglass catamaran sailboats. Wanting to get out of debt, MacCready recollected an eighteen-year-old challenge conceived by British industrialist Henry Kremer in 1959, offering £50,000 to the first group that could fly a human-powered aircraft over a figure-eight course covering 1.15 miles that included a ten foot pole that the aircraft had to fly over at the start and the finish.

Early attempts to build human-powered aircraft had concentrated on wooden designs, which were too heavy. In 1961, Southampton University's Man Powered Aircraft (SUMPAC) took off at Lasham Airfield on 9 November, piloted by Derek Piggott, who flew 2,145 ft. (650 m). A week later, on 16 November, the Hatfield Puffin flew for 2,996 ft. (908 m), but was too difficult to turn. In June 1972, the Jupiter flew 4,089 ft. (1,239 m). The Nihon Stork B flew over 1.6 miles (2,000 m) in 1976 without making sufficient turns. In the early 1970s, Drs. MacCready and Lissaman of AeroVironment Inc. designed the unconventional Gossamer Condor using hang glider concepts, increasing wing area so that the drag of the wire bracing needed would be reduced. The Gossamer Condor was built around a large wing with a gondola underneath for the pilot and a canard control surface on a fuselage extension in front, and was mostly built of lightweight plastics with aluminum spars. The canard configuration, using a large horizontal stabilizer forward of the wing, was similar to the Wright brothers' successful Flyer. The first version, known as the Pasadena Version, was a proof-of-concept aircraft which flew only once in the parking lot of the Rose Bowl in Pasadena. The first aircraft carrying the name Gossamer Condor, known as the Mojave Version, was flown at Mojave Airport by MacCready's sons on 26 December 1976. The record breaking version, known as the Shafter Version, included improvements allowing the aircraft to fly long distances, as well as maneuver. The aircraft, piloted by amateur cyclist and hang glider pilot Bryan Allen, won the first Kremer prize on 23 August 1977, by completing a figure-eight course specified by the Royal Aeronautical Society at Minter Field, Shafter, California. The Condor is on display at the Smithsonian National Air and Space Museum.

Gossamer Condor

Gossamer Albatross

The Gossamer Albatross was the second human-powered aircraft designed and built by AeroVironment's Paul MacCready, this time as a response to the second £100,000 Kremer challenge to be awarded for a flight across the English Channel to mark Louis Bleriot's cross-Channel flight seventy years earlier. The Gossamer Albatross was similar to the Condor, constructed with a carbon fiber frame, with the wings rib fabricated from expanded polystyrene and the entire structure wrapped in a thin, transparent Mylar plastic. The aircraft was powered using pedals to drive a large two-bladed propeller. The Albatross had very long tapering high aspect ratio wings like those of a glider, which supposedly required a minimum of peddling power to maintain the seventy-one pound aircraft in flight.

On 12 June 1979, amateur cyclist and pilot Bryan Allen powered the Albatross to the rehearsed speed of seventy-five revolutions per minute and took off from a point near Folkestone, England, under ideal, windless conditions. Soon problems began. Allen's radio malfunctioned and he was only able to communicate with the escorting boats via hand and head movements. Next, the Albatross met unexpected, slowing headwinds and Allen's water supply ran out, as it was intended for two hours flight, and Allen suffered from dehydration and leg cramps. The time extension affected the onboard instruments supplied by batteries (the airspeed instruments and acoustic altimeter), so Allen no longer knew his height or airspeed. The headwinds increased, causing concern that the flight would have to be aborted with the Albatross secured to an escorting vessel. Allen increased his altitude, found less turbulence, and continued to pedal doggedly toward France, requesting to be allowed five more minutes of peddling, and then another five minutes, and as the surface wind calmed Allen asked for another five minutes. The exhausted Allen peddled for twelve five-minute segments and finally landed on a beach at Cape Gris-Nez, completing the 22.2 mile crossing in 2:49 hours and achieving a maximum speed of 18 mph and an average altitude of five feet.

The Albatross II was built as a backup to the record breaking Albatross, and except for some minor design changes was identical to the Channel-crossing Albatross. The Albatross II later took part in NASA-funded low speed stability tests and was the first human-powered aircraft to make a controlled flight inside an enclosed structure, the Houston Astrodome. The Gossamer Albatross, conceived and built by Paul MacReady, is on display at the National Air and Space Museum in Washington, DC, while the Gossamer Albatross II is on display at the Museum of Flight in Seattle, Washington.

Gossamer Albatross II

MIT Daedalus

The MIT Aeronautics and Astronautics Department's Daedalus was a human-powered aircraft that on 23 April 1988, flew a distance of 71.5 miles in 3:54 hours from Iraklion, Crete, to Santorini. The flight holds official FAI world records for total distance, straight-line distance, and duration for human-powered aircraft. The craft was named after the mythological inventor of aviation, Icarus' father Daedalus, who escaped from Crete using wings. Three aircraft (Light Eagle, Daedalus 87, and Daedalus 88) were constructed at the MIT Lincoln Lab Flight Facility at Hanscom Field, outside Boston, Massachusetts, by a team of undergraduate students, faculty, and recent MIT graduates.

Under the leadership of graduate student John Langford, the project began as a partnership between MIT and the Smithsonian Institution's National Air and Space Museum. Following a successful feasibility study, the 92 lb. Light Eagle (originally Michelob Light Eagle) prototype was built and tested at Lincoln Laboratory's Flight Test Facility and the NASA Dryden Flight Research Center. Pilots Lois McCallin and Glenn Tremml set four world records for human-powered flight in January 1987 at Edwards AFB. Tremml set a closed-course distance record, while on 22 January 1987, the Light Eagle, powered by Lois McCallin, set the straight distance, the distance around a closed circuit, and the duration world records for the female division in human powered vehicles.

With support from United Technologies and other concerns, both Daedalus aircraft were constructed with a framework of carbon fiber tubes. Airfoil shape for the wing and tail elements was maintained with a thin polystyrene foam leading edge, polystyrene ribs, and a Kevlar trailing edge. Wing skin was a Mylar plastic approximately 0.3 mil thick. The bottom of the fuselage and the majority of the pilot seat were also made of Kevlar. Horizontal and vertical stabilizers were "all moving" control surfaces. Daedalus 87 and Daedalus 88 both had a wingspan of 111.5 ft. and a wing area of 322.8 sq. ft., a length of 28.2 ft., an empty weight of 70 lbs., and a loaded weight of 230 lbs.

Daedalus 87 crashed during testing at Rogers Dry Lake (NASA Dryden Flight Research Center) on 17 February 1988 and was rebuilt as a backup. After the crash the Daedalus 88, which later set the world record, was shipped from MIT to continue the 87's research flights, and for general checkout procedures. Due to the accident, flight testing was extended four weeks and ended in mid-March 1988, after having achieved the major objectives of the program. The information obtained had direct applications to the later design of many high-altitude, long endurance aircraft.

After completing its tests as Daedalus 87's substitute, Daedalus 88 was shipped to Greece to recreate the mythological flight of the craft's namesake from Crete to Santorini. Piloted by Greek Olympic cycling champion Kanellos Kanellopoulos, Daedalus 88 flew seventy-four miles from the main airport in Iraklion, Crete, with a horizontal launch under the pilot's own power as governed by FAI rules. During the flight the Daedalus flew mostly between fifteen and thirty feet in altitude and was accompanied by several escort vessels. A tailwind aided the aircraft's crossing, but also made a head-on landing approach to the narrow beach hazardous, especially with throngs of spectators there. The pilot maneuvered the aircraft to land more into the wind and parallel with the length of the beach.

As the right wing extended over the beach, the heat rising from the beach lifted that wing and swung the aircraft back toward the sea, and the Daedalus headed about twenty-five feet off shore. Then increasingly gusty winds caused a torsional failure of the tail boom, and lacking control, the airplane pitched nose-up; another gust caused a failure of the main wing spar and the pilot swam to shore. Pieces of Daedalus 88 are now in storage at the Smithsonian's restoration facility.

MIT *Daedalus*

ORNITHOPTERS: MANNED WING-FLAPPING AIRCRAFT

There are two types of manned ornithopters: human muscle-powered and engine powered. People often associate the ornithopter with Leonardo da Vinci, the true Renaissance Man who sketched some ideas for wing-flapping machines, or Icarus, the son of master craftsman Daedalus, who attempted to escape from Crete by means of wings that his father fashioned from feathers and wax to fit over his arms.

About 1894, Otto Lilienthal also studied bird flight and constructed an ornithopter, but its complete development was prevented by his untimely death in a glider accident.

In 1929, a man-powered ornithopter designed by Alexander Lippisch flew a distance of 800 to 1,000 ft. using an aircraft tow launch, leading to speculation that his ornithopter did not fly on its own, instead making an extended glide. Most of the subsequent human-powered ornithopters likewise used a tow launch and flights were brief simply because human muscle power diminishes rapidly over time.

In 1942, Adalbert Schmid built an ornithopter that weighed 135 lbs. with combined fixed and flapping wings. The larger fixed wingspan was 41.6 ft., and each human-powered flapper was 10.5 ft. long. Only the powered flappers enabled lift for the fixed surfaces, while the larger wings acted as stabilizers. Unlike the conventional up-and-down flapping movement preferred by other ornithopter designers, Schmid selected a rotary movement that imitated a bird's wing upstroke. Schmid's ornithopter flew on 26 June 1942, outside Munich. After being towed aloft it travelled a distance of about 3,000 ft. while maintaining a height of sixty-five feet throughout most of the flight. The deteriorating war situation in Germany caused the Nazis to deem his ornithopter as having no military value and Schmid was forced to abandon his tests. During 1947, Schmid modified a two-seat Grunau-Baby sailplane with flapping outer wing sections and installed a 3 hp Sachs motorcycle engine to power the flappers. This ornithopter was capable of flying for as long as fifteen minutes. Using a 10 hp engine, the craft was capable of speeds estimated at 60–75 mph (120 kph).

Adalbert Schmid's Ornithopter

In the mid-1990s, Russian Vladimir Toporov tested a human-powered ornithopter with four flapping wings that showed with much greater wing area it was possible to greatly reduce the ornithopter's body oscillation, an important step toward a practical manned aircraft.

Yves Rousseau attempted his first human-powered ornithopter flight with flapping wings in 1995, and finally, on 20 April 2006, on his 212th attempt, he succeeded in flying 211 ft. observed by officials of the Aero Club de France. Unfortunately, on his 213th attempt a gust of wind caused a wing to fracture, resulting in Rousseau being gravely injured and becoming a paraplegic.

Yves Rousseau's Ornithopter

On 2 August 2010, University of Toronto graduate students Todd Reichert and Cameron Robertson flew their ornithopter *Snowbird* to a record 476 ft. at about 10 ft. altitude at an average speed of 16.5 mph at the Great Lakes Gliding Club in Tottenham, Ontario. The Snowbird weighed only 94 lbs. and had a wingspan of 105 ft., being built from kevlar, foam, and balsa wood. Reichert, the pilot, lost 17 lbs. while maintaining a special diet during a strin-

Snowbird Ornithopter

gent daily training regimen. Snowbird was towed aloft by an automobile, after which the pilot turned a set of pedals with his feet, causing the wings to flap. Unlike previous attempts, the Canadian group was able to provide telemetry data to prove that their craft actually flew under its own power.

TRIVIA: LONGEST TIME IN THE AIR FOR AN UNMANNED FOLDED PAPER AIRPLANE

On 19 December 2010, Takuo Toda threw a paper airplane into the air in Hiroshima, Japan, and it landed 29.2 seconds later.

AIRCRAFT WITHOUT ENGINES

BALLOONS: HOT AIR AND HELIUM

Notable Balloon Flights 1709–1914

1709: 8 August: First recorded balloon flight: Bartolomeu de Gusmão, in a balloon filled with heated air at the hall of the Casa da India in Lisbon.

1783: 21 November: First recorded manned flight: Jean-François de Rozier and Marquis d'Arlandes piloted a hot air balloon (built by the Montgolfier brothers) from the Chateau de la Muette to the Butte-aux-Cailles, Paris. This was the first free manned flight; de Rozier had flown in a tethered balloon on 15 October 1783.

1783: 1 December: First manned gas balloon flight: Professor Jacques Charles and Nicolas-Louis Robert flew from Paris to Nesles-la-Vallée in a hydrogen filled balloon.

1784: 20 May: First women in a flight: The Marchioness and Countess of Montalembert, the Countess of Podenas, and Miss de Lagarde ascended in a tethered balloon over Paris.

1784: 4 June: First woman in an untethered balloon: Elizabeth Thible flew over Lyon, singing arias to entertain Gustav III of Sweden.

1784: 23 June: Jean Pilare de Roziere and L. J. Proust (France), first flight to exceed 50 km (thirty-one miles).

1784: 19 September: Marie-Noel Robert and Anne-Jean Robert (France), first flight to exceed 100 km (186 km/116 miles)

1785: 7 January: French aeronaut Jean-Pierre Blanchard and American John Jeffries successfully crossed the English Channel for the first time, taking about 2½ hours flying from Dover Castle to Guines. Blanchard was awarded a substantial pension by Louis XVI for the flight.

Jean-Pierre Blanchard and John Jeffries

1785: 15 June: Jean Roziere and his companion, Pierre Romain, died when their balloon crashed in the Pas-de-Calais during an attempt to fly across the English Channel, becoming the first known fatalities in an air crash. For the Channel crossing, Roziere's *Montgolfier* balloon would require large stores of fuel for hot air and he developed the Roziere Balloon, which was a combination hydrogen and hot air balloon. The modern hybrid gas and hot air balloon is named the Roziere Balloon after his pioneering design.

Jean Pilare de Roziere

1785: 26 August: Jean-Pierre Blanchard and Chevalier de Lepinard (France) first flight to exceed 200 km (124 miles).

1803: 4 October: Andre-Jacques Garnerin and M. Aubert (France) first flight to exceed 300 km (186 miles).

1805: 18 August: First woman to pilot her own balloon: Sophie Blanchard flew solo from the garden of the Cloister of the Jacobins in Toulouse.

1835: 8 April: Richard Clayton (US) first flight to exceed 500 km (311 miles).

1836: 7 November: Englishman Charles Green flew with passengers in the Great Balloon of Nassau 800 km (500 miles) from London to Weilburg, in Germany, in 18 hours, which involved flying throughout the night over France and Belgium. Green pioneered the use of coal gas (methane) to inflate his balloon and took thousands of passengers aloft without an accident.

1849: 2 September: Francisque Arban (France) crossed the Alps by hydrogen balloon, a feat that was not repeated until 1924.

1852: 24 September: First successful steerable powered balloon: The Giffard dirigible was invented by Henri Giffard, who piloted it from the Hippodrome in Paris to Trappes.

1859: July 1: John Wise and John LaMountain fly from St. Louis to Henderson, New York, about 1,300 km (800 miles).

1900: 9–10 October: The Aero-Club de France held a long-distance balloon race coinciding with the World's Fair and Olympic Games in Paris. Six balloon teams competed for the Grand Prix, including that of the Comte Henri de la Vaulx and Comte de Castillon de Saint-Victor, co-founders along with several others, including writer Jules Verne. The two Comtes flew 1,193 miles in 36.75 hours from Vincennes, France, to near Kiev, Russia (to be the longest balloon flight recorded until 1912). He received the 1900 Grand Medal of the Aero Club of France for exceptional contributions to the progress of aviation.

1905: Jacques Faure and his cousin Hubert Latham flew from London to Paris by balloon. Faure had originally intended to steer the balloon (the Aero-Club 2) with twin propellers and a 7 hp engine, but made a free flight instead under a 4,650 cubic foot envelope. The two aeronauts left Crystal Palace at 1845 on 11 February, and threw out ballast over Hastings at 0800 to climb to 3,000 ft. for the Channel crossing; they crossed on to the French side of the Channel at Dieppe at 2200, and seeing the lights of Paris on the horizon, they landed at Saint Denis at about 0100, after about six hours in the air.

Aero-Club de France long-distance balloon race of 1900

1906 and 1907: On 3 February 1906, balloonist C.F. Pollock with Mr. Dale, a fellow member of the Aero Club, crossed the English Channel from Britain to continental Europe. Although flown in winter weather, winter's north winds made the flight from England possible. Pollock flew from Wandsworth in a balloon called *Vivienne III* to the French coast near Dieppe in 3:20 hours. The next year, he repeated the performance by piloting the Hon. Mrs. Harbord in her balloon, *Nebia*, on 21 February 1907, from Chelsea to Stavelot, in Belgium, taking more than hours. On both flights the aeronauts landed in violent snowstorms.

1906: The first Gordon Bennett Balloon Race was held under the patronage of the Aero-Club. These annual races were sponsored by American newspaper tycoon James Gordon Bennett Jr. This was not the first competition Bennett had sponsored, as there had already been Gordon Bennett steamboat, horse, and motor races, and in 1908, Bennett would add airplanes to the list. The rules of the Coupe Aeronautique Gordon Bennett were simple. The race would be won by the balloon that traveled the farthest distance from the starting point and then next year's race would be held in the winner's home country. The inaugural race was held on 30 September 1906, from the Tuilleries Gardens in the center of Paris, and 200,000 watched an American balloon flown by Frank Lahm (pilot) and Henry Hersey (co-pilot) as it lifted off to fly 402 miles in 22:15 hours from Paris to the north of England. The longest duration was 73 hours set in 1908 by Swiss Col. Theodor Schaeck and Lt.Col. Emil Messner in the balloon *Helvetia*, which was a world record for sports balloons, with 48 of the 73 hours spent over the North Sea. This time was unbeaten until 1995, when another Gordon Bennett team led by Wilhelm Elmers (Germany) remained aloft for 92 hours. By 1909, the race became so popular that 400,000 spectators again watched from Tuilleries. In 1910, the race was held in St. Louis, Missouri, with the winners flying 1,173 miles to northern Quebec. After landing it took the winning pilots four days to hike back to civilization. The Bennett Balloon Race continued 1906–1938, but was interrupted by WWI and not run in 1931, then was suspended in 1939 by WWII. The race was not resumed until 1979, when American Thoma Heinsheimer, an atmospheric physicist, was authorized to host the race. The record time is held by Wilhelm Elmers and Bernd Landsmann (Germany), who remained aloft for more than 92 hours in 1995, taking off from Switzerland and landing four days later in Latvia. The distance record is held by Robert Berben and Benoit Simeons (Belgium) in 2005, when they flew their balloon 3,400 km (2,100 miles) from Albuquerque, New Mexico, to Squatec, Quebec, Canada. The most successful pilot is Austrian Josef Starkbaum, who won the trophy seven times between 1985 and 1993, while American teams have the most victories with twelve.

Bennett Balloon Trophy

1907: 12 October: Augustus Gaudron crossed the North Sea in a hot air balloon named *Mammouth*, flying 1,160 km (721 miles) from the Crystal Palace, London, to Lake Vanern, Sweden.

1912: 7 January: Emile Dubonnet and Pierre Dupont (France) rose from near Bordeaux and landed the next day in Sokolowka, Western Russia (now Poland). His Condor III balloon had traveled 1,954 km (1,213 miles), beating the Comte de La Vaulx's existing 1900 record by only eighteen miles. Dubonnet was the son of the wealthy distiller Marius Dubonnet and had previously represented

France in the 1908, 1909, and 1911 Gordon-Bennett Cup balloon race.

1912: 19 October: Alfred Leblanc's (France) first flight to exceed 2,000 km (1,243 miles).

1912: 27 October: Maurice Bienaime (France) set a new distance record of 2,191km (1,361 miles) in the Bennett Race.

1913: 19–21 June: Rumpelmager and William Goldschmidt (Germany) flew 1,600 miles from Brenil, Germany, to Kharkoff, Russia.

1913: 13–17 December: Kaulen, Schmitz, and Kwefft (Germany) flew 1,756 miles from Saxony to the Ural Mountains, and also set the endurance record with 87 hours in the air.

1914: 10 February: Hans Rudolf Berliner, Alexander Haase, and A. Nicolai (Germany) first flight to exceed 3,000 km (1,864 miles).

1914: 8–10 February: German Aeronaut Hans Rudolph Berliner and passengers Alexander Haase and A. Nicolai departed Bitterfeld, Germany, aboard Berliner's hydrogen balloon *Berliner* and flew 1,897 miles in 47 hours across the Baltic Sea, into Russia, and over the Ural Mountains to about 110 miles from Perm, Russia. The Russian government accused the three Germans of espionage and sentenced them to six months solitary confinement and a fine. They were released on 8 May 1914, and allowed to return to Germany with their balloon. By the outbreak of WWI in August 1914, Germans had taken all the major balloon records from the French.

TRANS-ATLANTIC BALLOON ATTEMPTS

1873: *Daily Graphic*: Washington Donaldson, with Alfred Ford and George Lunt, took off from Brooklyn, New York, on 7 October 1873, purportedly to fly across the Atlantic, but flew about 45 miles before being forced down by a thunderstorm, landing in Connecticut. The flight of the mammoth, two-story balloon was sponsored by the newly established *Daily Graphic* newspaper as a publicity ploy.

1958: *Small World*: A group of four British balloonists (Colin Mudie, his wife Rosemary, Bushy Eiloart, and his son Tim) planned to use their sailing experience to cross the Atlantic under the patronage of the Duke of Edinburgh. Disregarding the traditional west to east route, they decided to take an east to west route, leaving from Tenerife, Canary Islands, and heading toward the central US East Coast. A 15 ft. × 8 ft. gondola (basket) was specifically designed made from reinforced polystyrene, and was attached to the envelope 46 ft. in diameter and containing 53,000 cubic ft. of hydrogen with quick release cables in case of an emergency. The *Small World* lifted off on 12 December 1958, and on the third day rose quickly in a thermal through mist and cold rain to 3,400 ft. before the release of gas sent them rushing down to bounce off the ocean. They traveled 1,200 nautical miles, breaking all balloon duration records, but despite being caught in a violent storm they floated another 1,450 miles and arrived in Barbados on 5 January 1959, as the first major crossing from east to west, though not to mainland North America.

Small World

1963: First "Modern" Hot Air Balloon Across the English Channel

On 13 April 1963, Americans Edward Yost and Donald Piccard completed the first flight across the English Channel in a hot air balloon in a government sponsored project to demonstrate the range and endurance capabilities of the hot air balloon, which was new at the time. Air traffic control did not allow them to cross the Channel at the shortest point near Calais, as there was too much air traffic there. Yost had twelve hours of fuel on board, which was calculated to be more than sufficient. They took off on 13 April 1963, despite unfavorable winds, because the KC-97 transport that carried the balloon from America to England was scheduled to pick them up in France the next day and return them to the US. After lift-off the winds at low altitudes pushed the balloon inland toward London. Yost took the balloon up to 13,500 ft., where he finally found winds heading toward France, despite never before flying the balloon above 3,000 feet. When he was ready to descend, he "turned off everything and screamed out of the sky." To slow his descent he intermittently used the single burner can, finally turning it on wide open at 1,500 ft. to make his final descent, which

The Channel Champ

happened to be Calais. The same balloon later won the Catalina Channel race and the balloon was subsequently named *The Channel Champ*.

Free Life

1968: *Mapleleaf*: Mark Winters and Jerry Kostur launched from Halifax, Nova Scotia, and ditched after flying about 70 miles.

1970: *Free Life*: In 1970, English balloon pioneer Malcolm Brighton and Americans Rodney Anderson and his wife, Pamela Brown, actress daughter of prominent Kentucky politician and attorney John Y. Brown Sr. and sister of Kentucky Fried Chicken entrepreneur and future Kentucky Governor John Y. Brown Jr., took off on 20 September 1970 from Springs, New York, in perfect weather. The Americans hired experienced English aeronaut Malcolm Brighton, who had built the *Bristol Belle*, the first modern hot air balloon in Europe. Thirty hours after launch a hot air mechanism designed to maintain the balloon's altitude at night failed, and when the balloon encountered a high-altitude cold front and a severe rainstorm, the *Free Life* was forced to ditch in the Atlantic, about sixty miles southeast of Newfoundland, radioing the message: "We are ditching, we request search and rescue." No bodies or wreckage were found during the search. The *Free Life* balloon was the first use of a Roziere-type balloon for a trans-Atlantic attempt built by Mark Semich, using a combination of helium and hot air. Below the spherical helium gas cell was a conical sleeve where air could be heated by burners in the same manner as a normal hot air balloon. By varying the hot air temperature, altitude could be maintained without having to release helium or to drop ballast. The burners were mainly used to compensate for the lack of solar heating at night.

1973: *Yankee Zephyr*: On 7 August 1973, Bobby Sparks set off from Bar Harbor, Maine, in the *Yankee Zephyr*, but the flight was terminated by a violent storm after twenty-three hours with Sparks rescued.

Col. Thomas Gatch

1974: *Light Heart*: *Light Heart* was constructed and flown by Col. Thomas Gatch, who intended to fly the Atlantic (solo) from Harrisburg, Pennsylvania, to "somewhere in Western Europe" in two days using the Jet Stream, flying at 39,000 ft. *Light Heart* took off on 18 February 1974, but Gatch reported that one of the ten helium balloons had burst during the ascent; the balloon was able to continue in this circumstance, being forced to jettison water ballast to continue climbing. Gatch maintained radio contact with passing airliners until the balloon drifted southward out of the main transatlantic airway route. A freighter last saw Gatch drifting 1,000 miles west of the Canary Islands toward Africa. The US Department of Defense and the Spanish Army in West Africa conducted extensive search operations both at sea off West Africa and over the Spanish Sahara, but no trace of Gatch was ever discovered.

1974: *Spirit of Man*: In 1974, the *Spirit of Man* suffered a gas envelope burst at 6,000 ft. over the Lakehurst, New Jersey, launch site, killing pilot Robert Berger.

1975: *Windborne*: Malcolm Forbes used design, planning, and money for his cluster of helium balloons, *Windborne*, on his Atlantic crossing attempt on 6 January 1975, accompanied by Tom Heinsheimer. The balloon became uncontrollable at take-off and the cluster of helium filled balloons was cut loose to save the pilots' lives.

1975: *Odyssey*: Undeterred by his first failure while flying the *Yankee Zephyr*, Bobby Sparks lifted off in the *Odyssey* on 21 August 1975. Unfortunately, he was accompanied by a stowaway—his chief ground crewman—who added unforeseen weight to the balloon, and after only two hours Sparks and his balloon were once again in the ocean!

1976: *Spirit of '76*: Karl Thomas obtained the *Odyssey's* recovered gondola and attached it to a nine-story-high, helium-filled envelope. On 25 June 1976, the *Spirit of '76*, named in honor of the American Bicentennial, lifted off from the Lakehurst, New Jersey, Naval Air Station with Thomas as its only passenger. For the first thirty-one hours the balloon drifted eastward, but 400 miles south of Newfoundland Thomas ran into violent thunderstorms and a vicious downdraft forced the *Spirit* into the Atlantic. After four days and nights Thomas was rescued from the sea by a Europe-bound Russian freighter which took him to Rotterdam.

1976: *Silver Fox*: On 6 October 1976, pioneer balloonist Edward Yost lifted off from Milbridge, Maine, in a helium balloon, *Silver Fox,* that he designed and built partly in his home garage. It featured a gondola that was shaped like a boat in case he was forced down at sea, which is indeed what happened. Although he had traveled far in excess of the distance needed to reach Europe from his launch point, his flight path began to head south rather than the hoped for easterly direction due to inaccurate weather forecasting. On 10 October 1976, after a flight of 107:37 hours covering a distance of 2,474 miles, the balloon landed in the Atlantic 200 miles east of the Azores and only 700 miles from the coast of Portugal, breaking the eighteen-year-old record set by the *Small World* and the closest to crossing the Atlantic thus far. Yost was one of modern ballooning's pioneers. In October 1955, he developed and flew the prototype of the modern hot air balloon in a tethered flight. The envelope was plastic film, and heat was provided by burning kerosene. On 22 October 1960, Yost made the first-ever free flight of a modern hot air balloon from Bruning, Nebraska, flying untethered for 1:35 hours. The hot air was generated by a propane burner that pushed hot air into the balloon's forty foot special heat-resistant fabric envelope. In 1963, after further refining and improving of designs and materials, Yost piloted the first modern balloon flight across the English Channel with crew member Don Piccard in a balloon later named the *Channel Champ.* In 1978, Ben Abruzzo, Maxie Anderson, and Larry Newman made the first complete crossing of the Atlantic in a balloon designed, built, and launched by Ed Yost.

Edward Yost

1977: *Double Eagle*: On 9 September 1977, the combined team of Maxie Anderson and Ben Abruzzo made their first attempt to cross the Atlantic, launching from Marshfield, Massachussetts. After being blown off course by stormy weather, the team was forced to ditch three miles off the coast of Iceland on 12 September, 65.5 hours after taking off some 2,950 miles before. They named their balloon the *Double Eagle* in honor of Charles Lindbergh, the first man to successfully fly solo across the Atlantic in 1927.

Double Eagle

1977: *Eagle*: The third Yost-built envelope to be used on an Atlantic crossing attempt lifted off from Bar Harbor, Maine, on 10 October 1977, piloted by Dewey Reinhard and Charles Stephenson. They only flew 220 miles in 46 hours before crashing in another storm.

1978: Zanussi: On 26 July 1978, Don Cameron and Christopher Davey left St. Johns, Newfoundland, and after flying 1,780 miles came closest to crossing the Atlantic in a balloon when a tear developed in their envelope, forcing them to ditch in the Bay of Biscay only 110 miles from France. They had planned another trans-Atlantic attempt, but canceled it when the *Double Eagle II* succeeded.

1978: *Double Eagle II*: First Successful Trans-Atlantic Balloon Flight. In 1978, designer Edward Yost built the *Double Eagle II* with a 160,000 cubic ft., helium-filled balloon that towered 112 ft. high and 65 ft. in diameter that supported a gondola, *The Spirit of Albuquerque*, that measured 15 × 7 × 4.5 ft. Anderson and Abruzzo added Larry Newman to the crew. They left Presque Isle, Maine, on 11 August 1978. The flight went well, except for early radio problems, and on 16 August atmospheric conditions forced the balloon to drop 19,500 ft. to its voyage low point of 3,500 ft. Careful ballasting and then the superheating from the sun that afternoon caused the balloon to rise to its highest point, 24,950 ft. As they approached the coast of Ireland they began jettisoning equipment, and once over France began to look for a landing area. After sailing 3,099 miles in 137:06 hours they set down in a barley field near Evreux. The gondola is displayed at the Steven F. Udvar-Hazy Center of the Smithsonian National Air and Space Museum annex at Washington Dulles

Double Eagle II

International Airport. Anderson was killed on 27 June 1983, near Bad Bruckenau, West Germany, when he was in the air with co-pilot Don Ida. Not wanting to wander across the East German border, Anderson attempted to release the gondola from the envelope at touchdown, but the bolts failed to fire and a gust re-lofted the gondola; when the explosive bolts went off Anderson and Ida were killed in the fall.

1984: Joseph Kittinger: Solo Trans-Atlantic Flight Helium Balloon

Joseph Kittinger certainly experienced the highs of ballooning. He completed five high altitude flights in stratospheric balloons while conducting tests in preparation for America's forthcoming space program. In 1957, as part of Project Manhigh, Kittinger set an interim balloon altitude record of 96,760 ft. in helium balloon *Manhigh I*. The 1958 Project Excelsior was established to study and resolve the problems involved in very high-altitude escapes from high-flying jet aircraft and possibly space capsules. As Excelsior test director, Kittinger personally investigated the use of a parachute for escape from a space capsule or high-altitude aircraft. During November and December 1959, he piloted balloons *Excelsior I* and *Excelsior II* to 76,000 ft. and parachuted back to earth. In 1960, he set two major aviation records. On 16 August 1960, Kittinger flew to 102,800 ft. in *Excelsior III* and jumped out; his freefall lasted for 4:36 minutes and approached the speed of sound at 614 mph before opening his parachute at 14,000 ft. after free-falling about 16 miles. His records for highest parachute jump and fastest velocity stood for fifty-two years, until they were broken in 2012 by Felix Baumgartner as part of the Red Bull Stratos Project. Kittinger advised Baumgartner on his 14 October 2012 free-fall from 128,100 ft. that reached 843.6 mph.

Joseph Kittinger parachutes from a then-record 102,800 ft.

Kittinger later served three combat tours of duty during Vietnam, flying 483 combat missions, and then he volunteered for a third tour. On this tour he was shot down over North Vietnam and held prisoner for eleven months in the infamous Hanoi Hilton. After his retirement from the Air Force in 1979 as a colonel, Kittinger's interest in ballooning continued. Kittinger was the first to make a solo gas balloon trans-Atlantic crossing. On 14–18 September 1984, he flew from Caribou, Maine, to the Italian Riviera near Savona, Italy, in the 105,944 cubic foot helium-filled *Rosie O'Grady's Balloon of Peace*. His trip covered 3,535 miles in 86 hours. He participated in the Gordon Bennett Cup in ballooning in 1989.

Joseph Kittinger with the Trans-Atlantic *Rosie O'Grady*

1987: Virgin Atlantic Flyer: First Trans-Atlantic Hot Air Balloon

On 2–3 July 1987, Richard Branson's *Virgin Atlantic Flyer* lifted off from Sugarloaf, Maine, headed for Limavady, Northern Ireland, to become the first and only hot air balloon to cross the Atlantic, covering 3,075 miles in 31:41 hours using the Jet Stream to become the fastest manned balloon with an average crossing speed of 97 mph and reaching a maximum speed of 153 mph. Problems for Branson and co-pilot Per Lindstrand arose just after take-off, when one of the six pairs of large external propane fuel tanks broke free and one of the packs of sandbags used to anchor the balloon was carried aloft, but was cut loose. The balloon climbed rapidly to its cruise altitude of 27,000 ft. and reached a maximum of 166 mph, breaking all the hot air speed records on its way to Ireland. The balloon descended over Ireland to jettison the three unused full fuel tanks, and as the balloon broke through the cloud cover at about 2,000 ft. Limavady was ahead. The balloon did not respond to the burners due to its massive envelope and hit the ground heavily; the three remaining fuel tanks weighing 5,000 lbs. broke free. The suddenly lighter balloon was propelled back into the sky and headed toward Scotland. Lindstrand fired the explosive bolts to release the uncontrollable envelope, but nothing happened, as the battery was depleted. Lindstrand jumped from the capsule into the sea and the lightened balloon took off again with Branson on board. The balloon descended again and went into the sea, where Branson was rescued by a helicopter that was then guided to Lindstrand.

1992: Chrysler Trans-Atlantic Race: Duration Record Broken

On 16 September 1992, five teams of American, British, German, Dutch, and Belgian balloonists took off from Bangor, Maine, during the night to race across the Atlantic. The Belgian team (Wim Verstraeten and Bertrand Piccard) finished first, flying over the coast of Portugal and landing in Peque, Spain, at 0348 on 22 September, after flying 114.5 hours at about 28 knots over 2,580 miles. They were followed

Virgin Atlantic Flyer

by the British team Donald Cameron and Robert Bayly, who landed on coastal Portugal. The American team Richard Abruzzo (Ben Abruzzo's son) and Troy Bradley landed near Casablanca, Morocco, after 145 hours, breaking Richard's father's record (with Larry Newman and Maxie Anderson) of 137:05 set in 1978. However, this record was not officially recognized by the FAI. In 2010, the bodies of American balloon team Richard Abruzzo and co-pilot Carol Davis were recovered two months after being lost on 29 September, in a fierce Adriatic Sea storm while participating in the fifty-fourth Gordon Bennett Gas Balloon Race.

1980: DOUBLE EAGLE IV SETS ENDURANCE RECORD

Double Eagle IV, piloted by Ben Abruzzo and Larry Newman, set a new world endurance record of 75:10 hours, leaving Taft, California, at 2115 on 26 April, and landing in Fountain Valley, California, at 0025 on 30 April, as part of the Gordon Bennett Balloon Race.

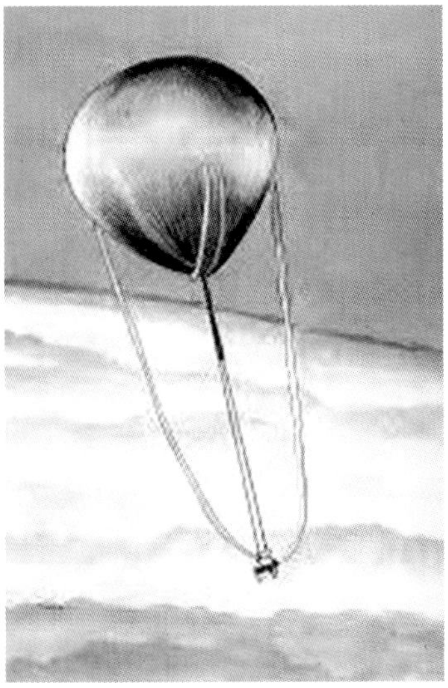
Kitty Hawk

1980: *KITTY HAWK:* FIRST TRANS-NORTH AMERICAN BALLOON FLIGHT

Maxie Anderson, along with his twenty-three-year-old son Kristian, made the first non-stop trans-North American balloon flight. The helium *Kitty Hawk* departed Fort Baker, California, 8 May 1980, and landed on 12 May in Sainte-Felicite, Quebec, after a journey of 2,823 miles that took just under one hundred hours. The *Kitty Hawk* sailed mostly at an altitude of 25,000 ft., with its pilots wearing oxygen masks. At that altitude the weather was mostly comfortable during the day, but was very cold at night; despite closed doors and a propane heater, the temperature inside the gondola often fell to minus thirty degrees at night.

TRANS-PACIFIC BALLOON RECORD BALLOON FLIGHTS

1981: Double Eagle V: First Trans-Pacific Balloon Flight

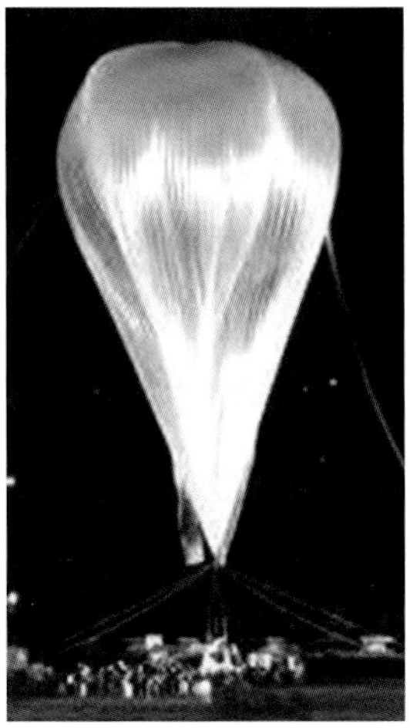
Double Eagle V

After winning the 1979 International Gordon Bennett Race in the *Double Eagle III* with Maxie Anderson, the next year Ben Abruzzo piloted the *Double Eagle IV* with Larry Newman to set a new world endurance record. *Double Eagle V* was the first balloon to complete a successful crossing of the Pacific Ocean, launching from Nagashima, Japan, on 10 November 1981, and landing in Mendocino National Forest, California, on 14 November in 84:31 hours, flying a record 5,768 miles. The four-man crew consisted of Albuquerque balloonists Ben Abruzzo, Larry Newman, and Ron Clark, and multi-millionaire adventurer/restauranteur (Benihana) Rocky Aoki, who helped fund the flight. Abruzzo and Newman had previously been two of the pilots of *Double Eagle II*, which in 1978, became the first balloon to cross the Atlantic. *Double Eagle V's* record did not draw the media attention the earlier flight did because it was overshadowed by the concurrent Space Shuttle mission.

1991: Virgin Pacific Flyer: First Trans-Pacific Hot Air Balloon

In January 1991, the *Virgin Pacific Flyer*—the largest hot air balloon ever built (2,600,300 cubic feet)—piloted by Per Lindstrand and Richard Branson, completed the longest flight in a lighter-than-air balloon in history when they flew 6,761 miles from the southern tip of Japan to Lac la Matre, Yukon, northwestern Canada, on 17 January 1991.

Their flight set two new world records for distance and duration, and they broke their own ground speed record, recording 245 mph. After ascending to the Jet Stream, half the fuel was lost by mistake and the balloon rose to 42,500 ft.—just below the maximum 43,000 ft., where the glass dome would explode, causing the crew's lungs to burst—but the balloon began to descend. The radio malfunctioned next and the weather closed in, obscuring vision. Soon the crew saw burning lumps of propane falling around the glass dome and realized they had to ascend quickly toward 43,000 ft. to deprive the fire of oxygen to put it out. They discovered the balloon was off course and headed north toward Canada instead of California, caught in the Jet Stream at 200 mph. They landed in the vast Yukon wilderness 300 miles from the nearest habitation and in extremely cold temperatures. After eight hours they were rescued to celebrate their new record.

Virgin Pacific Flyer: Richard Branson (L) and Per Lindstrand

Troy Bradley (L) and Leonid Tiukhtyae

2015: New Record Trans-Pacific Non-stop Balloon Flight

American Troy Bradley and Russian Leonid Tiukhtyae left Saga, Japan, on 26 January, in their gas balloon *Two Eagles*, and six days later they landed in Baja, California, just off western Mexico. They had traveled a record 6,646 miles and spent 161:17 hours aloft. The planned route was to take the pilots from Japan, across the Pacific Ocean, and toward the Pacific Northwest before they encountered shifting weather patterns that swept them south along the California coast toward a Mexican landing. Since they were flying at an altitude of at least 15,000 ft., they needed to wear oxygen masks and clothing to cope with the fifty degree capsule temperature. The balloon's capsule was 7 ft. long, 5 ft. wide, and 5 ft. tall, and contained sleeping bags, a small onboard heater, and a simple toilet. Their 6,646 mile flight broke the previous 1981 record of 5,208 miles for distance traveled by a gas balloon set by Ben Abuzzo's *Double Eagle V*. Their flight time of 161:17 hours broke the unofficial endurance record of 145 hours set by Richard Abruzzo and Troy Bradley in 1992 and the FAI record of 137:06 hours set by *Double Eagle II* flown by Maxie Anderson, Ben Abruzzo, and Larry Newman during their 1978 record trans-Atlantic flight.

FIRST AROUND-THE-WORLD BALLOON FLIGHT

Unsuccessful Attempts

Jules Verne: 12 January 1981: Maxie Anderson and Donald Ida launched from Luxor, Egypt, but the balloon steadily lost gas and landed in Hansa, India, 2,676 miles and 48 hours later.

Jules Verne: 20 December 1981: Maxie Anderson and Donald Ida continued their quest, launching near their previous landing spot, but their balloon developed an early serious leak that caused it to land after only 20 miles.

Jules Verne: 7 November 1982: Maxie Anderson and Don Ida made their third attempt, this time from Stratobowl, South Dakota, but the balloon again developed a leak and the flight was terminated after flying 1,162 miles, 16 hours before crossing the Atlantic.

Earthwinds: 13 January 1993: Larry Newman, Vladimir Dzhanibekov, and Don Moses launched from Stead Airfield, near Reno, Nevada, but after 30 minutes and seven miles, the flight was terminated when the lower ballast balloon was torn when the balloon did not clear a mountain top. The *Earthwinds* used a tandem balloon layout called the Sky Anchor system for a planned circumnavigation record attempt using the Jet Stream. This system was developed at Texas A&M University in 1976, and was usually used on unmanned balloons, but the concept was also applied to a piloted balloon. Sky Anchor is a system of two balloons in tandem, with a "zero pressure" lifting gas balloon tethered to a "superpressure balloon anchor." The gas balloon is filled with a lifting gas and provides buoyancy, while the superpressure balloon is filled with air and is pressurized to provide the desired ballast weight. The system was prone to frequent failures, as the tandem arrangement made launching difficult and its complexity led to in-flight failures.

Earthwinds

Earthwinds: 12 January 1994: Larry Newman, Richard Abruzzo, and David Melton took off from Stead Airfield on another circumnavigation attempt, but the flight ended because a valve in the lower ballast balloon froze after 202 miles and 6:54 hours.

Earthwinds: 31 December 1994: For the second time in a year Larry Newman, David Melton, and George Saad took off from Stead Airfield, but when they reached 31,000 ft., the ballast balloon burst after one hundred miles, four hours.

Earthwinds: 1 January 1995: Larry Newman, David Melton, and George Saad took off from Stead Airfield and the *Earthwind's* fifth abort was blamed on a failure of the lower ballast balloon.

Global Challenger: 15 January 1996: Steve Fossett's first around-the-world attempt encountered problems soon after take-off from Stratobowl, South Dakota, when the envelope's Mylar skin began to peel off; Fossett landed in Newfoundland after other problems developed two days later.

At the beginning of 1997, several balloon teams gathered at various launch sites in a race to become the first to circle the earth. Weather experts determined winter flights gave the advantage of faster Jet Streams and there were fewer thunderstorms and damaging winds.

Virgin Global Challenger: 7 January 1997: The *Challenger* was the largest balloon ever built, with a capacity of 1.1 million cubic feet and a height of 195 ft.; its gondola was large enough to support a crew of three in comfort. Richard Branson, Per Lindstrand, and Alex Ritchie were warned that after launching from Marrakech, Morocco, the ground crew had not unlocked fittings to the fuel tanks. Branson descended that night to depressurize and repair the problem, but was caught in a severe downdraft; to keep from crashing Branson depleted almost all the ballast and landed in Algeria after dawn after twenty hours in the air.

Breitling Orbiter I: 12 January 1997: Bertrand Piccard and Wim Verstraeten met problems soon after launching from Chateau d'Oex, Switzerland, when a simple metal hose clamp broke, leaking kerosene fumes into the gondola. The pilots decided to ditch into the Mediterranean, after which the envelope was jettisoned and the capsule and crew were towed to port.

Solo Spirit: 13 January 1997: Steve Fossett lifted off from Busch Stadium, St. Louis, Missouri, and traveled the longest distance of any previous attempt when he landed in Sultanpur, India, after 10,361 miles and 146:54 hours, setting new absolute balloon records for distance and duration. The *Solo Spirit* was a simpler and smaller 350,000 cubic foot balloon in which he could fly at about 20,000 ft. in an unpressurized gondola using portable oxygen supplies and wearing thermal underwear to keep warm, rather than air conditioning.

Virgin Global Challenger: 9 December 1997: Upon leaving Marrakech, Morocco, the Virgin crew ventured that they could attach the gondola to the inflated 195 ft. high envelope in negligible conditions, but the envelope broke its moorings and drifted away into Algerian airspace and crashed.

Solo Spirit: 31 December 1997: Steve Fossett took off from Busch Stadium, St. Louis, Missouri, on his third attempt and completed the fastest balloon crossing of the Atlantic, but was forced to dump one-tenth of his fuel to climb over bad weather. When trying to maneuver around the politics of Libya he lost the best weather track. After one of his burners and a heater malfunctioned he had no option but to put down in Russia near the Black Sea after flying 7,300 miles in 146:44 hours.

J. Renee: 31 December 1997, Kevin Uliassi launched from Rockford, Illinois, just hours after Fossett, but as soon as he reached 19,000 ft. the gas cell of his balloon ruptured and he was barely able to make a dramatic night landing aided by a helicopter and ground personnel.

Hilton Global Challenger: 9 January 1998: Dick Rutan and David Melton launched from Albuquerque, New Mexico, and when they reached their cruise altitude of about 29,000 ft., their gas cell—the same design as Uliassi's—ruptured. After two hours of discussions and deliberations the pilots bailed out, but after hitting the ground the balloon flew onward and eventually hit power lines and was destroyed in a fire north of Dallas, Texas.

Breitling Orbiter 2: 28 January 1998: Bertrand Piccard, Andy Elson, and Wim Verstraeten lifted off from Chateau d'Oex, Switzerland. During their voyage *Orbiter 2* encountered many problems. On the way over the Mediterranean, Elson made a daring repair on the outside of the capsule. The crew also had to ballast some fuel over water. On nearing China they were first denied permission to fly in that country's airspace and then the

Breitling Orbiter 2

balloon stalled in low winds. After China eventually granted permission *Orbiter 2* no longer had the necessary capability to circle the globe and landed in Thailand, setting a new duration record of 233:55 hours.

Solo Spirit: 7 August 1998: Fossett took off from a sport stadium near Mendoza, Argentina, for his fourth around-the-world attempt and the first Southern Hemisphere flight. Despite an early onboard fuel fire Fossett was able to continue over the Indian Ocean and then crossed Australia in record time, but the flight ended when the balloon was unable to climb over a thunderstorm and a ripped envelope caused a very hard water landing in the Coral Sea.

Solo Spirit

ICO Global Challenger: 18–25 December 1998: On 18 December, formidable balloon veterans Richard Branson, Per Lindstrand, and Steve Fossett took off from Marrakesh in the *ICO Global Challenger*, the best balloon that Branson's money could buy. The *ICO Global* was 160 ft. high and 120 ft. in diameter. The envelope was fabricated from tough aramid fabric panels joined with more than four miles of welds and coated in plastic to prevent helium escaping. The top of the balloon was white to control the sun's heat input and control the temperature of the helium. The cone was coated with a thin layer of reflective aluminum, keeping the heat of the burners sealed into the cone at night. The capsule was a pressurized and well-insulated aluminum cylinder almost 10 ft. in diameter and slightly more in height. The capsule was divided into two floors, with the three pilots' stations in the upper deck surrounded by a ring of small portholes. Each pilot had a comfortable seat facing computer screens and TV monitors fed by video cameras. On the lower deck there was a single sleeping bay, toilet, CD player, and video player. The flight progressed without much difficulty, except when they entered Tibetan air space without permission and then continued north over central China, explaining it was impossible to obey Chinese demands to land because of the high mountainous terrain. Then, on Christmas Day, the balloon was carried southward by a low pressure trough and missed the winds that would have carried the *Challenger* to the US West Coast. After discussions via satellite phone with the control center staff in Uxbridge, United Kingdom, the balloonists decided to "conduct a controlled sea landing" (ditch) in the sea near Hawaii. When the balloon landed in the water ten miles from Hawaii on Christmas Day, the mechanism that was to release the flying cables and separate the envelope from the capsule failed to function and the capsule was dragged along the ocean surface by 20 mph winds. Fortunately, the crew managed to escape and were rescued by the Coast Guard, but the gondola and envelope were lost at sea.

ICO *Global Challenger* crashes into the Pacific.

Cable & Wireless: February 1999: Andy Elson and Colin Prescot launched from Almeria, Spain, and broke the world endurance record, flying more than 12,000 miles from Spain, around China, to ditch in the Pacific after 17 days, 17 hours. Elson built and signed the *Cable & Wireless* balloon after being the designer and chief engineer of all the balloons and capsules for the American world record attempts, including Steve Fossett's. During the previous January Elson designed, built, and co-piloted the *Breitling Orbiter 2* (see previous). *Cable & Wireless'* envelope's skin was made from reinforced polyester film with a gross volume of more than one million cubic feet, most of which was used by the gas cell and only 24,000 cubic feet by the hot air cone. The bubble-like gondola was fabricated from special aluminum bonded in a honeycomb construction for added strength, with unique insulation that made the gondola resistant to fire. The high ceiling provided each pilot with his own bunk. There was a small galley with a special kettle for rehydrating food after the fresh food for the first four days was depleted

Cable and Wireless crashes into the Pacific.

and was replaced by dehydrated food. Eighty solar panels provided power for charging on-board batteries. Previously, Elson piloted the first balloon over Mount Everest, setting seven ballooning records, including the first balloon flight over the world's highest mountain, highest take-off by a balloon (15,000 ft.), and highest landing by a balloon (16,000 ft.). Elson was the pilot, project director, designer, and builder of *QinetiQ 1*, the mission designed to break the manned world altitude record, along with Colin Prescot. The attempt was originally planned for 2002, but unfavorable high altitude conditions halted several attempts. During 2003, the launch attempt was aborted due to a failure in the balloon and two years later the project was abandoned.

1999: *BREITLING ORBITER 3*: FIRST SUCCESSFUL AROUND-THE-WORLD FLIGHT

By 1999, the around-the-world prize was becoming the most sought after record in the ballooning world. The *Breitling Orbiter 3* was built by upgrading the balloons used on two previous attempts (*Breitling Orbiter 1* in 1997 and *Breitling Orbiter 2* in 1998). The Breitling team of pilots (Swiss Bertrand Piccard and Brit Brian Jones) developed dependable flight and living systems, and a plan in which they would guide their balloon up to altitudes of 36,000 ft., where Jet Stream winds would propel it across the Pacific and could average 100 mph. (Note: Bertrand Piccard is the grandson of Auguste Piccard, record setting balloonist and submersible research hydronaut, and the son of Jacques Piccard, who built and piloted a submersible that held the depth record of 35,815 ft.)

Breitling Orbiter 3 was a 180 ft. tall Roziere balloon combining the features of a hot air balloon and a gas balloon, with a helium cell inside the hot-air envelope. The helium cell was initially filled to approximately forty-seven percent of its maximum capacity and during ascent, warming by the sun caused the helium to expand even more than the surrounding air, which subsequently helped the balloon gain altitude. The two pilots lived inside a special Kevlar and carbon fiber gondola measuring 17.8 ft. long by 10.3 ft. high. After take-off the gondola was pressurized with a nitrogen-oxygen mixture to reduce the risk of fire, with enough reserves carried to repressurize the gondola four times. The forward cockpit contained the controls and instruments needed to monitor and control the balloon and various operating systems. The crew used satellite based systems to communicate and navigate. Solar panels under the gondola recharged the onboard lead batteries providing electrical power. The central portion of the cabin contained a single bunk and storage area with an inventive pressure operated toilet at the rear that was screened off with a curtain. Each pilot flew six hour shifts so that each was at the controls for part of the night, while the other was navigating or slept in a sleeping bag. The pilots were dressed in insulating synthetic fiber clothes suitable for the inside temperature of forty degrees (15°C). When it was time to sleep crew members removed some of their clothes before getting into the sleeping bag. Food for the twenty-plus day trip was "fresh items" for the first six to seven days, after which their diet was dried food. The gondola carried more than 200 liters of water.

The balloon took off from Chateau-d'Oex, in the Swiss Alps, on 1 March 1999, after which the pilots flew southwest to North Africa to meet a favorable Jet Stream flowing eastward, marking the official beginning flight the westernmost point the balloon reached before heading east. The pilot's first concern was to fly far enough south to avoid communist China's absolute non-fly-over air restrictions. Successfully evading Chinese air space, they maintained course, and after eleven days they reached the Pacific. They proceeded west uneventfully until they approached the Caribbean, where their balloon began to rapidly lose speed. Their only option was to use a huge amount of propane fuel to help them climb back up into the favorable west-to-east wind currents, which they accomplished. On 20 March, *Breitling Orbiter 3* crossed the last meridian as its lifting gas cooled and caused the balloon to descend slowly toward the ground in the direction of Libya, where a team was waiting to pick them up. Since they had more than a day's supply of propane fuel aboard they extended the flight toward the Nile desert, where they planned to set down near the pyramids, but the winds took them too far south. After 19 days and 2:55 hours in the air, they successfully landed in Mauritania, North Africa. They became the first balloonists to circumnavigate the globe with a non-stop, non-refueled flight, having traveled a record distance of 26,756 miles. Aside from establishing the paramount record in ballooning history, the *Breitling's* crew received $1 million from the Anheuser-Busch Brewing Company, as well as the Budweiser Cup, offered to the first balloonists to circumnavigate the earth without landing.

Breitling Orbiter 3 capsule

2002: STEVE FOSSETT/*THE SPIRIT OF FREEDOM*: AROUND-THE-WORLD SOLO BALLOON FLIGHT

Steve Fossett is known for being one of the greatest aviation adventurers, setting numerous records and becoming the first balloonist to voyage solo around the world in a hot air balloon on his sixth attempt. Fossett had made an attempt to set the around-the-world solo record after the 1999 Breitling success. His fifth solo was launched in Notham, Australia, and landed short in Bage, Brazil, after 12 days, 12:57 hours.

While Fossett self-financed his five previous attempts, the sixth attempt was sponsored by Bud Light. His balloon, the *Bud Lite Spirit of Freedom*, used the Roziere combination of hot air and helium, with an envelope 140 ft. tall and 60 ft. wide. The basket (gondola) was extremely cramped, and on average Fossett got only about four hours of sleep each day, divided into forty-five minute naps. The temperature outside the balloon was often much below zero, and Fossett would have had to regularly climb outside to change fuel tanks or to check on the burners. A special onboard autopilot system (Comstock Autopilot) could maintain the balloon at a constant altitude by using a computer to control the burners. The control center for the flight was at Washington University in St. Louis. The balloon was launched from Northam, Western Australia, on 19 June 2002, and the projected flight was to cross the Pacific first and then fly across South America via Chile and Argentina, then cross the Southern Atlantic Ocean toward South Africa, over the Indian Ocean, and would finally land back in Queensland, Australia, on 3 July 2002, at a longitude equal to or farther east than where the flight began. As Fossett reached touchdown at the end of the flight in Queensland, the balloon dragged him along the ground for 20 minutes. The trip covered 13 days, 12:05 hours (14 days 19:50 hours to landing) over 20,482.26 miles. Other records set on the flight included:

The Bud Lite *Spirit of Freedom* and pilot Steve Fossett

24 Hour Balloon Distance Record: 30 June–1 July 2002: 3,186.80 miles
Fastest Speed by Manned Balloon: 1 July 2002: 200.24 mph

Only the capsule survived the landing and is on display at the Smithsonian Institution, Washington, DC.

JAMES "STEVE" FOSSETT

American Steve Fossett, like his British counterpart, Richard Branson, was a multi-millionaire record setting aviator, sailor, and adventurer, having made his fortune in the financial services field. Besides his record breaking achievements as a balloonist Fossett set ninety-one aviation world records ratified by FAI, of which thirty-six stand (2015), plus twenty-three ocean sailing world records ratified by the World Sailing Speed Record Council. A fellow of the Royal Geographical Society and the Explorers Club, Fossett set 116 records in five different sports, sixty of which still stood when he disappeared.

As a glider pilot Fossett, with co-pilot Terry Delore, set ten of the twenty-one Glider Open records, including the first 2,000 km Out-and-Return, the first 1,500 km Triangle, and the longest Straight Distance flights. On 29 August 2006, he set the world altitude record for gliders over El Calafate, Argentina, at 50,720 ft.

His achievements as a jet pilot in a Cessna Citation X include records for US Transcontinental, Australian Transcontinental, and Round-the-World westbound non-supersonic flights. Prior to Fossett's aviation records, no pilot had held world records in more than one class of aircraft; Fossett held them in four classes. (Fossett's records flying *GlobalFlyer* will be recounted later.)

Steve Fossett

On 3 September 2007, Fossett was reported missing after the plane he was flying over Nevada's Great Basin Desert area failed to return. Despite a month of searches by the Civil Air Patrol (CAP) and other privately funded and directed search efforts, Fossett was not found and the search was called off on 2 October 2007. On 29 September 2008, a hiker found Fossett's identification cards in California's Sierra Nevada and the crash site was discovered on 1 October 2008, sixty-five miles south of where he took off.

SIR RICHARD BRANSON

English businessman and multi-billionaire investor Sir Richard Charles Branson is the founder of the Virgin Group, which comprises more than 400 companies, including Virgin Atlantic Airways and the space tourism company Virgin Galactic, which will license the technology behind *Spaceship One*. Branson is

Sir Richard Branson

also well known for being an adventurer, using his millions to finance them. His first record breaking attempt occurred in 1985, when he attempted the fastest Atlantic Ocean crossing in the *Virgin Atlantic Challenger*, which capsized in British waters and he was rescued by RAF helicopter. In 1986, in his *Virgin Atlantic Challenger II*, along with sailing expert Daniel McCarthy, he beat the Atlantic crossing record by two hours. His accomplishments as a balloonist and aviator have been previously chronicled.

2013: JONATHON TRAPPE: PARTY BALLOONS ACROSS THE ATLANTIC

On 13 September 2013, Jonathan Trappe, emulating the Disney movie *UP*, began the first attempt to cross the Atlantic Ocean suspended by 370 helium balloons, setting off from Caribou, Maine. Trappe expected to arrive in Europe sometime between three and six days. The last time the Atlantic was crossed by helium balloon was in 1984, by Joe Kittinger, who advised him for this trip. The craft ascended by the dropping of ballast and was intended to drift at an altitude of up to 25,000 ft., following the westerly wind currents toward Europe, or even North Africa or Norway, depending on the whims of the winds. To descend Trappe would have popped or released some of the balloons. Twelve hours and 350 miles into the trip Trappe was forced down in Newfoundland.

Jonathon Trappe: Party Balloons Across the Atlantic

ZPB-2 SNOW BIRD: NON-RIGID AIRSHIP UNREFUELED ENDURANCE RECORD

On 4 March 1957 the ZPB-2 *Snow Bird* (BuNo 141561), a non-rigid N-Class ("N" for non-rigid) airship popularly known as the Nan ship, lifted off from Naval Air Station South Weymouth, Massachusetts, with a crew of fourteen specially selected volunteers. The pilot in command was Cdr. Jack Hunt, supported by two co-pilots, Cdr. Ronald Hoel and Lt.Cdr. Robert Bowser. The huge Goodyear-built patrol airship was 343 ft. long, 76 ft. in diameter, and 107 ft. high, and its envelope contained just over one million cubic feet of helium. It was powered by two 800 hp Wright R-1300 air-cooled radial engines. The car was 83 ft. long and 11.5 ft. wide, and was divided into two levels. The upper deck contained bunks and a wardroom equipped with a galley, while the lower level housed the operational portion of the car, with all the flight controls and radio and navigation equipment. Extensive preparations were made for the flight. When planning the dietary requirements of the 1,017 lbs. of food for the flight, variety, space requirements, and preservation were taken into consideration. It was necessary to establish a food ration system to ensure an adequate supply for the entire trip by placing each day's rations in separate bags. Fuel consumption was carefully calculated, with every article taken aboard carefully weighed to ensure the *ZPG-2* would be within the weight limits necessary for correct fuel consumption and lift rate. Weather reports and communication links were carefully planned. A portable mooring mast was carried by a Super Constellation that was to fly ahead of *Snow Bird* and be available at designated landing sites if needed. The intended route was to cross the North Atlantic toward the southwest tip of Portugal and turn south and pass between the Canary Islands and Cape Yuta, on the African coast, passing Casablanca and on to the Cape Verde Islands, which was the turning point back 2,500 miles west across the Atlantic toward Puerto Rico and Cuba, finally landing in Key West. On 13 March, after 200:12 hours, *Snow Bird* officially eclipsed the previous endurance record set in May 1954 by Cdr. M. Henry Eppes, who piloted the first of the *ZPG-2s*, flying from NAS Lakehurst, New Jersey, to Nova Scotia, Bermuda, Nassau, the Caribbean, and the Gulf of Mexico before recovering at NAS Key West. (Eppes was awarded the Harmon Trophy for the flight.) On the thirteenth, *Snow Bird* passed the 6,980 mile mark, breaking the distance record established by the *Graf Zeppelin* in August 1929. On 15 March 1957, *ZPB-2* landed at NAS Key West after 264.2 hours, covering 9,448 miles without refueling. *Snow Bird's* commander and pilot Cdr. Hunt was awarded the Harmon Trophy on 12 November 1958 by President Eisenhower. Despite this impressive demonstration of endurance there followed a slow reduction in the USN airship force. *Snow Bird's* control car is on display at the National Naval Aviation Museum, Pensacola, Florida. After leaving the Navy Jack Hunt became the founding president of Embry-Riddle Aeronautical University, Daytona Beach, Florida.

ZPB-2 Snowbird

2013: JON HILTON: FIRST TRANS-ATLANTIC FLIGHT AND THEN RETURN IN A MICROLIGHT

Between 24 May–10 June 2013, Jon Hilton became the first pilot to fly a Microlight aircraft across the Atlantic (from Britain to Canada). Hilton flew his 600 lb., two-seat CTSW Microlight *Samson* for eighteen days on a 5,500 mile round trip, beginning in Manchester, England, and continuing to Iqaluit, in far

Jon Hilton and his CTSW Microlight Samson

northeastern Canada, via Scotland, the Faroe Islands, Iceland, and Greenland. The flight was divided in seven-hour sections, with Hilton conserving fuel by gliding when weather allowed. His longest leg of the trip was on his first day, when he flew 1,000 miles from Manchester to Iceland via Wick, Scotland, and the Faroe Islands. The trip was delayed for seven days along the way. He was delayed three days when Danish officials in Greenland refused to let him fly until he increased his insurance to allow them to recoup the costs of recovering his body from his estate if he crashed; he lost two more days in Greenland when he found that the airports were closed on Sundays; and then was unable to fly for two days due to windy conditions. At one point, because the CTSW was unable to fly through clouds, he was forced to descend to thirty feet above the sea and evade massive icebergs with no cabin heating. He then returned to Manchester via the same route. Hilton was awarded the 2013 Britannia Trophy by Prince Andrew for excellence in aviation.

GLIDERS/SAILPLANES

Lift is a meteorological occurrence used as an energy source by soaring aircraft and soaring birds. The three human sporting aerial uses of lift for soaring flight are gliding, hang gliding, and paragliding. Lifting energy can be gained by using rising air from five natural sources:

Ridge Lift: air is forced upward by a slope
Wave Lift: mountain produces a standing wave
Thermals: air rises due to heat
Convergence: two air masses meet
Differences in wind speeds rather than rising air to gain energy (dynamic soaring)

Aero tow is the most commonly used method of getting a glider airborne in the US today. The sailplane is pulled aloft by a 200 foot nylon or polypropylene rope secured by a special hook to the tow plane. The sailplane pilot can release the tow rope at any desired altitude.

Auto launches are sometimes used by connecting a 1,000 foot rope to the sailplane and to a special hook on the towing automobile. To start the procedure, the tow vehicle drives down the launch runway and the glider pilot flies the glider up to an altitude of about 800 feet, then releases the tow line, which falls to the ground. This method is commonly used when the airstrip is atop or along a large hill or mountain to catch ridge or wave lift. Many European clubs launch their sailplanes using a stationary ground-based winch run by a large diesel engine, though hydraulic fluid engines and electrical motors are also used. The winch pulls in a 3,000–5,500 foot cable made of high-tensile steel wire or a synthetic fiber attached to the glider. The cable is released at about 1,300–2,200 ft. after a short and steep stomach-churning ascent.

A BRIEF HISTORY OF GLIDING AND SOARING AIRCRAFT

1490: Leonardo da Vinci drew his concepts of a flying machine inspired by the wings of bats and birds.

1799–1853: Sir George Cayley spent much of his life devising and building gliding aircraft, and is considered the "Father of Aerodynamics," as the first to understand the underlying principles and forces of flight. In 1804, Cayley's model glider flew successfully. His glider had the layout of a modern aircraft, with a kite-shaped wing toward the front and an adjustable tailplane at the back comprised of horizontal stabilizers and a vertical fin. The model's center of gravity was adjusted by a movable weight. By the middle of 1809, Cayley had explored the improved lifting capabilities of cambered wings, the movement of the center of pressure, longitudinal stability, and the notion of streamlining. He determined the use of inclined, rigid wings to provide lift and roll stability and steering by rudder control. After these experiments with models he constructed what is considered to be the first true airplane. This glider, which was basically a kite on top of a pole, was about five feet long, with a fixed wing set at an angle of incidence of six degrees and a cruciform tail attached to the fuselage by universal joints. Movable ballast controlled the center of gravity. An assistant made a few hesitant hops into the air while clasping the fuselage. After these early glider experiments Cayley spent years in the English Parliament and also contributed in the fields of prosthetics, air engines, electricity, theatre architecture, ballistics, optics, and land reclamation, and believed his findings should be available without charge. Sir George Cayley's so-called "Boy Glider" of 1849 was similar to his 1799 glider. It was the first inherently stable full-sized heavier-than-air craft, being capable of lifting a ten-year-old boy off the ground for a few yards on two test runs. Lift was provided by the fixed triplane wing assembly and stability

Sir George Cayley 1853 Glider replica

by two cruciform tail units: one fixed and one operated by the pilot, who sat in the boat-shaped car below the wings. Once it was in the air the glider was propelled by hand-pumped flappers. Cayley's next major contribution to gliding occurred in 1853, when he designed and built a large but fragile (to keep weight at a minimum) aircraft. The wing was made in the shape of a diamond from linen sheet shaped by cane and held together with string, with a tailplane at the back. Below the wing was a seat with a three-wheel undercarriage. Since Cayley was seventy-nine years old he volunteered his coachman, John Appleby, or his resident engineer, Thomas Vick, to sit in the glider, which was pulled with ropes by farm workers down the Brompton Dale slope until it flew into the air. It flew across the Dale over about 200 yards before it crash landed.

1884: Gliding flight by John Montgomery at Wheeler Hill near San Diego, California.

1891–1896: Otto Lilienthal, known as the "Glider King," investigated the principles of winged flight to design and build gliders he would fly to become the first person to make well-documented, frequent, and successful flights. Between 1891 and 1896, he completed about 2,000 flights in at least sixteen types of gliders; photographs of Lilienthal flying aboard his gliders from an artificial hill he built near Berlin appeared in newspapers and the illustrated magazines of the time throughout the world. Lilienthal's gliders were designed to distribute weight as evenly as possible, ensuring a stable flight. They were controlled by changing the gliders' center of gravity by shifting the pilot's body, similar to controlling the modern hang glider. However, his gliders were difficult to maneuver and to recover from their inclination to pitch downward. Lilienthal made many attempts to improve stability, but with varying degrees of success, culminating on 9 August 1896, when his glider pitched downward and he fell from about fifty feet, breaking his back and dying in a hospital the next day.

Otto Lilienthal

1894–1897: During 1894, French immigrant to America Octave Chanute began experimenting using Lilienthal-type gliders and determined that "automatic stability" was the solution, and that wing pivoting would provide better control than shifting the pilot's weight. In 1895, he began building gliders of his own design, and over the next several years, with the assistance of civil and mechanical engineer Augustus Herring and pilot William Avery, Chanute designed, built, and tested gliders. To attain automatic flight control he built gliders with up to six tiers of wings, some that had either moveable wings or tail control surfaces, and others that pivoted on a central frame. Later he decided on rigid wings held in place by trusses similar to those used in the braced-box structure in bridge construction. In 1896, Chanute designed and commissioned five gliders constructed by Avery. The *Katydid* featured multiple wings that could be shifted on the fuselage to facilitate experimentation. The frame was made of spruce and the surfaces were varnished Japanese silk. The craft underwent several changes in its wing configuration that improved its flying ability. In its final configuration it weighed 33.5 lbs., with a "supporting surface" (wing) at the front of 143.5 sq. ft. It was flown for over 200 glides on the shores of Lake Michigan at Miller Beach, near Gary, Indiana. Wilbur and Orville Wright acknowledged that the *Chanute* glider provided them with a starting point for their own structural designs.

Octave Chanute Katydid

1902–1903: Wright Brothers obtained control by flying their glider from the low dunes at Kitty Hawk, North Carolina. This 1902 glider design would become the basis for their "Flying Machine" patent.

1906: The first American glider meet was sponsored by the Aero Club of America on Long Island, New York, with about ten to twelve club members sharing three biplane gliders.

1909: In September 1909, Raymond Hekking flew his Lilienthal-type biplane in a 20 mph wind at Larcouet, near Havre, for five minutes, which was only reported in the *Petit Havrais* of 7 September.

1911: Glider began to become popular, with intercollegiate meets held in the United States, Europe, and Australia.

1911: Orville Wright establishes the first world soaring duration record of 9:45 minutes at Kitty Hawk, North Carolina.

Wright 1911 Glider

1920–1939 Germany

After WWI, the public became captivated with flying and soaring, and the allure of motorless flight proliferated, particularly among poor and enthusiastic air-minded youth, especially in defeated postwar Germany. Germany was banned from developing or building powered aircraft, first under the Treaty of Versailles and later by additional restrictions. These limitations did not apply to gliding, and a substantial gliding program began in Germany, where meets were held on the Wasserkuppe, the highest peak in the Rhoen Mountains. As many as 60,000 spectators and seventy glider clubs from Europe sent their best gliders and pilots to compete for duration, altitude, and distance prizes held in these mountains. In 1921, Dr. Wolfgang Klemperer broke the Wright brothers' 1911 soaring record with a 13 minute flight. At the 1922 meet on 17 August, Arthur Botsch first revealed how to soar in a slope up-current. The next day Arthur Martens, in the sailplane *Vampyr*, soared over the west slope of the Wasserkuppe for 42 minutes and climbed 355 ft. in a wind varying between 8 and 18 mph, then flew out over the valley and glided down to a landing six miles away after flying 1:06 hours, of which the first 53 minutes were above the starting level. Next day F. H. Hentzen flew the *Vampyr* for two hours, and on 24 August, he raised the record to 3:06 hours, climbing over 1,000 ft. in the up-current and landing higher than where he had taken off.

In 1926, German newspaper *Grune Post* offered a RM 5,000 prize for the first glider pilot to fly 100 km. In 1929, Austrian Robert Kronfeld launched by bungee in a glider of his own design named *Wien* (Vienna) and flew for more than five hours, landing near Detmold, 102.5 km away. He then set three world distance records, the last between the Wasserkuppe and Marktredwitz, a distance of 164 km (102 miles) flown on 24 August 1930. During these noteworthy flights Kronfeld would free glide from its dependency on using mountain slopes for gaining altitude and distance by making short out and return flights into thermals to gain altitude that became widely known, and showed the gliding world the potential of cross-country soaring by a sailplane. On 20 June 1931, Kronfeld was the first pilot to fly a glider across the English Channel (210 miles from London to Paris) in less than five hours and then make the return flight the same day. However, Kronfeld's glider was powered with a 5 hp motorcycle engine, which he used to maintain course and height over the water. In 1933, the new Nazi government prohibited Jews from flying and Kronfeld fled to England. In 1933, wave lift was discovered by Wolf Hirth and one of his students. Hirth and Martin Schempp were co-founders of a still-renowned sailplane manufacturer, Sportflugzeugbau Schempp-Hirth. Their prewar *Go 3 Minimoa* was a distinctive sailplane with an elegant gull wing design that was used to break several world records and win championships around the world. From 1945, his company manufactured furniture until glider production could begin again in 1951. Hirth had a heart attack while flying an aerobatic glider in 1959 and died in the subsequent crash. In 1937, Heini Dittmar won the first recognized World Soaring Championships flying the *Sao Paulo* at the Wasserkuppe, in Germany, using wave flights to gain high altitudes. During the Nazi regime gliding was basically controlled by the state, and for Hitler Youth pilots and their instructors proficiency in gliding was access to the Luftwaffe. Sailplane research was also nationalized under the *Deutsche Forschungsanstalt für Segelflug* (DFS: German Research Institute for Sailplane Flight). Due to their emphasis on prewar gliding, the Germans were the first to use gliders in warfare, most famously during the assault of Eben Emael fortress and the capture of the bridges over the Albert Cana in the invasion of Holland on 10 May 1940. Consequently, the British, American, and Japanese quickly became aware of the methods used and began active glider programs. Hitler used his combat gliders in Greece in April 1941, and soon thereafter in Crete in May. Although the Germans won the battle for Crete with the use of 13,000 glider infantry and paratroopers, they suffered more than 5,000 casualties and Hitler never again used paradrops or gliders on such a massive scale. The Germans began the development of larger gliders, such as the Gotha Go 242 (twenty-three troops) and the massive Messerschmitt Me 323 (130 troops and later to be motorized) to transport troops and heavy armaments to reinforce combat fronts, but these gliders were found to be very vulnerable after their introduction and were subsequently abandoned.

Robert Kronfeld

Wolf Hirth

1929: National Glider Association founded in Detroit, Michigan.

1930: First USA National Glider Contest, Elmira New York, where all pre-WWII (up to 1941) Nationals were held.

1931: Lt. William Cocke of the 19th Pursuit Squadron set the world duration record in a single place sailplane of his own design (*Nighthawk*), sailing 14:07 hours on 17 December. On 19 December, Cocke's *Nighthawk* launched from the John Galt Gliderport and sailed 21:34 hours and an unofficial 600 miles, near Honolulu, Hawaii, at the International Glider Meet. Illuminating the path for Cocke along the cliff face during the night was the US Army's 64th Coast Artillery Battery. Cocke was killed during the Japanese attack on Clark Field, Philippines, on 8 December 1941. The Los Angeles County Museum of Natural History owns the *Nighthawk*.

William Cocke

1939: The US distance record was 263 miles, flown by Woody Brown in June 1939, with a flight from Wichita Falls, Texas, to Wichita, Kansas. At the time the world distance record was 465 miles flown by Ms. Klepikova in July 1939 in the USSR.

1950–1956: Paul MacCready was the first American to compete in the World Soaring Championships, flying in a Weihe sailplane to second place in Orebro, Sweden. He was a three-time winner (1948, 1949, and 1953) of the Richard du Pont Memorial Trophy awarded annually to the US National Open Class Soaring Champion. MacCready pioneered wave soaring, in which a sailplane uses strong lifting currents of air to reach extreme heights. He also invented the MacCready speed ring, an instrument still used by glider pilots to select the best flight speed between updrafts. In 1956, he became the first American to win the World Soaring Championships in Saint Yan, France, and then retired from active soaring for other safer pursuits. MacCready was a brilliant aerodynamicist, receiving a BS in physics from Yale in 1947, an MS in physics from CalTech in 1948, and a PhD in aeronautics from Caltech in 1952. In the mid-1970s, with Dr. Peter Lissaman, he created a human-powered aircraft, the *Gossamer Condor*, and won the first Kremer prize in 1977. In 1979, he built its successor, the *Gossamer Albatross*, which won the second Kremer prize for successfully flying from England to France. He later created solar-powered aircraft, such as the *Gossamer Penguin* and the *Solar Challenger*.

Paul MacReady, 1948
World Champion

MODERN SOARING: 1957–PRESENT

A better understanding of weather and atmospheric forces; advances in instrumentation technology (global positioning technology and electronic glide computers) combined with new composite materials (the prototype of the first lightweight composite sailplane, the *Phoenix*, first flew in Germany in 1957); and highly refined aerodynamics have created high performance sailplanes, leading to the expansion in the number of FAI competitive classes to eight. There are an estimated 150,000 glider pilots worldwide, with the majority in Europe, where the sport has national attention in many countries. In the United States there are more than 180 soaring clubs, with nearly 40,000 licensed glider pilots and more than 5,000 registered sailplanes.

Selected Current World Soaring Records

The FAI has established eight glider competition classes with records for each:

Standard Class (No flaps, 15 m wing-span, water ballast allowed)
15 Meter Class (Flaps allowed, 15 m wingspan, water ballast allowed)
18 Meter Class (Flaps allowed, 18 m wingspan, water ballast allowed)
Open Class (No restrictions except a limit of 850 kg for the maximum all-up weight)
Two Seater Class (maximum wing-span of 20 m)
Club Class (This class includes a wide variety of older, smaller gliders with different performances adjusted by handicapping. No water ballast.)
World Class: Low-cost gliders with moderate performance
Ultralight Class: Gliders with a maximum mass less than 220 kg.

1956: Endurance Record Any Class Glider: Charles Atger

The endurance records for any class glider is 56:15:00, set between 2–4 April 1952 by Charles Atger, flying an Arsenal Air 100 Glider over Romanin les Alpilles, near Saint-Remy-de-Provence, France. In 1954, another pilot in a different sailplane was killed attempting to beat Atger's record; the crash was attributed to pilot exhaustion and the FAI prohibited further duration record claims for gliders, so Atger's record still stands.

Atger's time broke Ernst Jachtmann's unofficial record of 53:52 hours set during wartime (22–24 September 1943) over

Baltic East Prussia in a Weihe sailplane. Also during 1943, another flight of 53 hours was flown by pilot Juez over Monflorite, Huesca, Spain, in a pre-production Weihe sailplane.

Charles Atgar's Air 100

Ernst Jachtmann

1963:Paul Bikle established two certified world soaring records on 25 February 1961 while flying his Schweizer SGS 1-23E near Lancaster, California, achieving an altitude of 46,267 ft. and a total altitude gained mark of 42,300 ft. He flew a Prue Standard sailplane to a world record distance of 557 miles in 1963, the longest ever made by a sailplane up to that date. He became a member of the Soaring Hall of Fame in 1960, and was awarded the FAI Lilienthal Gliding Medal, the highest award in international soaring, in 1962.

2000: Longest Glider Flight in All Categories: Ohlmann and Urbancic

At 0630 on 26 November 2000, pilot Klaus Ohlmann and co-pilot Alois Urbancic took off from San Martin de los Andes, Argentina, in a Stemme S-10 VT Glider, attempting to surpass the 2,045 km record set by Terry Delore of New Zealand. They landed at Malargue Airport, Argentina, at 2050, after flying 2,463 km over 14:20 hours at an average speed of 172 km/h.

Klaus Ohlmann

2002: Two Distance Records Set in One Day

On 13 December, Terry Delore and co-pilot John Kokshoorn set a new world record in New Zealand with a flight of more than 14 hours and a distance of 2499.2 km at an average speed of 227 kph around a course with three turning points that took them across Cook Strait twice. Later that day in Argentina, Delore's rival, record setting pilot German Klaus Ohlmann, beat his distance by 12 km to regain the record.

2007: Oldest Standing Distance Record Broken

On 12 July, multiple world record-holding glider pilots Steve Fossett and Terry Delore flew a 777-mile triangular course in 8:23 hours at an average speed of 92.73 mph, finally breaking a two-decade-old record set by German Hans Werner Grosse's 777-mile record of 89.14 mph flown from Alice Springs, Australia, on 10 January 1987.

2009: Longest Glider Flight in All Categories: Terry Delore and John Kokshoorn

Terry Delore

Terry Delore and John Kokshoorn took off from Omarama, New Zealand, in an Ash 25 Glider and flew to Ward, in Marlborough, back to Clyde, near Alexandra, and then back up and level with Taihape, in the North Island, before turning around and landing back at Omarama. Gliding as high as 28,000 ft., they glided 2,501 km, breaking the previous record by Klaus Ohlmann by about 80 km. Delore bought the glider from Steve Fossett's estate after his death. Previously Fossett and Delore set eleven glider world records between 2002–2007.

1992–Present: Airbus Perlan Mission II

In 1992, Perlan's founder and NASA test pilot Einar Enevoldson discovered an unknown weather phenomenon called "stratospheric mountain waves," which are huge waves of air caused by strong winds blowing over the tops of high mountain ranges like the Andes, or the New Zealand Alps, that then zoom up toward space. As a pilot Enevoldson continued his research as the Perlan Project (1992–1998), hoping to use a glider to ride these waves to the edge of space, all the way up to near space. In 1998, meteorologist Dr. Elizabeth Austin proved that it is the stratospheric polar night jet and the polar vortex that are the principal factors enabling these mountain waves to reach up to 130,000 ft.

into the middle stratosphere. In 1999, Steve Fossett decided to fund the Perlan Project and became one of its sponsors and pilots. Meanwhile, the NASA Dryden Flight Research Center analyzed the flight dynamics and aerodynamics of sailplane flight up to 100,000 feet. A DG 505M sailplane was modified to remove all engine and related equipment, and the space was used for the storage of liquid oxygen and a large number of LiSO2 primary batteries. Most of the instruments and electronics were replaced with equipment suitable for the extreme altitudes the sailplane would encounter. NASA requested that the USAF loan full pressure suits, while Duncan Cummings built special lightweight, efficient, reliable faceplate heat controllers. The Butler Parachute Company fabricated special high-altitude stabilized parachutes.

During Spring 2002, Enevoldson and Fossett flew the sailplane from California City for shakedown and preliminary high-altitude flights in the California Sierra Nevada, climbing to over 42,000 ft. In Summer 2002, the sailplane was shipped to Omarama, New Zealand, where it flew during three winters without reaching the stratosphere. In 2005, the sailplane was shipped to the Southern Hemisphere and El Calafate, Argentina, a small town at the base of the Andes. Five attempts were made in unfavorable weather conditions, all unsuccessful. On 28 August 2006, under very favorable conditions, the sailplane climbed strongly to 33,000 ft., where Fossett's pressure suit inflated too early and too much and the promising flight was aborted. The next day weather conditions continued to be promising, and after a four-hour climb in the atmospheric waves Enevoldson and Fossett reached record altitude. On 30 August, Fossett and Enevoldson shattered the existing altitude record for gliders by soaring up to 50,671 ft. in a standard glider using these stratospheric waves of air.

After Fossett's untimely death in 2007 the Perlan Project languished for a time, but Enevoldson gathered a new team and secured new partial funding. In 2014, Airbus Group agreed to become the sponsor and provided sufficient funding for completion of the aircraft, flight testing, and the altitude flights as the Airbus Perlan Mission II. RDD Enterprises, an aviation research, design, and development company based in Redmond, Oregon, assumed sailplane manufacture. The *Perlan II's* new lightweight and highly efficient carbon fiber aerodynamic design and 84 ft. wingspan is calculated to fly up to 90,000 ft. in a near vacuum, where air density is less than two percent of sea level. At such low air density the glider has to fly at almost supersonic speeds to create enough lift to remain aloft. The *Perlan II* has a pressurized cabin so the pilots do not have to wear pressure suits. It has an oxygen breathing system similar to those of scuba divers, with oxygen tanks, CO_2 scrubbers, and rebreather systems. It has a comprehensive, fully advanced electronic cockpit and a science payload bay for high-altitude atmospheric experiments. Initial flight testing was conducted in Redmond, Oregon, in Summer 2015, and continued over the Sierra Nevada Mountains near Minden, Nevada, in Fall and Winter 2015. During Summer 2016, the *Perlan II* arrived in southern Argentina's Patagonia Andes mountain region, which is known to have excellent polar vortex formations and mountain waves for a brief period in August and September every year. The 2016 Argentina wave season ended with strong wave conditions never materializing, but the *Perlan II* was flown to 90,000 ft.

Steve Fossett (L) and Einar Enevoldson

Airbus-Perlan II

HANG GLIDERS

Some of Otto Lilienthal's gliders of the 1890s were rigid wing hang gliders, but the hang glider lost prominence with the introduction of wing warping by the Wright brothers in 1902. Many of the gliders flown in 1920, particularly in the German Wasserkuppe glider competition, were hang gliders, in that they were controlled by the pilot's weight shift alone.

There are two types of hang gliders: the Flexible Wing and the Rigid Wing. In 1948, NACA aeronautical engineer Francis Rogallo invented a self-inflating wing that he patented on 20 March 1951, as the Flexible Wing (Rogallo Wing); a simple, inexpensive method of recreational flying with its capability of slow flight and its gentle landing characteristics.

There have been several rigid wing hang gliders since Otto Lilienthal took his first flights in the 1890s and are of the most modern type.

The basic hang glider, with the essential elements that most modern gliders are based on today, was conceived by Australian engineer John Dickenson in 1963. After seeing an image of a Rogallo Wing airfoil in a magazine, Dickenson decided to build a water skiing kite called the Ski Kite, that could be released at an altitude for a glide to safely drop in the water. He successfully flew his first hang glider on 8 September 1963, in Grafton, Australia. His revolutionary airframe, pendulum weight shift control method, and the triangular control bar became the prototype for the tens of thousands of hang gliders that have since been produced to supply the worldwide spread of a new sport.

First modern hang glider

In the early 1940s, aeronautical engineer Donald Mitchell first became involved with flying wing glider design and construction, but WWII interrupted his research. The first high-performance modern rigid wing hang glider was based on the Mitchell Wing. It would not be until 1974, with the beginning of hang glider "mania," that Mitchell's wing was resurrected by Dr. Howard Long. Long asked Don Mitchell to design and construct a refined flying wing hang glider, and the product was the foot-launched Mitchell Wing. The Mitchell Wing's structural design was simple, very strong, and light (less than 80 lbs.). It had a single "D" spar with a birch plywood torsion proof leading edge and three-axes control. Foam ribs were placed every 4.5 in. to maintain the D shape, and the built-up truss ribs aft of the spar were covered with fabric. When the foot-launched Mitchell Wing B-10 flew in the 1977 USA Nationals, it astonished the hang gliding world and would subsequently set and hold every world record in its class. In 1980, George Worthington soared to 17,000 ft. and glided 105 miles, setting two new rigid wing records.

Donald Mitchell and his Mitchell Wing

THE MODERN HANG GLIDER

Flex Wing hang gliders are the most closely related to the original early 1970s hang gliders. They have a basic tube frame and a flexible wing made of sailcloth stiffened into an aerofoil shape by aluminum battens. They are usually wire-braced and controlled by shifting the pilot's weight. Many of the most recent advanced wings use cantilever composite structure and advanced aerodynamics. Rigid Wing hang gliders resemble airplanes without tails, and are built from carbon fiber and epoxy for strength and light weight. They generally have better performance than flex wings, and though designed to be launched and landed on foot have a very good glide. In both flexible and rigid wings the pilot hangs below the wing without any additional fairing. For competitive purposes, there are three classes of hang glider:

Class 1: Flexible wing hang glider, having flight controlled by a wing whose shape the pilot changes by shifting his weight.

Class 5: Rigid wing hang glider, having flight controlled by spoilers, usually on top of the wing.

Modern hang glider

Class 2: (designated by the FAI as Sub-Class O-2) where the pilot is integrated into the wing by means of a fairing.

2012: Longest Hang Glider Flight: Dustin Martin

Dustin Martin (USA) and Jon Durand (Australia) launched simultaneously on 4 July 2012 from Zapata, Texas, with Martin flying his Wills Wing T2C and Durand his Moyes Delta Litespeed. Both men beat the previous record of 700.6 km (435.33 miles) set on 17 July 2001 by Manfred Ruhmer, but after 11 hours at 69 mph Martin landed 3 km (1.8 miles) farther than Durand near Lubbock, 761 km (4,72.8 miles) from the starting point.

Dustin Martin

2013: Out-and-Back Distance: Thomas Weissenberger
3 November 2013, Austrian Thomas Weissenberger set a new hang gliding record while ridge-soaring his Moyes Litespeed along the cliffs of Chile's Cordillera coast, where the Atacama Desert and the South Pacific meet. He was unsuccessful during the four previous years due to difficult flying and weather conditions on the coast of Chile. When he landed eight hours later he had beaten the official out and back record of 332.5 km set by George Stebbins (USA) on 5 July 2007, and his recent FAI-pending record also set on the Chilean Coast a week earlier on 27 October of 339.5 km.

Thomas Weissenberger

2
INTERCONTINENTAL BOMBERS OF THE COLD WAR AND BEYOND

IN-FLIGHT REFUELING

WORLD WAR II

B-24 Tankers and B-17 Receivers

Once America entered the war, the USAAC initiated studies on an aerial refueling solution and three primary refueling concepts were deliberated by US air planners. The first was launching B-17 Flying Fortresses from Midway Island against Japan using modified B-24 Liberators as tankers; the second used B-24s from Hawaii with tanker support from Navy seaplanes; and the third used B-17s to tow fuel-laden gliders to serve as tankers. But it would be Sir Alan Cobham's prewar use of aerial refueling that was resurrected. Washington looked to contact FRL, whose employees had dispersed, but RCAF Wing Commander Hugh Johnson, who was in charge of the tanker operations at Gander, was located and assigned to the American project. While organizing the project it was discovered the FRL equipment left at Gander was all for tankers and none for receivers. Johnson was flown to Britain and collected the FRL equipment, drawings, and several FRL technicians.

It was not until June 1943 that in-flight refueling testing was begun using a B-24D tanker and a B-17E receiver at Eglin Field, Florida. Hugh Johnson was in command; Percy Allison, British Air Commission, was the technical adviser; Capt. Fred Bretcher and 1Lt. M. K. Norton were pilot and co-pilot, respectively, of the B-24D tanker; and Capt. Ralph C. Hoewing and 1Lt. John Kelting were pilot and co-pilot, respectively, of the B-17E receiver. Refueling was accomplished at 150 mph, and by the seventh refueling flight, the receiver's tanks were filled to 101 percent and fuel was seen flowing out of its tank vents. It was found that loaded with three tons of bombs, the B-17's radius was extended from 1,000 to 1,500 miles by refueling.

Although the tests were considered successful, the equipment for squadrons of B-24 tankers and B-17 receivers would have to be refined and manufactured by the country's already over-extended aircraft manufacturers, the tankers and receivers modified, and the crews trained. By summer 1943, B-29s were beginning to come into inventory and B-29 units were in training and expected to enter combat by early 1944. Since the B-29 carried more than twice the bomb load of a B-17 and had a round trip combat radius of 1,500 miles carrying twice the bomb load of the B-17, the costly effort to form squadrons of B-24s for the in-flight refueling of B-17s was no longer viable.

June 1943, B-24D tanker and a B-17E receiver at Eglin Field, Florida.

Refueling a Lancaster of Tiger Force trailing its drogue.

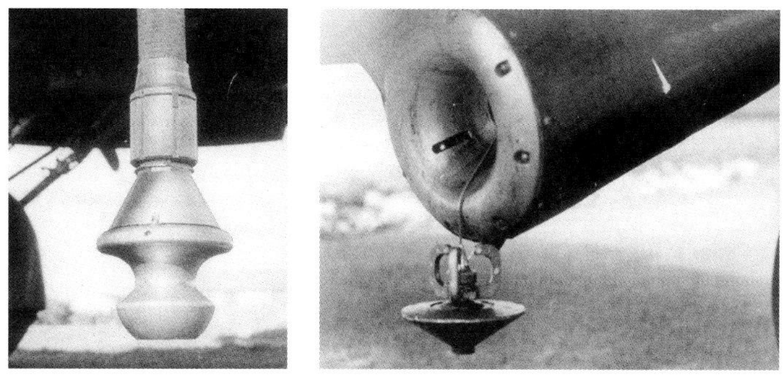

The refueling hose ended with a ball (L) and cone-shaped nozzle (R), with the ball engaging the receiver's reception coupling. This method was the basis for Cobham's postwar refueling efforts.

Extending the B-29's Range

In 1944, the AAF initiated a study on the feasibility of equipping B-29s with an in-flight refueling capability. Wright Field determined it was possible to modify the bomber, but the B-24 tanker's 1,500 gallon capacity only extended the B-29's range by 830 miles and the project was abandoned.

Other AAF In-flight Refueling Tests

The AAF also investigated a possible refueling method for smaller aircraft and engaged contractor All American Aviation to equip and test a specially modified P-38 Lightning and a B-24 tanker. In the test, the B-24 suspended an external fuel tank on a cable, with the P-38 maneuvering to catch the cable, securing it into a device mounted on the forward fuselage. The twin-engine fighter was then to descend to the tank, which was to lodge into the securing device while the cable broke away. A nitrogen bottle discharged, forcing the fuel into the fighter before ejector springs released the tank. The tests were not at all successful, and in March 1945, the AAF canceled the method; thus, the AAF would not use air refueling operationally during WWII.

Late-War British In-flight Refueling

During February 1944, the British Air Ministry informed Sir Alan Cobham of RAF plans to bomb Japan using aerial refueling after the defeat of Germany. Some fifty Lancaster bombers were to be converted into tankers to refuel fifty Lincoln bombers of the Long-range Force in an operation to be known as Tiger Force, with an eventual force of 500 or more of each. However, the Lincoln prototype would not be ready until 9 June 1944, and was then expected to have the usual new aircraft developmental problems. Meanwhile, Cobham's refueling project was granted increased status by the Air Ministry and the FRL was accorded industrial priorities to produce the equipment, assigned three airfields, and a school was established for training hundreds of aircrews. The prototype Lancaster tanker and receiver were flown successfully in November 1944. The tanker equipment consisted of two 640 (Imp.) gallon cargo tanks installed in the forward end of the bomb bay, along with a hydraulically driven hose drum and a hydraulically driven contactor reel for retrieving the tanker's contact line. The operator's compartment contained all the necessary controls for the refueling process. The refueling hose ended with a ball and cone-shaped nozzle, with the ball engaging the receiver's reception coupling. A drogue (parasheet) and its shroud lines, which were to stabilize the hose when extending or retracting it, were at a point about four feet from the nozzle. The contact reel wound in the receiver's hauling line once contact had been established with the tanker's line. The contactor engaged the receiver's sinker weight at the trailing ends of the receiver's hauling line and was a shaft with three claw-like prongs. The tanker's line-throwing gun fired the contactor cable from the port side of the tanker operator's compartment. The receiver refueling installation consisted of a bell-mouthed reception coupling that engaged the tanker's nozzle during the operation at the aft end and lower starboard side of the receiver's fuselage. A windlass controlled the trailing and winding of the receiver's hauling line. The refueling process was completed in three stages: contact between the tanker and receiver; transferring fuel; and breaking contact after fuel transfer, which would be the basis for Cobham's postwar refueling efforts. In June 1945, US amphibious forces captured Okinawa in a bloody battle that placed AAF heavy bombers less than 360 miles from southernmost Japan and 950 miles from Tokyo, cancelling the British refueling project.

POSTWAR REFUELING

Cobham Rekindles His Prewar Refueling Project

Once the war ended Cobham sought to return to his prewar plan of selling FRL's aerial refueling services to commercial airlines. He realized that American airlines were poised to develop trans-Atlantic aircraft capable of carrying up to one hundred passengers and substantial freight, and the capability for aerial refueling. Cobham purchased six surplus Lancaster bombers to be modified into tankers and receivers. During winter 1946–1947, FRL used its Lancaster tankers in association with British South American Airways (BSAA), which used Lancaster receivers. A rigorous series of forty-three demonstration flights (twenty-six in daylight and seventeen at night) flew over Britain, between Dover and Land's End. Each Lancaster tanker could deliver approximately 2,800 gallons using a FRL design innovation consisting of the probe/drogue method. The tanker simply trailed a hose with a stabilizing drogue on the end which served as a conical guide for a rigid forward-pointing pipe or drogue (i.e., a hose with a funnel on the end) that fit into a probe on the receiving aircraft. A very similar method is in use today.

In early 1947, these trials were expanded to include flights between London and Bermuda. Later that year FRL, in association with British Overseas Airlines Corporation, began winter refueling trials. For these operations FRL purchased four Lancastrians from Trans-Canada Airlines and converted them to tankers. (During the war some Canadian-built Lancaster bombers were converted into Lancastrian passenger carrying airliners and were especially prized because they were already fully winterized.)

Two Lancastrian tankers were based at Shannon, with another at Goose Bay and the fourth at Gander. For the trials, the receiver was a B-24 Liberator that BOAC had converted to carry cargo. Because of help from prevailing winds only one midair refueling was necessary for an eastbound flight, generally when the Liberator had passed 200 or so miles east of either Gander or Goose Bay. Two refuelings, one at each end, were required for the westbound trip. Between 4 February and 30 May 1948, fifteen flights each way were serviced by in-flight refueling, permitting the Liberator to fly 3,240 miles non-stop from London to Montreal (Dorval).

In 1947, BSAA prepared to modify the new four-engine Avro Tudor IIs that it intended for use on the North Atlantic route using in-flight refueling. The Tudor II suffered from design and construction problems and accidents that caused it to be withdrawn from passenger service and forced BSAA to suspend operations and have BOAC assume control of the company. BOAC had no interest in in-flight refueling and it seemed like Cobham's project would die.

Avro Lancastrian

Sir Alan Cobham (R) and Donald Bennett posing by their Avro Tudor passenger aircraft.

The USAF Buys Cobham's Refueling System

In early 1948, with relations between the US and USSR rapidly deteriorating into the Cold War, Gen. Carl Spaatz, the first chief of staff of the new United States Air Force, and Gen. Curtis Lemay, recently appointed commander of Strategic Air Command (SAC), recognized that the new jet-powered bombers coming into inventory required far more fuel than piston-engine bombers and would also have to fly farther from their American bases to targets deep inside the Soviet Union and return, so LeMay made aerial refueling a major objective. On 18 March 1948, a USAF contingent from Wright-Patterson AFB, Ohio, arrived in London and visited Cobham's FRL Littlehampton offices. The USAF purchased two sets of FRL's in-flight refueling equipment, manufacturing rights, and a contract to have FRL manufacture forty refueling sets and provide technical support. The sets were immediately installed in two B-29s, with plans to equip eighty B-29s.

B-50A, the postwar B-29 conversion, receives fuel via the telescoping boom with "ruddervators."

KB-29M Tanker, the B-50 Receiver, and the Boeing Boom System

On 19 July 1948, the first air refueling units in the USAF (43rd and 509th Air Refueling Squadrons) were activated at Davis-Monthan AFB, Arizona, and Roswell AFB, New Mexico, to prepare for their role as tanker aircraft using modified B-29s to carry and dispense fuel. These dedicated tankers and crews allowed SAC to extend the range of its B-29 and B-50A bombers, and all future USAF and SAC bombers were to be equipped with an in-flight refueling capability. The first FRL loop-hose refueling system proved unwieldy and difficult, particularly in bad weather and at night. The hoses were unable to transfer large amounts of fuel (only 110 gallons per minute) and could not operate at the higher operating speeds and altitudes of the new jet bombers.

Boeing KB-29M Refueling Tanker refueling a Boeing B-50A bomber.

At the time Boeing began testing the Boeing Boom System, consisting of a large-diameter "flying boom" connected to the rear of a KB-29M tanker. The boom featured a telescoping large diameter pipe with wing-like fins at the nozzle end dubbed "ruddervators," because they functioned as rudders and elevators. The tanker would fly above and forward of the receiving B-50A and the boom operator, in the B-29's converted tail turret, lowered and "flew" the boom's four-inch diameter pipe into a receptacle on the upper fuselage of the B-50A. This refueling system permitted fuel transfers at higher speeds and, significantly, at more than six times per minute fuel flow. The single-point refueling system on receiving aircraft allowed all of its several fuel tanks to be refilled from a single point instead of from multiple nozzles elsewhere on the bomber. The crew of the receiving aircraft would extend an apparatus designed to snag the trailing hose from the rear of the aircraft. Once the crew captured the fuel hose, they connected it to the refueling manifold, completed the transfer, and released the hose for recovery by the tanker crew.

Later, SAC converted several aircraft to a probe and drogue system using a design created by Flight Refueling International. This system used a refueling hose mounted on an electrically-driven reel inside the tanker, with the receiving bomber accepting fuel through a fixed refueling probe. Originally this system was tested with bombers, but later the design was particularly effective for refueling fighter aircraft.

1948: Lucky Lady I Around-the-World Flight

On 22 July 1948, three B-29s from the 43rd Bombardment Group took off from Davis-Monthan AFB, Arizona, in an attempt to complete an around-the-world flight in fourteen days. 1Lt. A. M. Neal commanded *Lucky Lady* and Lt.Col. R. W. Kline commanded *Gas Gobbler* (the third B-29 crashed in the Arabian Sea). After eight stops and flying 20,000 miles in 103:50 hours of actual flight time, *Lucky Lady* and *Gas Gobbler* landed back at Davis-Monthan on 6 August 1948, a day past their objective. The noteworthy flight was made by the fledgling USAF as a demonstration of America's long-range airpower capabilities.

B-29 *Lucky Lady I*

1949 B-50A Lucky Lady II First Non-stop Refueled Around-the-World Flight

On 26 February 1949, B-50A *Lucky Lady II* (46-010), piloted by Capt. James Gallagher, left Carswell AFB, Texas, with a crew of fourteen and flew eastward to start the first non-stop flight around-the-world. *Lucky Lady II* was refueled four times in flight by KB-29Ms of the 43rd Air Refueling Squadron, and after flying 23,452 miles in 94:01 hours, she completed her flight on 2 March 1949. For this outstanding flight *Lucky Lady II's* crew received the Mackay Trophy and the Air Age Trophy: "The success of the mission of the *Lucky Lady II* demonstrated even more rapid flight capability, supported by the fledgling ability to refuel in flight, and the ability to project global power through the USAF's Strategic Air Command." (Mackay Trophy citation)

B-50A *Lucky Lady II.*

KC-97 Stratotanker

The restrictions of the KB-29M's limited fuel offload capability and its mature, late 1930s B-29 airframe design had always made the aircraft considered an interim tanker (even though the last of the KB-29s were not retired from SAC until November 1957). Boeing developed the KC-97 based on its Model 377 Stratocruiser trans-oceanic airliner and C-97 Stratofreighter, which was a "fatter" version of the B-29. Boeing added the required fuel storage tanks, transfer plumbing, and boom arm apparatus required to convert it into a strategic tanker. The KC-97's interior was divided into two decks, with the upper deck carrying oversized cargo, while the lower deck contained transfer fuel tanks. Originally the aircraft, designated the KC-97G, was equipped with only four Pratt & Whitney R-4360 radial engines, but later two J-47 turbojet engines were added to allow the redesignated KC-97L to refuel B-47 and B-52 jet aircraft. A KC-97 with an offloading capacity of 53,000 lbs. of fuel could effectively refuel two B-47 Stratojets. The first KC-97 entered service with the 306th Air Refueling Squadron at MacDill AFB, Florida, in 1951. By 1953, SAC operated nearly thirty air refueling squadrons flying 502 tankers, with the majority of the squadrons equipped with KC-97s, and nearly every B-47 Wing had a KC-97 air refueling squadron assigned to it. The KC-97 Stratotanker was an instrumental factor in providing SAC's B-47 Stratojets with legitimate intercontinental capability.

Boeing KC-97 Stratofreighter refueling a Boeing B-47 Stratojet.

KC-97 fueling apparatus looking up from a B-47 pilot's view.

Boeing B-47 Stratojet

The B-47 Stratojet was a long-range, six-engine, jet-powered strategic bomber designed to meet a 1944 requirement to fly at high subsonic speeds and at high-altitudes to avoid enemy interceptors and incorporated many advanced qualities making its performance much better than its competitors, foreign and domestic. The first XB-47 prototype flew in December 1947 and was introduced into the Strategic Air Command during May 1951, replacing the propeller-driven B-29s and B-50s in SAC's medium bomber units, serving admirably both as a nuclear bomber and a reconnaissance aircraft. It was a mainstay of SAC's bomber strength and was America's first line of strategic nuclear deterrent during the late 1950s and early 1960s, and remained in use as a bomber until 1965. By 1956, the USAF had twenthy-eight B-47 bomber wings and five RB-47 reconnaissance wings, totaling 1,357 B-47s and 175 RB-47s. During the decade between 1947 and 1957, Boeing, Douglas, and Lockheed built more than 2,000 Stratojets, phasing out its last B-47 bombers in 1965 with the much larger B-52 becoming the mainstay of the USAF.

Boeing B-47 Stratojet

KC-97 Found Wanting

The KC-97 was found to have several limitations: while a single KC-97 could sufficiently refuel a B-47, the B-52's much larger fuel tanks (243,000 lbs.) and higher fuel consumption meant more KC-97s would be required to support the USAF bomber fleet. The speed and altitude disparity between the piston-powered KC-97 and the receiving turbojet B-52 bomber was the biggest problem. Because a fully loaded KC-97 required an extended time to climb to its cruising altitude, SAC had to deploy its tankers for prolonged periods to strategic locations in Canada and Alaska, along routes the bombers would fly to bomb Cold War Russian targets (with sufficient warning, of course). To reach the refueling location, the B-52s had to slow and descend to the KC-97's altitude, called "tobogganing." Once the two aircraft connected, to allow the bomber to maintain enough air speed to remain airborne the tanker had to dive to gain speed. But then, as the receiver acquired more fuel it became heavier, making tobogganing even more difficult, especially in poor or marginal weather. Once the two aircraft completed refueling the B-52 had to climb back to its cruise altitude, burning a considerable volume of the fuel it had just received. For instance, the three B-52s of Operation Power Flite (see below) required the support of seventy-eight KC-97s, plus several more standing on alert at bases along the route in case of adverse winds. The operation showed that eight KC-97s were required to provide the refueling requirements of one of the B-52Bs during its around-the-world flight.

B-58 Hustler

The delta wing Convair B-58 Hustler was the first operational supersonic jet bomber capable of Mach 2 flight. The aircraft was designed by Convair engineer Robert Widmer and developed for service in SAC during the 1960s. It was powered by four General Electric J79 engines in pods under the wing, and also had a large pod under the fuselage that carried fuel and a nuclear weapon, rather than in an internal bomb bay. It replaced the vulnerable Boeing B-47 Stratojet and was originally intended to fly at high altitudes at supersonic speeds to evade Soviet interceptors. The Soviet introduction of highly accurate surface-to-air missiles obligated the Hustler to function as a low-level penetration bomber, which significantly limited its range and strategic value, and it never delivered conventional bombs. This limitation caused it to have only a decade-long operational career during the 1960s, when it was succeeded by the smaller, swing-wing FB-111 in 1970.

Although the B-58 is probably more well known to the public for its window-rattling sonic booms, it set nineteen world speed/distance records, including US coast-to-coast records and one for the longest supersonic flight in history.

On 26 May 1961, a B-58 flown by Lt.Col. William Payne set a New York-to-Paris record of 3:19 hours at 1,089.4 mph. (Payne was subsequently killed in an accident in a B-58 in Paris.)

1962: B-58 Hustler Sets All Transcontinental and Return Records

On 5 March 1962, during Operation Heat Rise, two Convair B-58 Hustler supersonic bombers—call signs Tall Man Five Five and Tall Man Five Six, from the 65th Bombardment Squadron of the 43rd Bombardment Wing, based at Carswell AFB, Texas—took off at sunrise and headed west to Los Angeles. Off the Pacific coast they refueled from a KC-135A Stratotanker, then headed east at maximum speed to start the race. To make the race official they were to enter a radar starting gate at Los Angeles, but the radar did not pick them up, so they returned to the tanker, topped off their fuel tanks again, and then raced eastward once again after their entry was visually confirmed. The FAA assigned both B-58s a block altitude of Flight Level 250 to Flight Level 500 (between 25,000 and 50,000 ft.), and all other aircraft were cleared from those altitudes along the course as the Hustlers streaked from Los Angeles at 50,000 ft. at speeds over Mach 2. The two B-58s descended to 25,000 ft. toward their third refueling (first during the race) over Kansas, but the first B-58 (Tall Man Five Five) had a problem with its navigation radar and they had difficulty locating their tanker; they were finally able to refuel. Over a twenty-one minute period they received 85,000 gallons of fuel and then climbed back to 45,000 ft. to continue on to New York. *Cowtown Hustler* (Tall Man Five Six/sn 59-2458), flown by Capt. Robert Showers, Capt. Robert MacDonald, and Capt. John Walton, crossed the radar gate at New York with an elapsed time of 2:00:59 hours (the old record was 2:47 hours set by a McDonnell F4H-1) for the west-to-east flight, averaging 1,214.65 mph. Tall Man Five Six was only a minute behind. Passing over New York, the Hustlers flew over the Atlantic Ocean and rendezvoused with tankers for a fourth aerial refueling, then turned back toward the West Coast. At this point Tall Man Five Six developed mechanical difficulties and had to withdraw from the round-trip record attempt. Over Kansas *Cowtown Hustler* refueled for a fourth time, then continued west to Los Angeles. The east-to-west leg from New York to Los Angeles was completed in an elapsed time of 2:15:50 hours (the old record was 3:36 hours set by a McDonnell RF-101C), averaging 1,081.81 mph. The total round trip time was 4:41 hours (the old record was 6:46 hours set by a McDonnell RF-101C), and the round trip average speed was 1,044.96 mph at a cruising altitude of approximately 50,000 ft. with one aerial refueling. This still-standing record setting flight won the Bendix Trophy and the Mackay Trophy for its crew.

Bendix Trophy-winning crew of the B-58 Hustler *Cowtown*: Capt. Robert Showers, Capt. Robert MacDonald, and Capt. John Walton

During mid-October 1963, Operation Greased Lightning was being prepared to test the limit of its honeycomb construction method. The speed of the flight was to be limited only by the speed at which the honeycomb panels would theoretically delaminate. Convair B-58A-20-CF Hustler (61-2059B-58) *Can Do* was taken from an operational unit (305th Bombardment Wing, Bunker Hill AFB, Indiana) and had not been modified in any way. *Can Do* was flown to Kadena AFB, Okinawa, where it waited four days preparing for the flight. On 16 October, the mission was OK'd for takeoff to be flown by a crew of three: Maj. Sidney Kubesch, Maj. John Barrett, and Capt. Gerard Williamson. The route included five in-flight refuelings: between Tokyo and the Aleutian Islands; over Shemya; over Anchorage, Alaska; near Thule, Greenland; and off the southeastern coast of Greenland. Except to slow down to rendezvous with the tankers for refuelings, the B-58 would accelerate to supersonic cruising speeds. It flew over Tokyo to London (RAF Greenham Common), traveling 8,028 non-stop miles in 8:35:20 hours at an average speed of 938 mph; the speed from Tokyo to Anchorage, Alaska, was 3:09:42 hours at an average speed of 1,093.4 mph; and its speed from Anchorage to London was 5:24:54 hours at 826.9 mph. It was the longest supersonic flight in history and a record that still stands. The three crewmen were awarded the Distinguished Flying Cross. *Can Do* is displayed at the Strategic Air and Space Museum, Offutt AFB, New England. Over its career B-58s were awarded the Bleriot Trophy, the Thompson Trophy, the Mackay Trophy, the Bendix Trophy, and the Harmon Trophy. (Note: Folk singer John Denver's father, Col. Henry Deutschendorf Sr., set several speed records as a B-58 pilot.)

B-58 Hustler *Can Do* crew: (L-R) Maj. Sidney Kubesch, Maj. John Barrett, and Capt. Gerard Williamson

KC-135 Stratotanker

The KC-97's liabilities and the increasing demands of SAC led to the procurement of the Boeing KC-135 Stratotanker. The KC-135, the first dedicated jet-powered tanker, was similar (but not identical) to the commercial Boeing 707 airliner. The KC-135 was initially designated to refuel strategic bombers, but was used extensively in Vietnam and the later Gulf War to extend the range and endurance of US tactical fighters and bombers. The Air Force placed an initial order for twenty-nine KC-135As in 1954, the first of an eventual 820 of all variants of the basic C-135 family. The first KC-135 first flew in August 1956; the initial production Stratotanker was delivered to Castle AFB, California, in June 1957; and the last KC-135 was delivered in 1965. Analyses have concluded that many KC-135s could be flown until 2040, although their maintenance costs have greatly increased. The aircraft will eventually be replaced on its ninetieth birthday by the Boeing KC-46 Pegasus.

After its introduction the KC-135 set several speed/distance records:

On 8 April 1958, a Boeing KC-135 Stratotanker established a world non-stop unrefueled record for a flight from Tokyo to Lajes Air Base, in the Azores, in 18:45 hours that covered 10,229.3 miles.

Brig.Gen. W. E. Eubank piloted a KC-135, setting a world speed record of 13:46 hours between Tokyo and Washington, DC (492.26 mph).

On 12 June 1958, a KC-135 set an unofficial American coast-to-coast record of 3:42:45.

Boeing KC-135 Stratotanker refueling a Boeing B-52 Stratofortress.

During the Vietnam War, KC-135 tankers flew 194,687 sorties, averaging 21,631 sorties per year and carrying out 813,378 in-flight refuelings, an average of 90,375 per year, 7,531 per month, and 251 per day; total flying time was 911,364 hours, delivering almost 1.4 billion gallons of fuel weighing almost 9 billion pounds.

During the Gulf War (2 August 1990–28 February 1991), USAF tankers flourished. During the thirty-two days of Desert

Shield (2 August 1990–17 January 1991), USAF tankers flew 4,967 sorties, logging more than 19,700 hours flying time, offloading 28.2 million gallons of fuel (183 million lbs.), and making 4,588 hookups.

During the forty-three days of Desert Storm (17 January 1991–28 February 1991), USAF tankers flew 15,434 tanker sorties, a daily average of 358. The refuelers logged 60,000 flying hours and made 45,995 fueling contacts, delivering approximately 110.2 million gallons of fuel. During the operation nearly one-in-five (eighteen percent) of aircraft in the air on any one day were tankers. During the first day of Desert Storm, the 2nd Bomb Wing launched seven B-52s from Barksdale AFB, Louisiana, against enemy targets in Iraq using the first combat launching of conventional Air Launched Cruise Missiles (ALCM).The 14,000 mile round trip mission took thirty-five hours and set a record for longest distance combat mission, breaking the record previously held by an RAF Vulcan bomber in 1982 during the Falkland Campaign.

On 2–3 September, during the 1996 Operation Desert Strike—the US air component of the Kurdish Civil War—two B-52Hs struck Baghdad power stations and communications facilities with thirteen AGM-86C conventional air launched cruise missiles (CALCMs). At that time this was the longest distance flown for a combat mission involving a 34 hour, 16,000 statute mile round trip from Barksdale AFB, Louisiana.

KC-10 Extender

During the Vietnam War, there were concerns regarding the KC-135 fleet's ability to meet the needs of America's global commitments. At that time the aerial refueling fleet was deployed to Southeast Asia to support tactical aircraft and strategic bombers while also maintaining US-based support of its deterrent nuclear bomber fleet. Consequently, the Air Force sought an aerial tanker with greater capabilities than the KC-135. The result was the McDonnell Douglas KC-10 Extender, the modified military version of the three-engined DC-10 jet airliner. The KC-10 first flew on 12 July 1980, and flew its first aerial refueling sortie in October. Sixty KC-10s were manufactured by McDonnell Douglas for the USAF to supplement its KC-97s.

The KC-10 can transport up to seventy-five personnel and about 170,000 lbs. of cargo over about 4,400 miles unrefueled. In addition to the three main DC-10 wing fuel tanks, the KC-10 has three large fuel tanks under the cargo floor, one under the forward lower cargo compartment, one in the center wing area, and one under the rear compartment. The combined capacity of these six tanks is more than 356,000 lbs. of fuel, nearly twice that of the KC-135 Stratotanker. Utilizing either an advanced aerial refueling boom or a hose and drogue centerline refueling system, the KC-10 can refuel a wide assortment of US and Allied military aircraft within the same mission, and is equipped with lighting for night refueling operations. The KC-10 boom operator controls refueling operations through a digital, fly-by-wire system. Sitting in the rear of the aircraft, the operator can see the receiver aircraft through a wide window. During boom refueling operations, fuel is transferred to the receiver at a maximum rate of 1,100 gallons per minute, while the hose and drogue refueling maximum rate is 470 gallons per minute. The automatic load alleviation and independent disconnect systems greatly enhance safety and facilitate air refueling. The KC-10 can be air-refueled by a KC-135 or another KC-10A to increase its delivery range.

Analyses indicate the KC-10 is expected to serve until 2043. The USAF requires 480 tanker aircraft in its refueling fleet, which primarily consists of KC-135s dating from the 1950s, with several dozen KC-10s dating from the 1980s. The Air Force's chief

Boeing KC-10 refueling a B-2 Spirit.

Boeing KC-46 refueling a B-2 Spirit.

refueling priority is to accept the new Boeing KC-46 Pegasus to replace about one-third of its KC-135s. Boeing developed the KC-46 from its 767 jet airliner, and in February 2011, the tanker was selected the winner in the KC-X tanker competition to replace older KC-135s. The first eighteen combat-ready tankers are scheduled to be delivered by August 2017.

Despite all the technological developments, commercial aircraft designers have never embraced aerial refueling, preferring aircraft with large internal fuel tanks as less expensive than operating a dedicated fleet of refueling aircraft. Aerial refueling is now exclusively a vital military operation, greatly extending the range of bombers and making intercontinental fighter aircraft possible.

Robert Timm, John Cook, and their modified Cessna 172 Skyhawk

LONGEST MANNED FLIGHT: DAYS AND MILES

With all the in-flight military refueling records previously described, the record for the longest refueled manned flight is held by a civilian light aircraft. On 4 December 1958, a modified Cessna 172 Skyhawk piloted by Robert Timm and John Cook set the world record for continuous manned flight by flying more than 150,000 miles without landing for 64 days and 22:19 hours. The publicity flight was sponsored by the Las Vegas Hacienda Hotel to raise money for cancer research. A ninety-five gallon belly tank was installed and an electric pump was equipped to transfer fuel to the wing tanks. Plumbing was installed through the firewall so that engine oil and oil filters could be changed without shutting off the engine. Except for the pilot's seat, the aircraft interior was removed and a folding accordion-style door replaced the co-pilot's side door. The co-pilot's seat was replaced by a 4×4 ft. foam pad for sleeping and a small sink was installed, enabling the two-man crew to wash and shave. A small platform could be lowered out of the co-pilot's door to provide additional footing during refueling operations. The two pilots flew in four-hour shifts and descended once a day to twenty feet above a desert highway to receive ninety-five gallons of fuel from a tanker, or occasionally a Ford Thunderbird. The flight was forced to end on 7 February 1959, when the aircraft's performance deteriorated to the point where the Cessna had difficulty climbing away from the refueling vehicle. The record breaking Cessna 172 hangs from the ceiling of the baggage claim area at Las Vegas' McCarran International Airport. Perhaps this record should be retitled the longest sub-orbital manned flight, considering the manned space station, which for its occupants is more of a ride than actual flying.

THE INTERCONTINENTAL BALLISTIC MISSILE (ICBM)

Intercontinental Ballistic Missiles (ICBMs) were first deployed by America in 1959, relegating large, long-range nuclear-armed bombers obsolete. ICBMs had ranges between 6,000–9,300 miles, effectively making any target in the world vulnerable. The view of the western powers on ICBM deployment was they were considered a strategic defensive weapon, although they were obviously an offensive weapon, not defending anything. ICBMs' supposed defensive character was based on the concept of "mutually assured destruction," in which any nuclear attack on the United States would result in swift retaliation and overwhelming destruction of the attacker. This threat of complete annihilation of the attacker and defender helped maintain an uneasy peace during the Cold War.

The 1972 SALT treaty froze the number of US and Russian ICBM launchers at existing levels, while subsequent SALT II talks held 1972–1979 reduced the number of nuclear warheads held by both adversaries. While SALT II was never ratified by

Intercontinental Ballistic Missiles (ICBMs)

the US Senate, its terms were nevertheless honored by both sides until 1986, when the Reagan administration withdrew from its terms after accusing the Soviets of violating the pact. During the 1980s, President Reagan launched the Strategic Defense Initiative, as well as the MX and Midgetman ICBM programs, resulting in an arms race that the Soviet Union could not afford. In 1991, the United States and Soviet Union agreed to the START I treaty, reducing their deployed ICBMs and warheads and effectively ending the Cold War. To use ICBMs to deliver conventional bombing weapons in a strategic or tactical role was too expensive, as the Germans found using their V-2 rockets to inaccurately deliver a ton of explosives on London.

Thus, large intercontinental, nuclear-capable bombers had regained their place in American air strategy, as they were required in a tactical role in various "skirmishes" in Vietnam and the Middle East. Former military power Britain sat back and watched the Americans continue to fly their B-52s and then develop their immensely expensive Rockwell B-1-B and Northrop Grumman B-2 stealth bombers.

BOEING B-52 STRATOFORTRESS

After it became operational in 1955, the B-52 remained the principal USAF long-range heavy bomber throughout the Cold War, and the Gulf and Afghan Operations, Kosovo War, and after sixty years continues to be an important part of the USAF bomber force. The B-52H had a crew of five (pilot, weapon's system officer, navigator, electronic warfare officer, and tail gunner) until the removal of the tail gun in 1991. The huge bomber has a wingspan of 185 ft. (wing area 4,000 sq. ft.), a length of 159.3 ft., height of 49.7 ft., an empty weight of 185,000 lbs., and a maximum take-off weight of 488,000 lbs. (including almost 48,000 gallons of fuel). Its eight Pratt & Whitney TF-33 Turbofans drive the B-52 to a maximum speed of 650 mph (cruising 525 mph) over a combat range of 4,480 miles and a ferry range of 10,145 miles. The use of aerial refueling gives the B-52 a range limited only by crew endurance. A total of 744 B-52s were built, with the last, a B-52H, delivered in October 1962; only the H model remains in Air Force inventory.

Boeing B-52 Stratofortress being refueled.

The B-52 has completed sixty years of continuous service, and after being upgraded between 2013 and 2015, it is expected to serve into the 2040s. Other aircraft having more than fifty years of continuous service with its original operator are the KC-135 Stratotanker, C-130 Hercules, Northrop T-38 Talon, Lockheed U-2 Dragon Lady, Tupolev Tu-95 Bear, and the English Electric Canberra.

OPERATION POWER FLITE AND LUCKY LADY III

On 16 January 1957, five B-52Bs, including two spares, departed from Castle AFB, California, to begin their circumnavigation of the globe under the command of Maj.Gen. Archie Old of the 15AF. One of the three B-52s was the third USAF aircraft named *Lucky Lady*, a B-52B commanded by Lt.Col. James Morris who had served as co-pilot on B-50 *Lucky Lady II* when it set the world's first non-stop (refueled) circumnavigation of the globe in 1949.

During the flight one bomber, unable to take on fuel at the first in-flight refueling rendezvous with KC-97s, landed in Goose Bay, Labrador. The second spare continued with the main flight until after it received the second in-flight refueling over Casablanca, Morocco, when it left the group and landed at Brize Norton RAF Station, England, according to plan. After a midair refueling rendezvous over Saudi Arabia, the three Stratofortresses flew along the coast of India to Sri Lanka, and continued on to make a simulated bomb drop south of the Malay Peninsula before heading toward the next air refueling rendezvous over Manila and Guam. The three B-52s crossed the Pacific Ocean, and after flying for 45:19 hours landed at March AFB, Base Riverside, California, on 18 January. The 24,325 mile flight was completed at an average speed of 525 mph and was completed in less than half the time required by *Lucky Lady II* when it made the first non-stop circumnavigation.

SAC Commander Gen. Curtis LeMay personally attended the landing to congratulate the crews and to present each with the Distinguished Flying Cross. In his welcome speech LeMay noted that the flight was a "demonstration of SAC's capabilities to strike any target on the face of the earth.... (and)....its capability to drop a hydrogen bomb anywhere in the world." Later, the National Aeronautic Association recognized Operation Power Flite as the outstanding flight of 1957 and awarded the 93rd Bombardment Wing the MacKay Trophy.

B-52 *Lucky Lady III* during Operation Power Flight.

Crew of B-52 Stratofortress *Black Widow*, led by Col. Clyde Evely (pilot 2L), Maj. Robert Carson (second pilot), and Capt. Henry Sienkiewicz (co-pilot).

OPERATION PERSIAN RUG

On 11 January 1962, USAF Col. Clyde Evely (pilot), Maj. Robert Carson (second pilot), and Capt. Henry Sienkiewicz (co-pilot) and crew from Minot's 4136th Strategic Wing flew their newly introduced H-model Boeing B-52 Stratofortress *Black Widow* from Kadena AFB, Okinawa, to Torrejon Air Base, Spain. Operation Persian Rug was an unrefueled 21:52 hour flight that covered 12,532.30 miles at an average 604.44 mph to set an official FAI distance and eleven other FAI non-stop distance and course speed records for its aircraft class and time. The previous record for the longest non-refueled flight (Class C Powered Aircraft) was held by an air refueling plane, the KC-135 Stratotanker. Operation Persian Rug was one of several planned formidable exhibitions intended to demonstrate the B-52H's dominion as a nuclear deterrent. SAC Commander Gen. Thomas Power stated the more than 12,000 mile unrefueled flight demonstrated the intercontinental capabilities of the B-52H Stratofortress: "The flight proved that SAC aircraft have the capability of reaching target destinations in any area of the globe." President John F. Kennedy personally congratulated them at the White House.

B-52S IN THE VIETNAM WAR

After months of study on how to use a huge, nuclear-capable bomber in a tactical role in what was essentially guerilla/partisan war, air planners decided that B-52s could be used most effectively against enemy logistics centers. The target selected for the first B-52 strike on 18 June 1965 was a typical Viet Cong jungle sanctuary, measuring about a mile by 2.5 miles, northwest of Saigon. Two bombers collided during refueling and crashed into the South China Sea and one aborted, but twenty-seven bombed the target. After the strike ground reconnaissance reported no VC casualties, nor significant damage to facilities. Subsequently, carpet bombing was instituted and refined, and the B-52s were modified to increase the size of their bomb load to up to 60,000 lbs. A postwar AAF analysis found that due to the sheer tonnage of bombs dropped, the main contribution of B-52s was the "constricting effect the bombings have had on the enemy's freedom of movement and range of action. Emphasis then focuses on the psychological effect on the enemy of being bombed—or what is perhaps almost as disturbing, the threat of being bombed—and its debilitating effect on enemy plans for major operations."

America's last large-scale air combat without stealth and the largest since the end of WWII was Linebacker II, late in the Vietnam War (18–29 December 1972). Linebacker was intended to heavily bomb the North Vietnamese to induce them to negotiate for a peace settlement. The US air emphasis shifted from attacks by smaller tactical fighter aircraft to attacks by B-52 Stratofortress heavy bombers on industrial, military, transportation, petroleum, and electrical utility targets. During the daily attacks the seventy-mile-long column of B-52s required up to fifty support aircraft to jam, blind, and destroy surface-to-air-directing radars. Even so, over the eleven-day bombing operation barrages of Soviet-built missiles shot down twenty-seven aircraft (fifteen B-52s). The B-52s flew 741 sorties and combined with 1,274 other USAF, USN, and USMC sorties, caused severe damage to North Vietnam targets, particularly its infrastructure. The US claimed that Linebacker succeeded in forcing the Democratic Republic of Vietnam (DRV) Politburo to return to the negotiating table, with the Paris Peace Accords signed shortly after the operation. The agreement plainly benefited the People's Army of Vietnam (PAVN) in the end. Also, while the bombing did severe infrastructure damage in North Vietnam, it did not break the stalemate in the South, nor did it stop the continuous stream of supplies flowing down the Ho Chi Minh Trail into the south; the war would continue until 30 April 1975, when NVA troops entered Saigon.

B-52s in Linebacker II

CRUISE MISSILES

A cruise missile is basically a small, pilotless aircraft that can fly 500 to 1,000 miles, depending on its configuration, and with modern guidance systems permits very accurate attacks. There are a number of variations of cruise missiles, and their importance in the intercontinental sense is that they can be stored and carried over long distances by submarines, surface vessels, or aircraft and then launched. The warhead is integrated into the cruise missile, which is destroyed when its bomb explodes. Since cruise missiles cost $500,000–$1,000,000 each, it is a somewhat expensive means to deliver a relatively small payload. Thus, the most common mission for cruise missiles is to attack relatively high-value targets, such as command bunkers, ships, large electrical complexes, bridges, and dams. They are distinct from unmanned aerial vehicles (UAVs), in that they are used only as weapons and not for aerial reconnaissance.

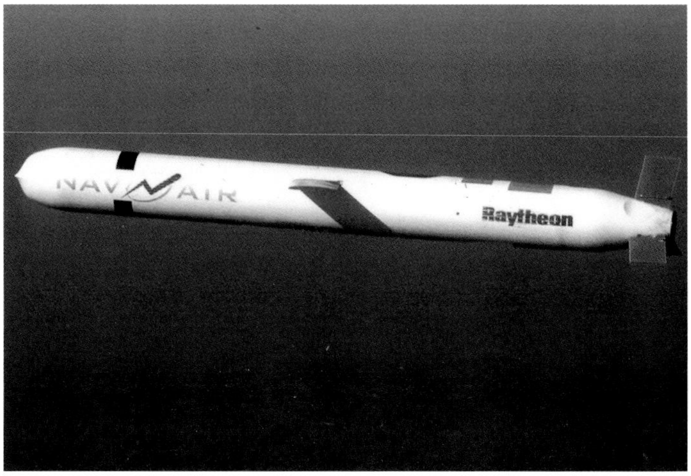

McDonnell Douglas Tomahawk long-range, all-weather, subsonic cruise missile

ROCKWELL B-1/B-1A/B-1B LANCER

The Rockwell B-1 Lancer is a four-engine supersonic variable-sweep wing, jet-powered USAF strategic bomber. The B-1A was first envisioned in the 1960s as a supersonic bomber with Mach 2 speed and sufficient range and payload to replace the B-52 Stratofortress. With the development of anti-aircraft surface-to-air missiles (SAMs), SAC began assigning its bombers to low-level penetration missions and developed the B-1B as primarily a low-level penetrator with long range and Mach 1.25 speed. Huge cost overrides ($100 million per aircraft) made the B-1A a political issue, and in 1977, President Carter canceled the program in favor of ICBMs, Submarine-Launched Ballistic Missiles (SLBMs), and a fleet of modernized B-52s armed with Air-Launched Cruise Missiles (ALCMs). Upon taking office President Regan resumed the program in 1981 as the B-1B, which was a revised B-1 design with reduced radar signature and a maximum speed of Mach 1.25 otherwise optimized for low-level penetration. The Lancer has a wingspan of 136.7 ft. extended forward and 78.2 ft. swept aft, a length of 150.2 ft., a height of 33.6 ft., and a normal operating weight of 389,800 lbs. The four General Electric F-101 GE-100 turbofan engines with afterburners give the bomber a maximum speed of Mach 1.2 at sea level (900+ mph) and a cruising speed of 560–650 mph over a range of 6,100 miles unrefueled. A total of one hundred B-1Bs were produced, and the Lancer continues to be deployed today, flying missions in support of continuing operations. With upgrades the bomber is projected to remain in service until approximately 2038.

NORTHROP B-2 SPIRIT STEALTH BOMBER

The Northrop B-2 Spirit Stealth Bomber is a flying wing aircraft with a wing span of 172 ft. (5,140 sq. ft. wing area), 69 ft. length, 17 ft. height, an empty weight of 158,000 lbs.,

Rockwell B-1/B-1A/B-1B Lancer

and a maximum take-off weight of 376,000 lbs. (including 167,000 lbs. of fuel for its four GE turbofans). The B-2 combines stealth technologies with great aerodynamic efficiency and a large payload. Its stealth characteristics provide a greater freedom of action at high altitudes, increasing range and field of view for onboard sensors. It has a range of approximately 6,900 miles at cruising altitude on its internal fuel load. Its four General Electric F118-GE-100 non-afterburning turbofan power plants give the Spirit a maximum speed of Mach 0.95 (630 mph) at 40,000 ft. and a cruise speed of Mach 0.85 (560 mph) at 40,000 ft. with a service ceiling of 50,000 ft. and a range of 6,900 miles. The B-2 requires refueling every six hours at its ideal cruising altitude to extend its range to more than 11,000 miles. During refueling fifty tons or more of fuel is transferred at a time in midair meetings that take a half hour or more. Flying round trip to Iraq takes thirty-eight hours, requiring at least four refuelings by KC-135s or KC-10s. Each B-2 represents about a $2.2 billion investment, and because of their specific and specialized maintenance requirements, particularly to retain their stealth characteristics, the B-2s are based in special hangars at Whiteman AFB, Montana. Whiteman press releases state it requires an average of nine to ten hours of maintenance for every hour of B-2 flight time.

Northrop B-2 Spirit Stealth Bomber

The B-2's combat debut was on 24 March 1999, during the Kosovo War in Operation Allied Force, a NATO mission to re-establish peace in Kosovo and Serbia. Two B-2s flew more than fifteen hours from Whiteman, refueling midair over the Atlantic to attack multiple targets, dropping satellite-guided 2,000 lb. bombs, and then returned directly back to Whiteman, again refueling. It was the first time the USAF carried out a sustained bombing campaign from its own soil, with the Whiteman B-2s

The B-52 and the B-2 could be flying together in 2040.

flying less than one percent of the total missions, but destroying thirty-three percent of the targets in the first eight weeks of US involvement in the war.

In response to the 9/11 terrorist attacks six B-2s were committed to Operation Enduring Freedom, the American intervention in Afghanistan. During Enduring Freedom these B-2s flew a total of six missions on the first three days of the war, including the longest combat mission in history. On 7 October 2001, six B-2s took off from Whiteman and headed west, refueling four times before arriving over Afghanistan to drop their sixteen JDAMs carried in the two B-2 bomb bays. JDAM (Joint Direct Attack Munition) is a guidance kit that converts unguided bombs ("dumb bombs") into all-weather "smart bombs." That night, the B-2s conducted bombing runs on multiple targets throughout Afghanistan, with the primary mission being to secure air superiority for air forces that would conduct subsequent attacks. After 44:20 hours in the air the six stealth bombers landed on Diego Garcia Island in the Indian Ocean with their pilots' missions ended. With their engines running the six Spirits were refueled and serviced, and forty-five minutes later six new crews began the thirty-hour journey back to Missouri; the B-2s operated flawlessly for more than seventy hours with their GE turbofans never stopping.

During the March/April 2003 Operation Iraqi Freedom campaign, B-2s operated from Diego Garcia and an "undisclosed forward operating location," flying twenty-two sorties, as well as flying twenty-seven sorties from Whiteman AFB and releasing more than 1.5 million pounds of munitions

During March 2011, B-2s were the first US aircraft to fly combat in Operation Odyssey Dawn, the UN mandated enforcement of the Libyan no-fly zone. Three B-2s flew from Whiteman across the Atlantic Ocean to Libya, being refueled four times on each leg of the twenty-five hour, 11,418-mile round trip mission.

During March 2013, two B-2s flew a 13,000 mile round trip from Whiteman to South Korea, dropping dummy ordnance as part of the annual South Korean-United States military exercises.

Twenty B-2s remain in USAF service, with plans to operate them until 2058.

3
THE FUTURE: INTERCONTINENTAL TO INTERSTELLAR

First man to orbit the earth Yuri Gargarin (USSR) aboard the *Vostok* on 12 April 1961.

First man to orbit longer than twenty-four hours Gherman Titov (USSR) aboard the *Vostok 2* on 6–7 August 1961.

Longest consecutive time in space: Valeri Polyakov (USSR) spent 437.7 days aboard Mir Space Station 1 September 1994–22 March 1995.

There were six US moon landings (Apollo 11, 12, and 14–17) over a forty-one month period beginning on 20 July 1969, with Neil Armstrong and Buzz Aldrin on Apollo 11 and ending on 14 December 1972, with Gene Cernan and Jack Schmitt on Apollo 17. A total of twelve men landed on the Moon, with two US pilot/astronauts flying a Lunar Module and a third crew member who remained on board the Command Module. The last three missions had a rover for increased mobility. In December 1972, Harrison Schmidt and Eugene Cernan of NASA's Apollo 17 mission spent just under seventy-five hours, and also completed three moonwalks that lasted a total of more than twenty-two hours.

The first space shuttle was *Columbia*, which was launched on 12 April 1981 from Florida. The other US space shuttles were *Atlantis*, *Challenger*, and *Discovery*.

The International Space Station, the $100 billion orbiting lab, has been continuously occupied since 2 November 2000 for the record.

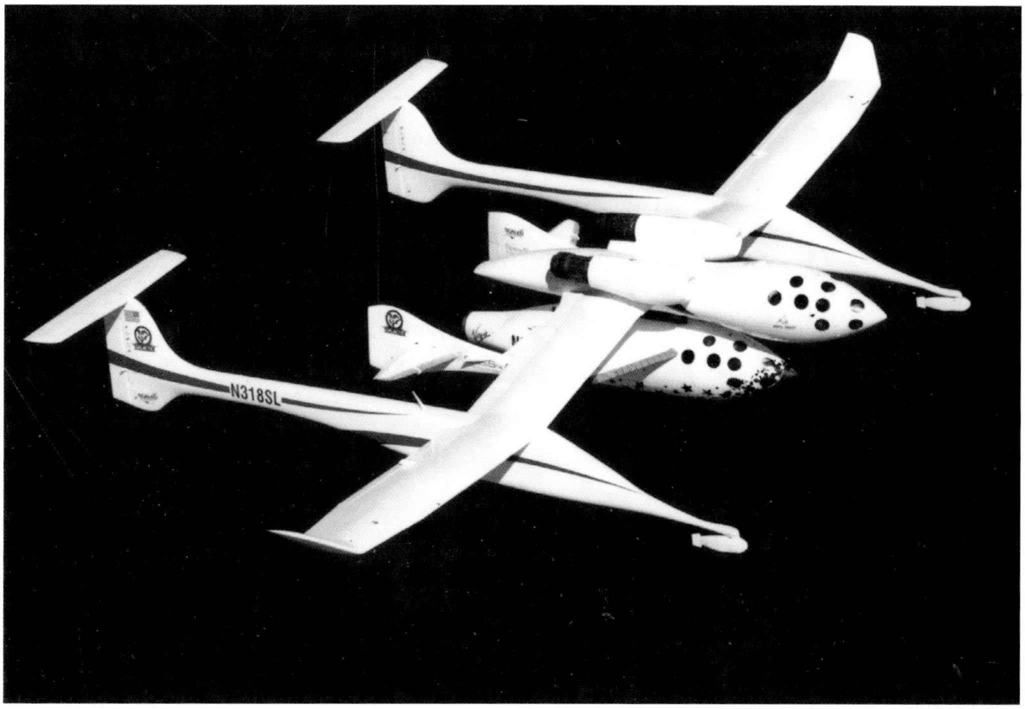

SpaceShipOne was a suborbital air-launched US spaceplane that completed the first manned private spaceflight in 2004. That same year it won the US$10 million Ansari X Prize and was immediately retired from active service. Its mother ship was named *White Knight*.

Virgin Galactic is a US spaceflight company that is developing commercial spacecraft to offer suborbital spaceflights to space tourists, suborbital launches for space science missions, and orbital launches of small satellites. The launch vehicle, *SpaceShipTwo*, is air launched from beneath a carrier known as *White Knight Two*. Virgin Galactic's founder, Sir Richard Branson, had initially hoped for a maiden flight by the end of 2009, but this date has been delayed on a number of occasions, most recently by the October 2014 in-flight loss of *SpaceShipTwo*.

Starship *Enterprise*—"Warp speed Scotty"

Close Encounters

APPENDIX

AVIATION TROPHIES

HARMON TROPHY

The Harmon Trophy was established in 1926 by Clifford Harmon, a wealthy real estate developer, balloonist, and aviator, as "American awards for the most outstanding international achievements in the arts and/or science of aeronautics for the preceding year, with the art of flying receiving first consideration." It was a set of three international trophies to be awarded annually to the world's outstanding aviator, aviatrix, and aeronaut (balloon or dirigible). A fourth trophy, the National Trophy, was awarded 1926–1938 to "the most outstanding aviator" in each of the twenty-one member countries, and again 1946–1948 to honor Americans who contributed to aviation.

Harmon Trophy

COLLIER TROPHY

The Robert Collier Trophy was awarded annually "for the greatest achievement in aeronautics or astronautics in America, with respect to improving the performance, efficiency, and safety of air or space vehicles, the value of which has been thoroughly demonstrated by actual use during the preceding year." In addition to being an aviator, humanitarian, and sportsman, Collier was a prominent publisher, whose family created popular *Colliers Weekly*. While president of the Aero Club of America, National Chapter—later named the National Aeronautic Association (NAA)—Collier commissioned the huge 525 lb. trophy in 1910. Originally called the Aero Club Trophy, it was renamed in his honor in 1922, after Collier died at forty-two of a heart attack in 1918, after completing his military service in WWI. When the Aero Club dissolved the award was assumed by the National Aeronautic Association. The Collier Trophy name became official in 1944, and was presented once a year by the NAA president, with the trophy on permanent display at the National Air and Space Museum in 1951. Collier was the first person to purchase an airplane from the Wright brothers for personal use. Shortly thereafter, he loaned his aircraft to the US Army for flight evaluations at Fort Sam Houston, in San Antonio, Texas, which led to the first military orders for a flying machine.

Collier Trophy

MACKAY TROPHY

The Mackay Trophy is administered by the United States National Aeronautic Association and is awarded yearly by the USAF for the "most meritorious flight of the year by an Air Force person, persons, or organization." The award was established on 27 January 1911 by Clarence Mackay, a prominent American industrialist, philanthropist, and aviation enthusiast. The trophy is held in the Smithsonian Institution's National Air and Space Museum.

MacKay Trophy

BENDIX TROPHY

The Bendix Trophy was an American aeronautical racing trophy for a transcontinental, point-to-point race sponsored by industrialist Vincent Bendix, founder of Bendix Corporation. It began in 1931, as part of the National Air Races, with an initial $15,000 prize for the winners. The purpose was "to interest engineers in building faster, more reliable, and durable aircraft." Bendix competitors flew from Burbank, California, to Cleveland, Ohio, except for two years when the contest began in New York and ended in Los Angeles. The last Bendix Trophy Race was flown in 1962.

Bendix Trophy

Bendix Balloon Trophy

THOMPSON TROPHY

The Thompson Trophy race was established in 1929, emphasizing low-altitude flying and maneuverability at high speeds over a ten mile long closed course, with the turns marked by fifty foot high pylons. The races were held for the next ten years, ending in 1939. Further races in this series were precluded by the onset of WWII and the original trophy was retired. After the war advances in aircraft technology required the establishment of a new series of races for a piston engine division flown by civilians and a jet-powered division flown by military pilots and administered by the USAF. Roscoe Turner, the last winner of the prewar trophy, refused to relinquish it, but the original molds were located and two additional casts were made: one for the piston division and the other for the jet-powered division. Piston Division races were held 1946–1949, while Jet Division races were held 1951–1961, except for 1952 and 1960, with the last race held in 1961.

Thompson Trophy

BRITANNIA TROPHY

The Britannia Trophy is a British award presented by the Royal Aero Club for aviators "accomplishing the most meritorious performance in aviation during the previous year."

In 1911, Horatio Barber, who was a founding member of the Royal Aero Club, was given £100 for a commercial flight; not wanting to taint his amateur status, he presented the money to the Club for the trophy. The first award was presented in 1913, but the trophy has not been awarded every year, particularly during WWI and WWII, and has been awarded jointly and to teams, as well as individuals. In 1952, the Royal Aero Club presented plaques to all the surviving holders, who previously only held the trophy for one year and were not given a permanent keepsake.

Britannia Trophy

LONG-DISTANCE RECORDS 1903–2015

Year	Date	Distance*	Pilot	Aircraft	Notes
2006	February 12, 2006	41,467.46 km/25,767.40 mi	Steve Fossett	GlobalFlyer	Absolute record holder all classes
1986	December 23, 1986	40,212.14 km/24,987.57 mi	Richard Rutan and Jeana Yeager	Rutan Voyager	Circumnavigation. Federation Aeronautique Internationale record holder up to 2006 (current class holder)
1962	January 10-11, 1962	20,168.78 km/12531.81 mi	Major Clyde Evely and crew	Boeing B-52H Stratofortress	From Kadena AB, Okinawa to Torrejon AB, Spain, via Tokyo, Seattle, Fort Worth, Washington DC and the Azores[4]
1946	September 29 -October 2, 1946	18,083.6 km/11,236.3 mi	Cdr. Tom Davies (pilot), Cdr. Eugene Rankin (co-pilot) and 2 crew	Lockheed P2V-1 Neptune	From Perth, Australia to Columbus, OH
1945	November 20, 1945	12,739.6 km/7,915.6 mi	USAF; C. S. Irvine and 9 crew	Boeing B-29 Superfortress	From Guam to Washington DC
1938	November 5-7, 1938	11,520.4 km/7,158,2 mi	RAF Long-range Development Unit; R. Kellett, H.A.V. Hogan and A. N. Combe (first pilots) and crew of two (also qualified pilots) in each aircraft	Vickers Wellesley	From Ismailia, Egypt to Darwin, Northern Territory in Australia; three aircraft flew in formation, Hogan landed to refuel at Koepang (500 miles short of Darwin), the other two landed at Koepang (500 miles short of Darwin), the other two landed at Darwin, Northern Territory
1938	May 13-15, 1938	11,651.0 km/7.239.6 mi	Yuzoh Fujita + crew (Japan)	Koken-ki	Three-corner course over Japan. Closed-circuit record
1937	July 12-14, 1937	10,148.5 /6,305.7 mi	Mikhail Gromov + crew (Russia)	Tupolev ANT-25	From Moscow to San Jacinto, CA
1933	August 7, 1933	9,104.7 /5,657.0 mi	Maurice Rossi and Paul Codos (France)	Bleriot110 F-ALCC	From Floyd Bennett Field, NY to Rayack, Syria
1933	February 8, 1933	8,544 /5,300 mi	RAF Long-range Development Unit; O. R. Gayford and Gilbert Nicholetts	Fairey Long-range Monoplane K1991	From Cranwell, UK, to Walvis Bay, South Africa
1931	July 28-31	8,066 /5,012 mi	Russell Boardman and John Polando	Bellanca J-300 Special	Cape Cod From Floyd Bennett Field, NY to Istanbul, Turkey
1929	December 15-19, 1929	8,029 /4,989 mi	Dieudonne Costes and P. Codos	Breguet 19 Super Bidon Point d'Interrogation	Closed-circuit record.
1929	September 27-29, 1929	7,905 /4,912 mi	Dieudonne Costes and Maurice Bellonte	Breguet 19 Super Bidon Point d'Interrogation	Paris to Qiqihar, China.
1927	June 28-29	3,862 /2,400 mi	Albert Hegenberger and Lester Maitland	Fokker F.VII	From California to Hawaii, the longest open sea flight up to that date, in the "Bird of Paradise". They received the Mackey Trophy
1927	May 20-21, 1927	5,809 km	Charles Lindbergh Ryan NYP,	Spirit of St. Louis	New York to Paris
1926	October 28-29, 1926	5,396 /3,610 mi	Dieudonne Costes and Jean Rignot	Breguet 19 GR	From Paris–Le Bourget Airport to Djask, Iran

(Long-distance records 1903-2015 continued on following page)

Year	Date	Distance*	Pilot	Aircraft	Notes
1926	August 31-September 1, 1926	5,174 /3,215 mi	Leon Challe and Rene Weiser	Breguet 19 GR	From Paris–Le Bourget Airport to Bandar Abbas
1926	July 14-15, 1926	4,715 /2,930 mi	Andre Girier and François Dordilly	Breguet 19 GR	From Paris to Omsk
1926	June 26-27, 1926	4,313 /2,680 mi	Ludovic Arrachart and Paul Arrachart	Farman F.62 Goliath	From Paris to Basrah, Iraq
1925	August 7-9, 1925	4,400 /2,734 mi	Maurice Drouhin and Jules Landry	Breguet 19	Closed circuit Chartres–Etampes–Toussus–Chartres.
1925	February 3-4, 1925	3,166 /1,967 mi	Ludovic Arrachart and Henry Lemaitre	Fokker T.2	Distance in a straight-line record. Etampes–Villa Cisneros.
1923	April 16-17, 1923	4,050 /2,517 mi	Oakley Kelly and John Macready	Farman Goliath	Closed circuit around Dayton, OH
1920	June 3-4, 1920	1,915 /1,190 mi	L Boussoutrot and J Bernard	Mercedes Aviatik-Pfeil	Closed-circuit record
1914	February 7, 1914	1,699 /1,056 mi	Karl Ingold		Flew continuously from 07:35 until 23:55 pm covering 1,056 miles in 16 hours and 20 minutes.
1903	December 17, 1903	279 m 915.35 ft	Wilbur Wright	Wright Flyer	59 seconds
1903	December 17, 1903	39 m127.95 ft	Orville Wright	Wright Flyer	12 seconds

ENORMOUS MID-30S AND WWII AIRCRAFT DESIGNS
(by 100 foot+ Wing Span)

First Flight	Wing	Span	Wing Area	Length Gross Weight	Engines US Post-War
Bombers and Seaplanes Hughes H-4 Spruce Goose* 1947	320 feet	11,290 sqft.	219.66 ft.	400,000 lbs.	8 x3,000 hp P&W R-4360
Consolidated B-36 Peacemaker 1946	230.0 ft.	4,772 sqft.	161.1 ft.	256,300 lbs.	6 3,800 hp × P&W R-4360
Northrop YB-35 Flying Wing 1946	172.0 ft.	4,000 sqft.	51.1 ft.	209,000 lbs.	4 x 3,000 hp P& W R-4360
US PRE-WAR AND WARTIME BOMBERS AND AIRLINERS					
Douglas XB-19 1941	212.0 ft.	4,492 sqft.	132.0 ft.	164,000 lbs.	4 x 2,000 hp R-3350
Boeing XB-15 1937	149.0 ft.	2,780 sqft.	87.58 ft.	70,700 lbs.	4x 1,000 hp R-1830
Boeing 314* 1938	152.0 ft.	2,607 sqft.	106.0 ft.	82,000 lbs.	4x 1,200 hp R-2600
Boeing 307 Stratoliner 1938	107.2 ft.	1,486sqft.	74.25 ft.	42,000 lbs.	4 x 900 hp R-1820
Boeing Model 299 1935	103.8 ft.	1,420 sqft.	68.75 ft.	38,000 lbs.	4 x 750 hp R-1690
US WWII BOMBERS AND FLYING BOATS					
Boeing B-29 Superfortress 1942	141.3 ft	1,736 sqft.	99.0 ft.	135,000 lbs.	4 × 2,200 hp R-3350
Consolidated B-24 Liberator 1939	110.0 ft.	1,048 sqft.	68.7 ft.	55,000 lbs.	4 x P&W 1,200 hp R-1830

First Flight	Wing	Span	Wing Area	Length Gross Weight	Engines US Post-War
Boeing B-17 Flying Fortress 1935	109.8 ft.	1,420 sqft.	72.3 ft.	65,500 lbs.	4 x 1,200 hp R-1820
Martin JRM-3 Mars* 1942	200.0 ft.	3,686 sqft.	117.25 ft.	165,000 lbs.	4 x 2,500 hp R-3350
Martin PBM Mariner* 1939	118.0 ft.	1,408 sqft.	79.0 ft.	41,000 lbs.	4 x 1,700 hp R-2800
Convair PB2Y Coronado* 1937	115.0 ft.	1,780 sqft.	79.0 ft.	63,000 lbs.	4 x 1,000 hp R-1830
ALLIED WWII BOMBERS					
Avro Lancaster 1941	102.0 ft.	1,297 sqft.	64.3 ft.	68,000 lbs.	4 x 1,280 hp RR Merlin
Tupolev Ant-20bis 1940	206.7 ft.	5,231 sqft.	111.92 ft.	99,200 lbs.	6 x 1,200 hp M-34FRNV
Tupolev Maxxim Gorky+ 1934	206.7 ft.	5,231 sqft.	107.92 ft.	92,600 lbs.	8 x 900 hp M-34FRN
Petlyakov Pe-8 1936	128.3 ft.	2,031 sqft.	76.0 ft.	77,000 lbs.	4 x 1,340 hp Mikulin
AXIS WWII BOMBERS FLYING BOATS TRANSPORTS					
Bloom & Voss BV 238* (German) 1944	197.5 ft.	3877 sqft.	142.25 ft.	198,416 lbs.	6 x 1,900hp BB 603
Messerschmitt Me 323+ (German) 1942	181.0 ft.	3,228 sqft.	92.3 ft.	94,815 lbs.	6 x 1,180 hp Gnome-Rhone
Junkers Ju 390++ (German) 1943	165.2 ft.	2,730 sqft.	112.2 ft.	166,400 lbs.	6 x 1,700 hp BMW 801G
Bloom & Voss BV 222* (German) 1940	150.9 ft.	2,740 sqft.	121.5 ft.	101391lbs.	6 x 1,000 hp Ju Jumo 207C
Junkers Ju 290++ (German) 1942	137.8 ft.	2,191 sqft.	93.9 ft.	99,141 lbs.	4 x 1,700 hp BMW 801G
Heinkel 177 (German) 1939	103.3 ft.	1,076 sqft.	72.2 ft.	70, 548 lbs.	2 x 2 duo 2,900 hp DB 610
Piaggio P. 108 (Italy) 1939	105.0 ft.	1,453 sqft.	73.1 ft.	65,865 lbs.	4 × 1,500 hp Piaggio P.XII RC
Kawanishi H8K* (Japan) 1941	124.7 ft.	1,721 sqft.	92.3 ft.	71,500 lbs.	4 x 1,850 hp Mitsubishi Kasei
Nakajima G8N (Japan) 1944	106. 8 ft.	1,205 sqft.	75.3 ft.	70,900 lbs.	4 x 2,000 hp Nakajima

* Flying Boat + Transport ++Transport/Patrol/LR Bomber

A

Abruzzo, Ben: 350, 352, 354
Adamowicz, Benjamin and Joseph: 232
Alcock, John: 145, 146-147, **146**(2), 199
Aldrin, Eugene "Buzz": 382
Alington, Cyril: 175
Allen, Bryan: 343
Ambrus, Jan: 141, 142
Amundsen, Roald: 94-95, **94**, 224
Anderle, Jan: 141
Anderson, Kristian: 352
Anderson, Maxie: 350, 352
Anderson, Rodney: 349
Andrews, Frank: 268, **268**, 269, 274
Andrews, W. H.: 150
Arban, Francisque: 346
Archbold, Richard: 233, **233**
Archdeacon, Ernst: 12, 15, 42
Armstrong, Neil: 382, **382**
Arnold, Henry "Hap": 195, 212, 264, 267, **267**, 278, 284, 286, **292**, 296, 302, 304, 305
Arnold, Leslie: 204
Arrachart, Ludovic: 119
Asboth, Oszkar: 334
Assolant, Jean: 123
Atcherley, R.L.R.: 150, 243, 245
Atger, Charles: 362-363, **363**
Atwood, Harry: 39
Aubert, M.: 346
Aubrun, Emile: 33
Audemars, Edmund: 27, 47, **47**
Avery, William: 360

B

Bagshaw, Jack: 175
Bahya, Jan: 332
Bailey, Honorable Lady: 130, 131, 132, 169, 170-171, **170**
Baidukov, Georgy: 190-191, **191**
Baines, J.K.: 164
Bajan, Jerzy: 132, 140, 141, 142, **141**
Balbo, Italo: 66-67, **67**
Balcer, Jan: 141
Balchen, Bernt: 88, 220, 224, **224**
Baldwin, Frederick: 17
Barber, Horatio: 389
Barberan, Mariano: 120
Barling, Walter: 263, **264**
Barnes, Pancho (Florence Lowe): 31, 230
Barnier, Joseph: 52, **52**, 53
Barrett, John: 373, **373**
Bartlett, John: 307, **307**
Basser, Gustav: 55
Bastie, Maryse: 126, **126**
Batten, Jean: 126, 131, 163, **163**, 178-179, **179**
Baur, Karl: 107
Bayer, Kurt: 141
Bayly, Robert: 352
Beachey, Lincoln: 31
Beaumont, Andre (Conneau, Jean): 37, **37**, 38, 39, **39**(2)
Beaumont, Roland: 314, **314**
Bedel, Rene: 30
Bedford, Duchess of (Mary Du Caurroy Tribe): 171, **171**, 173
Beil, David: **337**
Beinhorn, Elly: 90-93, **93**
Bell, Alexander Graham: 10, 17
Bellanca, Giuseppe: 227, **227**, 228
Bellinger, Patrick: 199
Bellonte, Maurice: 120, **120**, **157**, 232
Bendix, Vincent: **253**, 387
Bennett, D.C.: 164
Bennett, Donald: 246
Bennett, Floyd: 88, 100, 125, 210, 214, 223, 224, **224**, 226
Bennett, Gordon: 26, 332, 347
Bentley, Richard: 168-169, **168**
Benton, John: 207
Berben, Robert: 347
Berliner, Hans Rudolf: 348
Bernard, Frank: 149, 391
Bernard, Jean: 55, 118
Bert, Paul: 337
Bertram, Hans: 90, **90**
Bibesco, Prince George: 35
Bider, Oscar: 48, **48**
Bielovucic, Juan: 24
Bienaime: Maurice: 348
Bikle, Paul: 363
Black, Tom Campbell: 158, 160, 162, 165, **166**, 174, 175, 178
Blair, Charles: 317, **317**
Blake, W.T.: 150
Blakeslee, Donald: 314
Blanchard, Jean-Pierre: 346
Blanchard, Sophie: 346
Bleriot, Louis: 12, 15, 16, 19, 21, 22, **23**, 26, 28, 32, 35, 39, 46, 343
Blyakov, Alexandre: 190-191, **191**
Boardman, Russell: 231-232, **232**, 390
Boehm, Reinhold: 55, **55**, 56
Boll, Mabel: 227-228, **228**
Bonnier, Marc: 52, **52**, 53
Booth, P.A.: 175
Borschberg, Andre: **342**
Botsch, Arthur: 361
Bottalla, Batista: 129
Boussoutrot, Lucien: 55, 117-118, **117**, 255, 391
Bower, Joe Ronald: 339
Bradley, Troy: 352, **353**
Brand, Quintin: 167-168, **168**
Branson, Richard: 350, 352, **353**, 354, 355, 357-358, **358**, 384
Breese, James: 199
Bregi, Henri: 33
Breguet, Jacques and Louis: 331
Brereton, Lewis: 92
Bretcher, Fred: **366**
Brighton, Malcolm: 349
Broad, Hubert: 129, 130, 131, 132, 133, **133**, 149, 162
Broadbent, Harry (Jim): 163, **163**
Brock, William: 216, **216**, 234, **234**
Brook, H.L.: 163, 165, 167, **167**
Brookins, Walter: 27, 28
Broome, Frank: 167-168, **167**
Broome, L.E.: 150
Brossy, Frederic: 235, **235**(2), 294, 340
Brown, Arthur Whitten: 145, 146-147, **146**(2), 199
Brown, Janice: 341
Brown, Winifred: **150**
Brown, Woody: 362
Bruce, Hon. Mrs. Victor: 160, **160**, 243
Buczynski, Jan: 142
Burkhart, Robert: 321
Busson, Guillaume: **29**
Butler, Alan: 131, 132, 133, **132**
Byrd, Richard: 210, 223-224, **224**(2)

C

Cabral, Sacadura: 154-155, **155**
Calderara, Mario: 20
Callard, A.: 314
Cameron, Don: 350, 352
Campanelli, Ernesto: 64, **64**
Cappannini, Gino: 62-63, **63**, 64
Caproni, Count Gianni: 59-60, **59**
Carberry, John: 129, 130, 131, 132, 133, 134
Carney, Linton: 317
Carr, Reginald: 45, **45**, 46
Carr, Roderick: 155
Carroll, Wes: 242, **242**
Carson, Robert: 375, **375**
Carter, C.H.: 214, **214**
Casparenthus, Rhinie: 170
Castaldo, Gustavo: 129
Cave-Browne-Cave, Henry: 155
Cayley, Sir George: 331, 359, **359**
Cecconi, Fausto: 61-62, **62**, 122
Cernan, Gene: 382
Chadwick, Roy: 182
Challe, Leon: 119
Chamberlin, Clarence: 227, **227**, 324
Chandler, Capt. Charles: 36
Chanute, Octave: 360
Charles, Jacques: **346**
Charteris, R. L: 44
Chavez, Jorge: 24, **24**(2)
Cheremukhin, Alexei: 334
Chichester, Sir Francis: 157, **157**
Chidlaw, Benjamin: 300
Chkalov, Valery: 189, 191, **191**, 192, 194, 224
Claisse, Maurice: 334
Clayton, Richard: 346
Clouston, A.E.: 175-176, **176**
Coan, Richard: 336
Cobham, Alan: 151-154, **152**(2), **153**(2), **154**, 168, 243-244, **243** (2), 313, 367, 368, **368**
Coburn, Jay: 338, **338**
Cochran, Jackie: 164
Cockburn, George: 26
Cocke, William: 362, **362**
Cockerell, Stanley; 167-168, **167**
Codos, Paul: 62, 120-122, **121**, 123-124, 191, 232, 390
Cody, Samuel: 20, **20**, 21, 39, 44, **44**
Coffyn, Frank: 27
Coli, Francois: 125, **125**, 126
Colliex, Maurice: 35
Collyer, Charles: 217, **217**, 218, **218**
Colombo, Ambrogio: 135
Combe, Andrew: 180-181, **181**, 390
Comte de Lambert: 12, 20
Coningham, Arthur: 151, **151**
Conneau, Jean (see Beaumont, Andre)
Connor, Harry: 255
Conroy, John: 321, **322**
Cook, John: 375, **375**
Cornu, Paul: 332, **332**
Corrigan, Douglas: 254-255, **255**
Costes, Dieudonne: 62, 70, 119-120, **120**(2), 157, 232, 390
Councill, William: 318, **318**
Courtney, Frank: 149
Coutinho, Gago: 95, 154-155, **155**
Covell, George: 214
Crocker, H. G.: 202
Crombez, Henri: 29
Crooj, Louis: 238
Cross, Alexander: 39
Crosson, Marvel: 230
Cuno, Otto: 136
Curio, Capt. Mario: 68, **68**
Curtiss, Glenn: **17**, **18**, 22, 26, **26**, 27, 30, **30**, 35, 36

D

Dargue, Herbert: 207
Darius, Stephen: 232
D'Arlandes, Marquis: 346
D'Ascanio, Corradino: 334
Da Vinci, Leonardo: 358
Daucourt, Pierre: 30, 52, **52**
Daugherty, Earl: 237
Davey, Christopher: 350
Davies, C.G.: 165
Davies, Eleanor Trehawke: 24
Davies, Thomas: 294-295, **295**
Davis, Carol: 352
Day, Charles Healy: 225-226, **226**
De Barros, Joao Ribeiro: 66, **66**
De Beires, Sarmento: 95, **95**
De Bothezat, George: 333, **333**
De Castillon de Saint-Victor, Comte: 347
De Forest, Maurice Arnold (Baron): 35
De Gusmão, Bartolomeu: 346
De Havilland, Geoffrey: 130, 150, 151, **151**, 152, 202
De Laroche , Baronne Raymonde: 47, **47**
De Launoy, Christian: 331
De Lepinard, Chevalier: 346
De Lesseps, Jacques: 27, 28, 33
DeBona, Joseph: 317, **317**
De Pinedo, Count Marquis Francesco: 64-66, **64**, **66**
De Ponton d'Amecourt, Gustave: 331, **331**
De Ranssay, Le Lasseur: 38
De Rozier, Jean-François: 346
De Roumanet, Bernard: 29
De Vitrolles, Rene: 119
Defaux, Armand: 20
De la Vaulx. Comte Henri: 347
Del Prete, Carlo: 61-62, **62**, 64
Delagrange, Leon: 12, 15, 16, **16**, 18, **18**, 19, **19**, 20, 22, 25, **25**, 47
Delmotte, Raymond: 129
Delore, Terry: 363, **363**
Demmler, Charles: 320
Deutsch de la Meurthe, Henri: 15, 38, 42, **42**
Deutschendorf, Henry: 373
Dickenson, John: 363
Dinort, Oskar: 132, 133
Dittmar, Heini: 361
D'Oisy, Georges Pelletier: 119, **119**
Donaldson, Washington: 348
Donati, Renato: 135
Doolittle, James "Jimmy": 31, 68, 92, 132, 202, **202**, 229, 248, 269
Doran, Mildred: 214
Dordilly, Francois: 119
Doret, Marcel: 124, 124, **124**
Dornier, Dr. Claude: 86, 87
Dose, Robert: 320, **320**
Douglas, Donald: 204, **204**, 261, 276, 284
Douglas, John: 17
Douglas, Roger: 148
Drexel, Armstrong: 27
Drummond-Hay, Lady Grace: 93
Dubonnet, Emile 347
Ducrocq, Maurice: 41
Dudzinski, Piotr: 141

Dupont, Pierre: 347
Durand, Jon: 365
Dzhanibekov, Vladimir: 353

E

Eaker, Ira: 207, 238, 239, **239**, 274
Earhart, Amelia: 57, 92, 169, 179, 192, 217, 219-222, **222**(3), 228, 230, 231, 252, 254
Ebel, Ken: 257, 258
Eberhard, Kraft: 141
Eckener, Dr. Hugo: 93
Edison, Thomas: 332
Edwards, E.C.T.: 150
Edwards, George: 182
Edwards, Glen: 316, **316**
Edzard, Cornelius: 88
Eielsen, Carl Ben: 223, **223**
Elder, Ruth: 216, **216**, 231
Ellenhammer, JCH: 20, **21**, 332
Ellsworth, Lincoln: 94, 224, 249
Elmers, Wilhelm: 347
Elson, Andy: 354, 355
Emery, E. G. "Giff": 272
Emmons, Delos: 274
Endo, Ryokichi: 76
Enevoldson, Einar: 363-364, **364**
Erickson, Beryl: 305, **305**, 306, 307
Erwin, William: 214
Espanet, Gabriel: 49
Estes, Thomas: 322
Eubank, W. E.: 373
Evely, Clyde: 375, **375**, 390

F

Fabre, Henri: 35, **35**
Fahy, Claire: 230
Fairchild, Muir: 200, 201, 207, 217, 217, 224, 233, 263
Farman, Henry: 12, 15-16, **15**, **16**. 18, **18**, 19, 21, **21**, 24, 26, 31, **31**, 33, 42, 43, 47, 56, 113, 117
Farman, Maurice: 24, 113, 117
Farman, Richard: 117
Faure, Jacques: 347
Ferrarin, Arturo: 61-62, **62**, 63, **63**
Ferber, Ferdinand: 20
Ferry, Robert: 337, **338**
Fickel, Lt. Jacob: 36
Findlay, Maxwell: 175
Fitzmaurice, James: 88, **89**
Flettner, Anton: 335
Florine, Nicolas: 334
Florjanowicz, Stefan: 141
Flying Hutchinsons: 233, **233**
Forbes, Malcolm: 349
Ford, Alfred: **348**
Ford, Henry: **103**
Ford, Robert: 260
Forlanini, Enrico: 331
Fossett, Steve: 339, 340-341, 354, 355, 357, **357**(2), 363, 364, **364**, 390
Fougier, Gen. Rino Corso: 68
Foulois, Benjamin: 267, 268, **268**, **200**
Fourny, Geo: 47, **47**
Ford, Robert: 260
Fowler, I.G. Vaughan: 44
Fowler, Robert: 41, **41**, 148
Francke, Carl: 192
Franco, Ramon: 94-95, **95**
Frantz, Sgt. Joseph: 36
Fraser, George: 148
Fretz, Robert: 136
Frey, Andre: 29, 37, 38
Frost, Jack: 214, 219
Fujita, Yuzo: 71, **71**
Furnas, Charles: 19, **19**

G

Gallagher, James: 370
Gardner, Charles: 150, 178
Gargarin, Yuri: **381**
Garnerin, Andre-Jacques: 346
Garros, Roland: 27, 37, 38, 46, 48, 49, 50, **50**, 51, 54
Gatch, Thomas: 349
Gaudart, Francois: 21
Gaudron, Augustus: 347
Gayford, Oswald: 157, **157**, 390
Gelmetti, Umberto: 129
Gentry, Viola: 229, **229**
Gerstenhauer, Hulmut: 335
Geysendorffer, G.J.: 164
Giedgowd, Ignacy: 141
Giffard, Henri: 346
Gilbert, Eugene: 38, 42, **42**, 44
Giles, Barney: 291-292, **292**
Gill, Howard Warfield: 31
Gillmann, L.E.M: 155
Gilman, H.D.: 164
Girenas, Stanley: 232
Girier, Andre: 119
Glenn, John: 320, **320**
Goble, Stanley: 155, **155**
Goddard, Norman: 214
Goebel, Arthur: 203, 214-215, **215**, 217-218, **218**(2)
Goering, Hermann: 98, 99, **99**, 103, 104, 105, 107, 108, 210
Goldschmidt, William: **348**
Goodier, Capt. Lewis: 36
Gordienko, Mikhail: 194
Gordon, Louis "Slim": 219
Gordon, Richard: 321
Grade, Hans: 20
Graham, Stewart: 336, **336**
Grahame-White, Claude: 27, 28, **28**(2), 30, **31**, 33, 34, 39
Green, Charles: 346
Green, G. S. "Gus": 305, **305**
Gresswell, Clement: 41
Grieve, Kenneth Mackenzie: 145, **145**
Griffin, Bennett: 214
Griffin, J. L.: 214
Groenen, Victor: 238
Gromov, Mikhail: 70, 180, 187, **187**, 188, 190, 191-192, **192**, 390
Guazetti, Federico: 129
Guillaux, Maurice: 30
Gulick, William: 252
Guthrie, Giles: 158, **175**, 177, 178

H

Haase, Alexander: 348
Hackett, John: 319, **319**
Haizlip, Jimmy: 248, 251
Haizlip, Mary: 230, 231
Haldeman, George: 61, 216, **216**, 217, 234,
Halley, Robert; 143
Halliburton, Richard: 91, 225, **225**
Halse, Stanley: 175
Halverson, Harry: 238-239, **239**

Hambrick, George: 336
Hamel, Gustav: 24, 28, 41, 46, **46**, 48
Hamilton, Charles: 31
Harding, Jack: 204
Harman, Leonard "Jake": 268, 269
Harmon, Clifford: 31, 34, **34**, 387
Harriman, Averell: 281-282, **282**
Harvey, Alva: 204, 281-282, **282**
Hawker, Harry: 44, **44**, 45, **45**, 49, 50, **50**, 145, **145**, 226
Hawkins, Donald: 320
Hawkins, Kenneth: 214
Hawks, Frank: 241, 248-249, **249**, 252
Hayes, Caleb: 274, 280, **281**
Hearst, William Randolph: 39, 40, 41, 93, 214
Heath, Lady Mary: 169-170, **169**
Hegenberger, Albert: 212-213, **213**, 214, 215, 390
Heinkel, Dr. Ernst: 98, 111, 112
Heinsheimer, Thoma: 347
Hekking, Raymond: 360
Helen, Emmanuel: 42, **42**, 43, 44
Hemsworth, Geoff: 164
Henderson, Cliff: **230**
Henshaw, Alex: 150, 176, 177, 179, 180, **180**
Hentzen, F. H.: 361
Herndon, Hugh: 72, 235-236, **236**
Herring, Augustus: 360
Hersey, Henry: 347
Hertel, Heinrich: 101, 110
Hewitt, J.D.: 165
Hill, P. P. "Pete": 272
Hillwood, Peter: 314, **314**
Hilton, Joe: 358-359, **359**
Hinkler, Bert: 158, **159**
Hinton, Walter: 199
Hiroshi, Abe: 119, **119**
Hirth, Wolf: 135, 136, 361, **361**
Hoewing, Ralph: 366
Hoffman, Siegfried: 338, **338**
Hogan, Henry: 180-181, **181**, 390
Homma, Cdr. Kiyoshi: 72
Hooe, Roy: 238-239, **239**
Hope, W.L.: 149, 150
Horten Brothers (Reimar and Walter): 114-115, **115**
Howard, Ben: 252, **252**
Howell, Cedric: 148
Hoxsey, Archibald: 27
Hughes, Howard: 250, 254, 255-246, **256**, 261, 264
Humphreys, Lt. Francis: 36
Hunter Brothers (John, Kenneth, Albert, and Walter): 240, **241**

I

Ida, Donald: **353**
Iinuma, Masaaki: 74, **74**
Ingalls, Laura: 252, 253-254, **253**
Ingold, Karl: 55
Irvine, Clarence: 293, **293**, 390
Irving, Gilson: 214

J

Jachtmann, Ernst: 362-363, **363**
Jackson, Dale: 240, **240**, 241, **241**
Jacobson, Joe: 252
Japy, Andre: 73, **73**
Jeffers, Harry: **336**
Jeffries, John: 346
Jenkins, N.H.: 157
Jensen, Martin: 214, 228
Jeschonnek, Hans: 99, **99**, 107
Johnson (Mollison), Amy: 160-162, **161**(2), 173, **173**, **174**, 177, 178
Johnson, Hugh: 244, 366
Johnstone, Ralph: 27, 28
Jones, O. Cathcart: 163, **163**, 165, **166**, 172, **172**
Jones-Williams, A.G.: 157
Junck, Werner: 139, 141, 142
Junkers, Dr. Hugo: **89**, **103**. 104, 108, 186, 188

K

Kalinin, Konstantin: 187
Kaman, Charles: 335, **336**
Kanellopoulos, Kanellos: 344
Karkow, Jon: 340-341
Karpinski, Tadeusz: 131
Kasprowicz, Scott: 339, **339**
Kauper, Harry: 49, 50, **50**
Kazuhiko, Kawachi: 119, **119**
Kellett, Richard: 180-181, **181**, 390
Kelly, James: 239, **239**
Kelly, Oakley: 200-201, **201**, 202, **202**(2), 218, 391
Kelsey, Benjamin: 254, **254**
Kelting, John: 366
Kerr, R.Adm. Mark: 147, **147**
Kesselring, Albert: 98, 99, **99**
Kessler, Ulrich: 109
Key Brothers (Fred and Al): 242, **242**
Kidston, Glen: 172, **172**
Kilpatrick, Robert: 320
Kimura, Hidemasa: 70, 76, 78
Kilpatrick, Robert: 320
Kirby-Green, Betty: 175, **176**
Kittinger, Joseph: 351, **351**
Klatt, Gustav: 321
Klemperer, Dr. Wolfgang: 361
Kleps, Frantisek: 129
Kline, R.W.: 369
Klingensmith, Florence: **230**
Knabenshue, Roy: 31
Knight, Arthur: 44
Kohl, Hermann: 88, **89**
Kokkinaki, Vladimir: 194, **194**
Kokshoorn, John: 363
Koltsov, Michael: 188
Kono, Fumihiko:73
Koodrin, B. N.: 193
Koppenberg, Dr. Heinrich: 97
Kostur, Jerry: 349
Kronfeld, Robert: 361, **361**
Kruger, Ernst: 132, 133
Kse-Tiang, Col. Tsuo: 119
Kubesch, Sidney: 373, **373**
Kunz, Opal: 230

L

La Chappelle, Duval: 27
Lacy, Clay: 322
Laddon, Isaac: 264, 278, 302, **302**
Lahm, Frank: 347
Lamb, Dean Ivan: 36
LaMountain, John: 347
Landmann, Werner: 55, **55**, 56
Landsmann, Bernd: 347
Langer, Bernard: 55
Langley, Samuel: 10, **11**

Latham, Hubert: 12, 22, **23**, 26, 27, 347
Le Blanc, Alfred: 27, 28, 348
Le Brix, Joseph: 120, **120**, 122, 123, 124, **124**
Lees, Walter: 235, **235**(2), 294, 340
Lefebvre, Eugene: 20, **20**
Lefevre, Rene: 123
Legagneaux, Georges: 20, **21**
Lemaitre, Henry: 119
Lemartin, Leon: 19
LeMay, Curtis: 274, **281**, 292, **292**, 308, **308**, 368, 369, 377
LePage, Lawrence: 335
Levanevsky, Sigismund: 190, **190**, 192-193, **193**, 226
Levine, Charles: 227, **227**, 228, **228**, 324
Leyba, Antonio: 319
Light, Dr. Richard: 232-233, **233**
Lilienthal, Otto: 20, 345, 360, **360**, 364
Lindbergh, Anne Morrow: **211**, 232
Lindbergh, Charles: 57, 65, 71, 120, 156, 158, 192, 208-213, **211(6)**, 232, 248, 254, 255, 257, 273. 278, 284, 315, 324, 350, 390
Lindstrand, Per: 351, 352, **353**, 354, 355
Lippisch, Alexander: **345**
Llewellyn, David: 174, **174**, 175
Lombardi, Francesco: 129, 135
Lomonosov, Mikhail: 331
Long, Dr. Howard: 365
Lundgren, Theodore: 214
Lusser, Robert: 129, 132, 136

M

Macready, John: 200-201, **201**, 202, **202**(2), 218, 391
MacCready, Paul: 342-343, **362**
MacDonald, Robert: 372, **372**
Mack, John Henry: 260
Mackay, Clarence: 387
MacLaren, A.C.S.: 143, **144**
MacLaren, Stuart: 150, **150**
Macmillan, Norman: 150, **150**
MacPherson, Walter: 141
Madariaga, Modesto: 120
Maddalena, Umberto: 62, **62**, 87, 122
Magni, Dr. Publio: 68, **68**
Mailloux, Louis: 122
Maitland, Lester: 212-213, **213**, 214, 215, 390
Malins, Geoffrey: 150, **150**
Maloney, Daniel: 20
Mantz, Paul: 316-317, **317**
Marchetti, Alessandro: 61-62
Marienfeld, Walter: 136
Markham, Beryl: 133, 162, **162**, 175, 177
Marmoz, Jean: 122, 123, **123**
Martens, Arthur; 361
Martin, Frederick: 204-205
Martin, Dustin: 365, **365**
Martin, J.V.: 41
Masiero, Guido: 63, 64
Masson, Didier: 31
Mattern, James "Jimmie": 190, 193, 226, **226**
Matthews, George Campbell: 148
Maughan, Russell: 203, **203**
May, Wesley: 237, **237**
McAuliffe, Robert: 336
McCallin, Lois: 344
McCardle, William: 27
McCarthy, L. D.: 257
McClean, Francis: 49, 53-54, **53**
McCurdy, Alexander: 17
McDaniel, Arthur: 207
McEwan, AVM N.D.K.: 143
McGovern, Vincent: 336
McGregor, M.: 165, **166**
McIntosh, John: 149, **149**
McIntyre, Ivor: 155, **155**
Mears, John: 217, **217**
Melrose, Charles "Jimmy": **163**, 164, **164**, 165
Melton, David: 354
Mendell, Loren: 240, **240**
Mesmin, Rene: 123, **124**
Messner, Emil: 347
Messerschmitt, Willy: **103**, 104, 107, 128
Milch, Erhard: **103**, 104, 107, 108, 109
Miles, Lee: 252
Miller, Allister: 175
Miller, Paul: 320, **320**
Millikan, Willard: 318, **318**
Milling, Lt. Thomas de Witt: 36
Mitchell, Dr. Chalmers: 167-168
Mitchell, Donald: 365, **365**
Mitchell, Roy: 240, **240**
Mitchell, William "Billy": 200, 203, 212, 262, **262**, 263, 269, 273
Mitscher, Marc: 199
Moisant, John: 23, **23**, 27, 28, 32
Moll, J.J.: 165, **166**
Mollison, James: 157, 160-162, **161**(2), 164, **166**, 173, **173**, 174, 177, 178
Moneypenny, Peter: 319, **319**
Montgomery, John: 360
Moore, Harold: 336
Moore-Brabazon, John: 21, **21**, 44, **44**
Morgan, C.W.F.: 145, **145**
Morris, James: **375**
Morzik, Fritz: 129, 130, **130**, 131, 132, 133, 136, 140, 141
Moscatelli, Lt.Col. Antonio: 68-69, **69**
Moses, Don: 353
Moulinais, Marcel Brindejonc: 30, 48, **48**
Mudie, Colin and Rosemary: 348
Musick, Edwin: 257

N

Nakao, Sumitoshi: 75, **75**
Neal, A. M.: 369
Nehring, Johannes: 129
Nelson, Erik: 204
Neuenhofen, Willy: 88
Newcomb, Byron: 240, **240**
Newman, Larry: 350, 352, 354
Nicholetts, Gilbert: 157, **157**, 390
Nichols, Ruth: 220, 226-227, **226**, 231, **231**, 252, 253,
Noonan, Fred: 221-222, **221**
Northrop, John (Jack): 204, 219, 295-298, **295**
Norton, M. K.: 366
Notz, Oskar: 131, 132, 133
Novak, Josef: 129
Noyes, Blanche: 230, 252-253, **253**
Nungesser, Charles: 125, **125**, 126
Nurmi Carl: 339

O

O'Brine, Forest: 240, **240**, 241, **241**
O'Donnell, Emmett: 291-292, **292**
O'Donnell, Gladys: 220, 230, **231**
Oehmichen, Etienne: 333, **333**

Ogden, Henry: 204
Ogilvie, Alec: 27
Ohlmann, Klaus: 363, **363**
Old, Archie: 375
Olds, Robert: 273, 274, **274**, 280, **280**, 282
Olieslagers, Jan: 56
Oliphant-Hope, Simon: 339
Omlie, Phoebe: 230
Orlinski, Boleslaw: **119**
Orteig Prize: 65, 125, 208, 224, 227, 228
Osterkamp, Theo: 91, 132, 133 139, 141, 142

P

Paillard, Antoine: 122
Pallavicino, Cesare: 135
Pancherz, Hans: 110
Pangborn, Clyde: 72, 165, **167**, 216, 231, 235-237, **236**, 250
Paradisi, Lt.Col. Amadeo: 68, **68**
Parer, Ray: 149, **149**, 164
Paris, Neva: 230
Parker, John: 244
Parmentier, K.D.: 165, **166**
Patrick, Mason: 204, 212
Paulhan, Louis: 31, 32, **32**, 33, 34, **34**
Payne, William: 372
Peck, Paul: 28
Pedlar, Augy: 214
Peltier, Therese: 18, 19, **19**, 47
Penaud, Alphonse: 331
Percival, Edgar: 176-177, **177**, 178
Peroli, Max: 69
Perot Jr., H. Ross: 338, **338**
Perry, Margaret: **230**
Pescara, Raul Pateras: 333, **333**
Pethybridge, John "Tommy": 160
Petlyakov, Vladimir: 194
Piazza, Capt. Carlo: 36
Piccard, Bertrand: 342, 354, 356
Piccard, Donald: 348
Piccard, Jacques: 355
Pierson, Reginald: 144
Pilcher, Percy: 20
Piper, Harold: 244
Pixton, Howard: 51, **51**, 52, **52**
Plenderleith, William: 150
Plonczynski, Stanisław: 132
Polando, John: 231-232, **232**, 390
Pollock, C.F.: 347
Polte, Willy: 131, 132, 133
Polyakov, Valeri: **381**
Pond, George: 232
Poss, Reinhold: 130, 131, 132, 133, 135, 136, 137
Post, Wiley: 57, 222-223, **223**, 231 235, 255
Pottelsberghe de la Potterie, Mlle. P. Van: **18**
Poulet, Etienne: 55, **55**,
Pourpe, Marc: 53, **53**, 54
Powers, Edward: 304
Pratt, Conger: 268, **268**, 269
Pratt, Wesley Smith: 164
Prescot, Colin: 355
Prevost, Maurice: 27, 28, 29, **29**, 49
Prier, Pierre: 37, **37**
Ptacek, Steve: 342
Puffin, Hatfield: 343
Pulford, C.W.H.: 168
Purvis, William: 332
Putnam, George: 170, 219-222, **221**(2), 228
Putt, Donald: 272

Q

Quenalt, Corp. Louis: 36
Quesada, Elwood: 238-239, **239**
Quimby, Harriett: 24 , **24**

R

Radcliffe, Chester: 337
Rader, Philip: **36**
Radley, James: 27
Rankin, Eugene: 294-295, **295**
Rapp, Karl: 20
Rasche, Thea: 230
Raynham, Frederick (F. P.): 44, 45, 46, 145, **145**, **146**
Read, Lt.Cdr. Albert: 146, 199, **199**
Reichers, Louis: 281-182, **282**
Reichert, Todd: 345
Reinhard, Dewey: 350
Reinhardt, Curtin: 315, **315**
Reinhart, Roland "Pete": 240, **240**
Renaux, Eugene: 43, **43**, 51
Rendle, V.: 148
Rhoads, Eugene: 199
Richter, John: **237**, **237**(2), 238
Rignot, Jean: 120, **120**, 390
Risner, Robinson: 315, **315**
Risztics, Johann: 62, 88, **89**, 132
Ritchie, Alex: 354
Ritchie, William: 313
Robbins, Reginald: 239, **239**
Robert, Nicolas-Louis: 346
Robida, Henri: 124
Robinson, Charles: 207
Rodd, Herbert: 199
Rodgers, Calbraith (Cal): 40, **40**, 41
Rodgers, James: 339
Rodgers, John: 205-206, **206**(2), 215
Rolls, Charles: 23, **23**
Rose, Tommy: 150, 173, **173**, 174
Rosemeyer, Bernd: 92
Ross, J.S.L.: 148
Rossi, Maurice: 121, **121**(2), 122, 123, 191, 232, 390
Rousseau, Yves: 345, **345**
Rothrock, James: **280**
Rumpelmager, ?: 348
Rutan, Dick: 340, 354
Rybko, Nikolai: 196

S

Saad, George: 354
Sabelli, Cesare: 232
Sadi-Lecointe, Joseph: 27, 29
Salaman, Peggy: 172-173, **172**
Samson, C.R.: **168**
Santos Dumont, Alberto: 12, 14, **14**
Schaeck, Theodor: 346
Schairer, George: 289
Schempp, Martin: 361
Schilling, David: 313, **313**, 314
Schlee, Edward: 216, **216**, 234, **234**
Schlesinger, I. W.: 174
Schlieper, Clyde: 242, **242**
Schmid, Adalbert: 345
Schmidt, Otto: 189
Schmitt, Jack: 382
Schneider, Jacques: 49
Schofield, Harry: 150

Schrecengost, Ray: 320
Schwiebold, Jack: 337, **337**
Scott, C.W.A.: 157-159, **157**, **158**(2), 160, 162, **162**, 165, **166**, 175, **175**, 177
Scott, George: 147
Scott, Lt. Riley: 36
Scott, Robert: 318, **319**
Selfridge, Thomas: 12, 17, 19
Seidemann, Hans: 136, 139, 140, 141, 142
Senouque, Albert: 43, **43**
Serra, Joaquin Collar: 120
Shaw, G.: 164
Sheik, Steve: 339, **339**
Showers, Robert: 372, **372**
Sikorsky, Igor: 184, **184**, 185, 233, 335, **335**
Simeons, Benoit: 347
Skrzypinski, Henryk: 142
Smith, Charles Kingsford: 72, 91, 157, 150-160, 160, 162, 176, 177
Smith, Elinor: **169**,229, **229**, 230, **230**
Smith, Elton: 336
Smith, Ernie: 214, **214**
Smith, Lowell: 204, 237, **237**(2), 238
Smith, Ross and Keith: 148, **148**
Snook, Anita "Neta": 219
Sopwith, Thomas: 35, **35**, 44, 45, **45**, 46, 49, 145
Spaatz, Carl: 238-239, **239**, 306, 313
Sparks, Bobby: 349
Spooner, Winifred: 129, 130, 132, 133, 134, 135, 137, 170-171, **170**
Stanley, G.R.: 293
Stein, Wolfgang: 136, 141
Stephens, Moye: 91, 225, **225**
Stephenson, Charles: 350
Stinson, Edward: 61, 216, 217, 234, **234**
Stodart, K. & D.: 165
Stone, Elmer: 199
Store, Gordon: 172-173, **172**
Streett, St. Clair: 199, **199**
Stultz, Wilmer "Bill": 219, 228
Sullivan, James: 322
Sullivan, R.O.D.: 257
Sweet, Robert: 321

T

Tabuteau, Maurice: 32, 43, 56
Takahashi, Fukujiro: 70, **71**
Tank, Kurt: **100**, 113, 114, **114**
Teleki, Adam: 338, **338**
Thaden, Louise: 169, 220, 230, **231**, 252-253, **253**
Thieffry, Edmond: 119, **119**
Thomas, Karl: 349
Thomas, Royal: **228**
Thompson, Bernard: 207
Thorn, Sidney: 131, 132
Timm, Robert: 375, **375**
Tissandier, Paul: 12
Titov, Gherman: **381**
Tiukhtyae, Leonid: 353, **353**
Toda, Takuo: 346
Toporov, Vladimir: 345
Tower, Les: 272
Towers, John: 199, 200, **200**
Train, Andre: 38, **38**
Trappe, Jonathan: 358, **358**
Tremml, Glenn: 344
Trout, Bobbie: 229, **229**, 230, **230**
Tsukagoshi, Kenji: 74, **74**
Tucker, Harry: 217, 218
Tupolev, Andrei: 186, **186**, 187, 189, 190, 192, 194
Turner, Roscoe: 165, **166**, 218, 248, 249, 240, 250-251, **251**, 252, **252**, 389

U

Udet, Ernst: 98, 99, **99**, 102, 105, 128
Uliassi, Kevin: 354
Ulm, Charles: 158, 163
Urbancic, Alois: 363

V

Van Caudenburg, ?: 242
Vandenberg, Hoyt: 306
Van Der Schrouff: 21
Van Heijst, Floris Albert; 333
Van Ryneveld, Pierre: 167-168, **168**
Vedrines, Jules: 27, 28, 29, **29**(3), 30, 37, 38, **38**, 39, 52, 53, **53**
Verrier, Pierre: 41, 46
Verstraeten, Wim: 354
Vick, Dewain: 322
Vida, Joseph: 322, **323**
Vidart, Rene: **29**, 37
Villa, Alberto: 69
Vodopyanov, Michael: 189, **189**
Voisin, Charles: 16, 35, 47
Voisin, Gabriel: 16, **16**, 35
Voisin, Henri: 35
von Baumhauer, Albert: 333
von Dungern, Wolf: 129
von Gronau, Wolfgang: 95-96, **96**
von Hunefeld, Freiherr: 88, **89**
von Koenig-Warthausen, Friedrick: 89-90, **90**
von Koppen, Joachim: 132
von Mach, Mary: 230
von Massenbach, Dietrich: 132, 133, 136
von Ribbentrop, Joachim: 100
Vuia, Trajan: 14, 15, **15**

W

Wade, Leigh: 204
Waggener, R. S.: 214
Walker, H.C.: 165, **166**
Walker, Vera Dawn: 230
Waller, K.F.H.: 163, **163**, 165, **166**
Walton, John: 373, **372**
Ward, James (Jimmie): 40
Watson, Dennis: 314, **314**
Weddington, Leonard: 207
Wedell, Jimmie: 250, 252, **252**
Weiser, Rene: 119
Weiss, Pierre: 242
Weissenberger, Thomas: 366, **366**
Wells, Edward: 272
Westover, Oscar: 268, **268**, 277, 278, 326
Wever, Walther: 97, **97**, 101
Weymann, Charles: 27, 28, **28**, 33, 49
Whitehead, Lt. Ennis: 207
Whitehead, Gustave: 10, **10**
Widdifield, Noel: 322
Wigura, Stanisław: 134, 135, 136 137, **137**
Wilcockson, A.S,: 246
Willard, Charles: 24, 31
Willard, William: 24
Williams, John: 339
Williamson, Gerard: 373, **373**
Williamson, Ron: **338**
Williford, James: 337

Willkie, Wendell: 283, **283**
Wilkins, Sir Hubert: 223, **223**
Wilson, Charles: 332
Wilson-MacDonald, D. S.: 313, **313**
Wimmer, Wilhelm: 97, 98
Winters, Mark: 349
Wirth, Hans: 129
Wise, John: 347
Witchell, Doc: 307
Wlodarkiewicz, Andrzej: 141
Woods, J. ; 164
Woolsey, Clinton: 207
Worthington, George: 365
Wright, J.H.: 164
Wright, Orville: 11-13, **11**, **12**, **13**, 14-15, 17, 19, 22, 30, 31, 40, 147, **202**, 326, **326**, 331, 360, 387, 391
Wright, Wilbur: 11-13, **11**, **12**, **13**, 14-15, 17, 19, **19**, 20, **20**, 22, 30, 31, 40, 43, **43**, 47, **212**, 331, 360, 387, 391
Wyndham, Jill: 174

Y

Yeager, Jeana: 340
Yielding, Raymond: 322, **323**
Yoshihara, Seiji: 72
Yost, Edward: 348, 349, 350
Young, Arthur: 333, **332**
Young, Bobbie: 321
Yumashev, A.: 190
Yuriev, Boris: 334

Z

Zhukovskii, Nikolai:186
Zimmermann, Wilhelm: 62, 88, **89**
Zipfel, Edmond: 21
Zwirko, Franciszek: 132, 134, 135, 136, 137, **137**

R34
D-AURE